Ronald Reagan:
Revolution Betrayed

Ronald Reagan:
Revolution Betrayed

Richard C. Thornton

St. James's Studies in World Affairs

Academica Press
Washington~London

Library of Congress Cataloging-in-Publication Data

Names: Thornton, Richard C. (author)
Title: Ronald Reagan : revolution betrayed | Richard C. Thornton
Description: Washington : Academica Press, 2021. | Includes references.
Identifiers: LCCN 2021931249 | ISBN 9781680539189 (hardcover) | ISBN
9781680539202 (paperback) | ISBN 9781680537987 (e-book)

Contents

Chapter 2
Where Will the Missiles Go? Moscow's "Analogous" Threat

Chapter 3
How Close to Breakout? Krasnoyarsk and KAL 007

Acknowledgements

Ronald Reagan was among the most consequential of American presidents and thus a close examination of his strategy and policies is mandatory. Fortunately, a great deal of data is available, and I have attempted to avail myself of it. This book is based on the work of a generation of diligent print journalists, now mostly gone, who were the first chroniclers of the events of the Reagan years. It was they who uncovered the mysteries, plots, and conspiracies that swirled constantly around international politics in those days and this book could not have been possible without their efforts. I am also indebted to the many members of the Reagan administration who wrote of their experiences, as well as countless scholars who have tried their hand at interpreting the events. I want to express my sincere thanks to Soumyadev Bose and Sophie Judge for their thorough and thoughtful editing, and to Christopher Johnson for compiling the index. My deepest appreciation and gratitude, however, I reserve for my wife, Joanne, whose meticulous organizational and research contributions have made this two-volume revision of my original four-volume study much improved. Needless to say, all errors of omission and commission are mine alone.

Illustrations

Introduction

Ronald Reagan: Revolution Ascendant and this sequel, *Ronald Reagan: Revolution Betrayed*, were drawn from an earlier four-volume draft, revised and reorganized into two books. A new preface, included in *Revolution Ascendant*, contains an outline of that book. Additionally, the introduction places the Reagan years in historical perspective—what I see as four distinct eras of American strategy and politics.[1] Reagan entered office confronted with an economy in recession, an alliance in a state of collapse, and the Soviet Union on the march. *Revolution Ascendant* is my account of the president's decisions to jettison the failed strategy of détente and adopt a strategy that would rebuild the Western Alliance and achieve victory in the Cold War. To that end, he set about righting the economy, broadening the economic base so that it could produce both guns and butter. Not only would he set the economy on the path of rapid growth, he would also expand America's military power. Much greater economic and military strength was required to confront and defeat a Soviet Union that was reaching the pinnacle of its military capability, and actively attempting to change the global balance of power.

Confronting the Soviet challenge was a formidable task, not least because of the opposition the president encountered from those within his own administration who continued to advocate an accommodation with Moscow. These men, from Henry Kissinger's new world order faction, had acknowledged the failure of the previous attempts at détente, and now argued for "hard-headed détente," a compromise that gained them entry into the administration and permitted cooperation in the short run. But the long-term objectives of Reagan and the new world order faction remained opposed.

Thus, the Reagan administration, like all American governments in the modern era, was a coalition government comprised of two broad factions: the president and his supporters, who rejected détente and sought a strategy of victory in the Cold War; and the new world order faction, which pressed for what they viewed as a realistic accommodation with the Soviet Union. The president's strategy would find expression in NSDD-75, "US Relations with the USSR," signed on January 17, 1983. It was the first formal change in American strategic

---

[1] The original four volumes were: *The Reagan Revolution, I: The Politics of US Foreign Policy* (Victoria: Trafford, 2003); *The Reagan Revolution, II: Rebuilding the Western Alliance* (Victoria: Trafford, 2005); *The Reagan Revolution, III: Defeating the Soviet Challenge* (Victoria: Trafford, 2009); and *The Reagan Revolution, IV: From Victory to the New World Order* (Arlington: DJT Analytics LLC, 2013).

doctrine since NSC-68 in 1950, but would be honored more in the breach than in the observance.

The *leitmotif* recurring throughout the president's time in office was the running battle between the two groups, despite the president's clear decision to abandon détente. The new world order proponents, first under the stewardship of Secretary of State Alexander Haig, then under his successor, George Shultz, were determined to keep open all possible avenues for détente. They opposed every attempt by the president to defeat Soviet strategy (even while claiming that they agreed with him and he with them).[2] Their struggle and its outcome would have far-reaching consequences for the American nation and the world.

In this volume, I discuss the period from early 1983 when President Reagan promulgated NSDD-75, his blueprint for the defeat of Soviet strategy; and his offer to establish a new strategic order based on defense rather than on mutual assured destruction. By the spring of 1984, Reagan transformed the strategic weapons environment with the introduction of the Strategic Defense Initiative (SDI). He denied Moscow strategic weapons superiority over the United States, Western Europe and Japan by increasing the mobility of strategic forces, preempting the Soviet missile deployment to Grenada, and completing the deployment of the Pershing II/cruise missile package to Western Europe. And he defeated Soviet strategy toward Iran.

These Soviet setbacks were not irreversible, however, and in his second term President Reagan would attempt to turn them into enduring American wins. The president would seek to make permanent the change in the arms balance with a new arms control regime based on defense (SDI) rather than offense (Mutual Assured Destruction, or MAD). He would seek to stabilize Europe through a total elimination of intermediate-range weapons, the zero option, and he would attempt to complete the reconstruction of the containment structure through the re-establishment of a strategic relationship with Tehran.

Perceiving that the Soviets no longer possessed a strategic weapons advantage, were economically depleted and geopolitically overextended, the president commenced a vigorous support program for resistance movements in Afghanistan, Poland, Angola, Mozambique, Cambodia, and Nicaragua. While the initial purpose essentially was to harass and raise the cost to Moscow and its clients for their involvement, during the second term the president would seek to gain the initiative for these movements, defeating Soviet clients and the Soviets themselves. In short, the president sought to shift to the geopolitical offensive and achieve victory for the United States and its allies.

There were reasons to be optimistic about prospects for success. By mid-1984, not only had the president thwarted Soviet external aims, the Russians appeared to be teetering on the brink of general political and economic crisis.

---

[2] See Alexander Haig, *Caveat: Realism, Reagan, and Foreign Policy* (New York: Macmillan, 1984); George Shultz, *Turmoil and Triumph: My Years as Secretary of State* (New York: Scribner, 1993); and Ronald Reagan, *An American Life* (New York: Simon & Schuster, 1990).

Economic sanctions imposed pursuant to the imposition of martial law in Poland, the strengthening of COCOM technology transfer rules, and the tightening of credit restrictions on loans, had significantly impacted Soviet economic performance. Furthermore, the Yamal Siberia-to-Western Europe gas pipeline, now restricted to one strand instead of two, had yet to be completed.

The Soviet economy had ground virtually to a standstill, with growth hovering between 1 percent and zero.[3] Agricultural production was dwindling. The 1984 grain harvest of 170 million tons was the sixth successive year in which production fell substantially short of the projected target. Even with record imports of 55.5 million tons of grain during the 1984-85 marketing year, which drained hard-currency earnings, there remained a persistent shortfall. (The 1985 harvest would come in only marginally better at 190 million tons.)[4] The United States appeared to be the only producer with sufficient and consistent long-term excess capacity to meet Soviet grain and oilseed needs, although Moscow attempted to diversify imports.

Soviet hard currency earnings from the sale of oil and gas had fallen sharply, as the president's long-term objective of reducing oil prices began to bite. New sources of petroleum and gas were coming on line, from the North Sea, Nigeria, Mexico, Alaska and Canada, increasing overall supply. Oil prices were softening amid moderating global demand, even in the face of cutbacks by OPEC. The global energy market, on which Moscow depended for nearly three quarters of its hard-currency earnings, was unstable and trending lower. The president was determined to keep the pressure on the Soviet economy by effecting the continued reduction of energy prices.

Indeed, the energy price drop had double-barreled effect. Not only were the Soviets earning less, but also the increase in global supply of oil and gas prompted West European countries to renegotiate high-priced contracts for future delivery from the not-yet-completed Yamal gas pipeline. The hard currency needed to finance imports from agricultural commodities to high technology was drying up, forcing increased reliance upon Western credit markets. In 1984, Moscow and its East European clients had nearly tripled their formal borrowing from Western Europe and Japan to just under $3 billion, raising total bloc indebtedness to the West to close to $35 billion.[5]

By 1985, the Soviet Union had managed to run down its annual hard-currency trade surplus from over $4 billion to $534 million. This shrinkage had occurred despite a determined effort to increase energy exports and reduce imports. Moscow also attempted to compensate for its earnings shortfall by

---

[3] Henry Rowen and Charles Wolfe, *The Impoverished Superpower: Perestroika and the Soviet Military Burden* (San Francisco: ICS Press, 1990).
[4] *USSR Situation and Outlook Report* (Washington, DC: US Department of Agriculture, May 1986).
[5] Roger Robinson, "Financing the Soviet Union," *Wall Street Journal*, March 10, 1986, 36.

increased gold sales, which doubled to 200 tons in 1984.[6] But there was a clear limit to this approach.

In short, the costs to the Soviet Union of financing its empire, supporting client military operations across the globe, maintaining pace with the American buildup in high technology weapons, and providing for its own people, were exceeding earnings. Long-term trends indicated that conditions would grow worse, rather than improve, raising the fundamental question: what is to be done?

What was clear to both the American and Soviet leaderships was that their countries were moving in opposite directions—American power was waxing, and Soviet power was waning. Plotted on a graph their respective trends would be viewed as a giant strategic scissors. The problem for the American leadership was how to manage the transition to US supremacy and for the Soviet, how to reverse the trend, or at least arrest it.

It was precisely that prospect that prompted the Soviet leadership under Mikhail Gorbachev to change strategy from nuclear coercion to détente in hopes of stalling the American advance while sustaining progress toward fundamental Soviet objectives. These were the maintenance of strategic weapons dominance over the United States, military superiority over its Eurasian neighbors, and the establishment of decisive leverage over Persian Gulf oil by drawing Iran into the Soviet orbit. Soviet aid to so-called anti-imperialist movements was a growing drain on resources, and incongruent with the détente strategy. It would have to be written off, though not immediately. An effort would be made to leave Soviet clients with the best possible political prospects, but highly visible Soviet backing for what they termed "wars of national liberation" would end.

The Soviet turn was not apparent at the outset. Gorbachev's rise was accompanied by a major increase in military spending, an intensification of support for revolutionary conflict, and a quantum leap in the level of international terrorism—all directed against the West in general and the United States in particular. Although this prompted some in the Reagan administration to interpret early Soviet policy under Gorbachev as "politics as usual," in retrospect the military emphasis was but prelude to a major shift consistent with the adoption of the strategy of détente.[7] What initially appeared to be politics as usual was an effort to develop an improved bargaining position with the United States on those elements the Soviets were resigned to change or liquidate.

Soviet support for international terrorism was in a different category, however. Since the establishment of communist rule, the Russians had championed state support for international terrorism as an instrument of foreign policy. During the Gorbachev era Moscow would expand and develop an international support base, even while disguising its hand, somewhat in the

---

[6] Clyde Farnsworth, "Soviet Borrows Heavily as Oil and Dollar Fall," *New York Times*, December 3, 1987, A15.

[7] See Robert Gates, *From the Shadows: The Ultimate Insider's Story of Five Presidents and How They Won the Cold War* (New York: Simon & Schuster, 1996), 559-66, for a defense of CIA analyses of Gorbachev.

manner in which Stalin had transformed the Comintern during the era of cooperation with the West in World War II. International terrorism, from Moscow's point of view, was a cheap and effective means of keeping the West in general and the United States in particular off balance and would become one of Moscow's most important, if unacknowledged, successes.

The issue of Soviet support for international terrorism provoked a never-ending debate within the Reagan administration—a debate that intensified following the October 1983 attack on the US Marine Barracks in Beirut. Reagan and his supporters, especially CIA Director William Casey, wanted to publicly identify Moscow's role. Shultz and his supporters, while recognizing the need to combat global terrorism, were eager to identify and take action against Moscow's allies as state supporters of terrorism, advocating the use of military force against them; they strongly opposed labeling Moscow as a state supporter of international terrorism.

Secretary of Defense Caspar Weinberger vehemently opposed any use of US military power against terrorists, preferring more discreet means. The division within the administration over whether to name Moscow as a state supporter of international terrorism as well as the issue of the use of US military power against terrorists represented a major fault line in the administration. The high-leadership standoff resulted in a decision not to identify the Soviet Union as a state sponsor of international terrorism and *ipso facto* precluded the adoption of a successful strategy to deal with it to the present day.

President Reagan saw Soviet economic deterioration and leadership transition as an opportunity to bring about a fundamental change in the global order. Therefore, he sought to engage the Soviets in hopes of parlaying growing American power into a peaceful transition from Soviet strategic weapons superiority to a new global order based on mutual assured defense, rather than mutual assured destruction. A limited détente, success of the Strategic Defense Initiative, and the negotiated reduction of nuclear weapons were central to his goal of a powerful and secure America and a much weaker and compliant Soviet Union.

Secretary of State Shultz agreed with the idea of engaging the Soviets, but sought a much more equitable outcome for the Russians, the establishment of a mutually beneficial détente relationship. For him and the new world order faction the ultimate objective—to be pursued above all others—was to end the Cold War stand-off and develop the Russians as partners, rather than as subdued adversaries. For him, the failure of Soviet strategy and economic weakness combined with the emergence of a new leadership offered an opportunity to move toward this objective.

Thus, in the short term and on the issue of the growing American strategic advantage, the president's and the secretary's objectives were alike. However, their long-term objectives were fundamentally different. For Shultz, a negotiated strategic weapons reduction and the maintenance of mutual assured destruction remained the basis of accommodation, and he hoped to leverage SDI as a bargaining chip to get it. The new world order faction sought the further, if not final, deconstruction of the containment structure and the negotiation of what was the unacknowledged fact of a spheres of influence agreement with Moscow.

On the Soviet side, new leader Mikhail Gorbachev recognized that strategic trends were adverse and sought through détente with the United States to buy the time he needed to bring about a recovery of his country's political and economic fortunes. Toward this end he was willing to reach arms control agreements with Washington, but only on condition that the United States forgo, or at least marginalize, SDI, which would reinforce existing Soviet military strength, especially superiority over Western Europe.

The faction associated with the late General Secretary Konstantin Chernenko, led by Marshal Nikolai Ogarkov, opposed the strategy of détente and arms control with the United States as the means to buy time to reinvigorate the Soviet economy. They preferred the continued pursuit of current objectives, apparently even at the cost of further domestic privation. They clung to the outside chance that the effort to build a nationwide missile defense would be successful. Overruled, they appeared to attempt to disrupt the move toward détente by promoting terrorist attacks against American assets in Europe.

Through 1985 and most of 1986, President Reagan moved systematically toward his goals, in the face of Shultz and the new world order faction's attempts to undermine his policies in favor of their preferred alternatives.[8] Gorbachev, too, made sufficient concessions both to the United States and his internal opponents, while trying to foster economic recovery and preparing to cut losses in foreign policy.

The fall of 1986 witnessed the climax of a six-year struggle between the president and the new world order faction, which the president lost. Similar to the manner in which the political establishment had entrapped President Nixon in scandal in 1972, President Reagan would be entangled in 1986. That scandal, known as the Iran-Contra Affair, resulted in the transfer of control over foreign policy from President Reagan to George Shultz, who, from late in 1986, fundamentally altered American strategy from victory to the new world order.

---

[8] Peter Schweizer, *Victory: The Reagan Administration's Secret Strategy That Hastened the Collapse of the Soviet Union* (New York: Atlantic Monthly Press, 1994).

Part I:

The Soviet Challenge

Chapter 1

Andropov's Gamble:
Strategic Dominance and Missile Defense

The years 1983–84 witnessed a climactic global confrontation between the United States and the Soviet Union, eventually won by the United States. In a highly charged atmosphere in which each side accused the other of preparing for nuclear war, and as regional strife was escalating in the Middle East, Central America, Africa, and Southeast Asia, Moscow sought to engineer an advantageous shift in the correlation of forces. The means to this end were audacious, varied, and complex, but centered on efforts to establish permanent strategic weapons superiority over the United States by replacing the US-designed arms control regime with its own and activating a nationwide missile defense.

The Soviets sought to parlay strategic weapons superiority into geopolitical gains in several regions, bringing to fruition policies in development since 1971. Three areas were crucial: Europe, where the objective was to split the NATO alliance, exclude the United States, and establish total dominance over Western Europe; Central America and the Caribbean, where Moscow sought to reinforce already-strong positions of leverage and deploy medium-range missiles to Grenada; and the greater Middle East, where the plan was to obtain a stranglehold on oil by drawing Iran into Moscow's orbit.

The Russians would fail on all counts. This occurred for a variety of reasons—primarily due to President Reagan's determined counter strategy, but also inept policy management by a Soviet leadership in disarray after Brezhnev's death. Other reasons include steps taken by regional leaders to counter Soviet machinations, meaning the Russians would succeed in achieving neither their strategic nor geopolitical objectives. When failure was complete by the middle of 1984, the Soviets, while still under the nominal leadership of Konstantin Chernenko, would reverse strategy, abruptly drop the protracted confrontation with the Reagan administration, and brazenly embrace "détente" to continue pursuit of most of these same ends with far greater success.

Under the steady hand of President Reagan, the United States took up the Soviet challenge. The president progressively whittled away at what appeared to be an unmatchable Soviet strategic weapons advantage, gradually increasing US power in both strategic and conventional weapons. Reagan changed the *de facto* US strategic doctrine from mutual assured destruction, which excluded any defense, to an explicit inclusion of missile defense, focusing on space-based defense. In shifting the strategic competition into the realm of high technology, he played to America's strength and the Soviet Union's weakness.

Geopolitically, Reagan strengthened the US position in Western Europe by deploying intermediate-range nuclear forces (INF) and reinforcing the Western Alliance. The invasion of Grenada preempted the Soviet plan to deploy missiles there and the limited support provided to the Contras effectively contained Nicaragua and brought the Sandinistas to the negotiating table. The Iranian leadership, forewarned of the danger to their regime, took steps to suppress the Soviet surrogates in their country—the Tudeh Party. Throughout, Reagan kept US policy on track in the face of several diversionary moves in Lebanon and Nicaragua, which were designed to keep Washington off balance and disguise the main thrust of Soviet policy.

At stake in the American-Soviet confrontation was nothing less than the structure of the global balance of power, as both sides moved to the brink of nuclear war in their respective efforts to succeed. The worldwide struggle left the Soviets financially spent, their objectives unfulfilled, on a battlefield littered with political debris that smoldered for years afterward.

As the confrontation was global, it can only be understood in global terms. As it was total, it can only be analyzed in terms of the totality of instruments at the disposal of the protagonists. Indeed, at all levels—political, military, economic, and psychological—each side's use of power was wrapped in deception and disinformation in attempts to influence outcomes, making it impossible for the average citizen then and even many informed analysts now, looking back on those years, to comprehend the breadth and depth of the struggle.

Andropov Prepares His Challenge

In late 1982, Yuri Andropov, carrying forward the strategy charted by his predecessor, Leonid Brezhnev, presumed that the Soviet Union could achieve permanent strategic weapons ascendancy over the United States, coerce Washington into docility, and change the global correlation of forces to advantage. In the context of a dangerous nuclear war scare, Andropov's plan was to activate a nationwide ballistic missile defense system and counter the deployment of the US Pershing II missile into West Germany with an "analogous" deployment of missiles into the Caribbean. With American power thus effectively neutralized, continued SS-20 intermediate-range missile deployments would give the Soviet Union strategic dominance over the entire Eurasian landmass, including decisive leverage over Iran and Middle East oil.

Andropov focused on two major initiatives. The first was to alter decisively the European arms balance to Soviet advantage, in what can fairly be described as "Cuba in reverse." The key to this plan was the deployment of intermediate-range missiles to Grenada and possibly Suriname. Then, presumably, in return for the US withdrawal of nuclear missiles from Western Europe, Moscow would withdraw its missiles from the Caribbean. Such, at least, was the suggested *quid pro quo*. The result would leave the Soviet Union with permanent strategic weapons dominance in the Eastern Hemisphere.

Second, he sought to parlay strategic weapons dominance into a decisive shift in the Soviet control of global energy by acquiring significant leverage over Middle East oil. The means to this end was to broker a peace settlement between Iran and Iraq and thereby create the conditions for drawing Iran into the Soviet orbit. Andropov calculated that, weakened by its war of attrition against Iraq, an isolated and embattled Iranian leadership would accept a mediated settlement, rather than face revolutionary upheaval as Tehran's inability to defeat Iraq became apparent.

Geopolitical success, however, depended upon strategic success. Moscow could only expect to succeed in its aggressive efforts to transform the global balance of power in Europe, Iran and elsewhere, if it could gain and maintain strategic dominance and deter the United States from taking counteraction. Thus, Andropov's gamble hinged upon Soviet ability to maintain its strategic weapons advantage over the United States. Strategic success, in combination with tactical diversionary actions across the global field of struggle, in Lebanon and Central America, would neutralize Washington's efforts to defeat Soviet objectives—or so the record of Soviet policy suggests.

The US deployment of Pershing II missiles to West Germany would threaten Soviet strategic preeminence and had to be countered.[1] Contrary to Western assumptions, the Soviets had no interest in an American-designed arms control agreement that would require reducing SS-20 missiles. Rather, the Soviets sought to deploy countervailing weapons against the United States, which would lead to a settlement of Moscow's design. That design was to neutralize Washington's Pershing II deployment with the deployment of SS-20 missiles to Grenada (and possibly Suriname), regardless of the outcome of the arms control talks, reinforcing Moscow's overall nuclear supremacy.

The possibility for this strategic riposte had only emerged with the Maurice Bishop coup in Grenada in March, 1979, and Dési Bouterse's coup in Suriname in February, 1980. Moscow's decision to execute this strategy had been made before arms control talks with the United States began, no later than the spring of 1981. The decision was probably made just as NATO had finalized its INF decision and was represented by the beginning of construction of the Point Salinas airport in Grenada, both of which occurred in late 1979. As will be discussed in the next chapter, the Point Salinas airport was the crucial linchpin in Soviet strategy.

The plan to deploy nuclear missiles into the Western Hemisphere was as provocative and audacious in 1983 as it had been in 1962, the difference being

---

[1] Peter Vincent Pry, *War Scare: Russia and America on the Nuclear Brink* (Westport: Praeger, 1999), 16, argues that "more than any other single event, it was the decision by the United States and other NATO members to deploy Pershing II nuclear missiles in Western Europe that led Soviet political and military leaders to conclude that the West was preparing to launch a nuclear surprise attack."

that in 1983, the Soviets held far more powerful nuclear cards. Although the Soviets planned to present Washington with a *fait accompli*, they had to assume that Reagan would attempt to counter the Soviet move and that, therefore, Moscow would have to be prepared to face down the United States in a confrontation. This time, unlike in 1962, the Soviets would force the United States to back down in the face of the USSR's weapons supremacy; they sought to wrap the justification of their coercive ploy in the charge that the United States was planning a nuclear attack against the Soviet Union.

This was the reason why the Soviet leadership, in May 1981, instituted the intelligence alert known as RYAN, an acronym for *raketno-yadernoye napadenie*, or nuclear missile attack. The date of the alert's institution is significant. May 1981 was obviously too early to be in reaction to the new Reagan administration's plans, which were still in the formative stage, and must have been the function of a decision made earlier. In any case, the decision, announced in a speech by Andropov at a KGB conference, was to pool the capabilities of both the KGB and the GRU to cooperate in a global monitoring effort to provide the earliest possible warning of US plans to attack the Soviet Union. Forewarned, the Soviet Union could then preempt the United States.[2]

Soviet leadership had not conveyed the rationale for the decision to the intelligence rank and file expected to execute it, generating great skepticism. The vast majority with knowledge of the nuclear balance and American policy considered this decision as "seriously alarmist,"[3] for it was evident that the Soviet Union held the advantage in the nuclear balance, something the United States could not overcome in the short run. That meant that an American nuclear strike would be self-defeating. Nevertheless, while instructing its intelligence officers to be alert to US nuclear preparations, Moscow launched a parallel worldwide propaganda campaign charging that the United States was preparing a nuclear war.

In Europe, the true focus of the Soviet propaganda campaign to block deployment of the Pershing II/ cruise missile package was to condition public opinion against deployment of US missiles and, once deployed, was to develop sentiment against their retention and thereby drive a wedge between the United States and its West European (especially West German) partners.[4] At the same time, Moscow was preparing to break out of the arms control regime through

---

[2] Benjamin Fischer, "A Cold War Conundrum: The 1983 Soviet War Scare," CSI 97-10002 (Langley: Central Intelligence Agency, September 1997), 4.

[3] Christopher Andrew and Oleg Gordievsky, *KGB: The Inside Story* (New York: Harper-Collins, 1990), 583.

[4] Christoph Bertram, "Europe and America in 1983," *Foreign Affairs* 63, no. 3 (1984): 621-22, conjectured that "the Soviets never wanted an agreement in Geneva anyway but instead intended to use the issue to exploit to the full the strains visible in the Western Alliance, both between Europeans and Americans and between West Germany and its major allies."

deployment of a nationwide ABM system: one of the final, crucial components of which—missile-tracking radar—was on the verge of becoming operational.

Moscow's original strategy toward Iran appeared to center on weakening Tehran in its war with Iraq, then triggering a takeover from within, but the Soviets were never able to correlate all of the parts of this intricate plan. As described in Book I, the first attempt in mid-1981 by the Mujahedin and Fedayeen had failed badly, producing a vicious Iranian counter-terror campaign which suppressed the threat from these revolutionaries.

Israel's 1982 invasion of Lebanon and neutralization of Syria had foiled Moscow's second attempt, exposing as a sham the so-called "war-winning" strategy of an Iranian-Syrian pincer against Iraq. Preemptive Iranian action in early 1983, described in this chapter, following tips from British and American intelligence leading to the mass arrest of the Tudeh Party leadership and expulsion of numerous Soviet KGB agents, would frustrate Moscow's third attempt at forcible takeover from within and force a change of tactics toward Iran.

That the Soviets were never serious about supporting Iran against Iraq was made manifest when Moscow resumed large-scale arms deliveries to Iraq just prior to Iran's invasion in mid-1982. The depth of Moscow's treachery lay in the Soviet provision of weapons, supplies, and military advice to Iran in preparation for the invasion. The sudden Soviet resumption of support for Iraq made Iranian victory impossible, as long as Iran remained isolated, a circumstance Moscow strove to ensure.

But the larger picture was not black and white. By late 1982, after Iran's first three invasion thrusts had failed with heavy losses and Israel's invasion of Lebanon had failed, the Soviets began to reinforce Syria, raising anew the dubious possibility of a Syrian-Iranian combination against Iraq. Thus, with both Israel and the United States sidelined, conditions seemed to be ripening for a successful Iranian invasion of Iraq, recreating the conditions for a Soviet-style "revolution" from within—or so it seemed.

The new Soviet leadership was not united behind Andropov's management of Soviet policy. The defeat of Soviet arms in Syria had spurred a debate over the means of matching the sophisticated technological challenge posed by American weapons; and a faction had emerged under Constantin Chernenko and Chief of Staff Nikolai Ogarkov in opposition to Andropov's approach. As a result, Soviet policy toward the United States swung erratically through the year 1983, from attempts to cooperate to total rejection of relations; similar swings occurred in the execution of policy on other fronts. Indeed, by the fall of the year, as Andropov vanished from the Soviet political scene, the Chernenko/Ogarkov faction gained the upper hand, and US-Soviet relations careened toward crisis.

Reagan's Dilemma

By the end of 1982, President Reagan had achieved remarkable success in rebuilding the Western Alliance, potentially even augmenting it through improved relations with China. The US military modernization and buildup continued, enabling the president to pursue American foreign policy objectives with increasing confidence. In the great game with Moscow, however, the United States was struggling to close the gap that had opened in the strategic weapons balance and had clearly slipped to disadvantage in key geopolitical arenas.

At the strategic weapons level, the president was faced with a situation that was the reverse of the 1960s, after the Cuban missile crisis. Moscow held a strategic weapons advantage that the United States could not erase in the short run, although long-term measures were in place to reestablish US supremacy. Ultimately, deployment of the MX missile, B1 and Stealth bombers, and the Trident II submarine fitted with the D5 missile, would regain the strategic weapons lead for the United States (as it turned out, indefinitely). However, the administration had not yet devised a satisfactory deployment scheme for MX; the new bombers would not begin deployment until the latter half of the 1980s, if all went according to plan; and the D5 missile was not scheduled to become operational on Trident boats until after Reagan had left office.

The question was how to counter or neutralize Moscow's immediate advantage. The deployment of long range, nuclear-armed cruise missiles in air, land, and sea modes gave the United States a growing all-directional, precision strike capability, which, however, could only function as a retaliatory weapons system because of the relatively slow speed of cruise missiles. Moscow's determined efforts to develop a nationwide anti-aircraft/anti-ballistic missile shield raised questions about the penetrability of the cruise missile and therefore its value as a strategic deterrent.

The Pershing II intermediate-range missile was a weapon of far different caliber, combining both speed and accuracy to add a prompt retaliatory, if not preemptive, capability to the US arsenal. Although part of the 1979 NATO medium-range upgrade package, the Pershing II possessed strategic capability in that it could reach targets in the Western USSR in nine minutes. Although vehemently denied by US spokesmen, Soviet leaders believed that the Pershing II missile would be deployed in greater numbers than publicly planned and had the range to strike Moscow itself. The Soviet Union had no defense against the Pershing II, which was publicly targeted against Soviet command and control facilities, that is, the Soviet leadership.

The Pershing II, barring an arms control agreement, was scheduled for deployment into West Germany late in the fall of 1983, but questions abounded. Would West German leaders remain constant in support of deployment in the face of a growing nuclear freeze movement? Could the Soviets succeed in persuading or bullying the West German leadership into abandoning deployment? The coming West German elections in March would provide a key indicator of the popular mood and political direction. Would Moscow negate deployment by agreeing to an arms control treaty, or an easily negotiable interim agreement? Finally, there were questions that surrounded the weapon itself. Would it be ready for deployment on time? Test results to date raised questions about reliability.

President Reagan's ability to cover the gap until the strategic weapons balance had been righted hinged upon deployment of the NATO package in the fall of 1983 and the pressures that Washington and Moscow generated against the West German and NATO leaderships would produce heat and turmoil through the year. The two crucial arenas of geopolitical competition continued to be the Central American/Caribbean region and the greater Middle East; the president found himself in an unenviable position in both areas. There was growing domestic opposition to US intervention that constrained policy choices with respect to Nicaragua and also Grenada; and the president had only limited and indirect access to the Iranian leadership as it prosecuted its war with Iraq, giving the advantage to Moscow in both places.

The Iran-Iraq war had polarized the region and although the Soviets and the Americans attempted to support both sides, Moscow was having the better of it. The Soviets had deftly isolated Iran, leaving the United States with no immediate entrée except to side with Iraq. The Soviets were in the process of rearming Syria, raising anew the prospect of a Syrian-Iranian pincer against Iraq, and leading Iranian leaders to believe that further offensive action would bring victory.

In fact, however, this plan was a large-scale trap that would only weaken Iran and leave it vulnerable to takeover from within. Moscow was resuming supply of weapons to Iraq, ensuring that Iran could not win the war. The Soviets had executed a clever scheme, but not without help. As noted in Book I, US secretary of state, Alexander Haig, with the assistance of Israeli prime minister, Menachem Begin, had contributed mightily to the Soviet scheme. Haig's successor, Secretary Shultz, had continued with Haig's strategy, insisting that the United States maintain a military presence in Lebanon, and continue support of Iraq but provide no assistance to Iran.

For Shultz, pushing Iran into the arms of the Soviet Union by supporting Iraq was ideologically consistent with the new world order strategy that mandated the dismantling of the containment structure, of which Iran had been a large part. However, this made no strategic economic sense. Ideology aside, actively alienating Iran simply strengthened Moscow's leverage in the drive to gain control over the West's petroleum resources in the Middle East. Iraq, already Moscow's ally, had developed ties to Saudi Arabia with the encouragement of the United States, giving the Soviets influence over three of the world's largest petroleum producers.

The president strove mightily to play both sides in the war because that was the only hope of defeating Soviet strategy and keeping alive the possibility of reestablishing relations with Iran. In this regard, Israel played an important, if paradoxical, role. Even though Reagan had opposed the entire Haig-Begin scheme in Lebanon and even though Begin had destroyed the president's plan for a Middle East peace and an independent Lebanon, the president and Begin had common interests in the war. Iraq was Israel's main enemy in the region and Israel was quietly assisting Iran in delivering spare parts for Iran's US-supplied arsenal.[5] Begin's strategic failure in Lebanon had crippled his leadership, however, raising questions about his continued political longevity.

Entering into 1983, therefore, the president faced uncertainties at both the strategic and geopolitical levels, not to mention within his own leadership, at a time when the Soviet Union was reaching the zenith of its military power. Reagan's response was to codify his strategy and embark upon a counteroffensive designed to spoil Moscow's plans. Central to his counteroffensive was his plan to shift the strategic competition onto a higher, more financially costly level that the Soviets could not hope to match—the Strategic Defense Initiative—and to press forward with the technological modernization of American conventional arms.

At the same time, the president continued to exert pressure on the Soviet economy, which was beginning to show signs of serious disintegration, while probing to determine the extent of Soviet progress on missile defense. During these months, the president deflected a series of widely spaced diversionary moves in Lebanon, Chad, and elsewhere that were designed to draw US attention away from Moscow's main objectives and give the Soviets the freedom to manipulate events in Europe, Iran, and the Caribbean.

While the larger objective of Soviet strategy was the shift of Western Europe and Iran into the Soviet orbit, that could only occur in the context of Soviet strategic superiority. Therefore, the president's focus of action during 1983 was the struggle over the strategic correlation of forces, as the United States sought to deploy the NATO weapons package on schedule and to prevent the Soviet Union from countering that deployment. All through the year, the Soviets employed the threat of nuclear war as an instrument of policy, accusing the United States of preparing for Armageddon.

Soviet Leadership Dissension

Brezhnev's death in November, 1982, brought about an immediate change in leadership, but this only temporarily resolved the succession crisis which had been underway for several years. As Brezhnev became increasingly indecisive during the last months of his life and Soviet policy became immobilized, the Soviet leadership coalesced into two main factions, centering around heir-apparent Konstantin Chernenko and KGB chief Yuri Andropov. They reached an agreement to oppose all other claimants to power and to a tentative order of succession between them. The immediate consequence of their agreement was the elimination of Andre Kirilenko from contention just before Brezhnev died.[6]

---

[5] Shahram Chubin, "Israel and the Iran-Iraq War," *International Defense Review* 18, no.3 (1985): 303-04.

[6] John W. Parker, *Kremlin in Transition,* vol. 1, *From Brezhnev to Chernenko, 1978-1985* (Boston: Unwin Hyman, 1991), 170-71. Jonathan Steele and Eric Abraham,

Chernenko held the support of the old guard, while Andropov gathered around himself the younger generation of Soviet leaders, including Mikhail Gorbachev. The two factions also received the support of high-ranking members of the Soviet military high command, which was also divided. Chief of the General Staff, Marshal Nikolai Ogarkov, supported Chernenko; while Minister of Defense Dmitri Ustinov supported Andropov. In selecting Brezhnev's successor, it was Ustinov, along with Foreign Minister Andrei Gromyko who tipped the balance in the Politburo in favor of Andropov, with Chernenko named second secretary and next in line.[7]

In retrospect, the Andropov and Chernenko factions differed over execution of the several lines of Soviet foreign policy in play since 1971. There appeared to be general agreement on strategic goals—the Soviet version of détente; the intimidating use of the war scare; the establishment of strategic weapons superiority; missile defense breakout; regional military dominance over the Soviet periphery, particularly over Western Europe; and incorporation of Iran into the Soviet orbit—but not on the timing and sequencing of these disparate policies as they entered their decisive phases.

Marshal Ogarkov, for example, appeared to disagree with the policy of attempting to divide NATO. In his pamphlet, published in the spring of 1982, *Always in Readiness to Defend the Homeland*, he declared that differences in NATO were overstated. The implication was that the Soviet Union was wasting precious time in attempting to drive a wedge between the United States and its West European allies:

> On the main thing—in their anti-Sovietism and anticommunism,
> in the struggle against socialism, democracy and social
> progress—they basically adhere to a common policy.[8]

For Andropov, things could not be rushed. If geopolitical success depended on strategic success, then the culmination of Moscow's policies would occur sometime in 1984, when the Soviet Union expected to have an operational nationwide missile defense system, establishing its strategic weapons dominance, and to have deployed countervailing missiles into Grenada. With missiles based in Grenada, Moscow could reinforce its strategic supremacy by confronting the United States with a short flight-time-to-target weapon similar to the threat that the United States would pose to Moscow with the Pershing II deployment in West Germany.

Andropov in Power (New York: Anchor Press, 1984), 168, assert it was solely Andropov's doing.

[7] Parker, *Kremlin in Transition* 1: 178-79.

[8] As quoted in Parker, *Kremlin in Transition* 1: 111.

These developments would occur only *after* the United States had deployed its Pershing II/cruise missile package into Western Europe in late 1983.[9] For Andropov, this was both a political and technological necessity. Prior American deployment of weapons to Western Europe would "justify" Soviet counter-deployment in Grenada. Neither the Daryal long-range missile-tracking radar at Krasnoyarsk, which was the final piece in the ABM system, nor the airfield and port construction at Grenada, the site for Moscow's "analogous" missile deployment, would be completed and operational until sometime in 1984.[10]

Resolution of the strategic question was the *sine qua non* for everything else and it was over the sequencing of missile deployments that differences were sharpest, as the Chernenko faction pressed for the ideal outcome over the most feasible. The optimum outcome was for Moscow to deploy an "analogous" missile into Grenada *before* Washington deployed the Pershing II into West Germany. (Soviet missile deployment to Eastern Europe and submarine deployment off the American coasts were not subject to a time constraint.) This, however, would require either inducing the United States to postpone deployment of the Pershing II package, or convincing the West German leadership to reject or postpone deployment, which would provide time for the installations in Grenada to be constructed.

If Washington postponed deployment, then Moscow could deploy first to all three areas and be in a strong bargaining position, perhaps even to prevent the US deployment. Failing that, the Soviet Union could offer to trade withdrawal of its missiles in Grenada for withdrawal of the Pershing II from West Germany— Cuba in reverse— leaving the SS-20s balanced against the weapons of Britain and France. If the United States refused, then Washington would be faced with the same threat from Grenada that the Soviet Union would face from West Germany. In either case, Moscow would retain its SS-20 missile force ranged against Western Europe, the Far East, and everywhere in between.[11]

Sometime in 1982, before Brezhnev's death, the Soviet leadership appeared to have reached an uneasy compromise over these two sequencing approaches. Moscow would escalate the war scare rhetoric, charging the United

---

[9] Steele and Abraham, *Andropov in Power,* 181, argue that "Andropov appeared to calculate that it would be better to let NATO deploy its weapons and take whatever countermeasures might seem appropriate rather than 'legitimize' them by reaching a formal agreement at Geneva."

[10] For Soviet ABM planning, see William T. Lee, *The ABM Treaty Charade: A Study in Elite Illusion and Delusion* (Washington: Council for Social and Economic Studies, 1997), 97-105. Lee's views were based on those of Colonel General Yuri Votintsev, who was in charge of the Soviet Union's ballistic missile and space defense command from 1967-1985. See his "Unknown Troops of a Vanquished Superpower," *Voennaya Istoricheskaya Zhurnal,* nos. 8, 9, 10, 11 (1993).

[11] Perhaps more ominously, once Moscow's Grenadian *fait accompli* had succeeded, the Soviets would simply deploy additional SS-20s to Cuba and Nicaragua.

States with preparing for Armageddon, and intensify its propaganda campaign in Europe against deployment of the Pershing II package. A victory by SPD candidate Hans-Jochen Vogel over CDU Chancellor Helmut Kohl would be the easiest path to postponement, or outright refusal to deploy the Pershing II package; but it would complicate Andropov's larger scheme of a European-Caribbean trade-off. The Soviets were poised to deploy countervailing weapons against the United States regardless.

Either outcome would enable Andropov to deal from a position of strength. In Europe, he proposed an arms control agreement that would leave the United States with nothing, perhaps splitting NATO, and the Soviet Union in a dominant position based on the SS-20. With the SS-20, Moscow could threaten the entire Eurasian periphery and from that position of strength, Andropov would be able to dictate the political orientation of every nation of interest. High on the agenda was a Moscow-brokered peace in the Iran-Iraq war, which would enable the Soviets to develop relations with Tehran, perhaps something akin to the settlement Moscow had arranged between India and Pakistan in 1965, the so-called "spirit of Tashkent."[12]

From the summer of 1982, Soviet negotiators in Geneva explored the prospects of postponing deployment. Once Andropov came to power, he would mount a massive propaganda campaign in the Western media to move toward the same result. It was evident, however, that the Chernenko faction disagreed with the thrust of Andropov's approach, which in essence was to attempt first to obtain postponement and, if that failed, to deploy an "analogous" missile afterward. This appeared to be the line of Soviet policy until the end of August 1983, when the KAL 007 crisis, combined with Andropov's sudden disappearance from the political scene, completely upset whatever timetable he may have been pursuing. At that juncture, the Chernenko group assumed control over Soviet foreign policy and shifted to a much tougher approach.

Exploring the Postponement Alternative

Andropov, like Brezhnev before him, hinted at willingness to compromise in the INF missile negotiations in a long-term effort to shift West Germany out of the US orbit, but in fact wanted no agreement on US terms. For Moscow, all possible outcomes of the INF negotiation would mean a reduction in the deployment of Soviet missiles to zero, or to some number below current levels. This would degrade the existing Soviet missile advantage over Western Europe achieved by the deployment of over 250 SS-20s, each with three warheads. An additional 100 SS-20s were deployed east of the Urals and construction of launcher sites was underway in Soviet Central Asia.

The Soviet Union sought an arms control agreement involving a much broader conception of the nuclear balance extending beyond Europe, which would

---

[12] In that instance, Moscow utilized its access to both parties to manipulate the power balance against Pakistan, which enabled India to dismember its neighbor in 1971.

strengthen its overall position. Ironically, Jimmy Carter had established the precedent for this approach. The United States had broadened the scope of the nuclear balance, when the Carter administration intermingled strategic and intermediate-range missile systems in the decision to deploy the Pershing II intermediate-range missile into West Germany as part of the NATO upgrade. This decision opened the door for Moscow to intermingle strategic and intermediate-range systems too.

The coming deployment of the quick-strike Pershing II, with its nine-minute flight time to Soviet targets, meant that the only way Moscow could maintain its advantage would be to deploy a comparable weapon system close to the United States. In fact, Brezhnev himself tipped the Soviet hand in this regard, during a speech to the 17th Trade Union Conference on March 16, 1982. There, he introduced a shift in position in the intermediate-range arms talks, from the demand for a mutual freeze, the position held since the 26th Party Congress of February 1981, to a declaration that the Soviet Union was unilaterally placing a "moratorium" on the deployment of medium-range missiles into the European part of the Soviet Union.[13]

Furthermore, Brezhnev said, beginning that year, the Soviet Union intended "to reduce a certain number of its mid-range missiles on its own initiative." This was reference to Moscow's older SS-4 and SS-5 missiles, which the SS-20 was replacing. The Soviet Union, he said, would undertake this reduction "unless there is a new aggravation of the international situation." Elaborating on what would constitute a "new aggravation," he asserted that if the United States and NATO proceeded with the deployment of the Pershing II, "this would compel us to take retaliatory steps that would put the other side, including the United States itself, its own territory, in an analogous position."[14]

Brezhnev's disclosure of Soviet intentions may have been a slip of the tongue brought on by deteriorating health (he would suffer a minor stroke a few days later, on returning from a trip to Tashkent), or it may have been the deliberate revelation of a new approach. The hurried efforts of Soviet spokesmen to "explain" his remarks suggested the former. The obvious implication in Brezhnev's remark was a threat to deploy missiles to Cuba, raising the specter of another Cuban missile crisis; or to Nicaragua, Grenada, or Suriname, three other possibilities in the Western Hemisphere.

The following week, Georgy Arbatov, head of the Institute for USA and Canada Studies, specifically denied any intent toward Cuba, declaring in an interview in London that "Brezhnev said nothing about our intention to violate the 1962 agreement." This apparently left Nicaragua, Grenada, and Suriname; but a few days later, General Nikolai Chervov, Defense Ministry spokesman on arms control matters, ruled out these three possibilities, too. Chervov said that "to take adequate retaliatory measures...there is no need to bring other territories into

---

[13] "Brezhnev speech to the 17th Trade Union Conference," *Foreign Broadcast Information Service (FBIS) Daily Report, Soviet Union,* March 16, 1982, R 1-9.
[14] Ibid.

play," suggesting that the "analogous" deployment would be an increase in submarines deployed off the coasts of the United States.[15] Subsequent Soviet actions would belie these words.

In private, it was different. When the Geneva negotiations resumed in the fall of 1982, Soviet officials pointedly referred to Cuba and Central America as the place or places where Soviet missiles justifiably could be deployed. A member of the Soviet delegation, Vladimir Pavlichenko, declared that deployment of American missiles to Western Europe would be a violation of the 1962 agreement on Cuba. That agreement, he maintained, involved President Kennedy's decision to remove US Jupiter missiles from Italy and Turkey, in return for the removal of Soviet missiles from Cuba. Therefore, he said, if the United States sought to increase the threat to the Soviet Union from Western Europe, Washington would have to contend with an increased Soviet threat to the United States from "Cuba and other Central American countries." Pavlichenko asked: "how would you like [us] to have missiles there?"[16]

Soviet negotiators also began to probe various sequencing alternatives. One was to protest against what they termed the "automatic deployment" of weapons in November, suggesting the possibility that if deployment were postponed, negotiations would continue. Another was that the Soviet Union might make counter deployments on its own timetable, but keep on talking, ignoring the deadline. Still another, was the possibility of a trade after deployment of US weapons. Soviet negotiator Vasily Popov asked "whether it would be possible for the US to withdraw missiles from Western Europe once they had been positioned there, assuming an agreement was reached that required their removal." Chief negotiator Yuli Kvitsinsky likewise posited the possibility of a trade of SS-20s for Pershing IIs on several occasions. [17] US negotiators declined to respond to these suggestions.

Andropov's INF Gambit

As soon as Andropov assumed power, he quickly intensified the propaganda campaign to portray the United States as the aggressor preparing for war and the Soviet Union as the aggrieved party seeking only peace. Moscow was willing to compromise in the interest of détente, he said, but the United States was reckless on security issues and inflexible on arms control. The thrust of this campaign clearly was designed to sway West European opinion, in an effort to drive a wedge between the United States and its NATO allies. While its immediate focus was the upcoming West German election in March 1983, Soviet actions indicated less concern about the election of SPD challenger Hans-Jochen Vogel over CDU leader Helmut Kohl, than about conditioning West German, and indeed West European, public opinion against the presence of US missiles on their soil.

---

[15] Parker, *Kremlin in Transition* 1: 117.
[16] Strobe Talbott, *Deadly Gambits* (New York: Vintage, 1985), 158.
[17] Ibid., 159.

A few days after Brezhnev died, in mid-November 1982, Soviet negotiators placed before their counterparts in Geneva a new proposal. The main points were: (1) to reduce Soviet medium-range missiles to 162, equal to the number of British and French missiles, "in return for cancellation of the planned US deployment"; (2) to redeploy missiles withdrawn from the European part of the Soviet Union "to positions running roughly along the east slope of the Ural Mountains"; and (3) to separate "land-based missiles from nuclear-capable bombers in the negotiating arithmetic." There was also the suggestion that the Soviet Union "might be prepared to count warheads rather than missiles."[18]

The proposal was a blatant attempt to eviscerate the US position in Western Europe except at sea, to weaken the NATO alliance, and to leave the Soviet Union with nuclear superiority not only over Europe, but also over every other country around the Eurasian periphery. Given the 3,000-mile range of the SS-20, the provision to redeploy European-based SS-20s to the eastern slope of the Urals changed nothing. No European targets would be out of range of the missile, but additional Chinese, Japanese, and Southwest Asian targets would be in range. Finally, the so-called concession to the United States, separating land-based missiles from bombers, was hedged out of existence by Foreign Minister Gromyko's subsequent clarifications.

The United States rejected the Soviet proposal at Geneva and presented it to the NATO "special consultative group" of all member countries except France, at a Brussels meeting on November 24, 1982. They, too, "decided that the Soviet proposals...were unacceptable."[19] The NATO rejection came two days after Andropov began to present these very proposals publicly, kicking off the campaign with his first formal address as General Secretary to the Central Committee plenum on November 22.

Although most of his remarks were dedicated to domestic economic affairs, he made a pointed reference to foreign policy, announcing continuity of strategy, but a change in policy. Declaring continuity with the past, he said Soviet foreign policy "will remain exactly as it was determined by the decisions of the 24th, 25th and 26th Congresses of our party," that is, since 1971. Détente, he averred, "is not a past stage at all. The future belongs to it." However, "we will not agree" to "pay for it by preliminary concessions." Speaking of the arms control negotiations with the United States, he said that the USSR "favors accord, but it must be sought for on the basis of reciprocity and equality." We are in favor of curbing the arms race, he said, "but let nobody expect us to disarm unilaterally. We are not naïve." Then, he announced a change in policy, proposing that "as the first step towards future understanding, both sides should 'freeze' their arsenals and by so doing create more favorable conditions for continuing the talks on their mutual reduction." In these remarks, Andropov dropped the unilateral moratorium

---

[18] Hal Piper, "Words, Reality of Arms Control Can Differ," *Baltimore Sun*, February 6, 1983, A2. Talbott, *Deadly Gambits*, 160-61, discusses the Soviet negotiating ploy without noting that it was a specific proposal, or that the United States had rejected it.
[19] Piper, "Words, Reality of Arms Control Can Differ."

and reverted to the mutual freeze idea that was the Soviet position prior to Brezhnev's March 16 speech—which of course meant a postponement of the Pershing II deployment.[20]

Andropov's first comprehensive pronouncement on the arms control talks came December 21, on the occasion of the 60th anniversary of the founding of the USSR. It was a major effort to tar the United States as an aggressor nation. Charging the United States with war preparations on an "unheard-of, record scale," he warned that "wherever and however a nuclear whirlwind arises, it will inevitably go out of control and cause a world-wide catastrophe.... [A] nuclear war—whether big or small, whether limited or total—must not be allowed to break out."

Building on the proposal for a mutual freeze, Andropov declared that the Soviet Union favored the mutual reduction of weapons "of all types." In addition to the unilateral commitment not to be the first to use nuclear weapons, Moscow was prepared for both sides to agree to the renunciation of the first use of conventional weapons, as well. This was not the position of the United States, he claimed. The United States "would like to leave a free hand in building up strategic armaments. It is absurd even to think that we could agree to this." The Soviet Union seeks "an honest agreement that will do no damage to either side and will, at the same time, lead to a reduction of the nuclear arsenals."

"We are prepared to reduce our strategic arms by more than 25 percent. US arms, too, must be reduced accordingly, so that the two states have the same number of strategic delivery vehicles." We also propose, he said, that nuclear warheads "should be substantially lowered and that improvement of nuclear weapons be maximally restricted." While this proposal played well with European public opinion, it was not new, nor was it as equitable as he implied. Since the Soviets already possessed more weapons with multiple independently targetable reentry vehicles (MIRVs) than the United States, a 25 percent reduction in strategic delivery vehicles to the "same number" on each side would still leave the Soviet Union with the same relative advantage in warheads.

Andropov damned as "a deliberate untruth" the allegation that the United States lagged behind the Soviet Union in arms. Furthermore, he charged, the notion that new weapon systems such as the MX missile were meant to "facilitate disarmament negotiations" was altogether absurd. No arms buildup would ever force the Soviet Union to make unilateral concessions, he insisted. "We will be compelled to counter the challenge of the American side by deploying corresponding weapon systems of our own—an analogous missile to counter the MX missile, and our own long-range cruise missile, which we are now testing, to counter the US long-range cruise missile." In these remarks, Andropov omitted any reference to the Pershing II missile.[21]

---

[20] For a compilation of Andropov's major speeches, see Martin Ebon, *The Andropov File* (New York: McGraw-Hill, 1983), 146-268.

[21] For the December 21 speech, see Ibid., 260-63.

Andropov's clever use of the term "analogous" was designed to redefine and move discussion away from Brezhnev's threat to place US territory itself into an "analogous position," if Washington deployed the Pershing II and cruise missile to Western Europe. He sought to divert attention away from a possible Soviet deployment of missiles into Central America and the Caribbean—the clear thrust of Brezhnev's remarks in his March 16 speech. Andropov used the term only in connection with the MX and long-range cruise missile, neither of which involved a deployment into the Western Hemisphere.

The Soviet leader dismissed Reagan's zero option proposal as a "mockery," envisaging the "elimination of all Soviet medium-range missiles, not only in the European, but also in the Asiatic part of the Soviet Union, while NATO's nuclear-missile arsenal in Europe is to remain intact and may even be increased. Does anyone really think that the Soviet Union can agree to this?" He went on to proclaim that the Soviet Union "will continue to work for an agreement on a basis that is fair to both sides." Then, he said:

> We are prepared…to agree that the Soviet Union should retain in Europe only as many missiles as are kept there by Britain and France—and not a single one more. This means that the Soviet Union would reduce hundreds of missiles, including tens of the latest missiles known in the West as SS-20.

For the Soviet Union and the United States, he claimed, "this would be a really honest 'zero' option as regards medium-range missiles." And later, if British and French missiles are scaled down, the Soviet Union would reduce its missiles by an equivalent amount. In this "really honest" proposal, Andropov expressed his actual objective: to lock in a Soviet advantage over and exclude US weapons from Western Europe.[22] Under his proposal, the United States would cancel its deployment, while the Soviet Union would retain missiles aimed at Western Europe—missiles that were far superior to those of France and Great Britain.

The proposal to equate Soviet missiles with British and French weapons immediately met with the expected response. Not only did the United States, Britain, and France reject Andropov's proposal, but Japan did as well. Washington made the obvious response that Andropov's plan would leave the United States with no deterrent in Western Europe. Britain and France replied that their deterrent forces existed independently from that of the United States and were not in any way related to US-Soviet arms control negotiations. And Japan

---

[22] As William Safire, "Site Unseen," *New York Times,* January 10, 1983, A19, put it: "Having tipped the balance in their favor in strategic missiles, and having taken a major jump ahead in European theater missiles, the new leadership is now ready for a deal that will lock in its current advantages. That explains the current flurry of public arms-reduction offerings, summit calls and proposal for grandiose non-aggression pacts."

objected that Andropov's proposal, confined to Europe, offered nothing to Japan. The Soviet Union had nearly 100 SS-20s deployed in Siberia, along with several squadrons of Backfire bombers, and the number of missiles would increase if Moscow withdrew missiles from European Russia and redeployed them to Siberia. The absence of US missiles from Western Europe would simply increase Soviet leverage against Japan and West Germany.[23]

Andropov's INF ploy was clearly aimed at public opinion, with the objective of splitting the United States from its West European allies and also dividing the allies against themselves. Although couched as a serious, "really honest" proposal, it was anything but, because the United States and its West European allies had already rejected it. Indeed, demanding that British and French weapons be included in the INF talks guaranteed that there would be no agreement. Therefore, the only purpose in putting forward publicly what had already been rejected privately was to take the issue to the streets in the hope that public opinion would force either postponement or rejection of deployment.[24]

As West German political campaigns heated up, heading to the March 6 election, Andropov's proposal also seemed designed to support SPD candidate Hans-Jochen Vogel, who was trailing incumbent chancellor Helmut Kohl in the polls. Indeed, Vogel had arranged to visit Moscow (and also Washington) in mid-January in an effort to strengthen his credentials as a leader who could deal with both superpowers to West Germany's benefit.

Andropov's next step was to give the European propaganda campaign a boost. Taking his first (and what would turn out to be his last) foreign trip, Andropov traveled to Prague in early January for a meeting of the Warsaw Pact. The product of their meeting was the "Prague Declaration," a statement repackaging numerous past Soviet proposals centering on Andropov's call for a non-aggression pact.[25] Its immediate impact, however, was to reinvigorate Western European and United States public opinion against the "automatic" deployment of the Pershing II/cruise missile package. In other words, the objective was postponement of deployment and the instrument of pressure was an intensification of the peace offensive.

Grappling with the "Peace" Question

Determined not to leave the "peace" field to the Soviets, West European leaders publicly expressed "interest" in Moscow's proposal for an East-West non-

---

[23] "Japan Joins the Atlantic Allies in Spurning Soviet Arms Plan," *New York Times*, December 31, 1982, A4.

[24] See Wynfred Joshua, "Soviet Manipulation of the European Peace Movement," *Strategic Review* 11, no. 1 (Winter 1983): 9-18.

[25] Dusko Doder, "Soviet Bloc Urges Nonaggression Pact With NATO," *Washington Post*, January 6, 1983, A1. See also "How to Respond to Mr. Andropov," *Nature*, January 13, 1983, 30, which discusses the specific proposals contained in the declaration.

aggression treaty, but "in private" described the proposal "as another Soviet effort to hinder the possible deployment of new NATO nuclear missiles at the end of the year." Their interpretation was that the Soviets seemed to believe that "enough talk of peaceful intentions can convince enough West Europeans that deployment of the missiles is a provocation, rather than a response to the more than 300 Soviet SS-20s now in place." [26]

West German Foreign Minister, Hans-Dietrich Genscher, promised that the Bonn government would "examine the proposals very seriously," but Chancellor Kohl was more skeptical, pointing out that "there are clauses renouncing force in all the existing treaties between his country and those of the Soviet bloc," none of which held any meaning against the reality of the Soviet invasion of Afghanistan, Soviet pressures on Poland, and the invasion of Czechoslovakia. Vogel, the SPD challenger, hoping to keep the door open on the eve of his trip to Moscow, was more receptive. While acknowledging that Moscow's proposals were nothing new, Vogel put forward the hopeful view that the non-aggression proposal "could represent progress." [27]

President Reagan, attempting to put the best face on it, reacted with "guarded optimism" at the "encouraging words" from Moscow and announced that he would send Vice-President George Bush on a twelve-day trip to meet with America's West European allies at the end of the month. [28] Andropov's main proposals—for an INF agreement and a non-aggression pact—required a response from Washington, if only not to leave the public relations initiative in Moscow's hands in Western Europe. The challenge was to respond in a manner that would support and not undermine Helmut Kohl's election chances.

Meanwhile, after a quiet trip to Washington, where the president received him without publicity, Bonn challenger Vogel traveled to Moscow, where Andropov welcomed him with great fanfare. Vogel and his advisers spent two and a half hours conferring with Andropov, including a fifteen-minute session when the two men held a private discussion with only interpreters present. [29] When asked by reporters what had transpired, Vogel declined to divulge the contents of his discussions with Andropov, until after he had returned to Bonn and relayed them first to Kohl. However, the Russians had a different objective, and immediately let some of what Andropov had proposed become known to the Americans.

Soviet arms control negotiators, Victor Karpov and Yuli Kvitsinsky, meeting with a visiting thirteen-man congressional delegation from Washington

[26] John Vinocur, "Allies Privately Unsure of Bloc's Offer," *New York Times*, January 10, 1983, A3.

[27] Ibid. See also, "NATO Nations Express Doubts on Warsaw Pact Offer," *Washington Post*, January 7, 1983, A15.

[28] Francis X. Clines, "US Sending Bush to Europe to Meet the Allies on Arms," *New York Times*, January 9, 1983, A1.

[29] Dusko Doder, "Bonn Politician Encouraged by Talks in Moscow," *Washington Post*, January 12, 1983, A1.

led by Thomas Lantos (D-CA), divulged that Andropov had "mentioned the possibility of dismantling the weapons it would withdraw from Europe as opposed to re-siting them in Asia or putting them in storage." They also declared that Moscow would "consider destruction of the missiles" entirely. Everything, of course, "would be contingent on the North Atlantic Treaty Organization's shelving plans to deploy new US medium-range missiles in Western Europe."[30]

When that news broke, Vogel affirmed that "his discussions with Andropov and other senior officials 'do not contradict' statements by the US congressmen." Still, he would wait until returning to Bonn before making "detailed comments."[31] At a press conference upon his return, Vogel affirmed that Andropov had, indeed, proposed new positions. He was willing to negotiate a reduction in weapons aimed at Western Europe—not only missiles, but warheads. The Soviet Union was also willing to destroy "some" of its missiles, perhaps even SS-20s, although they would have to be "issues of negotiation." Moreover, the Soviets were willing to count aircraft separately from missiles, a long-standing American demand. Finally, he said, Andropov knew that British and French weapons could not be included in the negotiations with the United States, but "insisted that these arsenals be counted in any overall assessment of the nuclear balance in Europe."[32]

Vogel averred that Moscow was "moving in the right direction," and "the United States should follow up on this initiative." In his view, the "zero solution" was "an ideal goal but not feasible." He declared that "experience shows that negotiations rarely reach a final result that is identical with the starting position of one of the parties." Vogel had taken a step back from Helmut Schmidt's zero option, which strengthened his standing in the polls; but his position remained consistent with it. He declared that "we don't want any missiles pointing at us from the east nor do we want missiles on our soil posing a threat to the Soviets." Indeed, polls indicated that Vogel's image had been burnished as a result of his trips and the SPD had "enhanced their standing…as the party best suited to mediate between the superpowers."

It was the Reagan administration that appeared disoriented at the moment. SPD arms expert, Egon Bahr, who had accompanied Vogel to Washington and Moscow, noted that the dismissal of Eugene Rostow the previous week from his position as Director of the Arms Control and Disarmament Agency reflected serious policy differences within the Reagan administration. Although he found this "not particularly reassuring," Vogel thought that Paul Nitze's views were "on the same line as Rostow's" and he expected the US to remain flexible in its approach when talks resumed.

---

[30] "Soviets Offer to Dismantle Some Missiles in Arms Deal," *Washington Times*, January 12, 1983, A1.

[31] Dusko Doder, "Soviet Said to Offer to Destroy Some Intermediate Missiles," *Washington Post*, January 13, 1983, A21.

[32] William Drozdiak, "Moscow to Bargain on Warheads, Says Bonn Challenger," *Washington Post*, January 14, 1983, A1.

President Reagan strove to respond to Moscow's proposals in a way that would support Helmut Kohl's reelection bid without undercutting his own position.[33] Kohl held publicly to the zero position, but privately suggested that Reagan indicate some flexibility, out of concern that Vogel was making gains with German voters. His coalition partner, Hans-Dietrich Genscher, however, was publicly suggesting that the two sides move toward an interim solution, agreeing to deployment numbers higher than zero and below 572, but continuing negotiations.[34]

Both positions were calculated to strengthen the CDU-FDP appeal to the voters and split the electoral opposition. Kohl stressed alliance solidarity, contrary to the SPD, which called for West Germany to pursue its own interests; Genscher sought to undercut the popularity of the Greens, who stood to the left of his Free Democrat Party and were gaining in the polls by calling for no US deployments. The "interim solution" strengthened the appeal of the current coalition. Furthermore, the idea of a compromise solution seemed to be spreading. Margaret Thatcher, too, joined in to suggest that although the best balance was zero, "in the absence of that," there must be compromise.[35]

Soviet Foreign Minister, Andrei Gromyko, in Bonn on the invitation of Helmut Kohl, immediately threw cold water on the growing calls for compromise and undercut Vogel. He made no mention of Moscow's presumed new-found willingness to negotiate parity of warheads and not merely missiles, and simply reiterated Andropov's December 21 proposal to limit Soviet missiles to those deployed by Britain and France. While warning that "West Germany would be caught in a sharpened nuclear confrontation if a new generation of American medium-range missiles was stationed in Western Europe," he added a "new element" to the Soviet position. Moscow was prepared, he said, to "negotiate a reduction of its shorter-range SS-21, SS-22 and SS-23 nuclear weapons systems targeted on Western Europe on the basis of 'mutuality.'"[36]

During a dinner speech, Gromyko sharply attacked the Reagan administration, while claiming that "in the nuclear age the Federal Republic of Germany and the Soviet Union are, figuratively speaking, in one boat." The United States, he said, led by "gamblers and con men" who were "not capable of seeing things as they are," were "ready to plunge humanity into a nuclear catastrophe for the sake of their ambition.... Who gave them the right to pull all of the people who want to live down the abyss with them?" Carrying out the

---

[33] Hedrick Smith, "The Need Emerges to Respond to the Russians on Arms," *New York Times*, January 11, 1983, B8.

[34] Drozdiak, "Moscow to Bargain on Warheads [. . .]."

[35] Talbott, *Deadly Gambits*, 172-3.

[36] James Markham, "Gromyko Warns Germans of Risk If New US Missiles Are Deployed," *New York Times*, January 18, 1983, A1. These were tactical missiles with ranges between 75 and 500 miles and were comparable to the Pershing IA and Lance missiles.

NATO plan would mean "for the whole world an extended nuclear confrontation with all its consequences." He said he hoped:

> [that] the federal government; the political parties, independent of their current role in governing the state, and the entire West German public would soberly judge the present situation and do everything to avert the danger of a nuclear arms race in Europe.[37]

Chancellor Kohl would be criticized for excessive deference to his Soviet visitor, but, if Gromyko thought he had shaken the Bonn government, he miscalculated. Foreign Minister Genscher replied to Gromyko by defending the zero option, although he rejected the idea of an "all or nothing" approach and insisted that a compromise was possible.

At a news conference the next day before departing, Gromyko bluntly rejected the zero option: "We will in no case accept this zero option." Furthermore, the "rumor" that American and Soviet negotiators had reached an informal understanding the previous summer, the so-called walk in the woods proposal, "absolutely does not correspond to reality." He reiterated his view that Bonn and Moscow were "under the same European roof" and urged that Bonn steer an independent course and not "listen to what is dictated by another side if it does not serve good Soviet-German relations."[38]

Responding to press accounts that charged him with meddling in German internal politics and attempting to support Vogel against Kohl, Gromyko denied it. "We came here to explain our policies, to support the potential elements of the Federal Republic that aim at good-neighborly relations between our countries, toward maintaining peace, détente, and toward achieving disarmament." He said that at the end of his meeting with Chancellor Kohl he "asked if he could report to Moscow that the new Christian Democratic-led Government was in favor of 'continuing détente.'" Kohl, he said, had answered with "an unqualified yes."

That was not how Kohl saw it. As soon as Gromyko had departed, the chancellor acted immediately to correct any misimpression of his own views generated by the Soviet foreign minister's remarks. In a speech in Hanover, Kohl "spoke rather coolly" of Gromyko's visit. He said that "he had told the Soviet visitor that 'the negotiations in Geneva are taking place at the negotiating table, not before the eyes of the German or international public.'" Bonn, he said, would not be "coerced" by Soviet pressure and there should be "no doubt about our belonging to the West."

---

[37] Markham, "Gromyko Warns Germans [. . .]."
[38] James Markham, "Gromyko Rejects the 'Zero Option,'" *New York Times*, January 19, 1983, A11 and William Drozdiak, "US Thwarts Arms Pact, Gromyko Says in Bonn," *Washington Post*, January 19, 1983, A1.

Searching for a Way Forward

As the Reagan administration began to prepare its positions for the resumption of the Geneva negotiations in February, a leak to the *New York Times* seemed to confirm impressions of an administration in disarray. Paul Nitze, chief INF negotiator, was said to be arguing for a major departure from the president's zero position. He was quoted as saying that "in the end western Europeans will not support deployment, no matter what the United States does, and therefore the United States should try for the only politically realistic solution now—zero for the United States and a sharply reduced number for the Soviet Union." Nitze proposed that the United States "forgo all planned deployments of missiles if the Russians were to reduce their missiles aimed at Western Europe from 500 to 50 and freeze at 100 the missiles aimed at China and Japan." In effect, Nitze was advocating the acceptance of Andropov's recent proposal![39]

The article went on to emphasize that while Reagan was looking for ways to reach an acceptable agreement, he could make no change in the zero-option position until after the West German elections. "The judgment is that any American move before then would work in favor of the opposition Social Democratic Party" and against Helmut Kohl. Furthermore, it would "legitimize left-wing Western European attacks on American policy." It was felt that "Western European leaders would settle for less, but do not want to assume the responsibility for proposing anything less than the total elimination of Soviet missiles." Said one Pentagon official: "they want us to take the heat for them."

This leak to the press had several objectives. First, it was, as stated in the account, "to counter…what is widely seen as an increasingly successful Soviet peace offensive," which suggested that the Soviets were ready for an arms control agreement and the Americans were not. Moscow has been "grabbing the headlines in Western Europe and putting Washington on the defensive." It was important to take the initiative and show that Reagan was ready for an agreement, too, and not standing rigidly and inflexibly on zero. Second, it was designed to elicit a response from Helmut Kohl, who would have to suggest flexibility to enable Reagan to act, but which would also signal to German voters that he was ready for an agreement, too.

Third, it was also an obvious trial balloon to test Andropov's intentions. The fact was that Nitze's "proposal," if taken seriously, would amount to the US abandonment of Western Europe, the defeat of Helmut Kohl in the coming election, and the achievement of Soviet domination of Western Europe in a single play. If Andropov truly wanted to reach an agreement there would be a prompt response to this trial balloon, which, from Moscow's point of view was a major improvement on the "walk in the woods" proposal of the previous summer. The

---

[39] Leslie Gelb, "US Aides Report Arms-Talks Views Remain Unchanged," *New York Times*, January 19, 1983, A1. There seems little doubt that these discussions actually occurred. Talbott, *Deadly Gambits*, 162-67, also reports on them. Their significance, however, lay in the fact that they were made public.

walk in the woods formula had called for equal numbers on both sides and no deployment of the Pershing II. The new Nitze position posited no deployment of US weapons at all.

The Soviet reply came immediately, and it was a resounding "NO." The "so-called interim solution," being pushed forward by West German Foreign Minister Hans-Dietrich Genscher and British Foreign Secretary Francis Pym, TASS said, was "absolutely unacceptable to the Soviet Union." The quick public rejection undercut Vogel and the SPD, who were claiming that the Soviet Union would be receptive to compromise. TASS ridiculed the concept of a smaller deployment of US missiles than originally planned as like the joke "that a woman cannot be slightly pregnant." The "placement of the first Pershing II on West German territory and the first cruise missile in Sicily creates a new situation," which would deprive the Geneva talks "of the realistic basis upon which they are now being conducted."[40] Moscow had openly decided to embark upon a zero-sum gamble, even at the cost of a slowdown in momentum.

French President François Mitterrand also chimed in to offer support for Kohl, contributing to the turnaround in momentum. Speaking to the West German parliament the day after Gromyko left, he sternly warned against "any attempts to break Western Europe's defense alliance with the United States." Mitterrand "defended NATO's decision to deploy US-built Pershing II and cruise missiles in Europe at the end of the year if no arms control deal is achieved. He endorsed the US position that NATO will forego deployment only if the Soviet dismantles its medium-range nuclear missiles aimed at Western Europe." He also insisted that France's deterrent "could not be taken into account" in negotiations between the United States and the Soviet Union.[41]

Mitterrand's very presence in Bonn was intended to show support for Kohl's coalition, but his speech raised issues that went beyond the politics of the moment. In effect, Mitterrand moved the debate away from a focus on the mathematical formulas needed to determine the desired balance of power, to the deeper question of the direction of Europe itself, about the "struggle going on for the future of Europe"—a struggle in which he saw West Germany as the "weak point." Increasingly, French officials saw "segments of the West German political class dominated by a desire for accommodation with the Soviet Union in order to move, in the long term, toward German reunification."[42]

The issue went beyond the SPD's leftward movement, and the rise of the Greens, which had been under way for some time. French concern was over the general West German disinclination, including the Kohl coalition, to "take any kind of strong stand" against the Soviet Union and hinted at something more

---

[40] Dusko Doder, "Soviets Condemn 'Interim' Basing of Missiles in Europe," *Washington Post*, January 21, 1983, A1.

[41] William Drozdiak, "France Adamant against US, Soviets Negotiating Its Missiles," *Washington Post*, January 21, 1983, A1.

[42] John Vinocur, "Mitterrand Sees Test for the West's Unity," *New York Times*, January 24, 1983, A1.

fundamental—the prospect of the de-coupling of Western Europe from the United States. Gromyko's visit provided but the latest example. A French diplomat saw it nothing less than "extraordinary that the Christian Democratic-led coalition was not more aggressive in pointing out what he saw as the lack of novelty and contradictions of Mr. Gromyko's presentation. 'They reacted as if they were in a trance,' he said."

The thrust of Mitterrand's remarks was to raise for public discussion the question of West Germany's fundamental allegiance to the West. If West Germany refused to deploy the Pershing II and cruise missiles, "it will be hard to refute the argument of those Americans who believe that Europe will not defend itself and is not worth defending." If the United States diminishes its support for Europe, this would have dire implications for France, its independent deterrent, and global role. The French, and everyone else, were now "waiting to see if the United States considers the problem, regardless of its discomfort, as one meriting public discussion on the highest level."

Reagan Stands by Kohl

As Paul Nitze was returning to Geneva for the resumption of the arms control negotiations, he stopped in Bonn to join Helmut Kohl in an expression of mutual support for the zero option. Their joint statement, however, was low key and defensive, almost apologetic, declaring that "the object at the negotiations is to achieve a real breakthrough with a concrete negotiating result at the earliest possible time, bearing in mind the firm and valid accord on the NATO twin-track decision."[43] If Nitze and Kohl dared not face the wrath of German public opinion, there was another West German leader who would, and who would reveal that the emperor had no clothes.

Franz Josef Strauss, the Bavarian conservative leader, in an interview published in *Die Welt*, declared that he had long regarded the zero option as "utopian." He declared that the zero-option had "been invented by Helmut Schmidt" and adopted by the United States "only to soothe the German ally." In his view, US missiles must be deployed to counter the Soviet Union. "I take the view," he said, "that refusal of the Europeans to contribute their share to the military balance—that is, to accept intermediate-range missiles on European territory—would be an irreparable break within NATO. If we act as if we are living on neutral territory, we will be treated by America as neutrals."[44]

When Nitze and Kvitsinsky arrived in Geneva, each called upon the government of the other to make the next move, promising to give due consideration to whatever was put on the table as long as the result would be "an equal balance of forces." Indeed, Nitze went further, declaring that the United States was "not locked into the zero option," thereby indicating that the president

---

[43] James Markham, "US Missile Negotiator Confers in Bonn," *New York Times*, January 25, 1983, A3.
[44] Ibid.

was flexible.[45] However, in Washington, Hans-Dietrich Genscher, after meeting with the president, reaffirmed the zero option as "the best solution for Europe, for West Germany and for the West as a whole."[46]

While hoping that the Geneva talks would produce a "concrete result," Genscher stressed that NATO must be ready to deploy if the Soviets were not forthcoming. Furthermore, he said, referring to calls for postponement, "it must be clear that the date of schedule for deployment would not be changed, and no doubt should be cast about delay of that date." With these words, the foreign minister firmly aligned himself with his chancellor, removing the doubts about his position raised by his discussion of an interim solution. On the other hand, he disputed the idea that the United States should not offer new proposals until after the election. "What to do and when depends entirely on the negotiating situation, and we do not want it linked any way to the German elections."[47]

But, of course, it was. Despite all attempts by President Reagan, Chancellor Kohl, President Mitterrand, and others to beat back Andropov's peace offensive, the results had been meager. Scarcely more than a month before the West German elections, a *Newsweek* public opinion poll indicated that a 57 percent majority of the West German electorate believed that Western Europe "would be safer" if West Germany "moved toward neutralism," that only 37 percent believed that deployment should proceed on schedule if no agreement was reached by November, and 43 percent found neither Reagan nor Andropov "credible."[48]

The coming election, according to US officials, was a "toss up." The European peace movement was in full voice, flustered only briefly by Reagan's 1981 offer of the zero option. As an American commentator put it, "the protesters continue to seek safety in *no* numbers (for the West, that is) while condemning 'zero' as unfair to the Soviets. The majority of Germans 'appear virtually convinced that the Soviets are ready to negotiate seriously but that Reagan is not. In that sense, the Soviets have been winning the propaganda battle in West Germany.'"[49]

---

[45] William Drozdiak, "US Indicates Possible Shift in Missile Stance," *Washington Post*, January 26, 1983, A1.

[46] John Goshko, "Genscher Says Germany Backs US on Missiles," *Washington Post*, January 27, 1983, A26.

[47] Ibid.

[48] *Newsweek*, January 31, 1983, 17. This international poll, covering the US, France, West Germany, the Netherlands and Great Britain, was conducted by the Gallup Organization and its affiliates in Europe during January 17-19. Results also were reported in Frank E. Armbruster et al., *The Environment of the Long-Range Theater Nuclear Force Program, Its Opponents and the Effects of Specifics of the Program on Opposition* (Washington, DC: Defense Nuclear Agency, June 7, 1983), 147-148.

[49] James McCartney, "West Germany Deeply Torn by Debate over US Missiles," *Philadelphia Inquirer*, January 30, 1983, 1.

The Reagan administration had "put all its chips" on deployment, potentially courting "disaster," should Kohl be defeated. Kohl, struggling to conduct himself as the leader in charge of Bonn's destiny, but acutely sensitive to public opinion, was waffling. As he declared in an interview: "we don't want American missiles and we don't want Soviet missiles. We want negotiations." According to German commentator Joe Joffe, Kohl was "bravely holding on— but with crossed fingers. Who knows what the next intra-administration row (or campaign of leaks) will bring from Washington?"[50]

Regaining the Public Relations Initiative

At the end of the month, Vice President Bush began his twelve-day, seven-nation tour with the first stop in Bonn. Reading a statement at the airport, Bush affirmed the United States' commitment to Europe's security, genuine arms reductions, and openness to dialogue. Nevertheless, Kohl and his advisers were uncertain what to expect from Bush, but hoped that he would *not* make a major departure from the zero option. As one of the chancellor's closest advisors explained in an interview, "It's enough to give the impression that the Americans are ready to go forward. Our people are interested in détente with the Soviet Union. They are also interested in friendship with France and the United States."[51]

At his second stop in West Berlin, at the end of a televised dinner speech, Bush "unexpectedly" pulled out a letter from President Reagan. "An open letter to the people of Europe," it was an offer from the president to meet with Andropov "wherever and whenever he wants in order to sign an agreement banning US and Soviet intermediate-range, land-based nuclear missile weapons from the face of the earth." The president stated, "I make this offer out of a conviction that such an agreement would serve the interests of both sides and, most importantly, that the people of Europe want nothing more. I urge Mr. Andropov to accept it."[52]

Reagan's letter was no more than a restatement of the official US position, but it conveyed the impression of a president "ready to go forward." Kohl, in attendance, immediately applauded the offer and declared that he could speak for a majority of West Germans and many in East Germany in hoping that Reagan's offer would find "an open ear and outstretched hand" in Moscow. Reagan did not suggest a full-blown summit, something that Kohl had suggested, but Bush observed that it could not be "ruled out." For the moment, however, the main impact of Bush's trip was the welcome effort by the United States "to seize

---

[50] Josef Joffe, "Revising the 'Zero Option' in Europe," *Wall Street Journal*, January 27, 1983, 26.

[51] James Markham, "Bush Starts 7-Nation Trip in Bonn; Aim Is to Reassure Allies on Arms," *New York Times*, January 31, 1983, A7.

[52] "Reagan's Letter to Europeans," *New York Times*, February 1, 1983, A8.

the initiative from the Soviets in the battle for public opinion in western Europe."[53]

Andropov replied immediately to Reagan. In an interview with *Pravda*, he declared that "there is nothing new in President Reagan's proposal.... It is all about...the same 'zero option'" that the Soviet Union had already rejected. Asked whether he was willing to meet with Reagan to sign his proposed agreement, Andropov responded: "summit meetings have special significance to resolving complicated problems," but must not be a "propaganda game." A meeting would be useful, but not on condition that the Soviet Union consent to a "patently unacceptable" proposal. This, he concluded, "can only be regretted."[54]

In Brussels, after a stop in The Hague, Bush replied to Andropov. So far, he said, "the only argument I've heard against the zero option...is that the Soviet Union doesn't like it." That was not enough of a reason to abandon the proposal, the vice president insisted. He asserted, "If the Russians have another plan that would seriously address this question, President Reagan has said we would give it serious consideration. But, so far, all we have been offered is a policy that allows only a Soviet monopoly on these weapons and no western counterbalance."[55]

Bush's stop in Geneva, on February 4-5, however, was one of the most important stops of the trip, aside from the general intention to regain the public relations initiative. It had been arranged for him to meet privately with Soviet negotiators, Karpov and Kvitsinsky, who, with their delegations, each spent an hour with the vice president. The discussion with Kvitsinsky was crucial. Bush rejected the notion that if the United States deployed its weapons in December in the absence of an agreement, a "point of no return" would have been passed. "My answer to that...is that what goes in can come out."[56]

Asked about the possibility of an "intermediate step"—an "interim solution"—Bush responded: "If a sensible proposal is brought by the Soviets that fits that description, so be it." Heretofore the administration had avoided terms like "interim," "compromise," or "alternative" to focus attention on the zero-zero solution, which it considered to be best. Both the American delegation and European officials "were pleased" to hear Bush take the position that the administration was indicating a clear willingness not only to be flexible on achieving the maximum security with its allies, but also that the deadline at the end of the year would not terminate the negotiations.

Bush's statement that "what goes in can come out" was calculated to respond directly to the questions that the Russians had put to the American arms

---

[53] Michael Getler, "President Offers to Meet Andropov on Missiles Ban," *Washington Post*, February 1, 1983, A1.

[54] "Text of Andropov's Reply to Reagan's Letter," *New York Times*, February 2, 1983, A8.

[55] Michael Getler, "Bush Presses 'Zero-Zero' Arms Control Plan," *Washington Post*, February 3, 1983, A28.

[56] Michael Getler, "Missile Deployment Not Irreversible, Bush Tells West Europeans," *Washington Post*, February 6, 1983, A17.

control delegation the previous year. The thrust was to reaffirm the notion that deployment would be the next stage of the negotiation and not the end of it. There was, in short, no "point of no return." The response may have had a different impact than intended, encouraging the Soviets to proceed with their own plan to deploy missiles to Grenada, in the expectation that a negotiated removal of missiles from these locations would be the logical next step.

Meanwhile, Bush continued on his trip with visits to the Pope, where he emphasized the morality of the president's position, and with Mitterrand and Thatcher, whom he praised as staunch allies. While in London, he attempted to sum up his impressions. Without exception, he noted, "allied leaders had told him of their interest in an interim agreement…as a first step toward a total ban." At the same time, this position signaled a "rejection of demands for the total abandonment of deployment." Opposition leaders on the other hand, held a wider range of positions, but differences were not "frustratingly deep," and all "voiced allegiance to common Western values."[57]

There was no sense among them, Bush said, that Andropov was "soft," or "reasonable," but there had been "enormous skepticism" that he would be forthcoming with a compromise offer. Bush also felt that he had dispelled notions that President Reagan was not serious about arms control. His trip, he said, had "shored up the alliance in that regard." Finally, he concluded that the Soviets would "not be able to stop deployment through a public relations campaign." In his view, "this was not a viable option for the Soviet Union, not a viable possibility."

A few days following Bush's return, the president, having weighed the vice-president's report and recommendations, decided to "stick to his original proposal for banning all medium-range missiles from Europe at least until the March 6 West German elections." He may not offer a compromise "even then," White House officials said. A most important factor in the president's decision was Helmut Kohl, who was "understood not to have asked for anything specific from Washington by way of a new proposal before his election test." The president felt that "if Kohl is returned to office the Soviets will believe that the Allies are determined to deploy the new missiles and thus will negotiate more seriously at Geneva."[58]

Moscow's Pre-election Quiescence: Sacrificing a Pawn?

Meanwhile, following Bush's trip, the Soviets grew conspicuously silent on the question of the intermediate-range missile negotiations, though periodically raising proposals on matters related but not central to them. It became

---

[57] John Vinocur, "Europeans' Mood Depicted by Bush," *New York Times*, February 11, 1983, A3.
[58] Michael Getler, "President Firm on Arms, Eyes German Voting," *Washington Post*, February 16, 1983, A1.

increasingly evident that the Soviets would do nothing to assist Vogel's election challenge by taking a more flexible stance, instead holding adamantly to the position that Moscow would not compromise and that if the US deployed missiles, the risk of war would grow. The effect was to keep up pressure on popular sentiment against deployment but offer no reason to vote for Vogel over Kohl.

The case for US deployment and the realization that Moscow would not compromise was made powerfully clear by Bavarian premier Franz Josef Strauss. He saw deployment as "unavoidable" because "not the slightest progress has been achieved so far in Geneva." It was "necessary" to prevent "Soviet blackmail of Europe in the 1980s." If missiles were not deployed, "the rift between Bonn and Washington would be incurable." Furthermore, unless the missiles were deployed as scheduled, the Soviets would "hold the negotiating keys in their hands."[59] Strauss recounted that a conversation in Bonn the prior month with Soviet foreign minister Andrei Gromyko had convinced him that "Moscow had no intention of destroying any of its SS-20s." [60]

Reaffirming his support for Chancellor Kohl, he declared: "I say what Kohl thinks and he thinks what I say." As for the Social Democrats, it was putting it far too politely to say that Vogel was simply a "middle-class Philistine." He would take Germany "down the road toward de facto neutralization." A West Germany ruled by the SPD would mean "a farewell to democracy and a return to primitive forms of life." Reserving his harshest criticism for the Greens, he railed that they were "dropouts from school, society and human competition," whose only aim is to disrupt the parliamentary system that has ensured a long era of postwar political stability for West Germany.[61]

Attempting to present a more agreeable face, Moscow publicized an offer to withdraw 20,000 troops against 13,000 for the United States from Central Europe, as part of long-deadlocked Mutual and Balanced Forces Reduction talks that had been going on since 1973. In a rare move, Deputy Foreign Minister Victor Kompletkov held a news conference to make the announcement, leading Western diplomats to conclude that Moscow was attempting to influence the coming West German election by its offer. Western experts were quick to point out that Moscow's offer was not new and evaded the key issue that had deadlocked the talks for a decade.[62]

Moscow had refused to respond to long-standing Western estimates that there were 160,000 more Warsaw Pact troops deployed in Central Europe than Moscow admitted. Furthermore, the current offer fell short of an earlier 1979 US proposal that the Soviet Union withdraw 30,000 troops to 13,000 for the US.

---

[59] William Drozdiak, "Deployment of Missiles in Europe Is 'Unavoidable,' Strauss Says," *Washington Post*, February 17, 1983, A30.

[60] James M. Markham, "Strauss Jumps Off on Campaign Trail," *New York Times*, February 17, 1983, A3.

[61] Drozdiak, "Deployment of Missiles in Europe Is 'Unavoidable,' Strauss Says."

[62] Serge Schmemann, "Soviet Announces Offer on Troop Cuts," *New York Times*, February 19, 1983, 3.

Worse, the Soviet offer was even less than it initially seemed. Moscow suggested that the pullback be made "by mutual example, outside the framework of an agreement." Of course, it was pointed out, as there was no agreement on the total number of troops deployed by the Warsaw Pact, it would be impossible to verify the number withdrawn and without a formal agreement, troops could be returned at any time.

The derisory nature of the offer, coming as it did when all attention was focused on the missile question and the Soviet approach to disarmament, only reduced confidence in Moscow's promises and further undercut Vogel, who strove to preserve some credibility. At a news conference in Bonn, Vogel declared that the SPD opposed the "automatic" deployment of missiles if the talks produced no agreement by November. Vogel's remarks were in reply to President Reagan's of two days before, to the effect that West Germany's refusal to deploy missiles "would be a terrible setback to the cause of peace and disarmament." Taking what he thought was an independent stand, Vogel declared that

> The American president represents the interests of his land, and I represent German interests. German interests (call for) a result at negotiations in Geneva that would make stationing of the missiles unnecessary…there is no automatic stationing.[63]

Soviet foreign minister Gromyko, hosting visiting French foreign minister, Claude Cheysson, clearly forecast what the "result" of the negotiations would be, reaffirming Soviet rejection of the zero option. Attacking American "imperial ambitions" and charging Washington with "international brigandage," Gromyko insisted that Andropov's offer to balance Soviet missiles against British and French missiles was the only acceptable way forward. Cheysson, of course, disagreed, instead criticizing the Soviets for repressive policies in Afghanistan and Poland. France would negotiate over its missile forces, he said, but only after the Soviet Union and the United States reached agreement to reduce their "gigantic arsenals."[64]

Turning Point in Europe

The Russians clearly were losing ground in the public relations campaign for the West German electorate. Now it was they who were inflexible and dodging the issue. President Reagan sought to maintain the momentum. In a speech to the American Legion's annual conference in Washington, D.C., he declared the absolute inextricable bond between the United States and Western Europe. "Let

---

[63] "Leader in Bonn Casts Doubts on Missiles," *Washington Times*, February 18, 1983, A7.
[64] "Gromyko Attacks American Policies," *New York Times*, February 18, 1983, A3.

there be no doubt on either side of the Atlantic: the freedom and independence of America's allies remain as dear to us as our own."[65]

Stressing his commitment to arms reductions and the zero option as the best outcome, he declared that "ours is not a take-it-or-leave-it proposal." Our negotiations in Geneva were premised upon sound principles "supported by all the allies after long and careful consultation." These principles were that the "fair basis" of any agreement must include "equality of rights and limits" between the United States and the Soviet Union; British and French strategic weapons systems cannot be included; Soviet proposals that "have the effect" of shifting the threat from Europe to Asia were unacceptable; and, any agreement must be verifiable.

The Soviets immediately howled, digging their own hole of inflexibility ever deeper. Defense Minister Dmitri Ustinov, in an Armed Forces Day speech, declared that the threat of war, and "above all nuclear war," was increasing through the fault of "imperialist circles of the USA and its allies." He claimed that Washington "purposely held an inflexible stance in nuclear arms negotiations at Geneva so that deployment of new US missiles in Western Europe can be started late this year." But, the "hawkish imperialist circles" will never be able to achieve military superiority over the Soviet Union, he said. "If they challenge us" and deploy medium-range missiles in Western Europe, "the Soviet Union will be able to respond to this additional threat effectively and promptly."[66]

Foreign Minister Gromyko, attempting to counterbalance Ustinov's harsh rhetoric, claimed in a *Pravda* interview that the United States had not changed its attitude, "despite talk about adopting a more flexible position." He said that "regrettably, while there is talk, one fails so far to perceive any headway toward greater realism." Responding to Reagan, he said:

> We are for an accord conforming to the principle of equality and equal security, and if Washington gives up its insistence on breaking parity and adopts a constructive approach, there can be no doubt that an agreement is possible. It is now the turn of the United States to speak up.[67]

Gromyko also made what was Moscow's final appeal to West German voters to support a "just solution" on the missile question and thus demonstrate their "political maturity." He also rejected once again the idea that the Geneva negotiations would continue if deployment of missiles occurred. US deployments would mean a "qualitatively new situation," which "would actually undercut the nuclear arms talks."[68]

---

[65] "Excerpts from Reagan's Speech to Legionnaires," *New York Times*, February 23, 1983, A8.
[66] "Soviet Defense Chief Hints Missile Buildup," *Washington Times*, February 24, 1983, A7.
[67] "Gromyko Asks US Missile Offer," *New York Times*, February 24, 1983, A8.
[68] "Gromyko Statement," *FBIS Daily Report, Soviet Union*, February 24, 1983, AA 4-5.

Vogel, too, sensing that he had gotten too far out on a limb, attempted to prod President Reagan into keeping the missile issue in the forefront of voters' minds. He sent a letter, which was promptly leaked, to the president asking that he "make a counter-offer."[69] Reagan ignored it. The fact was, however, that it was a matter of too little, too late. The missile debate had already begun to "wither" from "burn-out syndrome" and the West German electorate was "subsiding into the normal humdrum pattern by which the electorate votes its pocketbook fears, not its nuclear fears."[70] Indeed, that "humdrum pattern" gave the Social Democrats only the slimmest prospects of victory.

Entering into the final week before the election, Vogel's only chance was for the SPD "to do what never has been done before in West German politics—out poll the Christian Democrats." A few weeks earlier, it had seemed briefly that Vogel could pull it off. His ratings had risen to nearly equal Kohl's as the missile mania hit its crest, but he had "peaked too soon." From the middle of February, Vogel's standing in the polls began to fall back to five-to-six points behind Kohl, as the debates increasingly focused on the issue of which party could provide the best economic management for an economy with an unemployment rate of 10.4 percent.

The election outcome was a decisive endorsement of Chancellor Kohl and a resounding defeat for Herr Vogel and the SPD. The CDU/CSU/FDP coalition of Kohl, Strauss, and Genscher won a 55.8 percent combined majority, against a 38.2 percent vote for the SPD, a 4.7 percent drop from the 42.9 percent of the vote won by Helmut Schmidt in 1980. The radical Greens captured 5.6 percent, barely exceeding the 5 percent minimum to gain representation in the Parliament.

As the *New York Times* characterized it on its editorial page, "missile calculations aside, a new era of German politics is clearly at hand. Mr. Kohl's Christian Democrats return to preeminence after thirteen years in the wilderness."[71] Indeed, the Christian Democrats out-polled the Social Democrats in every region except the small city-states of Bremen and Hamburg, traditional strongholds of the German left. Even in North Rhine-Westphalia, heart of the Ruhr steel industry, where the SPD held an absolute majority in the state legislature, the CDU emerged as the biggest party.[72]

Chancellor Kohl viewed the election as a double endorsement. On the one hand, he said, it was "a clear mandate to continue our politics of freedom and peace and our close friendship with the US." The election's outcome would contribute to the West's resolve in the missile negotiations, and if "there isn't any success in the negotiations, then we will station the missiles." On the other hand,

---

[69] Henry Trewhitt, "For the West, a Test of Unity," *Baltimore Sun*, February 27, 1983, K1.
[70] Hal Piper, "Politics and Missiles," *Baltimore Sun*, February 27, 1983, K1.
[71] "German Votes and Chits," *New York Times*, March 8, 1983, 19.
[72] James Markham, "Bonn Voting: Second Look," *New York Times*, March 8, 1983, 1.

Kohl interpreted his victory as approval of his plans to stimulate the economy with investment incentives and cuts in government welfare spending.[73]

Moscow reacted to Kohl's victory with a barrage of commentaries denying the proposition that his election represented a warrant for deploying the missiles—only Andropov's plan offered a way out for West Germany to avoid the "nuclear gallows." Bonn was entering a very dangerous period, for Washington "might fire its missiles against the Bonn Government's will." In that case, "the population of West Germany becomes, as it were, a hostage of the Pentagon, which would decide its fate." In this way, "Washington would turn West Germany into a target for a retaliatory nuclear strike."[74] West Germany was a target perhaps, but it was also the foundation of the Western Alliance.

Reagan's Counteroffensive

Soviet and American sparring over respective positions in the arms control negotiations would continue during the months leading up to the November deadline, as war scare tensions rose. Each side periodically suggested flexibility, implicitly nodding to the growing nuclear freeze movement, but not altering fundamental policy positions. Both sides understood, however, that Kohl's election marked the placement of a strategic foundation-stone in the US position and that of the Western Alliance. It meant that barring an extraordinary turn of events, or an agreement, President Reagan could count on Helmut Kohl to carry out the NATO decision on missile deployment in the fall.

Based on Kohl's electoral victory in Europe, President Reagan now proceeded to implement the strategy outlined in NSDD-75, to "contain and over time reverse Soviet expansionism" and exploit Soviet weaknesses—internal and external, political and economic, military and psychological. Washington considered the most threatening elements of Soviet strategy to be a potential "breakout" from the ABM Treaty that would alter the strategic weapons balance; the prospective deployment of intermediate range nuclear missiles in the Caribbean; and an effort to incorporate Iran into Moscow's orbit. In the spring of 1983, Reagan put policies into play to counter each of these, and to upgrade American military readiness and war-fighting capability.

Each of the policies the president would activate had undergone lengthy gestation periods and had been telegraphed earlier. On January 17, 1983, for example, a major news story was leaked to the *Chicago Tribune*, disclosing the "secret nuclear strategy" of the United States. The document was immediately authenticated by Pentagon spokesman, Henry Catto, who deplored the fact that "people leak this kind of thing." Titled "Fiscal 1984-1988 Defense Guidance," the

---

[73] Roger Thurow, "Kohl Promises to Maintain Ties with Alliance," *Wall Street Journal*, March 8, 1983, 38.
[74] John Burns, "Soviet Says Kohl Received No Mandate on Missiles," *New York Times*, March 8, 1983, 8 and Morton Kondracke, "German Showdown: Reagan Sweeps, Andropov Weeps," *Wall Street Journal*, March 10, 1983, 31.

planning document discussed US rearmament and the need to be able to prevail in a "protracted nuclear war" against the Soviet Union. Major emphasis was also placed on the ability to be able to wage war "effectively" from outer space.[75]

Among its major points, the guidance declared that the United States would redress the imbalance of power with the Soviet Union, "if need be without arms control." Plans should be readied to provide the necessary men and equipment "to fight the Soviets on several fronts for an 'indefinite period.'" A "Soviet invasion of the vital Persian Gulf oil fields would ignite a 'major conflict' between the United States and the Soviet Union" and the United States should be prepared to deploy US forces "should it appear that the security of access to Persian Gulf oil is threatened," even without a Soviet invasion.

Anticipating "major economic difficulties" that will confront the Soviet Union in two to three years, the United States should exploit Soviet deficiencies by opening "new areas of major military competition," aimed at making Soviet arsenals "obsolete." An anti-satellite weapon "should achieve" operational status by fiscal 1987 and "space-based weapons" would "add a new dimension to our military capabilities." Regarding current weapons systems, in seeking a viable basing option for the MX missile, modification of the ABM Treaty "should not be ruled out." Finally, a nuclear war begun at sea would "not necessarily remain limited to the sea."

The defense guidance actually forecast three of the main areas on which the Reagan administration would focus in coming months: the strategic breakout issue—particularly missile defense—the Soviet threat to Iran, and, more subtly, Central America. The connection of a nuclear war at sea to Central America would become abundantly clear as the United States concentrated carrier task groups off the Caribbean and Pacific coasts of Nicaragua through the summer and early fall of the year and spoke frequently of the possibility of quarantine and blockade against Soviet arms deliveries to Managua.

The very day the defense guidance story appeared, the president signed NSDD-75, the first codification of American strategy toward the Soviet Union since NSC-68 laid out the Containment strategy in 1950. Reagan's strategy went considerably beyond the Containment strategy, however, explicitly emphasizing the aim of prevailing over the Soviet Union by actively weakening its economic base, which had not been part of Containment. NSDD-75 committed the United States to "contain and over time reverse Soviet expansionism"; "attempt to reach agreements which protect and enhance US interests…consistent with the principle of strict reciprocity" and "promote…the process of change in the Soviet Union toward a more pluralistic political and economic system."[76]

---

[75] "US Arms Plan Bared; Secret Nuclear Strategy Told," *Chicago Tribune*, January 17, 1983, 1.

[76] "US Relations with the USSR," National Security Decision Directive Number 75, January 17, 1983, in Norman Bailey, *The Strategic Plan That Won the Cold War* (Mclean, VA: The Potomac Foundation, 1999), 27-35. The directive can also be found in Christopher Simpson, *National Security Directives of the Reagan and Bush*

Arms control agreements, NSDD-75 declared, were not ends in themselves, but must serve US national security objectives to maintain a military balance. A main priority was to maximize restraining leverage over Soviet behavior. The United States must insist that internally, "Moscow address the full range of US concerns about Soviet internal behavior and human rights violations." Designed for the "long haul," that is, five-to-ten years, the president envisaged no early improvement in relations with Moscow. Indeed, his strategy was "unlikely to yield a rapid breakthrough in bilateral relations with the Soviet Union."

The objective of the United States was nothing less than victory. The nation would build up its military power to the point where "Soviet leaders perceive that the US is determined never to accept a second place or a deteriorating military posture." American military power must be "strong and flexible enough to affect Soviet calculations in a wide variety of contingencies." In Europe, for example, the Soviets will face a "reinvigorated NATO" and in the Far East be "unable to count on a secure flank in a global war."

The economic policy of the United States "must serve strategic and foreign policy goals as well as economic interests." Above all, East-West economic relations must not "facilitate the Soviet military buildup." The West must not subsidize the Soviet economy, "unduly easing the burden of Soviet resource allocation decisions." The West must "minimize the potential for Soviet exercise of reverse leverage on Western countries based on trade, energy supply, and financial relationships."

It must be American policy to break down the Soviet alliance system and "wherever possible to encourage Soviet allies to distance themselves from Moscow in foreign policy and to move toward democratization domestically." In Eastern Europe, the United States would seek to "loosen Moscow's hold on the region"; in Afghanistan, keep maximum pressure on the Soviets; and elsewhere "limit" the destabilizing activities of Moscow's third-world allies, like Cuba.

The United States would seek "enhanced strategic cooperation and policy coordination with China," which "continues to support US efforts to strengthen the world's defenses against Soviet expansionism." Toward these ends, the United States would continue to pursue a "substantially liberalized technology transfer policy" toward Beijing and to sell military equipment on a "case-by-case basis."

Ever mindful of the objectives of the new world order faction which opposed his strategy, the president inserted specific language into the directive to guard against "pressure" for a change in policy "in the absence of dramatic near-term victories in the US effort to moderate Soviet behavior." He warned that "there will be appeals from important segments of domestic opinion for a more 'normal' US-Soviet relationship," which must be resisted. Despite this specific

---

Administrations: The Declassified History of US Political and Military Policy, 1981-1991 (Boulder: Westview, 1995), 255-63, but its description, 227-28, bears little relationship to the document itself, claiming that "it left the door open to improved US-USSR relations if the Soviets met US terms."

injunction, however, demands for precisely that approach arose immediately from his secretary of state, George Shultz.

The Attempt to Harness Shultz

According to Shultz, it was at this moment in time that President Reagan had decided to take a more accommodating stance toward the Soviet Union.[77] The specific evidence for this claim is said to have been an impromptu dinner meeting on February 12, 1983, between the President, Shultz and their wives. A powerful snowstorm the night before prompted the president and his wife to cancel plans to spend the weekend at Camp David and, instead, invite Shultz and his wife to dinner in the family quarters of the White House. It was during this dinner that "it was clear to Shultz that the president was interested in undertaking personal negotiations with the Soviet Union and ready to move toward improved relations."[78]

While this seems unremarkable today, given the reversal of strategy toward accommodation with Moscow that occurred in 1987, when placed in the context of 1983, an altogether different interpretation emerges which is far more faithful to the record, and especially to the just-signed strategy document, NSDD-75.

The United States and the Soviet Union were on a collision course, as the events in this volume attest. The two countries were already entering the early stages of crisis, which would reach at least its first climax with the Pershing II deployment in November. No one could anticipate what other clashes would precede that scheduled for the fall, but everyone expected that Moscow would fulfill its promise to respond promptly to US actions in Europe afterward with bellicose moves at one or more places, including, as the Soviets had repeatedly threatened, in the western hemisphere.

One of the explicit charges of NSDD-75 was to arm for protracted confrontation with the Soviet Union. The president was determined to defeat the Soviet challenge without precipitating World War III and would use every arrow in the nation's quill to accomplish that task. Thus, as will be shown below, the president would shortly set in motion a myriad of policies designed to spoil, disrupt, divert, intimidate, and otherwise stymie Soviet endeavors. It was only natural to expect Moscow to do the same. To ensure that the war of nerves would not spiral out of control, it was imperative that the leaderships be in contact during this period of impending crisis to avoid any misunderstandings and the president sought to open the door to direct communication.

---

[77] George Shultz, *Turmoil and Triumph: My Years as Secretary of State* (New York: Scribner's, 1993), 164-65.

[78] Don Oberdorfer, *The Turn: From the Cold War to a New Era* (New York: Poseidon Press, 1991), 17, based on his conversations with Shultz, makes this identical argument.

It was in this sense and for this purpose that the president agreed to Secretary Shultz's suggestion during the dinner on February 12 that he bring Ambassador Dobrynin to see him. Reagan wanted to keep the meeting secret from the public, but declared that he intended to tell Dobrynin that "if Andropov is willing to do business, so am I." Members of the president's inner circle, particularly NSC chief Judge Clark, sought to dissuade the president from taking this step at this time, but he refused. When, three days later, he met with Dobrynin, the message he conveyed was: "if you are ready to move forward, so are we."[79]

Shultz, of course, immediately sought to use the opportunity to turn US policy toward the "more normal" course explicitly warned against by NSDD-75. "I drew up a set of ideas for the president presenting a longer-term view of our relations with the Soviets."

> I urged that we work to set up a systematic dialogue, consider renewing some languishing agreements, point toward a possible Reagan-Gromyko meeting, reopen the idea of reciprocal consulates in Kiev and New York, and consider a new agreement on cultural exchange. Above all, we had to devise a clear strategy on human rights. We could not continue simply to vilify the Soviets publicly and expect them to respond by doing the things we wanted. It was time to start some quiet diplomacy.[80]

The president, however, was not attempting to establish a "more normal" relationship with the Soviets. Regarding Andropov, as he notes in his memoir, he had indeed "decided to experiment with some personal diplomacy using back channels to the Kremlin, outside the spotlight of publicity, through which both sides could speak frankly without the posturing and attempts at diplomatic face-saving that usually accompanied formal dealings...." At the same time, in an effort to combat the growing influence of the nuclear freeze movement in the United States, Reagan was determined "to take our case to the people, only this time we are declassifying some of our reports on the Soviets and can tell the people a few frightening facts: We are still dangerously behind the Soviets and getting farther behind." [81]

Thus, the purpose of president's Orlando speech to the National Association of Evangelicals on March 8, in which he described the Soviet Union as an "evil empire," was not simply "to remind the Soviets we knew what they were up to," and "to let Andropov know we recognized the Soviets for what they

---

[79] Shultz, *Turmoil and Triumph*, 164-65. Shultz thought "my meeting with the president and Dobrynin had generated an internecine struggle in the White House between Clark, who saw it as bad policy, and Deaver, who saw it as good politics. I saw it as good policy and would leave the politics to the president."
[80] Ibid., 168.
[81] Reagan, *An American Life*, 567-68.

were," but also to "reach" those in the United States who were "being told the path to peace was via a freeze on...nuclear weapons that...would leave the Soviets in a position of nuclear superiority...." Reagan declared that the United States would rise to the Soviet "challenge" and closed his speech with these words: "I believe that Communism is another sad, bizarre chapter in history whose last pages even now are being written."[82]

Thus, contrary to the view that President Reagan had decided to change strategy and *improve* relations with the Soviet Union in the spring of 1983, and/or that he was surreptitiously abandoning his public position as well as his own people in the White House, the truth is he sought to enlist Shultz's, perhaps unwitting, cooperation in opening a back channel to Andropov to ensure that events would not spiral out of control as the two countries moved inexorably toward confrontation.[83]

It is telling that the day before his dinner meeting with Shultz on February 11, the president had met with the Joint Chiefs and instructed them to "develop a missile defense proposal and report the results of their work as soon as possible."[84] He had not conveyed this decision to Shultz, or included him in his thinking. Nor did he ask for his advice. As Oberdorfer notes, "the president mentioned the possibility of a defensive shield over the United States, but the secretary of state was not aware of the discussion with the Joint Chiefs of Staff and did not realize that Reagan's remarks had any immediate or operational significance."[85]

Star Wars Trumps Breakout

With the lines of communication open, President Reagan now began to put into play a series of policies designed to counter "what they were up to." A large component of these policies lay in their psychological impact. It was important to convey to Soviet leaders that the president understood what their objectives were and to demonstrate that the United States had the means and the will to thwart them. The first step was to meet the Soviet drive to missile defense breakout with a US one, and thereby throw into question the very basis of the strategy the Soviets had been pursuing since 1971: the attempt to parlay growing missile power into geopolitical gain, a strategy which depended upon an American commitment not to defend its own land-based missiles.

At the strategic weapons level, particularly in land-based missiles, the United States was at a severe disadvantage. While the nation still held a significant edge in long-range bombers and missile submarines, Moscow had acquired the

---

[82] Ibid., 568-70.

[83] Shultz, *Turmoil and Triumph*, 267, thought that "the president was a prisoner of his own staff," which was why he wanted to keep his Soviet initiative secret.

[84] Donald R. Baucom, "Hail to the Chiefs: The Untold History of Reagan's SDI Decision," Heritage Foundation *Policy Review*, no. 53 (Summer 1990), 72.

[85] Oberdorfer, *The Turn*, 27.

capability to destroy the U.S land-based missile system. The Soviets could not yet simultaneously destroy all three legs of the "triad," and the US air and sea-based weapons systems would survive an attack on the land-based missiles, but bombers and sub-launched missiles were not powerful and accurate enough to target Soviet missile silos.[86]

The growing danger in Moscow's drive toward a national missile defense system was the capability to defend against the entire triad of US retaliatory forces. If the Soviet Union were to hold not only the sword of Damocles, but also brandish the shield of Athena, the United States would no longer be capable of retaliating against a nuclear attack. Nuclear deterrence would have ended. As Baucom put it: "if the US did not respond in some way to the growing threat to its ICBMs, it risked sending a signal to the Soviets that America would acquiesce to an apparent Soviet drive for strategic dominance."[87]

There were only two ways the United States could respond—either attempt to erase the Soviet Union's offensive advantage by increasing its own missile force, or defend that force to preserve a prompt retaliatory capability with all legs of the triad. Attempting to catch up would not work because the Soviet Union could stay ahead by simply matching the US buildup. The decision to deploy a modest addition to the land-based force, the MX, was not designed to erase the Soviet advantage because it was not large enough, although it was accurate. Besides, it was beset with basing problems. There was no basing mode that would not leave the missile vulnerable to attack. Indeed, it may have been the realization that catching up was impossible that moved the American leadership away from MAD.

But there was a more serious objection. Adding to the land-based missile force contradicted long-term strategic weapons strategy, which was to shift the main deterrent force to the sea—that is, to the Trident II/D-5 weapons system. When deployed, the United States would have erased the window of vulnerability and reestablished a favorable nuclear balance. The catch was that this weapons system would not become operational until 1989. The question therefore was: what could be done now to deter the Soviets from acting on their advantage in the near term? Reagan's answer was to shift the strategic paradigm, with the decision to develop a ballistic missile defense.

This was the Strategic Defense Initiative, which President Reagan announced in a major speech on March 23. Mindful of the dangers of pairing offensive and defensive systems and insisting that his plan was consistent with the ABM Treaty, the president said that he was proceeding with a plan "to counter the awesome Soviet missile threat with measures that are defensive." Moving decisively beyond the strategy of mutual deterrence and the threat of massive retaliation, the president sought through the ingenuity of the scientific community to develop a defense which would "intercept and destroy strategic ballistic

---

[86] For discussion of the power and accuracy of American strategic weapons, see Richard C. Thornton, *Ronald Reagan: Revolution Ascendant*, chapter 5.

[87] Baucom, "Hail to the Chiefs," 69.

missiles before they reached our own soil or that of our allies." To that end, he was:

> directing a comprehensive and intensive effort to define a long-term research and development program to begin to achieve our ultimate goal of eliminating the threat posed by strategic nuclear missiles. This could pave the way for arms control measures to eliminate the weapons themselves. We seek neither military superiority nor political advantage. Our only purpose—one all people share—is to search for ways to reduce the danger of nuclear war.[88]

Those committed to deterrence and to mutual assured destruction as the basis for accommodation to the Soviet Union attacked and derided the decision as the president's harebrained idea, tagging it with the sobriquet of "Star Wars," and insisting that it would never work.[89] Secretary Shultz was among them, attempting to scuttle the speech at the last minute when he learned of the president's intention. Shultz rightly understood that the president's decision implied a revolution in America's strategic doctrine. He argued that the president's science adviser, Jay Keyworth, had only a "limited understanding of strategic doctrine," and that the Joint Chiefs of Staff were "in no position to make what amounts to a scientific judgment."[90]

As noted above, President Reagan had not kept the secretary informed of his plans. It had been precisely the monthly meetings with the Joint Chiefs, with whom he had explored the problems of strategic doctrine and come to the realization of American vulnerability, that caused him to agree that there was need to shift to strategic defense. Nor had he informed him of the briefings of his science adviser, Jay Keyworth, who had convinced the president that as a result of advances in computing power and systems, "the 1980s would see an explosive growth in America's ability to identify, track, and intercept incoming missiles."[91]

Thus, while Reagan's decision had seemed to be a bold gamble, it had been made on the basis of technology that had been under development for many years. Scientific research had reached the point where it was feasible to pursue the technology further. It was understood that it would take twenty years to produce a workable system, perhaps longer. Nevertheless, rather than compete with the Soviets in the area where they held the advantage—in land-based missiles—the president decided to emphasize the area where the United States held the advantage—in high technology.

---

[88] "President's Speech on Military Spending and a New Defense," *New York Times*, March 24, 1983, 20.

[89] See, for example, Francis Fitzgerald, *Way out There in the Blue: Reagan, Star Wars and the End of the Cold War* (New York: Simon & Schuster, 2000).

[90] Shultz, *Turmoil and Triumph*, 250-52.

[91] Thomas C. Reed, *At the Abyss: An Insider's History of the Cold War* (New York: Ballantine, 2004), 255.

Of course, the president could have said nothing, continued with the research, and waited until the technology had been further developed. The significance of announcing the decision in March 1983 was supremely political and psychological, to declare to the Russians that their strategy of attempting to employ missile power in a coercive mode had no future. The public discussion of US technology that ensued revealed the superiority of US technology, convincing the Soviet leadership that the United States could accomplish what the Soviets themselves were striving to accomplish, and do it sooner.

The essential public argument was not whether an ABM system would work, but how well it would work. While critics thought they had won the argument when they "proved" that a leakproof defense was impossible, they had demonstrated *inter alia* that Soviet strategy would not work because it depended upon the perceived ability to execute a massive strike against the United States, especially against its land-based missiles. Even a partial defense that protected the missile fields was enough to defeat Soviet strategy.

Andropov replied quickly to Reagan's announcement, correctly describing it as "a bid to disarm the Soviet Union," which Moscow would never permit. He warned that Reagan's decision to "sever" the relationship between "mutual restraint" in the field of missile defense and limitation of offensive nuclear missiles, if pursued, "would actually open the floodgates to a runaway race of all types of strategic arms, both offensive and defensive."[92]

Perhaps in an effort to distract attention from the runaway offensive and defensive buildups of the Soviet Union, Andropov resorted to a personal attack on the president, a rarity in discourse between national leaders. He charged that Reagan had told a "deliberate lie" that the Soviet Union had broken its unilateral freeze commitment on medium-range missiles. He referred to Reagan's "impudent distortions" of Soviet policy and characterized Washington's attempts to "fight and win nuclear wars as 'not just irresponsible, it is insane.'" Moscow was the aggrieved party.

The shrill response of Soviet leaders revealed a fundamental concern that would only grow over time. They were fully conversant with both their own missile defense efforts as well as American technology and soon became convinced that the United States could deploy a missile defense—a conviction that in little over a year would lead them to abandon the strategy of missile coercion. Before they made that monumental choice, however, they would go to the brink of war to wring every ounce of benefit from their huge, decades-long investment in missile power.

Intelligence Games

In July 1981, at the Ottawa summit, President Reagan had been the recipient of an unrequited gift of what would turn out to be of enormous

---

[92] John Burns, "Andropov Says US Is Spurring a Race in Strategic Arms," *New York Times*, March 27, 1983, A1.

significance. Newly elected President François Mitterrand, hoping to demonstrate his *bona fides* and ease Washington's concerns about his decision to include four members of the French Communist Party in his forty-four-man cabinet, had turned over information from a Soviet intelligence agent whom the French had recruited. The agent, Colonel Vladimir I. Vetrov, was assigned the task of evaluating the technology the Soviets were acquiring from the West.[93] It was a bonanza.

As a defector-in-place, Vetrov provided information on the vast Soviet technology collection program, designated Line-X, and supplied the names of hundreds of KGB agents stationed around the world as well as the names of many of their recruits in the West. Upon studying Soviet collection requirements, it became painfully clear, as NSC staffer Gus Weiss put it, "our science was supporting their national defense," especially in radar, computers, machine tools, and semiconductors. The information also showed the extent of Soviet penetration of Western and Japanese scientific laboratories, factories, and government agencies during the seventies period of détente.

Armed with the knowledge of what the Soviets were after, their "shopping list" as it were, Weiss devised a scheme whereby the United States could turn the tables on the Soviets. In early 1982, President Reagan authorized Casey to execute Weiss's plan to make available to the Soviets the technology they were searching for—but with a twist. Enlisting the enthusiastic cooperation of scores of America's corporate leaders in this top-secret project, computer chips were made with viruses buried deep inside and timed to self-destruct, or operate erratically, months after installation. Software programs were written in the same fashion and scientific and industrial plans were drawn deliberately flawed.

An early target was the highly computerized system running the new Soviet gas pipeline, which Reagan was determined to delay if not disrupt as part of his larger effort to curtail Soviet hard-currency earnings.[94] In mid-1982, just as the president was squeezing European and Japanese firms to prevent the sale of natural gas technology to the Soviets, an explosion occurred on the pipeline. Detected by US satellites, it was "the most monumental non-nuclear explosion and fire ever seen from space."[95] Over the next year and a half, other "unexplained" explosions followed, severely hampering Soviet domestic economic performance.[96]

At first the Soviets were confused, but soon realized that some of the technology their clandestine services were stealing from the West was in fact booby-trapped. They had no way of knowing which equipment was reliable and which had been tampered with. The very technology the Soviets thought would save them could ruin them—everything was suspect. How much of American

---

[93] Gus Weiss, "The Farewell Dossier," *Studies in Intelligence* 39, no. 5 (1996).

[94] For the account of President Reagan's efforts to derail the Soviet gas pipeline, see Thornton, *Revolution Ascendant*, chap. 9.

[95] Reed, *At the Abyss*, 269.

[96] "Additional Blasts Cited in USSR," *Washington Times*, July 12, 1984, A6.

computer technology had the Soviets incorporated into their own missile and anti-missile systems? Could it be relied upon? Checking and reprogramming would take months. Their only choice was to diversify.

And diversify they did. By the spring of 1983, the KGB, collaborating closely with their East German, Czech, and Polish counterparts, intensified their collection effort to satisfy more of their technology requirements in Europe and Asia, especially Japan. A West German counterespionage official observed: "we see a multiplication and an intensification in the technology sector that must reflect unusual pressure to perform.... It just wasn't there before in the same degree. They've become very aggressive."[97]

By the spring, President Reagan was ready to let the other shoe drop, as United States government representatives began informing allied counterparts of the identities of the KGB agents in their own countries tasked with the clandestine acquisition of technology. There followed the wholesale expulsion of over a hundred Soviet agents from the West, up by a factor of five over 1982, and the most in any single year since the United Kingdom expelled 105 agents in 1971. The total was probably higher because some countries, like West Germany, expelled agents quietly so as not to undermine *Ostpolitik*. There were also unconfirmed reports that Italy, which had quietly ejected eight Soviets on espionage in recent months, had "drawn up a list of 100 suspected spies."[98]

Moscow, which characterized the expulsions as "spy mania," and as a "US-orchestrated course of confrontation," was "stunned by Western actions that included the expulsions of Soviet personnel from France, Australia, Britain, Italy, the United States and Spain—all in a relatively short period. [Furthermore], there have been allegations of Soviet KGB secret police activities in other places in Western Europe, as well as Japan, Indonesia and Malaysia."[99] In France, which had expelled forty-seven diplomats on April 5, an official declared that "the Soviets were just getting too blatant. It's really a question of enough is enough. The Soviets are trying to steal anything they can get their hands on."[100]

In this context of worldwide expulsions of Soviet agents occurred significant developments in Iran. The previous year, in early June, Vladimir Kuzichkin, one of Moscow's high-level KGB agents stationed in Iran, had defected to the United Kingdom.[101] British authorities promptly shared his information on Soviet plans for revolution in Iran with the United States and the

---

[97] John Vinocur, "The K.G.B. Goes on the Offensive and the West Begins Striking Back," *New York Times*, July 24, 1983, A1.

[98] Peter Almond, "Ejection of Soviets for Spying Gathers Worldwide Momentum," *Washington Times*, May 20, 1983, A1.

[99] Dusko Doder, "Soviets See Western Spy Charges as US Attack on New Leader," *Washington Post*, April 27, 1983, A15; and "Webster Says Soviet Spies Total 1,000," *Washington Post*, April 25, 1983, A20.

[100] Almond, "Ejection of Soviets [...]."

[101] Vladimir Kuzichkin, *Inside the KGB: My Life in Soviet Espionage* (New York: Ivy Books, 1990), 369.

president, himself interested in rebuilding ties to Iran, decided to pass relevant information, particularly as it related to plans, agents, and the Tudeh Party, on to Khomeini.[102]

The result was entirely predictable. Having already succeeded in eliminating the threat to the regime from the Mujahedin and Fedayeen in 1981-82, and now armed with information supplied by American and British intelligence, Khomeini moved forcefully to decapitate the Tudeh (Communist) Party from early in 1983. Of a total Tudeh membership estimated at 10,000, over a thousand Tudeh Party leaders and rank and file were arrested. Many were brought before a military tribunal, promptly sentenced, and executed.[103] Over a hundred military and police officials were also arrested. All were charged with spying for the KGB and preparing to overthrow the regime. Arrests, trials, and sentencing continued through the year.[104]

In early May, Khomeini turned on Moscow, expelling eighteen Soviet diplomats and military attaches for spying. At the same time, Iran's revolutionary prosecutor-general announced that the Tudeh Party had been dissolved because of its espionage activities. There followed a series of televised trials of Tudeh Party leaders who confessed to "spying for the Soviet Union and conspiring to overthrow the regime of Ayatollah Ruhollah Khomeini."[105] The Soviet adamantly denied any connection to the Tudeh Party, and any intention to conspire against the regime, but took no retaliatory action.[106]

The roll-up of the Soviet apparatus in Iran along with its controllers was, perhaps, the most serious blow to date to Moscow's plans. It meant that for the third year in a row, the strategy of creating a revolutionary situation in Iran in which its minions, the Tudeh, could seize power had failed. The destruction of the Soviet apparatus inside Iran occurred just as the Soviet Union was building the capacity to isolate Iran from external influence, while also generating the ability to exert pressure on Tehran from all quarters—all while Iranian forces mounted yet another drive to invade Iraq.

On February 7, Iranian forces launched "Operation Before Dawn" a four-division thrust against the Iraqi Fourth Army deployed near the town of Faqih,

---

[102] Gary Sick, "Iran's Quest for Superpower Status," *Foreign Affairs* 65, no. 4 (Spring 1987): 709.

[103] "Tudeh Party Members Executed in Iran," *Xinhua Overseas General News Service*, February 25, 1983. See also Zalmay Khalilzad, "Islamic Iran: Soviet Dilemma," *Problems of Communism* 33, no. 1 (January-February 1984):1-20.

[104] "Arrests of Iran's Communist Party Leaders Confirmed," *Xinhua General Overseas News Service*, February 9, 1983; and "Trial of Tudeh Party Members Continues," *FBIS Daily Report, South Asia*, December 22, 1983, I 4.

[105] "Iran Orders Expulsion of 18 Soviets for Spying," *Baltimore Sun*, May 5, 1983, A4; and "More Iranian Tudeh Party Cadres Make Confessions," *Xinhua General Overseas News Service*, May 3, 1983.

[106] "Keyhan Responds to Pravda on Tudeh Links," *FBIS Daily Report, South Asia*, May 9, 1983, I 1-2

two hundred miles southeast of Baghdad. The objective was to drive a wedge
between Baghdad and Basra. Declared by Majlis Speaker Ayatollah Rafsanjani to
be "the final military operation that will determine the final destiny of the region,"
it failed. The Iraqi command claimed to have decimated two Iranian divisions,
killing 7,000 troops and destroying "large numbers of tanks."[107]

Meanwhile, the Soviet Union continued to strengthen its ring around
Iran. In Syria, in the context of doubling the size of Syria's armed forces following
the Israeli attacks the previous year, the Soviets deployed, for the first time outside
their home territory, the SA-5 anti-aircraft missile. The long-range missile could
attack aircraft attempting to enter the region from the Eastern Mediterranean. The
missile sites were manned by several thousand Russian personnel. By the spring
of 1983, an integrated air defense network composed of over 100 sites of SA-5s,
6s, 8s, 9s, and 11s, and deployment of MiG-27 interceptors had been activated in
Syria and controlled from Moscow.[108]

At the same time, the Soviets continued to build regional military
leverage, commencing construction in Soviet Central Asia of "two or three new
bases for SS-20 intermediate-range nuclear missiles." Each missile base housed
nine missiles armed with three warheads; three bases would give the Soviets 54
missiles and 81 warheads. With its variable range of 500 to 3,000 miles, the SS-
20 could target every significant objective in Iran.[109] Moscow would be able to
exert pressure from without, but no longer could expect to call upon faithful
followers within Iran to heed their call.

In Afghanistan, Soviet forces began a major offensive in the western part
of the country around Herat, near the Iranian border. The drive near the Iranian
border followed heavy air strikes by Soviet planes "on Herat areas suspected of
sheltering Moslem guerrillas opposed to the Government of President Babrak
Karmal." The Soviet action came amid a general upsurge of fighting in the country
in Kabul, Kandahar, Gazni, and Mazar-i-Sharif.[110] It was nevertheless evident that
the Soviet Union was able to direct military power from Afghanistan into Iran, a
threat which forced Tehran to maintain a substantial force along the Afghan
border.

By the spring of 1983, then, two developments were clear. On the one
hand, Iranian forces were unable to make headway against the determined
defenses of Iraq, which increasingly employed its air and artillery supremacy, as
well as mounted armored counterthrusts to disrupt Iranian positions. Although

---

[107] Richard Preece, *The Iran-Iraq War: Implications for US Policy*, Congressional
Research Service Issue Brief Number IB84016 (Washington, DC: Library of
Congress; Congressional Research Service, 1984), 6-7.

[108] Avigdor Haselkorn, *Evolution and Implications of Soviet Military Presence in
Syria* (Los Angeles: Analytical Assessments Corporation, 1984), 13-15.

[109] Michael Getler, "Soviets Building 2 or 3 SS20 Bases in Asia," *Washington Post*,
April 30, 1983, A2.

[110] "Major Soviet-Led Drive Is Reported in Afghan War," *New York Times*, April 21,
1983, A11.

Iran increased the use of regular army units in these attacks, they were still accompanied by "massed frontal infantry assaults on the Iraqi lines, without proper armoured, artillery or air support."[111] The second development was the successful round up of internal dissidents, which considerably dimmed, if not extinguished, the prospects for a pro-Soviet internal upheaval against the regime.

The United States had spoiled several key elements of Soviet plans. At the strategic weapons level, President Reagan had established the basis for defeating the Soviet drive for strategic weapons supremacy. The decision to pursue SDI meant that the strategy based upon nuclear coercion would not succeed. Indeed, the coming deployment of the Pershing II alone meant that the Soviet Union could not execute an all-out strike against US-land-based missiles without suffering prompt and substantial, hard-target retaliatory attacks. Thus, from both the offensive and defensive perspectives, Reagan's actions had begun to close the window of vulnerability, although it was not yet fully closed. Still, the president was sufficiently confident to declare, during a weekly radio talk, that "any Soviet quest for nuclear superiority will not work."[112]

At the same time, Moscow's plans for incorporating Iran into its orbit through a revolutionary takeover from within had suffered what would turn out to be the final blow. Moscow would never again be able to contemplate an internal takeover and would be forced by the following spring to alter strategy fundamentally toward Iran, supporting Iraq in the war with the objective of bringing about the military defeat of Iran. The Soviet shift would offer Reagan the opportunity to develop better relations with Iran. However, this opportunity was as yet over a year away and much would happen before it materialized.

Reagan had successfully taken steps to undercut Soviet strategy at both the strategic weapons levels and with regard to Iran by the spring of 1983, but the game was not yet over by a long shot. Three other areas would preoccupy the president in the second half of the year: the deployment of the Pershing II into West Germany, the Soviet plan to deploy SS-20 missiles into Grenada, and the prospect of the Soviet activation of a nationwide ballistic missile defense.

In the context of seeking improved relations with the Soviets, the president would authorize negotiations on opening additional consulates and extending cultural exchange agreements, actually signing a five-year grain agreement. At the same time, however, he put naval and air power into position to preempt the plan to deploy SS-20 missiles into Grenada and probed Soviet defenses to determine how close the Soviets were to activating a nation-wide ballistic missile system. By the fall of 1983, these efforts would lead to a protracted confrontation, which would move the two nations to the brink of war.

---

[111] Efraim Karsh, "The Iran-Iraq War: A Military Analysis," *Adelphi Papers* 27, no. 220 (Spring 1987): 27.
[112] "'US Arms Must Counter Soviets', Reagan Says," *Philadelphia Inquirer*, May 22, 1983, 4.

Chapter 2

Where Will the Missiles Go?
Moscow's "Analogous" Threat

From the moment Leonid Brezhnev articulated the threat to deploy an "analogous" weapon to the Pershing II, in March 1982, President Reagan focused his attention on the greater Caribbean region, the self-evident location of Moscow's promised deployment. As discussed in the previous chapter, Brezhnev's declaration was not inadvertent. Soviet spokesmen reiterated this threat at every opportunity, publicly in the press and privately to American officials during the INF arms control negotiations. This repeated threat made it mandatory for the administration to determine its feasibility.

Analysis quickly made clear that, although a high-risk maneuver, under the right circumstances, the Soviet Union could just make good on its threat. It was also evident that the moment when the Soviets would attempt to make their move was perhaps a year and a half off—sometime around the planned deployment of the Pershing II to West Germany. Nevertheless, once the nature of Moscow's "analogous" deployment became clear, from early April onward, the president subtly altered policies toward Central America and the states of the Eastern Caribbean in order to counter the Soviet move and to prepare the United States for coming crisis.

The administration declined to publicize the threat of a Soviet missile base in the Western Hemisphere, although cautious references were made to Grenada as a possible base from the beginning of 1983. Rather, the president focused public discourse on the existing and growing Cuban and Nicaraguan efforts to destabilize Central America. Lingering fears that a "secret war" was triggering another Vietnam-like involvement in Central America, and the growing disparity between the perceived magnitude of the Cuban-Nicaraguan threat and US countermeasures, fed public anxiety about Reagan's policies, which led to increased opposition, especially in Congress. This also created opposition within his own administration—from the secretary of state.

Analysis of the "Analogous" Threat

The overriding question was: how would the Russians make good on their threat? The administration strove to identify the nature of the deployment, its possible location or locations, and the weapon itself. What would the Soviets attempt to deploy and how and where would they attempt to deploy it? It was imperative to identify the threat in order to defeat it, and answers were not long in coming. Preliminary conclusions were reached in a few weeks, by no later than the end of March 1982, which led to an immediate change in policy toward the Caribbean Basin. By the time of Brezhnev's death, at the latest, the president had determined the basic outline of his policy response to the Soviet attempt to insert ballistic missiles into the Western Hemisphere. [1]

Analysis focused on the land-based missile as Moscow's weapon of choice, largely, but not entirely, discounting the submarine and bomber threats. The Soviets were already deploying missile-carrying submarines off both US coasts and were flying long-range bombers, reconnaissance and, more recently, anti-submarine patrols out of Cuba. But Soviet submarine-launched missiles were not very accurate, and the long-range bomber was not a quick-strike threat. To be truly analogous, Moscow would have to deploy a missile comparable to the Pershing II that had the range, speed of launch, quick flight-time, and accuracy to threaten US mainland targets.

Of all of Moscow's missiles, only one—the solid-fuel SS-20—had these characteristics. Moreover, it was easily portable by large cargo jet, and required no elaborately prepared launch sites, containing its own transporter, erector, and launcher, or TEL. The SS-20's range of over three thousand miles meant that it could threaten virtually all of the United States from a number of possible locations in the greater Caribbean region. Indeed, unlike 1962, there were four locations where the Soviets could conceivably deploy its analogous weapon: Cuba, Nicaragua, Grenada, and Suriname. Each location, however, presented Moscow with unique logistical problems. [2]

---

[1] "The Soviet Cuba Card," *Wall Street Journal*, March 31, 1982, 17. The paper's editors, evaluating Brezhnev's threat, linked the European arms control negotiations with Cuba, and demanded that the United States "not permit further Soviet intrusion into this hemisphere," including the possible deployment of SS-20 missiles to Cuba.

[2] Guyana, next to Suriname, also was a possibility but apparently was ruled out due to unsettled political conditions; infrastructural limitations (the airfield was only 7,500 ft. long); and Venezuelan and possibly Chinese influence. Years later, in 1985, Moscow took a much greater interest in Guyana after Grenada and Suriname had been eliminated.

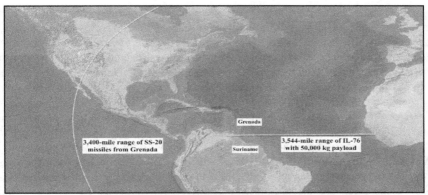

Optimum location for deployment of SS-20s to the Caribbean

The limiting factor was the range of Moscow's large cargo jets that would transport the missiles. Soviet cargo aircraft, including the An-22 and the Il-76, had a roughly three-thousand-mile range with maximum payload, somewhat longer with a lightened load. West Africa would be the logical departure point from which the Caribbean could be reached without refueling. Unless their payload was reduced significantly, these aircraft did not have the range to fly from West Africa to Cuba or Nicaragua without an intermediate refueling stop somewhere along the north coast of South America, or in the Eastern Caribbean. However, both Grenada and Suriname were just within non-stop range of Soviet cargo jets, particularly the IL-76, flying from an airfield in West Africa.[3]

The assumption was that the Soviet Union would not attempt to replay their slow-developing 1962 Cuban gambit of surreptitiously attempting to ship missiles by sea. Furthermore, Reagan was employing a resurgent US navy in a very aggressive manner, based upon a maritime strategy that dictated the forward engagement of the Soviet navy in all the world's oceans, including its home waters. The United States could concentrate a preponderance of naval and air power in the Caribbean-mid-Atlantic region, making it highly unlikely that the Soviets would risk the shipment of missiles to Cuba and Nicaragua, although Washington would obviously have to be vigilant against this possibility.

---

[3] Although the An-22 could carry a larger payload, it was an older aircraft and by the mid-1980s, there were more than six times as many Il-76s as there were An-22s available for airlift operations, making the Il-76 the primary Soviet air transport vehicle. One example of a West African airfield likely to be available at this time was Conakry in Guinea, which was a stopping point for Soviet transport aircraft en route to Angola. See *IL-76 Candid: Status and Outlook for the Soviets' Major Transport Aircraft Program: A Research Paper* (Washington, DC: Central Intelligence Agency, December 1985); and *Sub-Saharan Africa: A Growing Soviet Military Presence* (Washington, DC: Central Intelligence Agency, January 1985).

Thus, calculations based on geography, Soviet strategy and politics, and the limitations of Soviet technology led Reagan and his closest advisers to conclude that the Soviets were planning surreptitiously to deploy SS-20 missiles to Grenada and/or Suriname by air. Grenada, a small island at the southernmost tip of the Caribbean island chain off the coast of Venezuela, was already a Soviet client and Suriname, a small country on the north coast of South America between Venezuela and Brazil, was on the verge of becoming one.

The worst-case scenario that President Reagan sought to avert was one in which the Soviets surreptitiously inserted SS-20 missiles by air into Grenada and/or Suriname and presented the United States with a *fait accompli*. Brazenly, Soviet negotiators in the INF talks had spoken bluntly about deploying missiles into the Western Hemisphere and of a trade-off of Pershing II missiles for SS-20s.[4] However, the discussion was dangerously vague. If Moscow's initial deployment succeeded, other more ominous possibilities could arise, including deployment of additional Soviet missiles to Cuba and Nicaragua, employing Grenada/Suriname not only as missile bases, but also as refueling steppingstones.

As luck would have it, Moscow had not as yet consolidated its position in either Grenada, or Suriname. In fact, the situations that the Soviets faced in each country were almost exactly opposite. In Grenada, the political relationship was already established, with the existence of a Soviet-style client regime, or so it seemed; but the essential physical infrastructure, especially the Point Salines airport runway, was still under construction. The runway was scheduled to be completed in late 1983. In Suriname, it was the other way around. An 11,400-foot runway already existed at Paramaribo International airport, but the political relationship was still under negotiation. Thus, in both places, Moscow was months away from completing preparations before being able to commence with the analogous deployment scheme.

What undoubtedly focused the attention of American analysts on Grenada was the Soviet dispatch of General and Deputy Defense Minister Gennady Sazhenev to Grenada in April 1982, a month after Brezhnev's speech. According to intelligence sources, the presence of such a high-ranking Soviet general "sent shock waves through the CIA and the White House and signaled the strategic importance the Kremlin was placing on Grenada."[5] Later, in September, Sazhenev would be accredited to St. George's as the Soviet ambassador.

Evolution of US Caribbean Policy

Initially, the Reagan Administration's policy toward the region had tentatively focused on El Salvador—the result of the Carter Administration's belated decision to support El Salvador against a takeover attempt by Sandinista-supported FMLN rebels in January 1981. Having failed to coopt the Sandinistas,

---

[4] Strobe Talbott, *Deadly Gambits* (New York: Vintage, 1985), 158-59.
[5] Niles Lathem, "Top Red General Directed Isle Coup," *New York Post*, October 27, 1983, 3.

Carter had turned to aid El Salvador when the Sandinistas began to aid the Salvadoran guerrillas in what they proclaimed to be the "final offensive" to topple the government before Reagan entered office.[6] The offensive fizzled, however, failing to provoke a popular uprising and the government rallied behind US support.[7]

The fighting was still raging in El Salvador when the president-elect met with his national security team prior to taking office. During the first meeting, on January 7, Secretary of State Haig had pressed hard for a policy of direct action against Cuba, but the president had demurred.[8] He was not prepared to plunge the nation into war over and with Cuba as the first order of business. His immediate priorities were to restore the economic health of the nation, augment its military power, and rebuild the Western Alliance. Nevertheless, Haig would continue to insist that the United States focus on the Western hemisphere, drawing up plans to that effect to meet the region's problems "by going to the source."[9]

Despite Haig's insistence on a major confrontation with Cuba as the only way to stabilize the greater Caribbean region, the president decided on a far less visible course. Aside from continuing with the public assistance to El Salvador, he authorized a small, covert plan to bring together and support those who had fled the Sandinista regime out of fear or disgust. To this end, he signed a covert action finding (CAF) on March 9, 1981, authorizing the CIA to spend $19.5 million in an effort to support a Nicaraguan exile force.[10]

Over the next several months, agency operatives set up training camps in California, Texas, and Florida. Later that summer, CIA director Bill Casey arranged for CIA cooperation with Argentine leaders, who were themselves supporting a small anti-Sandinista band of former Somoza followers in Honduras, and named Duane "Dewey" Clarridge to head the effort.[11] In the fall of 1981, both Casey and Clarridge separately traveled to Argentina to discuss cooperation arrangements with General Leopoldo Fortunato Galtieri.

---

[6] For a discussion of Carter's policy toward Nicaragua and El Salvador, see the author's *The Carter Years: Toward a New Global Order* (New York: Paragon House, 1991), 363-76 and especially 510-16.

[7] US Department of State, Bureau of Public Affairs, Special Report no. 80, *Communist Interference in El Salvador* (Washington, DC, February 23, 1981); US Department of State, *El Salvador: The Search for Peace* (Washington, DC, September 1981); and US Department of State, Special Report no. 132, *Revolution Beyond Our Borders: Sandinista Intervention in Central America* (Washington, DC, September 1983).

[8] Caspar Weinberger, *Fighting for Peace: Seven Critical Years in the Pentagon* (New York: Warner Books, 1990), 30-31.

[9] Alexander M. Haig, *Caveat: Realism, Reagan and Foreign Policy* (New York: Macmillan, 1984), 122.

[10] For an analysis of the early discussions, see Leslie Gelb, "Argentina Linked to Rise in Covert US Actions against Sandinistas," *New York Times*, April 8, 1983, A10.

[11] Duane R. Clarridge, *A Spy for All Seasons* (New York: Scribner, 1997), 190.

The United States was pursuing a dual approach. On the one hand, the CIA was supporting the formation of an armed opposition force that the Argentines would manage and whose mission was to attack the flow of supplies moving through Nicaragua to El Salvador.[12] On the other hand, the Department of State was being tasked with exploring a political solution with Nicaragua, as well as with developing a more comprehensive plan for the vast Caribbean region bounded by Mexico and South America, Central America and the Caribbean Island chain. Thomas Enders was appointed Assistant Secretary of State to oversee these efforts.

Toward El Salvador, Honduras, and Guatemala, where insurgencies were growing, US strategy was to support reform-minded political leaders committed to democratic principles against the dictatorial aspirations of both the extreme right and the communist left. This would be combined with development of a strong military, capable of defending against foreign-based communist insurgency as well as the domestic-based right-wing death squads. In time, this strategy would meet with considerable success, but, in the beginning, the effort to build democratic institutions in states whose very existence was at risk tended to give preeminence to military over civilian leaders.

State Department officials were also engaged in developing a comprehensive plan for improving relations with the small states of the Eastern Caribbean, a plan which would ultimately be folded into the Caribbean Basin Initiative, launched the following February. Here, the idea was to enlarge the US presence in the region through the provision of incentives for economic development and to extend greater security assistance to enable the small island states to deal with the rising threat of subversion from Cuba and Grenada.

President Carter had quietly explored covert means of neutralizing Grenada when the Bishop regime began to turn the island into a miniature version of Cuba and openly supported the Soviet invasion of Afghanistan. Congressional objections persuaded him to rule out all but propaganda measures on the grounds that Grenada presented no imminent threat to its neighbors. Even the growing Cuban role on the island, especially assistance in the construction of the new Point Salines airport, and Bishop's decision to give Havana and Moscow landing rights, failed to change Carter's mind.

Covert action plans to "destabilize" Grenada were still on the books when Reagan entered office but suffered the same fate. In 1981 and 1982, the Senate Intelligence Committee "scuttled" proposals on the grounds that the threat was "exaggerated."[13] Through 1981, this was true enough. The possibility that Grenada could be a Soviet missile base did not arise until the spring of 1982. Until then, Reagan adopted a broad public policy approach toward the region, designed to isolate Grenada by strengthening the states around it.

---

[12] Leslie Gelb, "Argentina Linked to Rise in Covert US Actions Against Sandinistas," *New York Times*, April 8, 1983, A10.

[13] Patrick Tyler, "US Tracks Cuban Aid to Grenada," *Washington Post*, February 27, 1983, A1.

In early July 1981, Secretary of State Haig had met with the foreign ministers of Canada, Mexico, and Venezuela in Nassau, where they agreed to support a multilateral action program for the region. Meetings were held between the members of the so-called Nassau group and representatives of the Caribbean Basin countries, focusing on trade and security issues. Leaders of the island states, however, were already moving beyond their long-term association with Great Britain with its traditionally minimalist approach to security and had opened the door to strengthening security ties to the United States.

On July 4, 1981, the leaders of Antigua and Barbuda, Dominica, Grenada, Montserrat, St. Kitts-Nevis, St. Lucia, and St. Vincent & the Grenadines had agreed to replace the U.K.-sponsored West Indies States Association with the Organization of Eastern Caribbean States, headquartered at Castries, St. Lucia. Article 8 of the founding treaty charged its members with responsibility for collective defense and security against both external aggression and "the activities of mercenaries, operating with or without the support of internal or national elements."[14] Their decisions would be based on unanimity.

By the summer of 1981, the administration was not only becoming more involved in a broad-based effort to support allies and friends in the greater Caribbean Basin region, it was also enlarging its own presence. Between August and October, for example, in one of its largest naval exercises since WWII, US naval forces executed "Ocean Venture" on and around the Puerto Rican island of Vieques. In December, the Department of Defense established the Caribbean Command at Key West, Florida, its area of responsibility spanning the entire region from the Gulf of Mexico to the Caribbean, the mid-Atlantic and the Pacific, bordering Central and South America.

By the end of 1981, the US Congress had allocated the modest sum of $1 million in security assistance to OECS defense forces. In addition, the administration authorized the FBI to set up a Caribbean Police School in Puerto Rico to train police officers of the OECS, and the Puerto Rican National Guard were likewise training paramilitary security units for Barbados, Dominica and Jamaica. All of these measures were aimed at containing what seemed at the time to be the relatively small-scale threat of subversion from Cuba and Grenada.

Complementary Covert Action

On the Central American mainland, the approach was different, but equally small-scale. On August 11, Assistant Secretary Enders traveled to Managua to explore the possibility for normalization of relations with Nicaragua. Enders made plain that the United States accepted the revolution, but registered Washington's objections to the continued effort to destabilize neighboring El

---

[14] Rex A. Hudson, "Strategic and Regional Security Perspectives," in *Islands of the Commonwealth Caribbean: A Regional Study*, ed. Sandra W. Meditz and Dennis M. Hanratty (Washington, DC: Library of Congress, Federal Research Division: 1989), EPUB, 1694-95, https://www.loc.gov/item/88600483.

Salvador. The United States and Nicaragua, he said, had reached a "fork in the road." Depending on whether the Sandinistas would refrain from continued support for the rebels in El Salvador or not, future relations would be either one of accommodation or confrontation.[15]

For the next two-and-a-half months, the United States and Nicaragua engaged in a fitful and fruitless exchange. By the end of October, the Sandinistas ultimately rejected the US offer as "sterile," as they continued to funnel weapons to rebels in El Salvador and take decisive steps toward imposition of a Soviet-style communist regime in Nicaragua. By this time, too, the CIA had succeeded in building the *La Tripartita*, the tripartite command structure comprised of Argentines, Hondurans, and alienated Nicaraguans, which formed the basis of the effort to build a political and military opposition to the Sandinistas.[16]

On November 16, ten months after the Reagan Administration took office, the NSPG took up the question of policy toward Nicaragua for the first time—which indicated how low in priority the Sandinista issue was. The president was unenthusiastic about the idea of a covert action plan to support a rebel force against the Sandinistas. He was highly skeptical that a paramilitary effort would dissuade the Sandinistas from their aggressive course. But the alternatives were worse. After a week of inconclusive discussions, Reagan decided to act on the suggestion of Mexican President Jose Lopez Portillo, and explore a political solution with Cuba.

On November 22, Reagan sent Secretary of State Haig to meet privately with Cuban Vice President Carlos Rafael Rodriguez in Mexico City. Haig, however, uninterested in a political solution and continuing to prefer confrontation with Cuba, made no serious attempt to explore one.[17] There was, in any case, no indication that Castro was interested in ending his long-standing relationship with the Russians. Their meeting led to nothing but an exchange of views and a tentative agreement to meet again some months hence.[18]

As there was no political solution available with Nicaragua, and no interest in a confrontation with Cuba, the president signed NSDD 17 on November 23. Deciding on a covert operation put the CIA in charge and insured that it was kept out of Haig's hands. The plan, essentially Clarridge's creation, envisaged a low-profile operation in which the CIA piggybacked on the existing Argentine force of five-hundred ex-Somoza Guardsmen who had fled to Honduras. Calling themselves the *Fuerza Democratica Nicaraguense* (FDN), they were commonly referred to as the Contras, or those who opposed the Sandinista revolution.[19]

---

[15] Robert Kagan, *A Twilight Struggle: American Power and Nicaragua, 1977-1990* (New York: Free Press, 1996), 191-94.

[16] Clarridge, *Spy for all Seasons*, 210.

[17] For the doctrinal differences between the president and Haig, see Thornton, *Revolution Ascendant*, chaps. 1 & 2.

[18] Haig, *Caveat*, 133-36.

[19] Peter Rodman, *More Precious than Peace: The Cold War and the Struggle for the Third World* (New York: Scribner, 1994), 238.

Reagan allocated nearly $20 million to this effort, which included support for 1,000 additional Nicaraguan exiles whom Buenos Aires agreed to recruit for this force.[20] Reagan's objective was threefold: He wished to raise the profile of a political opposition to the Sandinistas, discourage Nicaragua's support for external subversion, and cripple Cuba's support presence inside Nicaragua. The Contra guerrillas were to interdict weapons' flows to El Salvador and attack targets of opportunity inside Nicaragua, such as bridges, power plants, fuel depots, and communications centers. It would be several months, however, before the CIA could train, arm, and deploy a small guerrilla force to battle.

To El Salvador and Honduras, the president allocated $50 million in security assistance and $250 million in non-military, economic support to strengthen their ability to contend with the insurgencies. Toward Nicaragua, the plan was to employ a multi-layered approach of diplomatic, covert and economic measures, including trade incentives, in an effort to influence Managua's policies. The Guatemalan government was also under pressure from rebel forces seeking its overthrow; but, as it was in no danger of immediate collapse, and exhibited little concern for the niceties of democratic practice, was not included in the president's plans at this time.[21]

On December 1, 1981, as required by the Hughes-Ryan Act of 1974, Reagan signed a "finding" authorizing the CIA's covert action program.[22] It specified three goals: interdicting the weapons flow from Nicaragua to El Salvador, forcing the Sandinistas onto the defensive, and making them more amenable to negotiations. This was, as Gutman observes, "an ambitious set of military, political, and diplomatic goals for a force of 500 men."[23] As noted above, however, the original plan was to support a force of fifteen hundred men, not five hundred—the existing five-hundred-man force, plus an additional one thousand the Argentines would recruit.

Also, as required by the FY1981 Intelligence Authorization Act, the director of central intelligence was statutorily responsible for briefing the Senate and House Intelligence Committee leaderships, known as the "gang of eight," on

---

[20] Questions were raised at the time about associating the CIA with Argentina, but it seems it was part of a parallel effort to show US support for Leopoldo Galtieri, who had just ascended to power in Buenos Aires. For that story, see Thornton, *Ronald Reagan: Revolution Ascendant*, chap. 6.

[21] Christopher Simpson, *National Security Directives of the Reagan and Bush Administrations: The Declassified History of US Political and Military Policy, 1981-1991* (Boulder: Westview, 1995),18, 53-54; and Clarridge, *A Spy for All Seasons*, 200-01.

[22] The CIA could undertake no covert operation unless specifically authorized by a presidential "finding."

[23] Roy Gutman, *Banana Diplomacy: The Making of American Policy in Nicaragua, 1981-1987* (New York: Simon & Schuster, 1988), 85.

all covert actions in a "timely fashion."[24] Casey's briefings on the Contra program, however, were notoriously vague and, in truth, barely comprehensible about what the administration expected to accomplish—its terms, objectives, and expected funding. The only thing obvious about the Contra program was the fact that it was the lowest budgeted operation of the US government.

At this point, the end of 1981, it was abundantly clear that Reagan's objective was neither to build up a Contra force to overthrow the Sandinista regime, nor to involve the United States militarily in a ground war against Nicaragua. Undoubtedly, those who were being supported hoped that American military power would eventually be brought to bear and those who objected feared that it would be. The difference in intentions between Reagan and the Contras and other allies in the region would provide ammunition for those who opposed the president's policy as the CIA effort unfolded.

Perhaps not so surprisingly, the CIA Contra program proved to be a force of attraction for thousands of disaffected and disenfranchised Nicaraguan citizens. This was mainly the result of the increasingly repressive character of the Sandinistas, as they began to institutionalize a Stalinist totalitarian "model." In the course of 1981, they collectivized agriculture, forced the Miskito Indians into internment camps, attacked the Catholic church, regimented urban life, including the schools, muzzled the press, and suppressed the workers and their labor unions.

By the end of 1981, the Sandinistas had moved decisively from the bourgeois-democratic to the socialist phase of their Soviet-style revolution. They had driven out members of the bourgeoisie, with whom they had cooperated to attain power, like Arturo Cruz, Alfonso Robelo, and Eden Pastora, and politically marginalized those who remained. Within months, by the early spring of 1982, as word spread that the United States was supporting the Contras, and aided also by the public adherence to the anti-Sandinista cause of several prominent ex-Sandinistas, the Contras had doubled in size to some eleven hundred men (which was still short of the fifteen-hundred level originally authorized), and the so-called "covert" CIA program had become an open secret.

Missiles to the Caribbean

Reagan's realization that the Russians were planning to deploy missiles into the Western Hemisphere led him to make the first of several adjustments to his policy there. (Brezhnev had publicly issued his threat on March 16 and preliminary analysis had shortly confirmed its feasibility.) The US policy change went largely unnoticed, however, because it was overshadowed by the outbreak of war between Great Britain and Argentina, when Argentine forces seized control

---

[24] Alfred Cumming, "Statutory Procedures under Which Congress Is to Be Informed of US Intelligence Activities, including Covert Action," Congressional Research Service Memorandum (Washington, DC: Library of Congress, Congressional Research Service, January 18, 2006), 2, 5.

of the Falkland Islands on April 2, and the United States became prominently involved in a mediation effort a few days later.[25]

In light of Moscow's expected ploy, the president gave up on plans to reach an accommodation with Cuba and Nicaragua—long shots in either case. Both would have to be contained. (The president sent former deputy CIA director Dick Walters to Havana in March with a warning for Castro and scrapped a planned mid-April trip to Managua by Enders for the purpose of further exploring normalization.)[26] The president decided to reinforce regional allies, now to include Guatemala, and to promote greater cohesion among the states of the Eastern Caribbean. Plans for all of this were hastily put in place in early April.

During what was termed a "working vacation" trip to Barbados, April 8-11, the president met with leaders of four of the Eastern Caribbean states (Dominica, Antigua and Barbuda, St. Kitts-Nevis, and St. Vincent and the Grenadines) and Barbados.[27] The ostensible purpose of his trip was to discuss the Caribbean Basin Initiative he had just announced in February, but, more importantly, it was to urge greater security cooperation among Grenada's neighbors. The press suggested that the main purpose of his trip was to see his former co-star Claudette Colbert, who lived on the island. The fact was, however, that the meeting in Bridgeton foreshadowed the effective future cooperation between Barbados, which was not a member of the OECS, and that organization.

In his after-luncheon remarks, the president noted the recent successful election in El Salvador in defiance of the efforts of "Communist guerrillas and terrorists" to prevent it. He warned: "El Salvador isn't the only country that's being threatened with Marxism, and I think all of us are concerned with the overturn of…parliamentary democracy in Grenada. That country now bears the Soviet and Cuban trademark, which means that it will attempt to spread the virus among its neighbors."[28]

For Fiscal Year 1983, which began in October 1982, not only had the United States "quadrupled" security assistance to Central America as expected, aid to the Eastern Caribbean nations near Grenada had unobtrusively jumped, as well.[29] For example, US military assistance to Dominica, where Prime Minister Eugenia Charles had beaten back an attempted coup the previous December, increased from an insignificant $12,000 in 1981 to $317,000; to Barbados, from

---

[25] For US policy toward the Falklands conflict, see Thornton, *Ronald Reagan: Revolution Ascendant*, chaps. 6 and 7.

[26] Haig, *Caveat*, 136.

[27] Lou Cannon, "Reagan Ties Aid Pledge to Warning," *Washington Post*, April 9, 1982. A3.

[28] Ronald Reagan, "Remarks in Bridgetown, Barbados, Following a Luncheon Meeting with Leaders of Eastern Caribbean Countries," *Public Papers of the Presidents of the United States, Ronald Reagan*, bk. 1, *January 1 to July 2, 1982* (Washington: Government Printing Office, 1983), 448.

[29] "US Has Quadrupled Latin Arms Aid," *Baltimore Sun*, December 2, 1982, A1.

$61,000 to $170,000; and to St. Vincent and the Grenadines from zero to $300,000.[30]

At the same time, the president broke off further negotiations with Nicaragua and authorized a major shift in strategy toward Central America. On April 8, while the president was in Barbados, US ambassador to Nicaragua, Anthony Quainton, delivered a new "eight-point plan" to Managua. Presented as the basis for further negotiations, in fact, it was intended to break them off. The central US demand was Sandinista commitment to hold free elections, which would be one of the "essential elements of the political context of future relations between our two countries." In addition, the United States demanded that Nicaragua reduce its armed forces to a level "appropriate" for defense purposes, reduce the number of "foreign military advisers," and halt the import of "heavy offensive weapons." As expected, the Sandinistas rejected the eight-point plan as an "ultimatum." [31]

In early April, the president put into place a broader strategy that went beyond containment of Cuba and Nicaragua, to the reinforcement of allies in the region. The strategy, leaked to the press a year later, declared that the United States would continue to improve the "military capabilities of the democratic states to counter subversion by the extreme left," while generating pressure on Cuba and Nicaragua "to increase for them the costs of intervention." Significantly, the objective was, "by 1984," to have strengthened the states of the region—economically, militarily, democratically—to the point where they could undertake "collective security action" through the O.A.S., the Rio Treaty, and the Central American Democratic Community. The goal was to strengthen allies and to gradually reduce Cuban and Nicaraguan "influence."[32]

US ability to exert "influence" on Nicaragua would be a function of the "full implementation" of NSDD-17, not all of whose provisions had yet been put into force. No US combat troops would be sent to Central America; the United States would seek to exercise its influence through security, economic, and political programs toward its allies and the Contras. The total cost of the entire Central American strategy was envisaged to be $1 billion, out of which the Contra program had thus far been funded at less than $50 million. Indeed, supplies had only just begun to arrive, and the Contras had only just begun to carry out small-scale, hit-and-run border attacks against Nicaragua.[33]

The abrupt US policy shift, as Gutman notes, left everyone—not only those in the field, but also many in the US government itself—"in a state of

---

[30] Hudson, "Strategic and Regional Security Perspectives," in *Islands of the Commonwealth Caribbean: A Regional Study*, ed. Sandra W. Meditz and Dennis M. Hanratty, EPUB, 1696-97.
[31] Gutman, *Banana Diplomacy*, 95-96. Haig claims that he was unaware of the eight-point plan, being immersed in the Falklands mediation at this time, a claim that rings true. He suspected that "a liaison had formed between Enders and Clark."
[32] Ibid.
[33] Clarridge, *Spy for All Seasons*, 219.

confusion about the aims of US policy."[34] In fact, Reagan was instituting a change in policy, whose true aims could not be disclosed. With the crisis estimated to be at least a year-and-a-half away, sometime coincident with the deployment of the Pershing II to West Germany, the administration sought to justify its actions in the context of policy toward Central America, while preparing to concentrate its response capability vis a vis Grenada and Suriname.

The fact was that the picture in Central America—at least at that moment—was improving. In March 1982, despite desperate rebel attempts to disrupt it, national elections were held successfully in El Salvador (with Alvaro Magana elected as provisional president in August). In Honduras, after a decade of military rule, the people elected Liberal Party candidate Roberto Suazo Cordoba as president and adopted a new constitution (by which the nation is still governed). Also, in March, Rios Mont executed a soft coup in Guatemala, which stabilized the government, opening up the prospect of closer relations with the United States, and enabled a firmer prosecution of the war against the guerrillas. Finally, a mini coup by Manuel Noriega in Panama brought a positive turn toward Washington, as well.[35]

These favorable political developments were buttressed by an improvement in the security situation, which was only temporary, as it turned out. The Salvadoran military appeared to be gaining control of the FMLN insurgency. Interdiction efforts were beginning to "hamper," although not yet close off, weapons re-supply to the rebels, and deteriorating economic conditions seemed to be forcing the Sandinistas to look inward. On the other hand, it was acknowledged that both Cuba and Nicaragua still "retain[ed] the ability to continue or even increase their support for insurgencies and terrorist groups."[36]

In mid-April, the CIA had managed to persuade the disillusioned former Sandinista, Eden Pastora, to declare his support for the Contra cause from his exile in Costa Rica. Although Pastora's actual role would be far less than the propaganda describing it, the declared presence of this former Sandinista on the side of the Contras not only heartened the rebels in the field, but it also theoretically at least established a southern front against Managua and raised the prospect of putting the Sandinistas in a two-front conflict situation.

Conflict Intensifies in Central America

President Reagan had put in place a strategy that he hoped would stabilize allies in the region, contain the expansionist aims of Cuba and Nicaragua, and put the nation in position to defeat Soviet plans. However, he had underestimated the will and resources the Soviets, Cubans, and Sandinistas were

---

[34] Gutman, *Banana Diplomacy*, 99.
[35] "National Security Council Document on Policy in Central America and Cuba," *New York Times*, April 7, 1983, A16.
[36] Ibid.

willing to expend on insurgency, as well as the drawing power of the Contras as they moved into action against the Sandinistas.

Far from moderating, the level of fighting surged through the year, forcing the president to attempt to contain it. Paradoxically, this meant that it would be necessary to tighten the leash on the Contras to make sure they would not precipitate a wider conflict in the region. Reagan wanted to keep the Contras viable as an opposition force, but he did not want them to draw the United States into the wrong conflict at the wrong time. Toward this end, the Congress played an unwitting role.

The Contras, who, up to this time, had only conducted hit-and-run attacks along the border, had just begun military operations inside Nicaragua in mid-March, blowing up the Somotillo and Ocotal bridges on the Pan American highway on the 14th. More serious was the scheme of Colonel Gustavo Alvarez, strongman of Honduras, later that summer. Alvarez was dismayed by the US failure to support Argentina against Great Britain in the Falklands war and, fearing that Washington would also drop its support for the Argentine presence in Honduras with the Contras, sought to precipitate a larger conflict with Nicaragua as a means of strengthening the U.S commitment.

Claiming that the Sandinistas were moving 2,000 troops, with tanks and artillery, toward the Honduran border, Alvarez put his own forces on "red alert." According to US officials who inquired, Alvarez declared that his plans were "to go to Managua. This is our chance." Alarmed at this unexpected, independent move by Alvarez which threatened to drag the United States into a larger conflict, US officials provided him with satellite photographs and other intelligence, convincing him that there was no threat to Honduran security, and he backed down.[37]

The fact was that from late spring, the CIA had been moving to "assume the leadership role in La Tripartita," raising the agency's "profile," not lowering it. Clarridge says that he had come to the realization of the need to do this before the outbreak of the Falkland's war, but acknowledged that "we didn't announce the change; we just did it over time."[38] Unfortunately, Alvarez misread the CIA's "command and control problems," springing from the withdrawal of Argentine advisers, as the early stages of disengagement from Honduras, persuading him to undertake his independent initiative.[39]

Congress and the Contras

The larger American "profile" and the growing risks of CIA involvement caused alarm in Congress, particularly in the Democrat-controlled House, which sought to place constraints on Contra policy. Opponents argued that the

---

[37] Gutman, *Banana Diplomacy*, 113.
[38] Clarridge, *A Spy for All Seasons*, 220.
[39] Don Oberdorfer and Patrick Tyler, "US-Backed Nicaraguan Rebel Army Swells to 7,000 Men," *Washington Post*, May 8, 1983, A1.

administration had secretly changed its objective from "arms interdiction," which they could tolerate, to "overthrow" of the Sandinista regime, which they opposed. The first of repeated congressional interventions, spearheaded by a vocal group of Democrats in the House Intelligence Committee, occurred in the spring of 1982.

Seeking to limit the CIA program to interdiction, Committee Chairman Edward Boland (D-MA) included language to that effect in a classified annex to the Intelligence Authorization Act for fiscal year 1983, enacted into law on September 27, 1982. It proscribed appropriated funds "for the purpose of overthrowing the government of Nicaragua, or of provoking a military exchange between Nicaragua and Honduras."[40] These, of course, were the two contingencies that the president, too, sought to avert. Nevertheless, from the spring, House Democrats incessantly voiced objections to the CIA's "secret war," and charged that what was occurring in the field in Nicaragua went beyond interdiction.[41]

Reagan's response to growing congressional opposition was to attempt to gain firmer White House control over the CIA's Contra program, work more closely with the Congress, and mount a stepped-up public information campaign to generate support. On May 28, the president signed NSDD-37 and 37A, which, reaffirming the limited objectives of NSDD-17, sought "immediately" to strengthen NSC chief Judge Clark's hold, establish an interagency Legislative Liaison group "to provide whatever support is required to obtain Congressional approval," and "internationalize" the public information campaign. Finally, Guatemala was formally included in US strategy with the authorization of an immediate injection of $10 million in military support funds and Foreign Military Sales credits.[42]

Despite the administration's efforts to constrain it, however, the clear trend was for an increase in the level of conflict and greater Cuban and Soviet involvement. The Contras continued to grow in size, if not capability, reaching some 4,000 men by the end of 1982, and more were signing on to the cause. Unfortunately, there was a parallel growth of so-called "revolutionary" forces. As the United States sought to employ the Contras to put pressure on the Sandinistas, attempting to draw Costa Rica into this effort with minimal success, the Sandinistas, with Soviet and Cuban assistance, were supporting rebel groups in Guatemala, Honduras, and El Salvador against those governments. By the end of the year, in each country there were "leftist" groups totaling between 5,000-6,000 men.

Meanwhile, in the Caribbean, preparations were under way to further contain Grenada. At the end of October 1982, under the auspices of the United States, the United Kingdom, and Canada, Barbados and four members of the

---

[40] Gutman, *Banana Diplomacy*, 117. See also Kagan, *Twilight Struggle*, 243-44.
[41] Gutman, *Banana Diplomacy*, 86. The irony was that neither "covert action," nor "interdiction," had ever been defined.
[42] Simpson, *National Security Directives*, 128-9.

OECS—Dominica, St. Lucia, Antigua and Barbuda, and St. Vincent & the Grenadines—signed a memorandum of understanding, establishing a Regional Security System. Grenada, St. Kitts-Nevis and Montserrat were not included. The members agreed to prepare contingency plans and the sponsoring authorities to provide material assistance with regard to the emergence of any threat to national security. Special service units were established in each of the signatory states.[43]

By the end of the year, military forces had grown throughout the region, but Nicaragua's had grown the strongest. Managua increased the size of its army to 22,000 troops, supported by a militia-reserve of 50,000, the largest in Central America. Assisting were some 2,000 Cuban "advisers" and numerous other Bloc advisers from the Soviet Union, East Germany, Libya, Czechoslovakia, and the PLO. It fielded 50 Soviet-made tanks, sixteen propeller planes (no jets), four helicopters, 7,000 French-supplied surface-to- air rockets, 100 anti-aircraft guns, and a few Soviet-supplied heat-seeking tactical missiles. [44]

The army was designed as a defensive force to protect the regime, like those of the Warsaw Pact, and was not an offensive army of conquest. Nicaraguan air power was severely limited, as was its potential for growth. As one military observer noted, "the country lacked the oil refineries and other facilities needed to support a large air force." The Soviet T-55 tanks were not well-suited to the rugged terrain and suffered frequent breakdowns. The ground force, however, was well-armed with the ubiquitous AK-47. Finally, Moscow's military supply program was increasing in size and intensity.[45]

The fact was, however, that despite the deficiencies of its army, the Sandinistas could not be overthrown except by US direct action. The likelihood that the four thousand US-supported Contras scattered in camps along the Nicaraguan border could overthrow the Sandinista regime, never high to begin with, had sharply receded. Yet, despite the lessening chances that the Contras could topple the Sandinista regime, their supporters in the US Congress charged increasingly vociferously that this had become the policy of the US government. This was partly because the secret war had now become quite public and the public was voicing increasing concern about policy toward Central America, punctuated by protests, demonstrations, and marches on Washington.[46]

Reagan Prods Congress

To avoid becoming mired in a Central American quagmire just as the Soviets were making a missile play into Grenada, President Reagan sought to place public limits on his policy, but without appearing to do so. He maintained a

---

[43] *Caribbean Islands—A Regional Security System*, Country Studies, Library of Congress.

[44] Raymond Bonner, "Behind Nicaraguan Buildup: Soviet-Bloc Aid Cited," *New York Times*, April 27, 1983.

[45] Ibid.

[46] Rodman, *More Precious than Peace*, 240-41.

public position of support for the Contras, even while acceding to limitations on that support—at least for the time being. At the same time, he moved to put American naval and air power in position to be able to deny Moscow its objective.

Given the growing opposition of congressional Democrats, the president decided to enlist their unwitting support for his position. CIA director Bill Casey played a key role in this effort, leaking information to "make the [Contra] program out to be bigger than it was . . . ." The director himself sat down with the staff of *Newsweek* twice to discuss the covert war, confirming "facts," "progress," "strengths," all on a not for attribution basis. The result was the November 8 cover story: "America's Secret War: Target Nicaragua."[47] US ambassador to Honduras, John Negroponte, was portrayed as being actively involved in covertly arming the Contras. When administration officials acknowledged the program and insisted, as Shultz noted, that its purpose was "to put pressure on, but not to overthrow, the Sandinista government.... This revelation set off loud alarm bells in Congress."[48]

As if on cue, congressional Democrats, who had strengthened their control of the House of Representatives in the mid-term elections, gaining 27 seats for a majority of 269 to 166, began to attack administration policy. The form their opposition took, however, was through the appropriations mechanism, which could only impose annual restraints, but would keep the issue before the public eye. For the Democrats, limiting the president's policy by attaching a rider to the defense appropriations bill was also a safe way to oppose the president because they reasoned that he would be loath to veto an appropriations bill.

Less than a month after the election, in early December, as the House deliberated over the annual defense spending bill, liberal Democratic members demanded an end to Contra support. Rep. Tom Harkin (D-IA) proposed an amendment to prohibit US aid to "any" non-governmental group carrying out military activities "in or against Nicaragua." This view found support in the Senate, where Sen. Christopher Dodd (D-CT) offered an even broader proposal to prevent US support for "irregular or paramilitary groups operating in the Central America region."[49]

Passage of these amendments, of course, would have completely shut down US support for the Contras and precipitated an immediate White House objection. Instead, the president proposed a compromise that House Intelligence Committee chairman Boland substituted for the Harkin proposal.[50] The Boland amendment, included in an omnibus FY 1983 continuing appropriations bill for the DOD and other agencies enacted December 21, 1982, provided that no authorized funds could be used by the CIA, or Department of Defense to furnish military equipment, training, or advice, to the Contras "for the purpose of overthrowing the government of Nicaragua or provoking a military exchange

---

[47] Gutman, *Banana Diplomacy*, 114-16.
[48] George Shultz, *Turmoil and Triumph: My Years as Secretary of State* (New York: Scribner, 1993), 288.
[49] *Congressional Quarterly Almanac-1983* (Washington, D.C.: CQ, 1984), 125.
[50] Ibid.

between Nicaragua and Honduras." This language made public the classified language Boland had formulated the previous spring.

The Boland amendment, which the White House helped to formulate, put the Congress on record as objecting to the president's covert support of the Contras, but stopped short of preventing it. Boland's formulation, *Congressional Quarterly*'s editors concluded, "gave the administration leeway to argue that it was not intending to overthrow the Nicaraguan government or to provoke a war between Nicaragua and Honduras." The fact was that the Boland amendment served the purposes of both the Congress and the president. Both accepted it as the "maximum step" that Congress could take at the time to curb the administration's policy. At the same time, it served the less obvious purpose of giving notice to the Contra leadership and Alvarez in Honduras that the United States Government would stop short of support for their ultimate goals.

Congress's actions "made it clear that they did not expect to stop US support for the anti-Sandinista rebels," which, however, failed to satisfy the left-wing fringe of congressional Democrats. Senator Dodd, for example, continued to complain that the Boland amendment was "the legislative equivalent of 'blue smoke and mirrors' and we should not have any illusions about it." Nevertheless, with these understandings in place, the president released his House supporters to vote in favor of the bill, which was adopted 411-0.[51]

Reagan and Andropov: The Pace Quickens

By the turn of the year, President Reagan was prepared to commence his counteroffensive against the Soviets, beginning, as noted in the previous chapter, with the codification of his strategy in NSDD-75, issued on January 17, 1983. On February 24, he signed NSDD-82, authorizing the establishment of a Central America Working Group with representation from State, Defense, JCS, CIA, and NSC. The group was to develop a detailed plan of action and to provide daily oral and written status reports to NSC adviser Clark. The directive envisaged that El Salvador would soon launch a "full scale country-wide counterinsurgency effort to include civic action and psychological operation."[52]

The president also began to identify Grenada as the location of Moscow's "analogous" deployment. The first effort along these lines came three days after he signed NSDD-82, by Nestor D. Sanchez, deputy assistant secretary of defense for inter-American affairs and a former CIA national intelligence officer for Latin America. In a speech to Florida Republicans, Sanchez disclosed the extent to which Grenada was being transformed into a "virtual surrogate" of Cuba.

If the Sovietization of Grenada continued, Sanchez said, Moscow "could literally place hostile forces and weapons systems capable of striking targets deep

---

[51] Ibid.
[52] "US Policy Initiatives to Improve Prospects for Victory in El Salvador," NSDD-82, February 24, 1983. Simpson, *National Security Directives*, 276-77.

in the United States." The new military facilities being constructed on the island "could provide air and naval bases...for the recovery of Soviet aircraft after strategic missions. It might also furnish missile sites for launching attacks against the United States with short- and intermediate-range missiles."[53]

The president himself took the ball from there. During a speech to the National Association of Manufacturers on March 10, describing his aid proposals for El Salvador, he focused on Grenada as a key element in Soviet and Cuban strategy. He ridiculed the arguments of some "experts" that the construction of air and naval bases on Grenada "and facilities for the storage of munitions, barracks, and a training ground for the military . . . [was] simply to encourage the export of nutmeg." His response was to say that "it is not nutmeg that is at stake in the Caribbean and Central America. It is the United States' national security":

> People who make these arguments haven't taken a good look at
> a map lately or followed the extraordinary buildup of Soviet and
> Cuban military power in the region or read the Soviets'
> discussions about why the region is important to them and how
> they intend to use it. [54]

Then, during the March 23 speech, in which he announced the Strategic Defense Initiative, the president prominently featured Grenada again. Although devoting the bulk of his speech to the budget and the growth of the Soviet threat, he allotted a substantial segment to a detailed description of the Soviet penetration into the Western Hemisphere. Employing several previously classified photographs to illustrate his points, he declared that the Soviets were "spreading their military influence in ways that can directly challenge our vital interests and those of our allies...very close to home [in] Central America and the Caribbean Basin."[55]

After displaying satellite photographs of the new Soviet signals intercept facility at Lourdes outside of Havana and a military airfield in western Cuba with MiG-23s parked on the apron, he showed a military airfield in Nicaragua, with MI-8 helicopters, anti-aircraft guns, and fighter revetments. Then he clicked to a photo of Grenada, where, he said, "the Cubans, with Soviet financing and backing, are in the process of building an airfield with a 10,000-foot runway." To what end, he asked? "The Soviet-Cuban militarization of Grenada . . . can only be seen as

---

[53] Patrick Tyler, "US Tracks Cuban Aid to Grenada," *New York Times*, February 27, 1983, A1.

[54] "Excerpts from President Reagan's Speech on His Proposals for El Salvador," *New York Times*, March 11, 1983, A8. Weinberger, *Fighting for Peace*, 106, says that the president "referred, warningly, to Grenada's apparent preparations to be a military base," a phrase which the *Time's* editors omitted from their "excerpts." For the full speech, see *Weekly Compilation of Presidential Documents*, 19, no. 12, March 14, 1983, 445.

[55] "President's Speech on Military Spending and a New Defense," *New York Times*, March 24, 1983, A20.

power projection into the region," a region, moreover, through which "more than half of all American oil imports now pass…"

The president had not mentioned the possible establishment of a *missile* base in Grenada, the way Sanchez had, nor had he discussed Suriname in any of his speeches, choosing to focus the national spotlight on the Soviet Union, Cuba and Nicaragua. The clear purpose of these multiple references to Grenada was a warning signal that the United States was cognizant of the island's threat possibility and was preparing to take action against Soviet inroads into the Caribbean region.

Moscow was attentive. Indeed, contemporaneous evidence indicated that the Soviets were accelerating efforts to strengthen positions in the region. As reported in the press in late July, "NSC and Pentagon officials said hints of the Cuban and Soviet buildups in Central America began flowing into US intelligence agencies 10 to 15 weeks ago."[56] In other words, sometime around the time between Kohl's victory and Reagan's SDI speech, the Soviets had decided to increase the pace of action. The Soviet plan for Grenada involved four steps: securing the allegiance of Bishop; pre-positioning of weapons on the island; sending Cuban troops to defend them; and, deploying SS-20 missiles there as soon as the airport was operational.

There began, in short, a Soviet-American race to objectives in the region and for both countries, there began to unfold public and secret plans. Moscow's public objective was to build up the military strength of Cuba and Nicaragua, while secretly rushing to complete preparations for the deployment of missiles into Grenada and/or Suriname. The majority of armaments delivered to Grenada was shipped from Cuba, arriving at night and unloaded during power outages that preserved secrecy. Washington's public objective, on the other hand, was to contain the spread of Cuban-Nicaraguan subversion, especially to El Salvador and Honduras, while privately positioning power to preclude the deployment of missiles into the hemisphere.

For Washington, however, there was a growing disconnect between the public and private. Outside the inner circle of the president's advisers, in Congress, in the media, and the public at large, the president's policy decisions were perceived as an overreaction to events. In truth, the administration had not been overly forthcoming in conveying its actual intentions either in private to congressional leaders, or more broadly to the public—a course of action that would prove costly in terms of public support. In retrospect, of course, it was perfectly understandable that the president would attempt to maintain the tightest security over his plans, as he sought to foil Moscow's attempts to deploy nuclear missiles into the western hemisphere, the gravest of threats to American security.

The president was faced with a difficult challenge. He could not accuse the Russians of *planning* to put missiles into Grenada; they would simply deny it. And he could not afford to wait until *after* the fact; it would be too late. The Point

---

[56] "Military Moves by Soviet, Cuba Said to Spur Reagan Actions," *Baltimore Sun*, July 29, 1983, A1.

Salines airport was under construction, with completion expected late in the year, when it was thought the crisis would actually begin. The problem was, as the SS-20s required no permanent infrastructure, there would be little advance warning by way of construction of missile sites on the island.

Aside from the obvious similarity of a surreptitious Soviet deployment of missiles into a Caribbean base, the current situation was unlike the Cuban missile crisis of 1962. In the Cuban case, Moscow had employed slow-moving ships, while in the Grenadian case the Soviets would be employing fast-flying aircraft. Then, as well, the key component was a fixed concrete launcher complex for the SS-5, whose construction could be monitored, while on this occasion, the SS-20 contained its own mobile launcher, which did not require a fixed site. Finally, where the Kennedy Administration had had more than adequate intelligence on Cuba, the Reagan Administration had limited intelligence on Grenada.

An airborne insertion of missiles would involve rapid deployment once begun, making the situation extremely volatile because it would be very difficult, if not impossible, to interdict the aircraft, although presumably, they could be tracked. Thus, in Grenada, Moscow could move very quickly to present the United States with a *fait accompli*. The only way to prevent deployment was to deprive the Soviets of a place, or places, to deploy. The only ways to do that were either by dissuading the Grenadian and Surinamese leaderships from cooperating with Moscow's plans, or, failing that, by taking direct action. Reagan would do both.

Suriname: Denial by Dissuasion

The president's first step was toward Suriname, a move that grew out of what, on the surface, appeared to be a botched Libyan attempt to deliver weapons to Nicaragua by air, but what was, in retrospect, a disguised Soviet test of an alternate airborne missile delivery route. In mid-April, a flight of four Libyan transport aircraft (one US-made C-130 and three Soviet Il-76Ts) en route to Nicaragua had requested a refueling stop in Venezuela. Caracas had turned down the request, but Brasilia granted permission on the claim that the aircraft were transporting medical supplies.

The four planes landed at Recife, on the northeast coast of Brazil, but the C-130, experiencing engine trouble, could not proceed; the three IL-76s continued on and landed at the inland city of Manaus. Based on a tip from the US ambassador, Tony Motley, that the aircraft were transporting arms, not medical supplies as claimed on the flight manifest, Brazilian authorities detained the planes and sequestered the forty-man crew.[57] Searching the planes, they discovered that the cargo included over one hundred tons of heavy arms,

[57]Bob Woodward, *Veil: The Secret Wars of the CIA 1981-1987* (New York: Simon & Schuster, 1987), 256.

missiles, Czechoslovak rifles, a dismantled Soviet training plane and at least five tons of bombs and grenades."[58] Most of the "crew" were soldiers.

Under tight security at both airports and over the objections of the crew, "Brazilian technicians forced open the planes and removed the equipment.... In Recife, the equipment, still in boxes, was placed in a tightly-guarded warehouse near the tarmac, while the cargo taken off the planes in Manaus was airlifted by military helicopters to an air force base 15 miles from the civilian airport." Foreign Ministry spokesman, Bernardo Pericas, said that Brazil would invoke international rules for the transport of undeclared cargo, confiscate the arms, and direct the planes to return to their point of departure.[59]

There seems little doubt that US intelligence, acutely conscious of Soviet and Soviet allies' arms shipments in general, but especially so in current circumstances, had surmised that Moscow was employing Libya, which had over forty IL-76 transports, to ship the weapons in a test of an air route Moscow could itself use later. Furthermore, there seemed little doubt that US authorities had not only provided the information upon which Brazilian authorities had acted in deciding to search the aircraft, but also obtained Venezuelan cooperation to deny the refueling request in the first place. Indeed, Casey had obtained a copy of the flight manifest "from a human source in Libya."[60]

Brazilian-US cooperation gave President Reagan "a tremendous gift," which he immediately parlayed into a more important, but secret, accomplishment in little Suriname, a recently independent, former Dutch colony located on the north coast of South America.[61] In February 1980, Sgt. Dési Bouterse had overthrown the democratically elected government and imposed a rigid dictatorship, driving "at least 80,000 of the country's 350,000 people into exile."[62] According to Shultz, "Bouterse had formed an alliance with the left-wing government of Grenada and was rumored to have reached an agreement guaranteeing him support from Fidel Castro."[63]

In fact, Cuba was merely Moscow's catspaw in relations with both Suriname and Grenada. Both the Soviet Union and Cuba had set up large embassies in Paramaribo and Cuban "advisers" had taken over key elements of the economy, including communications and airport facilities. Qaddafi, too, as Shultz notes, "was moving to support the new pro-Communist strongmen in

---

[58] Warren Hoge, "Old US Weapons among Arms Found on a Libyan Plane," *New York Times*, April 25, 1983, A1.

[59] "Brazil Stops Libyan Arms for Nicaragua," *Washington Post*, April 20, 1983, A26. See also Hoge, "Old US Weapons among Arms Found on a Libyan Plane," who attempted to downplay the incident.

[60] Woodward, *Veil*, 256.

[61] Michael Getler, "Grounding of Libyan Planes in Brazil a 'Tremendous Gift,'" *Washington Post*, April 28, 1983, A14.

[62] "The CIA and Suriname," *Wall Street Journal*, June 3, 1983, 17.

[63] Shultz, *Turmoil and Triumph*, 293.

Grenada and Suriname."[64] The emerging "secret deal" between Moscow and Suriname, reportedly worth between $70 and $80 million, would involve an enlarged Soviet presence, as well as "Cuban troops and Libyan support," including the provision of "arms and very sophisticated communications gear."[65]

If successful, the deal would have given the Soviet Union and Cuba their first base in South America proper, and the unfettered use of Paramaribo's first-class airport. The crisis broke in early December 1982, when Bouterse, seeking to clear the way for a move into the Soviet-Cuban camp, began eliminating those who were objecting to his plans. On the 8th, he sent troops to shut down opposition newspapers and radio stations, rounded up several dozen prominent labor, academic, and community leaders at Fort Zeelandia in the capital of Paramaribo, and murdered fifteen of the most obstreperous who refused to accede in his plan to change the national posture.[66]

American intelligence had learned of the Bouterse-Moscow deal and the crisis offered the president an opportunity to block it. As Suriname was a self-governing territory of the Netherlands, Washington first approached The Hague with an offer to use American naval power to deter Cuba from interfering, while Dutch forces reestablished civilian rule. Prime Minister Lubbers was alarmed by the course of events in Suriname, but was unwilling to contemplate the use of force. His professed concern was that Dutch leftists would use cooperation with the US in an "anti-Cuba" policy to topple his own government. That, he claimed, would place in jeopardy the INF deployment scheduled for later in the year. In other words, the Dutch would do nothing.

As the debate dragged on without resolution on both sides of the Atlantic, inside the US government, CIA director William Casey, who believed the Bouterse dictatorship to be extremely fragile, proposed a covert action plan to overthrow it, using a South Korean commando force staged out of Venezuela. When Casey presented this scheme to the House Intelligence Committee, Chairman Boland and other key members of the committee "objected that Suriname wasn't important enough and Cuban involvement not clear enough to justify such 'extreme' action."[67] Shultz, too, thought the plan was "crazy," and was "shaken to find such a wild plan put forward seriously by the CIA." He believed that "the best we could put together would be a combination of external economic pressure with, perhaps, some kind of covert support for Bouterse's remaining opponents in Suriname—if there were any."[68]

---

[64] Ibid., 293-94, provides an insightful discussion, but typically downplays Moscow's central role.

[65] Thomas C. Reed, *At the Abyss: An Insider's History of the Cold War* (New York: Ballantine, 2004), 271.

[66] Jay Mallin, "Pent-Up Pressures in Suriname Raise Fears of Another Grenada," *Washington Times*, January 17, 1984, A5.

[67] "The CIA and Suriname," *Wall Street Journal*, June 3, 1983, 17 and Shultz, *Turmoil and Triumph*, 296.

[68] Ibid., 296-97.

Rebuffed, but undeterred, Casey devised another approach to disrupt the Soviet scheme, which obviated any need to consult the intelligence committees, or Shultz. He suggested to the president that he simply disclose his plan for a US invasion of Suriname to the leaders of Brazil and Venezuela. Casey calculated that the threat of US military action would prod both governments to act on their own to preempt the lodgment of a Soviet-Cuban presence in South America on their respective doorsteps, rather than become complicit in the use of American military power in the hemisphere.

According to close presidential adviser Tom Reed, "Reagan loved the plan," and sent NSC chief Clark and a small group of NSC and CIA aides secretly to Brasilia and Caracas at the end of April to brief the presidents and defense ministers of the US plan. Shultz was not informed, nor were members of the president's own staff, including chief of staff Jim Baker. Using Air Force One, and conducting the meetings aboard the aircraft in out-of-the-way places on the tarmac to preserve secrecy, Clark and his aides disclosed plans for a quick strike employing US army forces from Panama, South Korean commandos, and planes and ships already in the area for an operation to overthrow Bouterse.[69]

As anticipated, Brazilian and Venezuelan leaders expressed deep concern, fearful of the political impact on their own countries of direct American military action. Rather than be faced with either an expanded Soviet presence or an American invasion, they volunteered to solve the problem on their own. "Clark respectfully deferred to their wishes."[70] The Brazilians, who considered Suriname within their sphere of influence, warned Bouterse of American plans and offered him military and economic assistance, if he would drop plans to shift Suriname into Moscow's embrace.[71]

Brazil offered Bouterse an economic and military aid package amounting to $300 million, which Anderson claims came mainly from the US Treasury.[72] Regardless of the origin of the funds, the threat that he might be ousted by force was sufficient to give Bouterse pause and he put the Moscow scheme on hold through the summer. When the United States invaded Grenada later in October, Bouterse realized that Reagan's threats were credible and immediately broke with Cuba, publicly expelling its ambassador, downgrading relations to the level of chargé d'affaires, and ended this scheme for a Soviet-Cuban base in South America.[73]

---

[69] Reed, *At the Abyss*, 272.

[70] Ibid. See also Paul Kengor and Patricia Doerner, *The Judge: William P. Clark, Ronald Reagan's Top Hand* (San Francisco: Ignatius, 2007), chap.10, for a similar analysis.

[71] Jay Mallin, "Pent-Up Pressures in Suriname Raise Fears of Another Grenada," *Washington Times*, January 17, 1984, A5.

[72] Jack Anderson, "Suriname Ruler Is Chastened by Grenada Assault," *Washington Post*, November 5, 1983, C12.

[73] David Harvey, "Caribbean: Suriname's Cuba Ties Broken?" *Defense & Foreign Affairs Daily*, October 28, 1983, 1.

Eliminating All Possibilities but One

The Suriname scam came off quietly, almost without a public ripple, and at no cost, although Suriname itself would remain an unstable dictatorial regime until civilian rule was restored in 1991.[74] There was nothing quiet about the rest of Reagan's plans that summer, however. The president's overriding objective was to prevent deployment of any Soviet missiles into the greater Caribbean Basin region. With Suriname on hold, there were only three remaining possibilities: Cuba, Nicaragua, and Grenada. As noted, administration analysts ruled out Cuba because they did not believe Moscow wished to run the risk of violating the 1962 agreements and triggering World War III. Besides, the United States was well-prepared to identify and prevent any such move at an early stage.

Nicaragua was a better possibility, but also unlikely, even though from the spring of 1983 the Soviets were shipping weaponry to Nicaragua at a rate comparable to that shipped to Cuba in 1962. The bulk of the buildup was occurring by sea, however, and was difficult to disguise. Although there were half-a-dozen paved airfields long enough to accommodate Soviet jumbo jets, and more were being constructed, Nicaragua was out of non-stop range for large Soviet cargo aircraft, which could only reach Nicaragua with a refueling stop in the Caribbean islands, like Barbados (and Grenada when the airfield construction was completed). There would be much difficulty in dealing with Barbados, and no secrecy.

More importantly, Moscow would have to consider that the United States had assets in place that could make any effort to deploy missiles into Nicaragua very risky. Indeed, the Contras, now nearly six-thousand strong, had recently begun to conduct guerrilla operations in-country, within seventy-five miles of Managua. In northeast Zelaya province, Nicaragua's Indian community, the Miskito, Sumo, and Rama tribes, had also taken up arms against the Sandinistas and in April, Eden Pastora had declared war once again against the Sandinistas from his base in northern Costa Rica.

At sea, the first of three planned several months-long naval exercises was already under way, prompting public discussion (and confirmation) of US ability to enforce a blockade. Thus, the United States was poised to squeeze Nicaragua on multiple fronts by land and by sea. Indeed, as armed clashes multiplied in the spring, an increasingly rattled Sandinista leadership took their case to the United Nations, where in an effort to force the United States to restrain its allies, they accused Washington of fomenting an invasion. [75]

The Reagan leadership decided that the only serious prospect for Moscow secretly setting up a missile base and creating an "analogous"

---

[74] Incredibly, Bouterse remained in power until 1991 and was not brought to trial for the "December murders," as they were called, until November 2007. See Simon Romero, "Long Memories May Ensnare a Dictator," *New York Times*, April 13, 2008, A7.

[75] Roy Gutman, *Banana Diplomacy*, 149-51.

deployment in the western hemisphere was in Grenada. Since the March 1979 upheaval, Maurice Bishop and his New Jewel Movement had turned the tiny island with a population of 110,000 into a Soviet-style dictatorship, and armed camp. Soviet bloc personnel were operating training camps for subversive purposes and Cuban personnel were well along in the construction of a major 10,000-foot-long aircraft runway, as well as building expanded, deep-water port facilities to accommodate large ship traffic, including submarines. The airfield was scheduled to be completed by the end of the year but would probably become useable sooner.

More important, as noted above, in terms of Moscow's promise to deploy "analogous" missiles near US territory, Grenada was just within the range of Soviet heavy transports operating out of airfields in West Africa. The Soviets could surreptitiously fly in SS-20 missiles, set them up in prepared sites, even parking lots, and present Reagan with a *fait accompli*. Grenada was also the perfect steppingstone for the Soviets to Central America, as well as in reverse for the Cubans to support positions in Africa. Grenada would be the site where Moscow could fulfill its promise to build the same kind of threat to the United States that the United States was preparing to deploy against the Soviet Union.

Grenada Signals and Soviet Diversions

President Reagan's condemnation of the Soviet Union as an "evil empire," the SDI announcement, and publicizing of Grenada as a possible Soviet missile base, prompted Moscow to accelerate its plans for the island and also to divert attention away from Grenada in a variety of ways. One was to deter through intimidation, raising anew "the possible advent of a second Cold War." Russian officials "have clearly indicated that the deployment of 108 Pershing II missiles in West Germany could lead to a crisis in relations that would be similar to the 1962 Cuban missile crisis." They see "Reagan as preparing for confrontation and applying pressure on the Soviet economy in order to weaken it and force a reduction of its military potential."[76] Of course, Soviet officials meant to convey the idea of the 1962 scenario in reverse, for at this point it was Moscow that held the high missile cards.

Another diversionary tactic was to suggest other deployment possibilities in the region. Georgy Arbatov, the Kremlin's America expert, in an article in *Pravda*, threatened that the Soviet Union would deploy medium-range missiles "near American borders," if the United States installed medium-range missiles into West Germany. Arbatov's threat was "the most explicit explanation so far of...Brezhnev's warning last year that if the new NATO missiles were installed in Europe, the Soviet Union would put the United States 'in an analogous position.'" However, unnamed "Western diplomats in Moscow insisted...that the Arbatov article probably does not herald installation of Soviet missiles in Cuba,

---

[76] Dusko Doder, "Crisis Seen in Moscow; Second Cold War Thought Possible," *Washington Post*, March 27, 1983, A1.

Moscow's only client state near 'American borders,' or in states like Nicaragua or Grenada, in the Caribbean. Such a move would undoubtedly trigger a second Cuban missile crisis. Instead, they believe that the Arbatov threat referred to Soviet submarine-launched missiles." [77] No doubt, these "Western diplomats in Moscow" were passing on the views their Soviet sources conveyed to them. The submarine missile threat, of course, was already a reality, as Moscow increased the number and frequency of patrols off the American coasts. But there was more.

A third diversionary tactic was the explicit Cuba-in-reverse threat. Chief of the General Staff Marshal Nikolai Ogarkov, in an interview with a Western correspondent, declared that if the United States deployed and ever used the Pershing II missiles against the Soviet Union, "the Russians would retaliate directly against the United States." It would be impossible, he said, to limit a nuclear war once it broke out.[78] Here again, Russian officials were attempting to persuade US officials that, contrary to 1962, the shoe was on the other foot. This threat was, of course, precisely that issued by President John F. Kennedy during the Cuban missile crisis of 1962.

A Cuban buildup was also occurring, as Moscow deployed two additional submarines, patrol craft, amphibious assault craft, and MiG-23s, as well as two TU-142 Bear Foxtrot long-range bombers. Up to now, the Soviets had deployed two Bear reconnaissance planes to the island. The two most recent aircraft were ASW versions of the Bear, but also "capable of carrying nuclear bombs and air-launched cruise-type missiles," a significant upgrade in capability. Moreover, revetments were being constructed to accommodate an entire squadron of bombers.[79] Cuba was rapidly being turned into an island fortress from which the Soviets could project power.

The presence of the Bear bombers was but the latest evasion of the 1962 agreement on Cuba that prohibited the Soviet deployment of offensive weapons to the island. The claim that they were solely anti-submarine hunters was unconvincing. Washington lodged no public protest, lending credence to the view that the United States would do nothing. Did this mean, one commentator asked, that the next step will be "Soviet missiles in Cuba? Or Nicaragua? Or Grenada?" To this author, "offensive weapon systems in Cuba would also provide handy umbrellas of protection for other pro-Soviet governments in the Caribbean..."[80]

Still another diversionary tactic was to draw attention to Nicaragua as a potential missile base. Nicaraguan defense minister Humberto Ortega, in an interview with the *New York Times*, averred that "Nicaragua would consider accepting Soviet missiles if asked." He went on to add that the Soviets had not

---

[77] Anthony Barbieri, "Soviet Union Threatens to Place Missiles Near American Borders," *Baltimore Sun*, March 18, 1983, A1.

[78] Leslie Gelb, "Soviet Marshal Warns the US on Its Missiles," *New York Times*, March 17, 1983, A1.

[79] Cleto Di Giovanni, "Sen. Symms and Cuba's Soviet Bears," *Washington Times*, April 5, 1983, C1.

[80] Ibid.

proposed to place missiles in Nicaragua, but "if they ask us, we will examine the proposal and make our own decision." These comments prompted Secretary of State Shultz to declare that "all of Central America" has become a target for subversion from Nicaragua, and he expressed concern that "the Soviet Union might use Nicaragua as a missile base."[81]

Given the Soviet attempt to divert attention away from Grenada, it is difficult not to interpret other events in the same light, including the bombing of the US embassy in Beirut on April 18, 1983. In March, snipers began to fire on the US-French-Italian multinational force deployed to Beirut the previous fall. Hezbollah took credit for the attacks and promised more. On April 18, a suicide bomber drove a truck loaded with 400 pounds of explosives into the entrance of the US embassy. The blast killed 63 people and injured 120. Seventeen of the deaths were Americans and eight of these were the CIA's top Middle East experts, including its chief Robert Ames.[82] Syria and Iran were both implicated as supporters of Hezbollah and the Islamic Jihad.

Overshadowed by the Beirut blast, on the same day, an unidentified Pentagon official said in obvious reference to Grenada that "if the Soviet Union sought to put nuclear missiles into the Caribbean area, the Reagan administration would take measures like those used by President Kennedy in 1962 to force withdrawal of Soviet nuclear missiles from Cuba." Although avoiding comment on specific measures to be taken, when asked whether it would involve steps similar to the naval blockade imposed by Kennedy, he replied, "I would think so."[83]

Indeed, the day before, Soviet minister-counselor Victor Isakov said on *Face the Nation* that the Soviet Union "might deploy medium-range nuclear missiles within striking distance of the United States if NATO nations proceed with plans to install new nuclear weapons in Europe this year." He refused to say where the Soviets might place missiles, but he and other Soviet spokesmen ruled out Nicaragua. Such blatant statements of intent that Moscow would deploy missiles "within striking distance of the United States" could not be allowed to pass without comment.[84] And, of course, the United States could be expected to heighten its vigilance.

[81] Don Oberdorfer, "Shultz Says Nicaragua Aims at 'All of Central America,'" *Washington Post*, April 16, 1983, A18.

[82] Herbert Denton, "Bomb Wrecks US Embassy in Beirut," *Washington Post*, April 19, 1983, A1.

[83] Hedrick Smith, "US Warns Soviet on Missile Threat," *New York Times*, April 19, 1983, A5.

[84] "Soviet Official Warns of Redeploying Missiles," *Washington Post*, April 18, 1983, A2.

Preparing for Crisis

Reagan's response was to invoke the Truman Doctrine for Central America before an unprecedented joint session of the Congress. Intending to "set the record straight," the president recounted the histories of US support for El Salvador against the Nicaraguan and Cuban support for "rebels" there, and the US support for the Contras against the Sandinistas of Nicaragua. He emphasized that the United States did not seek the overthrow of the Nicaraguan government, but only to compel its leaders to live up to their own promises of free elections. In contrast, he saw the Soviet goal as being "to destabilize the entire region from the Panama Canal to Mexico."[85] Paraphrasing Truman, President Reagan declared:

> I believe that it must be the policy of the United States to support free peoples who are resisting attempted subjugation by armed minorities or by outside pressures. I believe that we must assist free peoples to work out their own destinies in their own way. I believe that our help should be primarily through economic and financial aid, which is essential to economic stability and orderly political processes. Collapse of free institutions and loss of independence would be disastrous not only for them but for the world.

Although the president refused to believe that there was "a majority in the Congress or the country that counsels passivity, resignation, defeatism in the face of this challenge to freedom and security in our hemisphere...[or] is prepared to stand by passively while the people of Central America are delivered to totalitarianism and we ourselves are left vulnerable to new dangers," his appeal to the Congress fell on deaf ears. House Democrats led by Texas Rep. Jim Wright and Rep. Edward Boland of Massachusetts restricted further aid to the Contras on the grounds that the administration was violating the terms of the amendment passed the previous December.

In his speech, the president carefully sketched the role of Grenada in an airborne supply route to Nicaragua and Cuba, referring to the intercepted flight of Libyan cargo planes in mid-April. Describing the Caribbean Basin as a "magnet for adventurism," he observed that "if [the Point Salines] airfield had been completed, those planes could have refueled there and completed their journey." He did not mention that all of that could have been accomplished in complete secrecy.

There was another warning to Moscow embedded in, of all places, the Democratic response to the president's speech. In the context of criticizing Reagan's fundamental misunderstanding of the causes of conflict in Central America, Sen. Christopher Dodd noted that "the truth is never as simple as some would paint it." To him, it was not external subversion, but indigenous poverty,

---

[85] "President Reagan's Address to Joint Session of Congress on Central America," *New York Times*, April 28, 1983, A12.

political corruption, and death squads that were the causes of revolution there. Then, noting that nevertheless "on some very important things, all Americans stand in agreement," Sen. Dodd explicitly declared that "we will oppose the establishment of Marxist states in Central America." Furthermore, he continued, "we will not accept the creation of Soviet military bases in Central America. And we will not tolerate the placement of Soviet offensive missiles in Central America—or anywhere in this hemisphere." Finally, he said, "we are fully prepared to defend our security and the security of the Americas, if necessary, by military means."[86]

The message was clear. To Soviet intelligence analysts, who scrutinized every word coming out of Washington, despite all of the political posturing and ranting over the president's policies toward Nicaragua and the Contras, the American leadership was united against the Soviet threat in the hemisphere. Moreover, this message was being delivered by one of the administration's most vociferous critics.

As the president spoke, the United States was well along in a combined arms exercise employing 1,600 US personnel in Honduras, plus the deployment of a 77-ship battle group led by the USS *John F. Kennedy* and accompanied by a half-dozen British and Dutch ships. Although the president had largely ruled out a Soviet attempt to sneak SS-20s into either Cuba or Nicaragua by sea, he had to insure against that remote possibility. Therefore, even though the fleet maneuvers were discussed publicly in the context of the Honduran exercises, they were actually taking place off the east coast of Puerto Rico and directed at a different target.[87]

The Readex-1-83 exercise area off Puerto Rico was almost 1,500 miles from the Cuba-to-Nicaragua shipping lanes, but the carrier battle group was well-positioned to monitor Atlantic shipping lanes. The combat radius of the *Kennedy's* aircraft was a thousand miles, making the carrier group optimally placed for interdiction duty. The *Kennedy* battle group was in place to demonstrate that the United States could deter any Soviet attempt to slip weapons into the Western Hemisphere by sea.

However, while the carrier battle group monitored the sea lanes, no attempt was made to interfere with Soviet shipping into Cuba, which had accelerated dramatically in the past month. Eleven Soviet and Soviet-bloc ships had delivered cargo to Nicaragua and Cuba, twice the number of the previous year, and a dozen more were scheduled to arrive later in the year. It was unlikely, but not inconceivable, that Moscow would attempt to slip missiles in on one or more of these ships. Therefore, the president would guard against this possibility.

Washington also was reopening Ramey Air Force Base on Puerto Rico, which had been shut down for over a decade. In making the announcement, an

---

[86] "Democrats Respond to Speech by Reagan on Central America," *CQ Almanac—1983*, 31-32E.

[87] David Wood, "Combat Exercises Put Navy on War Footing," *Los Angeles Times*, April 3, 1983, A1.

Air Force spokesman said only that the base would be used for "training," but other sources said that "some type of Air Force unit will operate out of Ramey permanently," either a reconnaissance or fighter unit. Another factor in the decision, sources said, was "the construction by the Soviet Union and Cuba of what the administration calls a military air base on Grenada."[88]

The president would both guard against the unlikely possibility that Moscow might surreptitiously attempt to ship missiles to Cuba and/or Nicaragua; and also position US forces to prevent the more likely case of expected aerial deployment into Grenada. In light of what he had to anticipate would be a confrontation with Moscow, the president did not want to get bogged down in a major conflict in Nicaragua. Therefore, as he did late in the previous year, he submitted to—indeed, actually once again incited—congressional harangues against his policy. In doing so, he nevertheless drew the public's attention to the region.

As in the previous fall, Casey provided the spark, agreeing in March to permit news reporters for the *Washington Post* and *Newsweek* to travel to Honduras to spend ten days with the Contras. The result was fully predictable. Graphic accounts in the press of the fighting combined with reports that the Contras sought the overthrow of the Sandinistas "fueled concerns in Congress." There were cries that the administration had "violated the spirit of the Boland amendment. A House Foreign Affairs subcommittee voted a ban on further aid to the rebels, and in May the House Intelligence Committee voted to end the program."[89]

Crisis Indicators and a Play by Shultz

When, in May, an SR-71 overflying Cuba photographed Cuban troops practicing "sophisticated amphibious landings" on the beaches near Mariel harbor 35 miles west of Havana, the president and his close advisers realized they were entering the outer edge of crisis. Analysts speculated as to their purpose. Some thought that "the Cuban maneuvers [were] preparation for an invasion of some small Caribbean nation."[90] Combined with the earlier Soviet dispatch to Cuba of two amphibious assault ships, the maneuvers lent credibility to assumptions that Cuba was preparing to insert forces rapidly onto an island, presumably Grenada, should the necessity arise.[91]

At roughly the same time, one of the prime intelligence indicators that Moscow was preparing to deploy missiles triggered alarm bells. When Reagan

---

[88] "Rearming Island Against the Red Tide?" *New York News*, May 1, 1983, 62.

[89] Gutman, *Banana Diplomacy*, 154, says "the Agency agreed," which must be taken to mean Casey himself.

[90] "Military Moves by Soviet, Cuba Said to Spur Reagan Action," *Baltimore Sun*, July 29, 1983, A1.

[91] George de Lama, "US Eyes Soviet Build-Up in Caribbean," *Chicago Tribune*, April 4, 1983, 1.

decided that Moscow's analogous deployment would be SS-20 missiles to Grenada, analysts were tasked with carefully scrutinizing the key indicators that would tell when the Soviets were preparing to move. The more obvious of these were the state of airfield construction on the island, movement of Il-76 cargo jets, and the SS-20 missiles themselves, among others. Of course, the presence on Grenada of Soviet missile specialists would also be a prime indicator, but one presumably more difficult to track.

US intelligence, as a matter central to the arms control negotiations, kept track of the construction, deployment and movement of SS-20 missiles, which, were "clearly identifiable in their shelters from spy-satellite pictures that regularly photograph them." Suddenly, at mid-year, US intelligence "lost" and could not locate three regiments of SS-20 missiles. Each regiment had nine launchers; each missile had three warheads—three regiments meant that 81 missiles were missing. The sudden disappearance of such a large number of missiles was alarming; moreover, the Soviets refused "to identify the precise location of the missing regiments."[92]

Evans and Novak, who wrote the story, focused on improved Soviet camouflage procedures. "The missing regiments, however, have not been spotted, raising questions as to whether the Soviets have arranged new and unknown camouflage protection for them." The principal concern of intelligence analysts was not that the Soviets had devised better camouflage for the missiles, but rather that they had been withdrawn and were being made ready for transport to Grenada. And if that were the case, then the president should prepare for imminent crisis.

The end of May was a time of great and growing tension in the White House, relieved only by the hugely successful Williamsburg summit, which demonstrated the unity of the Western Alliance for all to see. Behind the scenes, a key question was whether the administration should go public with the information on Soviet and Cuban military involvement in Central America. Although not discussed in these terms, making public Soviet-Cuban military activities would establish the basis for Washington's own actions should it become necessary to move overtly over Grenada. In any case, Assistant Secretary Enders had opposed an exposé, while Reagan's key NSC aides had supported it.

The president decided to publicize the issue and also decided to replace Enders and appoint someone with enthusiasm for the task. Secretary Shultz announced Enders' reassignment as ambassador to Spain only hours after publication of the piece in question, on May 27, Langhorne (Tony) Motley, who as ambassador to Brazil, had worked successfully with Casey in exposing the Libyan cargo flight to Brazil discussed above, was named to replace Enders. The net effect of the personnel shift was to strengthen the president's control over policy, by installing at State someone who would cooperate with, and not oppose him.

---

[92] Rowland Evans and Robert Novak, "'Lost' Red Missiles," *New York Post*, June 9, 1983, 43.

Meanwhile, Shultz, perceiving the move against Enders as a power grab by Clark, made a play for control over Central American policy. This was his May 25 memorandum to the president, which has received widely divergent interpretations. Seeing a military solution in Nicaragua years away, Shultz declared that the only way to establish peace in Central America was "by regional negotiations leading to a reciprocal and verifiable agreement in which the Nicaraguans come to terms with the need for them to mind their own business." Shultz agreed that "we must not sell out the Nicaraguan patriots who wish their government to live up to the promises of free elections and a pluralistic society," but the United States must not support a military solution.[93]

Reagan, according to Kagan, wrote back to say that the secretary's "judgments regarding our policy toward the region are correct" and agreed that he was to have "full charge" of Central American policy. Kagan concedes, however, that Shultz "had to wait" before reaping the rewards of "bureaucratic victory," because as the situation in Central America deteriorated over the summer, "Reagan looked to [Clark and Weinberger], not to Shultz for answers."[94]

Gutman, on the other hand, disputes this interpretation, saying that Reagan's decision "reduced [Shultz] to one player in a free-for-all." He pointed out that Reagan went on to note in his response that "success in Central America will require the cooperative effort of several departments and agencies. No single agency can do it alone nor should it.... Still, it is sensible to look to you, as I do, as the lead Cabinet officer, charged with moving aggressively to develop the options in coordination with Cap, Bill Casey and others and coming to me for decisions." Concluding, Reagan said: "I believe in Cabinet government. It works when the Cabinet officers work together. I look to you and Bill Clark to assure that that happens."[95]

Like proverbial blind men groping to identify an elephant purely by touch, each author described part of the president's decision. Reagan did agree to put Shultz in charge of the negotiating track in Central America, but not the Caribbean. In essence, this meant the Contadora process, which had commenced the previous January when Colombia, Panama, Venezuela, and Mexico, meeting on the island of Contadora off the Pacific coast of Panama, proposed region-wide negotiations as a solution to the conflicts in Central America. The initiative had thus far gotten nowhere, but Reagan supported it, appointing a roving ambassador, Richard Stone, to move the process along. Moreover, as Reagan sought to moderate the conflict in Central America, placing emphasis on negotiations made obvious sense.

On the other hand, he reserved for himself control of the problem of Grenada, the full dimensions of which, from all available evidence, he had not yet

---

[93] Kagan, *Twilight Struggle*, 272.
[94] Ibid. Shultz, *Turmoil and Triumph*, 306, also claims that the president "approved all of my suggested rearrangements, which came down to my leading Central America policy . . . "
[95] Gutman, *Banana Diplomacy*, 133.

disclosed to his secretary of state. It appears that Shultz would not be brought into the president's confidence until later in the summer. Thus, Kagan and Gutman are correct to point out that Reagan leaned increasingly on Clark and Weinberger as the summer wore on "for answers." These answers, of course, were to questions about how to stymie Moscow's plans to insert missiles into Grenada. Shultz's behavior through the summer, his poisonous diatribes against Clark, his claim that Clark was usurping power, his repeated claims to have been "blindsided" by policy decisions, all reflected his frustration at being outside the loop.[96]

The simple fact was that Reagan didn't confide in Shultz because he knew that the secretary was pro-détente and would object vociferously to any plan that would lead to confrontation with Moscow. Shultz, like Haig before him and Kissinger, his friend and mentor, before that, strove to forestall the development of any situation that would place an impediment to an eventual accommodation with Moscow. The president already had given Shultz the green light to seek an improvement in relations with the Soviets for reasons noted in the previous chapter having to do with keeping the lines of communication open, but Reagan had no overriding ideological commitment to détente with Moscow the way Shultz did. Quite the reverse.

Grenada and Moscow's "Analogous" Deployment

Since coming to power in 1979, Prime Minister Maurice Bishop had slavishly followed the "advice" of his Cuban and Soviet masters. He emulated Communist practice in intimate detail, including the structure of his regime, its political practices, ideological tenets, even the jargon of the revolution—all of which had turned Grenada into a deadly Caribbean caricature of Communism, exhibiting the same failed-state characteristics of all Soviet satellites.

Long before taking power in 1979, Bishop had been enamored of Castro's form of communism, having visited Havana on many occasions. In fact, Bishop had carried out his coup d'état, as Ashby notes, with "the aid of a team of black Cuban commandos from the Cuban intelligence service's (DGI) Directorate of Special Operations."[97] Indeed, Cuban involvement in Grenada had begun immediately, when, three days after the coup, the Cuban freighter *Matanzas* arrived loaded with Soviet weapons and ammunition, and Cuban advisers.

Within a month, Cuba had established diplomatic relations with Grenada and assigned Julian Torres Rizo as chargé d'affaires. This senior intelligence officer of Castro's America's *Department* would become Cuba's ambassador later in October. From the start, however, Rizo attended "cabinet meetings, where he made policy 'suggestions,' which were rarely contested by Prime Minister

---

[96] See Shultz, *Turmoil and Triumph*, chap. 19, for the most rancorous attacks on a fellow high administration leader this author has ever read.

[97] Timothy Ashby, "Grenada: Soviet Stepping Stone," US Naval Institute *Proceedings* (December 1983), 30, offers a detailed brief history of the Grenadian People's Revolutionary Government, from which this account draws.

Bishop." Cuban advisers organized and trained the Grenadian army and militia, had a controlling presence in key ministries, and established a "training school" for the development of revolutionary cadre for infiltration into the other Caribbean states.

For the first year, the Soviet Union played a behind-the-scenes role, dealing with Grenada through Cuba. However, in March 1980, after Bishop had defended the Soviet invasion of Afghanistan, Moscow began tentatively to deal directly with the regime. Admiral Sergey Gorshkov, head of the Soviet navy, visited Grenada in March and Deputy Prime Minister Bernard Coard reciprocated with a visit to Moscow in May. In Moscow, Coard signed several trade agreements, including an agreement granting the Soviet Union landing rights at the Point Salines airport, on which several hundred Cuban workers had recently begun construction.[98]

In the fall of 1980, Bishop enthusiastically contributed Grenadian *Brigadistas* to the Communist causes in Namibia and Nicaragua and welcomed an expanded role and presence of Cuban and Soviet bloc personnel. The following year, Cuba began work on several new construction projects in addition to the Point Salines airport. Staking out a tightly guarded national security zone, they began construction of an auxiliary airfield, a docking area for patrol boats (three Soviet-built models were donated by Qaddafi), and a 75-kilowatt transmitter for the establishment of Radio Free Grenada.[99]

Moscow's interest and role increased dramatically in the summer of 1982, following, as we now know, the decision to utilize Grenada as the site for Moscow's "analogous" missile deployment. Reflecting the island's increased importance, the Soviets invited Bishop to Moscow in July, feting him for the first time as the "chairman of the Politburo of the Central Committee of the New Jewel Party." The Soviet media pulled out all the stops in covering his meetings with politburo members Mikhail Gorbachev and Nikolay Tikhonov. At the end of his visit, Bishop announced that he had "concluded substantial economic and political agreements with the Soviet Union to cut his country's dependence on the West."[100]

As part of a plan to develop the island's infrastructure, Moscow granted Grenada a $1.4 million credit to cover the purchase of 500 tons of steel, 400 tons of flour and other "essential" goods; extended a $7.7 million credit to finance the construction of a satellite earth station; and agreed to fund and construct a new port on Grenada's east coast. The Soviet Union also agreed to purchase substantial quantities of Grenada's main export crops—bananas, nutmeg and cocoa. Agreements were also signed, strengthening party-to-party relations, making Grenada a full-fledged member of the communist bloc.

Bishop tried to explain that the airport would be used for "tourism," that the satellite earth station was to enable his people to receive "TV and radio

---

[98] Ibid., 31.
[99] Ibid., 32.
[100] Ibid.

programs" from the Soviet Union, and that Soviet ships would be making "recreational calls" at the new port facility.[101] In fact, the Soviets also were constructing a satellite earth station in Nicaragua to accompany the one already in Cuba to facilitate real-time command and control communications between Moscow and its Caribbean satellites. It was also obvious that the airport and port would facilitate more than "tourism" and "recreational" activities.

In September 1982, the Soviets established formal diplomatic relations, appointing three-star general Gennady Sazhenev as ambassador. The embassy was staffed with 33 "diplomats," an unusually large number, considering that the Soviet Union conducted no direct business of any kind with Grenada.[102] Sazhenev was a pied piper, of sorts, of Soviet covert operations in South America, beginning with his assignment to Havana in 1961. From 1969-72, he was assigned to Bogota, Colombia, an assignment that coincided with an upsurge in urban terrorist activity by the M-19 guerrillas. In 1975, as head of a trade mission to Lima, Peru, Sazhenev arranged for the sale of Soviet jet aircraft to the Peruvian government, breaking into the South American market. In 1976, his last post before Grenada, Sazhenev served in Buenos Aires as minister-counselor, a posting which also coincided with an upsurge in urban terrorism by the Montoneros.[103]

While Moscow was gradually fixing its iron grip around Grenada, Bishop was strengthening ties with Castro and Suriname's Bouterse. In October 1982, while on a visit to Paramaribo, as opposition to the regime was growing, Bishop publicly cautioned Bouterse against being "too friendly to its enemies. You must eliminate them, or they will eliminate you." It was six weeks later that Bouterse executed his opponents at Fort Zeelandia and announced his intention to "study the possibility of inviting Soviet and Cuban troops in if the opposition resorts to foreign assistance."[104]

Bishop's Doubts

Despite the surface bravado, Maurice Bishop was privately beginning to have second thoughts about the benefits of his relationship with Moscow. According to Unison Whiteman, one of Bishop's closest allies, by late 1982, the prime minister had begun to realize that without normal relations with the United States, Grenada stood little chance of becoming economically solvent.[105] The promise of tourist wealth being generated by the new airport was meaningless if

[101] Ibid.

[102] Niles Lathem, "Top Red General Directed Isle Coup," *New York Post*, October 27, 1983, 3.

[103] Marvin Alisky, "Grenada's Importance," *Vital Speeches of the Day*, December 15, 1983, 160.

[104] Ashby, "Grenada: Soviet Stepping Stone," 33.

[105] Anthony Payne, Paul Sutton and Tony Thorndike, *Grenada: Revolution and Invasion* (New York: St. Martin's, 1984), 114-15.

the tourists did not come. Continued antagonism toward the United States was self-defeating.

Therefore, a growing conflict of interest began to emerge between Moscow and Bishop. The critical importance of Grenada to Moscow's missile scheme made the Soviets extremely sensitive to any possible vacillation on the part of the Grenadian leadership and they were prepared to secure their interests. Having dealt with the problem of vacillating leaderships many times, from the imposition of Soviet control over the regimes of Eastern Europe in the forties and fifties, to the most recent problems in South Yemen and Afghanistan in 1978, the Soviets were ready to strengthen their hold on Grenada.[106]

Standard Soviet practice was to build a loyal pro-Soviet faction within a bourgeois-nationalist leadership. In the Grenadian case, the immensely popular Maurice Bishop was their vehicle to power, but their staunchly pro-Soviet ally was the number two man, Bernard Coard. The Soviets cultivated Coard from the beginning, calling him to Moscow frequently after the New Jewel Movement came to power. Indeed, as Clark described it:

> A semisecret factional grouping or clique around Bernard Coard had managed, especially since mid-1982, to strengthen its influence and control inside the government apparatus, the officer corps of the army, and in the New Jewel Movement. It functioned more and more as a party within the party.[107]

In the fall of 1982, fearful that Bishop would attempt to loosen ties to the Soviet Union, Moscow instructed Bernard Coard to strengthen his position within the Grenadian leadership. No doubt, newly appointed Ambassador Gennadi Sazhenev and his aides guided him through the process. As his first step, Coard "suddenly resigned from the Central Committee," refusing to attend the October 12, 1982 meeting called to discuss his resignation letter.[108] In his absence, his allies on the Central Committee, led by his wife, Phyllis, turned the focus of discussion away from Coard's letter to the issue of Bishop himself.

At this point, the Politburo was roughly divided, with Bishop holding a slight eight-to-seven majority:

Maurice Bishop	Bernard Coard
Unison Whiteman	Selwyn Strachan
Kenrick Radix	Leon Cornwall

---

[106] See the author's *The Carter Years* for the parallels in Soviet orchestrated coups; 188-90 for Afghanistan and 200-03 for South Yemen.

[107] Steve Clark, "Grenada's Workers' and Farmers' Government: Its Achievements and Its Overthrow," in Bruce Marcus and Michael Taber, ed., *Maurice Bishop Speaks: The Grenada Revolution, 1979-1983* (New York: Pathfinder, 1983), xxix.

[108] Mark Adkin, *Urgent Fury: The Battle for Grenada* (New York: Lexington Books, 1989), 29.

Caldwell Taylor	Hudson Austin
Kamau McBarnette	Phyllis Coard
Fitzroy Bain	Ian St. Bernard
Ian Bartholomew	Christopher de Riggs
George Louison	

Coard's objective was to gain control of the Politburo by virtue of his strength in the Central Committee. Amid raucous debate about the necessity to build a disciplined Leninist party, the first step was to go after two of Bishop's staunchest supporters, Kenrick Radix for his "right opportunism" and Caldwell Taylor for his "ideological laxity," forcing them off the Politburo. At the same time, the Central Committee ordered Bishop's supporters Unison Whiteman, Kamau McBarnette, Fitzroy Bain, and Ian Bartholomew "to attend an eight-week crash course in Marxism-Leninism to be taught by Coard." Finally, three of Coard's allies—Ewart Layne, Liam James, and Chalkie Ventour—were promoted to the Politburo.[109]

Turning on Bishop, they moved to strip control of the people's militia from him (Coard already controlled the army through Austin). Criticizing Bishop's leadership shortcomings and his "general slackness...and analytical weakness in applying Marxist theory," Phyllis Coard prodded the Central Committee into removing Bishop from control over the militia. He was reassigned to oversee rural workers and to keep him in line, a watchdog personal assistant "of high political reliability" was assigned to him.[110]

It had been a major victory for the absent Bernard Coard. The new Politburo balance had been changed from an eight-to-seven majority for Bishop into a ten-to-six majority for Coard. In fact, Coard's position would shortly grow even stronger, as McBarnette would switch sides after undergoing ideological "instruction." The new lineup was as follows:

Maurice Bishop	Bernard Coard
Unison Whiteman	Phyllis Coard
Fitzroy Bain	Selwyn Strachan
George Louison	Leon Cornwall
Ian Bartholomew	Hudson Austin
Kamau McBarnette	Ian St. Bernard
	Christopher de Riggs
	Ewart Layne
	Liam James
	Chalkie Ventour

---

[109] Gregory Sandford and Richard Vigilante, *Grenada: The Untold Story* (New York: Madison Books, 1984), 151-52.
[110] Ibid., 152.

Even though their man was now in a commanding position, the Soviets faced a delicate problem. Like all Soviet client regimes, Grenada was built upon the charismatic appeal of an individual leader, in this case Maurice Bishop. Bishop personified the revolution in Grenada. To remove him would remove the sole source of revolutionary "legitimacy" of the regime. What the Russians directed Bernard Coard and his allies to do was to gain control of Bishop by strengthening their position within the ruling apparatus, not to depose him—at least not yet. It would take time to substitute the party for the individual as the source of political legitimacy. So, in the meantime, Bishop was necessary.

But, if Bishop had to be removed at some point, the legitimacy of the party had to be established. Accordingly, a major focus of discussion and decision during the October plenum was the establishment of "standards" for a "Leninist Chairmanship," creation of a disciplinary committee, and the formulation of a code of conduct for party members. It was also decided to draw up a party constitution, which would include rules for succession.[111] By the fall of 1982, Bernard Coard had put himself into position to control the policymaking apparatus, sharply diluting Bishop's power in the party. However, Bishop's main source of strength was his popular appeal and he would draw upon it in the months ahead as he sought to strengthen his own position and Grenada's independence by shifting the island toward the middle, which meant reaching an accommodation with the United States.

Maurice Bishop Visits Washington

Bishop's opportunity to open a dialogue with Washington came later in the year. In December, Vice-President Bush attended a conference in Miami devoted to a review of business opportunities in Latin America and the Caribbean. In his remarks, Bush described Grenada as an "economically weak," "repressive" regime, wholly "dependent" upon Cuba and the Soviet Union. The Grenadian government issued a low-key, diplomatically worded reply, rebutting the criticism and offering to send a high-level emissary to brief the vice president on the true state of affairs.[112]

American analysts would have been attentive to events in Grenada under ordinary circumstances as a standard approach of keeping track of country developments. Under the circumstances described above, they were especially attentive to the growing conflict within the leadership. Perhaps seeking to probe the possibilities for improving relations, in February 1983, Secretary Shultz replied to the Grenadian message with a conciliatory note to Bishop, the department's first communication with the regime since shortly after it took power.[113]

---

[111] Ibid., 152-53.
[112] Payne et al., *Grenada: Revolution and Invasion*, 115.
[113] Ibid., 115.

Carried by visiting congressman Mervyn Dymally (D-CA), a member of the Congressional Black Caucus, the ostensible purpose of the note was to inform the Grenadian government that all US embassy personnel in Barbados, except Ambassador Milan Bish, were to be accredited to St. George's. Dymally also passed on Shultz's invitation for Bishop to visit Washington. Bishop promptly responded in the affirmative, arranging for Trans Africa, a black American political organization closely tied to the Congressional Black Caucus, to sponsor his visit.[114]

Meanwhile, the Soviet-Cuban-Grenadian-Surinamese connection appeared to be developing. In March 1983, Bishop and Bouterse accompanied Castro to New Delhi for a summit meeting of the so-called "non-aligned nations." In March, too, a Soviet survey team visited the tiny, eleven-square-mile Grenadian dependency of Carriacou, home to 7,000 fishermen and farmers, deciding to build an airfield, naval port, cement plant, and electric power generating plant on the island. The port at Tyrrell Bay had been a sheltered anchorage used by the British fleet in the 18th century. Moscow offered a "gift" of 2,000 tons of steel as part of the developmental package.[115]

Grenada was being squeezed by the two superpowers and popular resentment against the Communist bloc presence on the island was growing, as economic conditions deteriorated. Moscow's pervasive presence, including personnel from Cuba, East Germany, Libya, Bulgaria, Czechoslovakia, and North Korea, were stifling any pretense of Grenadian independence. Then, there was also Reagan's public castigation of Grenada as a Soviet puppet, which was creating an adverse reaction among his people. (Three times as many Grenadians lived in the United States as lived in Grenada.)

It was thus under growing pressure from the superpowers that Bishop arranged for his visit to Washington, May 31 to June 10. Bishop may also have learned from Bouterse about Washington's secret plans to invade Suriname, which would have convinced him that he could face the same predicament. If the United States were willing to use force to overthrow Bouterse, whose regime as yet displayed few of the trappings of a Soviet satellite, what would Reagan be prepared to do about Grenada, which was already an avowed Soviet client? Bishop may also have begun to put two-and-two together and realized that Moscow had more than comradely interest in building extensive air and naval facilities on Grenada and Carriacou, which would have obvious uses beyond tourism and recreation.

Bishop anticipated that he would meet with President Reagan and Secretary Shultz, but when he arrived in Washington, both declined, instead arranging a lower profile meeting with Judge Clark and Kenneth Dam, Shultz's deputy, on June 7. Clark welcomed Bishop's proposal to "discuss differences," as well as to "discuss cooperation." He felt that the United States and Grenada "have

---

[114] Rowland Evans and Robert Novak, "Grenada's Marxist Chiefs Had Friends in Congress," *New York Post*, November 21, 1983, 39.
[115] Ashby, "Grenada: Soviet Stepping Stone," 33.

common strands of history" and hoped that this meeting could "lead to greater progress." Clark stressed that the United States needed to see deeds, not words, from Grenada and declared that "Soviet influence among our neighbors" was "not acceptable."[116]

Bishop complained about what he termed United States' "economic destabilization," because of Washington's determined efforts to block IMF and Caribbean Development Bank loans to Grenada. He also deplored the effects of "Reagan's attacks" on island tourism. Bishop wanted to reach an accommodation with the United States and "agreed to moderate his shrill anti-American rhetoric—and even his Marxist policies—in return for improved relations with Washington."[117] Clark said the administration "held out hope" that Grenada would abandon the communist model of government and "return to a 'basic form'—perhaps their post-colonial constitution of 1974."[118]

Afterwards, Bishop declared that he had been "encouraged...that they are willing to accept talks on the normalization of relations." For his part, he was able to "give the fullest assurance that we constitute no threat to the United States."[119] Possibly, he was also encouraged by the offer of a "small but significant loan from the International Monetary Fund," which he accepted as a sign of the administration's bona fides. According to one source, there had been "a second, off-the-record secret meeting between Bishop and US officials."[120] The upshot was that Bishop believed he had reached an "understanding" with the Reagan administration and had "struck a deal."[121] Both sides agreed, however, "that the content of their meeting should 'remain secret.'"[122]

Strategic Crisis Intensifies Factional Strife

When Bishop returned to Grenada, he attempted to fulfill his commitment to the United States, but only succeeded in intensifying the ongoing power struggle with Bernard Coard, who stymied his efforts. The Central Committee agreed reluctantly to Bishop's instruction to maintain the moratorium on anti-American rhetoric begun before his trip but was concerned that Bishop had exceeded his instruction and had held "unscheduled" and "sensitive" discussions with Clark and Dam "without prior reference and without guidance."

---

[116] Oswald Johnston and Robert Toth, "Notes on Bishop-US Talks Show Willingness for Ties," *Los Angeles Times*, November 22, 1983, A1.

[117] Jack Anderson, "Behind the Purge of Bishop," *Washington Post*, October 30, 1983, C7.

[118] Johnston and Toth, "Notes on Bishop-US Talks [...]."

[119] Ibid.

[120] Jiri and Virginia Valenta, "Leninism in Grenada," in Jiri Valenta and Herbert Ellison, ed., *Grenada and Soviet/Cuban Policy: Internal Crisis and US/OECS Intervention* (Boulder: Westview, 1986), 26.

[121] Anderson, "Behind the Purge of Bishop" and Jack Anderson, "Fateful Meeting," *Kansas City Star*, October 30, 1983, 10.

[122] Valenta, "Leninism in Grenada," 26.

Concern deepened when it was learned that Bishop was planning on reinstituting free elections.[123]

Bishop's next move increased their alarm. He "kicked out the 'diplomats' sent to Grenada by Libya's Colonel Qaddafi, giving them 24 hours to leave."[124] And he stopped the use of Grenada "as a transit point for radical youths from other Caribbean islands to travel to Libya for terrorist training."[125] Cutting the Libyan connection was one thing, but when he prohibited the Cuban ambassador, Rizo, from attending further cabinet meetings, the alarm bells went off in Moscow.[126]

Alarmed at Bishop's trip to Washington, the Russians demanded to know what had transpired there. All that Grenadian ambassador Richard Jacobs could tell Vladimir Kazimirov, Director of the First Latin America Department, was that "the results were confidential."[127] For the ever-suspicious Russians, this was the "turning point" in their relationship with Bishop. The Valentas thought that "given the traditional Soviet paranoia about the loyalty and orthodoxy of its socialist allies, the Soviet leadership had sufficient reason to lose confidence in Bishop."[128] Traditional Soviet paranoia played its part, but the issue was far more important. Having made the decision to use Grenada in its missile scheme and invested heavily in preparing the grounds for it, they were not about to let it all slip away because Maurice Bishop had suddenly gotten cold feet.

The Soviets suspected that Bishop had struck a deal with Washington, which left them with no choice but to accelerate Coard's timetable to take over the leadership. Responding to Moscow's decision to tighten its control further, Coard convened the Central Committee for its "first full-scale wholistic plenary," a marathon, six-and-a-half-day meeting, lasting from July 13 to 19. The results of the meeting, expressed in what were referred to as the July Resolutions, were that the party had failed "to transform itself ideologically and organizationally and to exercise firm leadership along a Leninist path."

Leadership work had "improved marginally," but "anti-communism and the ideological offensive of the church had been gaining ground." The economy had "stagnated," and the confidence of the masses had been "shaken." Worst of all, the plenum noted "the emergence of deep petty-bourgeois manifestations and influence" in the Party.[129] Still, while acknowledging the failings of the regime,

---

[123] Payne et al., *Grenada: Revolution and Invasion*, 116.

[124] Alisky, "Grenada's Importance," 160.

[125] Anderson, "Behind the Purge of Bishop."

[126] Ashby, "Grenada: Soviet Stepping Stone," 33, agrees that this decision "angered the Soviets and Cubans" and set in motion the chain of events that led to his death, but dates it in the previous fall. In my view, the fall of 1982 is when relations between Havana, Moscow, and St. George's, were closest and so keeping Rizo out then was unlikely.

[127] Document no.6, in Valenta and Ellison, *Grenada in Soviet/Cuba Policy*, 309.

[128] Ibid., 26-27.

[129] Ibid., 153.

Bishop had managed to insert language affirming his leadership role. The "July resolutions" maintained that the party's "line of march" was essentially correct.[130]

Coard's allies, no doubt under Moscow's prodding, strongly objected to the general conclusion of the July resolutions that the party's line was correct and demanded an emergency meeting, which was held on August 26. There, Coard's allies, Liam James and Selwyn Strachan, attacked the July decisions and implicitly Bishop. James pointed out that the situation continued to worsen to the point that "the party itself was now beginning to disintegrate." Strachan declared that "sections of the NJM had begun to rebel against the higher organs of the party." Unless properly handled, "this silent rebellion could easily turn into an open revolt."[131]

At the heart of the problem, said Strachan, "stood the fact that the Central Committee in July had not really criticized itself." Indeed, rank and file party members "did not dare to express their criticisms of the CC openly because of their feeling that certain committee members were hostile to criticism." It was decided to hold a full Central Committee plenum again in mid-September to rectify the party's failings. Bringing the meeting to a close, "Bishop agreed that the party was in danger of disintegration and that many party members were afraid to speak up."

Bishop's plan, it seems, was to mobilize the base of the party on his side as he urged the Central Committee membership "to rap with party members, leading mass organizations, activists, leading militia types, consistent participants in Zonal Councils, and party support groups,"[132] to prepare for the coming plenum. But, as we will see in the next chapter, Reagan's plan to draw Bishop over to the US side would fail, amid an international crisis that would superimpose itself on the factional strife occurring in Grenada, and Moscow's determination to keep control of the island would precipitate the demise of Maurice Bishop and his regime.

A Summer of Carrots

Meanwhile, as he had done time and time again during his presidency, Reagan offered both the carrot and the stick to an adversary. He had put Clark in charge of the arms control process—the Grenada problem—and the Middle East, which meant, of course, that he himself was in charge, even though Clark was increasingly portrayed as the real power in the administration. The president now authorized Shultz to offer to engage the Soviets in a "constructive dialogue," which the secretary did in testimony before the Senate Foreign Relations Committee on June 15. In its essence, Shultz's statement was a softened version

---

[130] Kai Schoenhals and Richard Melanson, *Revolution and Intervention in Grenada: The New Jewel Movement, the United States, and the Caribbean* (Boulder: Westview, 1985), 64.

[131] Ibid., 65

[132] Ibid., 65.

of NSDD-75, but to ensure that the proper message was sent, the president "went over it with him line by line."[133]

We do not accept "as inevitable," Shultz declared, "the prospect of endless, dangerous confrontation with the Soviet Union," which would only put "out of reach" many of the goals that the United States pursues in world affairs—peace, human rights, economic progress, national independence. A peaceful world order does not require that the United States and the Soviet Union agree on all matters of "morals or politics." Détente, "unfortunately" and "regrettably" did not lead to the kind of restraint that had been envisaged. Nor had containment succeeded. Our policy goes beyond both.[134]

"Our policy begins with the clear recognition that the Soviet Union is and will remain a global superpower." Unlike détente, however, "it assumes that the Soviet Union is more likely to be deterred by our actions that make clear the risks their aggression entails than by a delicate web of interdependence. The central goal of our national security policy is deterrence of war; restoring and maintaining the strategic balance is a necessary condition for that deterrence."

He described how the United States had begun accelerated programs to rebuild its strategic and conventional power and had rebuilt the Western Alliance. Furthermore, "we are helping our friends to help themselves and to help each other," politically, economically, and were assisting "our friends in the third world to build a foundation for democracy." Still, "strength and realism can deter war, but only direct dialogue and negotiation can open the path toward lasting peace."

"We have sought peaceful diplomatic solutions to regional issues," he said, in an "attempt to remove the obstacles that Soviet conduct puts in the way of resolving these problems," which are "central to progress." Thus, the United States sought to "encourage the departure of Soviet-backed forces" in the Middle East, withdrawal of Vietnam from Kampuchea, Soviet withdrawal from Afghanistan, a peace agreement in Namibia, as well as a peaceful solution to the "conflict and instability" in Central America.

Shultz also averred that "our policy is not one of economic warfare against the USSR." Trade in non-strategic areas "contributes to constructive East-West relations." Indeed, he said, "we have recently agreed . . . to extend our bilateral fisheries agreement for one year and have begun to negotiate a new long-term . . . grain agreement. Our grain sales are on commercial terms and are not made with government-supported credits or guarantees of any kind."

Toward the end of his remarks, Shultz attempted to rebut a recently published Senate Foreign Relations Committee analysis of US-Soviet relations that described the relationship as "worse than ever." While admitting that things were "serious" and "stormy," he cautioned against being misled by "atmospherics." To illustrate what he meant, the secretary referred to the Soviet decision to sign the Austrian state treaty in 1955, claiming that the "atmospherics"

---

[133] Shultz, *Turmoil and Triumph*, 276.
[134] "Excerpts from Shultz Statement on Soviet Relations to Senate Committee," *New York Times*, June 16, 1983, A16.

of the Cold War "did not prevent agreement." Soviet policy was affected by "our resolve and clarity of purpose. And the result was progress," which he hoped would be the case now.[135] Finally, Shultz declared:

> [There is] no certainty that our current negotiations with the Soviets will lead to acceptable agreements. What is certain is that we will not find ourselves in the position in which we found ourselves in the aftermath of détente. We have not staked so much on the prospect of a successful negotiating outcome that we have neglected to secure ourselves against the possibility of failure.[136]

Both the president and Shultz were satisfied with this statement. From Shultz's point of view, and that of the political establishment, he had "spelled out our requirements, and our hope, for a more constructive relationship with the Soviet Union." While Shultz emphasized "hope," the president no doubt emphasized "requirements." Most of all, for him, this statement established yet another marker that would justify taking strong action in the face of expected Soviet aggressive action in coming months.

Shultz wanted more, however, insisting on authority to negotiate additional agreements, and the president reluctantly acceded. As Shultz described it, "after a long battle inside the White House and NSC staff, President Reagan gave me the authority I was looking for." However, Reagan agreed only to permit Shultz to "start negotiations on a new cultural-exchanges agreement and on the opening of consulates in Kiev and New York."[137] If Shultz sought to offer carrots, the president insured that they were small carrots, and he took out a big stick.

Sticks in the Water

In the spring, as evidence grew of increased Soviet shipments to Nicaragua, the president had instructed the Pentagon to plan for ways to put American naval power into position to block them. Reportedly, plans for these "maneuvers were discussed in at least six inter-agency meetings since mid-June."[138] A few days after Shultz's speech, word promptly leaked that the "Pentagon has a sketchy contingency plan for deploying ships and aircraft to stop war supplies from entering and leaving Nicaragua by sea and air." The plan called for "stationing one US aircraft carrier and its protecting ships and submarines off

---

[135] This was a dubious argument, both as to accuracy and relevance. Most historians believe that the Soviet agreement to settle the Austrian dispute was a function of the post-Stalin leadership's larger decision to seek a neutral barrier between East and West Europe, of which Austria was a part.

[136] "Excerpts from Shultz Statement on Soviet Relations to Senate Committee."

[137] Shultz, *Turmoil and Triumph*, 281.

[138] Don Oberdorfer, "US Latin Policy Reflects a New Sense of Urgency," *Washington Post*, August 7, 1983, A1.

Nicaragua's east coast and a second carrier off its west coast." Castro's ability to "harass" supply ships was noted, but it was believed that the United States navy "could blockade Nicaragua."[139]

This rather sanguine outlook for a "contingency plan," implying no near-term development, was abruptly changed when intelligence identified the loading of a dozen Soviet and East bloc ships bound for Nicaragua. This represented a major jump in tonnage delivered to the Sandinista regime from 10,000 tons delivered in 1981 and 1982 to "a rate of 20,000 tons" this year. Moreover, the cargo consisted of heavier equipment. For example, in May, a Soviet vessel had unloaded some 350 trucks and the Soviets had "recently delivered eight to 10 Mi8 troop-carrying helicopters to Nicaragua and more appear to be en route." [140]

The increase in the rate of deliveries of more advanced weaponry presaged a sharp increase in the level of conflict. As sailing time for Soviet cargo freighters was about a month from Black Sea ports to Nicaragua's east coast, the president sought to get naval and air power into position to be able to deal with this problem. There was also the nagging suspicion that the Soviets just might, as in 1962, attempt to slip missiles into Nicaragua aboard one or more of the Soviet ships. More likely was the possibility they would attempt to deliver MiG-21s, which would also sharply raise the risk of open conflict.[141] Even more worrying were intelligence reports that Cuba had begun a reserve call-up and amphibious assault exercises, which suggested preparations for intervention.[142] Was Castro preparing to reinforce Grenada?

With an "increased sense of urgency," therefore, the president abruptly decided to convene an NSC meeting on July 8. Shultz, in the Middle East, deemed the session "so important...that he traveled 24 hours straight to get back in time."[143] Reconstructing from fragmentary data, it appears that the July 8 meeting was where the president roundtabled his options for dealing with the coming challenge in the Caribbean. A key issue was how to reverse the slide in public support. "Public support had slipped," the White House acknowledged, and had become a "negative drumbeat." The question was: how to reverse this trend? [144]

---

[139] "US Has Sketchy Contingency Plan to Curb Nicaragua Supplies," *Washington Post*, June 20, 1983, A4.

[140] Michael Getler, "Soviets Speed Up Nicaragua Arms, US Officials Say," *Washington Post*, July 2, 1983, A1.

[141] Clarridge, *Spy for All Seasons*, 243-44, notes that at both NSPG and RIG meetings officials were becoming "increasingly concerned about the possible introduction of MiG-21 aircraft into Nicaragua."

[142] "Military Moves by Soviet, Cuba Said to Spur Reagan Actions," *Baltimore Sun*, July 29, 1983, A1.

[143] Don Oberdorfer, "US Latin Policy Reflects a New Sense of Urgency," *Washington Post*, August 7, 1983, A1.

[144] "White House Says Public Support Is Slipping on Central America Aid," *New York Times*, June 25, 1983, 3.

At the NSC meeting, the "central point of disagreement...[was] the management of consent at home: how far and how fast the administration can go in Central America without exceeding the tolerance of the public and the political system in the United States." The president's answer was to pick up on an idea that had been floated earlier when polls began to show the slippage. He would establish a bipartisan commission on Central America in an attempt to forge some consensus. Tellingly, Reagan named Henry Kissinger to head it.[145] In fact, Kissinger would set up his office inside the State Department, where he could advise Shultz on how to proceed.[146]

The key topic, however, was the response to Soviet moves. After discussing a variety of "graduated military options," the president instructed Weinberger to bring forward the contingency plans he had prepared for naval and air exercises in the Caribbean, as well as ground exercises in Honduras. Shultz was skeptical. He doubtless pointed out that naval maneuvers would have little short-term impact on the ground in Nicaragua, but could lead to confrontation with Moscow. Obviously, Shultz was still not in the decision loop regarding the true purpose of the naval deployments. He thought that "President Reagan had made decisions about maneuvers and potential military actions on the basis of faulty intelligence," suggesting that Clark and Weinberger were operating behind his back.[147]

The president also wanted a new finding prepared to authorize greater support for a larger Contra force. The finding dropped "interdiction" as the main purpose behind support of the Contras. The new mission was "to force changes in Nicaraguan government policies."[148] According to Gutman, the "idea was to spread the notion that the United States was planning an invasion."[149] Looking at the broader chessboard, it was also decided to send Weinberger to China in an attempt to foster greater military cooperation with Beijing and send the message that in any US-Soviet conflict, Moscow would have to be concerned about multiple fronts.[150]

The president also wanted to step up the diplomatic pace, instructing roving ambassador Richard Stone to prod the dormant Contadora group into action, to bring the Central American foreign ministers together for broad discussions. He also instructed him to attempt to get the two sides in El Salvador talking. These "no agenda" talks were designed to explore the possibility of

---

[145] Lou Cannon, "Kissinger Will Head Latin Panel," *Washington Post*, July 18, 1983, A1.

[146] Shultz, *Turmoil and Triumph*, 309.

[147] Ibid., 312-14.

[148] Don Oberdorfer, "CIA Planning to Back More Nicaragua Rebels," *Washington Post*, July 14, 1983, A1.

[149] Gutman, *Banana Diplomacy*, 144. See also Fred Hiatt, "Administration 'Finding' Justifies Covert Operations in Nicaragua," *Washington Post*, July 27, 1983, A1.

[150] Charles Corddry, "Weinberger to Visit China; Expected to Discuss Military Sales," *Baltimore Sun*, July 12, 1983, A6.

inducing the rebels to put down their weapons and participate openly in Salvadoran electoral politics.[151]

As was his practice with contentious issues, the president deferred a decision on the naval maneuvers for four days. On the 12th (Gutman says the 13th), the president issued orders for "aircraft carrier exercises near Grenada and Suriname" and very large air and ground exercises in Honduras, involving between three and five-thousand US troops. The naval exercises were to continue for an unprecedented *six months*, beginning August 1. He also ordered preparation of detailed plans for quarantine and interdiction.[152]

Events would prompt the president to move sooner than he had planned, however. The dozen Soviet ships were now under way and the first was expected to reach Nicaragua by the end of the month, if not sooner. Fearing the worst, on the 15th, two weeks earlier than planned, Clark recommended diverting the aircraft carrier USS *Ranger* with its seventy aircraft and seven support ships, which were headed out to the Western Pacific, to Central America, instead. Top officials and the president had endorsed the recommendation, but there had been no time to inform Shultz or congressional leaders, who immediately complained.[153]

News of the *Ranger* diversion did not appear in the press, however, until the 20th, the day after the president's speech on Central America. A key line in the speech came after his description of the Soviet-Cuban buildup in Nicaragua: "This cannot be allowed to continue."[154] When news of the sudden shift of the carrier battle group to the west coast of Nicaragua appeared, press accounts opined that the ship movement "appeared to have stemmed from a recent high-level decision to use them as a signal that the administration is increasingly serious about safeguarding US security interests in that area."[155] It was also to put US ships into position to meet the Soviet ships that were heading for the port of Corinto, on the west coast of Nicaragua.

During a 12-minute press conference the next day, the president rebutted the charge that the United States was practicing "gunboat diplomacy," saying "we're conducting exercises such as we've conducted before in this hemisphere." The president acknowledged that naval exercises would be held off both the Atlantic and Pacific coasts of Nicaragua but dodged a question about a blockade. "A blockade is a very serious thing. I would hope that eventuality will not arise," he said.[156]

---

[151] Oberdorfer, "US Latin Policy Reflects a New Sense of Urgency."

[152] Ibid., and Gutman, *Banana Diplomacy*, 143, who says Weinberger laid out twelve exercise plans in a "top secret" memo to the president.

[153] Gutman, 146-7.

[154] "Excerpts from the President's Speech," *New York Times*, July 19, 1983, A6.

[155] "Carrier Heads Battle Group," *Baltimore Sun*, July 20, 1983, A1.

[156] Jeremiah O'Leary, "Reagan Says Navy Exercise Is Not Gunboat Diplomacy," *Washington Times*, July 22, 1983, A1.

It was also publicly disclosed that the carrier *Coral Sea* and its battle group, now in the Mediterranean, would arrive off the east coast in mid-August and the battleship *New Jersey* currently in Southeast Asia, would arrive in the Caribbean by the end of the month.[157] The US naval maneuvers, along with the exercises in Honduras, were expected to continue through the end of the year. In short, as time for the deployment of Pershing II missiles into West Germany drew near, the president was deploying naval and air power into the Caribbean to prevent Moscow's expected "analogous" missile threat.

Shultz Attempts to Soften the Edge

Just as US and Soviet ships were about to converge near Nicaragua, however, on July 25, Secretary Shultz precipitated a crisis within the administration by suddenly tendering his resignation. He claimed that over a several-week period he had been "blindsided" by Judge Clark, who had "without my knowledge and behind my back," obtained the approval from the president possibly based on "faulty evidence" to commence naval maneuvers in Central America and the Caribbean. He recounts:

> The biggest shock for me came with the revelation in late July that the United States was planning "Big Pine II," a six-month-long exercise off both the Atlantic and Pacific coasts of Nicaragua during which American and Honduran troops would conduct war games on Honduran territory. Three thousand or more US combat troops would be involved. The Pentagon had wanted to do it, and Bill Clark had approved it. I was totally blindsided, and I did not know the extent to which President Reagan had been involved. I knew that I had no chance to give him my views.[158]

Shultz's claim that he had been cut out of the decision-making loop on the naval maneuvers is highly dubious. Moreover, his own account does not support his claim that he had been "blindsided." Nor was there any basis for Shultz's charge that the president had acted on the basis of faulty evidence. Shultz clearly was not part of the president's inner decision-making circle, but he was included in all NSC meetings, including the key July 8 session where the naval maneuvers had been discussed at length. It appears likely, however, that he had not, as yet, been briefed on the deeper purpose of the maneuvers.

It was also true that the president had transferred the arms control negotiations, Central America, and Middle East issues to the White House, where they were being coordinated by Judge Clark. While that undoubtedly rankled the secretary, it cannot be said that he had had no policy input into these portfolios,

---

[157] Lou Cannon, "Maneuvers Part of US Strategies," *Washington Post*, July 22, 1983, A1.

[158] Shultz, *Turmoil and Triumph*, 310-11.

either. Indeed, he had been the point man on the Middle East since the previous fall, played a large role in the arms control negotiations, and was involved in the political side of Central America, especially the Contadora process.

Everyone understood that Clark spoke for the president and was not an independent actor in the policy process. Yet, Shultz argued as if Clark were an independent player with his own policy agenda, acting at variance to the president's interests. Indeed, Shultz portrayed the situation as a "fight" between himself and Clark for the president's ear. The truth was, however, that Clark was the president's man and Shultz's attacks on him were in fact attacks on the policy the president was pursuing, particularly regarding the Soviet Union.

Indeed, Soviet policy lay at the center of Shultz's decision to tender his resignation. He saw the crisis coming with Moscow over the naval maneuvers and sought to head it off. He told the president: "you can conduct foreign policy out of the White House if you want to, but you don't need me under those circumstances." He would not be an "errand boy," demanding that "no foreign policy moves should go forward that the secretary of state does not know about and weigh in on. I do not expect to get my way all the time.... That is not the point. The point is to know what is going on so that I can, at a minimum, give you the benefit of my advice."[159]

Shultz's own account of the decision-making chronology on the naval maneuvers belied his claim to have been blindsided, demonstrating a clear understanding of the steps taken during this period. His charge that "State did not see" a crucial memo until July 25 ignores the obvious process underway. His assertion that it was not until "shortly after" July 18, that "Defense got orders to proceed," was incorrect. The diversion of the *Ranger* occurred on the 15th and the president had issued his proceed order on the 12th. Indeed, anyone carefully reading the newspaper would have been reasonably well-informed about "contingency plans" for naval maneuvers, which first appeared on June 20, over a month earlier.[160]

Shultz was concerned about the maneuvers, less because he had been "blindsided" by Clark than because of what the maneuvers portended—a confrontation with the Soviet Union. There can be little doubt that Shultz made the case for continuing the "constructive dialogue" with Moscow and avoiding confrontation. He had received a reply from Anatoly Dobrynin, the Soviet ambassador, on July 15, that Moscow agreed to start talks on cultural exchanges and new consulates and pointed out that the ongoing negotiations regarding a new, long-term grain agreement were nearing completion.[161]

It was Shultz who had blindsided Reagan, and the president had been "visibly shaken" by Shultz's maneuver. To keep him on board, however, Reagan agreed to mute criticism of Moscow and allow Shultz to pursue negotiations. "He said he wanted me to do the job; he had no idea how these things had happened,"

---

[159] Ibid., 313.
[160] Ibid., 314.
[161] Ibid., 281.

yet "he could understand how they affected me," Shultz maintained. The fact is, that after the July 25 confrontation, the president did broaden his policy approach, and what Shultz termed a "mini thaw" with Moscow ensued, although Shultz claimed in his memoir that he had "left the Oval Office without a feeling that a definitive change would be made."[162]

He was correct. Two days later, the president reiterated his position, declaring that the naval exercises were intended to provide a "shield for democracy" in the region and were not a signal of a larger, permanent American role. But, he also reaffirmed his support for the Contadora process.[163] Then, in seeming defiance of the House of Representatives vote to cut funds for the Contras, which Democrats described as Reagan's "secret war,"[164] on July 28, he signed NSDD-100, which formally authorized a "program of expanded US military activities and exercises both in the Caribbean Basin and on the Pacific coast of Central America."[165]

These exercises were to "commence as soon as possible" and continue for "four to six months." Moreover, the directive stipulated, "the Secretary of State and the Secretary of Defense will prepare a coordinated legislative, diplomatic, and public affairs strategy that supports these initiatives." Finally, this "implementation plan should be provided to the Assistant to the President for National Security Affairs for Presidential review and approval by July 30, 1983." In other words, the president ordered Shultz and Weinberger to work together on a coordinated plan and submit it to Judge Clark in two days. For the time being, Shultz's role, and Clark's, would remain unchanged.

The Heat of August

Stepping unwittingly into this domestic imbroglio, Soviet Defense Minister Dmitri Ustinov said, in response to speculation that Moscow might acquiesce in the US deployment of Pershing II missiles, that Moscow was "determined to counter effectively" any deployment. He elaborated:

> We will take such countermeasures that will make the military
> threat to the territory of the United States and the countries on
> whose territories American missiles will be deployed the same

---

[162] Ibid., 281, 313.

[163] Steven Weisman, "Reagan Denies Aim Is Bigger Presence in Latin Countries," *New York Times*, July 27, 1983, A1.

[164] Don Oberdorfer, "House Acts to Bar CIA Rebel Aid," *Washington Post*, July 29, 1983, A1. The House vote was unlikely to withstand Senate scrutiny but placed the Democratic Party squarely in opposition to the president.

[165] NSDD-100, "Enhanced US Military Activity and Assistance for the Central American Region," July 28, 1983, in Simpson, *National Security Directives*, 313-14.

as the one the United States is trying to create for the Soviet Union and our allies.[166]

To Reagan administration officials, now including George Shultz, it was abundantly clear that Moscow was not backing down. Ustinov had precisely reiterated Brezhnev's statement of March 1982. There was no room for obfuscation. Making the *same* threat to the United States that Washington would make to Moscow meant missiles—SS-20 missiles—in the Caribbean. To conduct his own assessment as to the imminence of the threat, Bill Casey embarked upon a secret trip to Africa and the Middle East at the beginning of August.

Casey stopped first in West Africa, talking to the leaders of Senegal, the Ivory Coast, Nigeria, Zaire, Zambia, and South Africa—all nations whose airfields were possible transshipping points to Grenada—before streaking off to the Middle East.[167] There were doubtless many items on Casey's agenda, but one of the most important had to be a survey of air service arrangements currently available to Moscow. He would also want to explore the kind of cooperation the United States could expect to receive from these countries—would they cooperate the way Brasilia had?

Aside from the air transit scenario, there was also the more obvious possibility that missiles could be aboard one or more of the half-dozen ships now steaming for Nicaragua. Fortunately, Reagan's timely decision to divert the *Ranger* carrier battle group to the region put American power in position to thwart such a plan (and also quietly put to rest Shultz's charge that he had acted on the basis of faulty intelligence). The *Ranger* had only arrived in the region the previous week and its escorting destroyers began carefully scrutinizing each ship as it headed for port. There is no doubt that US surveillance systems also observed the unloading of cargo.

The first encounter set the tone for the rest when the US destroyer *Lynde McCormick* hailed the first Soviet freighter, *Alexander Ulyanov*, on July 30, after it transited the Panama Canal and headed for Nicaragua's Pacific port of Corinto. After inquiring by radio of the ship's cargo and destination, the destroyer followed the freighter to within twelve miles of the Nicaraguan coast before returning to its position with the battle group.[168] Moscow immediately complained that Washington was "planning a sea blockade of Nicaragua that…would amount to an act of piracy," and lodged a formal protest.[169]

The Defense Department also quietly gave notice that there would be three carrier battle groups deployed to the region, not two, as originally

---

[166] Dusko Doder, "Defense Minister Says Moscow Will Move to Counter Deployment of US Missiles," *Washington Post*, July 31, 1983, A21.

[167] Woodward, *Veil*, 267-68.

[168] Richard Halloran, "Pentagon Reports Encounter at Sea with Soviet Ship," *New York Times*, August 4, 1983, A1.

[169] "Soviets Charge US Plans to Blockade Nicaragua," *Washington Post*, August 4, 1983, A7.

announced.[170] The third group, led by the carriers *Independence* and *John F. Kennedy*, involved thirty-six ships, including six British and one Dutch vessel. Designated *Readex-2-83*, it would deploy in the Western Atlantic and Caribbean from the third week in August. Their exercises were described as "routine," but separate from the operations of the *Coral Sea* and *Ranger* carrier battle groups.[171] They were accompanied at the outset by eight B-52 bombers that conducted "maritime surveillance," tracking Soviet ship movements.[172]

In an unprecedented move, Reagan had deployed four carriers to the Pacific, Caribbean, and Western Atlantic, a massive display of firepower and national will, as if to challenge Moscow to make good on its threat. Should the Soviets attempt to do so, however, they would clearly be the aggressor and the United States the defender, a posture reinforced by the continued demonstration of good will toward Moscow. In this regard, President Reagan encouraged George Shultz, who pressed for the conclusion of a series of agreements with the Soviets, including a summit meeting between the two nation's leaders.

Once again, the president was sensibly employing both the carrot and the stick. Shultz pressed forward through the month of August engaging the Soviets in negotiations on several fronts. By the end of the month the two sides had agreed to reopen discussions on a new cultural and scientific exchanges agreement and on establishing consulates in New York City and Kiev. He concluded negotiations on a new five-year grain agreement and the president lifted his ban on Caterpillar Corporation's proposed sale of pipe-laying equipment to the Soviet Union.

There appeared, also, to be a possible breakthrough in the intermediate-range missile negotiations, when, on the 26th, Andropov declared that any SS-20 missiles included in the agreement would be destroyed and not merely moved to the eastern regions of the Soviet Union. There was less to it than it appeared, as Andropov tempered his offer by reiterating the threat to counter the Pershing II missiles if they were deployed:

> If the position of the United States at the negotiations continues to be unconstructive and lopsided and if it actually comes to the deployment in Europe of American Pershings and cruise missiles, we shall naturally be compelled to take appropriate countermeasures to preserve the balance of forces both on the regional, European and *on the global scale*. This should be quite clear to everyone.[173]

---

[170] "US Raises Number of Troops Set for Honduran Exercises," *Baltimore Sun*, August 4, 1983, A2.

[171] "3rd Major Naval Exercise Starts," *Washington Times*, August 23, 1983, A3.

[172] "B-52s Involved in Warship's Maneuvering," *Washington Post*, September 1, 1983, A11.

[173] John Burns, "Andropov Closes Loophole in Stand on Cuts in Missiles," *New York Times*, August 27, 1983, A1, emphasis added.

The Soviet side also renewed discussion of the "walk in the woods" formula that had been rejected a year earlier. It went nowhere. Finally, Shultz, aided by Mike Deaver in the White House, perhaps hoping to avert a crisis through personal diplomacy, began to press publicly for a summit meeting between Reagan and Andropov.[174] Andropov, however, dismissed it, declaring a summit meeting to be "meaningless" under present circumstances.[175] There was less to the "mini thaw" than had been hoped.

---

[174] Rowland Evans and Robert Novak, "The Push for a Summit," *Washington Post*, August 24, 1983, A27.
[175] Rudy Abramson, "Soviet Leader Sees Reagan Meeting as 'Meaningless,'" *Washington Post*, August 26, 1983, A22.

Chapter 3

How Close to Breakout?
Krasnoyarsk and KAL 007

The fall of 1983 saw American and Soviet strategies come into sharp and protracted conflict and their respective leaderships undergo fundamental shifts in composition and outlook. President Reagan sought to take the next and arguably most important step in eliminating the Soviet Union's strategic weapons edge, with the deployment of Pershing II and cruise missiles to Western Europe. The Pershing II, in particular, would not only make an important contribution to the defense of Western Europe, but it also would repair a major deficiency in the American strategic weapons arsenal, by giving the United States a small but significant precision, hard-target, quick strike capability against the Soviet Union.[1]

On the other hand, Yuri Andropov, seeking to maintain Moscow's strategic weapons advantage, was determined either to prevent US deployment, or neutralize it with an "analogous" deployment of missiles into the Caribbean. The Soviets were mounting a major West German-focused, European-wide campaign against deployment of US weapons, while offering their own plan for an arms control settlement. Rejecting Reagan's zero option, Andropov proposed a strictly Euro-strategic balance in which the number of Soviet weapons would be equal to those of Britain and France but requiring the cancellation of American missiles.

Needless to say, the Reagan administration was not at all interested in effectively handing Western Europe over to the Soviet Union but was acutely alert to the Soviet threat of an analogous deployment. As discussed in the previous chapter, Reagan had decided that the first step in the Soviet plan involved the deployment of SS-20s to Grenada; hence his deployment of four carrier battle groups, comprising over 60 ships and over 250 planes to the greater Caribbean area. Under existing circumstances, the United States could expect to deter or defeat any Soviet move to deploy missiles to the Caribbean, but there was an outside chance that the Soviets could surprise and turn the tables on the United States. It was the effort to guard against the worst case that would lead to one of

---

[1] For a discussion of the self-inflicted American nuclear dilemma, see Thornton, *Ronald Reagan: Revolution Ascendant*, chap. 5.

the most serious crises of the Cold War—the Soviet attack on Korean Air Lines Flight 007, on September 1, 1983.

Intelligence Discovery

Reagan administration officials had operated on the assumption that under existing strategic circumstances Moscow's repeated threats to deploy missiles to the Caribbean region were a bluff. Moscow would take no actions that would trigger an actual nuclear conflict, which would result in a national catastrophe for both sides. However, if the USSR could alter the strategic weapons equation and demonstrate that it could emerge victorious over the United States in a nuclear conflict, then the Soviet threat of analogous deployment took on a much more ominous dimension.

The only circumstance that offered Moscow the promise of fundamentally changing the nuclear balance was a breakout from the ABM Treaty. If the Soviet Union could hold not only a strategic weapons advantage, but also acquire the ability to defend against a nuclear attack, the Soviets would fundamentally alter the strategic weapons balance. Then, and only then, would Moscow be able to deploy missiles successfully to the Caribbean, in what would be the reverse of the strategic situation that obtained during the Cuban missile crisis of 1962.

In fact, from early in the Reagan administration, analysts focused on the possibility of an ABM breakout.[2] Central to the breakout scenario was Moscow's new phased-array battle-management radar system, the heart of any missile defense. The large phased-array radar (LPAR) was capable of identifying and tracking hundreds of incoming warheads and assigning interceptor missiles to destroy them. If an LPAR network was adequate to protect Soviet missile fields and thus Moscow's retaliatory capability, while the US lacked such a system, it would establish a decisive Soviet strategic weapons advantage.

The 1972 ABM Treaty permitted each side to have a single missile defense site, including a limited number of missiles, launchers and radars, either to protect its capital or a missile field.[3] The Soviets established an ABM system to protect Moscow, and in the early 1980s, were installing a phased-array radar at Pushkino—ostensibly to upgrade the defense against missiles aimed at the capital, but also potentially covering nearby missile fields. (The United States built an

---

[2] William Parham, "Will Soviets 'Break Out' of ABM Accord?" *Norwich Bulletin*, April 7, 1981, 1.

[3] The original treaty signed in May 1972 allowed each country to have two ABM sites, including one to protect the capital and one to protect a missile field; but a 1974 protocol changed the agreement to allow only one or the other. The ABM treaty, from which the US withdrew effective June 13, 2002, can be found in Gerard Smith, *Doubletalk: The Story of SALT I* (New York: Doubleday, 1980), 487-502; and at https://2009-2017.state.gov/t/avc/trty/101888.htm.

ABM site at Grand Forks, North Dakota, but shut it down in February 1976, just a few months after it became fully operational.)

An agreed statement accompanying the treaty prohibited either side from deploying new large phased-array radars except in a few circumstances: within the single permitted ABM deployment area; within permitted ABM test ranges; as early warning radars deployed along each country's periphery and oriented outward; or for space-tracking or national technical means of verification.[4] By late 1982, in addition to the Pushkino radar, the USSR had deployed or was constructing five LPARs around or near its periphery: one in the north at Olengorsk; one at Pechora near the Kara Sea; one at Mishelevka in the Far East; one at the Sary Shagan missile test range in Kazakhstan; and one at Lyaki in Azerbaijan.[5]

Reagan administration officials were concerned about Soviet testing of missile defense components, which generated growing discussion of Soviet treaty violations and fed concern about the possibility of a missile defense breakout. The Russians were probing the boundaries of the treaty by reportedly testing "a variety of surface-to-air missiles in an ABM mode, in violation of the treaty, including the SAM-10 and SAM-12." These missiles were also mobile, which was "another treaty violation," and were in "mass production." [6] But CIA estimates put the possibility of breakout several years away.

A February 15, 1983 CIA estimate of Soviet strategic nuclear capabilities, for example, was skeptical of any possibility of near-term deployment of a nationwide Soviet ABM system, as well as its viability, but declared that once activated, the Soviet system "would probably be more effective against SLBMs than against ICBMs, if adequate coverage of SLBM approaches were provided by battle management support radars."[7] The fact was, however, that the US missile threat against the Soviet Union was primarily sea-based, by a ratio of five at sea to two on land, which meant that a Soviet ABM system would be effective against the main US threat.

When, during a routine scan of Soviet territory, a reconnaissance satellite discovered yet a sixth large phased-array radar providing precisely such coverage, concern deepened, not only regarding the capability of the system, but also its projected date of operation. This sixth LPAR site was located not on the periphery, but in the Soviet interior near the village of Abalakovo in the Krasnoyarsk administrative area, and just north of the city of Krasnoyarsk. Press reports dated the discovery at mid-year, but there were indications that the complex had been discovered considerably earlier. President Reagan, for example, had mentioned in

---

[4] Agreed Statement F specifically limited deployment of LPARs.

[5] *Soviet Ballistic Missile Defense*, vol. 1, *Key Judgments and Summary*, NIE 11-13-82 (Washington, DC: Central Intelligence Agency, October 13, 1982), 19, and 20, fig. 6.

[6] "Soviet ABM Breakout," *Wall Street Journal*, August 16, 1983, 32.

[7] *Soviet Capabilities for Strategic Nuclear Conflict, 1982-1992*, vol. 1, *Key Judgments and Summary*, NIE 11-3/8-82 (Washington, DC: Central Intelligence Agency, February 15, 1983), 38.

a speech on March 31 that there were "increasingly serious grounds for questioning Soviet compliance" with the ABM Treaty, which, in retrospect, suggested that the discovery had been made some time before mid-year.[8]

Intelligence analysts were convinced that the Krasnoyarsk radar was "a dangerous new violation" of the ABM Treaty, which could transform the strategic weapons balance overnight. The radar was like the other five, an enormous structure 300 by 500 feet in size, and 100 feet tall. Larger than a football field and shaped like a decapitated pyramid, it was located deep inland and seemed to have been "built for only one discernible purpose: to protect the Soviet Union with an ABM system which both countries [had] agreed not to build." [9]

Officials explained that "peripheral systems can give early warning, but an inland system could be used to operate…anti-ballistic missile defenses," like the one permitted and operational around Moscow. The Krasnoyarsk radar faced outward toward Sakhalin, Kamchatka, and the Sea of Okhotsk and combined with the five existing phased-array radars, "would close a gap in Soviet coverage" to the northeast against incoming US missiles launched from submarines (see image below). "Sources said the new radar was 125 miles from a field of [SS-18] offensive missiles, close enough to become part of a second ABM system, if Moscow chose. [But] government officials said the evidence was insufficient to draw such a conclusion." [10]

Reagan's Quandary

Which was it? All of Moscow's new, phased-array radar complexes were built exactly alike, so there was no way to determine function from form. Yet it was vital to determine the purpose of the Krasnoyarsk radar: was it connected to Moscow's ABM missile network, or to other early warning radars, and how close was it to becoming operational? The worst was that if Krasnoyarsk were designed for missile defense, as suspected, then, combined with the system around Moscow, it would give the Soviet Union a nationwide, if rudimentary, ballistic missile defense and fundamentally alter the strategic balance.

---

[8] Hedrick Smith, "US Seeking Soviet Parley on Arms Violation Issues," *New York Times*, August 12, 1983, A3.

[9] Rowland Evans and Robert Novak, "New Soviet Radar Violates SALT Pact," *New York Post*, July 27, 1983, 35. See also *The Krasnoyarsk Radar: Closing the Final Gap in Coverage for Ballistic Missile Early Warning* (Washington, DC: Central Intelligence Agency, June 19, 1986). The Soviets claimed that the radar was for satellite detection and tracking, as permitted by the ABM treaty, but US intelligence analysts concluded that its primary mission was ballistic missile detection and tracking, and that it closed the final gap in the Soviet early warning and tracking network.

[10] Smith, "US Seeking Soviet Parley on Arms Violation Issues."

Chapter 3
How Close to Breakout? Krasnoyarsk and KAL 007

113

Ballistic Missile Early Warning, Target-Tracking, and Battle Management Radars

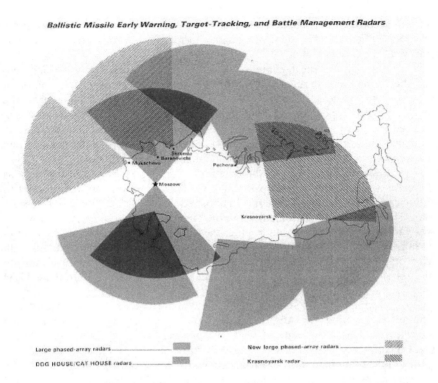

Source: Department of Defense, *Soviet Military Power, 1986*
(Washington, DC: US Government Printing Office, 1986).

The first question in assessing whether the Soviet Union was on the verge of ABM breakout, therefore, was to determine the status of the Krasnoyarsk radar. Was it ready to become operational? If it was, then the United States might well soon face another Caribbean missile crisis, as in 1962, only this time in reverse, with the Soviet Union holding the high card of missile superiority. The Soviets could deploy into Grenada and, once there, elsewhere in the Caribbean. In any resulting confrontation, the Soviets could threaten war, which would give credibility to their current rhetoric. Under these circumstances, there is no doubt that the president would find a reason to abandon his counteroffensive and seek an accommodation.

With the highest national security issues at stake, the president assigned to CIA Director Bill Casey the task of determining the status of Krasnoyarsk. As best as can be determined, this decision was taken in the context of the formulation of NSDD-75 the previous December when the president was preparing his counteroffensive against the Soviet Union. Much of what the president would be able to do would of course depend upon assessment of the strategic weapons balance and the issue of a Soviet breakout was therefore of the highest priority.

Indeed, according to Thomas Reed, one of the president's closest advisers of the time, Casey had been "implementing a plan to spoof the entire electronic nervous system of the Soviet Union."[11]

Spoofing is the technique whereby specially configured air and sea-based electronic countermeasure platforms manipulate the radar reception of an adversary to create false images on radar screens. They would confuse the location, number, position, and direction of aircraft penetrating Soviet airspace; jam radars, making them temporarily inoperative; disable weapons sensors and guidance mechanisms; and disrupt communications between radar stations and the weapons they support, and between command and control links.

Meanwhile, Secretary Shultz's threat to resign at the end of July, just as the crisis with Moscow developed in the Caribbean, prompted the president to fully brief the secretary on his concern about Krasnoyarsk, but not about Casey's plan. Then, once again, as he had numerous times, he sought to resolve a problem by negotiation before resorting to other means. Thus, as part of his agreement to authorize Shultz to proceed to negotiate economic and cultural agreements with Moscow, the president also instructed him to engage the Russians in forthright discussion about American concerns regarding a possible breakout from the ABM Treaty.

Secretary Shultz requested a meeting of the treaty's Special Consultative Committee meeting for August 11. The SCC was an agreed forum where American and Russian leaders could discuss sensitive treaty issues outside the glare of publicity. He proposed to discuss three issues: two had to do with the testing and deployment of ICBMs banned by the signed but not yet ratified SALT II treaty and the third was the radar at Krasnoyarsk. The president had wrapped the issue of Krasnoyarsk in the series of agreements Shultz was negotiating, the so-called "mini thaw," but the Soviets declined to take the bait. While they had readily agreed to resume negotiations on cultural exchange and consular agreements, signed the grain agreement, and were moving forward on the purchase of pipeline equipment from Caterpillar Corporation, they had stonewalled on the SCC.[12]

Hoping to prod the Soviets into an affirmative response, the administration and its allies blanketed the press with a spate of articles on the issue of Krasnoyarsk in August, revealing hitherto highly classified information. The first was an article in *Strategic Review* by Senator Malcolm Wallop (R-WY), who revealed that "a debate [was] unfolding in the United States over the facts and

---

[11] Thomas Reed, *At the Abyss: An Insider's History of the Cold War* (New York: Presidio, 2004), 240. Press reports stated that US intelligence had discovered the Krasnoyarsk radar only in the summer of 1983. That the "spoof" decision was made in December 1982, indicates that US intelligence had discovered Krasnoyarsk and worked through the implications before that time.

[12] Michael Getler, "US Asks Soviets for Special Meeting," *Washington Post*, August 13, 1983, 7.

implications of violations by the Soviet Union of existing arms control agreements." Referring to the missile defense issue and the ABM Treaty, he said:

> A nationwide ABM system must be served by a nationwide network of battle management radars. The treaty allows such radars only at one ABM site in each country. The Soviets have built five huge radars that are inherently capable of performing that [battle management] function. Are these radars intended to perform it? We will probably never have absolute proof short of their performance in actual battle.[13]

A few days later, the *Wall Street Journal's* editors pointed to a "Soviet ABM Breakout," identifying locations of Moscow's phased-array radars, including the one at Krasnoyarsk; and reporting that the Soviets had tested surface-to-air missiles in ABM mode, in contravention of the treaty.[14] This editorial was followed the next day by a piece in the *Washington Post* describing the Krasnoyarsk radar as a "smoking gun." Columnists Rowland Evans and Robert Novak claimed that the "massive new Soviet radar…looks like 'smoking gun' evidence of Soviet cheating on the Anti-Ballistic Missile treaty." Their contribution to the public information on the issue came with the revelation that the administration's internal differences on Krasnoyarsk had finally been resolved:

> What surprised hardline Reaganauts was not Clark but the fact that Secretary of State George Shultz and Foggy Bottom's Soviet experts are also convinced that the long-suspected smoking gun may now be in hand. That ends more than three months of high-level vacillation on whether Reagan should risk going to the mat with the Russians on SALT violations.[15]

By the end of August, there had been no response from Moscow and the anxiety level within the US Government was rising to a fever pitch. Soviet stonewalling on Krasnoyarsk, the earlier disappearance of eighty-one SS-20 missiles, the rush of Soviet ships to Nicaragua and the Caribbean, all fueled the president's fears that the critical moment was fast approaching. Would the Soviets attempt to fulfill their promise to deploy an "analogous" missile *before* the United States deployed the Pershing II to West Germany? If so, would that not require declaration of an initial operational capability for a nationwide ballistic missile defense to have any hope of success? Was there any indication that they had reached that level of readiness?

---

[13] Malcolm Wallop, "Soviet Violations of Arms Control Agreements: So, What?" *Strategic Review* 11, no. 3 (Summer 1983):18.

[14] "Soviet ABM Breakout," cited in n6 above.

[15] Rowland Evans and Robert Novak, "A 'Smoking Gun' in Siberia? *Washington Post*, August 17, 1983, A23. See also "Smoking Gun," *San Diego Union* August 22, 1983, 5.

Defense Minister Dmitri Ustinov and President Yuri Andropov fed the administration's fears, reiterating the "analogous" threat. On July 30, Ustinov had declared bluntly that the Soviet Union "will make the military threat to the territory of the United States...the same as the one the United States is trying to create for the Soviet Union..."[16] And on August 26, in the context of offering to liquidate any SS-20 missiles included in an arms control agreement, Andropov had reaffirmed that if the United States deployed the Pershing II to West Germany then the Soviet Union would "be compelled to take appropriate countermeasures to preserve the balance of forces both on the regional, European *and on the global scale*. This should be quite clear to everyone."[17]

Reagan and Andropov seemed to be eyeball-to-eyeball over issues that would determine the success or failure of their respective strategies. Before either could flinch, however, an event came literally out of the blue to raise tensions to the breaking point and move the building confrontation to the brink of full-fledged crisis.

The National Security Origins of KAL Flight 007

For President Reagan, it was imperative to determine whether Krasnoyarsk was soon to be activated. If so, it would create at least the putative basis for a Soviet claim of strategic weapons superiority. Even if a deception, under these circumstances, Moscow would most certainly attempt to deploy the SS-20 to Grenada. Would the United States be sufficiently confident to call Moscow's hand? Would the risk of confrontation prove to be too high? Moreover, with missiles in Grenada, would the Soviets attempt to unravel the US position in Western Europe? It would mean Cuba in reverse with all the manifold strategic implications of being consigned to the inferior position in the strategic weapons balance vis a vis the Soviet Union.

If, on the other hand, it was learned that Krasnoyarsk was still a long way from becoming operational, as suspected, then current Soviet bombast was bluff. The Soviets would not be able to break out of the arms control regime with activation of a nationwide missile defense before the Pershing II was deployed, and the president could move with confidence through the crucial period the nation was now entering. In its operational essence, Casey's task was to devise a means of prodding the Soviets into revealing their hand. Was Krasnoyarsk (1) simply part of an improved early warning system, (2) the final piece in Moscow's missile-defense system, or, (3) for the time being, still inoperable, and therefore nothing of immediate concern?

Such was the genesis of what became the tragedy of KAL 007. In one sense, the KAL 007 mission was a last, desperate step. A variety of moves had

---

[16] Dusko Doder, "Defense Minister Says Moscow Will Move to Counter Deployment of US Missiles," *Washington Post*, July 31, 1983, A21.
[17] Rudy Abramson, "Soviet Leader Sees Reagan Meeting as 'Meaningless,'" *Washington Post*, August 26, 1983, A22, emphasis added.

Chapter 3
How Close to Breakout? Krasnoyarsk and KAL 007

117

failed to produce the desired reaction. According to General John Chain, former chief of Strategic Air Command, "sometimes we would send bombers over the North Pole, and their radars would click on.... Other times fighter-bombers would probe their Asian or European periphery." Sometimes there would be several maneuvers a week, which would then abruptly be discontinued, only to be resumed later. "A squadron would fly straight at Soviet airspace, and their radars would light up and units would go on alert. Then at the last minute the squadron would peel off and return home."[18]

According to Soviet sources, there had been a dozen probes mounted in the Far East during the first eight months of 1983.[19] Perhaps the most intrusive, in late March, in the largest naval exercise held in the North Pacific since World War II, three carrier battle groups, a total of 40 ships accompanied by B-52 bombers, sailed off the Aleutian Islands in international waters off Kamchatka. As part of the "forward strategy" adopted by Navy Secretary Lehman, the United States had been sailing carrier battle groups into nominally Soviet waters north of the Greenland-Iceland-United Kingdom gap, the "GIUK gap," as it was called, and off the Soviet Far East coast—Kamchatka, Sakhalin, and into the Sea of Okhotsk. Washington was determined to demonstrate that the Soviet navy would not be safe in even its home waters in time of war.[20]

As part of the exercise in the North Pacific, on April 4, planes from the carriers *Midway* and *Enterprise* buzzed the Habomai islands, a small cluster located off the coast of Hokkaido, Japan. The Japanese claim Habomai, along with Shikotan, Etorofu, and Kunashiri as their "northern territories," which the Soviet Union seized in 1945 and refused to return. Two days after the flyover, the Soviets retaliated with an overflight of several islands in the Aleutian chain. But neither the aggressive fleet moves, nor the dozen aerial probes before and afterward had produced the response necessary to reveal the function of the Krasnoyarsk radar.

All of these probes had been relatively brief in-and-out border incursions, which produced only localized radar and interceptor reactions. They drew no reaction from the Krasnoyarsk radar sited 1,000 miles inland. From Washington's perspective, it was apparent that such "tickler missions," as they were termed, were inadequate and time was growing short. Pershing II deployment was scheduled for the end of November and it was vital that the US leadership know what to expect of Soviet response capability.

What was deemed necessary was a more prolonged penetration of Soviet airspace, which would produce a broader-based reaction. This was the genesis of

---

[18] Peter Schweizer, *Victory: The Reagan Administration's Secret Strategy That Hastened the Collapse of the Soviet Union* (New York: Atlantic Monthly Press, 1994), 8-9.

[19] V. Zakharov, "What Lies behind the 'Incident,'" *Pravda*, September 7, 1983, 4, in *Foreign Broadcast Information System (FBIS) Daily Report, Soviet Union,* September 7, 1983, C 3.

[20] Seymour Hersh, *The Target Is Destroyed* (New York: Random House, 1986), 17.

the idea of a commercial aircraft flying innocently off-course, traversing Soviet airspace and setting off a full-fledged air defense and radar reaction that would include Krasnoyarsk. Such a penetration would provide the needed information to enable the United States to determine whether Krasnoyarsk's communication links were to an early-warning, or a missile defense network and thus whether the Soviet Union was prepared to break out of the ABM Treaty and present the United States with a *fait accompli*.

Casey's Covert Probe

Even from the perspective of a generation after the event, it is still only possible to speculate about what transpired in the skies over the North Pacific the night of August 31/September 1, 1983. Both the American and Soviet governments consistently maintained and shaped what information was released to conform to a single intrusion, single interception, single-shootdown theory. The evidence, however, reveals a much more complicated sequence of multiple intrusions, multiple interceptions, and multiple shootdowns involving American and Russian aircraft.

Literally every presumed fact is contested. Working one's way through the labyrinth of information and disinformation put forth by the American and Soviet governments is thus a daunting task. My approach is to reevaluate the data from the hypothetical perspective of a US attempt to probe Soviet defenses to determine whether Moscow could credibly move to a nuclear war posture; and a Soviet effort to stymie the US probe. I evaluate and select the data from the technical point of view of how such a mission could have been executed and how the Soviet Union could have thwarted it.

Casey's plan, closely held even within the highest levels of the administration, was to employ a non-US commercial carrier, which would deviate from the normal flight path used by all airliners flying to and from the Far East and instead penetrate deep into Soviet territory, prompting a full-fledged electronic response. Korean Air Lines, which had a long history of cooperation with the US government, was selected for this vital mission.[21] Two planes were involved, one to perform the tickler role, and one to provide radio cover. As the tickler aircraft would be beyond radio range, flying over Soviet airspace, the cover plane would relay and misrepresent the penetrating aircraft's position to air traffic controllers monitoring its flight.

The most capable and experienced pilots were selected. Captain Chun Byung-in, who would pilot the tickler plane and Captain Park Yong-man, who would command the covering aircraft were friends, Park having been Chun's commanding officer during their days in the Korean Air Force. Captain Park would fly a standard course from Anchorage to Seoul serving as a radio contact

---

[21] For a succinct discussion of the history of Korean Air Lines, see Richard Rohmer, *Massacre 747: The Story of Korean Air Lines Flight 007* (Ontario: PaperJacks, 1984), chap. 4.

Chapter 3

How Close to Breakout? Krasnoyarsk and KAL 007

119

bridge between Captain Chun as he veered over 300 miles into Soviet airspace and air traffic controllers in Anchorage and Tokyo.

Even though the planes themselves would not be involved in any intelligence collection activity, there was an obvious risk in sending a commercial airliner filled with civilian passengers over Soviet territory. Under ordinary circumstances, such a means never would have been chosen; but given the magnitude of the issue at stake, it was deemed a necessary and acceptable risk. The risk was deemed acceptable because the Russians had never shot down a civilian airliner, although on two occasions in the recent past, 1968 and 1978, the Soviets had forced down commercial airliners that had wandered into Soviet airspace, including a Korean Air Lines plane in 1978.[22] Thus, the maximum risk was deemed to be that if the plan went awry, the Soviets would force the plane down on Soviet territory.

But Casey's plan had built-in protection that made even the worst-case prospect of a forced landing remote. He would station spoofing aircraft and ships at key positions along KAL 007's flight path and employ electronic countermeasures to confuse and deflect any Soviet air defense response.[23] They would safeguard the airliner by electronically blinding the Soviet air defense system, confusing Soviet defenders, delaying their recognition of what was occurring, and giving Captain Chun the time needed to traverse Soviet air space and exit without incident.

The plane's mission was to fly over Soviet territory, down the very center of the Krasnoyarsk radar's zone of coverage, which scanned Sakhalin, the Sea of Okhotsk, and Kamchatka. The entire US (and Japanese) intelligence collection system, especially a satellite hovering in geosynchronous orbit, would capture the Soviet response, from radar tracking, air and SAM defense, and communication links, including air-to-ground links and those between posts from local to regional to national levels. As Burrows notes, the United States had positioned an "antiballistic missile radar ferret code-named Jumpseat…[that] can 'hang' over Siberia for some eight hours as it soaks up the microwave pulses coming from there." Indeed, Jumpseat's "job is to take precise measurements of high performance phased-array ABM and space tracking radars (like the one at Abalakovo) by recording their microwave emissions…" In short, if Krasnoyarsk was operational,

---

[22] See David Pearson, *KAL 007: The Cover-Up: Why the True Story Has Never Been Told* (New York: Summit Books, 1987), 88-95, for discussion of the 1968 incident and 103-10 for discussion of the 1978 incident.

[23] John Burns, "Russians' Version," *New York Times*, September 6, 1983, 1. In its first full version of the incident, *Pravda* claimed that KAL 007 had been on a spying mission and that "Soviet forces had been tracking seven RC-135 reconnaissance planes on missions off the Soviet Far East coast in the period between 3:45 p.m. and 8:40 p.m. Moscow time on the day of the incident." It said there were three United States naval vessels just outside Soviet territorial waters in the area at the same time.

or about to become operational, it would become apparent to American intelligence.[24]

In the event, the flight of KAL 007 across Soviet territory enabled US intelligence analysts to construct an updated electronic map of the entire structure of the Soviet Union's air defense and command and control system in the Far East. US intelligence analysts were able to conclude from the Soviet response that Krasnoyarsk was not on the verge of becoming operational. Therefore, Moscow would not be able to break out of the arms control regime in conjunction with the coming Pershing II deployment, and any attempt to counter the Pershing II with an "analogous" deployment of SS-20s to Grenada would be quite risky. The president would be willing to call Moscow's bluff. He would preempt in Grenada and proceed to deploy to West Germany, without undue concern of a Soviet riposte.

However, from this flight and other intelligence collected later, American leaders also learned that they had been correct in assuming that Soviet leaders were planning on a missile defense breakout. The Krasnoyarsk radar was in fact designed as an integral part of a nation-wide missile defense system and was neither merely an early warning radar, nor a space-tracking mechanism, as the Russians claimed. Krasnoyarsk had simply not been ready for activation in time for the events of the fall of 1983. Indeed, years later, both Soviet Foreign Minister Eduard Shevardnadze and General Y.V. Votintsev, head of ABM and Space Defense Forces, confirmed Krasnoyarsk's intended role in a missile defense breakout scheme.[25]

In other words, the president's concerns in the summer of 1983 were genuine, not imaginary; and his efforts to determine the function of the radar justified, even if the means chosen were risky. By the spring of 1984, the CIA had changed its estimate. NIE 11-3/8, *Assessing Soviet Strategic Nuclear Capabilities*, revised the previous year's assessment, and concluded that "potential future developments in strategic defenses could be of great significance to the perceptions, and perhaps the reality, of the strategic balance. We are particularly concerned about the growing Soviet potential for widespread deployment of defenses against ballistic missiles well beyond the limits of the Antiballistic Missile Treaty using ABM systems currently in development."[26]

But, as is well known, Casey's plan did not work as expected. At the moment that the airliner was exiting Soviet airspace over Sakhalin, a Soviet fighter-interceptor attacked it, triggering one of the most volatile and prolonged

---

[24] William Burrows, *Deep Black: Space Espionage and National Security* (New York: Random House, 1986), 182, 223-4.

[25] William T. Lee, "Unlocking the Secrets of Krasnoyarsk," *Washington Times*, February 8, 1994, A19.

[26] *Soviet Capabilities for Strategic Nuclear Conflict, 1983-93*, vol. 1, *Key Judgments and Summary*, NIE 11-3/8-83, March 6, 1984, in Donald Steury, *Estimates on Soviet Military Power, 1954 to 1984* (Washington DC: Central Intelligence Agency, December 1994), 416, 431.

Soviet-American crises of the Cold War. The crisis would precipitate immediate internal conflicts in both leaderships, which underwent significant changes in composition and outlook, but in opposite directions. With respect to the crisis itself, both governments immediately mounted extensive cover-ups of their respective actions, which continue to the present.

Midnight Mission from Anchorage

Analyses based on American, Japanese, and Soviet radar data released years after the event show that Captain Chun intentionally deviated from his prescribed flight path along transoceanic commercial air route R-20 immediately upon takeoff from Anchorage and took KAL 007 onto a course over Kamchatka, the Sea of Okhotsk, and Sakhalin. [27] In short, the analyses refute the argument that KAL 007 wandered off course by accident, either through crew inattention, the inadvertent mis-programming of the aircraft's inertial navigation system, or by erroneously following a constant magnetic heading.

Commercial airliners are authorized to use only one speed, Mach 840 (490 knots) for transoceanic crossings. All changes in speed, altitude, and direction must be cleared with governing air traffic control for obvious safety reasons. Pilots, in regular communication with air traffic controllers, are required to report position at specified points en route (nine in the case of R-20). Failure to report position, even a missed report by three minutes, would prompt immediate commencement of search and rescue procedures. Yet, Captain Chun repeatedly and deliberately, in violation of international air traffic regulations and US air defense rules, changed airspeed, direction, and altitude in the passage through American airspace and the approach to Soviet airspace.

Captain Chun's many changes in speed, altitude, and direction raise the question of: to what end? The answer is that he timed the arrival of his aircraft over Kamchatka and then again over Sakhalin to rendezvous with US Electronic Security Command aircraft that would protect his passage over Soviet territory. These aircraft would confuse and disorient Soviet air defense efforts to identify, force, or shoot down the airliner. They would jam the radars attempting to track the airliner, deflect the interceptors sent up to identify it, and nullify SAM missile attempts to shoot it down. [28]

---

[27] Of the many accounts of the flight of Korean Air Lines 007, by far the most authoritative is that of James Gollin and Robert Allardyce, *Desired Track: The Tragic Flight of KAL 007* (Findlay: American Vision Publishing, 1995). Other invaluable accounts are Pearson, *KAL 007: The Cover-Up*; and R.W. Johnson, *Shootdown: Flight 007 and the American Connection* (New York: Viking, 1986).

[28] One theory, by P.Q. Mann (pseud.), "KAL 007: A New Theory," *World Press Review*, September 1984, 25-28, was that KAL 007 timed the arrival of his aircraft with an orbiting Elint "ferret" satellite, number 1982-41C. The ferret circumnavigated the earth every ninety-six minutes, moving from east to west over the Soviet Union on each pass. With its three thousand-mile viewing and collection range, the satellite monitored communication links throughout the Soviet Far East, and based on its

Captain Chun, in KAL 007, took off from Anchorage at 1300Z* after a delay of 40 minutes, ostensibly because of lighter than forecast headwinds en route, but actually to close the time distance with Captain Park in KAL015, which took off at 1315Z. A little over an hour and a half later, at 1437Z, KAL 007's deviation to the north toward Kamchatka first took it into the United States Distant Early Warning Identification Zone (DEWIZ), a restricted flying area that is the military buffer zone off the Alaskan coast between Alaska and Siberia (see map).[29]

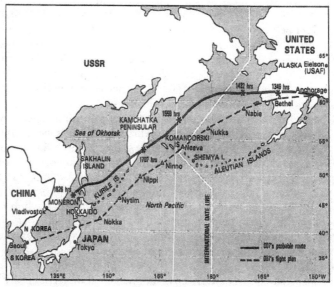

KAL 007's probable route, and the prescribed R-20 route with its waypoints marked. The route cuts the international dateline near the NEEVA waypoint. Source: R.W. Johnson, *Shootdown: Flight 007 and the American Connection* (New York: Viking, 1986).

---

information, analysts were able to determine Krasnoyarsk's function in the Soviet defense system. The problem with this theory is that the ferret would not have more than three minutes over the target area during which to capture vital communications occurring over longer periods of time, and therefore would not seem to have been able to glean the information necessary. It is far more likely that a satellite in geosynchronous orbit, hovering over eastern Siberia for as long as eight hours at a time, was the main intelligence instrument used for capturing Soviet communications, as noted above in Burrows, *Deep Black*, 180, 223-24.

* Military times are used here, with "Zulu" denoting UTC/GMT.

[29] Johnson, *Shootdown*, 10, provides this map, citing Allardyce and Gollin, "The Final Moments of KAL 007," *Pittsburgh Eagle*, May 23, 1985; and Eugene Kozicharow, "FAA Studies Upgraded Pacific Navaids," *Aviation Week and Space Technology*, September 19, 1983.

Fourteen distant early-warning and aircraft control and warning radars form a comprehensive tracking net that covers the Alaskan coast and Aleutian Islands. Operated by the US Air Force, this net is tied into the regional operations command center at Elmendorf AFB near Anchorage.[30] All commercial aircraft flying in the US DEWIZ are required to file flight plans with civilian air traffic control (ATC) in Anchorage, and with military air traffic control at Elmendorf. In addition, all aircraft entering the DEWIZ are required to perform an elaborate system of identification.

All unaccounted-for aircraft flying in this zone prompt an immediate scramble of interceptor jets to make a positive identification. The Alaskan DEWIZ was an area where Soviet aircraft routinely skirted to the edge of US airspace to probe US air defense procedures, force aerial identification, and be escorted back to international airspace. In fact, in 1983, Soviet aircraft probed Alaskan airspace 14 times, prompting scrambles of interceptors, all without incident.[31]

Captain Chun flew KAL 007 into and across the Alaskan DEWIZ for 185 miles during a span of twenty-five minutes without identifying himself or provoking an air defense reaction. But he was tracked.[32] At 1434Z, US Air Force controllers at Elmendorf AFB informed Anchorage Air Route Traffic Control Center that KAL 007 was in the DEWIZ buffer zone heading for Kamchatka. Tapes from the control center recorded the following conversation: "Okay, you guys got someone bumping into the Russians' air defenses over here." "Oh, you're kidding." "A person should warn him." "That's why you should've given the information here, instead of waiting."[33]

There are several points to be made about these fragmentary remarks. First, the tapes demonstrate military-civilian interaction. Second, the phrase ending "...instead of waiting," makes it apparent that tracking had been under way for some time. Indeed, "a controller unsuccessfully tried to contact Flight 007 five times between 14:32:21 and 14:34:37 to obtain a routine position report."[34] Third, controllers obviously recognized the aircraft as friendly. At 1445Z, Anchorage International Flight Service Station (IFSS) contacted and successfully executed a Selective Call, or Selcal check, identifying KAL 007.[35] Upon identifying the airliner, no alarm was sounded and no jets were sent aloft.

---

[30] Gollin and Allardyce, *Desired Track*, 36.

[31] "The Spreading Impact," *US News and World Report*, September 19, 1983, 26.

[32] Gollin and Allardyce, *Desired Track*, 42.

[33] Lawrence L. Porter, "Acoustic Analysis of Air Traffic Communications Concerning Korean Air Flight 007, August 31, 1983," (unpublished monograph, 1988), 5. See also Pearson, *KAL 007: The Cover Up*, 43-47.

[34] Douglas Feaver, "US Controllers' Role Questioned in KAL Case," *Washington Post*, August 31, 1985, A8.

[35] "Anchorage International Flight Service" transmissions 14:44 to 17:22Z. *Destruction of Korean Air Lines Boeing 747 On 31 August 1983, Report of the*

All commercial aircraft are equipped with secondary surveillance radar or transponders that can be electronically interrogated by ground radar performing Selcal checks. When interrogated, the aircraft automatically sends identifying information, including transponder number and altitude. This information then appears on the ground radar screen beside the tracking blip. Captain Chun had been assigned the transponder code number 6072 upon departure from Anchorage and US military ground radars monitoring the DEWIZ were able to identify him from filed flight plans.[36]

The "warn him" remark implicitly referred to the air traffic control interphone system, which enabled controllers to talk via landline to controllers at their own and other facilities in the network, including military personnel and personnel at the privately-operated International Flight Service Station, also located at Anchorage. The IFSS, utilizing high frequency (HF) channels would be called into service when air traffic control could not contact an aircraft using very high frequency (VHF) channels.

As Chun passed out of the Alaskan DEWIZ and headed for the sixty-mile-deep Soviet air defense buffer zone, he turned off his aircraft's transponder after the Selcal check at 1445Z. From this point, the airliner flew dark, preventing Russian ground-based radar from interrogating and identifying his aircraft as a civilian airliner. It was part of Casey's plan to confuse the Soviets about the identity of the aircraft, prompting them to light up their air defense radar system as jets scrambled to identify it. Casey counted on the Russians to follow their own intercept procedures, which required a positive visual identification before taking hostile action, to provide an additional margin of safety for the airliner.

As long as the aircraft remained unidentified, the Russians would not shoot it down with surface-to-air missiles, for fear that it was one of their own planes. They would first send up jets to identify the plane visually before taking any action. Casey, of course, had arranged for the spoofing of Soviet air defense to mislead them into "seeing" KAL 007 where it was not and making identification difficult if not impossible. And, if Soviet aircraft identified the plane as a civilian airliner, they would either escort it out of Soviet airspace, or, at worst, force it down. Spoofers would also jam Soviet surface-to-air missile radars to prevent any attempt to shoot the plane down.

Over Kamchatka

The lengthiest segment of the mission was the first. KAL 007 would spend the most time in Soviet airspace during the approach to and flight over Kamchatka. Soviet radar picked up and began tracking the aircraft while it was more than 200 miles from the air defense identification zone. The problems were how to prevent identification of the aircraft; and confuse Soviet air defenses long

---

Completion of the ICAO Fact-Finding Investigation (Quebec: International Civil Aviation Organization, June 1993), 30. (Hereafter referred to as ICAO-93).
[36] ICAO-93: 4.

enough to insert the plane into Kamchatka airspace and give it time to escape into international airspace over the Sea of Okhotsk. By turning off his transponder, Captain Chun had solved the first problem.

For the second, Casey employed one of the RC-135 electronic jamming platforms that routinely flew along the Soviet periphery to intercept Soviet radar and radio transmissions. There were two types of RC-135 aircraft, one designated Cobra Ball, based on Shemya and configured to monitor missile test telemetry data from Soviet missiles impacting on Kamchatka. The other, designated Rivet Joint, based at Eielson AFB near Fairbanks, Alaska, was an intercept platform capable not only of capturing ground and air radio/radar transmissions and communications, but also of spoofing/jamming Soviet air defense systems.

Part of the US cover-up afterward was to claim that the RC-135 off Kamchatka was a Cobra Ball on a routine unrelated deployment to track missile telemetry from a missile test scheduled for the night of August 31. The test, as the story goes, was canceled when KAL 007 appeared over Kamchatka and the RC-135 returned to base. There is, however, no unambiguous evidence that a missile test was in preparation for execution on that date and, in fact, the RC-135 in question was confirmed as having flown from Eielson Air Force Base, not Shemya, making it a Rivet Joint mission.[37]

It seems that the entire notion of a test, subsequently canceled, was concocted to explain the presence of an RC-135 in the vicinity of KAL 007—a plane, moreover, that, because it was configured to monitor missile tests, could have no relevance to the presence of KAL 007.[38] But its presence was crucial to the airliner's safe passage. According to one authority, "Not only do [RC-135s] know whether a MiG has been scrambled, but they can also tell you exactly what the pilot's orders are and probably even what his name is."[39] Knowing the enemy's flight plans in advance, of course, would make it possible to evade detection.

Exiting the Alaskan DEWIZ, KAL 007 approached the Soviet Union's Asian Coastal Buffer Zone off Kamchatka. Soviet radar had been tracking the RC-135 since at least 1522Z and twenty minutes later, at 1542Z, began to track KAL 007. It was on a flight path resembling that of RC-135s that routinely flew from Shemya to their orbit station in international airspace east of Karaginsky and the Komandorsky Islands. Indeed, Soviet radar controllers initially assumed that KAL 007 was either a replacement for the orbiting RC-135, a standard and

---

[37] George Wilson, "RC135 Was Assessing Soviet Air Defenses," *Washington Post*, September 7, 1983, A12.

[38] Hersh, *The Target Is Destroyed*, is the fullest expression of this cover story. In fact, Casey provided Hersh with much of his data and just before the book appeared threatened to sue the author for possible violation of federal law. The threat simply added credibility to Hersh, while distancing Casey from him. Edwin McDowell, "C.I.A. Said to Warn Publisher on Book," *New York Times*, June 25, 1986, C25.

[39] "The KAL Tragedy," *IEEE Spectrum* (December 1983), 22.

frequent rotation, or a refueling tanker. At this point, both aircraft were 250 miles from Soviet airspace.

When Soviet radars turn on to track overflying aircraft, US radio/radar intercept stations in Alaska and in Japan also turn on to read and record Soviet radar activity. Whatever they see, US and Japanese intelligence see. The two allies operate several ground collection facilities jointly, but each has its own independent system, the US system being worldwide in scope. The two most immediately relevant US intelligence collection stations were the 6981st Electronic Security Command at Elmendorf AFB and the 6920th at Misawa AB on northern Honshu, Japan.[40] The 6920th is the largest station outside the United States proper, with over 1,600 personnel on duty 24 hours a day.

The Japanese, of course, operated a technologically sophisticated system of their own, that was at least as efficient as the US system. Nine intercept stations manned by over a thousand personnel were located around the country, with headquarters in Tokyo. Informally referred to as *Nibetsu,* or "rabbit's ears," the system was linked directly to the prime minister's office, which meant that breaking news would get into the hands of Prime Minister Nakasone as quickly as it would to President Reagan.[41]

The US and Japan jointly operate an intercept facility at Wakkanai, on the very tip of Japan's northern island of Hokkaido, 27 miles across the La Perouse Strait from the southern tip of Sakhalin, a figurative stone's throw from the events that would take place during the early morning hours of September 1. Japanese radar tracking and radio intercepts of Soviet communications were crucial to deciphering the events, although Japanese authorities released only a small but critical portion of their findings covering the period from 1812Z to 1829Z.

At 1551Z, while still in international airspace, KAL 007 executed two course turns preparatory to making its run across Kamchatka. The purpose of the turns was to line up with the orbiting RC-135 Rivet Joint, which would spoof Soviet radar to provide safe passage across the peninsula.[42] It was also true that a ferret satellite, number 1982-41C, passed overhead just as the airliner turned to enter Kamchatka airspace.[43] Throughout, however, a satellite in geosynchronous orbit observed the entire proceedings.

KAL 007 flew on a southwesterly course parallel to the RC-135 reconnaissance aircraft for a time, the Russians say for ten minutes, but with some

[40] Gollin and Allardyce, *Desired Track*, 48, 55.

[41] Johnson, *Shootdown*, 104.

[42] *Destruction of Korean Air Lines Boeing 747 over Sea of Japan, 31 August 1983: Report of ICAO Fact-Finding Investigation* (Montreal: ICAO, 1983). See the flight diagram F-16. (Hereafter referred to as *ICAO-83*)

[43] Bhupendra Jasani and G.E. Perry, "The Military Use of Outer Space," *World Armaments and Disarmament, SIPRI Yearbook 1985* (London: Taylor & Francis, 1985), 138.

75 miles of distance between them.[44] When it unexpectedly turned north and headed toward Soviet airspace, instead of maintaining an orbit well off the coast, Soviet controllers attempted to interrogate KAL 007's transponder, but, as it was turned off, received no reply. They then redesignated the intruder as "81," on radar track 6065, to indicate that they were tracking an unidentified aircraft.

It was at this point that the RC-135 Rivet Joint did its work, which was to spoof Soviet air defense radar and communications systems to permit KAL 007 to pass safely through Kamchatka airspace and begin the process of spurring the Soviets to turn on their many and varied air defense radar systems in an effort to locate and identify the plane. What are termed air defense failures, malfunctions, and sheer incompetence in the Soviet air defense effort to intercept KAL 007 over Kamchatka should rather be interpreted as the spoofing success of the RC-135 Rivet Joint.[45]

Indeed, the description of what is asserted to be Soviet ineptitude is the exact response to have been expected from spoofing their system. First, the RC-135 jammed Soviet radar, blinding them to the entry of KAL 007 into Kamchatka airspace at 1630Z. Soviet procedures called for intercept of intruding aircraft well off the coast in the air defense identification zone, but Soviet fighters did not scramble to intercept KAL 007 until 1637Z, seven minutes after it had already penetrated 50 miles into Kamchatka airspace, indicating that initially they were unaware of its presence.

Second, when two pairs of interceptor aircraft did scramble, the RC-135 created a "ghost" image of the aircraft flying in a different place and at a different altitude. Soviet ground controllers vectored them "east...while KAL 007 was already well to the west," and onto an incorrect altitude lower than that which KAL 007 was actually flying.[46] Surface-to-air missile batteries placed on alert similarly could not obtain a lock on the aircraft.[47] This meant that Soviet ground controllers were not able to get a proper radar fix on the aircraft, and pilots could not get close enough to obtain a positive visual identification of the plane.[48]

---

[44] *ICAO-93*: 47 and "USSR Chief of Staff Ogarkov's Statement," *FBIS Daily Report, Soviet Union*, September 9, 1983, DD 1-3.

[45] See the highly informative piece by two former RC-135 crewmen, T. Edward Eskelson and Tom Bernard, "Former RC-135 Crewmen Question US Version of Jetliner Incident," *Baltimore News American*, September 15, 1983, 8.

[46] Gollin and Allardyce, *Desired Track*, 92.

[47] Pearson, *KAL 007: The Cover-Up*, 62.

[48] A report ordered by Senator Jessie Helms (R-NC) in 1991 concluded that "Kamchatka air defense forces were as much as 4 minutes late in communicating important location, speeds, and vectors for interception, communicated faulty radar tracking data, and experienced other communications problems, all leading to a serious break down in command and control..." *Did KAL-007 Successfully Ditch at Sea and Were There Survivors?* 31. This study, drafted by Senate Foreign Relations Committee Republican staff, is based largely on classified radio intercept data. It never was formally published, but subsequently leaked and is available online at

With their radars spoofed and KAL 007 flying dark, there could be little doubt in the minds of Soviet air defense personnel that they were dealing with a military aircraft on an intelligence mission. Kamchatka controllers experienced multiple communications malfunctions in attempts to make contact with other ground and air units resulting in a serious command and control breakdown, which delayed communication of information to control centers on Sakhalin and the Soviet mainland. The description of Soviet communication difficulties in intercepting KAL 007 was nothing if not the result of a successful spoof of "the entire electronic nervous system" of Soviet air defenses.

Having flown silently and at high speed for some 38 minutes over the entire Kamchatka peninsula, some 270 miles, without hindrance or identification by Soviet air defenses, KAL 007 exited into international airspace over the Sea of Okhotsk at 1708Z. At that point, co-pilot Son Dong-hwin radioed Tokyo Air Traffic Control at Narita airport six times in a span of two minutes, including a Selcal check, to confirm that he was on course and crossing Nippi, a mandatory reporting waypoint, which also demarcated the Anchorage and Tokyo Flight Information Regions (FIRs) of transoceanic operation.[49]

As KAL 007 was still well beyond Tokyo Control's radar range, the Selcal check was to establish contact and to assign a new transponder code to KAL 007 preparatory to its entry into the Tokyo FIR. Captain Chun turned on his transponder for the Selcal check, then either turned off his transponder again, or switched to what is called a nondiscrete code, giving data about his altitude but not his identity, as he flew with his running lights off and his aircraft darkened over the Sea of Okhotsk.[50]

Co-pilot Son reported that he was on R-20, where he was supposed to be, whereas in reality KAL 007 was 218 nautical miles north and west of R-20, just entering the Sea of Okhotsk.[51] At this point in the flight, KAL 007 had passed beyond US radar coverage and had not yet entered into Japanese radar coverage. Soviet radio/radar operators, of course, intercepted Son's radio calls, but could not reconcile his reported position with the unidentified aircraft they were tracking on their radar screens. When they sent two more fighters aloft from their base on Paramushir, an island in the Kuril chain adjacent to Kamchatka, these also failed to get close enough to make visual contact, let alone identify KAL 007.[52]

---

www.rescue007.org/republican_staff_study.htm. Unfortunately, while revealing much of Soviet activities, it also blatantly covers up the CIA's role.

[49] *ICAO-93*: 36.

[50] David Rogers, "Automatic Signal Marked 747 as Civilian," *Boston Globe*, September 10, 1983, 3. Aircraft entering the Japanese FIR are normally assigned a transponder code number in the 2000 series. Aircraft exiting Japanese airspace are assigned a number in the 1000s.

[51] Gollin and Allardyce, *Desired Track*, 100-01.

[52] Johnson, *Shootdown*, 19.

US experts later confirmed that "Soviet interceptor aircraft never came closer than 20 miles to the Korean Air lines 747 as it flew over Kamchatka."[53] (In fact, had KAL 007's navigation lights been on they could easily have been seen from that distance.) The same was true for passage across the Sea of Okhotsk, at least the early part of it. It appears that an EF-111 Raven, which the Soviets mistook for a P-3C Orion, was loitering off the Kurils to play the same electronic jamming role there for KAL 007 as it entered the Sea of Okhotsk that the RC-135 Rivet Joint had played earlier in facilitating Captain Chun's entry and passage over Kamchatka.[54]

Casey, Ogarkov and KAL 007

As KAL 007 sped across the Sea of Okhotsk toward Sakhalin, Casey's carefully crafted scheme fell victim to the determination of Marshal Nikolai Ogarkov, chief of the Soviet General Staff, to shift Andropov's policy onto a more confrontational course. The US intelligence director could not have anticipated the abrupt change that was occurring at that moment within the finely balanced Soviet leadership in late August, nor the opportunity that KAL 007 offered for Marshal Ogarkov to tip the balance in the leadership in his favor and push through his preferred, and much tougher, policy option.

Soviet commanders on Kamchatka, having regained control of their communications, reported back through the chain of command to higher authorities. By 1720Z, the 1993 ICAO report concluded, "the Sakhalin command center was aware of the intruder over Kamchatka."[55] Word of the intrusion was quickly forwarded to regional authorities at Khabarovsk, to the national air defense command center at Kalinin, some 100 miles north of Moscow, and to military headquarters at the Kremlin.

When word of the intrusion reached Ogarkov, he realized immediately that the plane, whether civilian or military, whether accidentally off-course or on a spy mission, would expose Andropov's carefully laid plans as illusory. If the aircraft veered onto a course that took it over Sakhalin, it would pass through the very center of the coverage area of the Krasnoyarsk radar. Ogarkov knew that American intelligence would pick up and analyze every aspect of the Soviet response to the flight. If Krasnoyarsk were operational it would be part of that response and American intelligence would be able to determine its function.

Ogarkov also knew that Krasnoyarsk was *not* yet operational and that the Americans would quickly draw the appropriate conclusion—that the Soviets were

---

[53] David Shribman, "US Experts Say Soviet Didn't See Jet Was Civilian," *New York Times*, October 7, 1983, A1.

[54] See *ICAO-83*, Flight Chart, F-16. The EA-6B Prowler, the EC-130H Compass Call, and the RC-135 Rivet Joint, all deployed to Japan at this time, are other aircraft that could have been used for this role.

[55] *ICAO-93*, 49.

engaging in an elaborate bluff.[56] Andropov's plan would not work without a credible threat of war, the point of the months-long cultivation of the war scare. Moscow would not be able to declare operational a nation-wide missile defense and therefore would not be able to fulfill the promise to respond to Reagan's Pershing II deployment to West Germany with an analogous threat against American territory, the deployment to Grenada.

Nevertheless, Ogarkov saw that the intruder aircraft offered him an opportunity to take control of Soviet policy—if he could propose an alternative that stood a chance of success. Ogarkov's plan was to force or shoot down the intruder plane and use the ensuing crisis of "an American spy flight," heightened by a war scare, to deploy missiles to the Caribbean before the United States could deploy to West Germany. In short, Ogarkov's plan was to trigger a crisis and present the United States with a *fait accompli.*

Afterward, when KAL 007 was discovered to be a civilian airliner, not a spy plane, high Soviet party and military leaders would deny any responsibility for the decision to attack. Party officials would claim that the decision was made solely by the Soviet military and that Andropov was informed of it only after the fact.[57] Military officials, on the other hand, would assert that lower-level officers made the decision, not the high command. Ogarkov himself publicly denied any responsibility, saying that "the order to the pilots was given by the commander of the Biya region."[58] Of course, he evaded the obvious question of who authorized the commander of the Biya region to give that order. Despite these bald-faced attempts to exculpate themselves from responsibility, the plain truth of Communist politics was that the party controls the gun.

But, at this critical moment, the question was: who was in control of the party? Yuri Andropov had quietly dropped from sight after a meeting in the Kremlin with nine US senators on August 18. According to them, "he seemed in good condition." Indeed, Soviet television had aired "film clips of the meeting."[59] He had told his visitors that he was about to go on vacation in the Crimea, the traditional vacation spot for Soviet leaders. There was no inkling that the Soviet leader had made the last public appearance of his life.

---

[56] It is interesting to speculate on the reason for the delay in bringing Krasnoyarsk to operational status. According to Lee, the Soviets had experienced delays in deliveries of the signal processing computers, which suggests that the Reagan administration's policy of secretly implanting destructive computer viruses in equipment exported to the USSR may have played a role. See William T. Lee, "Unlocking the Secrets of Krasnoyarsk," *Washington Times*, February 8, 1994, A19; and the section on "Intelligence Games" in chap. 1 of this book.

[57] John W. Parker, *Kremlin in Transition*, vol. 1, *From Brezhnev to Chernenko, 1978-1985* (Boston: Unwin Hyman, 1991), 295.

[58] "Ogarkov Statement and Excerpts from News Session," *New York Times*, September 10, 1983, A4.

[59] Bernard Gwertzman, "US Intelligence in the Dark about Andropov," *New York Times*, December 29, 1983, 9.

Initially, his disappearance was not noticed as he seemed to continue carrying out his duties. A week later, on August 26, in what was reported to be a major interview in *Pravda* Andropov offered to "liquidate" all missiles— including SS-20s—removed from the western USSR as part of an arms control agreement with the United States. These missiles would not merely be repositioned beyond the Urals, he said, but completely eliminated. Reportedly, his offer was intended to break the impasse in the negotiations as well as to serve as an opening bid to improve relations with China and Japan.

Andropov's offer stirred interest in Washington, but over the next several days, as US negotiators queried their Soviet counterparts in Geneva, they encountered a leadership in disarray. At first, Soviet spokesmen said that only "excess launchers," not the missiles themselves, would be dismantled. Pressed further, they said that "one missile associated with each excess launcher" would be liquidated.[60] The confusion in Geneva meant that either Moscow had not yet communicated instructions of the policy change, or Andropov's offer had been rescinded, because Soviet negotiators refused to confirm his carefully phrased offer to "liquidate all the missiles to be reduced."[61]

Where was Andropov?

If the arms control offer had been rescinded, this would raise questions about Andropov's health and the leadership issue. Early in the year Kremlin watchers had discerned that the Soviet leader had become ill. In February 1983, word had gotten around Moscow that Andropov had begun hemodialysis treatments for an undisclosed kidney ailment and his frequent prolonged absences from public view were attributed to the chronic nature of his illness.[62] American medical intelligence specialists thought it more likely that he had a serious heart problem. He had suffered at least two heart attacks and wore a pacemaker.[63] At public appearances through the spring and summer, Andropov displayed unmistakable signs of physical infirmity, although he remained mentally alert.

In early May, during the visit of East German leader Erich Honecker, Soviet television showed a "very tired" Andropov, whose "hands trembled" when he read the banquet speech. Early in June, during Finnish president Mauno Koivisto's visit, Andropov was unable to travel to the airport to meet his guest as protocol dictated; he had to deliver his welcoming banquet toast seated, instead of standing; and had difficulty walking the few steps to the table where he signed an extension of the Soviet-Finnish Friendship treaty. And in early July, during West German Chancellor Helmut Kohl's visit, Andropov had to put off his first two scheduled meetings because of a "slight health problem," but did attend the

[60] Parker, *Kremlin in Transition* 1: 289.
[61] John Burns, "Andropov Closes Loophole in Stand on Cuts in Missiles," *New York Times*, August 27, 1983, 1.
[62] Parker, *Kremlin in Transition* 1: 270.
[63] "How Sick Is Yuri Andropov?" *Newsweek*, July 25, 1983, 7.

third. Kohl's impression was that he was physically ailing, but mentally alert, and "spoke throughout [their] meeting without notes."[64]

Andropov's growing debility evidently explained a change in the power-sharing arrangement with Konstantin Chernenko that had occurred at the June party plenum. In return for acquiescing in Andropov's elevation as president (Chairman of the Presidium), Chernenko formally became second secretary, a hitherto ambiguous position with vague and undefined duties. As president, Andropov would be on an equal ceremonial footing with other heads of state. Chernenko, on the other hand, would now not only chair Politburo and Secretariat meetings when Andropov was indisposed, but he also became presumptive successor as the formal number two.

Further testifying to Andropov's debility, Chernenko delivered the main speech at the plenum, not Andropov. Nonetheless, both men promoted followers. Chernenko moved Grigori Romanov into the Politburo, a major step for him; while Andropov placed Mikhail Gorbachev, his closest aide, in overall charge of "cadre matters" in the Secretariat.[65] Moreover, rather than permitting Romanov to name his own successor in Leningrad as was the usual practice, Andropov sent Gorbachev there to name his choice, Lev Zaikov, as Leningrad first secretary.[66] Andropov had given some ground to Chernenko, but still appeared to be in overall command.

In retrospect, however, Andropov's "indisposition" appears to have been a key factor in the decision to attack KAL 007. Even if the Soviet leader had gone on "vacation" as he said to US senators, there should have been some evidence of his authority in Geneva and the crisis of the intruder aircraft should have prompted his immediate return to Moscow. It is inconceivable that a political leader would choose not to be seen to be in charge of his country during a national crisis. Extrapolating from his complete absence throughout the crisis-filled fall and winter, over five months in all, the only possible conclusion is that Andropov was either too weak to perform his duties, or that he had died.

From this time onward, Andropov was neither seen nor heard from, implying the latter. Furthermore, his total absence suggests that his demise was sudden and early, and then kept secret from even the highest party leaders. After August 26, there was not a single photograph, radio speech, recorded speech, or television news clip presented to show that he was alive. Had it been possible, there is little doubt that the Soviet leadership would have arranged to have pictures taken of Andropov propped up in front of a bank of telephones, or reading documents, or in discussion with colleagues, to show that he was in charge. In short, the evidence strongly suggests that Andropov died from a sudden heart attack.

---

[64] Parker, *Kremlin in Transition* 1: 276, 283.

[65] Ibid., 279.

[66] For more on the changes at the plenum, see Zhores Medvedev, *Gorbachev* (New York: Norton, 1986), 128.

Chapter 3
How Close to Breakout? Krasnoyarsk and KAL 007

133

Yet for months, third parties "vouched" that Andropov was alive, recovering, and in control. Trips and events were scheduled, only to be canceled at the last minute. Excuses were made, ranging from a persistent "cold," to a gunshot wound inflicted by Brezhnev's son, which prevented him from appearing in public.[67] Medvedev concluded from this that there had been "a deliberate medical deception aimed at misleading even Politburo members, and allowing Andropov to retain real power until his very last day of consciousness," but he does not date its beginning.[68] It is fair to conclude that this "medical deception" began from the first day of his disappearance in late August and continued until the day that his death was announced, on February 9, 1984.

Who Made the Decision to Attack KAL 007?

From the moment of Andropov's disappearance, Gorbachev controlled all access to him. In fact, aside from his personal doctor, V. Arkhipov and medical personnel, only Gorbachev and Andropov's personal aide V. V. Sharapov "saw" the fallen leader. No one else was permitted to see him, not even fellow Politburo members. In other words, like the man behind the curtain in the *Wizard of Oz*, Gorbachev manipulated Andropov's persona, and managed the affairs of state in his name. In the matter of the Korean airliner crisis, according to Medvedev, "a special triumvirate" consisting of Gorbachev, Chernenko and Defense Minister Dmitri Ustinov made all the decisions.[69]

Former General Dmitri Volkogonov, citing Russian presidential archives, tells a much different story, averring that Andropov, presumably returning from his vacation, "chaired his last Politburo meeting on 1 September 1983." Ustinov had told him that a plane had been shot down "just before the meeting." He further claims that Andropov returned to the Crimea after the meeting, authorizing Chernenko to be in charge of the Politburo to "work out a 'line,'" to deal with the crisis. Finally, he says that Chernenko "consulted Ustinov, [KGB chief Viktor] Chebrikov and [Foreign Minister Andrei] Gromyko about the immediate measures to be taken to meet Andropov's orders," omitting any mention of Gorbachev.[70]

---

[67] "Andropov Reportedly Shot in Arm," *Washington Times*, November 17, 1983, A5.
[68] Medvedev, *Andropov*, 224.
[69] Ibid., 217. Dusko Doder, *Shadows and Whispers: Power Politics inside the Kremlin from Brezhnev to Gorbachev* (New York: Random House, 1986), 197, relays a similarly incredible story that both exculpated Andropov from responsibility for the attack and placed him in charge. Doder reports that he "was told that [Andropov] had not been consulted about the incident until after the plane was brought down . . . He had returned to Moscow from Kislovodsk to deal with the crisis, but he remained in the background."
[70] Dmitri Volkogonov, *Autopsy for an Empire* (New York: Free Press, 1998), 362-69, and 376, also claims that these four, not Gorbachev, were "the only ones who saw him [Andropov] on a regular basis."

Volkogonov's account, in which neither Andropov nor Gorbachev bore any responsibility, is too conveniently exculpatory, and thus lacks credibility. First, by saying that Ustinov told Andropov of the shootdown *before* the meeting, he placed him in charge, yet exonerated him from responsibility for the decision to shoot. Chernenko, on the other hand, was saddled with responsibility for the consequences. And, by omitting Gorbachev from the decision-making process entirely, he relieved him of all responsibility for it, too.

Second, in his attempt to exonerate both Andropov and Gorbachev, he revealed the occurrence of a Politburo meeting around midnight, August 31. Tokyo time is six hours ahead of Moscow time and the plane was hit by a missile at 3:26 a.m. Tokyo time, 9:36 p.m. Moscow time. The Politburo meeting, which began sometime shortly after midnight and was preceded by preliminary discussions and presentation of policy proposals, thus looms as the decision-making locus in the matter of the attack on KAL 007.

Third, Volkogonov attempted to smooth over the obvious rivalry between the Andropov and Chernenko factions, even while placing blame on the latter. It was highly unlikely that Andropov would have authorized his chief rival, Chernenko, to deal with the crisis, if he himself were capable of managing it. Saying Andropov left *after* the meeting for the Crimea contradicted Andropov's own statement to the US Senate delegation almost two weeks earlier that he was leaving for the Crimea then. The entire story of a vacation in the Crimea was odd and must be doubted because, if his illness were acute renal failure, a "vacation" would have been out of the question. Besides, the specialized medical equipment and trained personnel required to treat it were in Moscow.

In other words, Volkogonov attempted the impossible: to show both that Andropov was in charge but not responsible for the decision to attack the airliner and that Gorbachev had no hand in it, either. Nevertheless, from Volkogonov's account, we know that the Politburo met that evening and discussed the budding crisis, which leaves the conclusion that it was the Soviet leadership, *sans* Andropov, that decided on the response, not a regional commander; a procedure entirely consistent with the arrangements made by the Andropov and Chernenko factions in June.

Ogarkov would have made the case to the top Soviet leadership for his proposed change of policy and immediate course of action once he had deduced the potential implications of the mysterious aircraft, sometime after it had penetrated Soviet airspace over Kamchatka. Emerging from Kamchatka, KAL 007's heading would have taken it over the La Perouse Strait, the 27-mile-wide body of water that separates Sakhalin from Hokkaido. Barring any change of course, KAL 007 would have remained in international airspace and would not have passed over Sakhalin. KAL 007's flight over Kamchatka showed conclusively that Soviet air defenses had been spoofed to enable the plane to fly into and out of Soviet airspace without being intercepted. But to what end? If it was one of the frequent intrusions of US military aircraft and the plane continued on its current heading, then no further compromise of Soviet air defenses would occur. However, if the plane veered into the air space over Sakhalin, as Ogarkov suspected it would, then a much more serious issue would arise. The full Soviet air defense network would turn on, revealing the true function of Krasnoyarsk, if only by default.

Ogarkov likely argued that if the intruder aircraft turned to violate Sakhalin airspace, it would mean that it was a spy plane whose mission was to force Soviet air defense to reveal its capabilities. American intelligence would deduce from the pattern of the Soviet response that Krasnoyarsk was inoperative and that the carefully crafted war scare was based on bluff. Thus, Ogarkov's proposal: if the intruder aircraft turned to cross into Sakhalin airspace, they should set aside standard procedures requiring positive identification before taking hostile action, and order Soviet interceptor aircraft to force the intruder plane to land or shoot it down.

Ogarkov's objective would be to precipitate a crisis and intensify the war scare. A Soviet-American crisis would permit Moscow to do two things: first, once they had possession of the aircraft, they would expose the American provocation, as in the U-2 incident of 1960. Ogarkov would have argued that, as in 1960, exposure of an American "plot" would give the Soviet Union tremendous political and propaganda advantage, which they could use to leverage public opinion against the deployment of the Pershing II. Second, they could also use the resulting international crisis as a smoke screen to carry out Andropov's plan to deploy SS-20s to Grenada before the Americans could deploy in West Germany, rather than after.

In Ogarkov's view, Andropov's original plan, which called for a response only *after* deployment of the Pershing II into West Germany, would not succeed because the Americans would perceive the bluff. The only hope was to advance the crisis and attempt to preempt the American deployment. Ogarkov was persuasive, especially as Andropov was not present to defend his own policy. Thus, Chernenko, acting under his authority as second in command in Andropov's absence, and with the concurrence of Gorbachev and Ustinov, made the contingent decision to bring down the intruder aircraft if it reentered Soviet airspace, and assigned to Ogarkov the responsibility to carry it out.

Foxhounds and Ravens over Sakhalin

Marshal Ogarkov proceeded to set a trap for the still unidentified aircraft heading across the Sea of Okhotsk toward Sakhalin. The Americans had spoofed the Soviet air defense system over Kamchatka, jamming and confusing radars and communications, preventing them from locating and identifying the intruder plane. Armed with this knowledge, Ogarkov's first task was to attack, shoot down, or drive off the spoofing aircraft, stripping the intruder of its protection and enabling his own interceptors a chance to bring it down.

For this task, the marshal held an ace in the hole. Earlier that month, the Soviets had secretly deployed an entirely new supersonic, mach-2 interceptor/jammer plane, the MiG-31, to the Far East. Later known as the Foxhound by its NATO designation, the MiG-31 was the most advanced, long-range interceptor ever fielded by the Soviet Union. A two-seater with pilot and weapons officer, it was configured similarly to the EF-111 Ravens escorting KAL 007, except that the Foxhounds carried weapons, whereas the Ravens did not.

At the time, however, US intelligence knew precious little about the new plane. Indeed, the Soviets would not admit to its existence for three more years. Washington knew only that in August, the Soviets had begun "flying special electronic warfare aircraft over Kamchatka....The purpose of these special electronic warfare flights was to broadcast a special masking or jamming signal which prevented US intelligence from intercepting and analyzing the electronic telemetry signals from their missiles..."[71] Unfortunately for Casey and KAL 007, the Foxhound could do much more.

The MiG-31 was the world's first operational fighter equipped with a phased-array radar, the Zaslon S-800, which enabled engagement of enemy aircraft at long range. Up to four of the aircraft could maneuver over 100 miles apart from each other, scanning a large area, and coordinate target tracking via datalink with each other and either a ground or airborne control center. Look-up/look-down radar enabled each plane to track up to ten targets while simultaneously attacking four of them. Each aircraft was armed with four air-to-air missiles guided with either semi-active radar homing, or inertial guidance warheads. The plane was also armed with an internal cannon capable of firing 8,000 rounds per minute.[72]

Of supreme importance for their mission, however, was the powerful electronics suite which enabled the MiG-31 to burn through the electronic countermeasures of enemy aircraft. The on-board radar capability gave the Soviets an interceptor capable of engaging the most likely US opponent at long-range without reliance on ground-controlled radar. The MiG-31, in short, was the first Soviet aircraft that could roam the skies to search out and attack enemy aircraft untethered from ground control.

Two separate but related aerial engagements thus took place in the night skies over Sakhalin. One was the MiG-31 Foxhounds attack on the US spoofer planes, the EF-111 Ravens and other aircraft protecting KAL 007; the other was the Soviet interception of the airliner, while the spoofers were being driven off. There was no possibility that Casey would have sent a tickler probe of any kind— let alone a civilian airliner—across Soviet territory without protection. The record of Soviet difficulty in tracking the airliner over Kamchatka and, as we shall see, initially also over Sakhalin, makes abundantly clear that spoofing planes were present to confuse Soviet radar and intercepting aircraft.[73]

The evidence for these two engagements, however, is almost exactly opposite. For the battle between the Foxhounds and Ravens there are no tapes of

---

[71] Republican Staff Study, *Did KAL-007 Successfully Ditch [. . .]*, 26.

[72] Wikipedia entry on the "Mikoyan MiG-31."

[73] One cannot exclude the possibility of different types of spoofer aircraft besides EF-111 Ravens being involved, such as RC-135 Rivet Joint, and/or EA6-B Prowler, both of which possessed powerful ECM capability.

pilot-to-pilot, or pilot-to-ground control conversations. These aircraft operated independently of ground control direction, although Brun claims that the Soviets had deployed two AWAC-type planes as airborne controllers. However, there are radar tracks and the wreckage of numerous (at least seven and perhaps as many as ten) aircraft shot down in the Tartar Strait.[74]

For the interception of KAL 007, on the other hand, there are air-to-ground tapes and radar tracks, but no aircraft wreckage. Despite persistent Soviet claims of the discovery and recovery of the 747's wreckage, it was never produced for public display. (Ten years after the event, the Russian government did return the luggage contained in the cargo hold of the airliner to families of the passengers and turned the cockpit and flight data tapes over to ICAO, subjects to be discussed in more detail below.)

Interception over Sakhalin

As KAL 007 approached the Sakhalin coastal buffer zone 60 miles off the coast, and now 365 miles off course, Soviet ground radar, having established contact, kept the track as 6065, but revised the earlier annotation from "81," to "91," to indicate that the intruder was now reclassified as a military aircraft. Interceptor pilots were scrambled to meet and confirm identification. At 1742Z, 1746Z, and 1754Z, three planes (call signs 805, 163, and 121) were sent streaking out to sea to intercept and follow the airliner. At 1753Z, Moscow issued the order to ground controllers that the contact was "a combat [military] target, which was to be destroyed if it violated the State border."[75] In other words, if the airliner turned to cross into Sakhalin airspace they would attack without prior identification.

American and Japanese sources differ on the kinds of aircraft that were involved in the interception of KAL 007 over Sakhalin. The Japanese maintained that the Soviets employed MiG-23s, based on analysis of radar tracks, intercepted communications, greater range of the aircraft, and the type of missile fired.[76] The United States, on the other hand, initially agreed that MiG-23s were involved, but later said that a Su-15 played the key role in subsequent events. A third view argues that the key aircraft were MiG-31s.[77] It seems that all three were involved in different capacities.

---

[74] Michel Brun, *Incident at Sakhalin: The True Mission of KAL Flight 007* (New York: Four Walls Eight Windows, 1995), 119-38, 29 and 217.

[75] *ICAO-93*:51.

[76] "Late Report: Kyodo Updates Rescue, Protest Reports," *FBIS Daily Report, Japan*, September 2, 1983, C 7; and "Radio Transcripts on Downed ROK Plane Released," *FBIS Daily Report, Japan*, September 7, 1983, C 1.

[77] Brun, *Incident at Sakhalin*, 222-23. Logically, MiG-31s would have been employed against US electronic spoofers, while MiG-23s would have been involved in the attack on KAL 007. Most versions of the Su-15 had no cannon and so could not have been the aircraft which tapes show to have fired a warning burst at the airliner, unless specially outfitted.

Although ground controllers attempted to vector the pilots to the airliner, it was not until 1805Z, a span of 23 minutes from the takeoff of the first interceptor plane, that they could locate it in the darkness, and then repeatedly lost contact with ground control.[78] The reason was because, as Johnson observes, the Soviets "were experiencing acute problems with their radar." They had "had difficulties until then in following [their] own fighters, let alone 'the target.'"[79] No doubt, the Soviets were having problems, but, for the most part, these were not of their own making.

Indeed, the transcripts are filled with exasperating commentary about Soviet controllers' inability to communicate with their pilots, and vice versa, or to observe the target. The 11-minute period between 1809Z and 1820Z, for example, was typical. Interceptor pilots could not contact their nearest ground controller at Burevestnik on Etorofu, just as the pilot of 805, Lt. Colonel Gennadi Osipovich, was making visual contact with KAL 007.[80] At 1820Z Colonel Gerasimenko, commander at Burevestnik, stated that "I cannot hear the radio transmissions." During that same span, the controller at Smirnykh said: "for some reason we cannot see it from Sokol, range of target is 20 kilometers, they are going away...." And then, "we have lost [them] from the screen, we are losing contact."[81]

Radar difficulties, of course, indicated the presence of US spoofer planes jamming Soviet radar and radio frequencies in an attempt to confuse and frustrate any attempt to intercept KAL 007. Soviet ground control and interceptor aircraft soon managed to coordinate their observations and actions toward the airliner, mainly by handing over control from one ground station to another to foil the jamming.[82] At the same time, their efforts were facilitated by the success of the Foxhounds in engaging and driving off or shooting down the Ravens and other aircraft attempting to protect the intruding airliner.

The critical time frame was from 1742Z when the first interceptor rose to contact and identify KAL 007, until about 1900Z when the Foxhound/Raven dogfight had ended. While Soviet ground controllers and interceptors from Sakhalin struggled to locate the intruder plane, the Foxhounds, sent from Postovaya, at that time the main Siberian airbase on the mainland coast near the Sovetskaya Gavan naval base, lay in wait for the Ravens. Attacking the US aircraft disrupted their jamming operations and allowed Soviet ground control and interceptors to coordinate their interception of the Korean airliner.

---

[78] *ICAO-93*, reel no.1: 59.

[79] Johnson, *Shootdown*, 20-21.

[80] The Soviets initially identified a Major Vasily Kasmin as the pilot of 805. It was not until eight years later, in 1991, that Gennadi Osipovich was named as the pilot.

[81] *ICAO-93*, track 2, reel 2, 111, 128-30.

[82] Ibid., track 1, reel no. 2: 51. In ICAO's view the "limitations in radar coverage necessitated the handover of control of the interceptors from one ground control station to another," but all of the radars in question were within a few miles of each other.

As KAL 007 approached the Sakhalin coastline, still paralleling it and on a course heading of 240 to pass south of it, at 1802Z, Captain Chun turned his plane to the right and flew to the northwest for five minutes, before turning left again, at 1807Z, an aerial jog-step that put him back on a course heading of 240, but now positioned to pass over the southern portion of the island. This zigzag maneuver also coordinated the arrival of his plane over Sakhalin with the arriving electronic countermeasures aircraft whose mission was to escort KAL 007 safely across Sakhalin to international airspace.[83]

It was at this point, at 1809Z, that Osipovich in 805, flying parallel to the airliner, made his first visual contact, reporting to controller Deputat at Sokol that the plane had turned and was "flying with flashing lights," that is, with its anti-collision and navigation lights on. Despite this unusual report, which signaled that what Osipovich was observing was clearly *not* a military aircraft, contrary to the earlier designation, Deputat instructed him to "set to lock-on mode," which he as well as the pilot of fighter 163, trailing behind, did. Two minutes later, Osipovich reported that "I see it both visually and on the screen." Ground control wanted confirmation of weapons status: "report lock-on," and Osipovich confirmed receipt of the order. At 1812Z, responding again to his controller, Osipovich declared: "I am locked-on."[84]

KAL 007 entered over Sakhalin airspace at 1816Z. Flying at 500 knots, or eight miles per minute, it would take the airliner no more than ten minutes to cross the island. As soon as the airliner crossed into Soviet airspace, a new ground controller, Karnaval, located at Smirnykh air base, came on the air to order fighter 805, trailing the plane, to "destroy the target," but in the same breath also asked: "are there navigation lights or not?" At 1818Z, in response to Osipovich's third reaffirmation that the intruder's navigation lights were on, Karnaval abruptly changed his instructions.

But Karnaval now also began to experience communications difficulties, as his frequency was being jammed. Reporting to Deputat and fighter 163 that he was losing contact, he ordered Osipovich in 805 to go through standard interception procedures to force the plane to "land at Sokol."[85] These procedures called for the pilot get close to the intruder, "flash the interceptor's lights," "interrogate" the intruder's transponder, and to "approach...rock [wings] at the...target...and force it to land." Then, a minute later, at 1819Z, Osipovich was instructed further to turn *off* his missile lock-on, "fire a warning burst with cannons and rock wings to show the direction to Sokol."[86]

The abrupt change in instructions reflected a growing concern by local commanders that what they were tracking in the dawning sky directly above them

[83] Gollin and Allardyce, *Desired Track*, 119-21.
[84] *ICAO-93*, reel no.1: 62-63.
[85] Ibid., track 2, reel 2: 126-28 and reel 1, 66-67.
[86] Ibid., track 2, reel 2: 126-28.

was not a military intruder, but a civilian aircraft.[87] Instructing Osipovich to execute interception procedures was not only standard procedure in that instance, but it also bought them a few precious seconds to decide what to do. In the air, Osipovich moved to within two kilometers of the aircraft in attempting to carry out his instructions. Indeed, as his cannon had a range of 3,000 feet, Osipovich would have had to close to within two kilometers for his burst to have had any effect.

  There was an additional reason for the abrupt change of instructions. From 1814Z, KAL 007 had been calling Tokyo Control to request a change of altitude and at 1820Z, Tokyo granted permission for an increase from 33,000 feet to 35,000 feet. More importantly, however, Tokyo carried out a Selcal check that positively identified KAL 007 as a civilian airliner.[88] At this point, Captain Chun had not only turned on all running lights, but also his transponder, to leave no doubt to trailing interceptors and interrogating ground radar that his was a civilian aircraft. As American officials later admitted, it was "apparent that the Korean crew realized that they were being intercepted."[89]

  We know from signals intelligence (SIGINT) intercepts that Soviet ground radar interrogated KAL 007's transponder "at least twice."[90] Soviet radio operators also overheard co-pilot Son's conversation with Tokyo Control and understood the significance of reports from Osipovich that the plane's navigation lights were on. All the indications were that they were dealing with a foreign civilian airliner that had overflown Soviet territory and was about to exit into international airspace.

---

[87] According to the NASA sunrise/sunset calculator, sunrise over Sakhalin on September 1, 1983 was at 5:12 a.m. local time or 1812Z.

[88] *ICAO-93* track 2, reel 2, "Radio Communications Recorded in Tokyo," 38. Japanese military radar showed that "the 747 jet was signaling an identification code used by civilian aircraft on international flights . . . [which] should have indicated to the Soviet command that the plane it was tracking was likely to be a civilian aircraft." See David Rogers, "Automatic Signal Marked 747 As Civilian," *Boston Globe*, September 10, 1983, 3.

[89] Philip Taubman, "Korean Jet Signaled Russians, US Says," *New York Times*, September 3, 1983, A2.

[90] According to NSA intercepts, "KAL-007 was electronically queried at least twice by Soviet Identification-Friend or Foe (IFF)-signals and KAL-007's failure to respond in code at least indicated to the Soviets that it was a non-Soviet aircraft." Republican Staff Study, *Did KAL-007 Successfully Ditch [. . .]*, 33. While there is little doubt that the Soviets interrogated KAL 007's transponder, the report is in error stating that there was no response. Tokyo Control had completed a Selcal check at 1820Z, indicating that the transponder was turned on, making a response automatic. *ICAO-93*, "Tokyo High Frequency Channel 3," 38. See also, David Rogers, "The Transponder Question," *Boston Globe*, September 8, 1983, 1, citing a Japanese military source who "understood" that "an identifying signal had been received from the airliner's transponder." Finally, a ground radar interrogation would have turned on a light in the airliner's cockpit to indicate his aircraft was being interrogated.

Their instructions were to destroy the target, but that was based on the presumption that KAL 007 was a military aircraft on a spy mission. What to do? What Soviet controllers should have done, but did not do, was "to seek help over the air traffic control link between Khabarovsk...and Sapporo..."[91] Instead, they called Moscow to obtain reconfirmation of their orders.

The Attack on KAL 007

The Soviets now knew for the first time that the plane they had been tracking for the past two and a half hours was most likely a civilian airliner in routine contact with Tokyo Control, but obviously well off course, and not a military plane.[92] On the other hand, the aerial dogfight going on around it indicated that it must be more than a mere civilian airliner on a routine flight. Time, however, was rapidly running out because KAL 007 was but minutes away from international airspace and the Soviets had to make an immediate decision whether to attack the plane or permit it to escape.

In a panic, General Ivan Tretyak, of Far East command, while urging both 805 and 163 to stay in position, called Moscow again for instructions.[93] The call reportedly went to Ogarkov, who, as noted above, had just received Politburo approval to force or shoot down the plane if it overflew Sakhalin. There is some dispute over who transmitted the actual authorization. Considering that the call went to Ogarkov's office and that it was Ogarkov who took command of the crisis afterward, handling both the public and private Soviet responses, it is likely that Ogarkov himself gave the order to shoot the plane down.[94]

At 1823Z, ground control Deputat, now also being jammed and unable to communicate directly with Osipovich in 805, called another controller, RCA, to ask whether he was in "contact with the target and Osipovich." RCA (radar-controlled approach?) replied that he was in "contact with all of them." Deputat

---

[91] *ICAO-93*: 13 and John Burns, "A Peek at Soviet Military," *New York Times*, September 11, 1983, 1.

[92] Clarence Robinson, "US Says Soviets Knew Korean Air Lines 747 Was Commercial Flight," *Aviation Week & Space Technology*, September 12, 1983, 18-21.

[93] Dusko Doder, "Soviets Said to Remove Air Officers," *Washington Post*, October 5, 1983, A1. According to party officials, "the Soviet Far East command had been in direct telephone contact with top military officials in Moscow on several occasions prior to the downing of the plane."

[94] Martin Sieff, "Akhromeyev: 'Shoot it down': General Who Killed Himself Blamed for Downing KAL Jet," *Washington Times*, August 30, 1991, A1. Quoting a retired, but anonymous, general, the central fact in the article is that Ogarkov was called for a decision "in the early hours of September 1, 1983." This fact was, however, wrapped in the incredible assertion that it was Akhromeyev, not Ogarkov, who ordered the shootdown. Doubt was cast on this assertion by "a senior European intelligence official [who] suggested that friends of Marshal Ogarkov may have put out the story to protect him from the wave of recriminations now sweeping the Soviet Union and to shift the blame onto the safely dead Marshal Akhromeyev."

then instructed RCA to "give the command to Osipovich, to 805, to move out to the target and destroy the target with missiles." Before RCA could act, however, Deputat regained contact with 805 and issued the order himself: "805, approach target and destroy target!" Osipovich replied: "Roger. Locked-on already."[95]

Radar tracking and aircraft debris recovered after the event add to our knowledge and understanding of what occurred during these few tense and frenzied moments. Japanese radar indicated the presence of multiple American and Soviet aircraft in the skies over Sakhalin between 1812Z and 1854Z, as illustrated in the map below.[96]

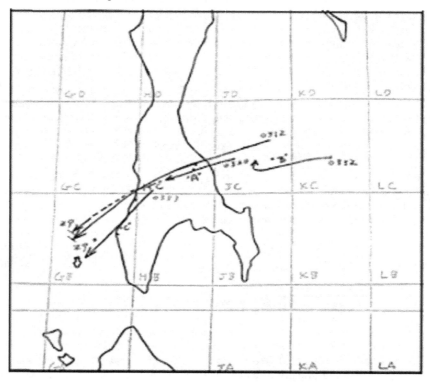

Japanese Defense Agency map distributed at 9:10 p.m. in Tokyo on September 1, 1983, indicating multiple US and Soviet aircraft over Sakhalin. Source: Michel Brun, *Incident at Sakhalin: The True Mission of KAL Flight 007* (New York: Four Walls Eight Windows, 1995)

---

[95] *ICAO-93*, transcript, reel number 1: 71.

[96] Brun, *Incident at Sakhalin*, 19, says there were three US and three Russian planes, though the map appears to show five in total. Later, on pages 226-27, he says Soviet radar showed nine different intruder aircraft.

Chapter 3
How Close to Breakout? Krasnoyarsk and KAL 007

143

Recovered afterward in the sea around Moneron Island (where KAL 007 was said to have crashed) were aircraft parts identified as coming from an EF-111 Raven, a RC-135 Rivet Joint, and an E2-C Hawkeye aircraft.[97] If true, then these planes were there to provide safe passage for KAL 007 over Soviet airspace. Collectively, they possessed the capability to intercept as well as to jam Soviet communications, create "ghost" images, and to disable air and ground missile targeting and radar. But they themselves were all unarmed.

As KAL 007 was exiting Sakhalin airspace approximately over the port city of Nevelsk and heading southwest in the direction of Moneron Island, and thus to safety, Soviet ground controllers were screaming the command to shoot down the airliner with missiles. SIGINT data show that controllers had to repeat the order "about six times before Pilot Osipovich heard and understood it."[98] Thus, by the time General Tretyak had relayed Ogarkov's order to shoot, KAL 007 was already into international airspace.

This was the most intense moment of the mission, as American ECM specialists aboard the spoofing/jamming aircraft, listening in to Soviet communications, also heard the orders to shoot, and were themselves frantically attempting to jam Soviet frequencies to prevent, deflect, divert, or defeat the attack. These were also the seconds when the Foxhounds stepped up their efforts to drive off the Ravens. While the efforts of the Ravens were not good enough to shepherd the airliner to safety, they were, as we shall see, quite probably good enough to prevent its destruction in the sky.

Meanwhile, KAL 007's climb reduced the airliner's speed relative to the interceptor, momentarily taking 805 out of firing position, and forcing Osipovich to execute a sharp banking "snake" turn to reposition his aircraft, a maneuver that also consumed valuable time in the process.[99] At 1824Z, ground controller Deputat, again commanded Osipovich to "approach target and destroy target!" After declaring that he was "locked-on" and closing on the target to a distance of eight kilometers, at 1825:31Z, Osipovich announced that he had "executed launch" and that "the target is destroyed."[100]

Osipovich had launched two missiles at KAL 007, the "a" and "b" versions of the Anab-3. The "a" was a semi-active, radar homing missile with a range of 20 kilometers, designed to head for the target and detonate by proximity fuse within forty feet of its largest part. The "b," on the other hand, was a heat-seeking missile, with a range of 5 to 10 kilometers, designed to follow the heat

---

[97] Ibid., 139. Brun also claims evidence of an SR-71, but this seems highly unlikely.

[98] Republican Staff Study, *Did KAL-007 Successfully Ditch* [. . .], 34.

[99] Gollin and Allardyce, *Desired Track*, 131-33, note the airliner's climb, but believe that it was from a lower altitude, suggesting that Captain Chun was making "a cunning use of limited resources" to evade attack. As noted above, Taubman, "Korean Jet Signaled Russians, US Says," quoted American officials, who observed that it was "apparent that the Korean crew realized that they were being intercepted."

[100] *ICAO-93*, reel no.1: 71-72. A variety of times have been given for the launch of the missiles, including 1826:02Z and 1826:20Z.

stream of a jet engine's exhaust and detonate inside it. At a distance of eight kilometers it would take only a few seconds for these missiles to reach their target.

Although Osipovich said that both missiles had hit the airliner, indeed, claiming that one ripped off part of the left wing, he was mistaken.[101] The aircraft's radio antenna was located in the left wingtip and Captain Chun's subsequent radio transmissions meant that that the wing was intact. Nor was the target "destroyed," which was simply Soviet military jargon for the target being "hit." In fact, the heat-seeking missile missed entirely, perhaps because it was out of range, or the missile failed to maintain lock-on or to detonate. Most likely, it had been diverted from its target by electronic countermeasures generated by the spoofer/jammer aircraft attempting to protect KAL 007.

But the radar homing missile successfully detonated within 40 feet of the 747, spraying shrapnel into the tail and rear section of the fuselage. The shrapnel burst knocked off a small piece of the tail section and punctured the main passenger cabin, making a roughly two-foot diameter hole and many smaller ones.[102] The resulting rapid loss of cabin pressure activated the release of oxygen masks and automatic public announcements that the plane was executing an emergency descent.

Amid the pandemonium, the cockpit voice recorder (CVR) transcript shows, flight attendants repeated instructions in English and Japanese for passengers to put out cigarettes and don oxygen masks, stressing that the plane was in an emergency descent. There were, however, no instructions to prepare for a ditching at sea, such as orders to remove shoes, eyeglasses, and other hard objects, or to take hold of flotation gear and put on life jackets.[103] In the cockpit the reaction was similar. Although Captain Chun and his crew struggled to control the aircraft, there was no May Day call, nor a switch of transponder-locator code to 7700, the standard signal to indicate that the plane was in danger of crashing into the sea.

In other words, if Captain Chun believed that he would have had to ditch, instructions to the passengers would have been evident in the transcript as soon as he had begun an emergency descent. This, of course, does not preclude the possibility that such instructions would have been issued later, after he had reached a lower altitude. It is quite possible that instructions would have gone out

---

[101] Andrey Illesh, "Interview with Lieutenant Colonel Gennadiy Nikolayevich Osipovich, Pilot of the SU-15," *Izvestia*, January 25, 1991, English translation in *FBIS Daily Report, Soviet Union,* February 6, 1991, 10.

[102] Body parts of three persons including a young child and a woman were found on the beaches of Hokkaido. Although none could be positively identified as having been passengers, the badly mangled corpses suggested that they had been sucked forcefully through a small aperture. If they had been flung from the airliner, the hole through which they were sucked had to have been at least two feet in diameter. See Pearson, *Cover-Up,* 234.

[103] *ICAO-93*, KE-007 CVR Transcript, 13-14.

to passengers then to prepare for a possible ditching at sea, as he looked for a place to land.

Captain Chun's Decision

Seconds after the captain and crew felt the impact of the explosion, the plane began to climb out of control. The explosion had destroyed three of the aircraft's four hydraulic control systems, but the main number four system remained operable. The number four system could actuate primary and secondary flight controls, including air brakes, and landing gear. The crew, double-checking all four of the engines, found them to be "normal."[104] After struggling for nearly a full minute to regain control of his aircraft, disengaging the autopilot and assuming manual control, Captain Chun began an emergency descent in accordance with airline procedures to an altitude which would permit breathing without oxygen masks, to around 16,000 feet.

At the beginning of his descent, at 1827:18Z, Captain Chun made a garbled transmission to Tokyo Control, which, because he was speaking with his oxygen mask on, was difficult to hear and has thus received widely different interpretations. One was that he was taking his plane to a lower altitude because of "rapid decompression." Although a logical reaction, voice analysis cannot verify this interpretation. Another was said to be the exclamation: "gonna be a bloodbath, real bad," said to describe his own circumstances of a plane hurtling to its doom. This, we now know, was not occurring. A third was that the "bloodbath" remark was a description of the dogfight occurring in the air at that moment.[105]

There were, in fact, three eyewitness accounts that corroborate a dogfight in the skies over Sakhalin at that moment. One was the excited utterance of one of the Soviet interceptor pilots, a second was Osipovich's own observation, and the third was the report of a Japanese fisherman in the sea directly below. According to Osipovich's later account, he said that Major Litvin, the pilot of the MiG-23, call sign 163, who was trailing behind him kept shouting: "I see a dogfight! I see a dogfight!," but Osipovich recalled that being focused on his own task, "I had no idea what dogfight he was talking about."[106] Osipovich himself noted that as he approached the airliner, ground control exclaimed to him that the images of both his plane and the airliner had "completely disappeared from [his] screen." Osipovich replied, "my radar did not show anything for me [either] it was a complete surprise." Then, he said, "someone had wedged into our conversation.

---

[104] Ibid.

[105] Porter, "Acoustic Analysis of Air Traffic Communications Concerning Korean Air Flight 007, August 31, 1983," 22. See also Brun, *Incident at Sakhalin*, 80.

[106] Illesh, "Interview with Osipovich," *Izvestia*, January 25, 1991, 1. The translation in *FBIS Daily Report, Soviet Union*, February 6, 1991, cited above in n101 offers a milder version in which Litvin, the pilot of 163 says "I am observing air combat. What combat was he seeing? It was difficult for me to understand."

A foreigner who knew Russian spoke on our frequency in order to create confusion and give false orders." In other words, "there was another intruder." [107]

Below, some 30 miles north of Moneron Island, there were approximately 150 Japanese fishing boats in the water trawling for cuttlefish. At about 1830Z, the eight-man crew of one of these, the Chidori Maru, no. 58, heard the sound of aircraft at "a low altitude" above them, followed by a muffled explosion, but, due to heavy clouds, saw nothing. The Captain, Shizuka Hayashi, said that "he heard a loud sound followed by a bright flash of light on the horizon, then another dull sound and a less intense flash of light."

The flashes of light, he estimated, were some distance away "in a southeasterly direction from somewhere south of the beacon light of Mys Lopatina on Sakhalin Island."[108] There occurred a second explosion, more flashes and a few minutes later he noticed the smell of burned kerosene. At a minimum, the Japanese fisherman had witnessed two widely separated events and possibly two missile hits (but not KAL 007, the location south of the Lopatina lighthouse being over 30 miles from them). Since light travels faster than sound, the fisherman should have seen flashes before hearing thuds. If his story is taken as literally correct, he may have witnessed four or more attacks.[109]

Soviet radar tracking showed that Captain Chun took KAL 007 down fairly rapidly in wide right and left spiraling turns over the first four minutes from an altitude of 35,000 feet to around 16,000 feet, then slowed his descent rate over the next eight minutes to a level of 1000 feet, before falling below radar coverage.[110] Calculating the descent in three segments shows that the maneuvering was deliberate rather than haphazard. Chun descended 19,000 feet in the first four minutes; 11,000 feet over the next four; and 4,000 feet over the next four—an unmistakable moderation of deceleration that indicated Captain Chun was in substantial control of his plane.[111] (Had KAL 007 been in freefall, as claimed, it would have taken the aircraft less than three minutes to crash into the ocean from an altitude of 35,000 feet.)

By the time Captain Chun had begun his emergency descent, KAL 007 already was four or five miles south of Moneron, roughly at 46.25N/141.20E, and in international airspace. Descending in wide circular turns, Chun would have

---

[107] Estatelite (website), "Life in Aviation Minus One Day. Aviation Lieutenant Colonel Osipovich Told How He Shot Down a Civilian Boeing," https://estatelite.ru/en/zhizn-v-aviacii-minus-odin-den-podpolkovnik-aviacii-osipovich-rasskazal-kak/

[108] *ICAO-93*: 5.

[109] Brun, *Incident at Sakhalin*, 27-29, In a more intricate interpretation, makes this same deduction.

[110] The *ICAO-93*: 53, report notes that after the missile strike "the target was reported to be descending and turning to the right, [but] the plotted radar information showed turns to the left."

[111] Bert Schlossberg, *Rescue 007: The Untold Story of KAL 007 and its Survivors* (Jerusalem: Xlibris, 2000), 46-54.

begun to search for the best place to set his aircraft down. He or his navigator would quickly have realized that the nearest airfield lay less than 30 nautical miles directly south, on the Japanese island of Rebun, located at 45.26N/141.02E, off the northwest coast of Hokkaido. There were two other Japanese airfields near Rebun, one on the neighboring island of Rishiri at 45.14N/141E and the other at Wakkanai at 45.24N/141.48E.[112]

Even at an airspeed of 350 miles per hour, a conservative estimate for this point in his initial descent, Chun was only five minutes flying time from Rebun, and safety.[113] Moreover, at his altitude Captain Chun could see the glow of lights from northern Hokkaido in the distance (low-lying clouds only would have magnified the illumination effect in the dawn sky). But Captain Chun did not continue southward in the direction of Rebun. Inexplicably, at 1828Z, he turned north, toward Moneron Island.[114] Less than five minutes from safety, in control of his aircraft, and over international waters, Captain Chun chose instead to return to hostile Soviet airspace.

Soviet base commanders were astonished by Captain Chun's decision, but the clues to why he turned north can be found in the cockpit recorder tape and the digital flight data recorder tape the Russians turned over to ICAO in 1993. Both the CVR and the DFDR tapes were cut at 1827:46Z, or one minute and forty-four seconds after the missile strike. Given the placement of the recorders—"black boxes"—on opposite sides of the fuselage near the tail; the fact that they were powered by separate cables; and that power continued to flow to them (as long as the engines were running there would be electrical power), there is a zero probability that the missile explosion would have severed the tapes in both boxes, let alone at the same instant. And if it had, the cutoff would have been much closer to the missile impact time of 1826:02Z

The fact that the plane continued to fly also meant that the recorders continued to record; indeed, the Russian controller record states that the plane flew for some ten more minutes before disappearing from radar.[115] Therefore, there is no technical reason for both tapes to have been cut off simultaneously at 1827:46Z. The Russians cut both tapes at that moment because they wanted to keep secret what occurred next, especially the fourteen seconds during which Captain Chun made the decision to turn north at 1828Z, and the communications that followed. The Russians cut the tapes at 1827:46Z because it was just after that that they contacted Captain Chun and compelled him to turn north. In short,

---

[112] *Flight Information Publication: Supplement Pacific, Australasia and Antarctica* (St. Louis: Defense Mapping Agency, 4 August 1983), B163-64, 202.

[113] Captain Chun could have been flying faster, but not much slower, because the stall speed of a 747, the speed at which it could no longer cruise, was just under 250 mph.

[114] *ICAO-93*, track 2, reel no. 2: 132. At 1828Z, the Commander of the air base on Etorofu (Burevestnik), Lt. Colonel Gerasimenko, reported to Anatoli Kornukov, commander of the air base at Sokol: "The target, the target turned north." "Say again." "The target turned north." "The target turned north?" "Affirmative."

[115] Ibid., track 2, reel no. 2: 136.

they wanted to keep secret what communications were recorded on the cockpit voice recorder and what aircraft movements were recorded on the digital flight recorder, as KAL 007 turned and flew north toward Moneron Island.

North to Kostromskoye

The geography of Sakhalin is an important factor in understanding what happened to KAL 007. Extending along the western side of the island is a mountain range varying in height from 2,000-5,000 feet. All of the Soviet ground control stations initially involved in the interception and attack on KAL 007 (Deputat, Karnaval, Trikotazh, and Plantatsia) were located east of the mountain range. As the action in the sky shifted west over the Tartar Strait and particularly as Captain Chun took his plane down below a level of 1,000 feet, the mountains blocked the radars located east of them from tracking the plane and low cloud cover prevented pursuing pilots from directly observing it. The position of the plane may also explain why KAL 007 dropped off the Japanese radar on Wakkanai at 1829Z.[116]

Thus, the Soviet claim that KAL 007 disappeared from radar coverage at 1838Z refers to the radars located on the east side of Sakhalin. However, other radars, located on the west coast of Sakhalin and on the mainland itself, were able to continue tracking the flight of the airliner. One Russian émigré, Valery Ryzhkov, offered such testimony. He was reportedly the "duty officer the night KAL 007 went down at Radio Technical Brigade 1845 at the town of Zavet Ilyicha on the mainland coast." In communication "with at least three other air defense radar sites," Ryzhkov tracked the plane's "controlled descent."[117] These other mainland coastal radars were reportedly units 67080 at Komsomolsk-na-Amure; 2112 at Edinka; 362 at Nelma; and 365 at Nakhtakhe.[118] From positions on the mainland, a hundred miles away, these radars could track KAL 007's descent, but not its actual landing.

The controller who would have been able to follow the landing was the one located at Kostromskoye on the western side of Sakhalin, just north of Kholmsk and about sixty-five nautical miles north of Moneron. Kostromskoye was also home to the only airfield on the southwest coast of Sakhalin. Referred to as Kostroma on the Russian tapes, this controller appeared in the record for the

---

[116] "KAL Airliner Observed Falling in 'Vast' Spirals," *FBIS Daily Report, Japan*, September 12, 1983, C 1. Japan Defense Agency sources claimed illogically that Wakkanai radar observed the airliner spiral down to an altitude of some 2,000 feet above sea level where it "blipped off" the radar screen and then plunged "almost perpendicularly to its death." It is elementary to observe that once the airliner disappeared from radar, its subsequent flight could not be determined.

[117] Republican Staff Study, *Did KAL 007 Successfully Ditch* [. . .]*, 76*. As the title suggests, the author of the study argues that the airliner ditched at sea near Moneron.

[118] Avraham Shifrin, Research Centre for Prisons, Psychprisons and Forced Labor Concentration Camps of the USSR, Press Release, July 11, 1991, Appendix 1. http://www.rescue007.org/docs/ShifrinPressRelease1991-07-11.pdf

first time at 1832Z, but it is evident that he had been involved for some minutes. Indeed, at that moment, the commander of Sokol air base, General Kornukov, was saying that "Kostroma must be involved. Eh."[119] It is how Kostroma was involved that is of supreme importance.

It is my view that the Russians tampered with and cut the CVR and DFDR tapes at 1827:46Z because it was just after that when the controller, Kostroma, communicated to Captain Chun, most likely on the international hailing frequency of 121.5MHz (more about that below), and compelled him to turn north, rather than continue south to safety. That communication commenced during the fourteen seconds between the cutoff of the CVR tape and Chun's observed turn north at 1828Z, and continued thereafter, until Captain Chun landed his plane safely on the airfield at Kostromskoye around 1900Z.

To enforce his demand, Kostroma would have threatened to blow Captain Chun's plane out of the sky with a surface-to-air (SA-5) missile. We know from SIGINT intercepts that a SAM missile battery located on the tip of Sakhalin was locked on his aircraft and authorized to shoot.[120] Cockpit lights would have confirmed to Captain Chun that his aircraft was being painted with target acquisition radar and so he turned north, rather than risk certain destruction. He would have complied in any case following airline rules, which instruct pilots to obey commands by hostile aircraft to follow them to a landing place, in order to preserve the safety of their passengers.

Subsequent events reinforce the thesis that the controller at Kostroma was in contact with and directing KAL 007 from this point. While the Sakhalin controllers east of the mountains clearly were acting on their original orders to direct their interceptors to shoot down the airliner, Ogarkov overrode them, now seeing the opportunity to capture it and prove that it was a spy plane. Initially, when Captain Chun took his plane into a controlled descent, and Osipovich turned for home base, controller Deputat vectored interceptor fighters 163 and 121 into position to continue the chase. These fighters were directed to go down after the airliner, then in the vicinity of Moneron, and shoot it down, but neither could locate it in the dense, low-lying clouds.[121]

When Kostroma entered the picture and commanded KAL 007 to turn north, the orders were changed, which created a moment of confusion among the controllers east of the mountains. As the ICAO report noted:

> ground control expressed concern that the target was still flying, despite being hit by missiles, and that having exited Soviet

---

[119] *ICAO-93*, track 2, reel no. 2: 134.
[120] Republican Staff Study, *Did KAL-007 Successfully Ditch* [. . .], *33-34* and Hersh, *Target is Destroyed*, 234. Given the presence of Soviet aircraft in the vicinity of KAL 007, the threat to bring it down with a missile was a bluff.
[121] *ICAO-93*, reel no. 1: 72-79.

airspace it was re-entering this airspace in the area of Moneron Island.[122]

Confusion was heightened momentarily when Kostroma lost sight of the airliner after making contact, until 1836Z, when he reported that he was once again observing it. At 1838Z, Colonel Gerasimenko informed General Kornukov that Kostroma was not only observing the target, but also "now has contact with the [MiG] 23."[123] In other words, with the switch in controllers from Deputat to Kostroma, Fighter 163's orders were changed from finding and finishing off the airliner to guiding it to a safe landing.

Others have noted this change without realizing its significance. Gollin and Allardyce argue correctly that "an examination of the flight pattern of the MiG-23 [call sign 163] tells us much about the action of Captain Chun and KE 007."[124] Pearson's depiction of 163's radar track tells us the most. In the map below, Pearson shows clearly that 163, after circling Moneron Island, flew up along the west coast of Sakhalin to the airbase at Kostromskoye.[125] A reasonable guess is that he either guided or followed KAL 007 all the way in.

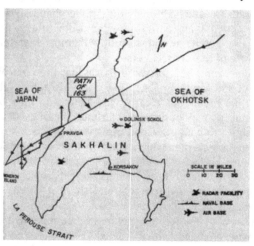

Radar track of Soviet MiG-23 jet "163" that may have directed KAL 007 to land at Kostromskoye on Sakhalin. Source: David Pearson, *KAL 007: The Cover-Up: Why the True Story Has Never Been Told* (New York: Summit Books, 1987)

---

[122] Ibid., 53.

[123] Ibid., track 2, reel no. 2: 136. In one of numerous contradictions, the Russians claim that KAL 007 disappeared from radar at 1838Z, but their own record indicates that Kostroma was at that moment observing the target on radar.

[124] Gollin and Allardyce, *Desired Track*, 142-43.

[125] Pearson, *KAL 007: The Cover-Up*, 81.

Chapter 3
How Close to Breakout? Krasnoyarsk and KAL 007

151

But how would the controller Kostroma have guided Captain Chun to his airfield in the dark of early morning? I believe that he ingeniously employed several lighthouses situated along the Sakhalin coast and on Moneron to guide KAL 007 to a landing. These lighthouses, easily spotted, all contained navigational beacons that would have permitted Captain Chun to orient his aircraft toward the Sakhalin coast and then northward toward Kostromskoye, where he would eventually have picked up the airfield's homing beacon.[126] That would appear to explain why, as Japanese fishermen testified and the Russians also later acknowledged, Captain Chun "circled Moneron Island twice," before turning north.[127]

If KAL 007's flight mirrored 163's radar track, after circling the Moneron lighthouse and establishing his position from its navigational beacon, Captain Chun flew northeast to the lighthouse on the coast at Lopatina point, just south of Nevelsk. Then, once reaching the coast he employed his ground mapping radar to fly north along the coastline to the lighthouse at Kholmsk, and thence to the airfield at Kostromskoye. The entire flight from Moneron would have been about sixty-five miles, which, at 350mph would have taken less than fifteen minutes. By this rough calculation, Captain Chun would have touched down at the airfield on Kostromskoye sometime around 1900Z.[128]

Co-pilot Son's Radio Transmissions

Is there any additional evidence that KAL 007 continued to fly after 1838Z when it is said to have dropped from radar coverage? Many accounts claim that after having dropped from radar coverage, the airliner then plunged into the sea. But this is a logical fallacy unsupported by evidence. It does not follow that once the airliner was no longer in view, it necessarily crashed. Out of sight cannot be taken to mean out of power, or control. Indeed, as we now know, Captain Chun had substantial control over his aircraft; all four engines were running; and he was flying below 1,000 feet on the outside of the mountain range along the western coast, which explains the disappearance of his plane from those radars east of the mountains. The better assumption is that the plane continued to fly, rather than suddenly and inexplicably crashed. Besides, as will be discussed in greater detail below, there is no evidence of a crash into the sea.

It is at this point that Michel Brun makes a most important contribution to the analysis, even though his interpretation of the events is completely at

---

[126] For the location and description of these facilities, see Igor Samarin, *Sakhalin Lighthouses* (online), cited with link at *Lighthouses of Russia: Northern Sakhalin* by Russ Rowlett https://www.ibiblio.org/lighthouse/sakn.htm; or consult the Tactical Pilotage Chart F10B for the data.

[127] Republican Staff Study, *Did KAL 007 Successfully Ditch* [...], 47. The dimensions of Moneron Island are one mile by four miles.

[128] In Tokyo, on the morning of September 1, the head of Korean Air Lines announced that the airliner had been forced to land on Sakhalin "at approximately four o'clock in the morning," that is 1900Z.

variance from the one presented here.[129] Brun engaged the services of acoustics and frequency expert, Dr. K. Tsuboi, director of the Iwatsu Laboratory outside Tokyo, to conduct a computer analysis of the Tokyo air traffic control tapes. Dr. Tsuboi positively identified the voice print of co-pilot Son in six transmissions to two KAL aircraft and to an unknown third party between 1830Z and 1913Z.[130] Five of these transmissions were made *after* KAL 007 was supposed to have crashed.

The first transmission, the single word, "Roger," at 1830:05Z, I take to be Son's reply to the instructions from Soviet ground controller Kostroma. According to Brun: "KAL 007 was responding to a call, transmitting only what was necessary to be understood by the caller but not enough to be detected by Tokyo."[131] Tokyo Control, meanwhile, unable to contact the airliner, asked other aircraft in the vicinity to attempt to do so. The first choice was to ask KAL 015, supposedly the closest to KAL 007. KAL 015 called on Tokyo's VHF frequency, 118.9 MHz, but, receiving no response, switched to the international calling frequency 121.5 MHz—and made contact. This obviously was the frequency on which Chun also was in contact with Kostroma.

KAL 015 called twice, at 1852:09Z and 1852:15Z: "zero zero seven, zero one five," and at 1852:40Z came co-pilot Son's reply: "zero one five." KAL 015 called back immediately five seconds later. Receiving no reply, he called again at 1854:35Z and 1854:45Z before Son responded with a short indecipherable transmission, to which KAL 015 answered: "Roger." However, even though the computer voice print analysis of the Narita tapes showed indisputably that KAL 015 had been in contact with KAL 007 twice, KAL 015 reported to Tokyo Control that there had been *no* contact. The explanation must surely be that Kostroma demanded secrecy, and the Korean pilots complied.[132]

A few minutes later, at 1908:14Z, when a third airliner, KAL 050, entered into the Tokyo Control zone, he was asked to contact KAL 007. After attempting to make contact on 118.9 MHz and failing, KAL 050 also switched to 121.5 MHz and made contact, KAL 007 responding at 1909:51Z with the common shorthand employed by pilots: "zero five...seven." KAL 050 immediately passed on Tokyo Control's message to contact it on 118.9 MHz. Ten seconds later, at 1910:04Z, co-pilot Son replied and "for three minutes they talked cryptically in Korean." As Brun notes: "obviously, KAL 007 did not want anyone to know that it had answered the call. It seemed caught between the desire to minimize radio contact and to calm the fears of other KAL people who were trying

---

[129] Brun, *Incident at Sakhalin*, 86-89, claims that KAL 007 never reentered Soviet airspace over Sakhalin, but that it continued to fly southward along the west coast of Honshu where it was mistakenly attacked by either a US or Japanese plane and crashed into the Sea of Japan off Niigata.
[130] Ibid., 86.
[131] Ibid.
[132] Ibid., 87.

to contact it."[133] But Son did not contact Tokyo Control; again, because he was under compulsion to remain silent.

KAL 050 advised 007 to "keep radio contact with KAL 015," to which Son replied: "we are in permanent contact with KAL 015."[134] That "permanent contact" was on the airline's private "chatter frequency" of 123.4MHz which was not monitored by air traffic control. Indeed, at 1911:01Z, KAL 015 then called KAL 050 to say that "you can contact KAL 007 at any time with our special apparatus. Just come in on one two three four." But KAL 015 was being overly optimistic. At 1913:16Z co-pilot Son made what was his last call to both KAL 015 and KAL 050.

According to Brun: "it is most likely that KAL 007, surprised by some unexpected event, transmitted a call to KAL 015 and KAL 050 at the same time," which was "cut short." Thirty-five seconds later KAL 050 radioed Tokyo Control to say that he, too, had been unable to contact Korean Air zero zero seven.[135] There is no record of the conversations that occurred between co-pilot Son and his colleagues aboard KAL 015 and KAL 050 on the chatter frequency, but we can be certain that he reported KAL 007's condition, circumstances, and whereabouts. In my view, however, the "unexpected event" that interrupted Son's call was the entry of Soviet troops into the cockpit, part of the contingent that boarded his aircraft on the tarmac at Kostromskoye and took control of it.

Co-pilot Son's transmissions show that KAL 007 continued to fly for over thirty-five minutes *after* he was said to have crashed into the sea and was in contact with KAL 015, KAL 050 and a third party, the one who guided his aircraft. The record shows that after the missile strike, Captain Chun was prevented from flying to safety and compelled to turn his aircraft around, returning to Soviet airspace. He was then directed up the west coast of Sakhalin by way of Moneron Island to a landing on the airfield at Kostromskoye. In fact, it was privately reported at the time that the radar at Wakkanai "followed Air Korea to a landing in Soviet territory on the island of Sakhalinska."[136]

Washington Offers a Way Out

If, as a Pentagon official reported on September 1, "nothing flies away, over, or close to Sakhalin, that we don't detect,"[137] then clearly American

---

[133] Ibid., 238

[134] Ibid., 87-88.

[135] Ibid., 90. Shifrin, in his press release cited above in n118, says that at 1915Z, "an officer on duty at the Japanese Narita Airfield heard on the radiophone the voice of KAL 007 Captain Chun Byung-in, who reported a safe emergency landing," and notes its confirmation by several officials.

[136] Pearson, *KAL 007: The Cover-Up*, 122.

[137] Wilhelm Bittorf and Anthony Sampson, "Sinken auf eins-null-tausend . . . " *Der Spiegel*, no. 42, October 15, 1984, 196. I am indebted to Ms. Anna-Marie Hetterich for the translation of this article. As one intelligence expert put it, "with the development of surveillance satellites, the ability of military intelligence to track

intelligence, indeed, if not Casey himself, given the vital importance of the mission, had followed the flight of KAL 007, and the air battle that swirled around it, from beginning to end. All were no doubt shocked, stunned, and outraged by the Soviet ambush over Sakhalin, in which several American aviators were lost, and the attack on KAL 007, followed by the forced landing on Sakhalin.[138] Casey quickly realized that his scheme had gone tragically awry, even though the flight itself had been a total intelligence success.[139] The immediate problems were to avoid an escalation of the Soviet military provocation into a major crisis and to bring the passengers to safety.

As the action was occurring, "critic" messages would have reached appropriate governmental authorities—no longer than ten minutes after their dispatch. If Casey were following the action by satellite in real time, however, he knew what had happened even before the critic messages had come in. Messages would have gone to the appropriate personnel at the National Security Agency, the Pentagon, the State Department, and the National Security Council. In other words, American leaders would have known within the hour that there had been an aerial battle in which several planes had been shot down, that KAL 007 had been attacked, and had landed on Sakhalin.

The attacks had occurred at approximately 11:30 a.m. California time, August 31, where President Reagan was with his wife at his ranch enjoying a leisurely morning. His aides, NSC director William Clark and counselor, Edwin Meese were with the presidential party, a few miles away at the Pacific Biltmore Beach hotel. Before noon (3:00 p.m. in Washington), a secure video conference link enabled Clark and Meese to confer with Casey and key officials at State: Secretary of State Shultz; Undersecretary of State Lawrence Eagleburger; and

---

aircraft movements and intercept messages has increased many fold . . . Military intelligence officials routinely have followed the passive radar emissions of both military and commercial aircraft, even on the ground, from as far as 10,000 miles away." See David Shribman, "Side Effect: Peek at US Intelligence Abilities," *New York Times*, September 2, 1983, A7.

[138] Through communications intercepts alone, setting aside satellite surveillance, if operators were monitoring Kostroma's transmissions on 121.5MHz, they could follow KAL 007's flight and, if also monitoring co-pilot Son's transmissions on KAL's chatter frequency, 123.4, they knew of his communications with other KAL aircraft.

[139] As Ernest Volkman, editor of *Defense Science*, put it: "As a result of the KAL incident United States intelligence received a bonanza the likes of which they have never received in their lives. Reason: because of the tragic incident it managed to turn on just about every single Soviet electro-magnetic transmission over a period of about four hours and an area of approximately 7000 square miles, and I mean everything . . . was detected—communications back and forth between Moscow, radar systems, computer tracking systems, communication systems, air defense systems, what one person has described to me as a Christmas tree, lit up. Everything you could possibly hope for. Now, admittedly that's a cynical statement, but we're talking about a very cynical business here." As quoted in Johnson, *Shootdown*, 265-66.

Chapter 3
How Close to Breakout? Krasnoyarsk and KAL 007

155

Assistant Secretary of State Richard Burt. There was, of course, every reason to inform the president, but sources claim incredibly that he was not disturbed at this point.[140]

The first decision the American leadership made was to attempt to limit the damage by offering the Soviets a way out of what clearly threatened to become a major crisis. No mention would be made of the Soviet attack on the US spoofer/jammer planes in the skies above Sakhalin. If word of the attack leaked, at the very least, US-Soviet relations would be damaged indefinitely; at worst, there could be war. Discipline had to be enforced in the field.[141] Washington would keep the focus on the Korean airliner, moving it away from a US-Soviet confrontation.

As for the airliner, there was a recent precedent; indeed, that very worst case that Casey had anticipated. In April 1978, the Soviets had forced down another Korean Air Lines plan that had drifted into Soviet territory over Murmansk after taking off from Paris on a flight over the North Pole to Seoul via Anchorage. In that instance, the Russians had arranged to return the passengers and their belongings within 24 hours, but held the pilots for a few days longer, releasing them only after they had signed statements acknowledging that they had been spying.[142]

No doubt American leaders' discussion included contingency plans and decisions to coordinate information with the Japanese and South Korean authorities. The Japanese had already communicated via satellite their early information, but they were proving to be recalcitrant, as we shall see. The KAL pilots informed South Korean authorities what had happened, and they immediately clammed up. In any case, by 9:00 p.m. Washington time (10:00 a.m. in Seoul), four hours after KAL 007 was due to land, and six and a half hours after the attack, the CIA put out the following information, made public simultaneously by both the Japanese and South Korean governments:

---

[140] Bittorf and Sampson, "Sinken auf eins-null-tausend [. . .]," 222. George Shultz, *Turmoil and Triumph: My Years as Secretary of State* (New York: Scribner, 1993), 361, claims that he first learned of the airliner's "disappearance" fifteen hours later, at 6:30 a.m. on September 1, a claim that is not credible because CNN, CBS, and NBC had run the story the previous evening.

[141] Hersh, *The Target is Destroyed*, 74, notes that "some senior Air Force and navy officers in the Pacific, who were provided with summaries of the NSA cable traffic, 'got emotional,' as one officer recalled, and began formulating action for retaliation against the Soviet Union, actions 'that could have started World War III.'"

[142] Milton Benjamin, "2 Dead in Russia As Korean Plane Mystery Deepens," *The Washington Post*, April 22, 1978, A1 and Steve Lohr, "Pilot in the '78 Incident Recalls His Experience," *New York Times*, September 9, 1983, A3.

The aircraft did not explode in flight and did not crash but is known to have landed on Sakhalin. The passengers and crew are safe, and the aircraft is undamaged.[143]

Clearly, the only way for the CIA to have known the specific details of the airliner's position and condition, as well as the circumstances of the passengers and crew, of course, was by satellite observation and communications intercepts. In fact, a KH-11 satellite was in geosynchronous orbit capable of transmitting images in real time and the 6920th intercept station at Misawa could feed back intercepted communications through a variety of systems, including the Fleet Satellite Communications system (FLTSATCOM), a global satellite communications network that "connects the president and the secretary of defense...to field commanders around the world."[144]

Alternatively, or perhaps additionally, Casey could have quickly dispatched an SR-71 and/or a U-2 to survey the scene. The SR-71, based on Okinawa, could reach Sakhalin in two hours flying at a speed of 2,000 mph and at an altitude in excess of 80,000 feet. Of this aircraft's capability, Burrows says suggestively, "an SR-71 tearing along the coast of Sakhalin Island...can photograph air bases, missile sites, and port facilities (including berthed submarines), while simultaneously eavesdropping on Soviet communication traffic and ferreting radar."[145] He could also have sent a U-2 aircraft from its base at Osan, outside of Seoul. It was reported that the US Navy had sent a submarine to the west coast of Sakhalin "within an hour" of the attack and several ships and aircraft moved to the scene shortly thereafter.[146] Thus, within a few hours, US leaders would have confirmed their intelligence.

It later came to light that "the story was developed and passed through both the State Department and the Pentagon—and even to the Soviets—that the plane was down and on Sakhalin."[147] Indeed, the "safe on Sakhalin" story was given worldwide distribution.[148] But it was precisely the point to convey to the

---

[143] Brun, *Incident at Sakhalin*, 5. Pearson, *KAL 007: The Cover-Up*, 122, also notes that the Japanese Defense Agency reported "Hokkaido radar followed Air Korea to a landing in Soviet territory on the island of Sakhalinska . . . " See also, Robert W. Lee, "KAL 007 Remembered: The Questions Remain Unanswered," *The New American*, September 10, 1991, and John McCaslin, "Pilot Probably Tried to Land KAL Jet, Study Finds," *Washington Times*, September 19, 1986, A5.

[144] KH-11 no. 5504 went into orbit on November 17, 1982 and remained there for over three years. Its camera was the equivalent of a television camera that could transmit images in real time. See Burrows, *Deep Black*, 245, 249, and n180.

[145] Ibid., 165-66.

[146] Pearson, *KAL 007: The Cover-Up*, 116.

[147] Walter Pincus, "The Soviets Had the Wrong Stuff," *Washington Post*, September 18, 1983, C5.

[148] See, for example, Clyde Haberman, "Korean Jetliner with 269 aboard Missing Near Soviet Pacific Island," *New York Times*, September 1, 1983, A1 and "Korean Jet

Soviets that the United States leadership knew in detail what had happened in the skies above Sakhalin and chose to focus on KAL 007. Washington wanted to convey, moreover, that it knew the plane had not exploded in mid-air, had not crashed, but was "known" to have landed on Sakhalin, be undamaged, and that the passengers and crew were safe.

The general assumption seemed to be that Moscow wished to resolve the issue in the same way it had in 1978. Thus, the vice-president of Korean Air Lines, Charles Cho, left for Japan immediately to arrange for the repatriation of the passengers from Sakhalin. At the same time, the head of the airline announced in Tokyo that KAL 007 had been forced to land on Sakhalin "at approximately four o'clock in the morning," that is at 1900Z—specific information suggesting that the Korean pilots in contact with co-pilot Son had informed their superiors of what had transpired.[149]

Moscow Rejects a Settlement

Ogarkov had no intention of "settling," having in hand the very object he intended to use to instigate a major crisis with the United States. The fact that Washington had immediately hushed up the aerial clash told him that the US had no desire to exacerbate Soviet-American relations and this would give him time to examine the aircraft, interrogate the pilot and crew, deal with the passengers, and go carefully over the flight recorders in hopes of being able to prove that the United States was spying on the Soviet Union. Once it was discovered that there were many Americans on board and that one of them was a US Congressman, Lawrence McDonald (R-GA), he realized that even the Soviet force-down of the airliner could easily be interpreted as a *casus belli,* and only reinforced the Soviet tendency to stonewall and deny everything.

Meanwhile, as soon as the plane landed, according to émigré reports, Soviet KGB border troops under the command of Major General Alexander Romanenko secured the plane and removed the pilots, crew, passengers, and luggage.[150] There had undoubtedly been significant loss of life from the missile's proximity burst and the scene in the passenger cabin could not have been pretty. Within four hours, according to SIGINT intercepts, the enormity of their act was clear. Soviet pilots were reported as saying that they had shot down a civilian airliner by mistake and ground commanders were reporting that Americans were among the passengers. They feared that "soon the Americans would be accusing them of killing Americans."[151]

Reported Downed in USSR.," *Baltimore Sun,* September 1, 1983, A1, and "Missing Airliner Reported Safe on Soviet Island," *Washington Post,* September 1, 1983, A1.
[149] Brun, *Incident at Sakhalin,* 5.
[150] Republican Staff Study, *Did KAL 007 Successfully Ditch* [. . .], 75. Émigré reports are of mixed quality. Most are based on rumors, and must be discounted heavily, but a few are purportedly direct experience.
[151] Ibid., 55.

To gain control of the situation and, perhaps, to enforce discipline for the difficult tasks that lay before them, Ogarkov immediately recalled those officers who had been involved in the affair and flew to Sakhalin himself with a "special maskirovka team from the deception department of the Main Operations Directorate and the Main Intelligence Directorate (GRU) of the General Staff to…cover-up the evidence of what really happened, and provide the cover story." This team was headed by General Valentin Varennikov, at whose direction the plane was stripped. "The luggage, the black boxes, the navigation and electronic and avionics equipment were all removed from KAL-007 and sent to Moscow aviation design institutes for analysis." [152] Of course, to have done this within a few hours would have been impossible if the airliner had crashed, or even had ditched, into the sea.

Ogarkov's response to the CIA report that the plane had landed on Sakhalin and to insistent demands by American and Japanese diplomatic personnel for a reply was to stonewall and deny everything. Thus, the first public reaction was a *Tass* statement that said:

> An unidentified plane entered the airspace of the Soviet Union over the Kamchatka peninsula from the direction of the Pacific Ocean and then for the second time violated the airspace of the USS.R. over Sakhalin Island on the night from August 31 to Sept. 1. The plane did not have navigation lights, did not respond to queries and did not enter into contact with the dispatcher service.

> Fighters of the antiaircraft defense, which were sent aloft towards the intruder plane, tried to give it assistance in directing it to the nearest airfield. But the intruder plane did not react to the signals and warnings from the Soviet fighters and continued its flight in the direction of the Sea of Japan. [153]

Soviet officials denied any knowledge of the plane's whereabouts, pointedly contested that it had landed on Sakhalin, and insisted that it had simply flown away "in the direction of the Sea of Japan." Clearly, Ogarkov knew perfectly well that US intelligence had followed the entire affair and that American leaders knew the truth. Goading by denial bought him the time to search for the spying apparatus, if there was one, analyze the flight data recorders, obtain confessions from the crew, and, perhaps, to rattle the Americans into making the same kind of mistake Eisenhower had made during the U-2 crisis in 1960, when he claimed that the spy plane was simply a meteorological craft. Then, with evidence in hand, he would spring the trap on Washington, throw the administration onto the defensive, and proceed with his plans under the growing cloud of a war scare.

---

[152] Ibid., 74-76.

[153] "Tass Statement on Incident," *New York Times*, September 2, 1983, A4.

Despite persistent later émigré reports that the Soviets had incarcerated the passengers in gulag concentration camps in Siberia, and some that claimed Congressman McDonald had been sent to a prison near Moscow, the greater likelihood is that the Soviets quickly decided to hide the evidence of their monstrous deed, and kill all the surviving passengers.[154] Indeed, spreading the rumor that they had imprisoned the passengers would tend slightly to ameliorate their brutality. The fact remains that as of this writing, there are no known survivors from the flight.

Washington: One Jump Ahead

If revealing KAL 007 as a spy plane was Ogarkov's plan, US authorities quickly turned the tables on him. After the attack, during the afternoon and evening of August 31, US leaders decided on contingency plans. First and foremost, Washington would suppress all knowledge of the Soviet-American dogfight. Second, the administration would offer to settle the airliner attack quickly. If the Soviets had been willing to settle and acknowledge their possession of the plane, arrangements would have been made to recover the passengers and crew, and the issue would have been allowed to fade. After the inevitable flare-up of criticism of Moscow's typically heavy-handed tactics, the "mini thaw" would have been allowed to continue.

If, on the other hand, the Russians declined to be responsive to the US offer, which would be evident within a few hours, Washington would implement plan "B," and charge them with the deliberate commission of a mass atrocity; and mount a worldwide campaign to impugn the Soviet Union, its leaders, and system. In that case, the propaganda victory would go to the United States and disarm those, especially in Western Europe, who were attempting to rally public support against the US deployment of missiles two months hence. It was a clever formulation of heads the United States wins, and tails the Soviet Union loses. Reagan's charge that the Soviet Union was an "evil empire" would become a self-evident truth.

By late afternoon Washington time, it had become clear that the Soviets had no intention of settling. When Soviet foreign minister Gromyko sent a note to the State Department repeating the *Tass* line, disclaiming any knowledge or responsibility, but adding that there were "signs of a possible crash" near Moneron Island, the die was cast.[155] State Department spokesman John Hughes informed the Soviet embassy that this reply was "totally inadequate" and reiterated the demand for a "satisfactory explanation." At this point, the administration quickly put plan "B" into action.

---

[154] Schlossberg, *Rescue 007*, 122-23.
[155] John Burns, "Moscow Confirms Tracking of Plane," *New York Times*, September 2, 1983, A1.

At 10 p.m. the State Department set up a "special operations group" under Assistant Secretary Richard Burt to manage the crisis.[156] Establishing the group in the State Department carried several implications. The president, acceding to Shultz's demands, assigned to the secretary, instead of to Bill Clark, the task of managing the evolving crisis. Shultz, of course, would to the extent possible, minimize the damage to US-Soviet relations, "coordinate" with Japan and South Korea, and control the search and rescue effort. At the same time, he assigned to Burt the task of maximizing the international impact of the crisis, especially on European public opinion, as it related to the impending missile deployment.

As Shultz prepared the US response, eighteen hours after the events, news from Tokyo sounded an alarm that threatened to sink his plan even before he got started. Intense back channel discussions with their American counterparts had failed to convince influential elements within the Japanese leadership of the wisdom of suppressing information about the Soviet-American air battle, perhaps because of its implications for Japanese security. Although Prime Minister Nakasone had agreed to keep silent, others within the JDA decided, subtly, to disclose some of the details about the incident.

At 9:10 p.m. on September 1 in Tokyo (8:10 a.m. in Washington), the head of the Japanese Defense Agency, Kazuo Tanikawa, held a press conference in which he presented an interpretation of the KAL 007 incident that threatened to blow away Shultz's plan for damage control and precipitate a most serious crisis in US-Soviet relations.[157] Tanikawa, in describing the Soviet attack on what "may have been the Korean airliner," in fact revealed that Japanese radar had tracked three Soviet and three unidentified (but obviously American) aircraft in an aerial battle over the skies of Sakhalin between 1812Z and 1829Z, in which at least one of the planes was destroyed in mid-air.

The time frame was that during which KAL 007 had traversed Sakhalin and also been attacked. Especially explosive was the map that the head of the Japanese Air Self-Defense Force, General Akihito Hayashi, distributed to those attending the press conference, which showed the Japanese radar tracking's of the six aircraft.[158] Here was hard evidence of a major air battle in the skies over Sakhalin. According to the Japanese version of the incident, "what was assumed to be the Korean airliner exploded in flight at an altitude of 32,000 feet at the moment when the plane's transponder, emitting code 1300 in mode A, stopped working."[159]

The subtlety in the JDA account lay in the revelation of the transponder data. Civilian aircraft flying into Japanese airspace are assigned a transponder number in the 2000 range, with a "mode C" designation. The 1300 number indicated a plane flying *out* of Japanese airspace, not into it, and the "mode A"

---

[156] Pearson, *KAL 007: The Cover-Up*, 126.
[157] Brun, *Incident at Sakhalin*, 18-19.
[158] Ibid.
[159] Ibid.

designation indicated that the aircraft was military not civilian, and therefore on two counts could not have been KAL 007. Most likely, it was a US plane sent in support of the spoofer/jammers that the Soviets were attacking and was itself attacked and destroyed. (Indeed, Japanese press accounts gave three different times for the shootdown: 1826:21Z, 1829Z, and 1839Z, which obviously referred to three different events.)[160]

Although couched in terms of KAL 007, Tanikawa and Hayashi had revealed the very information that Secretary Shultz sought to suppress—that a major US-Soviet aerial clash had taken place over Soviet territory in the skies over Sakhalin. What to do? Shultz quickly decided that the only answer was to go public and kill two birds with one stone. He would superimpose the US version of events over the Japanese in the context of a condemnation of the Soviet Union for shooting down the airliner. And he would use Japanese data to do it.

Limiting Damage by Escalating the Rhetoric

Thus, nearly twenty hours after the events, but only two and a half hours after the JDA press conference, at 10:45 a.m. Washington time on September 1, Secretary Shultz held what was described as an emotional press conference at which "he officially announced that Western intelligence had confirmed that a Soviet fighter had shot down a Korean Air Lines 747 jumbo jet."[161] The Soviets, he said, had tracked the airliner, which had "strayed" into Soviet airspace, for two and a half hours. The Soviet pilot, in "constant" communication with ground control, "reported visual contact" at 1812Z at 10,000 meters. Upon command, the interceptor pilot fired a missile at 1826Z, reporting that "the target was destroyed."

Radar tracked the plane at 5,000 meters at 1830Z and at 1838Z, "the Korean plane disappeared from the radar screen." Soviet officials had offered no information in response to inquiries. "The United States reacts with revulsion to this attack. Loss of life appears to be heavy. We can see no excuse whatsoever for this appalling act." In response to a question whether the Soviets had given any warning to this aircraft and request for it to land, or attempted to force it down before shooting it down, Shultz answered: "we have no evidence of that."

President Reagan, deciding to cut short his stay at his ranch in California and return to Washington, issued a strong statement through spokesman Larry Speakes, expressing his "revulsion at this horrifying act of violence." The entire incident, he said, "appears to be inexplicable to civilized people everywhere." Soviet statements "to this moment have totally failed to explain how or why this tragedy has occurred" and the president demanded a "full explanation for this appalling and wanton misdeed."[162]

---

[160] Ibid., 26.
[161] Bernard Gwertzman, "An Angry Shultz Says He Can 'See No Excuse,'" *New York Times*, September 2, 1983, A5.
[162] "Text of Statement by Reagan," *New York Times*, September 2, 1983, A5.

Once again, rhetoric aside, Washington had put the Soviets in a heads-I-win, tails-you-lose situation. If the Soviets now admitted to the US charge, they would verify the worst and the United States would occupy the moral high ground. The only way to refute the US charge would be to acknowledge that the plane and its occupants were safe, in which case the issue could be resolved but not without much loss of face for initially denying the attack. But the Soviets chose yet a third course—to counterattack and charge the United States itself with arranging a spy flight.

The Soviets were clearly taken aback by Shultz' charge. They knew that Washington knew the plane had landed on Sakhalin, but they responded immediately with a counter charge that was potentially ominous. The *Tass* statement of September 2 seemingly spoke of two planes, not one. The first, "an unidentified plane" which had violated Soviet airspace, refused to acknowledge all Soviet attempts to contact it, and "left the limits of Soviet airspace and continued its flight toward the Sea of Japan." The second plane was "a South Korean plane carrying out a flight from New York to Seoul," about whose "disappearance" the United States had raised a "hullaballoo."[163]

The second plane, the South Korean airliner, had also violated Soviet airspace, and the US side, *Tass* said, "cite[d] data which indicate that the relevant [intelligence] services followed the flight throughout its duration in a most attentive manner." Why then, *Tass* wondered, did US authorities neither warn the plane that it was off course, nor contact the Soviet side to inform them about this flight? There had been "more than ample time for this." Moscow, however, knew why Washington had said nothing:

> In light of these facts the intrusion into the airspace by the mentioned plane cannot be regarded in any other way than a preplanned act. It was obviously thought possible to attain special intelligence aims without hindrance using civilian planes as a cover.

Without admitting that it had attacked either the "unidentified plane," or the airliner, and expressly claiming that the first unidentified plane had flown off toward the Sea of Japan, the *Tass* statement expressed "regret...over the loss of human life," but condemned "those who consciously or as a result of criminal disregard have allowed the death of people and are now trying to use this occurrence for unseemly political aims."[164]

The suggestion that there was more than one plane in Soviet airspace and that Moscow had explicitly acknowledged that there had been a "loss of life" in

---

[163] "Text of Tass Statement on Downing of Airliner," *New York Times*, September 3, 1983, 4.

[164] In an accompanying article, reporter John Burns, "Moscow Response," *New York Times*, September 3, 1983, 1, omitted the fact that the *Tass* Statement referred to two different aircraft.

relation to the airliner, although not that they had attacked it, was instantly drowned out by Shultz's own counter charge, which appeared in the same edition of the *New York Times* as the *Tass* statement. Focusing on the Korean airliner, the secretary sharply attacked the Russians for their "continuing effort to cover up the facts of the inhumane Soviet attack on an unarmed civilian airliner." "No cover-up, however brazen and elaborate, can change this reality or absolve the Soviet Union of its responsibility to explain its behavior." The world, he said, "is waiting for the Soviet Union to tell the truth."[165]

Casey's Plan: Discovery and Cover-Up

The Soviets stood no chance against what Johnson termed Washington's "propaganda barrage," a well-orchestrated campaign that quickly ballooned into a worldwide condemnation of the Soviet Union's deliberate and callous act.[166] Internally, within the administration, however, the picture was decidedly different. On September 2, CIA and NSA briefers had said to Shultz that "they felt that the Soviets might have mistaken the identity of the aircraft" for an RC-135. The secretary was incredulous:

> It was obvious that our intelligence aircraft, the RC-135, bore no resemblance to the distinctive profile of KAL's Boeing 747. We also knew the Soviets had tracked and observed the 747 over a period of hours, so that a case of 'mistaken identity' was not remotely plausible. That the CIA was advancing such a theory made no sense and raised my suspicions. The intelligence community was being very elusive again. I had the feeling there was something they were not telling me.[167]

Shultz's reference to the CIA, of course, was in fact to its director, William Casey and his "suspicions" about what they were not telling him only grew as Casey himself elaborated on the possibility of a Soviet "mistake." At an NSC meeting later on the same day, while insisting that "there had been no reconnaissance planes in the area of the shoot-down," Casey allowed:

> that is not to say that confusion between the US reconnaissance plane and the KAL plane could not have developed as the Cobra Ball plane departed and the Korean airliner approached the area northeast of the Kamchatka Peninsula.[168]

Casey's assertion that "there had been no reconnaissance planes in the area of the shootdown," but that there had been one off Kamchatka, intensified Shultz's suspicions. He had not been privy to Casey's scheme to "spoof the entire

---

[165] Bernard Gwertzman, "Flight Ban Sought," *New York Times*, September 3, 1983, 1.
[166] See Johnson, *Shootdown*, 113, for discussion of the public campaign.
[167] Shultz, *Turmoil and Triumph*, 363-64.
[168] Robert Gates, *From the Shadows* (New York: Simon & Schuster, 1996), 267.

electronic nervous system of the Soviet Union"; indeed, only a handful on a strictly need-to-know basis had been. Only now, as his aides reviewed the intelligence data, did Secretary Shultz comprehend the enormity of the scheme. Investigating further, as he realized that the flight had been Casey's brainchild, he told his aides: "they [the CIA] have no compunctions about fooling you."[169]

Robert Gates, Casey's aide, later wondered "what possible ulterior motive CIA might have had in advancing the notion that the Soviets screwed up rather than intentionally attacked a civilian airliner...?" Why would Casey, the super-hardliner, "give the Soviets a break when they were in a corner...?[170] But the answer was straightforward. Damage control. It was Casey who had "screwed up," and now sought to distance himself and his agency from any complicity. As the way out, he put forward the thesis that the plane had been accidentally off course and Moscow had accidentally attacked it.

Adoption of this "twin accidents" interpretation would, and did, effectively stifle serious inquiry into the events, and would, in fact, become the US official position. As quickly and efficiently as it had advanced the safe on Sakhalin line, Casey activated the CIA's worldwide network to discredit its first story and put out the new story of a shootdown. Although this caused some difficulties with Tokyo, the Nakasone government quickly came into line with the US position.

But, for the moment, the issue was Moscow's reference to a second plane, which had to be dealt with lest the story of the accompanying spoofer/jammer planes "in the area of the shootdown" leak out. Out of the blue, however, the Soviets offered a golden opportunity for the administration to move more directly toward the "misidentification" idea. Colonel General Semyon Romanov, head of the Soviet air defense forces, suggested in an interview on September 4 that "a Soviet pilot could have confused the airliner with an RC-135 reconnaissance plane of the kind used by American forces off the Pacific coast of the Soviet Far East." This was doubly possible, he went on, because the airliner "flew with extinguished lights, and its outlines resemble much those of the American reconnaissance plane RC-135."[171]

The administration immediately seized upon the opportunity implicit in Romanov's statement to further define the event as a single penetration, single shootdown, even while acknowledging the presence of an RC-135. The administration, in short, would adopt Casey's interpretation (and Romanov's), giving the Soviets an out, which meant that the US response would be firm but not provocative, and allow for the possibility of misidentification. No effort would

---

[169] Shultz, *Turmoil and Triumph*, 364.
[170] Gates, *From the Shadows*, 269.
[171] John Burns, "A Soviet General Implies Airliner May Have Been Taken for Spy Jet," *New York Times*, September 5, 1983, A1.

be made to inflame US-Soviet relations, even while orchestrating a world-wide campaign of condemnation of Moscow for its action.[172]

That same evening, President Reagan, having returned from California, convened his top staff and congressional leaders to lay out the administration's case in order to reach "a genuine consensus on the president's approach." All agreed that sanctions would be limited and existing agreements kept, especially the recently signed grain agreement and pipeline sales.[173] The president played a selected portion of the tapes to confirm the charge that the Soviets had in fact deliberately attacked the airliner, but also disclosed that an RC-135 had been flying off Kamchatka.[174]

House Majority Leader Jim Wright, either inadvertently or by prearrangement, disclosed the presence of the RC-135 to reporters immediately after the meeting, prompting a flurry of comments by others who had attended and experts who volunteered their opinions, admitting to the presence of the plane, but denying that it had any relevance to the airliner. The next day, the administration released a statement on the plane, emphasizing that its "presence...some 1,000 miles from the scene of the shootdown in no way excuses or explains this act, which speaks for itself. In fact, the RC-135 in question, at the time KAL 7 was shot down, had been on the ground at its home base in Alaska for more than one hour."[175] In short, as Rohmer concludes, "the Americans laid it all out for them."[176]

No Resolution and No Agreement

The Russians, however, were still not cooperating and remained intent upon pushing the thesis of a US spy flight. Moscow's version of events appeared in the same edition as the administration's admission that a RC-135 had been in the area. According to *Pravda*, "Soviet forces had been tracking *seven* RC-135 reconnaissance planes on missions off the Soviet Far East coast...on the day of the incident. It [also] said there were *three* United States naval vessels just outside Soviet territorial waters in the area at the same time." Still declining to acknowledge that their forces had attacked the airliner, the account said only that "a Soviet fighter...fired tracer shells past a Korean Air Lines 747...[but] only after the airliner had changed course and altitude over southern Sakhalin Island in such a way as to carry it over a Soviet air base."[177]

---

[172] Bernard Gwertzman, "Reagan Sees Need for World Action in Plane Incident," *New York Times*, September 4, 1983, A1.

[173] Bernard Gwertzman, "Reagan Avoids Dramatic in Response to Shooting," *New York Times*, September 6, 1983, A15.

[174] Steven Weisman, "US Says Spy Plane Was in the Area of Korea Airliner," *New York Times*, September 6, 1983, A1.

[175] "Text of US Statement on Intelligence Plane," *New York Times*, A16.

[176] Rohmer, *Massacre 747*, 104.

[177] John Burns, "Russian Version," *New York Times*, September 6, 1983, A1, emphasis added.

Washington immediately moved to counter the Soviet argument. In the same article reporting the Soviet view, *New York Times* reporter John Burns also included the US denial. Pentagon spokesman Lt. Colonel Peter Friend "emphatically denied that seven RC-135 planes had been flying off the Soviet Far East coast during the period in question," but was not asked about the presence of other types of aircraft, and his response to a question about the presence of three US naval vessels off the Soviet coast was: "not to my knowledge."[178] At best, his response could be characterized as displaying a minimum of candor.

President Reagan's televised address to the nation on September 5, and ambassador Jeane Kirkpatrick's presentation before the United Nations the following day, during which both aired excerpts from Japanese tapes of the Soviet pilots' communication with ground control as they stalked and attacked the airliner, established the incontrovertible fact of the Soviet culpability for the attack.[179] Kirkpatrick, in particular, likened Soviet denials regarding the airliner to similar denials attending to the Cuban missile crisis 21 years before and observed that the photographic evidence then was "as irrefutable as the audio tapes we have heard today."[180]

Later that day, on September 6, Moscow, locked in a corner, finally admitted to the fact that its forces had "fulfilled the order of the command post to stop the flight" when the airliner refused to land after repeated attempts to contact it. The Soviets defiantly justified their action on the grounds that Soviet air defenses were protecting the border. Besides, there were extenuating circumstances. Soviet pilots "could not know that it was a civilian aircraft" because it flew without navigation lights in the dark of night under conditions of poor visibility.[181]

But, grudging admission aside, what was important was what the Soviets had declined to say. Moscow dropped reference to the previous assertion that KAL 007 had been accompanied during its flight by seven RC-135 reconnaissance planes and three US naval vessels; and instead focused solely on the flight itself as "a deliberate preplanned action" by the United States to spy on "strategically important" regions of the USSR. This was confirmed, Moscow said, by Washington's admission that an RC-135 "was in the same area near the Soviet border."

From the moment the Soviets gained possession of the airliner, their case depended on being able to show that it was a spy plane. The first surprise had been

---

[178] Ibid.

[179] Using the Japanese tapes also firmly committed Tokyo to Washington's version of events, for the moment eliminating a potential source of contradiction.

[180] Steven Weisman, "Reagan, Denouncing Soviet, Bars Series of Negotiations; Demands It Pay for Jet Loss," *New York Times*, September 6, 1983, A1; and "Transcript of Kirkpatrick Address on Korean Airliner to Security Council," *New York Times*, September 7, 1983, A15.

[181] "Text of Statement by Soviet Government," *New York Times*, September 7, 1983, A16.

the discovery that it was a South Korean airliner loaded with civilian passengers, not a US military plane. Now, after five days of scrutinizing the aircraft for spy apparatus, analyzing the black box recorders, and interrogating the pilot and crew, they had come up with nothing. Even the charge that seven reconnaissance aircraft and three ships were positioned along KAL 007's flight path amounted to nothing because they had all been flying in international airspace and sailing in open waters.

There was nothing to connect the airliner to the spoofer/jammer planes, or the ships. On the other hand, to admit that they had ambushed and shot down several US aircraft in international airspace would precipitate a major US-Soviet crisis and move dangerously close to war. The Russians were not ready for war; what they sought was strategic advantage and the political leverage that came with the threat of war. Their objective was to prevent the deployment of the Pershing II package, which would ensure Soviet domination of Western Europe, and to carry out a counter deployment in the Caribbean, which would insure leverage over the United States. For that, they needed a crisis, not a war.

To ensure that there would be no resolution of the incident, but no escalation out of control, either, General Ogarkov himself held an unprecedented news conference to press the case that KAL 007 was a US-engineered "espionage flight." Claiming to be reporting the results of a commission of experts who had investigated the incident, Ogarkov insisted that the intrusion of KAL 007 into Soviet airspace "was a deliberate, thoroughly planned intelligence operation...directed from certain centers in the territory of the United States and Japan."[182]

In going over the now familiar account of the flight, Ogarkov focused his attention on the flight itself, making no mention of accompanying aircraft or ships. However, on the large chart behind him showing the path of the airliner, there appeared five US aircraft—one RC-135 and four P-3C Orions—plus one ship, the USS *Badger*, implicit reference to a US intelligence presence around the airliner. The only explicit mention of this presence, however, was reference to the RC-135 the Reagan administration admitted had been flying off the coast of Kamchatka, which, Ogarkov maintained, "played the control...in the initial phase."

Asked what "hard evidence" he had that the airliner was a reconnaissance plane, Ogarkov spoke only of "the behavior of that aircraft, its route, the nature of its flight and our analysis...." In short, it was plain that Soviet specialists who had examined the aircraft had not found a single piece of incriminating spy paraphernalia. As to where the plane went down, Ogarkov lied that "we don't exactly know the area in which the plane came down." But, he said, "no bodies have been found and no survivors," although "some objects" have been found, as search operations continued.

---

[182] "Transcript of Soviet Official's Statement and Excerpts from News Session," *New York Times*, September 10, 1983, 4.

It was Ogarkov's intent to demonstrate that Soviet air defense forces only acted to "stop the flight" after exhausting "all cautionary warning devices at their disposal." As to who gave the order to terminate the flight, he evaded a direct answer and said that "the order to the pilots was given by the commander of the Biya region," although the air defense forces operated in "full contact" with government authorities. The actions of Soviet air defense forces, however, were in full compliance with Soviet law. Border protection, he averred, "is a sovereign right of each government." Their procedures were sound and defensive; there was no risk of an escalation to war. If any apologies were in order, he intimated, they should come from President Reagan.

Ogarkov's presentation moved the Soviet version of events firmly away from the suggestion made by General Romanov that Soviet pilots may have mistaken the airliner for an RC-135 reconnaissance aircraft. The decision to stop the flight, he said, was "not an accident or an error."[183] Instead, he reaffirmed the view that the flight was a spy flight instigated by the United States. In short, he sought not to resolve the crisis, but to intensify and prolong it. Still, there was perhaps a reluctant congruence of versions, in that all discussion focused on the thesis of a single intrusion/single shootdown event, which effectively limited the crisis.

A Necessary Mystery

Both sides covered up the facts, but for different reasons. Both sides agreed to cover up all evidence of the aerial clash and focus their differences on the issue of the airliner to avert a drift toward war, but, while Washington sought to limit the political fallout, Moscow sought to exacerbate it. Within each leadership, the crisis produced changes. In Moscow, the Chernenko faction backed powerfully by Ogarkov and leading elements of the Soviet military, rose to the ascendancy over the Andropov faction. The prominence of the Soviet military command during and after the KAL 007 crisis led to a belief in Washington that there might have been a military coup in Moscow.

In Washington, the crisis saw the ascendance of Secretary of State George Shultz over NSC adviser William Clark. Indeed, within six weeks of the crisis, Clark would have resigned his position and Shultz would have taken a strong step toward preeminence within the Reagan administration. Full control over strategy would elude the secretary for three more years, but henceforth, the president would be constrained in his pursuit of victory over the Soviet Union. Nevertheless, President Reagan would be able to press forward with the key lines of current policy—the prevention of a Soviet deployment of missiles to the Caribbean and the deployment of American weapons to Western Europe—acts that would fundamentally change the US-Soviet strategic balance.

---

[183] John Burns, "Soviet Says Order to Down Jet Came at a Local Level," *New York Times*, September 10, 1983, 1.

To forestall further deterioration of relations and keep open the door to accommodation, Secretary Shultz asserted State Department control of the incident, formally ordering the National Transportation Safety Board (NTSB) to conduct no investigation, although it was the appropriate body to do so; yet State undertook no investigation itself. Nor did Congress investigate. Instead, Shultz arranged for the UN's International Civil Aeronautic Organization (ICAO) to examine the incident, despite the fact that it was not an investigative body either and conducted its analysis only on the materials supplied by the United States and the Soviet Union.

Casey, in uneasy collusion with Shultz, stifled any investigation in the intelligence community. He, too, wanted to make the evidence disappear. His approach was to leak the notion that the plane had spiraled to its doom from a high altitude, obliterating all trace, despite the fact that this argument violated the fundamental laws of physics (and contradicted Shultz's testimony). The NSA's top secret, "conclusive" September 3 report, to make a catastrophic high-altitude crash credible, erroneously placed the airliner's altitude at 500 meters after its first four minutes of descent, instead of 5,000 meters as reported by radar tracking.[184] The error would not be corrected until October 19.

Meanwhile, Secretary Shultz also took command of the search and salvage operation, directing the US Navy in a two-month effort around Moneron Island, where the Russians claimed to have found evidence of a crash site. The massive US search, covering over 200 square miles and employing the latest in underwater detection technology, including side-scanning sonar and unmanned submersibles, failed to locate the wreckage even though the depth of the water around Moneron was relatively shallow, between 500 and 2,500 feet. Of course, no wreckage of the airliner was found because it had never crashed into the water.

The 747 was a huge aircraft weighing over half a million pounds before being loaded with fuel, passengers, and cargo. A crash into the sea would have produced an immediate and enormous debris field, several miles in radius. However, as the search effort commenced, a curious absence of any aircraft wreckage became evident. Indeed, aside from "cabin litter," the unsecured material that had been sucked out of the passenger cabin after the missile burst had gouged a hole in it, there was no debris of a kind that would result from a massive crash into the sea. Just over 1,000 small items were recovered, including the probable mangled body parts of three persons, and a small portion of the airliner's tail section, the size of a desktop.[185]

But salvage operations did recover debris of another sort: downed aircraft from an estimated nine or ten crash sites around Moneron Island. Soviet, American, Japanese, and South Korean ships scoured the waters to collect the wreckage. It seems that the Russians and Americans, in particular, operating in separate locations, were attempting to retrieve as much of the wreckage as possible from the planes that had gone down in the aerial dogfight. In fact, the

---

[184] Republican Staff Study, *Did KAL 007 Successfully Ditch* [. . .], 43-44, 48, 61.
[185] Lee, "KAL 007 Remembered: The Questions Remain Unanswered," 11, 17-18.

Soviet order to begin search and rescue operations was given at 1825Z, thirty seconds before Osipovich had launched his missiles at KAL 007.[186]

Brun reports that Japanese salvage operations and fisherman recovered parts from several different types of US military aircraft. Some debris washed up along the Hokkaido coast, as well. Items included pilot ejection seat parts, a life raft (which was not part of a 747's evacuation gear), titanium wing fragments, part of a variable-wing fairing, an engine cowling fragment, part of a wing flap, a missile fin, and many other smaller pieces. These materials were identified as coming from EF-111 Raven, RC-135 Rivet Joint, and P-3C Orion aircraft.[187]

Although the Soviets claimed to have located the airliner in the sea off Moneron, the plane was never raised from the depths and put on public display (as the U-2 was in 1960). Divers reportedly examined the plane but noted the absence of passengers and baggage and speculated that crabs had eaten all of the passengers, leaving no trace. It would take a decade and the demise of the Soviet Union before the Russians admitted to having the flight recorders and turning them over to the International Civil Aviation Organization. Moscow also returned a substantial portion of the luggage to the families of the survivors. ICAO quickly conducted a second investigation based on the CVR and DFDR data, and issued a second report, on which this analysis partly relies.

In June 1993, Russian authorities announced their intention to reveal that KAL 007's debris had been "buried in a deserted silo on Nevelsk District territory." Kostromskoye lies within the Nevelsk district. The district mayor also said that relatives of the dead had been invited to Nevelsk where a memorial stone would be unveiled. The ceremony was scheduled for the tenth anniversary of the event.[188] Thus had the Russians grudgingly revealed what had generally been believed: that they had possessed the aircraft and all of its contents from the start.

The burial site of KAL 007 solved one mystery, however. If the plane had plunged into the sea north of the La Perouse Strait, that is, in the area of Moneron Island, as the Russians claimed, the Tsushima current that flows from south to north through the Sea of Japan would have precluded any crash debris from washing up on the Japanese coast. Thus, the small fragments that had appeared on Japan's shore weeks after the event, some as far south as Niigata, had been planted by the Soviets to support their initial claim that the plane had not come down on Soviet territory, but continued its flight in the direction of the Sea of Japan.

Despite strenuous American efforts to back away from the airliner crisis and prevent it from affecting overall US-Soviet relations, the Russians would have none of it. They were determined to expand the incident into a crisis of the highest magnitude, marshaling a major anti-US propaganda campaign to prevent the deployment of the Pershing II package to Western Europe, while secretly

---

[186] *ICAO-93*: 153.

[187] Brun, *Incident at Sakhalin*, 42-44, 139, and chap. 10 passim.

[188] "Debris from ROK Plane Downed in 1983 Unearthed," *FBIS Daily Report, Central Eurasia*, June 10, 1993, 18.

preparing to make good on their threat to place the United States into an "analogous" position with a missile deployment to Grenada.

The crisis over KAL 007 was only the beginning of a downward spiral in US-Soviet relations that would stretch out over the next nine months, as the Soviets ratcheted up the tension and blew up the war scare to intimidate the West and justify their own actions. The United States, on the other hand, led by Secretary of State Shultz, took an extremely conciliatory stand, offering concession after concession, especially on arms control, while focusing on the need to deploy the Pershing II to Western Europe and to prevent any Soviet attempt to make good on its threat to place the United States in an "analogous" position.

Part II:

Defeating Soviet Strategy

Chapter 4

Denial in the Caribbean:
Pre-emptive Strike in Grenada

During a time of war or crisis, truth is the first casualty, and 1983 would be a year of crises. The truth about the Korean Air Lines tragedy was the precise opposite of the "twin accidents" theory. The United States had conducted a covert operation against the Soviet Union, that Moscow had disrupted and attempted to exploit. The Soviets had taken a huge risk in shooting down the spoofing aircraft accompanying KAL 007, but both sides had immediately covered up the Soviet-American aerial dogfight, focusing their attention on the airliner itself.

The KAL 007 mission, however, had generated intelligence of unparalleled importance. President Reagan now knew that the Soviets were not ready to activate a nationwide missile defense and that therefore their war-scare rhetoric was a bluff. He could proceed to forestall any Soviet attempt to install SS-20s in Grenada and he could probably deploy the Pershing IIs into West Germany without fear of precipitating war. These two steps alone would rectify the strategic weapons imbalance and deprive Moscow of any coercive leverage based on missile power.

But the mission had produced internal political consequences that were equally or more important, which thereafter changed the dynamics of the Reagan leadership. The evidence suggests that Secretary Shultz discovered Casey's covert mission and used the threat of its exposure to obtain greater leverage over policy. With Casey compromised, Shultz forced the removal of NSC adviser Judge Clark. Clark's removal, which the president orchestrated secretly in an attempt to disguise the outcome, shifted the locus of control over foreign policy to the secretary of state, who proceeded to turn American strategy toward an accommodation with Moscow.

With Shultz in charge of overall foreign policy, the president was reduced to working toward his international objectives by *ad hoc* means. Thus, he pursued his policy toward Iran and Nicaragua essentially by covert means through the NSC. From September 1983 onward, the US strategy shifted away from the course set in NSDD-75 toward accommodation with Moscow. However, while Shultz opened the door on the American side in the fall of 1983, it would not open on the Soviet side until nine months later, when the Soviet leadership concluded that its strategy could not succeed. And even then, Shultz got far less than he bargained for.

In Moscow, General Ogarkov had played a weak hand well, in leveraging the KAL crisis to propel himself and the Chernenko faction into power. Realizing that the "intruder" plane would reveal Soviet weakness to US intelligence regardless of its true identity and purpose, he had persuaded the Politburo to gamble that precipitating a crisis in US-Soviet relations and presenting Washington with a *fait accompli* was Moscow's only hope of advancing Andropov's strategy. Thus, Moscow sought to beat Washington to the punch in Grenada. Without a preemptive "analogous deployment," the Soviets would have no hope of preventing the Pershing II deployment to Europe and negotiating Andropov's proposed arms control trade-off.

In Grenada, Maurice Bishop's turn away from Moscow, followed by the KAL crisis, essentially determined the timing of the events that followed. The Russians had already begun to tighten their control in Grenada before the airliner crisis broke; its occurrence spurred them to accelerate the takeover by the hard-line faction before it was fully prepared. Ogarkov appeared to assume that the United States would not take direct action to prevent a Soviet deployment. For example, in discussion with Grenadian army chief of staff Einstein Louison in March 1983, Ogarkov had declared that Grenada, being close to US imperialism, would have to be vigilant, but that "there were no prospects for imperialism to turn back history."[1]

Whether Ogarkov actually believed his own rhetoric, or was merely attempting to instill confidence in his Grenadian protégé, is unknown. He certainly understood that unless the Soviets could present a *fait accompli* to the United States in Grenada, they would have no negotiating leverage to forestall deployment in West Germany, aside from the relatively weak reed of attempting to influence European public opinion through mass demonstrations.

In retrospect, in the context of a growing war scare, the three months following the KAL tragedy witnessed a US-Soviet race to accomplish mutually exclusive strategic objectives in the Caribbean and Europe. The first challenge for President Reagan was to foreclose any Soviet move to surreptitiously deploy SS-20s to Grenada. In this, both the Reagan and new world order factions were united, even as they struggled for control over the direction of overall foreign policy. Feigning indifference, Washington watched intently as events unfolded on the island, while secretly preparing to take whatever action was necessary to deny this option to the Soviets.

Of course, if Bishop were successful in disentangling himself and Grenada from the Soviet embrace, no action would be necessary. But, if he failed and the Soviets attempted to proceed with the missiles, then the United States would have to act first. As it turned out, of course, Bishop lost his struggle to maintain control and the United States invaded the island, preempting a Soviet move. The US strike, the first major military action since Vietnam, also persuaded Dési Bouterse in Suriname to reject any ties to Moscow or Havana, demolishing

---

[1] Charles Corddry, "Pentagon Unveils Document on Grenada-Soviet Meeting," *Baltimore Sun*, November 10, 1983, A8.

any Soviet prospects for an analogous deployment in the Western Hemisphere to counter the imminent Pershing II deployment to West Germany.

An Inexplicable Conciliatory Turn

The public US response to the KAL crisis was puzzling and self-defeating. On the one hand, the administration promoted a general, worldwide campaign to excoriate the Soviet Union for its heinous act; on the other hand, Washington progressively undercut every specific accusation made against the Soviets, seeming to offer them a way out. Secretary Shultz designed this conciliatory course to keep bilateral relations with Moscow from spiraling out of control but failed, and could not conceal the roiling internal dissent within the administration that erupted over his supine policy.

Indeed, as the rhetoric intensified, the Soviets and their agents of influence adopted an increasingly hostile approach toward the Reagan administration. By the end of September, the level of acrimony had reached the point where Soviet spokesmen at the highest levels were denouncing the president, his administration, and the United States in the most antagonistic of terms, much to the discomfiture of the Shultz camp.

The shift in the US position began shortly after the KAL crisis and was disguised by it. On September 5, the same day that the administration revealed the presence of the RC-135 at the point where KAL 007 entered into Kamchatka airspace, thereby introducing the possibility of mistaken identity, the president signed NSDD-102, *US Response to Soviet Destruction of KAL Airliner*.[2] While not imposing sanctions, the United States would "initiate a major public diplomatic effort to keep international and domestic attention focused on the Soviet action," demanding justice, a full accounting, an apology, compensation, and appropriate punishment for those responsible.

The president initiated the effort that same evening with a televised address to the nation, excoriating the Russians for their "crime against humanity [that] must never be forgotten, here or throughout the world."[3] UN Ambassador Jeane Kirkpatrick continued the campaign the next day, with her address before the Security Council. She quoted from the *TASS* statements of September 1 and 2 and then sought to refute the main points of the Soviet argument by playing a tape of Soviet air to ground conversations covering the period from 1756Z to 1846Z.* The Russians claimed that the plane flew without navigation lights, would not respond to repeated attempts to contact it, and that the Soviet pilot fired warning shots before firing missiles.

---

[2] Christopher Simpson, *National Security Directives of the Reagan and Bush Administrations: The Declassified History of US Political and Military Policy, 1981-1991* (Boulder: Westview, 1995), 320-23.

*Military time, with "Zulu" designating GMT/UTC.

[3] "Transcript of President Reagan's Address on Downing of Korean Airliner," *New York Times*, September 6, 1983, A15.

Claiming that "nothing was cut from this tape," in her commentary afterward she focused on these points, using the tape to show that the pilot saw and reported that he had seen the airliner's navigation lights "on three occasions," and therefore knew he was tracking a civilian aircraft; and that the pilot made "no mention of firing any warning shots," nor "made any attempt either to communicate with the airliner or to signal it…to land in accordance with accepted international practice." In short, Kirkpatrick declared: "the Soviets decided to shoot down a civilian airliner, shot it down, murdering the 269 persons onboard, and lied about it."[4]

Within days, however, even as the worldwide revulsion and condemnation of the Soviet attack developed momentum, US intelligence sources began to backtrack on all three of Kirkpatrick's main points and supplied other revisions that weakened the original story beyond reclamation. US officials acknowledged that the Soviet pilot's reference to navigation lights may have been to his own lights and therefore the Soviets may not even have known the plane was civilian. Then, a revised translation of the tape showed that the pilot had in fact fired warning bursts of cannon, and did attempt to communicate with the aircraft, before firing his missiles.[5]

Contrary to Kirkpatrick's claim that "nothing was cut from this tape," it turned out that the tape had been spliced together from fragments of the original.[6] Kirkpatrick had used a Japanese tape, which included only air-to-ground transmissions. The Japanese government admitted to having both air-to-ground and ground-to-air intercepts but refused to release the latter. The United States first denied having ground control tapes, then admitted to having them, but also would not release them. The obvious inference was that the ground control portions would contradict US assertions.

Sources admitted that what was first identified as an RC-135 Cobra Ball, whose mission was to monitor Soviet missile tests, was in fact an RC-135 Rivet Joint, whose mission was to probe Soviet air defenses.[7] Moreover, it was revealed that this aircraft could jam opposing radars, intercept Soviet communications, and relay information back to Washington in "no more than 10 minutes after the time

---

[4] "Transcript of Kirkpatrick Address on Korean Airliner to Security Council," *New York Times*, September 7, 1983, A15.

[5] David Pearson, *KAL 007: The Cover-Up: Why the True Story Has Never Been Told* (New York: Summit Books, 1987), 219; Robert Toth, "Airliner Reportedly Glided 12 Minutes before Crash," *Los Angeles Times*, September 8, 1983, B1; Michael Getler, "Soviet Fired Gun Toward Jet, New Analysis Shows," *Washington Post*, September 12, 1983, A1; and Richard Witkin, "New Tapes Show Korean Airliner Was Experiencing Radio Trouble," *New York Times*, September 13, 1983, A1.

[6] Seymour Hersh, *The Target Is Destroyed* (New York: Random House, 1986), 171-72; Brun, *Incident at Sakhalin*, 217.

[7] George Wilson, "RC135 Was Assessing Soviet Air Defenses," *Washington Post*, September 7, 1983, A12.

of transmission."[8] All of this tended to support Soviet assertions that Washington had doctored the tapes and raised questions about all aspects of the administration's charges.

Several accounts of this period spoke of the president's "turn" toward détente. Shultz himself attempted to place the president's "conversion" earlier in February, which was demonstrably not the case. Fischer, on the other hand, identified the president's "reversal" a year later, in a January 16, 1984 speech. Oberdorfer, whose book is based on interviews with Shultz, inexplicably argued for both dates.[9] In fact, the president's "turn," or "reversal," if that is what it was, occurred immediately after the KAL crisis and was a major political defeat, which was then quickly covered over.

Reagan's Woes

What accounted for this extraordinary turnaround, in which the United States literally repudiated itself? The short answer was George Shultz. In the aftermath of the KAL crisis, the secretary clearly assumed command of US foreign policy and Bill Clark, who throughout the summer had been paraded before the public as the dominant figure in the Reagan administration, was relegated to instant obscurity. Indeed, Clark literally disappeared from public view for two weeks after the incident, reappearing for a speech only in mid-September as his fate was being decided.

Given the prominent and central role Clark had played up to this moment and his identification as the president's alter ego, long-time friend, and close adviser, only a major behind-the-scenes development could have so abruptly and so totally led to his eclipse and to Shultz's equally dramatic ascent. That development was the secretary's discovery of Casey's covert mission, which, of course, like all covert missions, had been approved by the president. Its operational failure had led immediately to Casey's attempt to cover-up his role in the affair, which, as noted in the previous chapter, had made Shultz extremely suspicious. Shultz's discovery gave him the leverage he needed to gain control of the foreign policy process and effect at least a temporary change in strategy.

A brief comparison of the president's and his secretary's actions before and after the KAL crisis shows the dramatic change that occurred at this time. Beforehand, Reagan, in a mounting public challenge to Moscow based on NSDD-75, had centralized control over the policy-making process under NSC chief Clark. Clark was in charge of policy toward the Soviet Union, the arms control

---

[8] T. Edward Eskelson and Tom Bernard, "Former RC-135 Crewmen Question US Version of Jetliner Incident," *Baltimore News American*, September 15, 1983, 8.

[9] George Shultz, *Turmoil and Triumph: My Years as Secretary of State* (New York: Scribner, 1993),164; Beth A. Fischer, *The Reagan Reversal: Foreign Policy and the End of the Cold War* (Columbia, MO: University of Missouri Press, 1997), 3; Don Oberdorfer, *The Turn: How the Cold War Came to an End: The United States and the Soviet Union, 1983-1990* (New York: Poseidon, 1991), 20, 72.

negotiations, Middle East policy, policy toward Nicaragua, and the Caribbean. Media accounts broadly described this accumulation of power in the White House at the expense of the role and position of the secretary of state, who had threatened to resign on several occasions because of his exclusion from the policy-making process.

Shultz, as a cabinet member, had occupied a seat at the table—the NSPG and NSC—in all of these matters, except for the covert operations; but was subordinate to the president through Clark, as NIEs repeatedly show. He was not an "insider," had complained about being uninformed about key policies, and was unhappy about it. In particular, he opposed the president's challenging approach to the Soviet Union. Shultz's preference, as was well known, was to strive for an accommodation with Moscow. In this, he represented the new world order faction's strategic view within the Reagan administration. Indeed, Shultz openly turned for advice to Henry Kissinger, giving him an office in the State Department.

The KAL crisis changed everything, as Clark first became conspicuous by his absence and then abruptly was removed from power completely, and Shultz became equally conspicuous by his sudden elevation to the center of policy prominence. This fundamental shift had required the president's approval. In the several earlier instances where Shultz had gone to the president and threatened to resign unless given greater authority, Reagan had gently assuaged his ego, but rebuffed him. What was it that enabled him to succeed in early September? There are only two possibilities. Either Reagan had a change of heart, and willingly relinquished control over foreign policy, or he had been compromised and forced into it by a recent development.

The evidence suggests the latter. The president obviously realized the KAL crisis could escalate and wished to avoid the drift toward war implicit in a growing confrontation with Moscow. No doubt, Shultz emphasized the risks attendant to continued escalation of confrontation. The result was that while the president condemned the Russians verbally, he imposed only limited sanctions.[10] Reagan's refusal to impose sanctions was interpreted as a measure of his restraint. No one believed that the Russians would go to war because they were losing the propaganda contest, but their escalating belligerence was disquieting.

What was different and decisive this time, it seems, was that in demanding control over foreign policy, Shultz coupled that demand with a threat to disclose Casey's covert mission. The threat of exposure is the most likely circumstance that would have convinced the president that he had no choice but to comply. What Shultz claims to have been the president's desire to improve relations with Moscow was in reality his partial capitulation to the threat of political blackmail.

President Reagan agreed to pursue a more conciliatory approach toward the Soviet Union, and authorized Shultz to carry it out. In the immediate aftermath

---

[10] Benjamin Taylor, "Reagan Shuts Aeroflot Offices," *Boston Globe*, September 9, 1983, 1.

of the KAL crisis, this meant lending credibility to Moscow's justification for the attack on the airliner, as we have seen. On this issue, and only on this issue, Casey and Shultz had an uneasy meeting of the minds. Casey wanted nothing more than to make KAL disappear; Shultz did too, but for the purpose of keeping open the door to détente. Indeed, for the first time, the two men appeared together before the Senate Intelligence Committee.[11] Shultz, now clearly in control, authored compromises on arms control, on negotiations in Central America, and in the Middle East, systematically peeling back the Reagan counteroffensive.

At the same time, all agreed on the necessity to keep a close watch on events in Grenada and to prevent any effort by the Soviets to carry out an "analogous" deployment there. A second Cuban-style missile crisis in the Caribbean would be far more volatile than the first and, if successful, have disastrous, long-term consequences for United States-Soviet relations. Shultz wanted an accommodation with Moscow and would do everything he could to bring it about. He would strive hard to achieve an arms control agreement that would obviate the need to deploy the Pershing II/cruise missile package in November. He would not place American security in jeopardy to reach an accommodation, but he would limit the true extent to which the public was informed of Soviet machinations.

For Reagan's part, and much to the disappointment of his supporters, who knew nothing of the president's new and secret arrangement with Shultz, the president was willing to soften his approach in the face of Moscow's growing truculence. Perhaps he believed that, as he had in the past, he would be able to reclaim relinquished authority once the current crisis was surmounted. However, the president's subsequent use of the NSC to conduct policies toward Nicaragua and Iran, which were opposed by the Secretary of State, indicated his failure to reclaim lost authority.

Indeed, Shultz turned the tables on the president, locking in his new authority by restructuring the policy-making apparatus. Having obtained control, Shultz demanded that the president agree to restructure the decision-making process, returning to the arrangement proposed by Alexander Haig during the first days of the administration. Reagan's original "compact" with the new world order faction required assigning preeminence to the State Department in the policy-formulating process, downgrading the role of the national security adviser and removing him from the policy-making process altogether. [12]

President Reagan had voided that compact with the appointment of Clark to replace Richard Allen in January 1982 and established the NSC adviser as the primary policy coordinator in exactly the way Kissinger had been, except that Clark served as the president's interlocutor. The removal of Alexander Haig in mid-June of 1982 had only strengthened the president's hand. From then until

---

[11] Bob Woodward, *Veil: The Secret Wars of the CIA 1981-1987* (New York: Simon & Schuster, 1987), 276. They appeared on September 30 to explain the president's finding on Nicaragua four months earlier.

[12] See, Thornton, *Ronald Reagan: Revolution Ascendant*, chap. 1.

the KAL crisis, the president, through NSC adviser Clark, had pursued his preferred strategic course, which was codified in NSDD-75. Shultz, as this volume has demonstrated, repeatedly sought to change that course and enlarge the role of the secretary of state to no avail, until the KAL crisis.

Henceforth, the secretary of state would be the primary originator and coordinator of foreign policy. In any case, nothing could happen without the president's acceptance, a reality that Shultz recognized. Learning from Haig's many mistakes, Shultz wanted Reagan to agree with his accommodationist approach, and would proclaim that he and the president saw eye-to-eye on every possible occasion, but the fact was that the Department of State would chair the meetings of the senior interagency groups and interagency groups in all areas of concern. The national security adviser would revert to the low-level, managerial function Reagan had originally agreed upon—except that the new world order faction would now control that position.[13]

Prelude to Disaster in the Middle East

Reagan agreed to Shultz's demand, but, in what Cannon referred to as the "Byzantine battles" occurring within the "inner circle of the White House" at this time, and in an atmosphere Mike Deaver described as "semi-rampant paranoia," he did so in secrecy and employed misdirection to disguise the fact that he had suffered a major defeat and that there had occurred a struggle over strategy—even though that is exactly what occurred.[14] In what was, perhaps, one of the more bizarre of the byzantine battles, the president made an attempt to preserve the strong national security system he had created and along with it the role of Judge Clark, but failed.

The context of this struggle was the rapid deterioration of the situation in Lebanon. Recall, the previous fall Reagan had assigned the Lebanon problem to Shultz, but without allocating the resources to accomplish it. The Israelis, in the face of American opposition, had abandoned Begin's strategy of a pro-Israeli unified Lebanon and reverted to partition. In the spring of 1983, the Israelis were preparing to withdraw their forces to the Awali River from the Shouf mountains overlooking Beirut, where they protected the Multinational Force (MNF).

US policy was to arrange for the mutual withdrawal of Israeli and Syrian forces from Lebanon, while at the same time strengthening the Lebanese government and army to stabilize the country. Under the best of circumstances this would have been a lengthy, complex, and exceedingly daunting task and impossible to coordinate in any foreseeable timeframe. The Multinational Force of 1,200 US Marines and smaller numbers of French, Italian, and later British troops was deployed to show an international commitment to Lebanese

---

[13] Leslie Gelb, "Reagan's Foreign Policy Advisers Call a Truce," *New York Times*, November 27, 1983, E3, describes the new system in detail.

[14] Lou Cannon, *President Reagan: The Role of a Lifetime* (New York: Simon & Shuster, 1991), 423.

independence and to provide the semblance of a security guarantee, but it was not a fighting force.

Everything depended upon delaying the Israeli withdrawal, strengthening the Lebanese government, now under the command of Amin Gemayel, Bashir's brother, and gaining the cooperation of Syria's Assad. The United States, under Shultz's direction, accomplished none of these goals. The Israelis would withdraw in a manner and time of their own choosing, while superficially cooperating with Washington and extracting concessions. Amin was pro-Syrian, and though he professed adherence to the "American option," he made no attempt to unify his country. Syrian president Hafez al-Assad, playing an increasingly strengthening hand as Moscow rebuilt Syrian power, moved to defeat US strategy and dominate Lebanon.[15]

The larger purpose of the American presence was to have a position from which to ensure the continued stalemate in the Iran-Iraq conflict, in the event that Moscow resuscitated the Iran-Syrian pincer against Iraq. In this, Shultz sought to continue with Haig's approach to neutralize Syria, without, however, the benefit of Israeli participation. In fact, this approach meant that the United States would replace Israel, although for the moment the American presence was disguised within the MNF as part of the neutral buffer force interposed between the Israelis and Syrians.

Aside from the fact that this was not Reagan's approach, which was to act through Jordan and the Arabs to counter Damascus, the situations in both Syria-Lebanon and Iran-Iraq changed rapidly during the course of the year, rendering the Haig-Shultz approach pointless and the continued presence of US forces in Lebanon a dangerous liability. Shultz brokered the May 17, 1983 agreement to obtain Israel's coordinated withdrawal from Lebanon, and Israeli leaders insisted that the IDF would not withdraw until Syrian forces also withdrew. However, the agreement had been a dead letter from its inception because Assad rejected it. Other factors would determine Israel's actions.

Of course, all sides knew that neither Israel nor Syria would withdraw from Lebanon before the other, and possibly not even then. The considerable diplomatic effort expended to "persuade" Begin, Assad, and Amin to "coordinate" policies was merely a Kabuki play, although not so for the American officials directly involved. The May 17 agreement was in reality designed for another purpose: to maintain the status quo for as long as possible, in order to justify an American presence, enabling the United States to neutralize Syria, should Damascus attempt to cooperate with Iran against Iraq.

---

[15] Howard Teicher and Gayle Radley Teicher, *Twin Pillars to Desert Storm: America's Flawed Vision in the Middle East from Nixon to Bush* (New York: William Morrow, 1993), 227-28.

Shultz's Failure in the Middle East

By the summer of 1983, however, the circumstances had changed. The Soviet Union had not only replaced all of the arms lost by Syria in the Israeli invasion but had actually doubled the size of the Syrian army and air force. Moreover, in strengthening Syrian air defense, Moscow had augmented the surface-to-air missile force along the Syrian-Lebanese border, adding to it the newly developed long-range SA-5, a system managed by the Russians and integrated into the Soviet Union's overall air defense network. Thousands of Soviet advisers were pouring into Syria to manage the system.

Given this sharp accretion in power, there was no possibility that Assad would cooperate with the United States in "stabilizing" Lebanon, a state he considered a historical part of Syria. In the summer, anticipating Israeli withdrawal, Assad brought together and armed the fractious Druze, Amal, Shia, and Sunni dissident groups to form the National Salvation Front (NSF). Assad moved openly into opposition to the May 17 agreement and demanded the creation of a Muslim-dominated Lebanese government. At the same time, Iran dispatched around 2,000 revolutionary guards to Lebanon where, working in the shadows, they directed militant Lebanese Shiites, the Hezbollah, to do "most of the dirty work," infiltrating into the areas from which the IDF withdrew.[16]

Even more ominously, reports indicated that the Soviets were making plans for an intensification of the fighting. Small groups of Russian advisers were observed periodically moving through the area around the western slopes of Mount Lebanon, which commanded a broad view of Beirut. Western reporters were told by local residents that "the Soviets…typically arrived by helicopter and stayed for a day at a time, apparently collecting military information."[17] Moscow, too, had a larger purpose in Lebanon; it was an area where the Soviets could divert the United States, if not sink it in a quagmire.

Perceiving the change in the Lebanon situation, the Begin government now dropped its prior insistence that the IDF would wait to withdraw until Syria did, and prepared to depart forthwith. Desperate, Shultz and deputy national security adviser Robert McFarlane pleaded with Assad to cooperate and for Begin to delay the withdrawal of the IDF from the Shouf until the Lebanese Armed Forces could move in to replace them, but both knew the Lebanese forces would not be ready any time soon. US and French advisers had only been able to arm and train three brigades by the summer and they were no match for the many Syrian-backed armed groups facing them.[18]

From "late July," as the Israeli forces prepared to withdraw, the NSF, bolstered by Syrian artillery and under Syrian and Iranian direction, stepped up their activity. They attacked Israelis departing from the Shouf mountains, the

---

[16] Ibid., 228.

[17] Walter Mossberg, "Soviet Advisers Reported Near Beirut; US Concerned but Lacks Confirmation," *Wall Street Journal*, May 5, 1983, 2.

[18] Robert C. McFarlane, *Special Trust* (New York: Cadell & Davies, 1994), 250.

Lebanese Armed Forces coming in to replace them, and the Multinational Force in increasingly exposed positions around the Beirut airport.[19] By the end of August, the level of fighting intensified in the mountains above Beirut. The 24th Marine Amphibious Unit (MAU) deployed at the international airport was coming under attack, yet defensive response was limited under restrictive rules of engagement.

The result was four US Marines killed and twenty-five wounded. Seven French soldiers also were killed. In an effort to suppress the Druze mortar fire, the frigate *Bowen*, one of seven US ships in the Eastern Mediterranean, which included the carrier *Eisenhower* and the helicopter carrier *Tarawa*, sailed to within a mile of shore and fired four rounds.[20] US spokesmen insisted that the naval gunfire was retaliatory and did not signal an escalation, nor a change in the Marines' role. However, it did succeed in provoking additional Druze mortar and artillery fire on the Marines.[21]

The situation on the ground, however, was quickly escalating out of control as the exposed Marine positions around the airport took mortar fire. In response to American pleas, Begin, in a last act before resigning as prime minister, agreed to delay full Israeli withdrawal until September 3, while McFarlane made a frantic and fruitless attempt to co-opt the NSF into the Lebanese government. The escalation in shelling on the Marines raised concern that the United States was being drawn into a quagmire.[22]

Assad made sure that no agreement would be reached. To demonstrate the total ineffectiveness of US policy, he directed intensified artillery fire from the mountains against the MNF position in Beirut. Then, as soon as the IDF departed, on the night of September 3, he provided Syrian artillery support to Druze forces as they attacked and mauled the LAF 8th Brigade at the village of Suq al-Gharb, located on a ridge overlooking Beirut. Artillery and mortar fire hit the US ambassador's residence nearby, where McFarlane was staying while attempting to mediate a settlement.

The sharp intensification of the conflict in Lebanon, with the attacks on the Marines, coming hard on the heels of the KAL crisis, placed great pressure on the American leadership to arrive at a solution. Over the next several days, the argument centered around whether or not to authorize an expanded role for the MNF. Shultz and McFarlane argued that the Marines must be kept in place and supplied with greater firepower. Defense Secretary Weinberger, supported by General John Vessey and the Joint Chiefs of Staff, argued that they should be withdrawn as their mission was now compromised. Reagan, concerned about "how it would look to the rest of the world," deferred a decision, leaving the

---

[19] Teicher, *Twin Pillars*, 239-42.
[20] Herbert Denton and David Ottaway, "US Warship Fires to Halt Shelling of Marines in Beirut," *Washington Post*, September 9, 1983, A1.
[21] "A Lebanese Quagmire?" *Newsweek*, September 19, 1983, 50-51.
[22] George Wilson, "The Engagement and Disengagement of US Forces from Crises," *Washington Post*, September 9, 1983, A14.

Marines' mission unchanged, but did agree to send the battleship *New Jersey* to Lebanon.[23] The battleship would not arrive on station until September 26.

It was not until McFarlane's flash cable of September 11, commonly referred to as the "sky is falling" cable, claiming the "serious threat of a decisive military defeat which could involve the fall of the Government of Lebanon within twenty-four hours," that the president decided on the policy of "direct fire support, including carrier-based air strikes, if necessary, to bolster the Lebanese Army."[24] Although the fighting at Suq al-Gharb was brutal, the Lebanese forces held position. As the situation briefly stabilized, Marine commander Colonel Tim Geraughty held off a call for fire support until September 19, a full eight days later.

When the 5-inch guns from the cruiser USS *Virginia* commenced fire on the 19th, the American role in Lebanon changed from neutral protector to a participant in the conflict on the side of the Lebanese government, and the Marines became prime targets of the Syrian-supported enemies of the Gemayel government. Although the introduction of American firepower led to a ceasefire in Lebanon within a week, coincidentally on the day that the *New Jersey* arrived, it was only temporary and set the stage for one of the worst, if not the worst, foreign policy disasters of the Reagan administration within a month.

Reagan's Attempt to Save Clark

The president's decision authorizing a policy of direct fire support promptly leaked to the press and became the basis for his attempt to retain control of the foreign policy mechanism he had created. The leak itself, as Cannon noted, "served the useful purpose of warning Syrian and Druze gunners that they could no longer shell the marines with impunity."[25] Indeed, "high-ranking military officials" welcomed the leak, which was only the latest of many officially inspired revelations to the press for policy purposes. The president's reaction this time suggested that it was a pretext for him to take action against his opponents.[26]

The scheme was devised by Clark, who argued that the leaker had to have been among those present when the president made the decision on fire

---

[23] Caspar Weinberger, *Fighting for Peace: Seven Critical Years in the Pentagon* (New York: Warner Books, 1990), 160, says he proposed a compromise to keep the marines in Lebanon, but move them to ships offshore—a proposal which he says Clark supported. Shultz, *Turmoil and Triumph*, 226, skips over the events between August 28 and September 17 omitting all mention of this decision in his chapter on Lebanon. McFarlane, *Special Trust*, 249, claims that Clark "was adamant in support of my strategy."

[24] Teicher, *Twin Pillars*, 252-53, and McFarlane, *Special Trust*, 250-51.

[25] Cannon, *Role of a Lifetime*, 424.

[26] The articles in question were Lou Cannon and George Wilson, "Reagan Authorizes Marines to Call In Beirut Air Strikes," *Washington Post*, September 13, 1983, A1; and Hedrick Smith, "Reagan Upgrading Lebanon Presence," *New York Times*, September 13, 1983, A1.

support. That, of course, included Shultz. Clark and presidential counselor Ed Meese drafted a letter for Reagan's signature the morning the leak appeared. It was to order Attorney General William French Smith to take "personal charge" of an FBI investigation to find the source of the Lebanon leak. Smith would be authorized to use a polygraph test on anyone he suspected and "to ask for the resignation of whoever was found to have leaked the information."[27]

Late the next morning, September 14, Clark and Meese presented the order to the president in the Oval Office. Just as he was about to sign it, White House Deputy Chief of Staff Michael Deaver entered on routine business and asked what was going on. When Reagan showed him the order, Deaver immediately realized its ramifications and hastened to tell his boss, Chief of Staff Jim Baker, who was widely known as a leaker. Believing his own position to be in potential jeopardy, Baker went immediately to see the president, who was having lunch with Vice President Bush and Secretary Shultz.

Attempting to talk the president out of going forward with his plan, a highly agitated Baker pointed out that Reagan would be indicating a "lack of trust" in his closest associates, including the vice president, to subject them to lie detector tests. Baker also claimed that ordering Smith to conduct the investigation contradicted his own authority as chief of staff. However, the attorney general, not the chief of staff, served as the administration's top law enforcement officer, and he possessed the statutory authority to conduct investigations. Baker also said that Clark had never checked with him, which was true; but it implied that the president, who had already signed the letter, should have done the same.[28]

Baker's arguments were heated, but carried little weight, for the president clearly had the authority to direct his attorney general to investigate and to use polygraphs. It was the reactions of Bush and Shultz, however, that won the day. Shultz immediately spoke up and thundered: "Nobody'd better polygraph me...I'll only be asked to take one polygraph," a thinly veiled threat to resign. Baker said the same and Bush criticized lie detector tests as "a bad idea." Beleaguered, Reagan retreated and said: "Bill [Clark] shouldn't have done that." Calling Attorney General Smith on the spot, he said: "I want that letter back. I want you over here this afternoon. I want to roundtable this thing."[29]

That afternoon, the president met with the attorney general, Clark, Meese, Baker, and Deaver. Cannon says the vice president attended, but not Fred

---

[27] Cannon, *Role of a Lifetime*, 424. Hedrick Smith, *The Power Game: How Washington Works* (New York: Ballantine Books, 1988), 444, basing his analysis on consultation with "four top officials," says that French would ask for the resignations of "anyone who declined to take the lie-detector test."

[28] The accounts of Cannon, *Role of a Lifetime*, 425, and Smith, *Power Game*, 445, are at variance regarding this conversation. Cannon claims that the order to Smith "contradicted" Baker's authority as chief of staff, while Smith says that Reagan had designated Baker as the "official to decide when lie detectors should be used on high government officials."

[29] Smith, *Power Game*, 445; and Cannon, *Role of a Lifetime*, 425.

Fielding, the White House Counsel; Smith says Fielding attended, but not the vice president. Both agree that Shultz was not there. In a "tense session," Clark and Meese urged the president to press ahead with the investigation and polygraphs; Baker and Deaver opposed, saying that it would be a "terrible reflection on the president to order the polygraphing of his top advisers." Baker offered a compromise: "go ahead and have the investigation, but don't strap people up."[30]

The president, no doubt concerned about the threat of wholesale resignations, accepted Baker's compromise. The investigation would go forward, but there would be no polygraphs. Of course, without them, investigations would offer no leverage against the new world order faction. Clark, hopping mad, "stormed out of the Oval Office."[31] Cannon "was told that Shultz used the incident as the basis for privately expressing to the president his reservations about Clark's performance as national security adviser. Bush may have done the same, for he was now convinced that Clark was a divisive influence."[32] At this point, Clark's role as the president's point man was rapidly coming to an end.

Shultz Gains Added Power

The president's gambit had failed; Clark would have to go. Blame would fall on him for the leak, even though the most likely culprit, if culprit there was, was Baker. Although stories were put out that Clark had lost the favor of the president and incurred the wrath of the president's wife, the plain fact was that Reagan had lost a major battle with the new world order faction. Henceforth, policy initiatives would come from the State Department and Reagan would find himself increasingly isolated within his own government, including his national security staff.

That very evening of September 14, in what was described as "a rare public appearance," his first since the KAL crisis, Clark spoke to the Air Force Association convention where he accepted the General "Hap" Arnold award on behalf of the president. Clark denounced the Soviet Union for shooting down the Korean airliner and for contending that the plane was on a spying mission. The Soviets were, he said, "embarked on a 'big lie' campaign through their own statements and those of 'their apologists both here and abroad' to shift blame away from themselves and onto the United States…and, we believe, they will take further initiatives to cover up."[33]

"Already, they are stating…that the airline massacre was the result of strained US-Soviet relations…. They will…blame that relationship on our government's actions and suggest that a summit is called for to reach a 'greater understanding.'" The United States must resist the "big lie," he said, while also

---

[30] Cannon, *Role of a Lifetime*, 425.

[31] Smith, *Power Game*, 445.

[32] Cannon, *Role of a Lifetime*, 426

[33] Lou Cannon, "Clark Accuses Soviets of 'Mass Murder,'" *Washington Post*, September 15, 1983, A17.

demonstrating that aggression does not pay. Was Clark suggesting that something good might ultimately come of the disaster, as Johnson posits, or was it a warning to supporters about a Shultz takeover?[34] Copies of his speech "were distributed by the White House press office, calling attention to Clark's remarks as an expression of administration policy."[35]

If this was not Clark's parting shot, it was very close to it. Paralleling the leak investigation imbroglio was a battle over trade with Moscow. In the immediate aftermath of the KAL crisis, the president had sought to tighten controls on exports to the Soviet Union. On September 13, Assistant Secretary of Commerce Lawrence J. Brady, hoping to "strike while the iron is hot," had chaired an inter-agency meeting of the Advisory Committee on Export Policy which recommended the shift of 17 items of oil and gas exploration technology from foreign policy controls to national security controls.[36]

The recommendation would have moved control over this technology to the Department of Defense—that is, to Weinberger—from the State and Commerce Departments, and effectively denied exports of the items to the Soviet Union. The recommendation pushed Commerce Secretary Malcolm Baldridge and Secretary of State Shultz together on ideological and institutional grounds. Both favored increased trade with the Soviet Union and sought to protect their respective turf against the Defense Department. When, on September 19, Clark entered the picture with a letter instructing the two cabinet officers to carry out the advisory committee's decision, the battle was joined.[37]

Although Clark's letter was likened to "a grenade in the chicken coop," both Shultz and Baldridge fought back. In a telephone conference three days later, on September 22, which undoubtedly included the president, who would have to decide, they argued the case. Shultz and Baldridge warned that the export restrictions would only re-ignite trade frictions with the allies. Clark said this vital technology must be kept out of Soviet hands. The president sided with Shultz and Baldridge; Clark backed down. Both Brady and Under Secretary of State William Schneider, who supported him, were asked to resign. As Farnsworth put it, the "doves" had captured control of trade.[38]

For the next two weeks, the president worked to devise a means to keep Clark in the cabinet and thus close-by for advice. His solution, similar in structure to what he had done in installing Clark as national security adviser in the first

---

[34] R.W. Johnson, *Shootdown: Flight 007 and the American Connection* (New York: Viking, 1986), 196: and Bill King, "Soviets Use Passenger Planes to Spy on US, Clark Charges," *Washington Times*, September 15, 1983, A3.

[35] Cannon, "Clark Accuses Soviets of 'Mass Murder.'"

[36] Clyde Farnsworth, "Curb Asked on Trade to Soviet," *New York Times*, September 22, 1983, D1; and Farnsworth, "The Doves Capture Control of Trade," *New York Times*, October 23, 1983, F1.

[37] Clyde Farnsworth, "Soviet Oil Tool Curbs Ruled Out," *New York Times*, October 5, 1983, D1.

[38] Farnsworth, "The Doves Capture Control of Trade."

place, was to orchestrate Clark's lateral movement from the NSC to a lesser position in the cabinet, and to tab Clark's deputy, Robert McFarlane, who was part of the new world order faction, as his replacement. Indeed, Clark would arrange McFarlane's appointment. Public revelations of these decisions would occur sequentially weeks later and be obscured by further internal bickering, but most of all by the plunge of US-Soviet relations into deeper crisis.

Moscow Tightens the Screws

Secretary Shultz had misunderstood Soviet strategy, or, if he had understood it, he overestimated his ability to bring the Russians into line. It would be three weeks after the crisis before he realized that the Soviets were pursuing a confrontational course wholly incompatible with what he expected. They were not interested in "resolving" the KAL crisis, they were intent upon exacerbating it. The question was: why? To what end? It would soon become clear that while the Russians were acting on many fronts, it was the weapons deployment issue that stood foremost on the Soviet agenda. But, at first, Shultz proceeded according to a scenario of improving bilateral relations.

Shultz sought to steer US-Soviet relations back along the course set in August before the KAL incident. His plan was to meet with Foreign Minister Gromyko in Madrid, where they could put the airliner crisis behind them. Then, he expected Gromyko to visit the White House as part of his trip to the UN later in September. After that, Shultz would go to Moscow for a meeting with Communist Party leader Andropov. He expected to have to weather a "stormy period" in December when the United States would have begun deploying the Pershing II/cruise missile package to Western Europe, but, after that, "the scenario called for a meeting at the summit between Reagan and Andropov," where the elements of an arms deal could be certified.[39]

The Russians, however, did not follow the script. Shultz's meeting with Gromyko a week after the airliner incident produced an acrimonious exchange, despite Shultz's plea for a "serious dialogue."[40] Gromyko then canceled his trip to the UN. That step was provoked by requiring him to land at a military airport, instead of a commercial terminal; and by the president, who, in his Saturday radio broadcast, lambasted the Russians over the KAL incident, charging that "the world's outrage has not diminished." (Reagan retained control of his speeches, many of which he wrote himself, much to the discomfiture of Shultz.)

In any case, as Kraft observed, Gromyko's cancellation "shatter[ed] any hope of getting back on the pre-established diplomatic track soon."[41] Shultz and the new world order establishment figures around him were confused, and

---

[39] Joseph Kraft, "What's Going on With the Russians?" *Washington Post*, September 20, 1983, A15.
[40] Bernard Gwertzman, "Shultz Assails the Russians But Asks 'Serious Dialogue,'" *New York Times*, September 10, 1983, 6.
[41] Kraft, "What's Going On With the Russians?"

suspicious "of something gone wrong in the Kremlin." Andropov had not been seen for over three weeks and issued no public statements. "If he doesn't emerge soon," they said, "the United States will be convinced he has trouble asserting his primacy—especially in dealing with the Soviet armed forces." Indeed, the Soviet military was "out front," in the handling of the airliner crisis, exhibiting a "harsh," and "nasty tone."[42]

The American leadership had expected difficulty with the Russians over the Pershing II deployment, but now believed "the Russians will respond to nuclear deployment with a major escalation of Soviet forces at several levels." Already, the Russians were "pushing home their challenge to American power" in all the "usual trouble spots." They were attempting to cozy up to China, and intensifying military operations in Afghanistan, by sending planes (nominally Afghan, but actually Soviet) across its borders into Iran and Pakistan. They continued to send arms to Syria and to many PLO factions in Lebanon; and were spurring Libyan military incursions into Chad.

Transmitting the administration's concerns, Kraft concluded that "the central fact is that Washington is in the dark about the intentions of Moscow. Relations are bad and getting worse, and short of some move by Andropov himself, there is now no good way to get them back on course."[43] It was a plea for the Communist Party to reassert itself over the military. Ironically, that very day's edition of the *Washington Post* carried the summary of an article by Soviet General Piotr Kirsanov escalating the tension. Kirsanov charged that KAL 007 was part of a "'large-scale intelligence operation' involving several military planes and vessels as well as a spy satellite."[44]

The Soviet charge was that "the operation was carried out with the approval of the US administration and implied that President Reagan had been informed beforehand." This was the "first time the Soviet Union has accused the White House of direct involvement in planning a spy mission involving the Boeing 747, and it could herald further strains in relations between Moscow and Washington." Until now, the Soviets had blamed "American special services," leaving open the possibility that "they could have acted without formal US government approval."

Kirsanov maintained that KAL 007 was part of a mission supported by two RC-135 aircraft, an AWACS plane, two Orion aircraft, and the frigate USS *Badger*. The entire flight was monitored by US intelligence and synchronized with a Ferret-D satellite's three passes over the Soviet Far East. Its purpose was to gather and record as much information as possible on the Soviet air defense system. Kirsanov's theory, which received considerable attention, was plausible enough. The planes, ship, and satellite were present. The only proof suggested in the article was Kirsanov's claim that there had been eleven "intelligence

---

[42] Ibid.
[43] Ibid.
[44] Michael Dobbs, "Soviets: 747 Was Part of Spy Network," *Washington Post*, September 20, 1983, A1.

specialists" aboard the Korean passenger plane, in addition to the regular crew. Of course, how he could have known this unless he, or someone, had interrogated the passengers, was left unstated. In its essence, the article evoked the first detailed Soviet analysis of the incident, which claimed the presence of seven planes and three ships accompanying KAL 007.

If the article represented the state of the Soviet Union's understanding of American intelligence capabilities, it revealed ignorance of what had actually happened. Even a casual reading of US newspaper accounts would have afforded a much more sophisticated interpretation of the flight as an intelligence mission. Most important, Kirsanov had left out the presence of US satellites in geosynchronous orbit, which were able to make continuous readings of Soviet communications activity, not the mere communications snapshots that the so-called Ferret-D could take. Finally, the article betrayed no inkling of precisely what American intelligence had been after.

Reaffirmation of the "Analogous" Threat

The surge in Soviet geopolitical activity, however, was to one degree or another designed to divert US attention from the main event: the strategic weapons balance and specifically the Soviet determination to counter the US plan to deploy the Pershing II into West Germany. Throughout, the Soviets continued to be remarkably forthright, indeed, brazen, in declaring their principal objective. The latest statement came from Radomir Bogdanov, deputy director of the USA and Canada Institute. He said that the jetliner incident was over; it had "underscored the importance of Soviet-American relations," but that the arms control talks were crucial:

> We think that Geneva is the key to the international situation. How you turn this key will impact for a very long time on the international situation…If there is progress in Geneva, then there is progress in Soviet-American relations. All the other things are cosmetics, irrelevant to the substance of Soviet-American relations.[45]

Then came the threat. If the United States went ahead with its planned deployment of new medium-range missiles in Europe, he said, "we'll put the American mainland under the same threat as our mainland would be." The reiteration of the oft-stated "analogous" threat to deploy medium-range missiles close to the United States tended to pass little-noticed compared to the continuing drama being played out over the airliner incident, as the search of the waters around Moneron Island began to focus on the location of the plane's black boxes, which would identify its presumed location. Despite this, the threat was not ignored by the American leadership, especially with US-Soviet relations spiraling

---

[45] Antero Pietila, "Soviet Warns US on Missiles," *Baltimore Sun*, September 13, 1983, A2.

downward despite American efforts to reach accommodation, and as events on the island of Grenada took an ominous turn.

Andropov's first purported act since the shootdown of the airliner came in the form of a letter in response to an appeal from a group of West German Social Democrat deputies in the Bundestag. Ignoring the airliner incident, the gist of "Andropov's" reply was to assert a common interest against the United States on the missile issue. "People of our countries…cannot look indifferently on how attempts are being made in the name of interests alien to Europe" to destroy all the positive achievements in East-West relations.[46]

Andropov's letter was followed a day later by an article by Marshal Ogarkov in which he reiterated once again the "analogous" threat. Ogarkov warned that the Kremlin "would reply to new United States medium-range missile deployments in Western Europe with 'response measures' that would pose an equal military threat to the United States and Western Europe." Evaluating the threat, "Western strategists" opined that "one option open to the Russians was the siting of new SS-20 batteries in the extreme northeast corner of the Soviet Union, across the Bering Strait from Alaska," which would bring "the northwest corner of the United States within potential striking distance."[47] There was, of course, another option.

The "Western strategists" discussing Moscow's options mentioned only the extreme Soviet northeast as a site for the 3,000-mile-range SS-20, but anyone using the same range criterion would quickly conclude that the Caribbean would be a far better place to deploy these missiles. For those who remembered the history of the Cuban missile crisis, suggestions were made then that the Soviet Union would deploy SS-5s to the extreme northeast, rather than in Cuba. In neither case were American leaders fooled. From the Caribbean, the SS-20 would be able to target most of the United States. In fact, the Soviets would be able to cover more of the United States from the Caribbean than the United States would be able to cover of the Soviet Union from West Germany.

In the meantime, the American leadership, now led by George Shultz, began to back-pedal on Reagan's arms control position, hoping to bring Moscow around to agreement. Letters were sent to all NATO heads and to Andropov outlining the change in position. The changes, which were not yet made public, were welcomed by European leaders as a sign of US "flexibility," but dismissed by Moscow.[48] Nevertheless, in an effort to soften his image, Reagan broadcast an appeal directly to the Soviet people through the Voice of America. Then, on September 26, in an address to the UN, the president made public his proposals.

---

[46] Michael Dobbs, "Andropov Letter Cites Dangers of Stationing Missiles," *Washington Post*, September 21, 1983, A21.

[47] John Burns, "Kremlin Renews Missile Warnings," *New York Times*, September 23, 1983, A11.

[48] Andrew Rosenthal, "Tass Says New US Missile Proposal 'Smells of the Old' Zero Option Plan," *Washington Post*, September 23, 1983, A19.

Crafting his remarks in the context of his view that "a nuclear war cannot be won and must never be fought," he said that "I believe that if governments are determined to deter and prevent war, there will not be war." He went on to assert the importance of non-proliferation: "we must ensure that world security is not undermined by the further spread of nuclear weapons." Very carefully, President Reagan was putting the United States on record, and the Soviet Union on notice, that it was prepared to act in pursuit of those objectives.[49]

The president reviewed US proposals in the START and INF negotiations—the offers made to respond to Soviet concerns, while moving toward reductions in both areas. Despite Soviet rejections of American proposals, the president said, focusing on the INF talks, "we are determined to spare no effort to achieve a sound, equitable and verifiable agreement." Toward this end, he continued, he had given "new instructions" to negotiator Paul Nitze, designed to "advance the negotiations as rapidly as possible."

The new American proposals were: first, on the issue of global limits, "if the Soviet Union agrees to reductions and limits on a global basis, the United States...will not offset the entire Soviet global missile deployment through US deployments in Europe," but would reserve the right to deploy missiles elsewhere. Second, the United States was now willing to "limit aircraft as well as missiles." Third, "in the context of reductions to equal levels, we are prepared to reduce the number of Pershing II ballistic missiles as well as ground-launched cruise missiles." The door to an agreement is open, the president concluded. "It is time for the Soviet Union to walk through it."

A Hidden Move to the Brink

What produced this abrupt retreat in position? The answer, it seems, aside from the now-dominant views of George Shultz and the new world order faction, was a completely secret event that occurred just before the president spoke. When revealed 15 years later, it was described as a malfunction of the Soviet missile defense warning system, which indicated that the United States had launched a missile attack against the Soviet Union. Thanks to the quick thinking of the Soviet watch officer on duty, who realized that it was a computer malfunction and not an actual attack, the Russians did not launch a counterstrike and the world was saved from nuclear catastrophe.[50]

However, everything about this story smells of disinformation and when placed in contemporaneous context, takes on an entirely different and decidedly more ominous character, the opposite from how it was later portrayed. The presumed event occurred at the precise moment when the Soviets were attempting to ratchet up the tension in their war scare and its purpose was to cow the Reagan administration into backing down from its plan to erase the US nuclear deficit. In

---

[49] "Text of President's Address at U.N.," *New York Times*, September 27, 1983, A16.
[50] David Hoffman, "'I Had a Funny Feeling in My Gut,'" *Washington Post*, February 10, 1999, A19.

this context, the so-called false alarm was a completely staged event, aimed to send disinformation to American intelligence operators monitoring Soviet response capability. The message was that the Soviet Union was on hair-trigger alert, which could produce a Soviet attack on the United States. It most certainly reinforced the aversion of Shultz and the new world order faction to confrontation with Moscow.[51]

In any case, Moscow immediately refused the compromise offered by Reagan. The Soviets objected to the deployment of *any* US missiles. For them, the zero option meant zero for the United States. Speaking from Moscow, Gromyko termed the president's proposals "patently unacceptable" and reiterated the Soviet threat to take "countermeasures" if the US deployed the Pershing II and cruise missile package to Western Europe. Reports by *Tass* from New York, while concurring in Gromyko's view of Reagan's proposals as a "propaganda game," expressed surprise that he had "used the word détente without an abusive epithet for the first time in 10 years."[52]

Moscow's full response came the next day, in a statement described as an "assessment" by the Soviet leadership of US policy. Broadcast in Andropov's name, the statement lambasted the United States as pursuing "a militarist course that poses a grave threat to peace." Trying to assure for itself "a dominant position in the world," Washington was expanding its military presence to all parts of the globe and raising tensions worldwide. Dismissing President Reagan's address to the UN as just so much "talk," the Soviet leadership effectively wrote off any further possibility of cooperation with the Reagan administration:

> Even if someone had illusions as to the possible evolution for the better in the policy of the American Administration, the latest developments have dispelled them. For the sake of its imperial ambitions, it is going so far that one begins to doubt whether it has any brakes preventing it from crossing the mark before which any sober-minded person would stop.[53]

Clearly stung by the success of American diplomacy portraying Moscow as a maniacal, shoot-first regime, the statement attempted to turn the tables, reiterating the charge that it had been the "United States special services," who "masterminded and carried out the [KAL] provocation." Using a South Korean

---

[51] Months later, reflecting on the events of the fall and winter of 1983-84, CIA analysts decided that "we do not believe that Soviet war talk and other actions 'mask' Soviet preparations for an imminent move toward confrontation on the part of the USSR, although they have an incentive to take initiatives that discredit US policies even at some risk." *Implications of Recent Soviet Military-Political Activities*, SNIE 11-010-84 (Washington, DC: Central Intelligence Agency, May 18, 1984), iii.

[52] Michael Dobbs, "Reagan's Arms Proposals Unacceptable, Gromyko Says," *Washington Post*, September 28, 1983, A14.

[53] "Text of Soviet Statement on Relations with US," *New York Times*, September 29, 1983, A14.

plane was an "example of extreme adventurism in politics." Yet, it was these very same leaders, indeed the president himself, who "slanders" the Soviet Union, "smears" the Soviet people, and the socialist system, resorting to what "almost amounts to obscenities alternating with hypocritical preaching about morals and humanism."

On the "burning problem," reduction of nuclear armaments in Europe, the theme of turning the tables continued. While the Soviet Union sought to find "mutually acceptable solutions on a fair, just basis," Washington did not. "Their task is different—to play for time and then start the deployment in Western Europe of Pershing II ballistic missiles and long-range cruise missiles. They do not even try to conceal this. All they do is prattle about some sort of flexibility." Deployment would be "a step against peace of a fundamental nature" by the American leadership and those NATO leaders who, "disregarding the interests of their peoples and the interests of peace, help implement the ambitious militarist plans of the United States Administration."

Although there were those in the US who purported to glean from the Andropov statement a "signal" that all Moscow wanted was respect, to be "seen and treated as the other superpower," suggesting that all that was needed was for the United States to offer genuine concessions, the truth was much more ominous.[54] The Andropov statement was designed to disengage and to free the Soviet Union to take the countermeasures it had promised. In retrospect, Moscow and the United States had set the stage for the move that would present one or the other with a strategic *fait accompli*. That move would be on the tiny Caribbean island of Grenada.

The Attempt to Capture Bishop

The pace of events on Grenada had increased markedly. Deputy Prime Minister Bernard Coard used the September 14-17 extraordinary meeting of the ruling New Jewel Movement's (NJM) Central Committee to make his bid to gain control of the party, but again in absentia, as his allies led the attack. His wife, Phyllis, derided Bishop's July thesis that there had been an "improvement in work." The situation in the party, all agreed, was critical. Ewart Layne saw the party deviating onto a path of "right opportunism," which in Marxist jargon meant a readiness to work with the imperialists. But it was Liam James who attacked Bishop directly. The problem, James said, was "the quality of leadership of the party and the Central Committee, and in particular the leadership of Maurice Bishop."[55]

---

[54] Leslie Gelb, "Soviet Signal to the US," *New York Times*, September 29, 1983, A1.
[55] Gregory Sandford and Richard Vigilante, *Grenada: The Untold Story* (New York: Madison Books, 1984), 153-54; Anthony Payne, Paul Sutton and Tony Thorndike, *Grenada: Revolution and Invasion* (New York: St. Martin's, 1984), 118-19; and Mark Adkin, *Urgent Fury: The Battle for Grenada* (New York: Lexington Books, 1989), 36-37.

Charisma was not enough, James said. What was needed was a disciplined, Leninist party, which Bishop was not qualified to build. A lengthy harangue from the members of the Coard faction about Bishop's faults was accepted by Bishop's supporters, and Bishop himself, with grudging acknowledgment. George Louison replied with the counter argument that with all his faults, Bishop was "still the best leader the NJM had." James had the solution, proposing joint leadership, "with Bishop focusing on relations with the masses and Coard taking charge of the party organization." [56]

The proposal for joint leadership became the focal point of the struggle, as Coard's followers unanimously supported it and Bishop's allies questioned its workability, theoretical basis, and implications. Louison said that joint leadership wouldn't work and proposed collective leadership, instead, with Bishop remaining sole leader. Besides, he said, there was no theoretical basis for joint leadership. Bishop declared that he had never had a problem with sharing power, or accepting criticism, but he wanted to hear Coard's view. He feared that if the party moved to joint leadership "the world would see it as a power struggle and a vote of no confidence in him."[57]

James sought to reassure Bishop with the argument that he would "still be Prime Minister and Commander in Chief and sign all Central Committee documents." Coard "would not decide strategy and tactics 'all by himself.'" Layne said that there was a theoretical basis for joint leadership, and it was the commissar system in the Soviet army, which worked, but that, of course, was simply an example of a political control mechanism, not a leadership system. Nevertheless, put to a vote, the joint leadership proposal passed overwhelmingly with nine votes in favor, two against, and two abstentions.[58] Bishop played for time, wanting to "reflect" on the proposal and work through its ramifications.

A proposal was made to reconvene the next day with Coard present. Bishop would not be there, however, as he and Whiteman were to go to St. Kitts to attend their Independence Day celebration. Louison also would not be there, as he was to depart to lead the advance team for Bishop's forthcoming trip to Eastern Europe. It was agreed to hold a general meeting of the leadership on September 25, when Bishop returned from Eastern Europe. After Bishop's departure, the Central Committee convened with Coard present, briefing him about the meeting with Bishop. Coard supported the Central Committee's decisions and the need for a "fundamental package of measures" to salvage the situation. He accepted joint leadership, but insisted that Bishop accept it, too, "to save the party and the revolution."[59]

---

[56] Sandford and Vigilante, *Grenada: Untold Story*, 154.

[57] Payne, et al., *Grenada*, 120-21.

[58] Payne et al., *Grenada*, 121. Adkin, *Urgent Fury*, 37, says there was one vote against and three abstentions. Sandford and Vigilante, *Grenada: Untold Story*, 154, imply that there was one vote against and one abstention.

[59] Payne et al., *Grenada*, 122.

The Central Committee then elected Coard as its chairman and approved the decision to establish joint leadership. Over the next two weeks, Coard set about the task of reorganizing the party, deciding on the best way to build its image and legitimacy among the masses, involve more party members in the task of cadre selection and promotion, and instill more organization and discipline. The purpose of these actions was straightforward. It was to create an apparatus of which Bishop would be the figurehead, but whose *de facto* leader would be Coard.[60]

Although Bishop and Whiteman had returned from St. Kitts on September 22, the party's general meeting for the 25th had to be postponed a day because not all of the documents were prepared. When the meeting convened, however, Bishop declined to attend on the grounds that he still needed time to reflect on the concept of joint leadership. In that circumstance, Coard also decided not to attend. James presented the Central Committee's decision on joint leadership to the assembled party membership, declaring that their decision was simply the "formal recognition of the leadership of our party for the first ten years."[61]

On a vote, the party members insisted that both Bishop and Coard come to the meeting. When they arrived, Bishop was asked to explain his objections to the Central Committee decision on joint leadership. He said that the "concept of joint leadership did not bother him, but...some aspects of it required mature reflection." If he were "unfit to lead," then the joint leadership idea was an "unprincipled compromise." He was considering withdrawing from the leadership entirely but had not yet made up his mind. In the meantime, he wanted the Central Committee to "clarify its own position."[62]

Layne immediately charged that Bishop was showing "gross contempt for the intelligence of the Central Committee," by implying that "there was a conspiracy to remove him, but at this time for tactical reasons we are going halfway." Others, however, spoke up for Bishop. Whiteman put forward the collective leadership idea, while Bain warned that "'left opportunism' could replace 'right opportunism,'" and accused some members of "caucusing" against Bishop. Rank and file party members, unaware that there in fact *was* a conspiracy to harness Bishop, exhorted him to accept criticism "in a comradely way."[63]

The general tenor of the meeting was strongly in favor of the Central Committee and its decisions. Summing up, Coard said he "would work with Bishop...for the party, the revolution and the Grenadian working class." Listening to Coard, Bishop was moved. To great applause, he stood and embraced Coard, declaring that "since the meeting had endorsed the committee's analysis, 'this has satisfied my concern...I sincerely accept the criticism and will fulfill the decision in practice.'" Joint leadership would move the party and the revolution forward.

---

[60] Ibid., 122-24.
[61] Ibid., 126 and Sandford and Vigilante, *Grenada: Untold Story*, 155.
[62] Ibid., 155-56.
[63] Ibid., 156 and Payne et al, *Grenada*, 127.

He pledged to overcome his petty-bourgeois traits and devote his "whole life" to the revolution.[64] For the moment, it seemed, the crisis had passed, and the meeting ended on a high, emotional note with the singing of the *Internationale.*

Bishop Insists on Collective Leadership

Bishop, accompanied by his personal bodyguard Cletus St. Paul and Whiteman, arrived in Budapest and met with Louison. Briefed on the late September meeting, Louison was horrified to hear that Bishop had agreed to the plan for joint leadership, which he viewed as nothing but a "power grab" by Coard. They all agreed that collective leadership with Bishop as *primus inter pares* was the proper decision. During their trip, therefore, Grenadian representatives were informed that the leadership issue had not been settled and was still under discussion.[65]

Bishop and his party were to return to Grenada on October 6, but instead made an unscheduled two-day stopover in Havana. Although all authors agree that the prime minister had a "long meeting" with his friend Fidel Castro, they accept the Cuban leader's claim that Bishop "made not the least references in his conversations with Comrade Fidel and other Cuban leaders about the serious arguments and differences going on inside the New Jewel."[66] This is tantamount to believing the bromide about honor among thieves and ignores obvious Cuban and Soviet interests in Grenada.

That Bishop, in a life and death struggle with Coard, said nothing about it to Castro is implausible on the face of it.[67] Moreover, even if Bishop had said nothing, it should not be taken to mean that Castro was ignorant of the power struggle that had been raging for several months. Indeed, it would be surprising if he had not been fully informed of events by Cuban ambassador Julian Torres Rizo, who had returned to Havana for consultations. Bishop most certainly appealed to Castro for help. Otherwise, his unscheduled stop in Havana made little sense. The request would have put the Cuban leader in a position similar to an earlier episode in Nicaragua when he sought to resolve a factional dispute.[68]

Bishop was an old friend, but friendship would not be the governing factor in any decision Castro would make. He most certainly would have checked with Moscow. If the Soviets told him anything, they told him that Bishop was attempting to become more independent and that it was important to rein him in—

---

[64] Ibid., 128.

[65] Ibid.

[66] *Declaration of the Party and Revolutionary Government of Cuba Regarding the Events in Grenada* (Havana, October 20, 1983), 1. Alan Berger, "Grenada, According to Castro," *Boston Globe*, November 20, 1983, A23. See also Sandford and Vigilante, *Grenada: Untold Story*, 157; Payne, et al., *Grenada*, 128; Adkin, *Urgent Fury*, 40.

[67] "Bishop Appealed to Cuba to Aid Grenada," *Washington Times*, December 19, 1983, 7.

[68] For Castro's approach in the Nicaraguan case, see the author's *The Carter Years: Toward a New Global Order* (New York: Paragon House, 1991), 363-70.

the point of the joint leadership scheme. Collective leadership would accomplish the same result, so long as Coard controlled the Central Committee. In the event, what we do know is that Castro attempted to support Bishop in a way that would avoid a leadership split.

Cletus St. Paul called a member of the Central Committee from Havana. Castro, of course, had to approve such a call. He said that Bishop had rejected the notion of joint leadership and hinted that he would return to fight it. The clear implication was that Bishop would return to Grenada with Castro's backing for a showdown. Indeed, this was precisely the way Central Committee member Selwyn Strachan interpreted Bishop's move. He said to his cohorts of Bishop's "surprise visit to Havana":

> Maurice has now compounded the problem by taking the Party's business to the Cubans in an unfraternal and unprincipled way, using his personal friendship with Fidel.... As a show of support for Maurice, Fidel had given a reception for [him] at which eight members of the [Cuban] Politburo had been present, including Fidel and Raoul.[69]

Coard and his supporters also would not have failed to note that Castro had sent some 240 Cuban combat troops aboard the *Vietnam Heroica* to Grenada on October 6.[70] An additional, unspecified number of troops along with Ambassador Rizo accompanied Bishop on his return to Grenada. These troops spent the next several days camped out in the Cuban embassy, before moving to their barracks at the Point Salines airport.[71] Other Cuban vessels would arrive over the following days, loaded with arms.[72] At the very least, Castro was hedging his bet by having forces in place should they be required to coerce a solution.

Was there a dispute between the Soviets and Castro? After the invasion, Castro took the view that he had opposed the violent overthrow of Bishop. In a press conference on October 26, he declared that "we based ourselves on the fact that there was a division within the revolution. It was painful and unpleasant. We foresaw that great damage would be done to the country because of this division. We even addressed the Grenadian leaders, the central committee, and asked them to try to solve these problems peacefully, without violence. We said that violence would greatly damage Grenada's image."[73]

---

[69] Adkin, *Urgent Fury*, 41.

[70] Ronald Cole, *Operation Urgent Fury: The Planning and Execution of Joint Operations in Grenada, 12 October – 2 November, 1983* (Washington, DC: Joint History Office, Office of the Chairman of the Joint Chiefs of Staff, 1997), 15, 19.

[71] "Julián Enrique Torres Rizo," The Grenada Revolution Online, https://www.the grenadarevolutiononline.com/rizo.html.

[72] Cole, *Operation Urgent Fury*, 15,19.

[73] University of Texas Latin American Network Information Center (LANIC), "Fidel Castro's Press Conference on Grenada, October 26, 1983," http://lanic.utexas.edu/ project/castro/db/1983/19831026.html.

Despite Castro's insistence on a peaceful solution, Moscow was in a hurry and the Soviets controlled the events, orchestrating Coard's actions. Of that there is no doubt. On the morning of Bishop's murder, for example, in a pattern that must be assumed to have obtained throughout the developing crisis, a member of the Soviet embassy, either Ambassador Genady Sazhenev himself, or one of his staff, was directly observed in Coard's living room in animated discussion with his cohorts.[74] Other sources have noted that Sazhenev "masterminded" the events.[75]

At any rate, when Bishop and his group returned to Grenada on October 8, the usual welcoming committee was absent; only Strachan wearing a T-shirt was at Pearls airport to meet them. Bishop reaffirmed that he wanted the joint leadership issue put back on the Central Committee agenda and that he "insisted upon collective, and not joint, leadership."[76] Coard, however, was prepared for confrontation, having secured control of the army in Bishop's absence by moving Cornwall and Layne to top posts. General Hudson Austin, the army commander, was also with them, as were the security forces, but the militia remained largely pro-Bishop.

At the same time, Coard shunned Bishop, assembling the Central Committee in an emergency session without him on October 10. They decided against reopening the joint leadership issue and rejected the demand for collective leadership. Bishop found out about their meeting and sent his bodyguard St. Paul to it. He reported back their "deep anger."[77] Rumors began to fly about Coard and his allies holding "mysterious meetings" and party leaders not sleeping in their homes. There was talk of Bishop attempting to establish one-man rule and of consideration being given to an "Afghanistan solution," that is, the assassination of Bishop.[78]

The Battle Is Joined

The "storm broke" two days later, on October 12. Before the Politburo met that morning, Coard summoned Bishop's security detail, informing them that

---

[74] Adkin, *Urgent Fury*, 49. "Tony Buxo, a Sandhurst-trained former army officer of the West India Regiment, now an optician . . . was located in a house [with] . . . an unrestricted view down into the town, across to Coard's residence only 400 meters away . . . Focusing his telescope on Coard's house, he was able to see clearly right into the living room. A meeting between Coard and his close supporters was in progress. Apart from the Coards, Austin, Layne, Cornwall, McBarnette, James, Strachan, St. Bernard, Ventour, and later Redhead were present. Buxo spotted an Indian and a white, balding man with glasses in a Texaco T-shirt, neither of whom he recognized. It is quite possible the latter was from the Soviet embassy."

[75] Niles Lathem, "Top Red General Directed Isle Coup," *New York Post*, October 27, 1983, 3.

[76] Payne et al., *Grenada*, 129.

[77] Ibid.

[78] Sandford and Vigilante, *Grenada: Untold Story*, 157.

protection of the prime minister "was no longer their primary responsibility." At the same time, the People's Revolutionary Army held a secret meeting, passing a resolution supporting the Central Committee and calling for the expulsion of all those who did not accept its decisions.[79]

On the other hand, Bishop took his own precautions. Summoning his personal bodyguards, Cletus St. Paul and Errol George, he told them that Coard was planning to kill him and he wanted them to contact people they could trust to get the word out to his supporters. Bishop was attempting to play his hole card, his popularity with the people, to face down Coard and his party cohorts.[80] If Coard had the support of the party and the army, Bishop had the support of the people and the militia. At this point, he also appeared to have Castro's support, being in frequent contact with Ambassador Rizo.[81]

When the Central Committee convened, Coard stayed away, once again letting his followers mount the attack. First, they accused Louison of being a negative influence, blaming him for spreading rumors of a coup and lying to party members abroad about party decisions. When Bishop demanded to know why his personal bodyguard Errol George had been called to a meeting without informing him, James revealed that they had taken him into custody where he had confessed that Bishop had been responsible for the rumor that Coard was going to kill him. When James proposed arresting Cletus St. Paul, too, Bishop's ally, Fitzroy Bain threatened to march 3,000 people up to Mount Weldale where they were meeting.[82]

The Central Committee, on a proposal by Layne, voted to expel Louison from the party. Turning to Bishop, Strachan told him that he would have seven days to decide whether or not to accept the Central Committee's decision to establish joint leadership. Just as the meeting was concluding, word came that a group of Bishop's supporters in the St. Paul militia had taken up arms and were on their way to Mount Weldale to protect him from the Coards. Austin moved quickly to send army troops to disarm Bishop's supporters in the militia. The Central Committee demanded, and Bishop agreed, that he broadcast a denial of the assassination rumor.

Despite efforts to keep the internal conflict a secret, it was becoming evident, which spurred Coard and his Soviet handlers to move faster. Meeting that night at Coard's home, they plotted what they hoped would be the final step against Bishop. They placed the army on alert, confiscated all weapons at the St. Paul's and St. David's militias, and reinforced the People's Revolutionary Army units at St. Patrick's and Fort Rupert. The plan was to hold a meeting of the party membership the following day. Bishop would not be informed of the meeting and would be brought to it only after it had convened. To preserve secrecy and to

---

[79] Ibid., 158.
[80] Ibid.
[81] "Julián Enrique Torres Rizo," The Grenada Revolution Online.
[82] Sandford and Vigilante, *Grenada: Untold Story*, 159-60; and Payne et al., *Grenada*, 130.

ensure that Bishop did not go into hiding, his house was quietly placed under surveillance.[83]

The next morning, October 13, Coard convened a secret meeting of his Central Committee supporters at his home where it was decided to place Bishop under house arrest. They set up an armed guard around his house, which was next door. That evening, Bishop was brought under guard to a party meeting attended by some 250 members. The purpose of the meeting was to announce the decision to arrest Bishop and for the entire party to carry out the public denunciation of their former leader. In essence, it was an organized hate session to implicate the entire party in Coard's takeover. One participant described the meeting as "a horrendous display of militarism, hatred, and emotional vilification."[84]

Bishop spoke in his own defense, admitting to "petty-bourgeois weaknesses," but denied spreading the assassination rumor. Upon distribution of photocopies of George's confession, however, Bishop stood silent, which was taken as an admission of guilt. Layne denounced Bishop as a traitor, urging that he be expelled from the party and court-martialed. The Central Committee, with Coard present but with Chalkie Ventour in the chair, decided against that course of action. Instead, as agreed earlier, Ventour announced that Bishop would be placed under house arrest, with his telephone disconnected.[85]

The evident purpose of holding Bishop incommunicado and not court-martialing and executing him was to pressure the prime minister into accepting the joint leadership scheme. Coard needed Bishop's approval, for he was not perceived among the people as Bishop's equal, let alone his successor. Coard and his Soviet handlers were in a hurry, overestimating their ability to control events and underestimating Bishop's resourcefulness and popular support. [86]

The Coard faction had hoped to keep Bishop's arrest secret, but word had gotten out. At first, the news was met with "disbelief and amazement," as his followers began to arouse the people. Outmaneuvered, on October 14, Coard attempted to present a *fait accompli*. He sent Strachan down to the offices of the *Free West Indian* newspaper in the St. George's city center to announce before a crowd that Coard had replaced Bishop as prime minister. It boomeranged. The announcement precipitated a public outcry as the crowd shouted down Strachan, physically manhandled him, and chased him off the street.

The public rejection prompted Coard to issue an immediate press release announcing his resignation "to dispel the false rumors that he had plotted to kill Bishop."[87] He and he wife, Phyllis, who also resigned, immediately went into seclusion. Between October 15 and 17, with Bishop under house arrest, his

---

[83] Sandford and Vigilante, *Grenada: Untold Story*, 160; Payne, et al., *Grenada*, 130; and Adkin, *Urgent Fury*, 43.

[84] Adkin, *Urgent Fury*, 43.

[85] Payne et al, *Grenada*, 131; Adkin, *Urgent Fury*, 43; and Sandford and Vigilante, *Grenada: Untold Story*, 161.

[86] Payne et al, *Grenada*, 131.

[87] Sandford and Vigilante, *Grenada: Untold Story*, 162.

supporters Louison and Whiteman met "almost continuously" with Coard and Strachan at Coard's home in an attempt to work out a solution. At the same time, Radix had begun to mobilize popular demonstrations against Coard, and Castro reentered the fray on Bishop's side. Although Coard had control of the Central Committee, he most emphatically had no support among the people, who, moreover, were now aroused.

On October 15, Castro sent a message to the Central Committee declaring his "total non-intervention in the internal affairs of the [Grenadian] Party and of the country." Having disclaimed any intent to intervene, however, he then proceeded to do just that, warning the Coard faction to desist. He said that their actions would "considerably damage the image of the Grenadian revolutionary process both internally and externally." In Cuba, he said, "where Bishop was held in high esteem, it would not be easy to explain what was happening."[88]

In the negotiations, Coard tried to talk Louison into supporting him and the joint leadership line, but Louison refused, charging that Coard was destroying the party. The masses, he said, demanded Bishop's release. Coard said that if the masses wanted to march, he would let them. "They can stay in the streets for weeks; after a while they are bound to get tired and hungry and want peace." After all, the party and the army were with him. Just to make sure, however, when the negotiation foundered, Coard began to round up Bishop's supporters, arresting Radix, George Louison, Bishop's mistress Jackie Cleft, Vincent Noel, and George Louison's brother, Einstein.[89]

By October 18, events were slipping out of Coard's control, as Bishop's supporters, especially Whiteman, Fitzroy and Norris Bain, and Lyden Ramdhanny began to organize demonstrations and street protests. Ramdhanny was sending trucks and buses around the island to bring in as many people as possible from the outlying parishes. To one observer, it seemed as if "an underground telegraph system had worked all over the island...trucks and buses poured in from everywhere."[90] Between ten and fifteen thousand people congregated in the Market Square. The government had ceased to function, and businesses had shut down. The Cuban workers at the airport were also "inciting the local workers to go and get their Prime Minister."[91]

Death of a Revolution

The night of October 18, Coard sent Austin, Layne, James and Bartholemew to see Bishop with a "final proposal." Ostensibly a "compromise," it was a blunt demand that Bishop accept the role of powerless figurehead. Coard's

[88] Alan Berger, "Grenada, According to Castro," *Boston Globe*, November 20, 1983, A23.
[89] Payne et al, *Grenada*, 132-33, Adkin, *Urgent Fury*, 45
[90] Payne et al, *Grenada*, 133.
[91] Sandford and Vigilante, *Grenada: Untold Story*, 163.

terms were for Bishop to remain a full member of the party and continue as prime minister but be removed from the Central Committee and relinquish control over all military forces. Finally, he would publicly accept responsibility for the assassination rumor. Bishop would be reduced to placating the masses at home and interacting with foreign heads of state, while Coard decided policy.[92]

Bishop, perhaps sensing Coard's desperation, said he would consider the proposal, except for accepting responsibility for the assassination rumor, and reply the next day. He wanted to confer with Louison, Whiteman, and the Cuban ambassador, Rizo; this last request clearly indicating Castro's involvement, however peripheral. Coard brought Louison from his prison cell to Bishop's home the next morning, but would not permit Rizo to see him, for fear that he would bring Cuban troops in on Bishop's side. He could not contact Whiteman, who was in town helping to organize mass demonstrations against the universally "loathed" Coard and his Central Committee cohorts.[93]

The next morning, October 19, under the prodding of Bishop's allies—Whiteman, the Bains, and Ramdhanny—the masses had gathered in the St. George's Market Square and were ready for action, demanding the release of their prime minister. Whiteman, announcing his intention to march to Bishop's house to rescue him, led a crowd of some 3,000 up the hill to the prime minister's home shouting "we want Maurice." Coard was in his living room with his Central Committee and Soviet advisers, observing the crowd approach and arguing among themselves over the best way to handle the brewing confrontation. In a growing panic, Coard began to realize that the crowd might not only rescue Bishop—it might also turn on him.[94]

At 9:00 a.m. Whiteman led the large crowd to the gates of Bishop's house where they encountered a reinforced guard of some 100 troops blocking entry. They hesitated momentarily when warning shots were fired into the air, then surged past the guards into the house where they found Bishop and Creft in separate rooms, stripped to their underclothes and manacled to beds. Bishop was in a weakened state, having refused food for fear of being poisoned, and dazed from lack of sleep, but clearly exultant. With tears streaming down his face he kept praising: "The masses. The masses. The masses."[95]

Emerging from the house triumphant, Bishop led a makeshift motorcade down the hill toward the center of town but made a key decision that ultimately cost him his life. Against the advice of his supporters, perhaps because he was unwilling to test the loyalty of the troops at that moment, he decided not to order the immediate arrest of Coard and his men, who were only a few yards away in Coard's home, and instead drove off. En route, Bishop made two other decisions,

[92] Adkin, *Urgent Fury*, 47, Sandford and Vigilante, *Grenada: Untold Story*, 163.

[93] Sandford and Vigilante, *Grenada: Untold Story*, 163, Adkin, *Urgent Fury*, 47-48.

[94] Adkin, *Urgent Fury*, 48-49.

[95] Payne et al, *Grenada*, 134; Adkin, *Urgent Fury*, 51-52.

the first to head for Fort Rupert instead of Market Square; and the second to send a messenger to Ambassador Rizo, requesting Cuban assistance.[96]

Bishop and the accompanying crowd arrived at the fort around 11:00 a.m., taking control of it, disarming the garrison, and arming their own followers. The fort was ideally situated on a bluff overlooking St. George's and the harbor with only a single road leading to it. With its weapons armory and broadcast facilities, Bishop could buy time to recover, plan his next move, communicate to the Grenadian people, and wait for Cuban assistance. He hoped to counter Coard's army with the armed Cuban workers at the airport, less than five miles away. Unfortunately, events moved too fast for him to recover, plan, or speak to his people; and Castro turned against him.[97]

Upon receiving Bishop's message, Rizo immediately cabled Castro, who replied "within the hour." Rizo sent back Castro's reply to Bishop at the fort. It was negative: "Under no circumstances were Cuban personnel, civil or military, to become involved in the internal turmoil of Grenada." What had happened? Only four days earlier, Castro had warned Coard not to take action against his friend. He had armed forces waiting at the embassy. Why had he suddenly withdrawn his support? Even more striking, Castro himself later admitted that "our construction workers and all our other cooperation personnel in Grenada...could have been a decisive factor in those internal events."[98]

The answer was that the circumstances had changed dramatically in the interim. It was no longer a matter of persuading factions to cooperate or deciding on either a joint or collective leadership system. Now, it was Bishop versus Coard, with the victor determining Grenada's destiny. If Bishop won, the communist side lost. He would take Grenada out of the Soviet-Cuban orbit and normalize relations with the United States, a step that would quash Soviet plans to deploy missiles to Grenada. Therefore, Castro could "under no circumstances" support his old friend Maurice Bishop. The only question is why Bishop thought he would.

Meanwhile, Coard and his Central Committee allies, astonished at their good fortune in not being arrested, went quickly to Fort Frederick, three miles away. As soon as they arrived, they sought to enter into negotiations with Bishop, but were turned down. Bishop had failed to enlist Castro and fatally misjudged Coard, assuming that he would bow to the will of the people and accept his demand to surrender. For Coard, it was now a question of kill or be killed. Therefore, he immediately convened the Central Committee, which took the decision to act before Bishop could mobilize the people against them. Their plan was to send forces to assault Fort Rupert and kill Bishop in the process.[99]

---

[96] Adkin, *Urgent Fury*, 52. Payne et al, *Grenada*, 134, omits the request for Cuban assistance and Sandford and Vigilante, *Grenada: Untold Story*, 176, claim that it was Castro who offered assistance to Bishop.

[97] Adkin, *Urgent Fury*, 53

[98] Ibid., 53-54

[99] Ibid., 60-61

Fort Frederick was the headquarters of Military Region 1 and a motorized company of half a dozen Soviet BTR-60 armored personnel carriers. Assembling the most politically reliable men they could find from those at the fort and from troops stationed at nearby Camp Calivigny, they loaded some 35 troops into three APCs and sent them to Fort Rupert. Arriving at around 1:00 p.m., two of the vehicles set up blocking positions on the road in front of the fort, while the third stopped further back, disgorging ten soldiers who positioned themselves in a cordon around the fort to prevent any escape.[100]

As soon as they were all in position, the two forward APCs opened fire on the fort and the stunned crowd out front, raking the people with heavy machine-gun fire, and the fort with rockets and grenades. Although those within the fort attempted to defend themselves, they were no match for the heavy weapons wielded by Coard's troops. Within ten minutes the massacre was over. Bishop and his supporters had surrendered. Coard's troops had brutally gunned down between 30 and 40 people (some accounts double that number), and seriously injured some 40 more.[101]

Coard had turned defeat into victory, but it had not gone according to plan. The plan had been to kill Bishop in the assault on the fort, which would have made it easier to explain to the people. Instead, he and his supporters had surrendered and were being held in the upper courtyard of the fort awaiting their fate. Now, the Central Committee would have to issue an execution order, which would be impossible to conceal. Egged on by the Soviet ambassador, Coard and the Central Committee decided that Bishop and his supporters were to be "shot at once."[102]

Shortly after two o'clock in the afternoon, amid still-burning vehicles and dead bodies, Bishop and seven of his supporters were lined up against the wall in the upper courtyard of Fort Rupert and machine-gunned to death. That night, with the entire country under martial law and strict curfew, Coard's men piled the mangled corpses into a truck, drove to a large pit near Camp Calivigny a few miles away, and incinerated them beyond recognition. In the true Bolshevik tradition, to prevent any possibility of a political restoration, Coard and his men attempted to erase all evidence of the existence of Maurice Bishop. But even as they sought to consolidate their victory, trouble was already brewing on the horizon, causing a frantic change in plans.

---

[100] Ibid., 69.

[101] Ibid., 70

[102] Adkin, *Urgent Fury*, 74 and Niles Lathem, "Top Red General Directed Isle Coup," *New York Post*, October 27, 1983, 3.

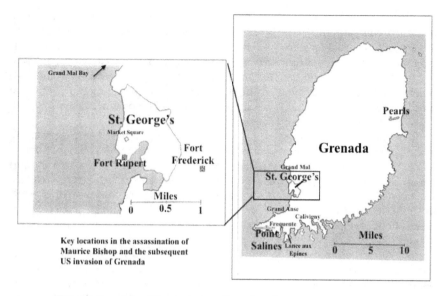

Key locations in the assassination of
Maurice Bishop and the subsequent
US invasion of Grenada

Washington Prepares for Action

American intelligence had been closely watching Grenada and, of course, the Soviet Union and Cuba, for months for any sign that missile deployment was imminent, a scheme which would be accompanied, or preceded, by the dispatch of Cuban troops. Secrecy, disinformation, and misdirection would be the hallmarks of US actions so as not to alert Moscow, or Cuba, before Washington was ready to act. President Reagan would preempt the Russians in Grenada at any cost, unless Bishop succeeded in winning his battle with the pro-Soviet faction and denied Moscow the opportunity on his own.

American intelligence focused on several key indicators. Regarding the Soviet Union and Cuba, radio intercepts and satellite observation of missile and aircraft movement, troop movement, and a command decision to deploy, would be crucial. In Grenada, employing technical as well as human assets, the key indicators were the progress of construction on the Point Salines airfield, the presence of Soviet rocket specialists, and of course, the evolution of the decisive factional struggle between Bishop and Coard.

In 1962, when the United States held strategic superiority, Washington could afford to wait until it had caught the Soviet Union red-handed with missiles deployed to Cuba, but not yet armed, before acting to force their removal. In 1983, the strategic situation was reversed. If Moscow succeeded in deploying missiles to Grenada before Reagan could act, the United States could not threaten war to force them out because the Soviet Union held the strategic weapons advantage. That is why it was absolutely imperative that the United States act before missiles were deployed, even though it would make later explanation of American action difficult.

Accordingly, the president signed a "get ready for action" directive, NSDD-105, "Eastern Caribbean Regional Security Policy," on October 4, 1983. Although its contents are heavily redacted, enough is available to indicate the thrust of US concern. "The principal objective…is to promote economically viable, independent democratic governments friendly to the United States and free of Cuban and Soviet influence." Grenada was singled out as a Cuban/Soviet "base for subversion" and "strategic outreach." Specific but redacted measures to meet US security concerns were to be undertaken "immediately" and "coordinated, diplomatic, military, intelligence, resource, and contingency plans" were to be forwarded for review by the President by October 15, 1983.[103] Thus, before Bishop even returned from his trip to Eastern Europe and the internal struggle was joined, the United States was preparing "contingency plans," in case Bishop failed.

By the second week of October, multiple indicators signaled that the crisis that the United States was anticipating had arrived. On the 10th, the State Department held an interagency meeting "to evaluate developments."[104] Both State and Defense commenced preliminary planning for their respective roles to come, and OECS allies were told to prepare a formal request for US assistance. Military planning was carried out in great secrecy at the Norfolk, Virginia Atlantic Command headquarters, instead of at Key West, as dictated by the US contingency plan for Grenada.[105] Indeed, contingency plan number 2360 for Grenada was never activated.[106]

Bishop's apparent defeat in the power struggle when he was placed under house arrest on October 13 prompted immediate calls to determine "what military resources could be mustered on short notice" for Grenada. The rationales for action being discussed were the possible rescue of Bishop, or the evacuation of the 800 American students attending the St. George's medical school on the island. In fact, the United States was preparing to preempt any Soviet move.[107]

First, however, the drama of Judge Clark's removal played out. Late on the same day that Bishop was arrested, Clark announced his resignation and decision to accept the post of Interior Secretary which had opened up four days earlier when the embattled James Watt had resigned. Regarded as the weakest of Reagan's appointments, and reportedly "out of favor" with the president's wife Nancy, Watt sacrificed for the president.

In a speech to the US Chamber of Commerce on September 21, reviewing the Interior Department's coal-leasing program, Watt had responded to a question about the ethnic composition of his department with the statement: "we have every kind of mix you can have. I have a black, I have a woman, two Jews

---

[103] Simpson, *National Security Directives*, 332-34.

[104] Shultz, *Turmoil and Triumph*, 326.

[105] "Joint Command in Key West Ignored in Grenada Planning," *New York Times*, November 9, 1983, A14.

[106] Adkin, *Urgent Fury*, 131.

[107] Cole, *Operation Urgent Fury*, 10-11.

and a cripple. And we have talent."[108] In the resultant furor over his remark, which offended almost every imaginable constituency, Watt sent a letter to the president on October 9 offering his resignation. Watt's resignation immediately opened up a place where the president could shift his old friend, Judge Clark.

Over the next three days the Reagan and new world order factions attempted to press their respective candidates forward as Clark's replacement, with Casey, Weinberger, and Meese arguing for Kirkpatrick and the new world order group arguing for Baker. The issue, however, had already been settled in favor of Robert McFarlane two weeks earlier, when Clark flew to Rome to meet with McFarlane to alert him about his appointment. The rest was simply an exercise in pure theater. The president announced his choice to replace Clark on October 17.[109] Shultz was now securely in control.

Meanwhile, by the middle of October, radio intercepts and spy photographs strongly suggested that the Soviet Union was about to make its move. A US agent on the island relayed photographs of "four thick-walled structures under construction about 800 feet from the new airport runway at Point Salines." The structures were identical to bunkers built in Eastern Europe and Cuba. When members of the Joint Chiefs of Staff saw them, they were convinced that they were "missile-storage facilities" and decided that "something had to be done about Grenada."[110] Had the United States allowed completion of the bunkers, the chiefs believed, "it would have been quite easy for the Soviets to offload some missile batteries from an aircraft and get them into the bunkers before our reconnaissance could get a look."[111]

Confirming these fears were "intercepts of communications from the Soviet Embassy in St. George's in which Soviet Rocket Forces advisers discussed their military construction project at the airfield." (The day after the invasion, congressional intelligence committee sources briefed key members of Congress that "Soviet missile experts" were included in the Soviet delegation to the island, but curiously, no missile specialists were publicly identified as being among the Soviets repatriated, nor were thick-walled bunkers found.)[112] Finally, reflecting communications intercepts from the Soviet high command, "analysts were telling the generals before the invasion that the Soviets might be getting ready to put missiles on Grenada."[113]

---

[108] Cannon, *Role of a Lifetime*, 428.

[109] Constantine Menges, *Inside the National Security Council: The True Story of the Making and Unmaking of Reagan's Foreign Policy* (New York: Simon & Schuster, 1988); 61-62, Cannon, *Role of a Lifetime*, 429-34; and McFarlane, *Special Trust*, 254-56.

[110] Frank Greve, "Spy's Photos Key to Invasion Decision," *Miami Herald*, October 28, 1983, A1.

[111] Frank Greve, "US Battling Defenders in Hills - Missile Sites Were Suspected," *Philadelphia Inquirer*, October 28, 1983, A1.

[112] Greve, "Spy's Photos [. . .]."

[113] Kent Bernhard, "US Sought Missile Link on Grenada," *Philadelphia Inquirer*, November 24, 1983, A24. Later in the spring of 1984, journalist Marvin Liebstone,

All of the above intelligence was leaked to the press in the days leading up to and just after the invasion. Shortly afterward, however, "the leaks stopped when it became apparent that the administration did not plan to dwell on the strategic implications of Soviet involvement."[114] Instead, the administration focused on its discovery of stockpiles of pre-positioned Soviet and Cuban conventional weaponry and the need to rescue the medical students, to explain its reasons for invading Grenada. Here, Secretary of State Shultz prevailed, just as he had in the KAL incident.

Determined to preserve the prospects for détente, which another Caribbean missile crisis would utterly destroy, Shultz downplayed the Soviet role, insisting that it was not "an East-West confrontation."[115] Denying any Soviet plan to deploy missiles into the Caribbean was imperative, because exposing it for what it was would foreclose any possibility of détente for the foreseeable future—it would be the Cuban missile crisis all over again. Moscow's plan to place missiles within decapitating distance of the American homeland would demonstrate the Soviet Union's blatant disdain for any kind of cooperative relationship with the United States, except that of victor over vanquished.

Outmaneuvering the Communists

On the assumption that Cuban troops would accompany if not precede the deployment of SS-20s to Grenada, it was imperative to preempt or deter Castro. Therefore, on October 17, the aircraft carrier *Independence*, loaded with 90 aircraft, and accompanied by 15 ships, departed Norfolk, headed, it was announced, for the Mediterranean. The next day, the helicopter carrier *Guam*, carrying a self-contained assault force, the 22nd Marine Amphibious Unit (MAU) with 1,900 Marines, a squadron of helicopters, landing craft, and five accompanying ships, departed Morehead City, N.C., also bound for the Mediterranean to replace the Marines in Lebanon "sometime next month."[116] They would both eventually fulfill these missions, but not until after they had performed another, more pressing task.

Given the ongoing contingency planning in Norfolk, and the need to get forces to Grenada on short notice, the story that the *Independence* and the *Guam* were actually intended to go directly to the Mediterranean was a clever bit of misdirection. In fact, both ship moves were designed to put US forces within striking distance of Grenada before either Castro or the Soviets could respond.

"Grenada Was a Soviet Dagger Aimed at US Interests," *Baltimore News American*, March 13, 1984, 4, would observe that "Moscow was considering basing SS-20 intermediate range missiles on Grenada, which accounts for the presence of 15 Soviet rocketry experts."

[114] Bernhard, "US Sought Missile Link on Grenada."

[115] Shultz, *Turmoil and Triumph*, 335.

[116] Fred Hiatt, "US Flotilla Stays Near Grenada in Wake of Lebanon Bombings," *Washington Post*, October 25, 1983, A4.

They succeeded. On October 20, the day after Bishop was murdered, and when invasion planning went into high gear, the Joint Chiefs of Staff directed the *Guam* / 22nd MAU to the vicinity of Vieques off Puerto Rico and the *Independence* carrier battle group to the vicinity of Dominica.[117] The news leaked immediately to the press.[118]

For Castro and the Soviets, the rapid appearance of American power precluded any Cuban scheme to send troops to Grenada and threatened to ruin the Soviet plan for the island. The only hope lay in dissuading President Reagan from using American power. Their response was threefold: to portray Grenada as a non-threatening, if repugnant, regime from which even fellow communists had drawn apart; present no hostage threat and offer to cooperate with the United States to evacuate the students; and create a significant diversion, which would focus American power elsewhere. Castro would attend to the first two issues; Moscow the third.

Castro had failed to prevent bloodshed and keep Bishop in power, even as a figurehead. Bishop's brutal elimination, the result of Moscow's haste, had given the United States the opportunity to intervene. It would be Castro's task to attempt to deter American intervention by suasion and keep revolutionary Grenada in the communist camp. Thus, Castro publicly distanced himself from the Revolutionary Military Council (RMC), yet gave them advice on how to avoid intervention; and offered to cooperate with the United States over the evacuation of the students. At the same time, he was at pains to avoid giving Reagan any pretext for attacking Cuba.

On October 20, while issuing a decree proclaiming three days of mourning for Bishop, Castro sent a message to the RMC decrying as totally unjustified "such brutal procedures as the physical elimination of Bishop and the prominent group of honest and worthy leaders who died yesterday." Castro wanted the perpetrators to be disciplined. "The death of Bishop and his comrades must be clarified; and had they been executed in cold blood, those responsible for it deserve exemplary punishment."[119]

Despite the decision to subject "political relations with the new Grenadian leadership" to a "serious and profound analysis," Castro declared that "we shall strictly abide by the principle of non-interference in the internal affairs of Grenada." In the interests of the Grenadian people" we will continue "economic and technical cooperation, where it is possible." Alluding to the approach of American naval forces, Castro warned that "Imperialism will now try to profit from this tragedy."

Two days later, with the *Guam* / 22nd MAU group "visible offshore [of Grenada] on the morning of October 22," Castro and the Grenadian leaders

---

[117] Cole, *Operation Urgent Fury*, 18.

[118] It would not be a surprise if the Walker spy ring, operating out of Norfolk, informed Moscow of ship movements.

[119] Adkin, *Urgent Fury*, 90.

panicked.[120] In response to frantic demands from the RMC for Cuban military support, Castro refused. He justified his decision on the grounds that "approaching" US naval forces could herald a "large-scale Yankee aggression," against not only Grenada, Nicaragua, and Angola, but also "right here in Cuba." If there was an attack on Grenada, it would have been because of the "gross mistakes made on the Grenadian side." Therefore, Castro concluded: "it is not of the new Government of Grenada we must think now, but of Cuba."[121]

Castro's advice was to "try to avoid pretexts for intervention." The regime must offer privately and reiterate publicly "basic guarantees and total facilities for evacuation of personnel from the United States, from England, and so forth." If this did not work and "should the invasion take place anyway, their duty is to die fighting." Castro acknowledged that the political situation created because of the "grave errors" committed by the Grenadian revolutionaries "considerably weaken the defensive capacity of the country." Nevertheless, "the sending of reinforcements is impossible and unthinkable."

Following receipt of Castro's message, a member of the RMC, Christopher Stroude, immediately went to the studio of Radio Free Grenada to announce the regime's new policy. After stalling State Department officials sent to Grenada the day before, Stroude now declared that "efforts made recently to better relations with the United States government would continue." He announced that a civilian government would be established "within ten to fourteen days," which would represent "all social classes and interests." Private investment would be welcomed, especially to build up the tourist industry. However, he made no mention of an offer to assist in the evacuation of the medical students.[122]

That same evening of October 22, apparently trying to remedy Stroude's omission, Castro made a direct appeal to the United States, desperately hoping to convince the American leadership that the students were in no danger and military action was unnecessary. In a message sent at 9:00 p.m., Castro declared:

> The US side is aware of the developments in Grenada, that it is also aware of our position on these developments and of our determination of not interfering in the internal affairs of that country. That we are aware of their concern for the many US residents there. We are also concerned about the hundreds of Cuban collaborators who are working on various projects and about the reports that US naval forces are approaching Grenada. According to our reports, no US or foreign citizen has run into any problems, nor has our personnel met with problems.[123]

---

[120] Clarridge, *Spy for all Seasons*, 250.
[121] LANIC, "Fidel Castro's Press Conference on Grenada, October 26, 1983."
[122] Adkin, *Urgent Fury*, 85.
[123] LANIC, "Fidel Castro's Press Conference on Grenada, October 26, 1983."

Castro then pledged to "maintain contacts" and offered to "cooperate if any type of difficulty arises and so that any measure regarding the security of these persons can be resolved favorably, without violence and without any type of interference in the country." Finally, belatedly heeding Castro's advice, on Monday, October 24, the RMC sent a note to the US embassy in Barbados saying that "Americans on the island were in no danger and would be permitted to leave if they wished."[124] Washington declined to respond.

Castro, of course, was playing the weakest of hands. As he admitted during his press conference, "we were willing to cooperate in any way to safeguard the citizens' security, without resorting to violence or intervention. We might add that this was a most unusual action on our part, to directly address the United States about a real situation." With a straight face, he continued: "I believe that we were doing the United States a service. We were trying to make them understand that this action was unnecessary, because we had information with which we were willing to cooperate in the search for a nonviolent solution, without resorting to intervention, thus guaranteeing the safety of the US citizens in Grenada."[125]

Castro's effort to deter the United States from acting against Grenada was too little, too late. American forces were in place in sufficient strength to defeat any Cuban attempt to reinforce Grenada (perhaps in the manner he had surreptitiously reinforced his ally Agosthino Neto in Angola when he was on the verge of defeat in 1975) and to remove the already disintegrating Communist regime on Grenada.[126] Indeed, one of the rescued students claimed that "had the US Army not intervened when they did, the rumor was that the Cubans would have. Their plan was perhaps a day or a day and a half behind."[127]

Decision in Grenada; Diversion in Beirut

By the time the Soviets and Castro realized that their only hope lay in persuading Reagan there was no need to intervene, the president already had decided to act. Although the approach of American naval forces was impossible to conceal, the administration was successful in dissembling as to the exact timing of American action, or, indeed, whether there would be any action. The president maintained his daily routine, leaving on Friday afternoon, October 21, on a previously scheduled trip to Georgia for a golf outing at the Augusta National Golf Club. Secretary Shultz and National Security Adviser McFarlane accompanied him.

---

[124] Ed Magnuson, "D-Day in Grenada," *Time*, November 7, 1983, 28.

[125]LANIC, "Fidel Castro's Press Conference on Grenada, October 26, 1983."

[126] For the Soviet-Cuban ploy in Angola, see the author's *The Nixon-Kissinger Years: The Reshaping of American Foreign Policy*, 2nd ed. (St. Paul: Paragon House, 2001), chap. 10.

[127] Ward Sinclair, "Student Evacuees Return, Praising US Rescue Effort," *Washington Post*, October 27, 1983, A1.

While the president gave no hint of the momentous decision that was approaching, his national security team was meeting in intense secrecy. Sensitive to Soviet surveillance efforts, as Menges notes, "cabinet members would arrive at the White House complex using different entrances. And none would use the entrance most visible to the White House press corps." Moreover, key meetings were held in the refurbished room 208 in the Old Executive Office Building adjacent to the White House, instead of the "more visible" Situation Room.[128] Security was complete. There were no leaks to the Washington press corps.

The president made the decision to strike early in the morning of October 22, while he was still in Atlanta, shortly after he received word that the OECS, joined by Jamaica and Barbados, voted to request that the United States send a multinational peace-keeping force to Grenada and the Governor General of Grenada, Paul Scoon, sent word asking the OECS "to free his country from the Revolutionary Military Council."[129] Later that morning, while he was on the golf course, the president formalized the decision in a teleconference with the NSPG gathered in the Situation Room.[130]

With requests for intervention in hand, the NSPG now "jettisoned the idea of a peaceful evacuation" of medical students in favor of "a military expedition to seize Grenada from local military forces." Accordingly, the mission statement now went beyond the safe evacuation of American citizens, to the restoration of democratic government in Grenada, in concert with the OECS, Jamaica, and Barbados; and the deterrence of any Cuban attempt at intervention.[131] This last consideration would in fact drive the timing of American action.

Just as plans were being finalized, however, Moscow made a desperate attempt to divert the United States away from Grenada. Early Sunday morning, October 23, in Beirut, two truck bombs, one driven into the US Marine barracks and the other into the French compound, exploded and killed 241 Marines and 56 French soldiers. Although the exact death totals were not immediately known, for the Marines it was the worst single-event loss of life in the history of the Corps.[132] (Although 246 Marines were killed during the Tet offensive in 1968, those losses were spread out over several days.)

Upon being awakened with the news of the bombing, the president immediately returned to Washington, arriving at 8:30 a.m., and plunged into NSPG discussions about the two events. Inevitably, as Adkin notes, "the main

---

[128] Menges, *Inside the National Security Council*, 73.

[129] Cole, *Operation Urgent Fury*, 22-23 and Shultz, *Turmoil and Triumph*, 329-30.

[130] Clarridge, *Spy for all Seasons*, 251.

[131] Curiously, Shultz, *Turmoil and Triumph*, 335, omits the objective of restoring democratic government in Grenada, declaring that the president's plan was to secure the airports and other key installations, rescue American citizens, and deter Cuban intervention.

[132] William Claiborne, "Beirut Blast Kills 146 Marines and 26 French Troops," *Washington Post*, October 24, 1983, A1.

question was whether the awful events in Beirut should affect the decision to intervene in Grenada." The president hesitated. "With so many American lives just lost, could Reagan risk more so soon in a military action he had the power to abort? Momentarily, he considered abandoning the invasion."[133] Then, he said: "If this was right yesterday, it's right today, and we shouldn't let the act of a couple of terrorists dissuade us from going ahead."[134] That evening, the president signed the final copy of the NSDD authorizing action in Grenada and initial, pre-invasion reconnaissance operations began.

Although the president had characterized the perpetrators of the Beirut attacks as "a couple of terrorists," the disaster not only spurred investigations by the Defense Department and Congress, but it also triggered a lengthy discussion about state sponsorship of international terrorism, in which the Soviet Union was perceived to be playing a major role.[135] The discussion would continue for nine months and result in a fateful decision not to label Moscow, but to focus on Syria and Iran as state sponsors of terror in the Middle East.

In view of last-minute intelligence that the Grenadians were attempting to mobilize some 2,000 reservists, combined with an estimated 1,500 regulars and supported by 600 armed Cubans, it was clear that a larger than planned force would be necessary. Accordingly, a multi-service force of 8,000 US troops, comprised of Rangers, Marines, Airborne, and Special Forces, was rapidly assembled to invade Grenada on October 25.[136] To discourage any interference by Castro, F-15s deployed earlier to Ramey Air Force Base in Puerto Rico flew conspicuous "aerial surveillance operations between Cuba and Grenada," beginning on the 24th.[137]

Providing Cover for Thatcher

On Monday evening, October 24, the president issued the final "go" order to set in motion the invasion, which would begin the next morning. Then, he set about the task of briefing the five top members of Congress on his decision. Careful not to alert reporters that "something unusual was astir," presidential aides quietly got in touch with House Speaker Tip O'Neill (D-MA), Majority Leader Jim Wright (D-TX), and Minority Leader Bob Michel (R-IL); and Senate Majority Leader Howard Baker (R-TN), and Minority Leader Robert Byrd (D-WV), telling them that the president wished to see them. They "quietly slipped

---

[133] Magnuson, "D-Day in Grenada."

[134] Adkin, *Urgent Fury*, 121

[135] For the investigations, see Margaret Shapiro, "Pentagon Report Said to Attack 'Poor Judgment' in Beirut Blast," *Washington Post*, December 23, 1983, A20 and "House Unit Faults US Security in October 23 Bombing," *Washington Post*, December 20, 1983, A1. For the beginning of the discussions about state-sponsored terrorism, see Thomas Friedman, "State-Sponsored Terror Called a Threat to US," *New York Times*, December 30, 1983, A1.

[136] Cole, *Operation Urgent Fury*, 23-26.

[137] Ibid., 3, 32.

into the White House through the old Executive Office Building to the White House basement and up a back stair" to the family sitting room in the president's quarters.[138] As Weinberger described it:

> The president opened with a brief but thorough summary of the situation, emphasizing the risks to the American students, the evidence we had of growing Cuban involvement, the increasing madness of the regime presently in power in Grenada, as exemplified in the twenty-four-hour shoot-on-sight curfew, the risk of extensive and violent civil war there, and the knowledge we had had for a long time of both Soviet and Cuban involvement in the island itself, beyond the building of the new airfield. And, of course, he emphasized the plight of our students and our fears they might all be held as hostages, or worse. The President reported on the urgent plea that had come to us from the neighboring Eastern Caribbean islands, and concluded, 'I feel we have absolutely no alternative but to comply with this request. I think the risks of not moving are far greater than the risks of taking the action we have planned.'[139]

Briefings by Secretaries Shultz and Weinberger, Bill Casey and Joint Chiefs of Staff Chairman Jack Vessey on various aspects of the invasion plan produced a predictable response. The Democrats "were cool," and the Republicans supportive, if understandably worried. O'Neill thought an invasion "premature," Wright thought the situation "wasn't clear enough yet." Byrd asked about the kind of opposition US forces would face. Michel deferred to the president's judgment, while Baker offered "full support."[140] Shultz, however, thought Baker "seemed worried."[141] The president enjoined them to secrecy.

During their discussion, Speaker O'Neill recounts how he asked the president: "What does Mrs. Thatcher think about all this?" The president replied: "She doesn't know about it." O'Neill wondered how the United States could "go into Grenada without informing her?" In his view, "in all their excitement about the invasion, the White House had overlooked the British connection." He goes on to observe that "sure enough, as we left the meeting, Bob Michel, the House Republican leader, told me that the president was already on the phone with Margaret Thatcher. We could hear Reagan's side of the conversation, and from his fumbling and his apologies it was obvious that she was enraged."[142]

---

[138] Magnuson, "D-Day in Grenada," 28.

[139] Weinberger, *Fighting for Peace*, 118-19. In Weinberger's account, the president makes no mention of a request from Gov. General Paul Scoon.

[140] McFarlane, *Special Trust*, 264.

[141] Shultz, *Turmoil and Triumph*, 335.

[142] Thomas P. O'Neill, *Man of the House: The Life and Political Memoirs of Speaker Tip O'Neill* (New York: Random House, 1987), 366.

In addition to O'Neill's, several other accounts allege that a conversation between the president and Mrs. Thatcher occurred. There is, however, substantial grounds for believing that the conversation, if it in fact occurred, was a staged event for the benefit of the Democratic congressmen to give plausible deniability to Thatcher. Aside from the significant variations about the event that participants in the meeting have offered, there is the most important fact of presidential protoColonel

It is unheard of for a president to permit outsiders, especially those of the opposition party, to eavesdrop on a privileged conversation, as the president's conversation with Thatcher most certainly was. Indeed, the Democratic leaders' knowledge of Thatcher's objections should only have strengthened their own, which they had been expressing. Could there have been a reason for the president to arrange for the congressional leadership to overhear a "livid" Margaret Thatcher dressing down the American president and rejecting any role in the coming invasion?

From the very beginning of the planning process regarding Grenada it was obvious that an American invasion would have negative political implications for the position of the United Kingdom within the Commonwealth. Barbados, a member of the Commonwealth, had granted the United States "unrestricted use" of its international airport.[143] Barbados and Jamaica, another member, were providing military contingents. There was no possibility that British intelligence would not have known of these developments as they were happening, even if Washington had deliberately chosen to keep the British government "in the dark" about its intention to invade Grenada.[144]

In fact, the United States had requested British assistance in the invasion, which was refused.[145] Thatcher would not agree to a second intervention in the Western Hemisphere within two years, and against a member of the Commonwealth. There being no completely satisfactory solution, I believe that the president, if not both Thatcher and Reagan, decided to minimize any erosion of British influence by demonstrating her ignorance of and opposition to US plans. The alternative, acknowledging complicity, would have severely damaged Britain's standing among the Commonwealth nations. The key issue was how to make credible the argument that Britain was "in the dark" about US plans.[146]

President Reagan provided the necessary political cover with the old ploy of having a supposedly privileged conversation overheard by third parties who could then "verify" its occurrence, if not its content. Support for this

---

[143] Adkin, *Urgent Fury*, 143, 122-23. The British high commissioner's office in Barbados kept London fully informed.

[144] Bill Proctor, "We'll Always Have Grenada," *Foreign Affairs* 85, no. 6 (November-December 2006). See also Payne et al., *Grenada*, 151-54; and Adkin, *Urgent Fury*, 96-98.

[145] Payne et al., *Grenada*, 151-54.

[146] Gary Williams, "'A Matter of Regret': Britain, the 1983, Grenada Crisis, and the Special Relationship," *Twentieth Century British History* 12, no. 2 (2001): 228.

interpretation lies in the differing accounts of when the congressmen arrived for the briefing, whether there actually was a phone call, who called whom, and when. On the first point, Reagan, Shultz, and O'Neill say the Congress members arrived around 8:00 p.m.; McFarlane says it was an hour later, at 9:00 p.m. and Weinberger mentions no specific time. Different recollections of arrival time could be attributed to faulty memory.

Differences widen on the second point. Reagan, Shultz, and McFarlane all say that Thatcher called while the congressional leaders were present. Weinberger, however, flatly contradicts them, saying not only that the phone call came "after they left," but also that Reagan called Thatcher.[147] Tip O'Neill supports Weinberger, implying that Reagan called Thatcher just "as we [the congressmen] left the meeting" and noted that "we could hear Reagan's side of the conversation, and from his fumbling and his apologies it was obvious that she was enraged."[148]

Thatcher herself says that she sent a cable and followed up with a telephone call around 7:00 p.m., which would have been well before the congressmen had arrived.[149] Among scholarly accounts, Smith places Thatcher's call even earlier, at 5:00 p.m..[150] Payne, Sutton, and Thorndyke say that Thatcher called Reagan much later, at midnight.[151] Adkin, on the other hand, delving into great detail, says that Thatcher sent a cable that evening, but did not place a telephone call until three o'clock the following morning, not the evening before.[152]

Thus, Thatcher's call on the evening of October 24, if it occurred, was a staged event to provide political cover for the United Kingdom to preserve its relations with the Commonwealth states. Without it, given the centrality of Barbados's participation in the invasion, Commonwealth leaders would have justifiably assumed British complicity. As Proctor, Clerk of the House of Commons Foreign Affairs Committee from 1982 to 1987, notes: "The United Kingdom's relations with most of the 'nonwhite' Commonwealth would have

---

[147] Ronald Reagan, *An American Life* (New York: Simon & Schuster, 1990), 454-55, says he briefed the congressmen "shortly after eight" and Thatcher's call came "just before nine." Shultz, *Turmoil and Triumph*, 334, concurring, says there was a call, which came mid-way through the briefing to congressional leaders, who had arrived "about eight o'clock." McFarlane, *Special Trust*, 264-65, implies that the congressmen arrived at nine and that "before the meeting was over, President Reagan was called out to the telephone. Prime Minister Thatcher was returning his earlier call from London."

[148] O'Neill, *Man of the House*, 366.

[149] Margaret Thatcher, *Downing Street Years* (New York: Harper Collins, 1993), 331, says she called the president about 7:00 p.m. Washington time, daylight saving time having begun the previous weekend.

[150] Goeffrey Smith, *Reagan and Thatcher* (New York: Norton, 1991), 126.

[151] Payne et al., *Grenada*, 153.

[152] Adkin, *Urgent Fury*, 122.

been seriously damaged had the British been suspected of having had any part in the operation. Thus, in the long run the White House did Downing Street a good turn."[153]

The Invasion of Grenada

The invasion of Grenada succeeded, thanks to the command decision to apply overwhelming force against a strategically isolated target. Within that context, the quick thinking of on-scene commanders, their ability to improvise as the action unfolded, and the ingenuity and mobility of the troops on the ground were key factors accounting for success. At the same time, the determination to put forces into Grenada as quickly as possible explained the greater-than-normal flaws in planning and execution, which at times conveyed the impression of a Keystone Kops routine.[154] Indeed, the troops themselves did not know they would be invading Grenada until the last minute, as "all participating units were…alerted for an exercise, not an operation, to help prevent leaks." [155]

Problems arose even before the first shot was fired. The invasion was supposed to occur at night, but air control and reconnaissance teams failed to make a pre-invasion landing, causing delays and loss of the advantage of darkness. Surprise, of course, had been lost days earlier, as an attack was expected. Nevertheless, at daybreak on October 25, 800 Army and 400 Marine air assault forces seized the two airports, Pearls in the northeast part of the island and Point Salines in the southwest. The Marines mounted a heliborne assault and quickly took control of Pearls against minimal resistance but Point Salines was a different story. Nearly all of the action in the invasion of Grenada occurred in the five square-mile area bounded by Point Salines and St. George's, the capital.

Army Rangers, originally intending to land in fixed-wing aircraft on the Point Salines runway, on approach found it blocked with construction equipment and other obstacles. In one of a string of improvisations, the Rangers parachuted in, but in doing so, encountered stiff resistance from Cuban troops dug in at several strong points around the airport and to the north. Despite Castro's later claim that the Cubans "were not the first to fire," the Rangers "jumped into a hail of red and green enemy tracers that cut through the air all around them. Although enemy fire damaged some of the planes, none of the men were hit."[156]

The Cubans were prepared. On the day before the invasion, Castro had flown in a small military advisory group led by Pedro Tortolo, who had recently

---

[153] Proctor, "We'll Always Have Grenada."

[154] Fred Hiatt, "Accidents, 'Friendly Fire' Blamed for Many US Casualties in Grenada," *Washington Post*, November 1, 1983, A1.

[155] Adkin, *Urgent Fury*, 134.

[156] Richard Meislin, "Castro Says the Coup in Grenada 'Opened Doors' to US Invasion," *New York Times*, November 15, 1983, A1; and General William W. Hartzog, *American Military Heritage* (Washington, DC: Center of Military History, US Army, 2001), 226.

headed Cuba's military mission to Grenada, to organize the defense. Despite the brief time for preparation, the Cubans constructed defensive positions at Point Salines, Grand Mal, Grand Anse, Frequente, and Fort Frederick, in addition to their barracks area at Camp Calivigny. To the extreme disappointment of General Austin, however, Tortolo reaffirmed that Castro would not send reinforcements and worse, that Cuban troops would not deploy with PRA units, but only defend themselves.[157] Militarily overmatched, Castro, it seems, wanted to avoid giving the United States any pretext for an attack against Cuba.

The Cuban force was a combination of combat troops (the 240-man contingent that had arrived aboard the *Vietnam Heroica* on October 6) and construction workers (the 500 workers building the airport). Including embassy and aid personnel, there were a total of 784 Cubans on the island.[158] The construction workers were from one of Cuba's Production and Defense Brigades, all of which are organized along military lines.[159] Captured table of organization charts, for example, depicted "company A and B, mortar company, and machine-gun company."[160] Most of the personnel were former combat veterans too old for military service. According to Cole, when interrogated, it was learned that "many of the Cubans had fought for Castro in Ethiopia and Angola."[161]

Under intense fire from Cuban forces dug in north of the airport, Rangers quickly improvised, hot-wiring a bulldozer and other vehicles to clear the runway, which permitted circling C-130 cargo planes protected by hovering gunships to send in the remainder of the 1,900-man invasion force and its equipment. Over the next several hours, fierce fighting ensued, but with ammunition stocks exhausted, 250 Grenadian and Cuban troops, whom Castro had ordered to fight to the death, had surrendered.

Although the Rangers had seized the Point Salines airport, the western end of the runway was still incomplete, surfaced only with gravel and oil, and there were no lights. This meant that C-130s could utilize the field, but the larger C-141 Starlifters, with longer runway requirements, could only fly in during the daylight hours.[162] Nevertheless, with the airport secure, additional troops, equipment, and supplies poured in. Over the next few hours, these aircraft flew in 4,000 more troops, including two battalions of the 82nd airborne division, and a

---

[157] Adkin, *Urgent Fury*, 205.

[158] Castro would later provide a detailed listing of 784 Cuban personnel, minimizing the military contingent, in order to refute the charge that Cuba was preparing to take over the island. See *Granma*, November 6, 1983. American officials decided not to contest the Cuban numbers, but consistently expressed the view that there had been more than a thousand Cubans on the island. See Richard Halloran, "US Won't Dispute Havana on Tally," *New York Times*, October 31, 1983, 1.

[159] More than 3.5 million Cuban citizens are organized into over 60,000 Production and Defense Brigades, roughly 600 to a brigade.

[160] Weinberger, *Fighting for Peace*, 124.

[161] Cole, *Operation Urgent Fury*, 43.

[162] Ibid., 223.

300-man Caribbean police contingent made up of troops from Jamaica, Barbados, Dominica, St. Lucia, Antigua, and St. Vincent, to secure victory.

A crucial objective was to ensure the safety of Governor-General, Paul Scoon, who was under house arrest. Scoon was considered to be the remaining source of political legitimacy and the essential building block for a post-invasion political system. It was also vital to gain his belated signature on the letter requesting the "assistance" of outside forces, including the United States, to restore order on the island. Toward this end, a dozen special forces troops parachuted into his residential compound, but, once inside, found themselves surrounded by Grenadian troops and forced to spend a harrowing night defending the residence and its valuable occupants.

Early the next morning, in yet another improvisation, two companies of the Marine assault force from Pearls, augmented with five tanks, and a dozen amphibious vehicles, were transported around the island to Grand Mal Bay, just north of St. George's, where they made an amphibious landing. Their mission was to rescue the governor-general and secure the capital. The noise of their tracked vehicles as they approached was enough to convince the Grenadian troops surrounding the governor-general's residence to beat a hasty retreat after firing a few shots.

Scoon and his wife were whisked off by helicopter to the USS *Guam*, and later in the afternoon flown back to Grenada and provided accommodations in a secure house near Point Salines. There, he signed the backdated letter, formally requesting military intervention.[163] Then, using a secret communications channel to London set up by the CIA, Scoon "received instructions establishing him as the nucleus of an interim regime."[164] He would shortly name an advisory commission comprised of bankers, lawyers, and other non-political Grenadians to act as an interim government until elections could be held.

Meanwhile, paralleling these developments, within two hours of the initial air drop, the Rangers secured the True Blue campus of the St. George's medical school, located just off the eastern end of the Point Salines runway. To their great relief, no hostages had been taken and no one was harmed. However, relief turned quickly to chagrin when they discovered that True Blue contained fewer than half of the students. The others, they were told, were at a second campus, at Grand Anse, a mile north on the coastal road leading to St. George's.

Setting off for Grand Anse, the Rangers encountered the Cuban strongpoint at Frequente, causing further delay, but producing another improvisation. Instructed to avoid civilian casualties to the extent possible, commanders decided to go around the Cuban strongpoint rather than charging through it, instead taking a detour by sea. Late the next afternoon, October 26, a combined Marine and Ranger force mounted a heliborne landing on the beach at Grand Anse, reached the school and safely transported over 200 students to the *Guam*.

---

[163] Ibid., 256.
[164] Ibid., 47.

In the process of evacuating the students, however, US troops learned of yet a third group of some 200 students scattered in off-campus housing on the Lance aux Epines peninsula southwest of the True Blue campus. These would not be evacuated, or many even located, until after the main combat operations had concluded on the 28th. As it was, many students never left Grenada. All told, US forces evacuated 599 American citizens of a reported 1,100; and 121 foreigners. The cost in casualties was low. For the US, there were 19 killed and 116 wounded; for Cuba, 25 killed, 59 wounded; and for Grenada, there were 45 killed and 358 wounded.

Denying Moscow the "Analogous" Option

The Reagan administration would struggle to justify the invasion against its critics, sliding from one rationale to another. The most persuasive vindication was the reaction of students who were returned to the United States. On October 27, when the first of the evacuees, Jeff Geller, landed at Charleston, South Carolina, he "dropped to his knees and kissed the runway," cheered the United States, and "thanked the US military for rescuing them from a chaotic and dangerous situation."[165]

This was enough to quell the administration's more vocal critics, and the actual reason for the invasion—to forestall a Soviet missile deployment—was never mentioned. Nor was the overriding fact that in a swift and bold strike, the United States had administered what Crozier described as the Soviet Union's "first strategic defeat," eliminating any possibility that Moscow could carry out its repeated threat to make an "analogous" deployment of missiles to counter that of the Pershing II.[166]

On the morning of the invasion, President Reagan announced that he had authorized it to "protect innocent lives [and] forestall further chaos," and to restore "democratic institutions" in the wake of the bloody coup by a "brutal group of leftist thugs." After receiving reports that "a large number of our citizens were seeking to escape the island…I concluded I had no choice but to act strongly and decisively." [167] Secretary Shultz, too, referred to an "atmosphere of violent uncertainty . . . that caused anxiety among US citizens." The president, said Shultz,

> felt that it was better under the circumstances to act before [Americans] might be hurt or taken hostage than to take any

---

[165] Ward Sinclair, "Student Evacuees Return, Praising US Rescue Effort," *Washington Post*, October 27, 1983, A1 and Fred Barnes, "Student Views Held Vindicating Reagan," *Baltimore Sun*, October 28, 1983, A1.

[166] Brian Crozier, *The Rise and Fall of the Soviet Empire* (Roseville, CA: The Forum, 2000), 370.

[167] Patrick Tyler and David Hoffman, "US Says Aim Is to Restore Order," *Washington Post*, October 26, 1983, A1.

chance given the great uncertainty clearly present in the situation.[168]

Shultz averred that US action did not violate the OAS Charter, which prohibits intervention in each other's internal affairs. The OECS mutual security treaty of 1981, he said, "justified the United States working in concert with Grenada's neighbors to eliminate the threat of a potentially more hostile government there." A senior White House official declared that "Grenada itself had acknowledged in recent weeks that it effectively had no government, thus providing a legal basis for triggering the collective security provision of the OECS treaty" without Grenada's participation.[169]

The administration's rationale quickly shifted to a "rescue mission" after discovery of a purported Cuban plan to take over the island and hold the students hostage. Captured documents, the administration said, showed that "Cuba planned to send hundreds of troops to Grenada within the next several weeks and expected to carry out a major expansion of its presence in Grenada before the end of the year." Some officials also suggested that the Cuban forces encountered in the invasion had been "rushed to Grenada last weekend after a flotilla of United States warships headed into the Eastern Caribbean."[170] This would of course explain the administration's determination to get there first.

But the president and his secretary of state differed sharply over the Soviet role in Grenada. Shultz declared that the action was not intended to "send a message" to the Soviets or Cubans.[171] He also declared that this was "not an East-West confrontation," by which he also meant to emphasize that it was not a US-Soviet confrontation.[172] That, however, was not how the president saw it. In his address to the nation on the 27th, when victory was certain, Reagan explicitly saw Moscow behind not only the events in Grenada, but also in Lebanon, and he saw them as "closely related."

> The events in Lebanon and Grenada, though oceans apart, are closely related. Not only has Moscow assisted and encouraged the violence in both countries, but it provides direct support through a network of surrogates and terrorists. It is no coincidence that when the thugs tried to wrest control of

---

[168] Tyler and Hoffman, "US Says Aim Is to Restore Order."

[169] Ibid.

[170] Philip Taubman, "US Reports Evidence of Island Hostage Plan," *New York Times*, October 28, 1983, A14.

[171] Jim Hoagland, "US Invades Grenada, Fights Cubans; Reagan Cites Protection of US Citizens," *Washington Post*, October 26, 1983, A1.

[172] Shultz, *Turmoil and Triumph*, 335.

Grenada, there were 30 Soviet advisers and hundreds of Cuban military and paramilitary forces on the island.[173]

In these brief sentences, the president raised, but understated, the multiple issues of the communist presence on the island, how Lebanon and Grenada were related, and Soviet state support for international terrorism. Moreover, no doubt at the insistence of Shultz, he made no mention of the SS-20 issue and sharply downplayed the communist factor. While Reagan had mentioned 30 Soviet advisers, there were actually 49, the difference probably being the rocket specialists who were never identified publicly. In addition to these, there were reportedly 784 Cubans, 24 North Koreans, 16 East Germans, 14 Bulgarians, and three or four Libyans.[174] There was a foreign Communist presence in every department of Grenadian government and armed forces.

The president juxtaposed but did not draw the obvious conclusion from the events in Lebanon and Grenada. Indeed, the Russians and their supporters quickly argued that the president acted in Grenada to offset the loss in Lebanon.[175] However, even a cursory glance at the chronology would demonstrate the invalidity of that suggestion. Rather, if Moscow were pulling the strings in both places as the president said, then it was the Soviets who had triggered the events in Lebanon to affect the president's decision in Grenada.

Although the president implied that Soviet state support for international terrorism was widespread, he limited his charge that Moscow provided "direct support through a network of surrogates and terrorists" to Lebanon and Grenada. In Grenada, he focused on the Cubans and their presumed plan to turn the island into a "Soviet-Cuban colony being readied as a major military bastion to export terror and undermine democracy." His conclusion that "we got there just in time," was likewise left undeveloped, but clearly implied that there had been a race to determine who would get to Grenada first, which, of course, was precisely the case.[176]

A large part of the difficulty in determining the truth was the veil of secrecy placed by the administration over the invasion. Except for the information released by the government itself, the general public received no independent

---

[173] "Transcript of Address by President on Lebanon and Grenada," *New York Times*, October 28, 1983, A10.

[174] "The Battle for Grenada," *Newsweek*, November 7, 1983, 76. Marvin Liebstone, "Grenada Was a Soviet Dagger Aimed at US Interests," *Baltimore News American*, March 13, 1984, 4, would observe that "Moscow was considering basing SS-20 intermediate range missiles on Grenada, which accounts for the presence of 15 Soviet rocketry experts."

[175] Dusko Doder, "Moscow Assails Reagan for Grenada Invasion," *Washington Post*, October 26, 1983, A22. "Soviet sources said privately they believe the decision to send American forces into Grenada was prompted by Reagan's efforts to obscure what they consider the failure of his Middle East policy."

[176] "Transcript of Address by President."

reporting and knew nothing of the tense and extremely significant drama that played out on Grenada. In an unprecedented decision, the press was excluded from the island. Those who managed to make their way there were promptly escorted to the *Guam*.[177] The Federal Communications Commission even prohibited the lone Ham radio operator on the island, one of the medical students, from sending information to the outside. Only after two days was a press pool, limited to 15 reporters, permitted to move about the island on "guided afternoon tours."[178]

The obvious question, asked by *New York Times* reporter Anthony Lewis, was: what was the president hiding? While Lewis asked the right question, he came up with the wrong answer. In his view, "Mr. Reagan was afraid that the facts on the ground would not support the reasons he gave for the invasion."[179] Yet the reverse would have been true, had circumstances allowed. However, during the two days in which US forces had complete control of the island, all evidence of Soviet/Cuban construction or infrastructure relating to the emplacement of missiles was either destroyed or removed.

Although censorship on the island was total, that was not completely the case in Washington. One enterprising journalist, Frank Greve, unearthed key details about the missile question. In an article appearing in the *Philadelphia Inquirer* on October 28, Greve quoted Pentagon and congressional Intelligence Committee sources, to reveal that there had been photographic evidence of "missile bunkers" on the island identical to those found in "Cuba, Poland, East Germany, and the Soviet Union." He also revealed the existence of radio intercepts in which "Soviet rocket-force advisers discussed their military construction project at the airfield."[180]

It would be almost two months before another article appeared on the missile question, also in the *Philadelphia Inquirer*. Kent Bernhard noted the pre-invasion "concern in some quarters of the government that facilities which could be used for missiles were being prepared." Reviewing the photographic and radio intercept data, he asked: "Did the United States expect to find the beginning of Soviet missile installations on the tiny east Caribbean island?" The answer was important, he said, because "it might add another facet to the motivation for the operation that President Reagan now calls a 'rescue.'"[181]

---

[177] Jim Hoagland, "US Troops Remove Reporters from Island," *Washington Post*, October 27, 1983, A19.

[178] William Farrell, "US Allows 15 Reporters to Go to Grenada for Day," *New York Times*, October 28, 1983, A13 and Fred Hiatt and David Hoffman, "US Drops Estimate of Cubans on Island," *Washington Post*, October 30, 1983, A1.

[179] Anthony Lewis, "What Was He Hiding?" *New York Times*, October 31, 1983, A19.

[180] Frank Greve, "Missile Sites Were Suspected," *Philadelphia Inquirer*, October 28, 1983, 1.

[181] Kent Bernhard, "US Sought Missile Link on Grenada," *Philadelphia Inquirer*, November 24, 1983, A24.

While "debate over eventual Soviet-Cuban intentions is still reported in the intelligence community," Bernhard said, the official explanation the administration settled on was that the Soviets and the Cubans planned to make Grenada a base for the export of terrorism. Why not truthfully explain the invasion as a preemptive strike to block deployment of missiles? The answer is that exposing the Soviet role would foreclose indefinitely any possibility of a move toward détente. It would be the Cuban missile crisis all over again, this time in Grenada, and reveal the Soviet intent to seek a strategic weapons advantage over the United States.

For the same reason, the administration would make no reference to the presumed 1962 "understanding" after the Cuban missile crisis. Shultz, in particular, wanted no suggestion that Grenada had been a US-Soviet confrontation. As Rowland Evans and Robert Novak, who raised the issue of the 1962 understandings observed, "the State Department, struggling to keep Washington-Moscow channels open amid renewed Cold War, objects to accusing the Soviets of treaty-breaking on the Caribbean, just as it does on arms control."[182]

But the game was not over. Whatever the secretary of state envisioned, reality had a way of seeping through. The US invasion of Grenada had preserved the status quo; the coming Pershing II deployment, if successful, would tip the balance in favor of the Western Alliance, not only ensuring Western Europe's security, but also America's. The question the Reagan leadership grappled with after Grenada was: would the Soviet Union find a way to preempt the Pershing II deployment? Would an arms control settlement negate deployment at the last moment? Would a military-dominated Soviet leadership, on the verge of losing strategic weapons superiority, resort to war in desperation to keep it? Finally, where was Andropov?

---

[182] Rowland Evans and Robert Novak, "Why Use Makeshift Rationales?" *Washington Post*, October 31, 1983, A13.

Chapter 5

Deployment to West Germany:
A Pershing Sword of Damocles

The US invasion of Grenada, the first defeat of a Soviet client, was not only a severe blow to Soviet strategy, but it was executed with a degree of strategic deception that shook the confidence of the Soviet leadership to the core. The Soviets had not expected the kind of response the Reagan administration had made. Indeed, Moscow had telegraphed its move so often that it seemed to have assumed that the United States would take little or no action to prevent the SS-20 deployment to Grenada, in advance of the US deployment of the Pershing II to West Germany.

Had it been successful, the Grenada deployment would have offered Moscow at least three possibilities. The first, a negotiated withdrawal of the SS-20 from the Caribbean in exchange for no deployment of the Pershing II to West Germany, which would have left Western Europe defenseless and the Soviet Union dominant in the region. The second, more ambitious but also more dangerous: an attempt to force cancellation of the Pershing II deployment under threat of war, which would give Moscow the advantage in both places. And finally, the deployment of weapons to both places, which would have left both countries with strategic swords of Damocles poised over each other, in effect a mutually neutralizing, if not paralyzing, outcome.

Instead, with the Grenadian option denied, Moscow now faced the worst of all possible situations. Once deployed, Washington would hold the Pershing sword of Damocles over Moscow, with Moscow wielding no analogous tool against the United States, and, moreover, dramatically reducing the Soviet threat to both Western Europe and the United States. Under this circumstance, Moscow's best option would be to accept the proposal Washington had been offering: to negotiate the withdrawal of both weapons, leaving both the Soviet Union and Western Europe with zero intermediate-range missiles, the object of the Pershing deployment in the first place.

The question was: would the Soviets attempt to prevent the deployment of the Pershing II in order to preserve their advantage, and, if so, how? The question went to the very heart of Moscow's response to the Reagan administration's efforts to eliminate the Soviet strategic weapons advantage. The president had publicly delineated a straightforward program to accomplish this objective in two ways: through the deployment of a variety of counterforce weapons, of which the Pershing II was the first; and through SDI, the construction of a ballistic missile defense, on which early testing was already beginning.

In short, the end of Soviet strategic weapons advantage, which Moscow had labored for two decades to build, was in sight. After the Pershing II/Cruise Missile deployments would come the MX, then the B1 bomber followed by the Stealth bomber, and the Trident II submarine armed with the D5 missile. Regardless of the Soviet response, by the late 1980s, the United States would have erased the Soviet Union's strategic weapons advantage. Indeed, the Soviet leadership was faced with the same situation that the American leadership had faced in the 1960s following the Cuban missile crisis, when the Soviet Union acted to eliminate the strategic weapons advantage the United States had then held.

There are four possible responses for the nation losing advantage. First, is to build additional weapons to maintain relative position. Second, is to strike preemptively before the adversary catches up. Third, is to acquiesce to the inevitable. And fourth, is to build a missile defense. The Soviet leadership had decided upon a mix of all of these. They would heighten the threat of war, including the prospects of a preemptive strike, in hope of deterring the United States from continuing its programs; build additional weapons, although resources were dwindling and technology lacking; continue to move as quickly as possible on their own missile defense system; but ultimately acquiesce in the elimination of their strategic weapons advantage.

Within the context of the war scare from fall 1983 through spring 1984, Soviet bluster against the United States and Western Europe over the Pershing II and Cruise Missile deployments screened Moscow's attempt to gain control over Middle Eastern oil—the geopolitical prize sought since the fall of the shah. The Soviets sought to use the war scare, the threat of war, in two principal ways: as a military deterrent against precipitate US action and as a political instrument to insert a wedge between Western Europe and the United States. Moscow's war scare had failed as a deterrent with regard to Grenada but would be attempted again in the end game over deployment of the Pershing II and, more so, when the Iran-Iraq conflict reached a climactic point in the spring of 1984.

To recapitulate: in the Iran-Iraq conflict, the Soviets were playing a double game, supporting both sides. Having fostered an Iran-Syria alliance, Moscow urged Iran to invade Iraq in a final attempt to destroy Saddam Hussein's regime. At the same time, with their position in Afghanistan and the active arming of Saddam, the Soviets ensured that Iran could not succeed. Thus, they could weaken Iran through attrition, then spur their allies in the Tudeh party to overthrow Ayatollah Khomeini's regime. Soviet military pressure along the Iranian border and SS-20 deployments also enabled Moscow to generate both conventional and nuclear weapons pressure against the Tehran regime.

By the spring of 1984, however, Soviet strategy had failed. Not only had Soviet bluster not inhibited Washington from deployment of the Pershing II, but also the Khomeini regime avoided the attrition trap set by Moscow. When the Soviets perceived the failure of their strategy, they promptly discarded it, switching to a new strategy of friendly relations with the United States, even while covertly continuing to pursue the same geopolitical objectives. Indeed, with no hope of succeeding in direct competition against the United States, the Soviets turned to the indirect strategy of supporting international terrorism against the United States and its allies, even while offering a friendly face.

Arms Control Negotiations Endgame

The Reagan leadership, of course, did not know how the Soviets would react to the gradual but ineluctable elimination of their strategic weapons advantage, and so had to be alert to all possibilities. The Soviets had immediately understood the strategic significance of the US invasion of Grenada and on its second day, put forward a seemingly conciliatory arms control offer. At the same time, they pulled out all the stops on the propaganda front in an effort to generate European popular revulsion against deployment that would cause its cancellation.

As a matter of negotiating strategy, Washington had expected a Soviet offer before deployment began, but was somewhat surprised that it came so soon. Some thought it was timed "to exploit the negative impact of the Grenada invasion in Europe," and it may have been partly that, but it was more likely that Moscow hoped to affect the deliberations of the NATO Nuclear Planning Group, then conducting a ministerial meeting in Montebello, Canada, to consider missile deployment.[1] (The NPG would issue its communiqué two days later on October 28.)

The Soviet statement, issued in Andropov's name, announced three new proposals. The first was that the Soviet Union was prepared to reduce its SS-20 deployment aimed at Western Europe to 140 missiles (420 warheads), down from the previous offer of 162. He reaffirmed an earlier pledge to "liquidate," and not merely redeploy, all missiles eliminated in an agreement. Finally, he said that Moscow was prepared to reduce the numbers of medium-range, nuclear-capable aircraft to levels "substantially differing from earlier proposals," which the United States had rejected.[2]

Although designed to demonstrate Moscow's "flexibility," the so-called offer still required that the United States cancel its deployment. In other words, Moscow's position was still zero for the United States. Moreover, the statement was ambiguous about the Soviet attitude toward the talks. On the one hand, it was categorical in declaring that the arms control talks would collapse when the

---

[1] Dusko Doder, "Andropov Offers New Cut in SS20s," *Washington Post*, October 27, 1983, A1.

[2] "Andropov Makes New Arms Offers for Geneva Talks," *New York Times*, October 27, 1983, A1. The proposals were published by *Pravda* as Andropov's replies to questions posed by the newspaper. The Soviet leader had not appeared in public since the previous August. For the full text, see "Andropov Replies to Pravda Questions on INF," *Foreign Broadcast Information Service (FBIS) Daily Report, Soviet Union*, October 27, 1983, AA 1.

United States began to deploy its missiles, but, at the same time, was ambiguous about the meaning of the terms "start" and "deployment." The statement said, "the Geneva talks can be continued if the United States does not start the actual deployment of the missiles."[3]

Clearly, the Soviets were hoping to induce a postponement of missile deployment, but the immediate question was: what was meant by "start"? In the Geneva negotiations, where the Soviet offer was scrutinized in detail, it soon transpired that it was the "de facto stationing" of the missiles, not the Bundestag vote to deploy them, that would trigger the end of the talks.[4] In other words, it would not be the West German vote to deploy that triggered the end of the talks, but when the United States deployed actual weapons—in fact a meaningless distinction, as the two actions would be closely connected, but it served Soviet interests to separate Bonn from the equation.

If the Soviets hoped that their latest offer would be seen as demonstrating "flexibility," they would be disappointed. The NATO final communiqué declared that compared to the flexibility of the US approach,

> the Soviet Union has not yet demonstrated similar flexibility. Each Soviet modification of their original proposal made so far would have the same basic outcome: the prohibition of any NATO LRINF missile deployments while the Soviet Union retained a monopoly in such missiles.[5]

Therefore, it was to be expected, as reiterated by the NATO ministers earlier in the communiqué, that "in the absence of a concrete arms control agreement...deployment of a mixed force of ballistic and cruise missiles as decided in the dual-track decision of 1979 will begin by the end of the year."

To demonstrate the West's own flexibility and "to help the West German government fend off rising political pressures" to postpone or cancel the imminent missile deployment, the Nuclear Planning Group announced that over the next six years, "1,400 of the 6,000 US tactical nuclear warheads now deployed with allied forces in Europe will be removed."[6] The Reagan administration also began to leak word that it would soon offer another compromise proposal, reportedly along the lines of the "walk in the woods" construct presented by US negotiator Paul Nitze the previous year.[7] All of this, of course, was designed to ensure a favorable vote in the West German Bundestag on November 22. As we will see below, the Soviets would attempt to turn this notion to advantage.

---

[3] Doder, "Andropov Offers New Cut in SS20s."
[4] Strobe Talbott, *Deadly Gambits: The Reagan Administration and the Stalemate in Arms Control* (New York: Vintage, 1984), 197-99. Nor was there any compromise in the rest of the proposal.
[5] NATO Nuclear Planning Group, *Final Communiqué*, October 28, 1983.
[6] "NATO Cuts Nuclear Dependence," *Los Angeles Times*, October 30, 1983, D4.
[7] "US May Offer New Arms Deal: Proposal Would Limit Each Side to 600 Warheads," *Chicago Tribune*, November 3, 1983, N8.

West German Chancellor Helmut Kohl, in Tokyo, also sought to show flexibility to undercut what was anticipated to be an "energetic protest movement" attempting to derail deployment. Kohl, reiterating Vice President Bush's statement earlier in the year, declared that even after the missiles were deployed, they "might be removed...if Washington and Moscow came to 'appropriate' terms on arms reduction." Therefore, he said, negotiations should continue even after deployment. He insisted that "it must remain our common goal to seek a balance between the free nations and an expansive hegemonic policy at the lowest possible level of armaments..."[8]

The cacophony of the West German protest movement was amplified by the concerns of Moscow's own East European allies. East German leader Erich Honecker appealed to Chancellor Kohl "in the name of the German people" to reconsider Bonn's commitment to deploy, a call that resonated powerfully with the West German Social Democratic left. Calling for a "coalition of common sense" to prevent a nuclear catastrophe, Honecker warned ominously that the Warsaw Pact would take "appropriate countermeasures" to maintain the strategic balance. Czechoslovak Party Secretary Vasil Bilak delivered a similar message, declaring that Western missile deployment would mean that the "wheel of armaments will start turning anew."[9]

The East German and Czech public statements about bloc solidarity were considerably undercut by the obvious discomfort that Moscow's "allies" were exhibiting regarding the "counter deployment" of additional nuclear weapons on their soil. Honecker and Czech Prime Minister Lubomir Strougal used nearly identical language in informing their own people that "there was no joy" in what was communicated to be "unavoidable" compliance with a decision in which they had played no part.[10]

In the Soviet Union, too, the leadership generated a war scare among its own people. The Kremlin organized mass "peace" rallies, sponsored "peace" classes in schools, briefed party activists on the "war danger," aired films of the horrors of war, and practiced civil defense measures. The Soviet media excoriated President Reagan as a "madman," an heir of Hitler; and depicted the United States as a militarist regime bent on world domination. The general thrust of the message was that the Russian people should be prepared for an attack by the United States at any moment.[11]

---

[8] Ibid.

[9] Ronald Asmus, "Soviet Bloc Intensifies Campaign against Euromissiles," *Radio Free Europe*, Background Report, no. 241, October 17, 1983, 2.

[10] Vladimir Socor, "INF Negotiations and Soviet Nuclear Missiles in the GDR and Czechoslovakia," *Radio Free Liberty Research*, Background Report, no 148, October 21, 1986, 5.

[11] Benjamin B. Fischer, *A Cold War Conundrum: The 1983 Soviet War Scare* (Central Intelligence Agency, Center for the Study of Intelligence, September 1997), 18-19; and John W. Parker, *Kremlin in Transition*, vol. 1, *From Brezhnev to Chernenko, 1978-1985* (Boston: Unwin Hyman, 1991), 294-95.

Despite Soviet efforts to generate a public groundswell, however, at this point the actual demonstrations in West Germany were, from Moscow's point of view, disappointingly mild, especially when compared to demonstrations two years earlier. This time, there were over two million participants, but they were overwhelmingly young, orderly, and peaceful. There were no pitched battles in the streets between rock-throwing demonstrators and police armed with water cannon; few windows were broken, or people injured. Indeed, the demonstrations had been rehearsed days in advance, which allowed both protesters and police to play their respective roles without incident. [12]

Moscow Signals Hair-Trigger Alert

Meanwhile, as the deployment date neared, the United States prepared to deal with the worst case—a Soviet attempt to somehow prevent deployment. Whether Moscow precipitated a major confrontation with Washington, or resorted to more spurious tactics, such as a Spetsnaz strike disguised as a terrorist attack against the missile bases in West Germany, the consequences were bound to be overlaid with the threat of war. It was therefore only prudent for Washington to take precautionary measures.

To ensure that it could respond promptly to a crisis, during November 2-11, the Reagan administration conducted a command post exercise to practice nuclear release procedures within the context of the large, annual Autumn Forge NATO maneuvers involving over 300,000 troops that had begun on October 31. Periodic command post exercises (CPX) are common to all military organizations to keep personnel up to date on current procedures and prepared to perform their duties, but this one, code-named Able Archer, would be the most comprehensive in recent years and the first to incorporate release procedures for the Pershing II missile.

The intelligence services of both sides routinely monitored each other's activities, and war gaming and other military exercises received special attention. Each side thus could communicate the depth of its concern by its conducting of these exercises and response to them. Perhaps that accounts for the manner in which the United States carried out, and the Soviet Union reacted to, Able Archer. There were in fact two notable aspects of the Able Archer affair: The Soviet reaction during the actual exercise and the politics of its aftermath.

The Soviets had analyzed the coming Pershing II and Cruise Missile deployments and understood clearly their strategic significance. According to a highly classified KGB analysis, once the missiles were deployed, the United States would have the capability to execute a "surgical strike against command centers in the Soviet Union [that could] destroy the system by incapacitating the

---

[12] Hal Piper, "Mostly Young Took Part in German Protest," *Baltimore Sun*, November 10, 1983, A15.

command centers."[13] Short of going to war, what was to be done? The Soviets, it seems, eschewing war but not the threat of war, decided to send a warning to Washington that they were able and prepared to respond to the new US quick-strike capability.

A crucial public clue to the Soviet scheme was divulged ten years after the event; but it seems that the maneuver was well understood at the time. Sergei Tarasenko, former adviser to First Deputy Foreign Minister Georgi Kornienko, disclosed that sometime in late 1983 "we were given the task of preparing a paper for the Politburo and putting forward some suggestions on how to counter this [missile] threat not physically but politically." The Foreign Ministry's proposed response was that "we should leak some information that we know about these capabilities and contingency plans, and that we are not afraid of these plans because we have taken the necessary measures." [14]

Moscow decided to leak information that it had adopted a launch-on-warning posture as its means of countering the quick-strike Pershing II threat.[15] And to lend added credibility to its warning, the information was leaked through a double agent, Oleg Gordievsky, then a KGB resident in London, as part of the Soviet response to the Able Archer command-post exercise. The warning was real enough. According to Blair's analysis, for the Russians, "launch on warning . . . became technically feasible in the early 1980s."[16]

Moscow's overt military reaction to the exercise was relatively restrained. American intelligence noted an increase in the number of fighter-interceptors placed on strip alert and the heightened readiness of a few Soviet air units in East Germany and Poland, but little else.[17] However, American and, especially, British intelligence noted an "unusually sharp increase in the volume and urgency of the Warsaw Pact [communications] traffic."[18] Then, four days into the exercise, British intelligence passed to Washington a cable from Moscow Center that they had received from Gordievsky.

As Andrew notes, Gordievsky had "provided the text of a directive from Moscow Center on November 5 that revealed, for the first time, what Moscow believed was the likely timetable for a Western first strike." The assumption was that the United States would commence a surprise attack on the Soviet Union under the guise of an exercise and its instructions were for their agents to "keep a

---

[13] William Wohlforth, ed., *Witnesses to the End of the Cold War* (Baltimore: Johns Hopkins University Press, 1996), 71. See also Fischer, *A Cold War Conundrum*, 21.
[14] Ibid.
[15] Washington came publicly to this conclusion a month later. See William Broad, "Pershings Stir Accidental-War Fears," *New York Times*, December 12, 1983, A16.
[16] Bruce Blair, *The Logic of Accidental Nuclear War* (Washington, D.C.: Brookings, 1993), 173.
[17] *Implications of Recent Soviet Military-Political Activities*, SNIE 11-10-84/JX (Washington, DC: Central Intelligence Agency, May 18, 1984), 4.
[18] Don Oberdorfer, *The Turn: How the Cold War Came to an End: The United States and the Soviet Union, 1983-1990* (New York: Poseidon, 1991), 65.

constant watch" on key individuals and locations for any signs that could signal preparations for an attack, which could come at any time within the next seven-to-ten days.[19] The implication was that any signs of preparations would justify Soviet preemption.

When Washington received the directive, its response was to signal that no attack was contemplated by removing all principals from the exercise. Initially, President Reagan, Vice President Bush, the Joint Chiefs of Staff, and Secretary of Defense Weinberger were to participate in the final phase of Able Archer, but, according to National Security Adviser Robert McFarlane, it was "scaled down and most of the top-ranking civilian and military officials were taken out of the exercise because of concern about the high state of Soviet nervousness."[20]

But Moscow was not yet satisfied that it had conveyed its message. Gordievsky further reported to British intelligence that, on the night of November 8-9, the KGB Center "had pressed what came close to a panic button," sending flash cables to West European residencies, advising them, incorrectly, that US forces in Europe had gone on alert and that troops at some bases were being mobilized.[21] The telegrams clearly implied that Moscow believed the American alert "marked the beginning of preparations for a nuclear first strike" and that the Soviet Union was itself preparing for a preemptive attack.[22]

If true, the superpowers were moving inexorably toward nuclear war. But it wasn't true. The exercise ended without incident and the war scare tensions abated for the time being. However, if Moscow had temporarily toned down the alarm, the furor within American and British intelligence had only just begun.

The Politics of Able Archer

The significance of Able Archer lay, perhaps, more in its repercussions in Western intelligence and in the Reagan administration, than in the event itself, having at least as much to do with the credibility of British intelligence as with the Soviet response to the US exercise. A few weeks after the exercise, British authorities passed on Gordievsky's view that Moscow had been "alarmed about the real possibility" of an attack and pressed for a reevaluation of the Soviet response to Able Archer in light of Gordievsky's information.[23]

There seems little doubt that the Soviets had played British intelligence, using Gordievsky as a conduit to send an alarming message to President Reagan, who at the time reacted prudently. Perhaps realizing that they had been used and

---

[19] Christopher Andrew, *For the President's Eyes Only: Secret Intelligence and the American Presidency from Washington to Bush* (New York: Harper Collins, 1996), 475-76.

[20] Oberdorfer, *The Turn*, 65.

[21] Gordon Brook-Shepherd, *The Storm Birds: Soviet Postwar Defectors* (New York: Henry Holt, 1989), 330.

[22] Christopher Andrew and Oleg Gordievsky, *KGB: The Inside Story of Its Foreign Operations from Lenin to Gorbachev* (New York: Harper Collins, 1990), 600.

[23] Oberdorfer, *The Turn*, 67.

hoping to avert further damage to the credibility of their intelligence service, the British decided to maintain that Gordievsky's information was genuine and that he was a bona fide defector. There was a widespread and perhaps unwarranted belief in intelligence circles that the Soviets had thoroughly penetrated British intelligence, based on the string of spy scandals that had plagued Britain in earlier years. The ability to produce a genuine defector would have gone a long way toward rebuilding credibility in its service. Whatever their reasons, the British decided to accept Gordievsky as genuine, despite the slim evidentiary basis for his claims at the time. Later, when he defected to the United Kingdom in 1985, Gordievsky appears to have brought considerable information and insight about the workings of the new Gorbachev leadership, but his status and role during Able Archer was another matter. Unfortunately, his later behavior tended to influence judgment of his earlier role.

The Soviets had for many years employed the ingenious strategy of sending false defectors to raise doubts about the credibility of genuine ones. Sometimes they sent several—one contradicting the other—to confuse Western intelligence. The most famous instance of the use of false defectors was the dispatch of Anatoliy Golitsyn and Yuri Nosenko, who tangled the CIA in knots for years. A testimony to the KGB's success was the CIA's conclusion that both men had been genuine defectors, when the reverse was probably true.[24] In this case, the Soviets had used a double agent as a conduit to add credibility to its message.

When the British pressed for a reevaluation of the Soviet response to Able Archer, some analysts questioned "whether the British were acting as analysts or spin doctors." [25] Nevertheless, the CIA agreed to review its findings, recalling a former official, Fritz Ermarth, to head the review process. Released the following spring, the overall judgment of the Special National Intelligence Estimate (SNIE) was that while the Soviets obviously were concerned about the overall trend of the American buildup, Moscow "does not perceive an imminent danger of war." [26]

The Soviets, the SNIE concluded, "have not initiated the military readiness moves they would have made if they believed a US attack were imminent." Although Moscow's reaction to Able Archer was "somewhat greater than usual, by confining heightened readiness to selected air units Moscow clearly revealed that it did not in fact think there was a possibility at this time of a NATO attack." In any case, American intelligence "would see preparatory signs which the Soviets could not mask."

Indeed, the estimate's key judgment was that Soviet war talk had been "consciously orchestrated across the board to achieve political effects through

---

[24] See David Martin, *Wilderness of Mirrors* (New York: Harper & Row, 1980), 225. For a first-hand account by Nosenko's handler, see Tennent Bagley, *Spy Wars: Moles, Mysteries, and Deadly Games* (New Haven: Yale University Press, 2007).

[25] Fischer, *A Cold War Conundrum*, 18.

[26] CIA, *Implications of Recent Soviet Military-Political Activities*, 3.

posturing and propaganda." The Soviet objective had been "to discredit US defense and foreign policies," and put Washington on notice that the Soviets were bent on pursuing "a hard—perhaps even dangerous—line, unless US concessions are forthcoming."[27]

Although the Estimate observed that, in private diplomatic exchanges, "the Soviets have neither made any direct threats . . . nor betrayed any fear of a US attack," this was not precisely true. Indeed, the very reason for commissioning the estimate was the Soviet threat conveyed by Gordievsky, which although neither "direct," nor formally "diplomatic," had in fact been made and certainly betrayed concern about an attack.

Ermarth had fudged the true purpose of the estimate, which did not directly deal with Able Archer alone, but included a string of other threat issues that occurred over the next several months.[28] The estimate referred only obliquely to Gordievsky himself in the phrase Soviet "internal communications," and only vaguely referred to the Soviet launch on warning decision in the following context:

> Soviet INF-related military activities have also been designed to convey an impression to the West that the world is a more dangerous place following US INF deployment and that the USSR is making good on its predeployment threats to counter with deployments of its own.

In a retrospective evaluation, Ermarth contended, "we got it right. The US did not intend to attack the USSR, and Moscow perceived no such intention. Moscow did not intend to attack nor start a confrontation that could lead to war."

However, the proper conclusion to be drawn from the alarm passed on to the American government was that it had been entirely a KGB-orchestrated maneuver. Gordievsky himself was never able to produce the anxious cables of November 8-9 and the gravity of the event rested largely on his word. From Mastny's later analysis of the vast East German spy network in NATO, it appeared that the Stasi found no evidence of plans for an attack and that the KGB had "acted on reports . . . from their own sources." Furthermore, the KGB "did not . . . pass its findings about the 'Able Archer' to the Soviet politburo or even the upper levels of the defense ministry."[29]

---

[27] Ibid., 2. Six years later, in completely different circumstances, the president's Foreign Intelligence Advisory Board (PFIAB) revisited the incident and gave Soviet concerns more credence. See Oberdorfer, *The Turn*, 66-67.

[28] See the statement by Fritz Ermarth, "Observations on the 'War Scare' of 1983 from an Intelligence Perch" (March 11, 2003), 27-30, Parallel History Project on NATO and the Warsaw Pact (PHP), Stasi Intelligence Collection, www.isn.ethz.ch/php.

[29] Vojtech Mastny, "Did East German Spies Prevent a Nuclear War?" Parallel History Project on NATO and the Warsaw Pact (PHP), Stasi Intelligence Collection (November 6, 2003), www.isn.ethz.ch/php.

Reinforcing the thesis of a KGB orchestration, when queried years later, high-ranking Soviet officials, who would have been intimately involved in any Soviet war preparations, knew nothing about the war scare. Both General Sergei Akhromeyev, who had been deputy chief of the Soviet high command, and Alexander Bessmertnykh, head of the American section of the Foreign Ministry at that time, "had no recollection of a special alert in November of 1983."[30]

Turnabout Is Fair Play

Moscow immediately followed up the Able Archer ploy with an arms control scheme designed to drive a wedge between Washington and its European allies over the imminent Pershing II deployment. Although constantly proclaiming that the United States wished no arms control agreement, in fact, the Soviet Union wished no agreement that would allow the deployment of US missiles, and so sought to head off any possible compromise. Time, however, was running out and Moscow was reduced to desperate and futile measures.

Its scheme, called the "walk in the park," was intended to tip the Bundestag debate against deployment by demonstrating that Washington was working behind the backs of its allies and against their interests. There was also a sense that the form it took was a payback to Paul Nitze for his "walk in the woods" ploy of the previous year, in which Washington had floated an attractive proposal to Moscow, which had been kept secret from Helmut Schmidt, in order to exert pressure on Japanese premier Zenko Suzuki.[31] If it was payback, however, it was one that backfired.

In his UN address of September 26, President Reagan had laid out a formula for compromise over the INF negotiations, without proposing specific numbers. The president had proposed "reductions and limits on a global basis," that is, limits on deployments in Europe and Asia and a commitment that Washington "would not offset the entire Soviet global missile deployment through US deployments in Europe." Furthermore, he said, in the context of reduction to equal levels "we are prepared to reduce the number of Pershing II ballistic missiles as well as ground-launched cruise missiles." Also, the United States was prepared to "limit aircraft as well as missiles." As the president said at the time: "the door to an agreement is open. It is time for the Soviet Union to walk through it."[32]

That, of course, was precisely what the Soviets did not want to do. The Andropov proposal of October 28, while appearing to be responsive, was designed to block an agreement. The proposal offered a reduction from 162 to 140 SS-20

---

[30] Oberdorfer, *The Turn*, 454. On the other hand, Pry, *War Scare*, 44, saw the Soviet response to Able Archer as the single most dangerous incident of the early eighties. The Soviets "probably came within a hair's breadth of ordering nuclear strikes against missile, bomber, and submarine bases in NATO and the United States."

[31] See *Ronald Reagan: Revolution Ascendant*, chap. 13.

[32] "Text of President's Address at U.N.," *New York Times*, September 27, 1983, A16.

missiles and 420 warheads, a commitment to liquidate and not merely redeploy missiles eliminated in an agreement, and a willingness to include nuclear-capable aircraft in an agreement. While this seemed to offer the possibility of compromise, the Soviet proposal was, as were all of its proposals, predicated on the basic demand that the United States cancel its entire deployment, which made it patently non-negotiable.

As the negotiations in Geneva neared the deadline when the West German Bundestag would vote on deployment, the Soviets strove to head off in advance the expected US counterproposal. In the Geneva discussions following the Andropov proposal of late October, Yuli Kvitsinsky had suggested to Nitze that he propose "equal reductions" as a settlement formula. What he meant by this term was that the United States would reduce to zero and, while the Soviet Union would make an equal reduction, the outcome would still leave the Soviet Union with an overwhelming advantage in weapons.

Nitze was skeptical, but at subsequent gatherings, receptions, and informal walks in the park adjacent to US offices over the next two weeks, Kvitsinsky continued to press this approach, offering the added inducement that the sticking point of British and French forces could be deferred to a future negotiation. Then, on Saturday, November 12, immediately following the end of the Able Archer exercise, Kvitsinsky called Nitze at his home late in the evening. He had just "received instructions from Moscow," he said, "and needed to meet . . . the next morning."[33]

When they met, Kvitsinsky gave Nitze the following proposal: "if the US government were to propose equal reductions from 572 to zero on your side and 572 from our side, my government would accept it." In addition, he said, the issue of British and French weapons, which Andropov had insisted on including in the agreement, could be deferred to a future, appropriate forum. Nitze's reaction was straightforward: "I'm certain that the US government will not convert a Soviet proposal into an American one."[34]

Nitze smelled a rat. During their discussions, Kvitsinsky had insisted that Nitze report the "equal reductions" proposal to Washington as his own, which the US negotiator refused to do, repeatedly reiterating that authorship of the proposal had been Kvitsinsky's, not his. Therefore, in reporting back Kvitsinsky's proposal, he recommended that the State Department "promptly inform our NATO allies of the Soviet equal reductions move," lest the Soviets "go to them behind our backs."[35]

Washington replied promptly with a proposal that filled in the numbers left out of the president's September UN speech. Asking Kvitsinsky to meet him on November 14, Nitze gave him a preview of the proposal he would present

---

[33] Paul H. Nitze, with Steven L. Rearden and Ann M. Smith, *From Hiroshima to Glasnost: At the Center of Decision: A Memoir* (New York: Grove Weidenfeld, 1989), 391.

[34] Talbott, *Deadly Gambits*, 202.

[35] Nitze et al., *From Hiroshima to Glasnost*, 392.

formally to the delegation the next day. (In fact, his proposal appeared in the press that day.)[36] The president proposed 420 warheads for each side in a global settlement. Furthermore, the United States would simply match what the Soviets deployed in Europe and reserve the right to deploy the remainder in Asia but would not do so.

President Reagan decided to take the numbers in the Andropov October proposal and meld them into his September proposal. Thus, the United States accepted Andropov's proposed limit of 420 warheads but applied it to Reagan's global formula for Europe and Asia, which would sharply reduce the Soviet deployments in Europe. The inducement was that, although the US called for deployment of equal numbers in Europe, it offered to deploy fewer Pershing II missiles than originally included in the overall weapons mix.

The US proposal offered the possibility of a genuine compromise at low levels of deployment and clearly raised the pressure for a settlement. As Nitze was informing Kvitsinsky of Reagan's proposal, British Defense Secretary Michael Heseltine announced the arrival of the first shipment of sixteen Tomahawk cruise missiles, flown to Greenham Common air base a day earlier than expected. Britain had committed to accept 160, but Heseltine made a point of saying that "if progress is made at Geneva," the missile deployment in Britain and elsewhere could be "halted, modified or reversed."[37]

That, for Moscow, was its drawback. As Moscow wanted no US deployments at all and therefore would accept no compromise, it would be necessary to discredit the US scheme. Therefore, on November 17, the day after the Italian parliament approved deployment plans for 112 cruise missiles by a 351 to 219 vote, in both Geneva and Washington the Soviets "began to circulate rumors that [Nitze] had made a proposal to the Soviet side, that Moscow had accepted it, and that Washington had rejected it."[38] As Talbott observed: "it was a transparent attempt . . . to make it look as though the walk in the park was a replay of the walk in the woods, to make it seem that once again Nitze had on his own hammered out a workable compromise only to be shot down as before by the hawkish, intransigent Reagan Administration."[39]

Fortunately, the State Department had forewarned the allies and publicly laid out the Soviet "equal reductions" proposal exposing the fact that they had

---

[36] Michael Getler, "Refined Arms Offer Planned by US as Deployment Nears," *Washington Post*, November 14, 1983, A1. Talbott, *Deadly Gambits*, 203, incorrectly slips the date of the instructions to Nitze to November 16, perhaps to make room to criticize his "counterproposal." Nitze presented Reagan's proposal on the 15th. See Robert Greenberger, "Reagan Spells Out Arms-Control Plans; Soviets Balk, Appear Ready to Quit Talks," *Wall Street Journal*, November 15, 1983, 3.

[37] Peter Osnos, "Missiles Delivered in Britain," *Washington Post*, November 15, 1983, A1.

[38] Nitze et al., *Hiroshima to Glasnost*, 394; and "Italians Approve Plan on Missiles," *New York Times*, November 17, 1983, A7.

[39] Talbott, *Deadly Gambits*, 204.

"asked the US to propose the plan."[40] Forewarned, the allies "treated the Soviet trick as exactly what it was" and turned it against them, Kohl declaring that the Soviet proposal "gives up a point that [they] have up to now considered essential: the inclusion of French and British weapons." Their ploy exposed, and desperate to return to square one, Dmitri Ustinov published an article in *Pravda* excoriating Kohl and reiterating the Soviet insistence that British and French weapons be included, and maintaining that it had been the United States, not the Soviet Union that had made the equal reductions proposal.[41]

Desperate Last Cards

The Soviets and their sympathizers played their last cards as the West German parliament prepared to vote, and now with no holds barred. First came a blatant effort to play on the sensibilities of the American people through the film media. An ABC-TV movie, *The Day After*, depicted the nuclear vaporization of Lawrence, Kansas, by Soviet missiles as part of a global nuclear conflict. The film "suggested that deployment of US cruise and Pershing II missiles in Europe to counter Soviet missiles stationed in the eastern USSR was viewed as a provocation by Moscow and some US allies. It suggested that the Soviets started a conventional war and that the United States escalated it to atomic war."[42]

The overt message was that American policy was provocative and if Washington only abandoned its deployment there would be peace. Determined to insure that the American people understood that United States' policy was to "reduce the possibility of nuclear conflict," not intensify it, Secretary Shultz appeared on ABC's *Viewpoint* after the conclusion of the movie to defuse its message and to emphasize the president's oft-stated view that "a nuclear war can never be won and must never be fought."[43] Vice President Bush, in an Op-Ed in the *New York Times*, rejected the notion that it was President Reagan who was the gravest threat to the peace. On the contrary, he said, "the gravest threat" was the Soviet Union, which has "embarked on an arms buildup so vast it lacked any parallel in history."[44]

The day following the film's airing, massive protests erupted in Bonn, even as the administration sought to allay Western fears. Clearly responding to European "political unease," US and European diplomatic "sources" stated that for "technical reasons," i.e., the relatively slow production schedules, there would be "nine months between the first deployment next month of new, American

---

[40] Robert Greenberger, "Soviets Offer New Missile Cuts in Europe; US Says Current Deployment to Proceed," *Wall Street Journal*, November 18, 1983, 2.

[41] Talbott, *Deadly Gambits*, 204-5.

[42] Michael Getler, "Fresh Look into Nuclear Nightmare," *Washington Post*, November 21, 1983, A1.

[43] George Shultz, *Turmoil and Triumph: My Years as Secretary of State* (New York: Scribner, 1993), 374.

[44] Hedrick Smith, "War Film Elicits White House View," *New York Times*, November 21, 1983, A1.

medium-range nuclear missiles in Western Europe, and the second round, which is scheduled for September 1984." The delay, it was said, will offer "the first real opportunity to see if the Soviets want to negotiate."[45]

Meanwhile, in Bonn, as the West German Parliament began to debate final authorization to deploy the Pershing II missiles, earlier peaceful demonstrations turned ugly. Three thousand demonstrators clashed with police in an effort to break into the parliament buildings and disrupt the proceedings. Speaking behind a cordon of hundreds of riot control policemen armed with water cannon and tear gas, Chancellor Kohl declared on the steps of parliament that his government was "prepared to do what is necessary to safeguard our freedom and security."[46]

Inside the parliament itself, the opposition was no less intense, if more restrained. Former chancellor Helmut Schmidt, making his first speech to the Bundestag since being ousted the previous October, "agreed that West Germany must deploy the missiles to prove its reliability as a NATO ally." Nevertheless, he "attacked Kohl for lacking the courage or will to prod the Geneva negotiations toward an acceptable agreement." He was particularly incensed that Kohl had failed to seize upon the "walk in the woods" formula when it became known. That formula was "clearly in German interests." (Schmidt, of course, omitted the fact that the "walk in the woods" scheme had been broached when he was chancellor, but had been kept secret from him.)

SPD parliamentary leader Hans Vogel repudiated Schmidt, opposed deployment of US missiles, and lamented the fact that Kohl had subserviently bowed to Washington's will. Moscow's offer of a reduced deployment, he claimed, was "worthy and qualified for negotiation." In his view, the Soviet proposal offered the possibility of breaking off the arms race. At least deployment should be postponed, in order to find out. "The arrival of new missiles in Western Europe," he warned, "will cause the Soviet Union to increase its missile force in Eastern Europe," increasing tensions which were already dangerously high.

Foreign Minister Hans Dietrich-Genscher rebutted Vogel, declaring that the missile question is the "litmus test" of "where West Germany will stand in the future—as a dependable alliance partner or one that drifts away to neutralism." It cannot be denied, he said, that "our allies are increasingly worried about an incalculable form of German nationalism . . . . This time it is not the strength but the weakness of Germany that creates dangers for Europe." West German identity was bound with the fate of Europe, he said, "and if we break our responsibilities and attempt to go alone, stability will be lost."[47]

---

[45] Walter Pincus, "Pause Set in Missile Schedule," *Washington Post*, November 21, 1983, A1. The next day State Department spokesman John Hughes took issue with this report, declaring to reporters "you would be misled if you thought there was a nine-month gap."

[46] William Drozdiak, "Kohl Defends Missiles as Protests Erupt," *Washington Post*, November 22, 1983, A1.

[47] Ibid.

The next day, the West German Parliament voted 286-226 to deploy US missiles to West Germany. Undoubtedly, part of the reason for the strong vote of approval was the recent Soviet softening of its position on the issue of West German-Soviet relations. Andropov earlier had threatened to bring down an "ice age" between the two Germanys, which would view each other through a "palisade of missiles," causing considerable anxiety in West German ruling circles. Partly as a result of the Kohl government's efforts to limit the possible fallout from the missile deployment and partly as the result of Moscow's own policy recalculation, which was conveyed by letter to Kohl, West German anxieties were allayed.[48]

A letter from Andropov had eased West German fears and a visit to Moscow by Economics Minister Otto Lambsdorff reinforced the view that trade relations would not suffer as a result of the missile decision. West Germany was the Soviet Union's largest trading partner, with total trade volume in 1982 reaching $7.7 billion and total West German trade with the East bloc at $19 billion, nearly 5% of West Germany's total foreign trade. The West Germans reached the conclusion that remaining a steadfast alliance partner would not impact negatively on relations with Moscow because the disruption of trade "would be a greater blow to the sputtering Soviet economy than to their own." Nevertheless, former Chancellor Willy Brandt predicted a "deep cut" in East-West relations and said that those who don't take Soviet threats seriously were "whistling in the dark."[49]

The Reagan administration wasted no time. Within 24 hours of the Bundestag vote, the United States flew in the first battery of nine Pershing II missiles to Ramstein Air Base. From there, they were to be transported by helicopter to the US Army's 58th Field Artillery Brigade at Mutlangen, near Schwäbisch Gmünd. Mutlangen had been the target of an anti-missile demonstration by 1,000 people in early September.[50] This time, amid freezing rain and high winds, protesters were much fewer in number; but they managed to tear down the barbed wire fencing that the US Army had erected around the base, resulting in dozens of arrests.[51] Nevertheless, Kohl held firm.

Moscow's Retreat
from "Analogous" to "Adequate"

Moscow, too, lost no time. As its delegation left Geneva declaring the current negotiating round "discontinued, without setting any date for resumption,"

---

[48] Roger Thurow, "West Germany Votes to Deploy US Missiles," *Wall Street Journal*, November 23, 1983, 35.

[49] Ibid.

[50] James Markham, "First US Pershing Missiles Delivered in West Germany," *New York Times*, November 24, 1983, A14.

[51] "Germans Rip down Fence at US Base," *Washington Times*, November 28, 1983, A6.

the Soviets issued a statement in Andropov's name (he had not been seen in public for 98 days) acknowledging the change in the strategic balance, although doing so in typically bombastic manner.[52] Due to the "new strategic environment," the statement read, the Soviet Union had been forced to adopt corresponding measures. The Soviets ended participation in the Geneva talks because to continue them "would only serve as cover" for Washington's policies.[53]

In addition, the Soviets canceled all "unilateral obligations designed to create a better climate for the Geneva talks," including the moratorium on deployment of SS-20 missiles in the European part of the Soviet Union. They would accelerate preparatory work for deployment of "operational-tactical" nuclear missiles in East Germany and Czechoslovakia and deploy new nuclear arms "in ocean areas and seas" near the United States. Implicitly acknowledging their failure to make an "analogous" deployment against the United States, the Andropov statement said that: "by their characteristics these systems of ours will be *adequate* to the threat which is being created for us and our allies by the American missiles that are being deployed in Europe."

At the same time, the statement contained recriminations and demands for withdrawal of US missiles. Andropov charged that the United States "from the outset did not want" an agreement and accused the governments of Britain, West Germany and Italy of "colluding" with the Reagan administration, saying that they, too, "knew all along" that Washington did not want an agreement. It was as if the massive Soviet deployment of SS-20 missiles, whose numbers were continuously being augmented and which was the reason for the Western counter deployment, had never happened.

On the other hand, the Soviet statement said, "should the United States and the other NATO countries display readiness to return to the situation that existed before the commencement of the deployment . . . of missiles . . . .our earlier proposals . . . would become valid again."[54] In other words, the Soviet position was that if the United States withdrew its missiles the Soviet Union would pick up where the negotiations left off—with the Russians holding a monopoly on nuclear missiles in Western Europe and the West having zero.

In a statement issued in reply from his ranch in Santa Barbara, President Reagan said that "we can only be dismayed at this Soviet statement. . . . It is at sharp variance with the stated wish of the Soviet Union that an agreement be negotiated." Nevertheless, "we are determined to renew our efforts to entirely do away with the land-based intermediate-range nuclear missile systems." The United States, he said, will "continue to seek negotiations in good faith."[55]

---

[52] Nitze et al., *From Hiroshima to Glasnost*, 397.
[53] Dusko Doder, "Andropov Warns Soviets Will Add Sea-Based Missiles," *Washington Post*, November 25, 1983, A1.
[54] Ibid.
[55] David Hoffman, "President Vows to Renew Efforts at Arms Control," *Washington Post*, November 25, 1983, A44.

Chancellor Kohl and President Mitterrand in "studied calmness" also issued a joint statement at a news conference, calling upon the Soviet Union "to return to the negotiating table as soon as possible." The "dispassionate reaction" of the two European leaders "reflected a widespread analysis in Paris and Bonn that the Andropov measures were neither unexpected nor harsher than earlier Soviet signals had presaged. Moreover, neither Mr. Kohl nor Mr. Mitterrand is eager to rush forward now with new negotiating formulas." In dinner remarks, Kohl also reinforced West German firmness, saying that he was aware that there was talk in France about "the spirit of Munich"—a concern that the Soviets would be appeased as Hitler was. The chancellor hastened to alleviate the worry. "Let me say in all clarity: The Federal Republic stands firmly in the Western alliance. The Germans will not endanger this adherence with unrealistic neutralist dreams."[56]

Although Soviet recriminations would continue over the next several weeks, the plain fact was that a fundamental tenet of Soviet strategy—its strategic weapons component—had failed. The Russians had been unable to secure strategic weapons dominance over the United States or Western Europe. Moscow's nearly two-decade drive to achieve strategic weapons supremacy and coerce favorable geopolitical change had backfired, as Reagan preempted the Soviets in Grenada and had taken the first step in reestablishing American preeminence with the deployments in Western Europe.

A top secret NATO analysis estimated that, once the Pershing II/cruise missile package was fully deployed, even at the declared ranges of 1,000 miles for the Pershing II and 1,500 miles for the cruise missiles, the United States and its allies would place "at risk approximately 87 percent of the high-priority targets, including Moscow itself." This translated into being able to strike over 2,000 of the 2,500 "high priority military targets" identified by NATO planners. In addition to military targets, for the first time, the European Target Data Inventory also included over 25,000 economic infrastructure targets. "Such installations historically have not been targeted by [NATO] forces."[57]

That was just from Western Europe. In a general nuclear war, US strategic nuclear forces would target "many additional military targets in the western Soviet Union which are not included in the European high-priority target list," such as ICBMs and heavy bomber bases. US forces would also strike economic and political targets such as industrial sites and leadership infrastructure. It was no wonder that the Soviets evinced such a "hysterical" reaction to the NATO deployment, but it had been the outcome of the Soviet Union's own calculated decision to attempt to attain a coercive first-strike capability against the United States and the West.

---

[56] "Kohl and Mitterrand Respond Calmly," *New York Times*, November 26, 1983, 6.
[57] Jack Anderson, "Euromissiles May Get Soviets to Talk Turkey," *Washington Post*, November 28, 1983, B31.

Dual Strategic Transitions

By the end of 1983, at the latest, Moscow had begun a major reassessment of its strategy. The paralyzing effects of the US deployments would not come into full force until a significant number of Pershing II and cruise missiles had been deployed some months hence. Moscow would move as rapidly as possible to mitigate these effects by pushing ahead with new types of mobile ICBMs, and most importantly, with its missile defense program. The near-term deployment of a successful missile defense system before the United States could do the same would enable the Soviet Union to maintain a significant advantage and perhaps continue with its current strategy. A lengthy delay, on the other hand, combined with US advances in missile defense, would force an immediate change in overall strategy.

In fact, over the next several months, behind a veil of obdurate bellicosity, the Soviets would gradually put into place the basis for a shift to the strategy of détente with the United States; not, it must be said, to enter into the kind of cooperative relationship desired by the new world order faction, but to disarm the United States and disrupt its strategy, while pursuing the same strategic objectives as before. However, the process was choppy, as opposing factions argued over how much of a change in strategy, if any, should be made. At the same time, Soviet leaders carefully assessed the changing political dynamic within the Reagan administration. They could not fail to observe the rise of Secretary Shultz to preeminence and realize the positive implications for themselves in his preferred strategy of détente with Moscow.

In the meantime, Moscow still possessed some maneuvering room over the next several months to attempt to salvage the most important element in current Soviet strategy, to bring about the capture of Iran in the Iran-Iraq conflict. The attrition strategy for Iran, recall, had been one of the three main Soviet foreign policy goals. The conflict was moving toward what was widely believed to be its decisive phase when Iran would mount a full-scale invasion of Iraq and Syria would assist in applying military pressure on Iraq's western front.

During this phase, the Soviet role would be to marshal its power to hold the ring and prevent US interference, and Iraq's defeat, as Moscow's allies inside Iran struck for power during the invasion. There was also the possibility that the Soviets would manufacture some pretext to intervene directly to facilitate a takeover.[58] To set the stage for this climactic development, the Soviets continued to emphasize the war scare, freeze US-Soviet relations, and intensify support of international terrorism.

A strategy shift was also occurring in Washington, in a similarly choppy manner, as American leaders pondered the meaning of Soviet behavior. As Secretary Shultz consolidated his position in the wake of Clark's removal and in response to Moscow's truculence, he pressed hard for a major effort to reach an

---

[58] "Moscow Maneuvers toward a Takeover in Iran," *Businessweek*, August 15, 1983, 46.

accommodation with Moscow.[59] A key factor persuaded Reagan to agree to make such an effort, without, however, changing his overall strategy toward the Soviet Union expressed in NSDD-75. This was the approaching election campaign, in which it would be vital to show that the president was on the side of peace.

The American leadership, including the president, was alarmed by the prominent policy role assumed by the Soviet military command after the KAL 007 affair, and by Andropov's protracted absence from view, which lent credence to the idea that a hardline faction might have taken control. Indeed, the president publicly expressed his concern about the Soviet military "seeming to enunciate policy on their own."[60] Bellicose Soviet behavior suggested that a major confrontation, if not war, was just around the corner. It was therefore only prudent to extend a conciliatory hand, if only to determine the true state of the Soviet leadership.

Meanwhile, Soviet sponsorship of global terrorism had reached the point where American officials began to discuss it publicly.[61] President Reagan had been concerned about the issue of Soviet state sponsorship of international terrorism from the beginning of his administration. In fact, one of William Casey's earliest steps as CIA Director was to commission a Special National Intelligence Estimate on the subject. Completed in late May 1981, the key judgment was that "the Soviets are deeply engaged in support of revolutionary violence worldwide."[62] Subsequent behavior had only served to intensify American concerns.

The veiled internal discussion about the proper way to respond to the widespread upsurge of international terrorist incidents was connected to the larger issue of relations with the Soviet Union and would continue for six months until the administration settled on its policy. Public accusation of the Soviet Union as a state supporter of terrorism would obviously be a major obstacle to an improvement in relations. The issue of international terrorism would loom in the background of events as US-Soviet relations lurched toward crisis over the Iran-Iraq conflict.

---

[59] As a mark of how far the locus of power had shifted away from the national security adviser, Clark's successor, Robert McFarlane, *Special Trust*, 277-78, said of this period: "no great overseas crises loomed in [1984] to challenge Ronald Reagan in his role as leader of the free world, to test his skills as a decision-maker, or to threaten his commitment to world peace and stability. The withdrawal from Lebanon put the Middle East, ever simmering but in no imminent danger of explosion, on the back burner."

[60] "Reagan Criticizes Soviet Brass," *Washington Post*, December 27, 1983, A8.

[61] Georgie Anne Geyer, "Shultz on America and the World," *Washington Times*, December 5, 1983, A10; and Allan Brownfield, "Moscow as Source of Funding and Training of Terrorists," *Washington Times*, December 20, 1983, C2.

[62] *Soviet Support for International Terrorism and Revolutionary Violence*, SNIE 11/2-81 (Washington, DC: Central Intelligence Agency, May 27, 1981), 1. Declassified February 28, 1994.

American intelligence had been closely following the course of the war and Soviet policy toward it, noting its twists and turns, but apparently mistaking the specific object of Soviet strategy. One CIA study completed in August confirmed Moscow's "clear tilt" toward Iraq but explained it as a defensive act. "If they did not aid Baghdad, Iraq might decide it had no choice but to accelerate its turn toward Western Europe, China, and even the United States."[63] In fact, Moscow was encouraging Saddam's ties to the West as a means of isolating Iran. Indeed, in the course of 1983, not only had France, West Germany, Egypt, and Brazil become major arms suppliers, there were many others eager to join in the arms sale bonanza.

The Soviet Union, too, had "reopened the arms pipeline to Iraq in a big way . . . replacing every piece of ground equipment Iraq had lost during the first two years of the war." In December, the Soviets concluded their first large arms deal since before the war, for "several thousand tank transporters," which gave Iraqi commanders the ability to move armor quickly "from one end of the battlefront to the other without being seen."[64] Iraqi ability to concentrate armor at points of Iranian attack would enable them to defeat all Iranian invasion attempts.

A second CIA analysis completed in December, focusing on the potential for a Soviet intervention in Iran, correctly deduced that "the major long-term Soviet goal in the Persian Gulf region is to move the Gulf states from a pro-Western to a pro-Soviet orientation. The Soviets seek to enhance their influence in the area to the point at which Moscow could exercise some degree of control over Persian Gulf oil, with resultant economic and political leverage over Western Europe and Japan."[65] The main point was left unstated, which was that if Moscow were able to exercise some degree of control over Persian Gulf oil, the Soviets would also be able to exert great political leverage over the United States.

While noting that the Soviet Union had not significantly modernized its force structure in the southern theater of operations along the border with Iran, the estimate omitted the improved power projection capability inherent in the deployment of SS-20 missiles to Soviet central Asia. While judging that the Soviets "might consider military intervention if a pro-Moscow group were to seize power and 'request' assistance, or if Iran were to fragment into a number of regional entities," the estimate doubted Soviet capability to seize the oil fields of Khuzestan province. While the studies had not advocated any policy response, American leaders were fully apprised of the range of Soviet policy options toward the region and the possibilities inherent in an expanded conflict.

---

[63] *Moscow's Tilt toward Baghdad: The USSR and the War Between Iran and Iraq*, an Intelligence Assessment by the Office of Soviet Analysis (Washington, DC: Central Intelligence Agency, August 26, 1983), 2. This assessment was heavily influenced by discussion with Soviet officials.

[64] Kenneth Timmerman, *The Death Lobby: How the West Armed Iraq* (New York: Houghton Mifflin, 1991), 184. For a list of contracts, see pp. 420-22.

[65] *Soviet Forces and Capabilities in the Southern Theater of Military Operations*, NIE 11/39-83 D (Washington, DC: Central Intelligence Agency, December 1983), 3.

The internal debate on US policy toward the Iran-Iraq war unfolded in the fall of 1983 in the complex context of multiple crises (the KAL crisis, the Grenada preemption, and Pershing II deployment) and as the war itself appeared to be moving into a critical phase. Indeed, although repeated Iranian human-wave attacks in the course of the year had appeared threatening, they had failed to do more than dent increasingly impregnable Iraqi defenses. As the ground war had subsided with the onset of the rainy season, it was the prospect that the war would soon expand to affect oil shipping from the Gulf that prompted debate.

Knowledge that France had sold five Super Étendard jets armed with Exocet missiles coupled with Iraqi threats to attack Iranian petroleum interests in the gulf had prompted Iranian counter threats to close the gulf to all shipping. Indeed, to reinforce this threat, in September, the Iranians had sent forces to Sirri Island located at the mouth of the Strait of Hormuz.[66] Some 50 tankers carrying close to 20 percent of the world's petroleum passed through the strait every day. The threat to this maritime choke point would directly impinge upon the president's overall strategy, as expressed in NSDD-75, a crucial part of which was the reduction of world oil prices as a means of spurring Western economic growth and undercutting Soviet hard-currency earning capacity. Closure of the gulf would send oil prices skyrocketing and had to be prevented.

The question of the US policy response produced a difference of opinion between the president and his Secretary of State that reflected their divergent strategic preferences—the president seeking to strengthen containment as the means of defeating Soviet strategy and the secretary pressing for the new world order faction's strategy of détente with Moscow. Iran, of course, had been a central part of the containment structure before the fall of the shah and the president sought to prepare the grounds for a restoration of close relations, if the opportunity arose. At this point, as long as Khomeini remained in power, the ultimate goal was out of reach, but it was vital to avoid taking positions which would preclude action later. Indeed, that was the problem, for an Iranian attempt to shut down the gulf could lead to a direct conflict with the United States and make rapprochement virtually impossible.

Shultz, on the other hand, basing all of his policy proposals on the new world order strategy that called for the dismantlement of the containment structure and the removal of any forward US positions around the Soviet Union in order to create the basis for détente, opposed any policy that was inconsistent with it. Thus, despite the fact that this strategy, pursued by Kissinger, Ford, and Carter had produced only setbacks and despite the fact that Reagan had rejected it, Shultz argued vociferously against any proposal that could result in the reestablishment of the containment structure, which meant his strong opposition to any prospect of reestablishing relations with Iran.

From Moscow's point of view, of course, the strategy of détente was a virtually cost-free means of facilitating a US withdrawal from the Eastern

---

[66] Edgar O'Ballance, *The Gulf War* (London: Brassey's, 1988), 127.

Hemisphere. Soviet leaders never tired of praising the virtues of this strategy for the obvious reason that it was the mirror-image of their own. One can only wonder at the determination of eastern establishment leaders to pursue this strategy. If carried to fulfillment, it could only redound to the grave disadvantage of the United States, especially as applied to Iran, for it would allow the Soviets to wield significant influence over the supply and price of oil, the very lifeblood of the American and international economy. There seemed, in short, to be a sharp contradiction in the new world order strategy as it applied to Middle East oil.

Policy Battle over Iran and Iraq

The Iranian threat to close down the gulf opened the door to greater US involvement in the Iran-Iraq war, as Washington deployed a carrier task force just outside the gulf to protect shipping. At the same time, a policy conflict that had raged since the beginning of the administration was brought to a head. From the outset, adopting a neutral position on the war, the president had sought to gain an opening to Tehran through indirect arms sales in a wide-open international arms market, in which over 30 countries, including key US allies, vied to sell weapons to both sides. [67] Secretary Shultz, on the other hand, sought to edge the United States closer to Iraq to foreclose an opening to Iran.[68]

Indeed, in early 1983, the president, considering a proposal for the CIA to provide weapons directly to Iran, had sought an opinion from the General Counsel of the CIA to ascertain whether any laws prevented it. The response, a memorandum from W. George Jameson, Assistant General Counsel to Stanley Sporkin, General Counsel, was that "there were no general legal restrictions that would preclude the CIA from providing equipment to Iran as proposed. Rather, the relevant constraints involve policy considerations that may have to be weighed before undertaking the activity proposed."[69] The proposed "activity" was the provision of arms, but action was deferred at that time due to "policy considerations."

Shultz, on the other hand, sought indirectly to align the United States with Baghdad through gradual improvement of relations, provision of battlefield intelligence, and extension of economic aid. Beginning in December 1982, according to Shultz, "we provided Iraq with $210 million in credits to purchase American wheat, rice, and feed grains, as well as access to Export-Import Bank

---

[67]See Kenneth Timmerman, *Fanning the Flames: Guns, Greed & Geopolitics in the Gulf War* (online), chap. 7. http://kentimmerman.com/krt/fanning_index.htm.
[68] Seymour Hersh, "US Secretly Gave Aid to Iraq Early in Its War Against Iran," *New York Times*, January 26, 1992, A1.
[69] "Restrictions on Exports to Iran," Memorandum for Stanley Sporkin, General Counsel, from W. George Jameson, Assistant General Counsel, January 7, 1983, *Digital National Security Archive-ProQuest*, DNSA Collection: Iraqgate. I am indebted to Colleen Gilbert for bringing this memorandum to my attention.

credits and continuing financing of agricultural sales by the Commodity Credit Corporation. Some intelligence was also provided to Iraq."

In the spring of 1983, Shultz claimed to want to "dry up the sources of weaponry" to both sides and to that end obtained the president's agreement to proceed with Operation Staunch. When implemented later in the year, however, it was biased heavily against Iran.[70] Operation Staunch was largely ineffective, as Timmerman notes, due to the "widespread perception abroad that the United States was pursuing a double-track policy: a public policy of cracking down on arms sales to Iran, and a private policy of seeking contacts with Iran."[71] Operation Staunch evidently was Shultz's attempt to close off any possibility of an opening to Iran through arms sales.

As it appeared that the war would be entering a more volatile phase, Shultz pressed to align the United States more openly in support of Iraq, but it was not an easy sell, even within the State Department. Asked to develop a plausible rationale for shifting from a position of strict neutrality to support for Iraq, Assistant Secretaries Jonathan Howe (politico-military affairs) and Nicholas Veliotes (Near East affairs) reluctantly came up with two circumstances that could justify a change. In their reply memorandum of October 7, which was addressed to Shultz's aide, Under Secretary Lawrence Eagleburger, they observed that the policy of strict neutrality had "served our objectives and interests well." It had "avoided great power involvement," "contributed to the current military stalemate," "prevented the spread of the war" to the gulf, and "preserved the possibility of developing a future relationship with Iran while minimizing openings for expansion of Soviet influence."[72] This last, of course, was precisely what Shultz now sought to avoid.

The two circumstances that could justify a shift, Howe and Veliotes thought, were: either an Iranian attempt to stop gulf shipping, or "sustained Iranian pressure . . . over the next year [that could] bring about Iraq's political collapse." It was, however, "in the context of keeping the Gulf open for international oil shipments" that "a possible tilt toward Iraq should be considered." They warned that as "the steps we have taken toward the conflict since [1982] have progressively favored Iraq," any further tilt would become obvious and "defer any improvement in our relations [with Iran] in the post-Khomeini period."[73] Nevertheless, this was the course Shultz embarked on.

In other words, the issue was strategic. Shultz's proposal for a tilt toward Iraq would close off any future opening to Iran. As Preece observed of this argument in the policy debate: "Iran remains the strategic buffer between the

---

[70] Shultz, *Turmoil and Triumph*, 236-37.

[71] Timmerman, *Fanning the Flames*, chap. 7.

[72] "Iran-Iraq War: Analysis of Possible US Shift from Position of Strict Neutrality," Information Memorandum to Mr. Eagleburger from Nicholas A. Veliotes and Jonathan Howe, October 7, 1983, 1. *Digital National Security Archive-ProQuest*, DNSA Collections: Iraqgate and US Policy and Iran, 1978-2015.

[73] Ibid., 6.

Soviet Union and the Gulf; closer US relations with Iraq would tend to draw Iran closer to the Soviet Union and weaken the nonaligned and anti-Soviet position held by many in the Tehran regime."[74] Nevertheless, Shultz drew upon the analysis of Howe and Veliotes to propose that a tilt was necessary because Iraq faced defeat, despite the fact that he must have known this was a false argument. Iraq was just then reaching a position of overwhelming military power vis a vis Iran with infusions of new weapons from Western powers such as France, and a major resupply of weaponry from the Soviets.

Shultz crafted a series of flimsy reasons to justify this change in policy. He claimed that the United States must act to forestall Iraq's collapse to maintain regional stability and to keep pressure on Syria. Otherwise, a Syrian Iranian axis would emerge to dominate the region. Saddam had changed, he argued, having indicated his willingness to support Washington's goals by supporting the US position in Lebanon, accepting Israel's right to exist, and ceasing his support for international terrorism by expelling Abu Nidal. Indeed, Saddam had even "invited Amnesty International for discussions over human rights issues in Iraq." Iran, on the other hand, not only supported "terrorism through training, financing and equipping various groups, and . . . is suspected for its complicity in the bombings in Lebanon and Kuwait," Khomeini's "human rights record is atrocious." The United States, he maintained, must "at all costs prevent Iranian success."[75]

The claim that Iran had been complicit in the Beirut bombing brought an immediate outcry from Weinberger, who realized that if Iran could be saddled with responsibility it would place yet another obstacle in the way of rebuilding relations. Thus, Weinberger put the blame on Syria, claiming that he possessed "intelligence data showing that Syria supplied and trained 20 Iranians to blow up the Marine headquarters in Beirut." The terrorist operation "could not be put together without some of the highest levels of the Syrian government knowing." Based on the intelligence data, Weinberger was "'absolutely sure' that Syria sponsored the October 23 attack."[76] Pointing the finger of responsibility at Syria, of course, also implicated the Soviet Union, Syria's close ally.

President Reagan, hoping to avoid closing the door on Iran, sought to take a neutral position, yet be partially responsive to Shultz. At the end of November, he signed NSDD-114, "US Policy Toward the Iran-Iraq War." Focusing on the protection of shipping through the Persian Gulf, and making no reference to Iran, the directive stated:

---

[74] Richard Preece, *The Iran-Iraq War: Implications for US Policy*, Congressional Research Service Issue Brief no. IB84016 (Washington, DC: Library of Congress: Congressional Research Service, March 8, 1984), 3.

[75] Ibid. In his memoirs, *Turmoil and Triumph*, 237, Shultz argued that the attack on the Marine barracks "was the work of Iran . . . . In this situation, a tilt toward Iraq was warranted to prevent Iranian dominance of the Persian Gulf."

[76] Charles Corddry, "Weinberger 'Sure' of Syrian Bomb Role," *Baltimore Sun*, November 27, 1983, A1.

It is present United States policy to undertake whatever measures may be necessary to keep the Strait of Hormuz open to international shipping. Accordingly, US military forces will attempt to deter and, if that fails, to defeat any hostile efforts to close the Strait to international shipping. Because of the real and psychological impact of a curtailment in the flow of oil from the Persian Gulf on the international economic system, we must assure our readiness to deal promptly with actions aimed at disrupting that traffic.[77]

Concluding, the directive mandated that Weinberger and the Chairman of the JCS, General Vessey, "in coordination with the Secretary of State . . . maintain a continuing review of tensions in the area."

Shultz did more than review the tensions. He appears to have set the stage to exacerbate them in a way consistent with his plan to tilt toward Iraq. First, in early December, in an act fully consistent with the president's decision, a State-Defense team headed by Deputy Assistant Secretary of State James Placke and Deputy Assistant Secretary of Defense Major General Edwin Tixier traveled to Saudi Arabia, Kuwait, Bahrain, Qatar, the United Arab Emirates and Oman to reiterate the president's "pledge to keep open the Strait of Hormuz." While "contingencies" were discussed, no guarantee was extended for "protection against Iranian attacks," but the presence of a naval task force in the Gulf was reassuring.[78]

On December 19-20, however, Shultz sent newly appointed Middle East envoy Donald Rumsfeld to the region, to meet with Saddam Hussein. He carried a letter from the president, whose contents were not divulged, and offered to reestablish diplomatic relations broken by Baghdad after the Six Day War in 1967. Rumsfeld informed Saddam of Washington's concern "if the Iranian revolution were to spread triumphantly in the strategic region." This was the reason, he said, the United States had decided to oppose the defeat of Iraq (a remark which no doubt bemused the Iraqi dictator, who was confident that defeat was unlikely).

Rumsfeld also apparently made "informal suggestions . . . that Iraq quietly begin 'trial basis' efforts to export some of its oil in tankers in the Persian Gulf." It would be a win-win situation for Iraq. If Iran did nothing, then Iraq's inability to increase oil exports, currently limited to pipelines through Turkey and Jordan, would be alleviated. But, if Iran attacked the tankers, then the United States could utilize its naval assets and make good on its pledge to keep open the Strait.[79]

---

[77] "US Policy toward the Iran-Iraq War," National Security Decision Directive 114, November 26, 1983. *Digital National Security Archive-ProQuest*, DNSA Collection: Presidential Directives, Part II.
[78] Don Oberdorfer, "US Moves to Avert Iraqi Loss," *Washington Post*, January 1, 1984, A1.
[79] Ibid.

Finally, in December, Shultz also named Richard Fairbanks as Special Ambassador and sent him to make the rounds of US friends and allies to urge them to stop all arms sales to Iran, but not to Iraq. According to Fairbanks, "it may not have been a 100% success, but we definitely managed to stop most major weapons systems from reaching Iran from US allies. By the time I returned to private law practice in September 1985, Iran's major suppliers were almost all Soviet Bloc countries."[80] (The reader may recall that the fall of 1985 marked the beginning of the president's Iran initiative to ship weapons to Iran.)

Shultz continued to press forward with his dual approach, tilting toward Iraq while isolating Iran. In the first week of January 1984, the tilt toward Iraq became public, as did his decision two weeks later to place Iran on the state sponsors of terrorism list. "A senior American official," actually Shultz himself, professed to be concerned about three Iranian threats: "mining of the Strait of Hormuz; attacks on oil shipping; and a decisive [Iranian] victory on the battlefield with Iraq." The US was also worried about "the growing danger of Iranian-supported terrorism in the region."[81] When Shultz placed Iran on the terrorism sponsors list, he justified his action based on his suspicion, never confirmed, that Iran had been responsible for the attack on the Marine barracks.

In fact, Shultz's tilt to Iraq concealed another purpose, not only to isolate Iran, but to align the United States with the Soviet Union to establish a presumed basis for cooperation. While the secretary's intent may have been to attempt to cooperate with Moscow on settling the war, that was manifestly not Moscow's objective, as would shortly become clear. The outcome of the Iran-Iraq war would go a long way toward determining the future shape of the world oil market, in both quantity and price. American leaders were not naïve; intelligence estimates clearly identified Soviet strategy as seeking to gain control over Middle East oil. Why assist in this process? This was not an issue that would be settled in cooperation with Moscow; rather, it could only be settled in contention, but Shultz would not be deflected from his quest.

Meanwhile, the running debate over state-supported international terrorism bubbled to the surface once again after another terrorist attack on the US embassy in Kuwait, and the release of the Long Commission report on the Marine barracks terrorist attack. It was well understood within the administration that the public identification of the Soviet Union as a state sponsor of terrorism would place a large obstacle in the way of any possible improvement of relations, which is why Shultz strove to keep the discussion on a theoretical level, not naming the Soviet Union. Other members of the administration were not so constrained.

In an interview Chief of Naval Operations Admiral James Watkins, citing the Long report, declared that unlike past random acts to make a political statement, the new international terrorism is supported by nation states and is "an

---

[80] As quoted in Timmerman, *Fanning the Flames*, chap. 7.
[81] David Ignatius and Gerald Seib, "US Tilts toward Iraq to Thwart Iran," *Wall Street Journal*, January 6, 1984, 24.

integrated part of a strategy in which there are well-defined political and military objectives." Adm. Watkins explained:

> For a growing number of states, terrorism has become an alternative means of conducting state business and the terrorists themselves are agents whose association the state can easily deny . . . . Armed with operational guidance and intelligence from their sponsor, there are few targets beyond their capability to attack. Consequently, they constitute a potent instrument of state policy.[82]

Watkins said that the United States must take "a hard look" at what can be done to cut off terrorism "at its source." While many things could be done defensively, such as building bunkers and higher fences, stringing barbed wire and wearing flak jackets, this was "just not good enough." He agreed with the commission's conclusion that "it make little sense to learn that a state or its surrogate is conducting a terrorist campaign or planning a terrorist attack and not confront that government with political or military consequences if it continues forward."[83]

The CNO had come as close as he could to naming the Soviet Union without actually doing so. Clearly, to anyone reading this report, the unnamed subject here, the "source," which had adopted terrorism as an alternative means of conducting state business—and which must be confronted if it continued forward—was the Soviet Union. Syria and Iran's agents operating in Lebanon were merely Moscow's surrogates, but identification of the Soviet Union as a state supporter of international terrorism was, as yet, prohibited by administration officials.

Syria, the Iran-Iraq War, and Moscow

If Shultz thought that his tilt toward Iraq and isolation of Iran had settled the question of US strategy, he was wrong. The president would attempt to reestablish relations with Iran over the vehement opposition of his secretary of state the following year, with disastrous results for himself, politically, and the United States, in what would become known as the Iran-Contra affair. However, at that moment, there was still another aspect of the coming Iranian offensive against Iraq he had to address. As in 1982, the Iranian offensive was expected to be a pincer that would include Syrian pressure against Iraq. The question was: how would the United States neutralize the Syrian prong?

There was no question of employing the Israelis to counter Syria as Haig had done in 1982. The failure of Israel's Lebanon War had led to a change of strategy, the abandonment of the goal of a unified Lebanon and acceptance of its

---

[82] Walter Andrews, "Halt Terrorism at Source, Watkins Says," *Washington Times*, January 2, 1984, A1.
[83] Ibid.

de facto partition, with Israeli forces in control of the southern tip of the country. Israel had justified holding a position in the south on the grounds that Syria had not yet withdrawn from the north, a position that Shultz had sanctioned in a side letter to the May 17 pact. However, there was little likelihood of a Syrian withdrawal as a newly fortified Damascus sought to exploit its opportunity to consolidate control around Beirut.

Following unsuccessful attempts to persuade both Yitzhak Shamir and Amin Gemayel to adopt a more robust policy in Lebanon (the Lebanese forces were too weak and the IDF refused), Shultz arrived at a course of action that involved using American power to neutralize Syria, should it become necessary.[84] First, hoping to avoid that step, he sought to reach an accommodation with Hafez Assad, dissuading him from cooperating in Moscow's presumed pincer scheme, offering a more representative Lebanese government under Amin Gemayal, which would include Syria's Druze and Muslim allies.

Before making Assad an offer, however, Shultz gave him a taste of what could be expected if he refused to cooperate, as well as to assess more precisely what capability Syria's newly refurbished air defenses possessed following the Soviet Union's massive replenishment of arms after the 1982 war. On December 4, 1983, two F-14 reconnaissance jets were sent over northern Lebanon drawing a heavy response from Syrian gun and missile batteries. Reportedly, "a combination of anti-aircraft fire and at least 10 surface-to-air missiles" were fired at the two US planes. All missed.[85]

The administration responded immediately, the next day, sending 28 attack bombers, A6E *Intruders* and A7 *Corsairs*, from the carriers *Kennedy* and *Independence* stationed offshore to strike targets at Syrian air defense and command headquarters east of Beirut. Receiving unexpectedly heavy anti-aircraft fire from SA-7 and SA-9 surface-to-air missiles as well as ZSU-23 anti-aircraft guns, however, two planes were downed and a third damaged in the attack, with one pilot killed and another, Lt. Robert Goodman, captured after bailing out.[86] Syrian-backed Druze militia forces immediately retaliated against the US Marines in Beirut, killing eight, and US warships responded with a heavy bombardment of Druze positions. It was the first US use of combat aircraft in the Middle East, marking the beginning of air strikes and naval bombardment that would continue in tit-for-tat fashion over the next several weeks and formed the backdrop for Shultz's efforts to persuade Assad.[87]

---

[84] Bernard Gwertzman, "US Bids Gemayel Broaden His Base to Unify Lebanon," *New York Times*, December 2, 1983, A1.

[85] David Ottaway, "8 Marines Killed After US Raid," *Washington Post*, December 5, 1983, A1.

[86] Goodman would be held for a month and released on January 4, 1984 as a sign of Syrian good faith.

[87] Thomas Friedman, "US Ships Attack Syrian Positions in Beirut Region," *New York Times*, December 14, 1983, A1. For an excellent survey of events, see Larry Fabian,

Controversy immediately surrounded the US action, with critics pointing out that with all of the satellite and communications intercept coverage focused on Lebanon, it was unnecessary to send F-14s to acquire more intelligence. And, if lessons needed to be administered, naval bombardment would have been more effective and less risky than an air strike. In their view, "the F-14s were employed to draw Syrian fire and thus provide a pretext for a major bombing attack the next day."[88] Of course, neither satellite photography, nor naval bombardment would have revealed as much of the capability of Syria's new air-defense system as an air strike.

Nevertheless, while denying devious intent, the president defended the use of force, declaring that "our days of weakness are over." "Now the world knows that, when it comes to our national security, the United States will do whatever it takes to protect the safety and freedom of the American people."[89] The message, of course, was to Moscow, not to the "world," and it was that the United States had decided to up the ante in its use of military force. Indeed, on December 5, President Reagan had signed NSDD-117 on Lebanon, authorizing US forces to use "*vigorous* self-defense against all attacks from any hostile quarter."[90]

Washington was pursuing a policy of carrots and sticks. While announcing the new policy of "instant retaliation" in the Middle East, and strengthening relations with Israel once again, Secretary Shultz was also sending Donald Rumsfeld to Damascus for talks with Assad. While US and Syrian forces were exchanging fire over Lebanon, Rumsfeld sought to convince Assad to cooperate with Gemayel in supporting a broad-based coalition government. However, Assad would not be intimidated by the demonstration of American power and felt no need to cooperate with Gemayal, who was already in his pocket. Thus, he adamantly refused to cooperate unless and until Gemayel formally repudiated Shultz's May 17 agreement between Israel and Lebanon and Israeli forces withdrew completely from Lebanon. [91]

Rumsfeld may also have intimated that the United States would be withdrawing its troops from Beirut. In any case, that is what would shortly occur, with some public loss of face for Shultz, whose policy would be labeled an abject

"The Middle East: War Dangers and Receding Peace Prospects," *Foreign Affairs*: *America and the World 1983*, 632-58.

[88] Drew Middleton, "US Flights over Lebanon: Their Value Called into Question," *New York Times*, December 10, 1983, 8.

[89] Juan Williams, "President Defends Using Force," *Washington Post*, December 13, 1983, A1.

[90] "Lebanon," NSDD-117, December 5, 1983, in Christopher Simpson, *National Security Directives of the Reagan and Bush Administrations: The Declassified History of US Political and Military Policy, 1981-1991* (Boulder: Westview, 1995), 355.

[91] Fred Hiatt, "US Initiates 'Instant Retaliation' Policy in Mideast," *Washington Post*, December 14, 1983, A1; and David Ottaway, "US Envoy Holds Talks with Syrians," *Washington Post*, December 15, 1983, 1.

failure. In other words, as Washington was demonstrating its willingness to project power from offshore with aircraft and naval bombardment to ensure that Syria was mindful of the consequences of cooperating with Moscow, the administration was also offering Assad an open invitation to strengthen his position in Lebanon as the Marines were withdrawn. Thus, Shultz's "solution" to the presumed Syrian prong against Iraq was to divert Damascus into Lebanon. The problem was that Syria was, at least on paper, now powerful enough to manage both.

Everything about this deal, from the "tilt" toward Iraq to the "diversion" of Syria, hinged on the very dubious assumption that Iran was militarily superior to Iraq, whose defeat was imminent. Furthermore, Shultz's scheme ignored Soviet strategy entirely. The massive Soviet resupply of Iraq, including Scud and longer-range missiles and precursor chemicals for poison gas, as well as helicopters, tanks, rocket launchers, and artillery, made unmistakable Moscow's determination to prevent Saddam's defeat. The equally massive resupply of Syria's air and ground forces, especially provision of the SA-5, the long-range air defense missile, strongly suggested a Soviet intention to establish an air defense shield over Syria and the Eastern Mediterranean.

Aside from the president's decision to keep open the strait, which addressed the larger question of oil supply and price, Shultz's isolation of Iran and support for Iraq and Syria could not have been better contrived to support Moscow's own strategy. That is, if the secretary understood what that strategy was, which seems highly likely. As some others were publicly declaring at the time, Moscow's game was to weaken Iran in a war of attrition, then promote a takeover from within.[92] The Soviets had no intention of actually assisting Iran to conquer one of their most valuable allies.

Indeed, the critical moment for Moscow was fast approaching with the imminent Iranian invasion. When it began, as we shall see, the Soviets themselves would encourage Assad to reap the benefits being offered in Lebanon, rather than join in with Iran against Iraq, and to strengthen Iraq further, but more about that below.

---

[92] "Moscow Maneuvers toward a Takeover in Iran," *Businessweek*, August 15, 1983, 46.

Chapter 6

Preserving the Oil Fields:
An Opening to Iran?

As the Iranian invasion date grew closer, the president decided to deliver a speech to extend a conciliatory hand to Moscow, presumably in hopes of dissuading the Soviets from pursuing their plans. Although Matlock claims that the president's intention was to set the stage for a serious negotiation of arms reductions in his second term, a year hence, there were more pressing objectives.[1] As he had done time and again during his presidency, when entering a crisis period, Reagan had spoken out to the Soviets to soften the blow, offer to negotiate a solution, and, most importantly, to contain the problem so that it did not escalate from into a superpower confrontation.

A speech by Defense Minister Dmitry Ustinov on December 14 moderating Moscow's war fever raised some hope that a presidential plea might receive a fair hearing. Ustinov had said that although the world situation was "very tense,"

> no matter how complicated the military and political situation, there is no point in dramatizing it. Soberly appraising the full seriousness of the current situation, we must see that imperialism is far from omnipotent and we are not frightened by its threats. The Soviet people have strong nerves. We people of the older generation have experienced much more difficult times than now.[2]

Ustinov's words were mildly encouraging, but it may have been a more ominous event two weeks later that clinched the president's decision to deliver the speech. In early January the KGB held a conference to review the previous year's work. KGB head Vladimir Kryuchkov's address to the conference warned that the risk of nuclear war had reached "dangerous proportions" and declared to his men that "the single most important task facing them" was to obtain "copies of the secret war plans of the United States and NATO." Accordingly, Moscow

---

[1] Jack F. Matlock, *Reagan and Gorbachev: How the Cold War Ended* (New York: Random House, 2004), 78-86.
[2] As quoted in Don Oberdorfer, *The Turn: From the Cold War to a New Era* (New York: Poseidon Press, 1991), 69.

Center had sent the London (and no doubt other) KGB residencies in Western Europe instructions to monitor steps to put Western military and civilian agencies on a war footing.[3]

Whether American intelligence was able to obtain Kryuchkov's speech, or was able to intercept KGB transmissions, no doubt Gordievsky passed on to British intelligence the instructions to the London residency about stepped up vigilance of Western activities. If so, the notion that the Soviets were prepared to preempt any signs of war preparations by the west, as in the signal sent during Able Archer scarcely two months before, would have removed any doubts on the part of President Reagan that it would be appropriate to extend a friendly hand to Moscow at this juncture.

Reagan's January 16 Speech: The Turn?

The president decided to deliver his speech just before the opening of the Stockholm disarmament conference in mid-January where Secretary Shultz would have an opportunity to reinforce the administration's position in talks with Foreign Minister Gromyko. Consequently, one of the president's main themes was a plea to establish a "constructive and realistic working relationship" with Moscow (a phrase he used four times in the speech). Reagan declared that his administration had "halted America's decline," with a now strong economy, a rebuilt defense, solid alliances, and a commitment to "defend our values" as never before.

> We're stronger in all these areas than we were three years ago. Our strength is necessary to deter war and to facilitate negotiated solutions. Soviet leaders know it makes sense to compromise only if they can get something in return. But America can now offer something in return.[4]

America's deterrence was making the world a safer place, but "to say that our restored deterrence has made the world safer is not to say that it's safe enough." We must "engage the Soviets in a dialogue . . . that will serve to promote peace in the troubled regions of the world, reduce the level of arms, and build a constructive working relationship." Reagan proposed a "major effort to see if we can make progress in three broad problem areas": the elimination of the threat and use of force in solving international disputes; reduction of the "vast stockpiles of armaments in the world"; and establishment of a "better working relationship," built on deeds not words.

The administration's approach to these three tasks, the president continued, would be based on three guiding principles: "realism, strength, and

---

[3] Christopher Andrew and Oleg Gordievsky, *KGB: The Inside Story of Its Foreign Operations from Lenin to Gorbachev* (New York: HarperCollins, 1990), 601-02.

[4] "Transcript of Reagan's Speech on Soviet-American Relations," *New York Times*, January 17, 1984, A8.

dialogue." Realism meant "we are in a long-term competition with a Government that doesn't share our notion of individual liberty at home and peaceful change abroad." Strength—military, political, and moral—was "essential to negotiate successfully and protect our interests." Strength and dialogue went "hand in hand." The United States, he said, was prepared to "work for practical, fair solutions on the basis of mutual compromise." Priority number one was to reduce the "risk of war," especially nuclear war.

Referring to Ustinov's speech in December, Reagan said "these are encouraging words, but now is the time to move from words to deeds." Our negotiators were "ready to return to the negotiating table to work towards agreements in INF, Start, and MBFR." We also seek to "reduce the chances for dangerous misunderstanding and miscalculation" and toward this end have put forward confidence-building measures, such as "advanced notification of missile tests and major military exercises." Last week, the president noted, there had been productive discussions with the Soviets in Washington designed to improve communication, including the hot line. Then, Reagan came to his immediate point, the Iran-Iraq conflict, saying that

> arms control has long been the most visible area of US-Soviet dialogue. But a durable peace also requires ways for both of us to defuse tensions and regional conflicts. Take the Middle East as an example. Everyone's interest would be served by stability in the region . . . . The Soviets could help reduce tensions there instead of introducing sophisticated weapons into the area.

Recalling a theme from John F. Kennedy's seminal speech at American University twenty years earlier: "let us not be blind to our differences but let us also direct attention to our common interests . . . ," Reagan challenged the Soviets to eliminate the risk of nuclear war. The president saw these differences as those of "Government structure and philosophy" and the common interests as "things of everyday life for people everywhere." He posed the hypothetical question of what a Russian and an American couple, Ivan and Anya and Jim and Sally, might do if they happened to find themselves sharing a shelter from a storm.

He doubted that they would debate differences between their governments. More likely, he thought, they would "compare notes" about their work, children, hopes, and hobbies. His point was that "people don't make wars," governments do, and concluded by saying "if the Soviet Government wants peace, then there will be peace." Together we can help "fulfill the hopes and dreams of those we represent and, indeed, of people everywhere. Let us begin now."

Much was made of this speech. Some writers of this period claim that the speech "was a turning point in the US attitude toward Moscow," asserting that Reagan had undergone a conversion akin to the biblical Saul's on the road to

Damascus.[5] But, Reagan underwent no such conversion; the speech was designed to change public perceptions, countering a ratings dip in the polls, and to set the tone for the president's re-election campaign. As Reagan described it, by early 1984: "the balance in the arms race had already changed." What was necessary was to "hang tough and stay the course" and bring about a change in public perception, which had the United States "on the defensive." With the speech, he maintained, "we went on the offensive."[6]

In devising the reelection campaign plan, Richard Wirthlin, the president's pollster, had concluded that with the economy booming, Reagan's main vulnerability would be foreign policy, particularly the "peace" issue, on which he had been attacked in 1980. The Soviet-generated "war scare" was clearly having an impact on public opinion. There was little doubt, he reported to the president, that the Democrats would focus their attacks there again. In Wirthlin's view:

> The claim that the Reagan administration has maintained the peace would be fortified if we could show some progress in negotiating an arms settlement.[7]

It was a somewhat ironic turnabout. Reagan had defeated Jimmy Carter on both the economic and foreign policy arguments, but especially on the argument that he had been too soft on the Soviets. Four years later, the Democrats, unable to criticize his successful economic policy, were expected to mount a challenge against him on the grounds that he had been too tough on the Soviets, so much so that his policies might lead to war. The irony was that he would have to become more like Carter, soften his approach, in order to be reelected. So, it was with the understanding his reelection campaign would be enhanced by seizing the "peace" issue that Secretary Shultz's constant refrain about seeking better relations with Moscow began to receive a more attentive hearing.

In other words, the January 16 speech, delivered two weeks before the president announced his decision to seek reelection, was intended to enhance that prospect by turning the corner on the "peace" issue. However, in extending Moscow a friendly hand, the president also raised a mailed fist. Little noticed in his speech was a reference to "mounting evidence" of Soviet violations of agreements and treaties. "In response to a Congressional request, a report on this will be submitted in the next few days. It is clear that we cannot simply assume that agreements negotiated will be fulfilled. We must take the Soviet compliance record into account . . . "[8]

---

[5] Oberdorfer, *The Turn*, 72; and Beth A. Fischer, *The Reagan Reversal: Foreign Policy and the End of the Cold War* (Columbia, MO: University of Missouri Press, 1997), 49; passim.

[6] Ronald Reagan, *An American Life* (New York: Simon & Schuster, 1990), 590.

[7] Oberdorfer, *The Turn*, 71.

[8] "Transcript of Reagan's Speech on Soviet-American Relations."

As pundits Evans and Novak saw it, Reagan had positioned himself perfectly. "If Soviet conduct permits Reagan to play his trump card of peace . . . the 1980 warmonger cry will strike deaf ears." On the other hand, "if the Soviets compel Reagan to make a campaign cause out of the cheating issue . . . the Democrats may find themselves unwittingly tainted by Soviet deeds that originated on their White House watch . . . "[9]

Moscow's "Turn"

Meanwhile, in Stockholm, the Shultz-Gromyko encounter was bruising and hostile. Although Shultz had "hoped" that the Stockholm conference would mark a "turning point in East-West relations," [10] in declaring that "the United States does not recognize the legitimacy of the artificially imposed division of Europe," he raised the entire question of the post-World War II political structure of Europe. On the other hand, he also sought "ways to make surprise attack more difficult, to make miscalculation less likely, to inhibit the use of military might for intimidation or coercion, to put greater predictability into peaceful military exercises . . . and to enhance our ability to defuse incipient crises."[11]

In reply, Gromyko could not have been more negative, continuing to accuse Reagan of banging the drums of war. In what the secretary termed a "truly brutal" litany of rejection, the Soviet foreign minister saw the president's speech as "hostile" to the Soviet Union and excoriated the administration as "thinking in terms of war and acting accordingly." "Militarism, enmity and war hysteria are being exported to Western Europe along with the missiles."[12] Gromyko viewed US policy around the world in the same fashion. In Lebanon, the United States was "sowing death and destruction," and in Grenada, the US had undertaken a "piratic, terrorist action." Washington was propping up a "regime of butchers" in El Salvador and sending "bands of mercenaries, terrorists against Nicaragua."[13]

The Russians, however, were doing a two-step of their own. Two weeks later, on the eve of the president's State of the Union speech, "Andropov," ostensibly from his sickbed, sent a "conciliatory" response, asking Washington to demonstrate "practical deeds" to open the way for a dialogue. However, a Soviet

---

[9] Rowland Evans and Robert Novak, "The Week Reagan Played His Trump," *Washington Post*, January 18, 1984, A21.

[10] David Ignatius, "Shultz Expected to Suggest Resumption of Arms Talks Using Confidential Forum," *Wall Street Journal*, January 18, 1984, 32.

[11] "Shultz: US Won't Accept The 'Artificial Barrier' Now 'Imposed on Europe,'" *Washington Post*, January 19, 1984, A29.

[12] "US-Soviet Clash of Ideas at Stockholm Conference," *Washington Post*, January 19, 1984, A29.

[13] George Shultz, *Turmoil and Triumph: My Years as Secretary of State* (New York: Scribner, 1993), 467-68. Remarkably, Shultz averred that he had perceived "a turn" at Stockholm where he and Gromyko had broken the ice. Incidentally, Shultz omitted from his account the sentence regarding the refusal of the United States to recognize the artificial division of Europe.

general, no doubt hoping to preempt and neutralize the sting of the noncompliance report just sent to Congress, charged at the same time that the United States had violated the honored but never ratified SALT II treaty by deploying the Pershing II/cruise missile package to Western Europe.[14]

Moscow defined as strategic any weapon that could hit the Soviet Union. However, State Department spokesman Alan Romberg immediately pointed out that the treaty contained a different definition of what was "strategic." The treaty defined as strategic those missiles with a range exceeding 3,400 miles, which neither the Pershing II, nor the cruise missile possessed, but it was true that they could strike Soviet territory.[15]

Then, the *Washington Times* reported that the Soviets had begun to base cruise-missile-carrying submarines at Cienfuegos, Cuba, and deploy them off the southeast coast of the United States.[16] A second alarming report from the same newspaper disclosed that American intelligence had discovered Soviet pilots in Cuba "practicing bombing techniques used to deliver nuclear weapons." The aircraft involved were MiG-23s and the Soviet Union's most advanced fighter-bomber, the MiG-27. Several dozen of these nuclear-capable aircraft were deployed to the island.[17]

President Reagan would not be intimidated, continuing to stir Moscow's worst fears, pressing forward with decisions to strengthen US positions in space and missile defense. While in his State of the Union address he assured the Soviet people that "a nuclear war cannot be won and must never be fought," in the same address he declared that he was "directing NASA to develop a permanently manned space station, and to do it within a decade."[18] Then, "administration sources" disclosed that two weeks earlier the president had signed NSDD 119, "formally setting in motion a stepped-up multibillion-dollar research program to determine if new space-based or other advanced defensive weapons can be developed to stop an enemy missile attack."[19] And, further demonstrating American technological prowess, the US Air Force announced the first successful test of an anti-satellite rocket launched at high altitude by an F-15 fighter.[20]

---

[14] Don Oberdorfer, "Soviet Says US Missiles Violate SALT II," *Washington Post*, January 25, 1984, A18.

[15] Timothy Elder, "US Denies Euromissiles Violate Pact," *Washington Times*, January 26, 1984, A6.

[16] Ted Agres, "Soviet Subs off US Bear Cruise Missiles," *Washington Times*, January 27, 1984, A1.

[17] Ted Agres, "Soviets Test A-Bombing over Cuba," *Washington Times*, January 30, 1984, A1.

[18] "Text of Message from the President on the State of the Union," *New York Times*, January 26, 1984, B8.

[19] Michael Getler, "Reagan Signs Anti-Missile Research Order," *Washington Post*, January 26, 1984, A1.

[20] "Reagan's ASAT Folly," *Boston Globe*, January 24, 1984, 27.

Meanwhile, in Washington, it was becoming increasingly evident that the president and his secretary of state were at odds over policy toward the Soviet Union, this time over the very report on Soviet treaty violations to which the Russians had objected. On January 23, the president delivered to Congress the report of a special review panel detailing Soviet cheating on arms control treaties and agreements dating from the 1925 Geneva protocol that banned the use of poison gas; and including every arms control agreement entered into with the United States—the ABM Treaty, SALT I Agreement, the Threshold Test Ban Treaty, the Biological and Toxin Weapons Convention, the Helsinki Final Act, and the (unratified) SALT II Treaty.

Secretary Shultz, in league with James Baker in the White House, soft-pedaled the charge of Soviet treaty violations; Shultz because it placed an obstacle in the way of his strategic goal of improving relations with the Soviets and Baker because it would presumably hamper Reagan's reelection campaign. Consequently, State Department briefings and press reportage downplayed the issue by stating that evidence for the violations was not "ironclad" and it was an issue better to be handled privately with Moscow.[21]

But the report was in fact the product of a major presidential decision, NSDD-121, which was intended to place an obstacle in the way of any attempt to make a dramatic improvement in relations with Moscow. As Evans and Novak pointed out, the report was "the gravest charge of treaty cheating ever sent to Moscow" and concluded that its dispatch to the Senate "was a defeat" for Shultz, who was trying "to promote a nonexistent warming trend with Moscow."[22]

NSDD-121 declared that Soviet noncompliance with arms control agreements "raises serious questions for US national security, our Alliances, arms control, and US-Soviet relations." Seven violations were identified. Most were not new, but all were serious, especially the charges that the Krasnoyarsk radar "almost certainly constitutes a violation of . . . the Anti-Ballistic Missile Treaty of 1972," that encryption of missile test data was a "violation" of the SALT II treaty, and that the new SS-X-25 missile's reentry-vehicle to throw-weight ratio constituted a "violation" of SALT II. In addition, the Soviets had violated the 1925 Geneva Protocol against the use of poison gas and the Biological and Toxin Weapons Convention of 1975 prohibiting the development of biological agents and toxins.[23]

Thus, while Reagan strove to position himself as the "peace" candidate in the coming election campaign, he also sought to raise the bar against any attempt to reach an accommodation with the Soviet Union. Indeed, Reagan

---

[21] See, for example, "Are the Soviets Cheating?" *St. Louis Post-Dispatch*, January 19, 1984, 31; and Joseph Harsch, "Nuclear Cheating," *Christian Science Monitor*, February 2, 1984, 6.

[22] Rowland Evans and Robert Novak, "Softpedaling the President's Alarm," *Washington Post*, February 3, 1984, 19.

[23] "Soviet Noncompliance with Arms Control Agreements," NSDD-121, January 14, 1984 (declassified February 8, 1996) *National Security Council*.

ordered the report on Soviet treaty violations briefed to all US allies to ensure that his concerns were understood. The Soviets interpreted the president's actions in precisely that way. Denouncing the president's State of the Union address, *Tass* and *Novosti* bitterly attacked the plan for a space station as "one more link" in US plans to militarize space. Furthermore, "the approaching elections in the USA compel the Reagan administration to change tactics to replace invectives against the USSR with more cautious words, and to use peace phraseology in official statements."[24]

The Russians were determined to keep the pressure on. Moscow not only sent a diplomatic note to the State Department charging the United States with multiple arms control treaty violations, it published the note in full, an extraordinary act which appeared "to symbolize a further deterioration in Soviet-American relations" and "placed into doubt the entire process of arms control." Aside from making the outrageous charge that Washington was "systematically" violating the principle of confidentiality in the arms talks and repeating its charge that the Pershing II/cruise missile deployment violated SALT II, the Russians raised a series of new charges, essentially projecting their own objectives onto the United States.

Among the charges were accusations that "shelters" built over Minuteman II and Titan II missile silos were designed "to conceal work to refit these launchers into MIRVed missiles." Washington was violating the ABM Treaty in the same way, using "shelters" to conceal a developing mobile ABM radar and Minuteman I as an ABM missile. The radar on Shemya Island in the Aleutians included "elements tested for ABM purposes" and the "new big Pave Paws radar stations" have the potential to support a nationwide ABM defense. [25] It was nothing less than the pot calling the kettle black.

Thus, on the eve of what promised to be a period of protracted crisis, as Iran prepared to undertake what it proclaimed would be the final offensive against Iraq, and the overthrow of Saddam Hussein, the United States and the Soviet Union traded barbs—the Soviets hurling invective and threatening war; and Reagan taunting the Russians with a show of American moral, technological, and military might. The trend toward confrontation was interrupted by that all was not well in the Kremlin, which immediately raised the question of whether there would be an imminent change of leadership and what that might mean for Soviet foreign policy.

---

[24] Andrew Rosenthal, "Address Is Denounced by Soviets," *Philadelphia Inquirer*, January 27, 1984, 7.
[25] Dusko Doder, "Soviets Say US Cheats on Treaties," *Washington Post*, January 30, 1984, A1.

The "Death" of
Andropov and "Rise" of Chernenko

The death of Andropov, announced on February 9, 1983 to the strains of funereal music on Moscow radio, ended at last the more than four months-long charade about the health of the Soviet leader. Four days later, in what was an apparently difficult if not contentious decision, Konstantin Chernenko, who had lost to Andropov after Brezhnev's demise, was named the new party chief. Chernenko's appointment contravened expectations in the West because his faction had lost significant power to the Andropov faction, most recently in a series of personnel shifts, appointments, and demotions during the Central Committee and Supreme Soviet sessions at the end of December.[26]

In retrospect, the timing of Andropov's death and the ascension of Chernenko, the last of the hardline Brezhnevites, signified that the Soviets had determined to press on with the final phase of a long-term strategy dating back to the 24th Party Congress in April 1971. That general strategy, which I have termed the "Brezhnev gamble," was to utilize growing Soviet nuclear and conventional weapons strength to alter the global geopolitical balance of power to advantage.[27] The focus of this strategy had shifted after the fall of the shah of Iran to embrace the now feasible goal of obtaining decisive leverage over Middle Eastern oil, and the main means of accomplishing this objective was the capture of Iran.

As demonstrated in this volume, by early 1984, the USSR's general strategy had failed in all of its crucial parts: The Soviets were failing to maintain strategic superiority, had failed to establish nuclear dominance over Western Europe, or Japan; had failed to disrupt the Western Alliance, and China was on the verge of shifting to the US side. Finally, they had failed in three consecutive attempts to capture control of Iran from within. The essential significance of Chernenko's ascension to General Secretary—a decision publicly supported by Foreign Minister Gromyko, Defense Minister Ustinov, and Armed Forces Chief of Staff Ogarkov, was that the Soviets would now make their fourth try.

Mikhail Gorbachev, leader of the Andropov faction clearly waiting in the wings, was designated Second Secretary; and three of Andropov's former aides, A.M. Alexandrov, P. Plaptev, and V.V. Sharapov, were assigned to "assist" Chernenko, who was only able to name two of his own men—V.V. Pribytkov and

---

[26] Dusko Doder, "Soviet Promotions Seen Important to Succession," *Washington Post*, December 30, 1983, A19. In early February, the publication of a new history of the CPSU, a revised version of the sixth edition that appeared eighteen months earlier, contained hints of what was to come. The new edition "gave unusual prominence to Konstantin Chernenko," and praised Brezhnev as a "leading revolutionary and peace champion, and greatest political and state figure of the mid-20th century." See Dusko Doder, "Soviet History Puts Brezhnev in New Light," *Washington Post*, February 6, 1984, A13.

[27] See the author's *The Nixon-Kissinger Years: Reshaping America's Foreign Policy*, 2nd ed. (St. Paul: Paragon House, 2001).

V.A. Pechenev—to his staff.[28] Thus, the decision to elevate Chernenko was a general leadership decision, not the victory of one faction over another. He would run out the string on the current strategy and Andropov's aides would be there to ensure that everything went according to plan; and if it didn't, they would be there to pick up the pieces.

President Reagan, perhaps sensing that the Soviets had made a major decision, decided "the time had come to explore holding a summit conference with Chernenko." He believed that while the Soviets had not changed their "secular religion of expansionism and world domination . . . something else had changed. I felt we could now go to the summit, for the first time in years, from a position of strength."[29]

The reason for the president's interest in direct contact was that the Iranian invasion of Iraq was just getting under way and the odds for a dangerous Soviet miscalculation were increasing. Indeed, the president became unusually active in seeking a meeting, engaging in an exchange of five letters with Chernenko through the spring, to no avail, and resorting to an attempt to make direct contact through a visit by former national security adviser Brent Scowcroft, which also was rebuffed.[30]

The reason for the Soviet Union's obdurate stance was to increase the president's doubts about the lengths to which the Soviets were prepared to go to achieve their ends and also to deflect attempts to influence their course. Turning a cold shoulder to Reagan was only one of several steps Moscow took in preparing the battleground for the endgame over Iran. Relations with the West, in general, as well as with China, iced over. The Soviets also began a major sweep against US assets in Moscow. Sources, secure for years, were being arrested, covers blown, and electronic intercepts blocked. "It was as if the KGB had been given a list of every source for the station and the name of every CIA official in the embassy."[31]

From early February, roughly coinciding with the announcement of Andropov's death, and continuing through much of May, the Soviets manifested a massive display of military power, in worldwide military exercises. These exercises included test-firing ballistic missiles; deploying of conventional air, ground, and naval forces; and the evacuation of an entire city, classic signals that suggested preparation for war with the United States.[32]

---

[28] John W. Parker, *Kremlin in Transition*, vol. 1, *From Brezhnev to Chernenko, 1978 to 1985* (Boston: Unwin Hyman, 1991), 341.

[29] Reagan, *An American Life*, 593-4.

[30] Shultz, *Turmoil and Triumph*, 473 and Matlock, *Reagan and Gorbachev*, 94-96.

[31] Peter Schweizer, *Victory: The Reagan Administration's Secret Strategy That Hastened the Collapse of the Soviet Union* (New York: Atlantic Monthly Press, 1994), 185-6.

[32] Jack Anderson, "War Game Gives a New Look at Soviet Missiles," *Washington Post*, July 3, 1984, C8.

Moscow's war games reached extremely threatening proportions in early April with the launching of intercontinental ballistic missiles from submarines into Pacific test ranges.[33] But it was the "first ever" firing of six SS-20 missiles from operational silos in the northern USSR that came as a "shock" to American leaders. A top official said that the administration had reached a consensus that the Soviets had decided to "turn up the fear factor to the max."[34]

The missiles were launched on a trajectory that would take them over the North Pole "toward the United States." Although the Russians had notified US authorities of the "test" and although the missiles were destroyed in flight over the Barents Sea, they had engaged the United States in the most serious form of international chicken imaginable—a nuclear missile attack that was only terminated in mid-flight.[35]

Soviet navies conducted drills in the Atlantic, the Pacific, the Mediterranean, the Indian Ocean, the South China Sea, and the Caribbean. By far the largest occurred in the North Atlantic, where without warning over 200 ships and submarines of the northern fleet poured out of Soviet bases in the Baltic and the Arctic into the Norwegian Sea north of the GI-UK gap.[36] Grouped around the 28,000-ton, nuclear-powered battle cruiser *Kirov*, the ships took part in extensive battle maneuvers, joined by some 50 Backfire bombers and Badger long-range reconnaissance aircraft.[37]

Further south, advanced Soviet Delta-class missile carrying submarines also moved from their polar redoubts to positions 500 miles off the Atlantic coast of the United States, joining Yankee-class cruise-missile carrying submarines already on station there.[38] As was their practice, Soviet attack submarines aggressively trailed US naval forces worldwide wherever they went.

The Soviets had given no advance warning to Washington of their plans, as was customary, but not required, which caught US commanders by surprise. Admiral Wesley L. McDonald, supreme allied commander for naval forces in the Atlantic said that he had been "surprised but not shaken" by the large-sale maneuvers.[39] Navy Secretary John Lehman, on the other hand, derided the Delta deployment, declaring that moving them so close to US shores not only

---

[33] Gerald Seib, "Soviet Maneuvers Puzzle US Analysts," *Wall Street Journal*, April 9, 1984, 38.

[34] Rowland Evans and Robert Novak, "A Soviet Fear Campaign," *Washington Post*, May 9, 1984, A31.

[35] Anderson, "War Game Gives a New Look at Soviet Missiles."

[36] R.W. Apple, "Soviet Is Holding Big Naval Games," *New York Times*, April 4, 1984, A4.

[37] "Moscow's Muscle Flexing," *Time*, April 16, 1984, 28.

[38] Robert Toth, "Advanced Soviet A-Subs Move to North Atlantic, Navy Secretary Asserts," *Los Angeles Times*, February 15, 1984, B13.

[39] Peter Almond, "Maneuvers by Soviets a Surprise to NATO," *Washington Times*, April 5, 1984, A6.

complicated their targeting tasks, but it also made it easier to sink them.[40] Lehman was not boasting.

In 1979, the US navy, in a skillful and audacious mission, had placed a tap on a Soviet undersea communications cable in the Barents Sea off Murmansk. (They had also tapped another in the Sea of Okhotsk.) Now, as the Soviets began their naval war games in the North Atlantic, the navy sent the submarine USS *Parche* to retrieve information collected on the tap. According to intelligence officials, the information represented Moscow's "crown jewels," the Soviet navy's nuclear command and control procedures for the submarines being deployed under the Arctic Ocean. In any actual conflict the United States would know where Soviet submarines were headed and be able to intercept them.[41]

In Europe, the Soviets deliberately stepped up provocative behavior against US forces, flying air exercises along the Berlin air corridors, and forcing commercial traffic to alter routine flight paths into the city.[42] Selected air units in East Germany and Poland went to "high alert" status.[43] At the same time, Polish premier Wojciech Jaruzelski also began another nation-wide effort to suppress Solidarity, the reformist workers' union.

Domestically, in one rather esoteric signal indicating a heightening of combat readiness, the Soviets ended the use of military vehicles to assist in bringing in the harvest, a move similar to one made in 1968 on the eve of the Soviet invasion of Czechoslovakia.[44] In addition, the evacuation of an entire Soviet city was a clear "test of civil defense measures that would accompany a nuclear strike."[45]

While holding the ring around Iran, the Soviets were also heavily involved in the Caribbean in an effort to build up Nicaragua and reinforce Cuba. By spring of 1984, Nicaraguan armed forces had reached 107,000 on the way to a projected force of 250,000 men. (By comparison, El Salvador had an army of 29,000 men.) Soviet shipping cargo volume to Nicaragua had doubled in 1983 to 11,000 tons and was on a pace to match that volume in 1984. There were over 3,000 Cuban military advisers and 9,000 "civilians" in country.[46] Arms shipments

---

[40] Toth, "Advanced Soviet A-Subs Move to North Atlantic [. . .]."

[41] Sherry Sontag, Christopher Drew, with Annette Lawrence Drew, *Blind Man's Bluff: The Untold Story of American Submarine Espionage* (New York: Public Affairs, 1988), 244-45.

[42] William Drozdiak, "Allies Protest Soviet Restrictions on Flights to Berlin," *Washington Post*, April 5, 1984, A33.

[43] *Implications of Recent Soviet Military Political Activities*, SNIE 11-10-84 (Washington, DC: Central Intelligence Agency, May 18, 1984), 1.

[44] Parker, *Kremlin in Transition* 1: 345.

[45] Anderson, "War Game Gives A New Look [. . .]."

[46] Jay Mallin, "Sandinistas Undertake Huge Military Buildup with Soviet, Cuban Aid," *Washington Times*, April 20, 1984, A6.

to Cuba continued at the rate of 60,000 tons per year, as Moscow was turning the island into a fortress bristling with weapons.[47]

At the same time, Soviet and Cuban naval forces conducted joint exercises in the Gulf of Mexico, coming as close as 75 miles to the Louisiana coast. For the first time, Moscow sent one of its largest warships, the 20,000-ton helicopter carrier *Leningrad*, accompanied by the 8,000-ton guided missile destroyer *Idaloy*, and an oil-supply ship. A Cuban Koni-class frigate in the Gulf joined them. The ships conducted what appeared to be standard anti-submarine warfare exercises, but the message being sent was that the Gulf of Mexico was no longer an American preserve.[48] The increased Soviet activity in the Caribbean was consistent with overall Soviet objectives; but in its timing, it served particularly as a diversion from events in Southwest Asia.

The same could be said of Soviet activities in other areas. The helicopter carrier *Minsk* conducted drills in the South China Sea and there were "reports of increased Soviet naval activity in the Mediterranean and the Indian Ocean." Analysts said that "the Soviets have not attempted such wide-ranging naval exercises since the 1970s," with the Atlantic portion of the maneuvers being "the largest Soviet exercise seen" there.[49]

Suspending the Syrian-Iranian Alliance?

The massive display of Soviet military power correlated with the events occurring in the Iran-Iraq war and its purpose was to "hold the ring" against US intervention there to enable Moscow's allies to act unimpeded. The battleground ring stretched well beyond Iran itself and involved Soviet policy moves toward all of the states in the region.

Even while exhorting Iran to attack Iraq and continuing to provide the Iranians with weapons and equipment indirectly through Libya, Syria, North Korea, and Vietnam, Moscow also was ensuring that any Iranian attack would fail, by reinforcing Iraq.[50] The Soviets sent tons of new weapons, including missiles capable of striking Iranian inland cities; raised the threat of attack against Iran from Afghanistan; and attempted to neutralize Pakistan.[51] Most importantly, the Soviets persuaded Syria to move into Lebanon, instead of hindering Iraq via a threat to the supply line through Jordan, as the Syrians had done in 1980 (and as the Iranians expected).

---

[47] Jay Mallin, "Soviets Bolstering Military Presence in Latin America," *Washington Times*, April 17, 1984, A11.

[48] "Cuba Joins Soviets in Exercise off US Coast," *Washington Times*, April 10, 1984, A2.

[49] Rick Atkinson, "Superpowers Maneuvering for Supremacy on High Seas," *Washington Post*, April 4, 1984, A1.

[50] Walter Andrews, "Soviets Reportedly Arm Both Sides," *Washington Times*, June 6, 1984, A5.

[51] David Ignatius, "US Is Cautious in Aiding Afghan Rebels," *Wall Street Journal*, April 9, 1984, 7.

As the rainy season was ending, US satellite intelligence traced the Iranian buildup of well over 300,000 troops, more than 30 divisions, deployed along a front from the central sector adjacent to Baghdad to the southern sector around Basra. Although five or six regular Iranian divisions were deployed, the overwhelming majority of the troops were lightly armed Pasdaran and Basij, mostly young teenagers and even some young children, who had received minimal training in human wave tactics.[52] In mid-February, following a small, but sharp attack in the northern sector with a combined Iranian-Kurdish force designed to pin down Iraqi forces in the Sulaymaniyah-Kirkuk area, the Iranians began what Karsh described as "the largest engagement of the war so far."[53]

On February 15 and again on February 21, Iran mounted attacks in the central sector with the apparent objective of gaining control of the Baghdad-to-Basra road that roughly paralleled the border. The actual objective of both attacks, however, was to draw Iraqi forces north toward Baghdad and away from the main target, the lightly defended Hawizeh Marshes, a natural water barrier just to the north and east of Basra. The marshes were a 120 square-mile watershed lying at the confluence of the Tigris and Karun rivers that flooded during and after the rainy season to an average depth of about five or six feet. The area was heavily dotted with reed clumps and small reed islets, and the foliage offered protective cover for an invading force.[54]

The Iraqis had considered it impossible to mount a large-scale attack through the marshes and therefore had not assigned a high defense priority to the area. But this was precisely where Iran struck. Operation Kheibar commenced on February 22 as thousands of Pasdaran and Basij troops maneuvered a flotilla of small watercraft stealthily through the marshes and sought to seize control of the southern end of the Baghdad-to-Basra road, which passed along the western edge of the marshes, and cut off Basra. The Iranians secured control of the undefended Majnoon Island petroleum platform in the marshes. A prompt counterattack by the Iraqi 3rd and 4th Corps, using tanks and helicopter gunships and employing poison gas, wreaked havoc on the onrushing Iranians, inflicting losses in excess of 20,000 men.[55]

By March 1, the Iraqis had recovered control of the marshes, except for Majnoon, and the battle was essentially over. Tehran's regular divisions had not been involved in the initial attacks and, even though Iran had absorbed very high casualties, according to Cordesman and Wagner, there remained overall between 250,000 and 330,000 troops "at the front and in position to attack."[56] Western

---

[52] Edgar O'Ballance, *The Gulf War* (London: Brassey's, 1988), 142.

[53] Efraim Karsh, "The Iran-Iraq War: A Military Analysis," *Adelphi Papers* 27, no. 220 (Spring 1987): 28.

[54] Cordesman and Wagner, *Lessons of Modern War*, 178-79.

[55] O'Ballance, *Gulf War*, 147-48.

[56] Anthony Cordesman and Abraham Wagner, *The Lessons of Modern War*, vol. 2, *The Iran-Iraq War* (Boulder: Westview, 1990), 183-85. Other sources claimed more. Robert D. Kaplan, "Bloodbath in Iraq," *New Republic*, April 9, 1984, 21-23, citing US

observers concluded that, as no regular divisions had been committed, "the final offensive had not yet taken place . . . [and they] continued to anticipate another major attack."[57]

Iran increased its deployment to the front to 500,000, and Iraq announced its intention to escalate air raids against Iranian shipping, but there was no attack. [58] Cordesman and Wagner thought that "costly" tactics and an inability to sustain attacks accounted for the break-off. O'Ballance, on the other hand, saw "hesitation and indecision" on the part of the Iranian leadership about whether to resume the offensive.

In retrospect, it is evident that the Iranian leadership was waiting for Damascus to join the attack, either by mounting a threat to cut Iraq's supply line that ran through Jordan from the port of Aqaba to the Iraqi border, or by attacking Iraq directly. This, recall, had been the role Damascus had played briefly in 1980, producing a Syrian- Jordanian confrontation. The Iranians had expected Syria to play the same role in 1982, as they mounted their first invasion of Iraq, but the Israeli invasion of Lebanon had neutralized Syria, forestalling a coordinated drive. Now, with major Iranian forces poised to attack, Tehran waited for Damascus to join in the pincer; and at this critical moment, the Soviets sent Politburo member Heydar Aliyev to Damascus.

Aliyev, leader of the Azerbaijan SSR and a Soviet Politburo member with responsibility for third-world clients, was scheduled to go to Damascus for a "working visit" in mid-February, but the trip was delayed until March 10 because of Andropov's death. Aliyev would be the "first senior Kremlin official to visit Syria in four years,"[59] it was said (but in fact the Soviets had been sending emissaries to Damascus regularly). In a speech given at his welcoming banquet, Aliyev attacked US policy for its "aggressive line and its terrorist and military methods," particularly with regard to its "intervention in Lebanon and its threats to Syria." US policy, according to Aliyev, had "brought the world to the brink of nuclear war."[60]

It is, of course, impossible to know what Aliyev discussed with his Syrian hosts, but if what occurred publicly in Damascus reflected anything of what transpired behind closed doors, Aliyev's recommendations precipitated a crisis within the Syrian leadership, while he was still there. Rifaat al-Assad, Hafez's brother and commander of what had become "an autonomous praetorian guard," suddenly put tanks in the streets and sealed off access to Damascus.

---

intelligence sources, said that the Iranians had massed four hundred thousand troops at the front.

[57] Karsh, "The Iran-Iraq War: A Military Analysis," 28.

[58] Don Oberdorfer, "Iran Moves 500,000 Up to Front," *Washington Post*, March 3, 1984, A1.

[59] Antero Pietila, "Key Soviet Aide Plans Syrian Visit," *Baltimore Sun*, February 9, 1984, A3.

[60] "Soviet Says US Uses 'Terrorist' Means in Mideast," *Baltimore Sun*, March 11, 1984, A15.

In response, two of Hafez al-Assad's confidants, General Ali Haydar, head of Special Forces Commandos, and Colonel Shafiq Fayyad, commander of the 3rd Armored Division, deployed their forces in opposition to Rifaat. After a brief armed confrontation, Hafez Assad ordered a stand down, ending the crisis. Clearly, a policy dispute had escalated to irreconcilable proportions and Rifaat had resorted to a show of force to win it, which failed.[61]

Hafez Assad would subsequently defuse the crisis by creating three vice presidents, one of whom was Rifaat. The other two were Foreign Minister Abdul-Halim Khaddam and Baath Party deputy chief Zuhair Masharqa. Assad had cleverly promoted his brother into a position that held no formal responsibilities, while removing him from command over his military force. Two months later he would send Rifaat to Moscow with Haydar and Fayyad to negotiate a new arms package. Analysts at first thought that Assad was sidelining Rifaat's rivals and would bring his brother back to succeed him, but it was Rifaat who was sidelined. Upon leaving Moscow, Rifaat went to Geneva for "medical attention," remaining there until November, while Haydar and Fayyad returned to Damascus.[62]

In the meantime, Assad decided, with evident Soviet approval, to project Syrian power into Lebanon, rather than to generate a military threat to Jordan as he had done in 1980 and was preparing to do now. It seems, in other words, that contrary to press reportage that the March crisis in Damascus was a struggle over the succession to Hafez Assad, it was over Moscow's proposal to dispense with Syria's four-year commitment to support Iran in the conflict with Iraq.

Later, on May 24, Assad would send his vice president Abul Khaddam to inform Iranian president Ali Khamenei personally of the decision: "Syria would not accept the establishment of an Islamic Republic in Iraq and that Syria might withdraw its support for Iran if the Iranians were to escalate the war."[63] But by then the Iranian leadership already had deduced the change in Moscow's policy, and its implications for themselves.

At the same time that Moscow was turning Assad away from Iraq and toward Lebanon, in March, a top-level Soviet delegation led by Yakov Ryabov, head of the State Committee for Foreign Economic Relations, traveled to Baghdad to extend a $4.5 billion weapons contract, "the biggest arms package the Soviets had ever proposed." Moreover, in addition to sending new SS-12 missiles with a range of 500 miles, Moscow was prepared to "rush deliveries of additional MiG-21 and MiG-23 fighters, Mi-25 Hind helicopter gunships, and 350 Scud-B missiles."[64]

---

[61] Loren Jenkins, "Swiss Exile for Syrian?" *Washington Post*, September 26, 1984, A18.

[62] Ibid.

[63] See Claude van England, "Iran's Doves and Hawks Disagree over Gulf War Strategy," *Christian Science Monitor*, July 20, 1984, 14.

[64] Kenneth Timmerman, *The Death Lobby: How the West Armed Iraq* (New York: Houghton Mifflin, 1991), 184-85; and Michael Sheridan, "Iraq Reportedly Gets New Soviet Missiles," *Washington Post*, June 8, 1984, A29.

The Soviets evidently had decided to suspend the Syrian-Iranian alliance and inject sufficient weapons power into Iraq to thwart any continued Iranian attacks. Correctly interpreting the Soviet decision, the Iranian leadership broke off their assaults. Had the Soviets blundered by acting prematurely? Did they assume that Iran, having committed its forces, would be unable to disengage, and would become caught in an attrition trap? If so, they erred. Iran eluded the trap, withdrawing their forces, with armies intact. The Iranians were no longer entangled in a war of attrition and could respond to other threats from within or even from the Soviets.

Despite the fact that Moscow had mismanaged its strategy, failing to entrap Iran in a position that would leave the regime vulnerable to an internal takeover, the Soviets continued through April to demonstrate their readiness for conflict, if not war, with the United States and hinted at the possibility of conflict with Iran. Having suspended Syrian cooperation with Iran, the Soviets now moved to strengthen the Afghan-Iraq position, paralleling the reinforcement of Iraq with a major campaign in Afghanistan to secure the main communications route from the Soviet border through the Panjshir Valley to Kabul.

Through April, the Soviets increased their ground force contingent to 130,000 and provided aerial bombing support from bases in the Soviet Union in what appeared to be an all-out effort to clear the area.[65] In the process, however, reports indicated that "Soviet forces have . . . carried out other air operations in lesser strength around Herat, in northwest Afghanistan, and around Kandahar," which suggested that the Russians might have something more in mind than merely securing the main transportation corridor into Afghanistan.[66] At the same time, threatening Pakistan with direct attack unless their interference in Afghanistan were stopped, it seemed that the Russians were attempting to strengthen the Afghan eastern front for any contingency.

Reagan's Riposte

The Russians got far more than they had bargained for, as President Reagan responded to the Soviet strategy of military intimidation with a matching world-wide display of American and allied power, but he did so in characteristically understated fashion. Asked at a news conference whether he thought the Soviets were sending a message, the president replied: "No, I really don't. Nor are we trying to send them a signal with our own war games."[67] With little fanfare, beginning in early March and continuing until mid-year, the United

---

[65] Fred Hiatt, "Soviets Use Bombers in Afghanistan," *Washington Post*, April 24, 1984, A1.
[66] Drew Middleton, "Soviet Said to Step Up Afghan Drive," *New York Times*, May 4, 1984, A3.
[67] "President's News Conference on Foreign and Domestic Issues," *New York Times*, April 5, 1984, B14.

States conducted numerous military and civilian exercises to demonstrate Western preparedness for war.

The US response, of course, was not merely a matter of gratuitous military muscle flexing. The CIA had long discounted the possibility that a US-Soviet nuclear war would begin with a surprise attack by either side. Instead, analysts assumed that "if a general war occurred, it would most likely result from the expansion of a theater conflict, preceded by a political crisis period that could last several weeks or longer."[68] As that was exactly the situation that was occurring, it was only prudent to be prepared.

Strategic Air Command commenced a worldwide exercise code-named Global Shield to provide "realistic training missions" for all 328 B-52 and FB-111 bomber crews and all 1,040 ICBM missile crews, "for nuclear war should deterrence fail." The exercise included test firing of two Minuteman missiles from Vandenberg Air Force Base and test launching of cruise missiles from B-52 bombers. Bomber and missile crews from all over the United States as well as bomber and aerial tanker crews from Guam and Okinawa were also involved, as were active duty and reserve units from the Air Force, Navy, and Marines. Canadian forces also participated. Moscow was notified in advance, although Pentagon spokesmen insisted that the exercise "bears no relationship to any aspect of current international relations."[69]

In Full Flow, an exercise designed to rehearse rapid reinforcement capabilities, the United States deployed 35,000 troops to Western Germany within a two-week period. At the same time the United States and its European allies conducted NATO-wide exercises named Elder Forest-84 designed to "test Britain's air defenses and the ability of NATO allies to protect their shipping lanes during a war."[70]

Exercise Team Spirit followed, focusing on the US navy's ability to secure sea-lanes of communication in the vast ocean areas from the North Atlantic to the North Pacific and crucial sea areas, like the Arabian and South China Seas, in between. Aside from close monitoring of the Soviet Union's naval surges in the Atlantic, five aircraft carriers deployed to the Pacific in the navy's most extensive fleet exercise ever held in that ocean. (Two carriers sailed to within 50 miles of Vladivostok).[71] The 80,000-ton carrier *Kitty Hawk*, serving as the flagship for Battle Group Bravo, forced a shadowing 5,000-ton Soviet Victor-

[68] *Soviet Capabilities for Strategic Nuclear Conflict, 1982-92*, NIE 11-3/8-82 (Washington, DC: Central Intelligence Agency, February 15, 1983), 29.

[69] "Air Units Start Vast Exercise," *New York Times*, April 4, 1984, A; and "SAC Starts its Readiness Test," *New York News*, April 3, 1984, A13.

[70] "Three-day NATO War Game Begins Today in British Skies," *Washington Times*, March 5, 1984, A7.

[71] Eugene Carroll, "US–Soviet Naval Competition: Dangers and Risks," in Richard Fieldhouse, ed., *Security at Sea: Naval Forces and Arms Control* (Stockholm: SIPRI, 1990), 65.

class submarine to surface under it. The submarine was disabled, losing a propeller screw that became lodged in the carrier's hull, causing minor damage.[72]

In the Caribbean, Ocean Venture, involving over 30,000 men would "demonstrate the capability of the US to protect and maintain the free use of the sea lanes of communication in the Caribbean Basin and the Gulf of Mexico."[73] The carrier USS *America* with its support vessels exercised with the 82nd Airborne Division; the 26th Marine Amphibious Unit; more than 250 aircraft from the Strategic, Tactical, and Airlift Commands; and the Coast Guard. The naval exercise would be paired with Granadero I, involving some 7,000 men in Honduras where air strips were under construction for the rising conflict with Nicaragua.

A great deal of attention focused on a CIA mining operation to discourage foreign, especially Soviet, shipping into Nicaraguan ports. When the mines damaged a Soviet tanker, Dutch and Japanese freighters, a Liberian cargo ship operated by a British crew, and Panamanian ships, a furor erupted in Congress at the "indiscriminate" nature of the CIA's operation. Congressional critics lambasted CIA Director Casey, charged that the United States was threatening "the principle of freedom of navigation," and demanded that the operation cease.[74]

In fact, the operation demonstrated the ease with which Soviet shipping to Nicaragua could be interdicted.[75] Later, Reagan would justify the CIA's mining operation as designed to interdict a "flood" of Soviet weapons going to Nicaraguan ports. He dismissed the congressional uproar as "much ado about nothing," describing the mines, called "firecrackers" by the CIA, as only powerful enough to damage, but not sink ships.[76]

From April 5 to 13, in tandem with Global Shield, US military and government officials tested the nation's ability to "defend itself from, and respond to, a nuclear attack from the Soviet Union." Cabinet personnel, and key members of Congress all participated, relocating the essential functions of government to designated areas outside of Washington, while the president moved to his airborne command post. In Night Train-84, the Joint Chiefs of Staff conducted a parallel worldwide command post exercise to test their communications links. The fact

---

[72] Fred Hiatt, "Soviet Salvage Ship Reported on Way to Aid Sub That Hit US Carrier," *Washington Post*, March 23, 1984, A17; and Rick Atkinson, "High Seas Diplomacy Is Own Saga," *Washington Post*, June 8,1984, A1.

[73] Bob Poos, "Large-Scale Maneuvers Planned for Caribbean," *Washington Times*, March 23, 1984, A2.

[74] Michael Getler, "Nicaragua Minelaying Said to Harm US Goals," *Washington Post*, April 13, 1984, A20.

[75] Hedrick Smith, "US Latin Force in Place If Needed, Officials Report," *New York Times*, April 23,1984, A1.

[76] David Hoffman, "President Says 'Flood' of Arms Justified Mining," *Washington Post*, May 30, 1984, A1.

that these tests were taking place at the same time as the Soviet war games was said to be a "coincidence."[77]

Drills designed to respond to a societal crisis affecting the continuity of government, like the devastation attending a nuclear attack, also were implemented. Readiness Exercise 1984 Alpha (Rex-84 Alpha) called upon FEMA to carry out a federal government-wide civil readiness exercise involving 34 departments and agencies. In Readiness Exercise 1984 Bravo (Rex-84 Bravo), FEMA and DOD led the CIA, Secret Service, Treasury Department, and FBI through an exercise to coordinate military assistance with civil defense measures, including the practice of martial law procedures and the arrest of previously identified subversives.[78]

In addition to the war games, in late April, President Reagan played an important diplomatic card against Moscow, traveling to China for a six-day visit. In a prepared statement made as he departed from Honolulu, the president said that he hoped that the United States and its Pacific neighbors "can go forward in a mighty enterprise to build dynamic growth economies, and make the world safer, by working for peace and jointly opposing expansionist aggression." That, he said, "is what our trip to China is all about."[79]

In China, the president signed agreements to spur American investment, further scientific and cultural exchange, and initiate cooperation on nuclear energy.[80] His trip built on the foundation established by the August 17, 1982 agreement and thus reinforced the strategic relationship that Nixon had initiated, but which had been allowed to atrophy during the new world order détente years.

Although the president acknowledged that their friendship was "not an alliance," he declared that as "friends and neighbors . . . . We can be such a force for good in the world." Chinese President Li Xiannian agreed, saying "your visit has been very successful." Although "there are differences but that doesn't matter . . . . We shall face them. It is good for two great nations to be friendly." [81] Li alluded to Chinese demands that Washington reduce arms sales to Taiwan, which Washington rejected on the grounds that the United States was adhering strictly to the August 17, 1982 agreement.

There were other differences. On two occasions when, during speeches, Reagan attempted to voice criticism of Soviet policies, the Chinese censored his remarks. They would not be drawn even implicitly into an anti-Soviet stance. On the other hand, a third speech to students at Fudan University in Shanghai was

---

[77] "Prez to Play Key Role in US War Exercises," *New York Post*, April 5, 1984, 4.

[78] Alfonso Chardy, "Reagan Advisers Ran 'Secret' Government," *Miami Herald*, July 5, 1987, A1.

[79] Lou Cannon, "Reagan Leaves Hawaii, Hits Soviet 'Expansionist' Policies," *Washington Post*, April 25, 1984, A3.

[80] Steven Weisman, "President to Sign Pacts with China in Peking Today," *New York Times*, April 30, 1984, A1.

[81] Lou Cannon, "Reagan Ends Trip with a 'Dream' of Friendship," *Washington Post*, May 1, 1984, A1.

carried live on television and was not censored, but was not translated either, which meant that only those Chinese who understood English would hear the president criticize the Soviets.

On balance, Reagan believed that his trip had raised US-China relations to a "new plateau," and the Chinese agreed. *Xinhua* called the visit "a significant step forward." Indeed, in addition to agreements to advance trade, cultural exchange, and nuclear cooperation, it was revealed that the Chinese would "send a military delegation to Washington to discuss possible purchase of US defensive weaponry."[82]

By early May the Reagan administration had demonstrated the national power, alliance cohesion, and the will to stand up to Soviet bellicosity. The net effect of American actions in the spring of 1984 was to further isolate the Soviet Union. The question was: how would the Chernenko leadership react?

From "Deep Freeze" to Fissures

In early May of 1984, the Chernenko leadership's reaction to the events of the spring was, in Parker's felicitous phrasing, "to put its relations with Washington, Beijing, and Bonn into various stages of a 'deep freeze.'"[83] But, it did not last. By the end of the month, signs of policy change began to appear. Almost totally isolated, the initial Soviet response was to dig itself deeper into a hole. Chernenko stood prominently in the forefront. At a banquet speech for visiting Polish premier Wojciech on May 4, Chernenko echoed Andropov's harsh dictum after the KAL crisis, saying of US policy: "he who could hope that realism and rationality are making their way here at long last would be profoundly deceived."[84]

Three days later, after insisting for months that the Soviet Union would participate in the Los Angeles Olympic Games, Moscow announced that Soviet participation was "impossible," because of the "anti-Soviet campaign launched by reactionary circles in the United States with the connivance of the official authorities."[85] Secretary Shultz, clearly reluctant to state the obvious, said, "we see the Soviet Union engaged in a tactic of negotiation that involves withdrawal, that involves a kind of scare campaign, and that involves a sort of deep freeze. We will not be intimidated."[86]

Despite vigorously denying any intent at payback for the US boycott of the Moscow Olympic Games in 1980, because of the Soviet invasion of Afghanistan, that is precisely what the Soviets attempted, but their boycott was

---

[82] "Looking Back on China" *Los Angeles Times*, May 2, 1984, C6.

[83] Parker, *Kremlin in Transition* 1: 361.

[84] "Speech by Secretary Chernenko," *Foreign Broadcast Information Service (FBIS) Daily Report, Soviet Union*, May 7, 1984, F 8.

[85] "Text of Soviet Statement on Olympic Games," *New York Times*, May 9, 1984, A16.

[86] Bernard Gwertzman, "Shultz Says Soviet Olympic Decision Is Part of Plan to 'Freeze' Ties," *New York Times*, May 12, 1984, A4.

ineffective. Claiming that "as many as 70 countries might join a Soviet-led boycott," in the end only 13 countries did so. Indeed, even some of those who were compelled to withdraw, like East Germany and Hungary, openly resented doing so. Romania participated, as did China, taking part in the games for the first time. All told, a record 142 nations joined in the games.[87]

On May 9, the day before Deputy Premier Ivan Arkhipov was to visit China, Moscow announced that his trip would be postponed.[88] His visit had been announced on the eve of President Reagan's trip to China and suggested that the Soviets would attempt to steal a march on the United States in developing better relations with China. Moscow may have thought the Chinese would go along with some scheme to embarrass Reagan but the Chinese refused, which left the Russians in the position of following in the president's footsteps to pay homage to China. So, the trip was canceled on the trumped-up excuse that the Chinese were making "armed provocations" against Vietnam.[89]

The Soviets had invited West German Foreign Minister, Hans-Dietrich Genscher to Moscow. The Kremlin leadership continued its scare and intimidation campaign right up to the moment of Genscher's arrival on May 20, tarring the West German government with charges of "revanchism and neofascism." Chief of General Staff Nikolai Ogarkov, in a May 9 interview, alleged that "fascist holdouts" and "reactionary imperialist forces" were openly preparing for a new world war, galvanized by "revanchist neofascist organizations." Upon arrival, Foreign Minister Gromyko condemned the deployment of Pershing II and cruise missiles as a "black page" and a "big military and political miscalculation," but underneath the bluster the West German delegation detected a "friendly" tone.[90] The Russians were at pains not to disrupt the highly valuable trade relationship with Bonn.

Indeed, within days the first crack in the Kremlin's façade began to appear. The signs were subtle and seemed to be the product of heated discussions within the Politburo. At a Politburo meeting in late May, Chernenko reversed the former long-term heavy emphasis on defense preparations to declare that the "people's prosperity" must be the "superordinate goal" of the next Five-Year Plan. The Politburo, reportedly, "fully supported" his position.[91] However, the fact that others preaching the defense-above-all-else line continued to be heard meant the issue had not yet been decided.

Iran's avoidance of the attrition trap and the robust response of the United States to Soviet war bluster prompted Soviet leaders to reconsider their strategy. A staccato-like series of events in June made clear that they had reached

---

[87] Parker, *Kremlin in Transition* 1: 368.

[88] "Arkhipov Postpones Visit to PRC for 'Some Time,'" *FBIS Daily Report, Soviet Union*, May 9, 1984, B 1.

[89] Parker, *Kremlin in Transition* 1: 368.

[90] Ibid., 370-71.

[91] "CPSU CC Politburo Examines Nation's Development," *FBIS Daily Report, Soviet Union*, June 1, 1984, R 1-2.

a dead end. First, on June 9, Chinese Defense Minister Zhang Aiping arrived in Washington for an unusually long 16-day visit. His arrival, just five weeks after the president's trip to China, was sooner than expected. Zhang met with the president and top administration officials; and toured West Point, army, navy, and air force bases, and several of the production facilities of major US defense contractors.[92]

While going out of their way to say that neither country sought an alliance, both sides made clear that relations were "warming," and that the "symbolic implication of Zhang's visit is seen as potentially more important than the substance of his business talks." US officials made clear that Washington was prepared to provide selected defensive weapons systems, especially in the areas of anti-tank and anti-air weapons, in view of the presence of 47 tank and mechanized divisions the Soviets had deployed along the Chinese border.[93] Agreements that would result in the first "direct sale of US military weapons to Peking's communist government" were expected to be signed just "before or shortly after" Zhang left the country.[94] In fact, an "agreement in principle" to sell weapons was announced on June 14.[95]

If drawing China into Washington's orbit were not devastating enough, at virtually the same moment, the Reagan administration stunned the Soviet leadership with accomplishment of a technological feat thought not yet possible. On June 10, "an experimental antiballistic missile . . . accomplished the first direct interception and destruction of an incoming dummy missile warhead." The non-nuclear vehicle, fired from Meck Island in the Kwajalein island group, intercepted a missile launched from Vandenberg Air Force Base in California thousands of miles away, destroying the warhead over 100 miles above the earth.[96]

In its announcement, the Army declared that the successful test "moved the United States a step closer to a non-nuclear defense capability against enemy strategic ballistic missiles." The Homing Overlay Experiment (HOE) was "a first for the United States and, as far as is known, for the world." An infrared sensor capable of detecting heat against the cold background of space at a distance of 1,000 miles maneuvered the interceptor to the incoming warhead.[97]

---

[92] Richard Halloran, "Weinberger and Chinese Aide in Accord," *New York Times*, June 12, 1984, A3.
[93] Rick Atkinson, "China's Defense Chief Here to Discuss Sales," *Washington Post*, June 12, 1984, A8.
[94] Roger Fontaine, "US-China Pact Expected on Weapons," *Washington Times*, June 12, 1984, A6.
[95] Rick Atkinson, "US Sets First Arms Sale to Peking," *Washington Post*, June 15, 1984, A1.
[96] Charles Mohr, "Army Test Missile Is Said to Destroy a Dummy Warhead," *New York Times*, June 12, 1984, A1.
[97] Walter Andrews, "Missile Intercept Test Succeeds, Army Says," *Washington Times*, June 12, 1984, A4.

A spokesman said that the test showed a "clear technological advantage by the United States in such vital missile defense fields as high-speed data processing by a computer carried on the defensive rocket and in the ability to maneuver a vehicle in space to hit an incoming missile." The interceptor maneuvered toward the warhead while traveling at a speed of 15,000 miles per hour and the interception occurred at a closing speed—that is, the combined velocity of the target and interceptor—of four miles *per second.*[98]

The next crack in Moscow's "deep freeze" occurred two days later when chief Kremlin spokesman Leonard Zamyatin said in response to a question at a news conference that Moscow wanted "to have negotiations with the United States on a whole complex of issues" and that a meeting between President Reagan and President Chernenko was "possible." A day earlier, Chernenko complained that Reagan had refused his proposals for a treaty banning the militarization of space.[99] Clearly, the Russians were very attentive to American advances on the ballistic missile defense front and wanted to head off any development that would compromise their own schemes, even if it meant lending symbolic support to Reagan's reelection.

There were other more obscure but still important reasons for Moscow's grudging turn. The focal point of Soviet strategy since 1979, the capture of Iran, was fast unraveling. Here, the signs were subtler, but no less real. The first sign occurred in the immediate aftermath of Iran's decision to call off the offensive against Iraq. On March 16, members of Hezbollah, Iran's terrorist cell in Lebanon, abducted the CIA's station chief William F. Buckley.

Within 24 hours, CIA agents in Beirut learned that the abduction had been carried out on the orders of Iranian officials and that Buckley was to be transported to Tehran and held there.[100] Someone in the Iranian leadership, it seems, had decided to open up a potential, if crude, line of communication to the CIA, although no immediate attempt appears to have been made to establish contact, and additional hostages were taken, which muddled the meaning of Buckley's abduction.

Nevertheless, Iranian leaders subsequently extended less ambiguous feelers to the West. In early June, for example, Iranian parliament speaker Hashemi Rafsanjani said that Iran wanted to avoid intervention by the Soviet Union and the United States: "As far as is possible we will prevent such a disaster for humanity from happening by diplomacy and by appropriate talks and

---

[98] Mohr, "Army Test Missile [. . .]" and Rick Atkinson, "Test of Missile Interceptor Called Success by Pentagon," *Washington Post*, June 12, 1984, A1.

[99] Dusko Doder, "Soviet Spokesman Conciliatory on Summit," *Washington Post*, June 15, 1984, A1.

[100] "Meeting with [Excised] Re: Beirut Kidnapping," March 17, 1984; and "Update on Contact with Iranian Terrorist Source," March 17, 1984, *Digital National Security Archive-ProQuest,* DNSA Collection: Iran-Contra Affair.

meetings."[101] As the main danger of intervention was from the Soviet Union, this seemed to be a signal of Iran's interest in having "talks and meetings" with the heretofore shunned "Great Satan."

As was perhaps standard practice in such matters, Iran extended feelers through intermediaries; in this case, West Germany, inviting Foreign Minister Hans-Dietrich Genscher for a formal state visit in July. Genscher was the first Western foreign minister to visit Iran since the revolution in 1979. While offering Bonn a long-term oil agreement, Rafsanjani made a point of urging "other countries" to help bring the war to an end by withdrawing financial support from Saddam Hussein. Although naming both the United States and the Soviet Union as the two countries that "supported Iraq at the beginning of the war," it was clear that his message was intended for the United States.[102] Indeed, a Kuwaiti newspaper said that Genscher had passed on a US proposal for an "amelioration" of relations with Washington.[103] Prospects for the president's long-awaited opportunity to seek an opening to Iran seemed to be promising.

The Soviet Union:
State Supporter of International Terrorism

While Iranian attempts to signal interest in making contact with the United States were subtle and perhaps ambiguous, there was nothing subtle or ambiguous about the president's efforts to damn the Soviets with the charge of being state supporters of international terrorism. The administration, recall, had been embroiled in a running internal debate over the issue of terrorism, particularly state-supported terrorism, since the attack on the Marine Barracks the previous October.

The unspoken question running through the debate was: should the United States name the Soviet Union as a state sponsor of international terrorism? Allegations about the Soviet role already were spreading publicly in the West. On April 21, Claire Sterling, noted author of *The Terror Network,* published an interview on a new volume exploring the plot behind the attempted assassination of Pope John Paul II three years earlier. She pulled no punches in accusing Brezhnev and Andropov themselves of issuing the order to the Bulgarian secret police to carry out the job.[104]

In her view, "any normal grown-up has to see that it's really not possible for the Bulgarians to have done this on their own, unless the Russians had told them to do it." It was time, she said, to hold the Russians accountable. "Public knowledge of this Russian accountability is in itself a strong deterrent." Up to

---

[101] Jonathan Randal, "Iraq Moves Tanks to Southern Front," *Washington Post*, June 3, 1984, A15.

[102] "Iran Said to Seek New Ties to West," *New York Times*, July 23, 1984, A1.

[103] "Kuwaiti Paper Reports Genscher Carried US Proposal," *FBIS Daily Report, South Asia,* July 27, 1984, I 2.

[104] "Why Is the West Covering Up for Agca?" *Human Events*, April 21, 1984, 1.

now, Western governments had concealed the Russian role in providing "weapons and sanctuary" for terrorist groups. "And that has encouraged them I think to ever bolder kinds of attack on the assumption that they were going to continue to enjoy the Western intelligence shield."

What was vital was "to take the shield away," she stressed; and to say that they would be held accountable from now on. "This will have to be part of our bargaining package when we sit down with [them] to talk about anything, to negotiate anything. This is a form of warfare, and therefore we have to negotiate a peace settlement that can hold, understanding who the interlocutor is and what form of warfare he is waging."105

Sterling's work had an impact, declaring in public what the president was saying in private. Indeed, just a few weeks before, he had signed NSDD-138 endorsing in principle both preemptive strikes and reprisal raids against terrorists. The decision was a first because the United States, as one State Department official noted, "never had a doctrine for dealing with low-level conflict where force is required."106

As the discussion continued, it was decided to raise the subject of state support for international terrorism at the upcoming meeting with the allies. Thus, the president, in London for a meeting of the G-7 economic summit, raised the issue first with Margaret Thatcher during a private dinner with no aides present.

A Thatcher aide observed that while the prime minister "most certainly intend[ed] to raise the issue of terrorism . . . at the summit," he was uncertain "precisely what will come out of it." Officials were pessimistic whether "France and Italy would agree to public condemnation of 'state-supported terrorism.'" A White House official, however, called Thatcher "our ace in the hole," meaning that "she could be relied upon to make a statement even if the other nations would not go along."107

In the end, however, the public statement on international terrorism was tepid, naming no specific countries and the "economic" summit focused on less divisive questions. Thatcher's statement focused on the shared democratic values of the West and Western determination to fully deploy the intermediate-range missile package; and Reagan called upon the allies to prepare "contingency plans to coordinate oil reserves in case of any serious disruption of supplies" caused by the Iran-Iraq war.108 The allies, it seemed, would not stand with the president on the terror issue.

Still, President Reagan refused to let the terrorism issue die. As internal discussions continued, at the end of the month Secretary Shultz himself leveled a

---

105 Ibid.

106 Stephanie Nall, "Move on Terrorism Ordered by Reagan," *Washington Times*, April 16, 1984, A1.

107 Lou Cannon, "US Seeks Allied Accord on Terrorism, Missiles," *Washington Post*, June 6, 1984, A18.

108 Michael Getler and Lou Cannon, "Reagan: Allies Must Cooperate on Oil Reserves," *Washington Post*, June 8, 1984, A1.

major blast, charging the Soviet Union with leading a global "league of terror" that included Syria, Iran, Libya, and North Korea and called upon the democratic nations to join to combat this insidious threat. While the Soviet Union "officially denounces the use of terrorism as an instrument of state policy," he said, "there is a wide gap between Soviet words and Soviet actions."[109] Leaving the Soviets with no escape, Shultz said:

> The international links among terrorist groups are now clearly understood, and the Soviet link, direct or indirect, is also clearly understood. The Soviets use terrorist groups for their own purposes, and *their* goal is always the same: to weaken liberal democracy and undermine world stability.

As one example, Shultz continued, "when Libya and the PLO provide arms and training to the communists in Central America, they are aiding Soviet efforts to undermine our security in that vital region." And "when the Soviet Union and its clients provide financial, logistic and training support for terrorists worldwide . . . they hope to shake the West's self-confidence and sap its will to resist aggression and intimidation."

Noting that the terrorist "epidemic is spreading," he said that "it is time to think long, hard and seriously about more active means of defense—about defense through appropriate preventive or preemptive actions against terrorist groups before they strike." Deterrence will require greater international cooperation, better intelligence, and the ability to penetrate terrorist organizations, although our collective response must be "within the rule of law, lest we become unwitting accomplices in the terrorist's scheme to undermine civilized society."[110]

Shultz's statement was the harshest accusation that any public US official had ever leveled against the Soviet Union. That Secretary Shultz, the man most publicly identified with pro-Soviet views, would take such a tough public stand was testimony to the extent to which the Soviets had cast themselves, their state, as an international pariah. But it was also an indicator of how close Reagan was to washing his hands of the Russians.

Although the Russians probably did not know it, there was less to Shultz's "turn" than it appeared. After the events of the spring, opinion within the administration was running heavily in favor of the president and Shultz was faced with the danger of becoming isolated himself, for up this point he had refused to name the Soviets publicly, charging only their surrogates.[111] Therefore, he seized

---

[109] Joanne Omang, "Soviets Using Terrorism, Shultz Asserts," *Washington Post*, June 25, 1984, A1; and "Shultz Urges 'Active' Drive on Terrorism," *New York Times*, June 25, 1984, A3.

[110] Ibid.

[111] David Hoffman and Don Oberdorfer, "Secret Policy on Terrorism Given Airing," *Washington Post*, April 18, 1984, A1.

the terrorist issue by the horns, as it were, as a way of staying out front and in the good graces of the president.

After Mikhail Gorbachev came to power and the United States and the Soviet Union became engaged in another effort to achieve détente, something very much like Sterling's recommendation to negotiate a "peace package" on the terror question must have come to pass, because Shultz's accusation that the Soviet Union was a state sponsor of international terrorism was the last such statement ever uttered by an American official from that time to the present. Needless to say, while the United States upheld its commitment, the Soviets did not, continuing to support terrorist movements worldwide. Like the Soviet commitment to all agreements, it was not worth the paper on which it was written.

The Russians were not, as one pundit put it, "driven by fear," but acting in the belief that they were powerful enough to flaunt every code of civilized conduct the Western world held dear.[112] But having played their hand and lost it, being the supreme pragmatists that they were despite all the ideological bombast to the contrary, the Soviets did the only thing possible in the face of the utter defeat of their strategy. They changed it.

Crisis and Response

While not immediately apparent, June 1984 was the crisis point in Soviet strategy. The Soviet leadership, led primarily by the Gorbachev-Ustinov faction, had reached general agreement that the two-decade-long strategy of openly contending with the United States in a worldwide effort to alter the balance of power by military coercion had reached the point of negative returns and needed to be changed. In addition to strategic and geopolitical failures, key assumptions that had underlain Soviet strategy had failed to hold true.

The Soviets had believed that strategic superiority was attainable and politically usable; that its cost was bearable; and that development along the single dimension of military power at the expense of the rest of society would not be harmful or dangerous to the nation. However, not only had the Soviets failed to alter the essential correlation of forces to advantage, they had stressed the essential fabric of Soviet society to the ripping point, if not shredded it entirely.[870]

Fundamentally, the decision to build military power at the expense of broad-based societal development was an extraordinary gamble that failed. The elementary failure to build a wealth-generating economic system meant that a substantial portion of the cost of the military buildup would have to be borne by the people in what was termed in an earlier day "primitive accumulation," the forceful expropriation of national wealth for the ends of the state.

Yet, Soviet leaders also understood that a massive military buildup could not be accomplished by reliance upon their own means and resources alone. They

---

[112] "Morton Kondracke, "What if the Soviets Are Driven by Fear?" *Wall Street Journal*, May 31, 1984, 31.

[870] See Henry Rowen and Charles Wolf, *The Impoverished Superpower* (San Francisco: ICF Press, 1990), especially 51-61.

gambled that by utilizing Western wealth and technology they could exploit the very system they planned to subvert. As their need for advanced technology increased, however, so did their dependence upon the West. By the spring of 1984, aside from the geopolitical failures described in this volume, the growing dependence upon the West boomeranged against them, crippling the financial and economic underpinning of Soviet society.

First came news of another bad harvest, the sixth in succession, requiring a record volume of grain imports (55.5 million metric tons of grain were imported during the 1984-85 marketing year). The 11th Five Year Plan (1981-1985) called for average annual grain output of about 240 million metric tons; the 1984 harvest was the second-worst of the overall disappointing period, at 170 million.[871] Thus even with imports, the Soviets were falling well short of minimum needs. Ironically, the United States appeared to be the only producer with sufficient and consistent long-term capacity to meet Soviet grain and oilseed requirements, although Moscow was attempting to diversify imports.

Second came the beginning of the oil shock, as Reagan's long-term strategy of bringing down energy prices began to take effect. In mid-1984, petroleum prices began to dip sharply, as new sources of petroleum came on line, increasing overall supply even in the face of cutbacks by OPEC. Almost three-fourths of Soviet hard-currency earnings were derived from the export of oil and natural gas, and the oil price drop affected both sectors. In 1984, hard currency earnings from petroleum exports amounted to $15.1 billion and from natural gas, $3.8 billion. This represented 58 percent and 14.5 percent, respectively, of total Soviet hard currency earnings.[872]

The energy price decline had a double-barreled effect. On the one hand, the Soviet Union began to feel the pinch in lowered earnings from reduced oil and gas prices. (Each one-dollar decline in the price of oil equated to a half-billion-dollar reduction in annual hard currency earnings.) On the other hand, the price fall triggered a reduction in West European demand for Soviet natural gas, leading to the renegotiation of contracts for gas deliveries from the not yet fully completed Yamal gas pipeline. The Soviets had expected to earn some $5 billion from natural gas sales. Instead, revised estimates projected earnings not to exceed half of that total.

The combined shock of persistent agricultural failure and the plunge of energy prices produced the beginning of a general economic crisis for the Soviet Union, which undoubtedly lay at the center of the decision to change strategy. The hard truth was the currency needed to finance imports of merchandise from

---

[871] *USSR Situation and Outlook Report* (Washington, DC: US Department of Agriculture, May 1986), 3, 13-15, 30-34; and John Hardt and Donna Gold, *The Soviets' 5-Year Plan (1981-1985)*, Congressional Research Service Issue Brief no. IB81025 (Washington, DC: Library of Congress, Congressional Research Service, May 19, 1983), Table 2.

[872] *USSR Situation and Outlook Report* (May 1986), 39.

agricultural commodities to high technology was drying up, forcing increased reliance upon Western credit markets.

In 1984, the Soviet Union and its East European clients nearly tripled their formal borrowing from Western Europe and Japan to just under $3 billion, raising total East Bloc indebtedness to the West to close to $35 billion, roughly half owed to Western banks and half owed in the form of export credits and official loan guarantees.[873] In short, mid-1984 marked not only the failure of a two-decades-long strategy to alter the global geopolitical balance to advantage, it also saw the beginning of a systemic crisis.

The enormous Soviet investment in strategic weapons had yielded great power but little leverage, as the United States had built sufficient countervailing power to neutralize the Soviet buildup. Thus, the Russians had failed to maintain the essential condition for the execution of an aggressive foreign policy—strategic weapons advantage, the *sine qua non* without which an aggressive strategy designed to change the balance of power could not be pursued. Locked into commitments on four continents in Nicaragua, Angola, Vietnam, and Afghanistan, with no prospect of seeing any one of them through to successful conclusion, the Soviets found themselves overextended. Most of all the strategy of isolating Iran and weakening it in a war of attrition had failed, as the Iranian leadership moved to establish contact with the West.

By mid-1984, too, the correlation of forces was clearly shifting in favor of the United States. Not only had the United States begun rebuilding its military power at both the conventional and strategic levels, but also President Reagan had opened a new level of competition in space, with the Strategic Defense Initiative. A powerful economy promised to provide the wealth and technology resources needed to prevail in a long-term competition with the Soviet Union. Even more, American growth was spurring global growth, except in the Soviet bloc, which was becoming progressively impoverished. In a real sense, Reagan was spending the Soviet Union into submission.

Still, the evidence suggests, not all of the Soviet leadership was convinced as to the timing of the decision to change strategy, although all were convinced of the need to do so. Continued differences over the question of timing most persuasively explains the zig-zag course of Soviet policy through June and July, when the Soviets first proposed talks on the "militarization of outer space," then backed away when the United States expressed interest. Once it became clear, however, that President Reagan would not cave in to Shultz's pleas for concessions, the Soviets moved. Defying all predictions that Moscow would never contribute to the president's reelection, the Russians did precisely that by deigning to deal with him at every opportunity.

The Republican National Convention, August 20-23, nominating Reagan as the presidential candidate, made official his candidacy and inevitable his reelection against Democratic challenger Walter Mondale, former President

---

[873] Roger Robinson, "Financing the Soviet Union," *Wall Street Journal*, March 10, 1986, 36.

Jimmy Carter's vice-president. The Politburo meeting that followed, August 24-30, evidently made the decision to resume talks with the United States. Chernenko was ill and hospitalized when the decision was made and Gorbachev and Ustinov pushed the decision through, authorizing Gromyko, one of the dissenters, to accept a US proposal for a meeting when the Soviet foreign minister went to New York for the annual resumption of United Nations sessions in September.[874]

In retrospect, the Soviet leadership realized that they possessed neither the resources, nor the technology to continue in a long-term competition with the United States and so decided to buy the time needed to retool the economy and acquire a high technology base, their only hope to become competitive. Therefore, the Soviets switched to a new strategy of friendly relations with the West, and especially the United States. They would progressively cut losses where overextended, but secretly continue to pursue the main geopolitical objective: the drive to gain decisive leverage over world oil. To keep Washington off balance, however, even as they offered a friendlier face, the Soviets turned full force to the indirect strategy of pitting their international terrorist network against the West in general and the United States, in particular.

US and Soviet negotiators secretly agreed on August 31, the day after the Politburo meetings ended, that Gromyko would visit the White House for a luncheon with the president on September 28, after his appearance at the United Nations.[875] The public indicator that the Soviets had decided on a change of strategy occurred on September 6, when, without fanfare, Marshal Nikolai Ogarkov, perhaps the principal figure behind the previous year's hard-line approach, was removed from both his positions as chief of the General Staff and as first deputy minister of defense. He was replaced by one of Gorbachev's supporters, Sergei Akhromeyev. Although described as a "transfer," Ogarkov's removal was tied to a decision to shift Soviet military doctrine to the defensive and to "phased arms reduction."[876]

Although the Reagan-Gromyko meeting produced no immediate breakthroughs, the fact that the Soviets had agreed to meet, publicly acknowledging that the president would be the leader with whom they would have to deal for the next four years, was its main significance. Thus, even before the election, US-Soviet relations were poised to enter into a new era. For President Reagan, on the other hand, defeating the Soviet challenge put him in position to pursue his long-sought objective of victory in the Cold War. He would press for a genuine reduction in nuclear weapons and a shift to the strategic defensive. He

---

[874] Parker, *Kremlin in Transition* 1: 398-400.

[875] Lou Cannon and David Hoffman, "Invitation Was Planned in Secrecy," *Washington Post*, September 30, 1984, A1.

[876] Parker, *Kremlin in Transition* 1: 404. Matlock, *Reagan and Gorbachev*, 106, says that in early September, Gromyko "sent word . . . that he would come to Washington . . . if the secretary of state and the president received him." Shultz, *Turmoil and Triumph*, 480, on the other hand, says that "hints" came from Soviet sources that Gromyko wanted to meet Reagan "in the first part of August."

would also attempt to reestablish relations with Iran, drive the Russians entirely out of Afghanistan, and eliminate Nicaragua as a threat to the peace. All of these objectives, however, would have to be pursued amid intensified struggle with the leaders of the new world order faction who pressed hard for a general accommodation with Moscow above all else, as Mikhail Gorbachev rose to power.

Part III:

Entrapment of the President

Chapter 7

Strategy and its Discontents

In many ways, President Reagan's 1984 reelection was a pyrrhic victory. Despite the public euphoria, the president's electoral landslide was not duplicated in the Congress. In the Senate, Republicans lost two seats, which narrowed their margin of advantage to 53-47. And even though picking up 16 seats in the House, Republicans still trailed the Democrats by a large 71-seat margin, 253-182. The continued legislative stalemate was only the tip of the political iceberg, as the division within the administration between the president and his secretary of state grew more pronounced.

Wholesale change within the White House itself also weakened the president's position. Immediately after the election all three members of what had been Reagan's management team, called the troika, began making plans to depart. The first to go was Chief of Staff James Baker, who, seeking a cabinet post, persuaded Treasury Secretary Donald Regan to switch jobs, a change that the president announced in February 1985.[1] At the same time, Counselor Edwin Meese left the White House to become Attorney General and, later in May, Deputy Chief of Staff Mike Deaver left government entirely to set up a public relations firm in Washington, DC.

The departure of Baker, Meese, and Deaver from the White House did not, however, mean that they had lost influence. According to Regan, Baker requested that both he and Meese be retained as members of the National Security Planning Group (NSPG), giving them a formal voice in policy decisions, and the president agreed.[2] Thus, the Baker-Meese-Deaver troika was not so much broken up as shuffled into new positions, except for Deaver, who attempted to tutor new Chief of Staff Don Regan until he departed. In consequence, as Cannon observes, "the president was left to fend for himself while Regan underwent on-the-job training in 1985."[3]

---

[1] Michael K. Deaver, *Behind the Scenes* (New York: William Morrow, 1987), 130, notes "the Treasury swap originated with Baker, but he found a willing buyer in Don Regan." Don Regan, *For the Record* (New York: Harcourt, Brace, Jovanovich, 1988), 220, claims that he proposed the swap.

[2] Regan, *For the Record*, 235.

[3] Lou Cannon, *President Reagan: Role of a Lifetime* (New York: Simon & Shuster, 1991), 565.

Although Regan attempted to keep a tight rein on White House affairs, multiple lines of private access to the president materialized. National Security Adviser Robert McFarlane, in addition to briefing the president daily, had virtually unimpeded access. Secretary of State Shultz had private access to him twice a week arranged by McFarlane, and CIA Director Bill Casey, as before, also had walk-in access as well as a private office in the Executive Office Building adjacent to the West Wing of the White House.[4] Even though Regan was present during most meetings held with the president, the chief of staff was not well versed in matters of foreign policy and strategy, and therefore much escaped him. When he asked McFarlane to explain issues, for example, the national security adviser would invariably demur on the grounds that the chief of staff had "no need to know."[5]

The battle lines were clearly drawn between the president and Shultz in the NSPG, which on paper seemed to favor the president. On one side were Reagan, Casey, Meese, Regan, and Defense Secretary Caspar Weinberger; on the other side were Shultz, McFarlane, and Baker. Vice president George H. W. Bush, as president-in-waiting, played what by all accounts was an enigmatic role, especially in meetings where he was reticent in voicing opinions that could be recorded. Reportedly, in private, he supported the president, but in fact he was part of the political establishment that opposed him.

Secretary of State Shultz was the big winner in the musical chairs game, moving to a position of great influence over the policymaking apparatus.[6] In addition to gaining weekly access to the president, he had reestablished State Department preeminence over the policy formulating process through the senior interagency groups (SIGs), and had a strong White House ally in McFarlane. He also reshuffled personnel to advantage, either firing Reagan's supporters, or moving them to less influential positions.[7] For example, Jeane Kirkpatrick, cabinet member and UN representative, sought a more important assignment in the second term; she was denied, and resigned at the end of January.[8] Kirkpatrick was replaced by Vernon Walters and the UN position was downgraded, removed from the cabinet, and subordinated to the secretary of state.

In the key area of arms limitation, Reagan had wanted to keep control of the negotiations with the Soviets in the White House, as he had with former National Security Adviser William Clark earlier, proposing to appoint an arms

---

[4] Robert C. McFarlane, *Special Trust* (New York: Cadell & Davies, 1994), 287.

[5] Regan, *For the Record*, 324.

[6] Don Oberdorfer, "Shultz Firmly in Command," *Washington Post*, February 8, 1985, A1 and James McCartney, "Shultz, With Minimal Fanfare, Moves to Strengthen His Role," *Philadelphia Inquirer*, January 27, 1985, A1.

[7] Bill Outlaw, "Conservatives and Shultz Reach Accord in Debate Over Diplomats," *Washington Times*, January 16, 1985, A1 and John McLaughlin, "Shultz's Purge," *National Review*, February 8, 1985.

[8] Bernard Weinraub, "Reagan Is Told by Kirkpatrick She Will Leave," *New York Times*, January 31, 1985, A1.

control "czar"; but Shultz strongly opposed it. He insisted that "he personally wanted to lead the American effort to improve Soviet-American relations and get arms talks back on track," and Reagan relented.[9] Shultz promptly reorganized the entire team, establishing his and the State Department's dominance. Thus, he forced out Reagan's man Ed Rowny, relegating him to advisor status, and replaced him with John Tower. At the same time, he appointed Paul Nitze as his personal arms control adviser, marginalizing Secretary of Defense Weinberger and Assistant Secretary Richard Perle.[10]

Shultz tried but failed to force Weinberger out of government entirely. Shortly after the election, both Shultz and McFarlane spoke disparagingly of him. Shultz insisted to the president that he could no longer "work congenially" with the defense secretary and suggested that one or the other would have to go, offering his own resignation. Reagan refused the suggestion as well as the secretary's resignation offer.

Then, just before the inauguration, McFarlane repeated Shultz's argument, but the president once again refused, insisting, "We can work with both George and Cap." McFarlane said that left only two choices: "either you delegate to someone within the White House," by whom he meant himself, or "you've got to expect to become far more involved . . . in decision-making." Reagan replied presciently: "fine . . . . If that's what it takes, then that's what I'll do."[11] In fact, as we shall see, McFarlane, too, became more involved in decision-making.

When McFarlane replaced Judge Clark as national security adviser in the fall of 1983, control over the NSC was removed from the president and shifted to the new world order faction, although initially McFarlane played the role of honest broker. By the beginning of the second term, however, he would support Shultz in all important issues and attempt to persuade the president to do the same.[12]

Mayer and McManus thought that McFarlane was acting independently. As they saw it, as the second term began, "McFarlane decided to make the decisions himself. In effect, he guessed what the president wanted, and acted on

---

[9] Hedrick Smith, "For Shultz, Arms Control Talks Offer Fresh Prominence and New Purpose," *New York Times*, January 7, 1985, A8. See also George Shultz, *Turmoil and Triumph: My Years as Secretary of State* (New York: Scribner's, 1993) 491.

[10] Don Oberdorfer, "Rowny's Replacement Picked in Stealth," *Washington Post*, January 20, 1985, A29. Edward L. Rowny, *It Takes One to Tango* (Washington: Brassey's, 1992), 159-60, says the decision was a "stunning blow," which he could not comprehend.

[11] Jane Mayer and Doyle McManus, *Landslide* (Boston: Houghton Mifflin, 1988), 55-56. McFarlane, *Special Trust*, 286, also discusses these conversations, but reverses their order of occurrence, placing his before Shultz's, and omits the last remark by the president.

[12] See Norman Bailey and Stefan Halper, "National Security for Whom?" *Washington Quarterly* (Winter 1986): 186-88, for an incisive discussion of McFarlane and Shultz's domination of the decision-making process.

that," including signing White House orders FOR THE PRESIDENT in his own name.[13] Reality was more complicated. That McFarlane was making decisions in Reagan's name was true, but that he was acting independently was not. His actions were part of the new world order faction's plans to gain control of the foreign policy decision-making apparatus. As McFarlane put it:

> I decided that the Soviet Union ought to be the leading priority, and Shultz agreed . . . . We devoted most of our efforts in 1985 to getting the two of us back to the table and developing an agenda that the American people might understand and support.[14]

With Shultz and McFarlane in position to affect the formal policy machinery, not only would the president find it difficult to have his policies enacted through normal channels, his authority over covert operations also was circumscribed. Shortly before the inauguration Shultz made a move to limit the president's authority over covert operations. According to Executive Order 12333 the president and Casey controlled covert operations, but, on January 18, shortly before the inauguration, the president was prevailed upon to sign NSDD 159. On paper, NSDD 159 significantly weakened the president's authority by requiring that a specially configured National Security Planning Group "provide a recommendation to the president on each proposed covert action, or proposed modification to an ongoing covert operation."

Where formerly the president and the CIA director decided on covert operations, now a ten-man committee would decide. The membership of the committee was: Reagan, Bush, Shultz, Weinberger, Casey, Regan, McFarlane, Chairman of the Joint Chiefs of Staff General John Vessey, Fielding, and Dawson. (Fred Fielding was counselor to the president, and Tom Dawson was Regan's deputy.) Even more important was the stipulation that "the president shall approve of all covert action findings in writing."[15]

Thus, although the president would attempt to implement the "Reagan Doctrine" of building pressure on the Soviet Union to reach agreements to bring the Cold War to an end on his terms, his actual ability to execute his plans was limited by George Shultz and Robert McFarlane, who were determined to cajole, pressure, and turn the president's plans toward the main objective of the new world order faction—a more favorable accommodation with the Soviet Union furthered by "negotiated" outcomes of issues in conflict. The fundamental

---

[13] Mayer and McManus, *Landslide*, 65, 61.

[14] Ibid, 65.

[15]"Covert Action Policy Approval and Coordination Procedures," January 18, 1985. Christopher Simpson, *National Security Directives of the Reagan and Bush Administrations: The Declassified History of US Political and Military Policy, 1981-1991* (Boulder: Westview, 1995), 493-97.

difference in strategy would have ramifications for virtually every proposed policy.

NSDD-159 had a major impact on the means the president chose to implement his two crucial covert policy objectives—aid to the Nicaraguan Contras and the opening to Iran. When Congress cut off funding for the Contras, insiders wondered why the president did not issue a covert action finding to authorize continued funding. After all, the initial program in 1981 was authorized with just such a finding and later actions in 1986 would be authorized the same way. The answer was that with Shultz and McFarlane both on the committee deciding on covert actions, they were in position to block any proposed covert action or proposed modification to an ongoing covert action, which left as Reagan's only recourse a private, off-the-books operation that skirted the edge of legality.

The same was true for the opening to Iran, but with a twist. There was no support from Shultz, or Weinberger either, for an opening to Iran in 1985, although McFarlane surprisingly supported it. Therefore, the president appeared to proceed toward Iran in the same unofficial manner he had with the Contras, running both operations out of the NSC. But appearances were deceiving, and the initial approach collapsed.

As we shall see later in this narrative, McFarlane cut Casey out of the action, brought the initiative to the brink of failure, and resigned. After he resigned, however, the president took control of the initiative, signed a covert action finding—three of them, in fact—authorizing arms sales to Iran; but he and his new national security adviser, John Poindexter, kept the findings secret from the secretary of state, or at least they thought they had.

The Reagan Victory Program

As the program unfolded in 1985, President Reagan sought to consolidate the gains of the first term and parlay them into a new global order based on American hegemony. What came to be known as the "Reagan Doctrine"[16] was the public articulation of NSDD-75, which the president had signed in January 1983. The main objective was to negotiate a new arms control regime with the Soviet Union based on the Strategic Defense Initiative (SDI). The president sought to gain Soviet agreement to make a transition to the strategic defensive, abandon the long-held doctrine of mutual assured destruction (MAD), and sharply reduce inventories of strategic and intermediate-range missiles. Such an agreement would strip Moscow of its military advantage.[17]

At the same time, Reagan wanted to keep the pressure on the Soviet Union, both economically and geopolitically, without which he knew there would be no incentive for Moscow to reach agreement. Economically, the president

---

[16] Charles Krauthammer, "The Reagan Doctrine," *Time*, April 1, 1985.
[17] For a succinct contemporaneous analysis of the doctrine, see Cord Meyer, "Reagan's Role on World Stage," *Washington Times*, January 11, 1985, C1.

sought to spur the growth of the United States and the Western allies, while undercutting further the Soviet Union's hard currency earning capacity, raising the cost of maintaining the Soviet empire. Saudi Arabia would be a secret lynchpin in this endeavor, as success would involve a sharp plunge in the price of oil. Low oil prices would spur Western economic growth while depriving the Soviet Union of needed hard currency earnings.

Geopolitically, the president sought to bolster opponents of Soviet regimes, especially in Afghanistan, Nicaragua, Poland, Angola, Mozambique, and Cambodia. With the supporting infrastructure put in place during the first term, Reagan now sought to turn up the heat and assist them to victory. Here, too, Saudi Arabia secretly played a major role in providing funds when the US Congress was slow to act, or refused to act, or where secrecy was vital.

The president also strove to complete the renewal of the global containment structure by reestablishing relations with Iran, the largest single part of that structure. Having blunted Soviet strategy toward Iran in the first term, he now sought to respond to persistent signals from the Tehran leadership of an interest in improving relations. Saudi money would play a "bridging" role in this endeavor, as well. Finally, the president was determined to take steps against the growing wave of terror against the United States and its Western allies. Libya, one of Moscow's surrogates, would be a key target.

The secretary of state and the new world order faction had a different agenda. Seeking accommodation with the Soviet Union rather than victory, to varying degrees Shultz opposed every one of the president's policies, while portraying his own policy positions as fully in accordance with the president's. Shultz could not survive politically in open defiance of his president, at least not yet. Alexander Haig's experience was testimony to that. Thus, whatever his actual position, he would assert unanimity with the president.[18] Besides, he believed that he could persuade the president to his point of view and, if he could not persuade him, he would outmaneuver him with and through the bureaucracy.

The secretary's most obvious opposition to the president was over the Iran initiative, where he publicly opposed Reagan, but on all other issues— including the nature of an arms control settlement with the Russians, the economic struggle with them, support for anti-Soviet resistance movements around the world, and the issue of international terrorism—Shultz's positions diverged from the president's in subtler ways.

Indeed, except for Iran, their differences were over the extent of pressure to be applied before coming to the bargaining table, and in all cases, Reagan took a tougher stand than his secretary. There was essential agreement between Reagan and Shultz on means, i.e., the application of pressure on the Soviet Union and its clients around the globe. Where they differed was on the ends, with Reagan seeking victory over the Soviet Union and its clients in the Cold War, while Shultz searched for issues on which to strike a negotiated accommodation.

---

[18] Shultz's memoir, *Turmoil and Triumph*, is a graphic demonstration of this tactic.

In practice, it meant that where the president sought to apply sustained and decisive pressure on the Soviet Union, whether with SDI, or support for anti-Soviet resistance groups around the globe, Shultz sought to continue the policies of *bleeding* the Russians and their clients sufficiently to bring them to the bargaining table where a solution could be negotiated to demonstrate the benefits of détente. The policy battle over support for the Afghan resistance was a clear manifestation of this divergence.

Shultz's approach predetermined the result of any ensuing *negotiation,* which was the legitimization and reinforcement of the Soviet-supported side. During the second term, and especially the last two years, when Shultz was in complete control, not a single communist regime would be displaced by means of negotiation. The political outcomes in Nicaragua, Angola, Ethiopia, Mozambique, Poland, and Cambodia reinforced pro-Soviet, communist regimes. Not even in Afghanistan, where the Soviets were driven out, was a pro-Western regime established.

Iran was a special case. Shultz's vociferous opposition to an opening to Iran was based on a fundamental difference in strategy. Restoring relations with Iran would reestablish the essential containment structure around the Soviet Union and involve American support for a pro-Western state on the Soviet border. The new world order faction was committed to dismantling the US forward global position and thus eliminating a presumed obstacle to détente, regardless of how that might impact on the question of the availability and price of petroleum supply and the security of the Persian Gulf.

Contemporaneous observers, the press, and participants in the policy process understood the conflict within the administration, but consistently portrayed it as either personal (Shultz versus Weinberger, or Casey), or institutional (State versus Defense or CIA), rather than fundamental and strategic, involving the struggle between the president and the new world order faction.

Ultimately, the president could always say no, as at Reykjavik where, against all odds, he maintained his stance to preserve SDI against the arguments of both Gorbachev and his secretary of state. He would often be advised by his supporters simply to dismiss Shultz, but Reagan knew that was not possible without major cause, such as with Haig, precisely because of the "compact" between the president and the political establishment. The administration was a coalition government made up of Reagan and his supporters and the new world order political establishment and theirs. Besides, Shultz was usefully engaged in what the president wanted, even if he did not want to go as far as the president did.

The Shift to the Strategic Defensive

There was no more important nor contentious an issue within the administration than arms control, because it would define the relationship with the Soviet Union, and tensions heightened when the Soviets shifted strategy and sought to resume negotiations. The Soviet decision galvanized Shultz into action.

As he viewed it, "we were smack in the middle of what was ever more clearly shaping up to be the endgame of the Cold War."[19] The president and his aides, especially Weinberger, wanted to tread cautiously, seeing no value in a precipitous agreement. The strategic tide was running with the United States and the president and his allies wanted to let it run until US power and position improved further, but not Shultz. As the secretary described it, referring to Weinberger:

> They feared agreements. They thought the Soviets would out negotiate us and then cheat. I disagreed. We could out negotiate them and catch them if they cheated. But it meant we would have to compromise and have to realize that nothing is perfect or airtight.[20]

Reagan, of course, clearly understood that having defeated the Soviet challenge in the first term, he would need to engage the Russians in the second, if he were to be able to forge a new global order based on SDI. Moreover, it would be vital to do so before the Soviets had become locked into a new strategy. And so, to the consternation of his supporters, who worried about a presidential change of heart, he sided with Shultz. Reagan, too, understood that they were approaching the "endgame of the Cold War," and wanted to end it on his terms.

Secretary Shultz and Soviet Foreign Minister Andrei Gromyko were scheduled to meet in Geneva, January 7-8, to decide on the structure, agenda, and time for resumption of arms control negotiations. In the weeks leading up to the meeting the maneuvering on both sides was intense. Although Weinberger objected to the meeting, the president agreed to it. He intended to bring the Russians back to the bargaining table. Without negotiations there would be no means to obtain his overarching objectives: Soviet agreement for a transition to strategic defense based on SDI and for a sharp reduction in nuclear missiles, both strategic and intermediate.

The president knew full well that Shultz saw arms control negotiations as an opportunity to use SDI as a bargaining chip and parlay a severely restricted system as the basis for an accommodation. According to Talbott, "Shultz said privately on a number of occasions that he was prepared to 'signal' that SDI was 'open for discussion' as long as Gromyko acknowledged that the Soviet superiority in ICBMs was also negotiable."[21]

To ensure that his secretary hewed to his objectives and would *not* attempt to indicate that SDI was negotiable, Reagan issued an unusually detailed and specific set of negotiating instructions for him to follow when he met Gromyko. NSDD-153, which Reagan signed on January 1, 1985, was the product

---

of the combined inputs of Shultz, Weinberger, Casey, the Joint Chiefs of Staff, and the Arms Control and Disarmament Agency (ACDA).[22] McFarlane's accompanying memo to the president highlighted the president's objectives, namely, to "open formal talks within a month or so," and to "begin a process of education and persuasion with regard to your view of how together we can agree on a road which will lead us toward less reliance on offensive systems and more on defensive systems. This latter goal represents a truly historic initiative."[23]

More than a simple set of instructions, the 16-page document presented a succinct analysis of the historical evolution of strategic weapons, how the balance had skewed toward Moscow, and how the US strategic modernization program was making it possible to "restore the nuclear balance . . . by the end of the decade." It explained why Reagan believed that it was important to make a transition to a new arms control regime based on strategic defense, instead of continuing to rely on mutual assured destruction. "If the promise of SDI is achieved, the Soviet advantage accumulated over the past twenty years at great cost will be largely neutralized."[24]

Nitze had drafted what was termed the "strategic concept," which Shultz was instructed to present to Gromyko when they met. A concise four sentences in length, it stated:

> During the next ten years, the US objective is a radical reduction in the power of existing and planned offensive nuclear arms, as well as the stabilization of the relationship between offensive and defense nuclear arms, whether on earth or in space. We are even now looking forward to a period of transition to a more stable world, with greatly reduced levels of nuclear arms and an enhanced ability to deter war based upon the increasing contribution of non-nuclear defenses against offensive nuclear arms. This period of transition could lead to the eventual elimination of all nuclear arms, both offensive and defensive. A world free of nuclear arms is an ultimate objective to which we, the Soviet Union, and all other nations can agree.[25]

However, the specific negotiating instructions to Shultz, beyond the presentation of the "strategic concept" were muddled and contradictory. Although the secretary was instructed to keep the START and INF negotiating fora substantively and procedurally "*separate*," and offer "corresponding negotiations

---

[22] Simpson, *National Security Directives,* 439, 469-84.

[23] McFarlane, *Special Trust*, 302.

[24] Simpson, *National Security Directives*, 472.

[25] Simpson, *National Security Directives*, 473. For Nitze's original draft, see Paul Nitze et al., *From Hiroshima to Glasnost* (New York: Grove Weidenfeld, 1989), 404-05.

on nuclear defensive forces," which referred to the Soviet missile defense system, not SDI, which was non-nuclear, he would not be bound by these instructions.

The president authorized him to agree to virtually any formulation that Gromyko proposed, including "a *merger* of talks on reducing medium-range and intercontinental-range nuclear weapons," to get the talks going.[26] However, anticipating that the Soviets would seek to gain agreement to "prevent the militarization of space," Shultz was instructed at all costs to avoid any pejorative reference to SDI as a "space" weapon. Indeed, he was specifically enjoined to ensure that "the word 'space' should not appear in the description of any negotiations . . . in a manner prejudicial to the US."[27]

To ensure that the president's views would not be easily circumvented and especially that SDI would not be viewed as a "bargaining chip," before Shultz left for Geneva, the White House issued a report entitled *The President's Strategic Defense Initiative* explaining the centrality of SDI in Reagan's defense concept. In addition, the gist of Shultz's instructions was telegraphed in a series of press articles based on conversations with "unnamed" administration spokesmen. One article outlined the intent to separate the offensive and defensive negotiations.[28] Another revealed that the United States would negotiate arms reductions, but "offer only to hold discussions on future defensive arms."[29] A third said that Shultz would confront the Russians about the ABM Treaty violation at Krasnoyarsk.[30] A fourth emphasized that "Reagan has closed the door . . . on any deals that would limit his 'Star Wars' missile defense program."[31]

The public campaign to keep pressure on Shultz had little effect on the secretary, however, and the negotiating instructions, as is usually the case, were of only marginal relevance to the actual course of the discussions. The same was true for the composition of the delegation that went to Geneva. Although he had been directed to take a large, 21-man arms control contingent with him to Geneva, representing all relevant institutional interests, the secretary excluded all but a select handful to "sit at the table" with him.

On January 5, the day of departure for Europe, Shultz held a meeting of the entire delegation and informed them that only he, McFarlane, Nitze, Ambassador to the Soviet Union Arthur Hartman, and Russian-speaking State Department note-taker Jack Matlock, would sit at the negotiating table with the

---

[26] Leslie Gelb, "Unused US Option in Geneva Related," *New York Times*, February 1, 1985, A4. (emphasis supplied)

[27] Simpson, *National Security Directives*, 478-9.

[28] Lou Cannon, "US Sees Dual Talks Covering Offensive, Defensive Weapons," *Washington Post*, January 1, 1985, A1.

[29] Bernard Gwertzman, "Shultz Instructed to Spurn Russians on Space Weapons," *New York Times*, January 3, 1985, A1.

[30] Walter Pincus, "US to Confront Soviets with Charge of Treaty Violation," *Washington Post*, January 3, 19895, A1.

[31] David Hoffman, "US Firm in Pursuing 'Star Wars,'" *Washington Post*, January 4, 1985, A1.

Russians. All of the others, representatives from the Defense Department, ACDA, CIA, and the Joint Chiefs, would be relegated to an adjacent room and would not be privy to what would occur.

Shultz further stunned the group by imposing a strict no press contact rule, declaring that only Press Secretary Bernard Kalb would be permitted to talk to the media.[32] Thus, while the contingent that accompanied the secretary to Geneva appeared to present a formidable, unified front, the delegates literally had no duties to perform except to sit in an adjacent room while the secretary and his aides negotiated with the Russians. Shultz briefed them after each session, called on them for their particular expertise when needed, but excluded them from the negotiations. Indeed, the members of the delegation were even kept in the dark about the meeting agenda. Ostensibly to preserve secrecy, they were handed copies of Shultz's talking points only when they boarded the aircraft for Geneva.[33]

The negotiations themselves were conducted in a complete news blackout. Although Shultz claimed that the Soviets accepted "our concept" of linking strategic, intermediate, and space negotiations in an independent, but interrelated fashion, it appears that this was Gromyko's idea, which Shultz accepted.[34] So much for Shultz's boast of being able to "out negotiate" the Russians. Their agreement bore no relationship to the "strategic concept" of a transition to the defensive, or to the secretary's negotiating instructions.

Indeed, Matlock characterized Gromyko's approach as one of "double linkage." As he described it, "there could be no agreement on INF . . . without one on START. Additionally, there could be no agreement on either of these weapons types without an agreement regarding 'space weapons.'"[35] Shultz weakly complained that to "hold up progress in one area until all three were resolved" was a formula for stalemate, but acquiesced.[36] Of course, as far as Shultz was concerned, as SDI was not sacrosanct, linkage was preferred.

As expected, it was the "space" issue on which Shultz and Gromyko differed most. Gromyko wanted to define SDI as a "space strike weapon," which Shultz rejected, while Shultz wanted to describe SDI as "space defense," which Gromyko thought a contradiction in terms. The talks appeared headed to failure over the Soviet insistence that the focus of the talks was to prevent an "arms race in space." Stalemated, Shultz consulted Richard Perle waiting in the anteroom. The Defense Department's arms control specialist suggested adding on to the phrase "preventing an arms race in space" the words "and terminating one on earth," a solution that both Shultz and Gromyko accepted.

Nevertheless, the Soviets managed to insert into the final communiqué the suggestion that SDI was an offensive weapon by claiming that the negotiations

---

[32] Jay Winik, *On the Brink* (New York: Simon & Schuster, 1996), 323.

[33] Shultz, *Turmoil and Triumph*, 512.

[34] Ibid, 515-16.

[35] Jack Matlock, *Reagan and Gorbachev* (New York: Random House, 2004), 104.

[36] Winik, *On the Brink*, 331.

would be about "nuclear and space arms." A following clarification ameliorated the point, stating as the objective:

> [to] work out effective agreements aimed at preventing an arms race in space and terminating it on earth, at limiting and reducing nuclear arms and at strengthening strategic stability.

The negotiations, it was agreed, would be conducted by a delegation from each side, divided into three groups. The subject of the negotiations was to be a "complex of questions" concerning nuclear and space arms, strategic and intermediate range missiles, "with all the questions considered and resolved in their interrelationship."[37]

Shultz could hardly have been serious in reporting to the president that "we got what we wanted" in the structure of the talks. Except for agreeing to recommence talks, which, in truth, both sides did want, the Russians had gotten their way almost entirely. For his part, the president declared that he perceived a glimmer of hope in the forthcoming dialogue with the Russians. However, he warned, "It takes two sides to have constructive negotiations . . . . For our part, we will be flexible, patient and determined. We now look to the Soviet Union to help give new life and positive results to that process of dialogue."[38]

To set a high bar for the upcoming negotiations, and, perhaps to satisfy critics on the right, on February 1, the president released a report on Soviet arms control violations. It was the third such report issued in the past thirteen months, the first having been issued on January 13, 1984, citing seven violations; the second on October 10, citing seventeen violations; and the current report, citing eleven violations out of thirteen findings.[39] Four violations involved the ABM Treaty, the most serious being the Krasnoyarsk radar, which suggested "the USSR. may be preparing an ABM defense of its national territory."[40]

In his letter of transmittal, the president said that for arms control agreements "to have meaning," there must be full compliance and "this administration will not accept anything less." His goal in the coming negotiations was to "reverse the erosion of the ABM Treaty and to seek equitable, effectively verifiable arms control agreements which will result in real reductions and enhanced stability." The Soviet Union, he noted, has "thus far not provided

---

[37] "Text of the Communiqué," *New York Times*, January 9, 1985, A11.

[38] Bernard Gwertzman, "Reagan Sees Hope of 'New Dialogue' With the Russians," *New York Times*, January 10, 1985, A1.

[39] "The President's Unclassified Report to the Congress on Soviet Noncompliance with Arms Control Agreements," February 1, 1985, in Simpson, *National Security Directives*, 502-12.

[40] Bernard Gwertzman, "US Says Soviet Violates ABM Treaty," *New York Times*, February 2, 1985, 3.

satisfactory explanations nor undertaken corrective actions sufficient to alleviate our concerns."[41]

Tass, the Soviet news agency, immediately replied by charging the Reagan administration with plans for a "crash militarization of outer space." Military analyst Vladimir Bogachev said that it was Washington, not Moscow that was preparing to "violate the ABM Treaty by developing a space-based antimissile system."[42] Not to be outdone, Defense Secretary Weinberger retorted that the United States was indeed considering the "partial deployment of a "Star Wars" anti-missile defense system without waiting for it to be fully completed." This would, he maintained, "strengthen our existing deterrent . . . . [and] could make a major contribution to the prevention of nuclear war before a fully effective system is deployed."[43] The exchange guaranteed that the coming talks would receive wide attention.

Arms control negotiations would resume on March 12 but would be immediately overshadowed by the death of Communist Party Chairman Konstantin Chernenko and the ascendance of Mikhail Gorbachev, who became personally involved in the negotiations thereafter. By that time, the president already had set in motion the other elements of the Reagan Doctrine.

Signaling Opposition to Moscow

King Fahd of Saudi Arabia was scheduled to visit the White House in the second week of February. As Reagan was counting on the King's support for much of what he planned to do, it was important to signal publicly the administration's second-term direction to him, as well as to the American people and other interested parties. First to sketch out what would soon be described as the "Reagan Doctrine" was Bill Casey. In a January 9 speech to the Union League Club of New York, Casey announced, "the tide has changed." He explained:

> Whereas in the 1960s and 1970s anti-Western causes attracted
> recruits throughout the Third World, the 1980s have emerged
> as the decade of freedom fighters resisting communist regimes.
> In many places, freedom has become as exciting and
> revolutionary as it was here in America over 200 years ago.[44]

Although the Soviets had acquired "surrogates in Cuba, Vietnam, Ethiopia, Angola, South Yemen, Mozambique, Nicaragua, and Afghanistan," he said, they were overextended. It was costing Moscow $8 billion annually to

---

[41] "Arms Control Violations—The 1985 Report," Heritage Foundation *National Security Record*, no. 77 (March 1985): 1-3.

[42] "Cheating on Arms Denied by Moscow," *Washington Post*, February 3, 1985, A18.

[43] James McCartney, "Weinberger: Early 'Star Wars' Deployment is Weighed," *Philadelphia Inquirer*, February 4, 1985, 7.

[44] Herb Meyer, ed., *Scouting the Future: The Public Speeches of William J. Casey* (Washington, DC: Regnery, 1989), 171.

support these regimes and they were running out of money. The good news was that "hundreds of thousands of ordinary people are volunteers in irregular wars against the Soviet army or Soviet-supported regimes." Oppressed people, he said, "want freedom and are fighting for it. They need only modest support and strength of purpose from nations that want to see freedom prevail . . . "[45]

On February 6, during his State of the Union address, the president picked up Casey's theme:

> We cannot play innocents abroad in a world that is not innocent; nor can we be passive when freedom is under siege. Without resources, diplomacy cannot succeed. Our security assistance programs help friendly governments defend themselves and give them confidence to work for peace.
>
> We must stand by all our democratic allies. And we must not break faith with those who are risking their lives-on every continent, from Afghanistan to Nicaragua-to defy Soviet-supported aggression and secure rights, which have been ours from birth.
>
> The Sandinista dictatorship of Nicaragua, with full Cuban-Soviet bloc support, not only persecutes its people, the church, and denies a free press, but arms and provides bases for Communist terrorists attacking neighboring states. Support for freedom fighters is self-defense and totally consistent with the OAS and U.N. Charters. It is essential that the Congress continue all facets of our assistance to Central America. I want to work with you to support the democratic forces whose struggle is tied to our own security.[46]

King Fahd's visit to Washington a few days later, February 11-15, marked the high point of a carefully nurtured, unwritten, and, as it turned out, short-lived alliance between the United States and Saudi Arabia. Its impetus had been the Soviet invasion of Afghanistan, and heavy military involvement in Ethiopia and South Yemen, which belatedly had convinced the Saudi leadership of earlier US claims that the Soviet Union was attempting to encircle the kingdom with a ring of pro-Soviet client states.

---

[45] Ibid, 172.

[46] "Address before a Joint Session of the Congress on the State of the Union, February 6, 1985," *Public Papers of the Presidents of the United States, Ronald Reagan, 1985*, bk. 1, *January 1 to June 28, 1985* (Washington: Government Printing Office, 1988), 130-136. See also Lou Cannon, "Reagan Hails 'New Freedom,'" *Washington Post*, February 7, 1985, A1 and Don Oberdorfer, "Reagan Declares US Again a Leader of the Free World," *Washington Post*, February 7, 1985, A18.

Earlier US efforts at policy suasion during the Carter years had been disastrous, alienating the Saudis who believed that Carter had not only abandoned the shah of Iran, but also had repudiated his own Camp David pledge to provide for Palestinian self-rule. In addition, during the South Yemen invasion of North Yemen, the administration's clumsy efforts to depict the Soviet threat as being greater than the Zionist threat had only deepened suspicion of American intentions. The result was that by mid-1979 the Saudis had turned away from Washington with a vengeance, sending oil prices sky high.[47]

The Soviet invasion of Afghanistan changed everything. Throughout 1980, the United States countered the Soviet thrust by constructing or refurbishing a string of bases and access points to the region from Turkey to Diego Garcia. Washington also sought to demonstrate its readiness to come to the aid of the Saudi kingdom, and a genuine coincidence of interest began to evolve. Carter's support of Iraq against Iran involved the Saudis as financier for Saddam Hussein's war. Riyadh now understood that the Shiite threat was genuine and that the Soviet threat was at least as great as the Zionist threat.

The Carter administration parlayed Saudi concern about the Shiite threat into greater cooperation as the Saudis granted to United States the use of territory and facilities in case of emergency. More importantly, they agreed to construct a massive $80 billion defense network according to US design and specifications. During the decade of the '80s the Saudis greatly expanded their defense infrastructure, building six major new air bases, nine new ports, dozens of airfields, and new pipelines linking Iraqi oilfields to export terminals on the Red Sea.

The purpose of the new defense infrastructure was to upgrade the kingdom's own defense capability and also to facilitate a seamless transition for American forces in the utilization of the bases, if and when it ever became necessary for the United States to come to the direct defense of Saudi Arabia. Few could have foreseen that when the emergency did arise in 1990 the threat would come not from Iran, but from Iraq.

Ronald Reagan sought to build on the relationship as soon as he came into office, consummating with some difficulty the AWACS sale in 1981. Washington had deployed a number of the aircraft to Saudi Arabia upon the outbreak of the Iran-Iraq war the previous September. The Saudis were so impressed with the technical capabilities of the planes that they insisted on acquiring them for their own defense. As the crisis over Lebanon erupted and Israel invaded in mid-1982, Reagan supported a greater peace-keeping role for the Saudis in the region, but with no success, as they were averse to assuming a public role in the peace process, especially one that involved negotiation with the Israelis.

By mid-1984, the beginning of a *quid pro quo* was nevertheless apparent. In return for substantial US support for Saudi national defense, the king broadened

---

[47] Richard C. Thornton, *The Carter Years: Toward a New Global Order* (New York: Paragon House, 1991), chap. 7.

his support for anti-Soviet resistance movements. The administration arranged to deploy an additional aerial refueling tanker to extend the range of the kingdom's fleet of F-15 aircraft, as well as to provide additional wing tanks for them. To assist in the Saudi air defense, Reagan authorized the unprecedented sale of 400 Stingers, the first time the highly advanced, man-portable missile launcher had been transferred to another country, and over two years before they were introduced into Afghanistan.

The Saudis already were supporting the Afghan resistance against the Soviets at a rate of one dollar for every dollar put up by the United States. At this point, their joint contribution was running over $1 billion annually. In the fall, the Congress had cut off funding for the Contras and the king had agreed to provide funding of $1 million per month for eight months, until the next congressional vote in early 1985.[48] Thus, by the time the king arrived in Washington for his state visit on February 11, 1985, the US-Saudi relationship was well on the way to an unofficial alliance. Reagan and the king would take it a giant step forward.

The President, the King, and the Reagan Doctrine: Lynchpin of Victory

King Fahd arrived in Washington as the crisis within the American leadership over strategy toward the Middle East-Southwest Asia region consumed the administration. Secretary of State Haig had sought to support Iraq as Carter had done and as the new world order strategy of dismantling the containment structure dictated, while Reagan was determined to hold open the possibility of a rapprochement with Iran, as called for by the strategy of rebuilding containment. Shultz's replacement of Haig had only intensified the differences between them, as Shultz's power grew and as the president moved forward toward his Iran initiative at the beginning of the second term.

In retrospect, President Reagan and King Fahd appear to have reached four major agreements in support of the president's strategy against the Soviet Union. The first was a $3 billion arms package, which initially included 42 F-15s to go with the 60 already in the Saudi fighter inventory. This part of the arms package would be canceled in May because of intense Israeli opposition expressed through the US Congress, but arrangements were made to provide a comparable aircraft through Great Britain.

The second agreement was for the Saudis to expand and broaden their support for anti-Soviet resistance movements. The kingdom would increase its support for the Afghan Mujahideen as congressional funding increased and triple its support for the Nicaraguan Contras, from $8 million to $24 million. In addition to increasing support for the Mujahideen and the Contras, the Saudis also agreed to provide funds for arms deliveries to Jonas Savimbi's UNITA forces struggling against the Soviet-backed MPLA regime in Angola and to support the

---

[48] Robert Kagan, *Twilight Struggle: American Power and Nicaragua, 1977-1990* (New York: Free Press, 1992), 340-41.

Mozambique resistance movement, RENAMO, against the Soviet-backed Maputo regime.[49]

There also appears to have been an agreement for the king to support Reagan's intended opening to Iran. What would make possible the opening to Iran would be Saudi financing of arms transfers, which may have reflected the assumption presumably made by the president and his aides that the best way to resolve the Shiite threat to the kingdom was by co-opting it, rather than contending against it. At the same time, the Saudis continued to funnel some American weapons to Iraq to ensure that no Iranian offensive would succeed.[50] The objective remained to perpetuate a stalemate in the war.

In any case, regarding Iran, Saudi involvement appeared in the person of businessman Adnan Khashoggi, who would not only establish contact with Iranian middlemen and Israelis, but also provide bridge financing for arms sales. His role would be similar to that played by Prince Bandar, who became the conduit for funds to the Contras. In both cases, there can be little doubt that action required the prior approval of the king.

The issue that would have the most decisive impact on Moscow would be the issue of oil. The oil price trend had been on a gradually downward sloping trajectory since 1981. OPEC had attempted to maintain prices by cutting output as non-OPEC production—North Sea, Mexico, Canada, the Soviet Union—increased. Saudi Arabia, as the swing producer, had cut production from 10 million bpd to 3.4 million bpd, in an unsuccessful attempt to prop up prices.[51] For Riyadh the result was a sharp drop in oil revenue from a 1981 high of $119 billion to a 1985 low of $26 billion. Foreign exchange reserves dwindled, and the country began to run a budget deficit, forcing the kingdom to cut back ambitious development programs initiated when income was at its height.[52]

Loss of revenue and market share began to marginalize Saudi Arabia's regional and global role. The Saudis were underwriting the policies of OPEC members who were circumventing agreed quotas for their own gain. For example, Iran and Iraq, attempting to pay huge war costs, were openly flouting OPEC quotas by heavily engaging in countertrade, bartering oil for arms. In effect, Saudi Arabia was losing money by propping up oil prices for the benefit of those who were cheating, including its enemy Iran.[53]

---

[49] Peter Schweizer, *Victory: The Reagan Administration's Secret Strategy That Hastened the Collapse of the Soviet Union* (New York: Atlantic Monthly Press, 1994), 217-19.

[50] "The Arming of Saudi Arabia," *Frontline*, February 16, 1993 (transcript of show number 1112).

[51] "Saudi Arabia Crude Oil Production by Year," *Index Mundi* (online), https://www.indexmundi.com/energy.aspx?country=sa&product=oil&graph=production.

[52] "Oil Price History and Analysis," *WTRG Economics*, www.wtrg.com/prices.htm.

[53] Daniel Yergin, *The Prize* (New York: Free Press, 1992), 728.

It is safe to assume that when the king arrived in Washington, he was ready to listen to any plan that would help alleviate his no-win situation. President Reagan and his aides offered just such a plan. In secret meetings behind all the pomp and circumstance that attend state visits, Reagan and his aides proposed what was in a nutshell a plan, as Ambassador Richard Murphy pithily phrased it, to "let the free market dictate prices."[54]

As it was obviously proving impossible to maintain high price levels and the Saudis were losing revenue by cutting production in an attempt to keep prices high, Reagan and his aides proposed to abandon the strategy. They pitched the idea of maximizing income by volume instead of price. This approach would allow market forces of supply and demand to determine prices, which meant that the growing abundance of supply would depress prices further. Lower prices were what the president wanted in order to generate Western economic growth and curtail Soviet hard-currency earnings, but they would also enable the Saudis to recover market share and increase income, regaining the kingdom's rightful place as the preeminent power in the gulf. As oil prices fell, the president's aides argued, the United States, Western Europe, and Japan would consume more and increase economic growth, while those dependent upon oil for hard-currency earnings, like the Soviet Union, Libya, Iraq, and Iran would suffer sharply reduced earnings. Simply put, their friends would gain, and their enemies would lose.

Once having acceded to this proposition, the next steps were to dismantle the framework that was in place to keep prices high. The Saudis brought the refiners on board by arranging netback deals guaranteeing per-barrel profits regardless of price. Refiners were given an incentive to maximize profits through volume of production, rather than by restricting production. It would not matter what the per-barrel price was. Their profit margin would be the same whether the price was $30 dollars a barrel, or $10 dollars a barrel. The netback deals meant that the Saudis would no longer cut production to support an official price. Once the Saudis decided upon a market share strategy, everybody else would be forced to do the same.

The agreement, it is said, was entirely based on "unwritten understandings," but these understandings would be reinforced by each party's public actions.[55] Reagan took the first step. Less than two weeks after King Fahd left Washington, Prime Minister Margaret Thatcher arrived, February 19-21. During that visit, Reagan convinced Thatcher that it was in Britain's interest, too, to go along with the plan to change oil strategy.

The issue was the role that the British National Oil Company, BNOC, played in setting prices. BNOC bought 51 percent of North Sea output at a specified price and resold it to refiners. In a market where demand was greater than supply this was a profitable enterprise, but a losing one when the reverse was

---

[54] "The Arming of Saudi Arabia," *Frontline*, February 16, 1993.
[55] Ibid.

true. Thus, as the market softened in the early '80s, BNOC found itself buying high and selling low, losing money for the British Treasury.[56]

Thatcher was therefore willing to consider proposals that would end market losses and here Reagan's proposal was simply that BNOC discontinue its price-setting role and let the free market determine prices. As Thatcher was outspoken in her support for free market solutions, this was an approach that appealed to her. Therefore, the prime minister later in May removed BNOC from the business of attempting to set prices.

But, of course, as everyone associated with the petroleum business understood, in a glutted oil market the removal of price restrictions meant that prices would go in only one direction—down—and fast. How fast depended on when Saudi Arabia began to increase production. But first the ducks had to be lined up. No doubt, the US-Saudi Joint Commission on Economic Cooperation, which met April 22-23 in Washington, played a role in working out details and timing. CIA Director Casey's trip to Riyadh in late spring may have been to signal that the time had come to move. The CIA director also conveyed information that would enable the Saudis to earn additional revenue when he divulged that the United States would commence a gradual dollar devaluation in the fall, which meant that non-dollar Saudi assets would rise in value.[57]

Whether or not Casey's visit was the trigger, the king clearly signaled his intentions at the June OPEC meeting a few weeks later when he said: "If member countries feel they have a free hand to act . . . then all should enjoy that situation and Saudi Arabia would certainly secure its own interests."[58] At that point, even though OPEC output had fallen to a 20-year low of 13.7 million bpd, prices continued to soften. In early September word began to get around that the price fall was coming.[59] Then, on September 13, oil minister Sheikh Ahmed Zaki Yamani announced that Saudi Arabia would no longer protect oil prices at all. The ducks were lined up.

Resigned to the inevitable, at the end of November OPEC convened and announced that its members had decided to compete as a group with non-OPEC producers to regain market share without regard to price. Over the next five months the price of oil plummeted. West Texas Intermediate dropped from its peak of $31.75 to under $10, with some cargoes selling for as low as $6 per barrel. A price correction would not come until May 1986 when prices would level and fluctuate in a new, much lower, $17-$19 per barrel range, which largely prevailed until the end of the century, except for a price spike in 1991 precipitated by the Gulf War and a price dip in 1999.

Needless to say, the sharp fall of oil prices devastated the Soviet Union's hard currency earning capability. In 1986 alone the Soviets lost over $20 billion

---

[56] Yergin, *The Prize*, 727.

[57] Schweizer, *Victory, 232-33.*

[58] Yergin, *The Prize*, 729.

[59] John Berry, "Saudi Oil Price Cut Rumored," *Washington Post*, September 5, 1985, E2.

in expected revenue, even though increasing production. Clearly, the change in the oil regime was one of the major factors that drove the Soviet Union into bankruptcy and contributed to its collapse in 1991.

By all accounts, however, this was not a foregone conclusion in early 1985 when the president initiated the Reagan Doctrine. Indeed, it was not evident that the "doctrine" would live up to its promise, as new Soviet leader Mikhail Gorbachev ascended to the Chairmanship of the Communist Party.

Shultz's Struggle with the President

On February 16, the president's weekly radio address described the situation in Central America within the broader movement to confront communism. Echoing Casey's views, Reagan declared:

> The move against communism and toward freedom . . . is sweeping the world. In the Soviet Union and Eastern Europe, we see the dissidents, in Poland, the Solidarity movement. We see freedom fighters in Afghanistan, Ethiopia, Cambodia, and Angola. These brave men and women are fighting to undo the infamous Brezhnev doctrine, which says that once a nation falls into the darkness of Communist tyranny, it can never again see the light of freedom.[60]

The president went on to plead for support for the Nicaraguan Contras, those "freedom fighters" who were seeking to restore democracy to their country in much the same way Americans themselves had done two centuries earlier. They were "our brothers. How can we ignore them? How can we refuse them assistance when we know that, ultimately, their fight is our fight?"

Secretary Shultz moved quickly but carefully to blunt the main thrust of the president's strategy. While Reagan had clearly articulated the anti-Communist, anti-Soviet emphasis of his policy during these early weeks of his second term, Shultz sought to deemphasize its anti-Soviet focus and, instead, underscore "independence, freedom, and human rights." In a speech to the Commonwealth Club of San Francisco six days later, on February 22, Shultz seemed to play off the president's speech, declaring that "a revolution is sweeping the world today—a democratic revolution." It was "fashionable in some quarters," he said, to claim that democracy was passé, yet, in fact, the great American experiment has "today captured the imagination and the passions of people on every continent." He listed various examples, some of which were pointedly different from Reagan's:

> The Solidarity movement in Poland; resistance forces in Afghanistan, in Cambodia, in Nicaragua, in Ethiopia and

---

[60] "Radio Address to the Nation on Central America, February 16, 1985," Ronald Reagan Presidential Library and Museum digital archives, www.reaganlibrary.gov.

Angola; dissidents in the Soviet Union and Eastern Europe; advocates of peaceful democratic change in South Africa, Chile, the Republic of Korea, and the Philippines . . . [61]

In the ensuing months, these different emphases would play out in the policy struggle between the president and the secretary of state. Shultz would drag his feet on support for anti-Soviet resistance forces, except in the special case of the Contras, while focusing his efforts on actively supporting "peaceful democratic change" for America's allies in South Africa, Chile, the Republic of Korea, and the Philippines. "Peaceful democratic change" was code for weakening Washington's relations with these countries. New Zealand, too, would receive special treatment, as part of the long-range plan to dismantle the containment structure in the South Pacific.

Nicaragua was a special case. Shultz had risked the president's ire by meeting directly with Daniel Ortega in mid-1984 and setting up direct US-Nicaragua talks paralleling the Contadora process, which only involved indirect contact. The discussions at Manzanillo, a small resort town in Mexico, showed some initial promise, but were broken off in December.

(The US invasion of Grenada had alarmed the Sandinistas and, it seems, they had agreed to talks in hopes of forestalling a possible attack on themselves. In any case, the outcome of the Nicaraguan elections, which the Sandinistas unsurprisingly won handily, and the US elections, with Democrats gaining in both chambers of Congress, persuaded the Sandinistas that they had little to fear from invasion and proceeded to stiff the United States. In short, as Kagan notes, Shultz had been "burned.")[62]

When the president took a strong public position of support for the Contras, and demanded that the Sandinista regime be "removed," Shultz decided to cut his losses for the time being. Reagan had made his demand at a nationally televised news conference the night before Shultz spoke to the Commonwealth Club. Asked if he wanted the Sandinistas removed from power, Reagan replied: "removed in the sense of its present structure, in which it is a communist totalitarian state, and it is not a government chosen by the people."[63] In other words, yes.

For Shultz, the prospects for engaging a new Soviet leadership far outweighed possible gains from talks with the Sandinistas, to whom, moreover, Reagan was viscerally opposed. Thus, on Nicaragua, he became, in Kagan's words, "a devoted and outspoken Hawk, following the lead of his president." Some astutely attributed his shift as an attempt to "mollify conservative critics . . .

---

[61] George Shultz, "America and the Struggle for Freedom," *US Department of State Bulletin* 85, no. 2097 (April 1985):16-29.

[62] Kagan, *Twilight Struggle*, 351.

[63] Lou Cannon, "Reagan Sees Change Due Nicaragua," *Washington Post*, February 22, 1985, A1. See also "President's News Conference on Foreign and Domestic Issues," *New York Times*, February 22, 1985, A14.

so that he might have a freer hand in dealing with the Soviet Union." [64] Shultz had not been "converted." He would continue efforts to reach a diplomatic settlement with Managua but do so in subtler ways and over a longer timeframe. Most importantly, he did not want to be seen as being in open opposition to the president on this highly visible issue.

Shultz's longer-term approach toward the Sandinista problem was to chip away at the foundations of the Contra program. Here, he was only partly successful. As we shall see, the president's promotion of an informal support program for the Contras, augmented by third country financial support from the Saudis and Israelis, translated into better military performance on the battlefield by late 1984.[65] But, it backfired. The timely Soviet supply of Mi-24 Hind attack helicopters, flying tanks they were called, to Managua emboldened the Sandinistas to take the fight to the Contras, driving them back across the border to their Honduran base camps in early 1985. The Soviets were willing and able to supply more advanced weapons to the Sandinistas than the Contras were receiving.

The strengthened presence of Sandinista forces on the border created great tension within the Honduran leadership, who demanded a "written guarantee" from the United States against Nicaragua in return for continued support for the Contras.[66] The turmoil in Tegucigalpa opened an opportunity for Shultz and McFarlane to undercut support for the Contra presence in the border areas, even as the secretary publicized his support for the president's policy.

In late January, for example, McFarlane went to Tegucigalpa ostensibly to reassure the Honduran leadership. Instead, he provoked a disagreement over the issue of a guarantee, which further roiled political waters. Relations were only patched over two months later when Vice-President Bush traveled to Honduras and publicly declared US support.[67] Increased aid, $88 million in military assistance and $142 million in economic aid ameliorated, but failed to dispel, Honduran concerns. Tension and rumors of a military coup persisted, along with questions about the US presence. A State Department official openly questioned

---

[64] Kagan, *Twilight Struggle*, 351.

[65] The Saudi contribution was only one factor accounting for improved Contra performance. Another was a sharp influx of weapons donated by the Israelis valued at well over $10 million. In a project initiated by Casey known as Operations Tipped Kettle I and II, and Project Elephant Herd, Israel donated to the DOD weapons they had captured from the PLO during the 1982 invasion of Lebanon. DOD turned the weapons over to the CIA for distribution to the Contras "as appropriated funds ran out." Major General Richard Secord negotiated the initial Israeli contribution and after he retired was later tapped to run the Contra supply program in 1984. See the "Stipulation of Fact" in *The United States of America v. Oliver I. North*, no.88-0080 02, US District Court, Washington, DC.

[66] Roy Gutman, "US Policy Squeezes Honduras," *Long Island Newsday*, February 8, 1985, 3.

[67] Kagan, *Twilight Struggle*, 349.

the value of a US presence: "It would be silly to go down for exercises if this turmoil continues . . . . If a coup takes place while we are there, we'd look bad."[68]

Shultz's main success was to engineer the "surprise" removal of General Paul Gorman, head of Southern Command and a major figure in provision of support for the entire program in Central America. Reportedly, "Shultz had actually lobbied the White House and the Pentagon to force the 57-year old general out of the critically important job." President Reagan, Secretary Weinberger and General Vessey "all tried to persuade General Gorman to remain at his post or take another government job," but the general said he was "disgusted with State Department opposition to his hard-line policies on communist guerrillas."[69] For Shultz, the retirement of Gorman, who was the administration's "major strategist" for Central America, was a positive development, especially as Gorman was being considered for promotion to either the Command of US forces in Europe, or to Chairman of the Joint Chiefs of Staff when Vessey stepped down.[70]

Shultz's objective was to remove or make very tenuous Honduras as a base for the Contras. Weakening the Contras by undermining their support base presumably would make them more amenable to compromise with the Sandinistas. The problem with this line of reasoning was that the Sandinistas were the more powerful party. Weakening the Contras would not hasten a negotiated settlement; it would simply ensure a military victory by the Sandinistas. Indeed, in early 1985 the Sandinista army was just reaching the point where it could go on the sustained offensive. The balance, thanks in great part to the congressional funds cut-off, was tipping against the Contras. This was, perhaps, the key reason that Shultz took a firm stand in support of the Contras early in the second term, for there would be no disguising the State Department's responsibility in a defeat.

Shultz and the Resistance Movements: Afghanistan

In addition to the Nicaraguan Contras, President Reagan had repeatedly declared American support for the "freedom fighters" of Afghanistan, Angola, Mozambique, Ethiopia, and Cambodia. In all of these cases, Shultz and the State Department dragged their feet, or actually opposed support for the anti-Soviet movements.

In Afghanistan, Congressman Charles Wilson (D-TX) leveraged his position on the House Appropriations Committee to become a major force in gaining increased funding for the Mujahideen. Obsessed with defeating the Soviets, Wilson moved out front in a personal campaign to provide better weapons

---

[68] Roy Gutman, "Turmoil Tests Key US Ally," *Long Island Newsday*, March 31, 1985, 5.
[69] Walter Andrews, "Tough US General Retires Early from Command in Latin America," *Washington Times*, January 11, 1985, A1.
[70] Bill Keller, "General to Leave Top Latin Position," *New York Times*, January 11, 1985, A4.

for the resistance fighters.[71] It was a common complaint, however, that increased congressional appropriations for the Afghan resistance fighters had been accomplished with "no help from the State Department," which continued its policy of "dragging its heels on providing aid."[72]

The State Department was only partly at fault for not responding promptly to the president's call. Support for the resistance had originated with former President Jimmy Carter, who had authorized a modest program designed to harass the Soviets in Afghanistan, but not to defeat them. Defeat was thought to be impossible and in truth undesirable because Carter naively harbored the hope that cooperation, even détente, with Moscow was still obtainable. President Muhammad Zia ul-haq of Pakistan, through whom the program functioned, was of a similarly cautious belief. Zia insisted that the US profile be minimized and that the program be run by the Pakistani intelligence service, ISI.

Reagan had inherited and tried to build on this program, but State Department and CIA officials assigned under Carter were still in place essentially to oversee and manage the program. The arrangement with Pakistan kept the US role masked and indirect. Washington supplied weapons to Pakistan and the ISI distributed them to the Mujahideen in Afghanistan at its discretion. While this enabled the United States to keep a low profile, and a pseudo plausible deniability, it fooled no one and gave ISI great latitude to distribute weapons favors to preferred recipients, not to mention siphon off a considerable percentage for themselves.

The downside to this arrangement was obvious. Even though the quantity and quality of weapons supplies increased by several times over the Carter levels during the first term, not only was there not a proportional increase in the distribution of supplies to the Mujahideen, but also the ISI funneled the bulk of what they did deem fit to distribute to only one of the seven resistance organizations, led by their favorite, Gulbuddin Hekmatyar.

Hekmatyar may have been an appropriate recipient from the ISI's point of view, but he was hardly the ideal choice for strengthening the resistance to the Soviet Union. Hekmatyar's men spent as much time fighting against the six other resistance organizations as they did against the Soviets. One source claimed that he "cooperated with Soviet troops in persecution and subsequent defeat of other resistance factions."[73] Although "loyalty" was a fragile concept, at best, among the resistance groups in Afghanistan, Hekmatyar, having been trained in the

---

[71] See George Crile, *Charlie Wilson's War* (New York: Grove Press, 2003) for an entertaining, informative, but critically flawed narrative of Wilson's efforts. The flaw in Crile's argument is the failure to acknowledge the president's and the CIA director's command role, attributing fundamental decisions to Wilson alone.

[72] Benjamin Hart, "Rhetoric vs Reality: How the State Department Betrays the Reagan Vision," Heritage Foundation, Backgrounder no. 484, January 31, 1986.

[73] Imran Akbar, "Gulbuddin Hekmatyar Had Links with KGB," *The News International* (Paris), October 8, 1992.

Soviet apparatus from his youth, was not someone in whom to place an inordinate amount of trust to fight the Soviets.

Several factors combined to produce the president's second-term call for increased support for anti-Soviet resistance fighters. By early 1985, Congressman Wilson had seen first-hand that the "system" put in place by State and the CIA to support the resistance was not doing the job. The personnel sent to manage it were firmly of the belief that bleeding the Russians was all that should be done, lest they get angry and retaliate against Pakistan.

Nor was the increased supply of weapons getting into the hands of the most effective resistance organizations. Finally, the stepped-up Soviet offensive early in the year, just as in Nicaragua, was succeeding. The Soviet winter attack took the Mujahideen by surprise. A combined-arms concept of aerial bombing, helicopter gunship assaults, armor attacks and Spetsnaz (special forces) strikes threatened to whittle down the resistance into ineffectiveness.[74]

Early in the year, however, Reagan was presented with crucial intelligence from a source on the Soviet General Staff. The report detailed Soviet plans for a general offensive of all of its client forces around the world and for the Soviets themselves in Afghanistan. In Afghanistan, with great fanfare, the Soviets assigned a new commander, General Mikhail Zaitsev, who was given two years to achieve victory.[75] Meanwhile, Valentin Varennikov, the general in overall command of Soviet third-world clients, took charge behind the scenes.[76] One wonders whether the knowledge that the Soviets were going on a general offensive in early 1985 played a part in Reagan's decision to publicize the "Reagan anti-Soviet resistance Doctrine."

In late January, at an NSPG meeting, when the discussion turned to Afghanistan, the president forcefully directed his aides to "do whatever you have to help the Mujahideen not only survive but win." The result was the formulation of a new directive, NSDD-166, which the president signed in mid-March, incidentally, just a few days after Mikhail Gorbachev had been named the successor to Chernenko. The directive fundamentally changed the objective in Afghanistan from Carter's goal of "harassing" the Soviets, to Reagan's goal of "victory."[77]

Yet, even though NSDD-166 formally changed US policy in Afghanistan and even though support for the "freedom fighters" was immensely popular in Congress, it would take months before the supply and distribution system was upgraded, personnel changed, training improved, and a more integrated weapons mix developed. And it would be over a year before the

---

[74] Mohammad Yousaf and Mark Adkin, *The Bear Trap: Afghanistan's Untold Story* (London: Leo Cooper, 1992), 134.

[75] Schweizer, *Victory*, 212-13.

[76] Crile, *Charlie Wilson's War*, 344-45.

[77] Schweizer, *Victory*, 213. Simpson, *National Security Directives*, 446-47, describes the thrust of the directive as supporting a "significant escalation," but does not use the term "victory."

decisive weapon of the war, the anti-aircraft Stinger missile was introduced. Simply put, key officials in the CIA, State Department, and in Pakistan's ISI deliberately dragged their feet.

John McMahon, number two behind Casey at CIA; Shultz, Pakistan station chief Howard Hart and ISI's Mohammad Yousaf, were particularly obstructive, for varying reasons. McMahon and Hart supported Shultz's strategy of merely bleeding the Russians and used "every bureaucratic trick in the book" to delay shipment of the Stinger, while Yousaf determinedly resisted all efforts by the CIA to gain greater control over the distribution of weapons.[78]

To some degree, their obstructionist efforts could be attributed to General Zia himself, who subtly resisted the introduction of Stingers until early in 1986. It was only when Reagan issued an executive order on provision of Stingers to Jonas Savimbi of UNITA that the dam broke, and Zia finally accepted their introduction into Afghanistan. McMahon resigned at the end of February 1986, clearing away the major obstacle within CIA. George Shultz, seeing the policy shift coming, jumped on board the resistance bandwagon. Casey removed Hart as station chief and replaced him with Milt Bearden; and Yousaf, who also saw the handwriting on the wall, suddenly became more accommodating.[79] The Stingers would deny Moscow control of the air and the Mujahideen would defeat them on the ground.

The president would attempt to follow a similar pattern of support for all of the resistance movements, but his main areas of focus would be on rebuilding a strategic relationship with Iran and on gaining Soviet agreement to shift to the strategic defensive. It is to the president's search for an opening to Iran that we now turn.

---

[78] On McMahon's role, See Jack Wheeler, "Charlie Wilson and Ronald Reagan's War," *To the Point News*, December 27, 2007, http://www.tothepointnews.com/content/view/3019/2/. For Hart's and Yousaf's roles, see Crile, *Charlie Wilson's War*, 351-53; see 417-18 for the author's attempt to downplay McMahon's obstructionism and opposition to supply of the Stinger.

[79] Ibid.

Chapter 8

The Origins of the Iran Initiative

President Reagan's defeat of Soviet strategy toward Iran would have profound consequences for both the president and the nation. Moscow shifted from a strategy of attrition in the Iran-Iraq war to support of Iraqi victory. As Iran sought to reach out to the United States, the Soviets activated their Middle East terror network to prevent it. The president saw an opportunity to reestablish relations with Iran, but his internal opponents, the new world order faction, did everything possible to sabotage it. These key developments unfolded in a highly complex milieu, involving parallel and competing Israeli interests, international arms sales to Iran and Iraq, and a highly developed terrorist contract network involving Iran, Libya, Syria, and the Soviet Union.

Moscow's strategy change regarding Iraq was wrapped in the larger strategy shift to détente. The shift was a change in means but not in ends and initially involved an increase in the use of conventional force virtually across the board. The Soviet Union continued to pursue its three main objectives: strategic weapons preeminence over the United States, regional military superiority over its Eurasian neighbors, and leverage over Middle East oil, specifically, by drawing Iran into its orbit. The fundamental purpose in the strategy shift was to disarm the United States politically, turning away from direct military confrontation, while moving stealthily toward the same objectives as before.

Thus, as Mikhail Gorbachev came to power proclaiming *perestroika* at home and détente abroad, Moscow's actual policies seemed to change little as the Soviet Union increased defense spending, continued to upgrade its weapons systems, continued work on elements of a nationwide missile defense, and intensified support for its client states around the world, including its occupation and suppression in Afghanistan. [1]

The big change was toward Iraq, where Moscow's strategy had failed. Whereas from 1980 to 1983 Soviet policy was to arm Saddam Hussein's forces sufficiently to prevent defeat in a war of attrition, from mid-1984, the Soviets began to provide Iraq with a major infusion of offensive weaponry that offered the prospect of victory. Compared to Saddam's armament levels when the war began in 1980, by mid-1984 the Soviets had dramatically increased his inventory. Moscow sent over 2,000 main battle tanks, raising Iraq's total from 2,750 to

---

[1] Robert Gates, *From the Shadows: The Ultimate Insider's Story of Five Presidents and How They Won the Cold War* (New York: Simon & Shuster, 1996), 331-37.

4,820. The Soviets more than tripled artillery pieces from 1,040 to 3,200; and increased Iraq's aircraft from 332 to 580. To utilize this infusion of new weaponry, Saddam increased troops from 535,000 to 675,000.[2]

Iran retained the battlefield initiative as it pressed human wave attacks across the Iraqi border in repeated but largely futile attempts either to seize Basra or Baghdad, or to cut the road connecting them. Thus, in the ground war, for many more months to come, Iraqi forces would remain on the defensive. From the summer of 1984, with deliveries of Mirage and MiG-23 strike aircraft, tanks, and Scud missiles, Iraq intensified military pressure on Iran from the air and at sea, striking cities and petroleum facilities and ships in the Gulf, while buttressing its ground defenses.

The large additions to Iraq's weapons inventory, especially in tanks and aircraft, presaged an eventual turn to the offensive and sent Iranian arms purchasers on a frantic worldwide search for materiel to counter Iraqi firepower. Indeed, Iranian leaders were concerned enough to reach out to potential Western—including American—arms suppliers in the fall of 1984.

These same battlefield developments had registered on US analysts, who, perceiving an opening to Iran, began to propose a change in American policy toward the war. The failure of Soviet strategy toward Iran and the Iranian extension of feelers to the United States, as described in volume three of this series, generated high-level interest in the possibility of a rapprochement with Tehran. The president saw the prospects unfolding of not only restoring relations with the Iranian regime, but also of completing his strategic goal of replacing what was perhaps the most important single part of the containment structure in his drive for victory in the Cold War.

Unfortunately, neither the president nor his advisers anticipated the means and the lengths to which Moscow would go to prevent a US-Iranian rapprochement. The new world order faction, led by Secretary of State Shultz, in strongly opposing the president's initiative toward Iran, wittingly or unwittingly supported Soviet strategic objectives.

The Strategic Issues in Dispute

President Reagan and the new world order faction had been engaged in a struggle over US strategy since taking office. As demonstrated earlier in this study the president sought to pursue a strategy of victory in the Cold War by expanding American economic power and undercutting that of the Soviet Union; reestablishing hegemony through a shift to the strategic defensive combined with a sharp reduction in nuclear weapons; restoring alliance relationships in a new containment structure that also included China; and fracturing the Soviet alliance system by raising the cost of its maintenance. These were very large structural objectives that required the implementation of myriad policies, which, by the end

---

[2] Anthony Cordesman and Abraham Wagner, *The Lessons of Modern War*, vol. 2, *The Iran-Iraq War* (Boulder: Westview, 1990), 192.

of the first term, had been largely successful, or were on the verge of being successful.

Policymaking is an inherently messy process and there were continuous policy disputes in the administration over the implementation of the president's strategy. This was, however, the essentially healthy argument of how best to pursue the president's objectives. There also were principled disagreements, such as the Secretary of Defense's strenuous objections to the actual application of US military power. The fundamental conflict within the administration was strategic: a struggle between the president's strategic vision and that of the new world order faction.

The new world order faction, led first by Secretary of State Haig and then by Secretary Shultz, pursued a strategy whose central objective was détente and accommodation with the Soviet Union, not victory over it. They envisioned that the United States and the Soviet Union would become equal partners who would cooperate to maintain a new, peaceful, world order. They sought to counter, undermine, and otherwise oppose any policy that contradicted this strategic conception.

In truth, the mere articulation of the strategy of détente exposed its incongruity. A new world order based on a cooperative global condominium was without historical precedent and in reality, suggested more surrender than cooperation. Worst of all, it rested on the very fragile assumption that the Communist rulers of the Soviet Union sought the same objective. Yet, this was the strategic framework that Shultz sought to press on the president at every policy opportunity.

The three public issues in dispute between the president and his secretary of state that carried over into the second term were: the nature of the relationship sought with the Soviet Union, a dispute that played out in the arms control negotiations; the structure of the global balance of power, which centered on the issue of relations with Iran; and the approach to the Soviet system of alliances and client regimes, which involved the Reagan Doctrine of bolstering opposition to them. The strategic differences between Reagan and Shultz were fundamental. Over the long term there could be no compromise, although there could be short-term, tactical cooperation until decisive policy points were reached.

With regard to the Soviet Union, for example, the president sought a new balance of power based on defense rather than offense. He sought a transition from a system based on mutual assured destruction to one based on strategic defense, with a sharp reduction in offensive weapons. The Strategic Defense Initiative was the centerpiece of this strategic concept.

Shultz and the new world order faction sought to perpetuate the balance of power based on mutual assured destruction, or MAD; some offensive missile reductions were acceptable, even desirable, to assure a balance, but there could be no missile defense, which they viewed as destabilizing. Shultz saw value in SDI solely as a bargaining chip to gain agreement, but not as the basis for a new strategic paradigm, as the president did. In his view, SDI was simply an instrument to be dispensed with as part of an arms control bargain.

There were similar rifts concerning the structure of the global order. Reagan was intent upon rebuilding the global containment structure, adding China to it, and reestablishing close relations with a post-Khomeini Iran. Iran had been the largest single state in the containment structure whose loss had not only fractured it, but also weakened the security of the Persian Gulf and its oil supplies. Reagan sought to rebuild the structure and restore security over the gulf. He had reestablished close relations with King Fahd, as we have seen, and Moscow's policy change toward Iraq had opened up the slimmest possibility of engaging Iran.

Shultz was totally opposed to rapprochement with Iran. Dismantling the containment structure was in the new world order faction's view the necessary pre-condition to entering into a détente relationship with Moscow. Reestablishing relations with Iran would reverse that strategy. They did not perceive a Soviet threat either to Iran or to gulf security. Here, too, Reagan and Shultz could cooperate on the short-term goal of promoting a stalemate in the war, but their long-term goals were totally opposed, as Shultz saw American interests best served by an alliance with Saddam Hussein's Iraq.

On the Reagan Doctrine, too, the president and Shultz were opposed, but differences varied by case. Shultz initially opposed but came around to support military assistance to the Contras as the president made such support a litmus test within his administration. In Afghanistan, Shultz supported a policy of bleeding the Russians against the president's goal of defeating them and driving them from the country. On Angola, Shultz and the president differed over the goals and means of forcing the Cubans to withdraw. In all cases, as opportunities presented themselves, Shultz sought to achieve negotiated settlements with the Russians, rather than their defeat.

Early Maneuvering over Iran

Anticipating the time when it would become feasible to attempt to reestablish relations with Iran as part of his general strategy of rebuilding containment, the president had twice during the first term explored the legal ramifications of providing arms to Iran, while Shultz sought to foreclose any opening. The first instance was in 1981 when Attorney General William French Smith asked the Department of State counsel for a ruling on the sale of arms to Iran, as Tehran was not then eligible for arms sales under the Foreign Assistance Act, or the Arms Export Control Act.[3]

The State Department's legal adviser, Davis R. Robinson, informed Smith that "the United States could sell weapons to foreign countries outside the Foreign Assistance Act and Arms Export Control Act . . . .The president could

---

[3] *Report of the Congressional Committees Investigating the Iran-Contra Affair* (Washington, DC: US Government Printing Office, 1987), 176, 189n42. [Cited hereafter as "*Congressional Report on the Iran-Contra Affair*."]

instead use the Economy Act and the National Security Act."[4] Both the FAA and the AECA contained provisions for prior public notification of Congress and set a low $14 million threshold over which congressional approval would be required. Under the Economy Act and National Security Act, if weapons were first transferred between agencies, such as from DOD to CIA, the reporting requirements did not apply. In this way the president could legally skirt the restrictions of the FAA and AECA.

Then, in early 1983, after information was passed from KGB defector Vladimir Kuzichkin regarding Soviet plans to subvert the Iranian government and in anticipation of the Iranian government's crackdown on the pro-Soviet Tudeh party and its potentially disruptive consequences, the president sought again to ascertain whether there were any legal impediments that would prohibit the provision of arms to Iran in case the situation deteriorated and action had to be taken quickly.[5] Responding to the president's inquiry regarding the use of the Economy Act or the Foreign Assistance Act, W. George Jameson, Assistant General Counsel of the Central Intelligence Agency, issued a memorandum on January 7, 1983, maintaining that "there were no general legal restrictions that would preclude the CIA from providing equipment to Iran as proposed. Rather, the relevant constraints involve policy considerations that may have to be weighed before undertaking the activity proposed."[6] The proposed activity implicit in Jameson's reply was the clandestine provision of arms. Indeed, arms sales as a means of gaining access to the Iranian leadership was the crux of it. (It should be noted that all this preceded the taking of a single hostage and makes clear the president's intent to reestablish relations with Iran.)

Later in the spring, using his discretionary authority, Secretary Shultz sought to close off any government sales by instituting Operation Staunch, which he justified as a means of drying up weapons sales to both sides. When implemented later in the year, however, the State Department's efforts were heavily biased in favor of Iraq and against Iran.[7] Indeed, the secretary would go to great lengths to build support for Iraq *against* Iran.[8]

Over the next two years Special Ambassador Richard Fairbanks and his staff cajoled, jawboned, and threatened Washington's allies and friends against continued involvement in the estimated "$3 billion to $4 billion" per year Iranian

---

[4] Theodore Draper, *A Very Thin Line* (New York: Hill and Wang, 1991), 247-48.

[5] Vladimir Kuzichkin, *Inside the KGB* (New York: Ballantine, 1990), 369, and Gary Sick, "Iran's Quest for Superpower Status," *Foreign Affairs* 65, no. 4 (Spring 1987): 709.

[6] "Restrictions on Exports to Iran," Memorandum for Stanley Sporkin, General Counsel, from W. George Jameson, Assistant General Counsel, January 7, 1983, *Digital National Security Archive-ProQuest*, DNSA Collection: Iraqgate.

[7] George Shultz, *Turmoil and Triumph* (New York: Scribner's, 1993), 236-37.

[8] See section on "Policy Battle over Iran and Iraq" in chap. 5

arms market.[9] As 39 countries were involved in arms sales to Iran, this was a Herculean task and obviously the effort was not completely successful. US laws, the Munitions Control List and technology transfer licenses, and the threat of a cut-off from the US market were effective levers in persuading allied governments, in particular, to curtail direct sales.[10]

The evidence suggests, however, that while other governments did curtail direct sales, they deftly shifted operations to less identifiable grey market operations, clandestine sales to illegal destinations using fake documentation, and/or to private arms dealers operating on the black market.[11] In the meantime Iran had set up purchasing offices in key cities throughout Western Europe. Some of the largest were in London, Madrid, Paris, Hamburg, Rome, Malmo, Brussels, Lisbon, and Zurich.

London, in particular, was a major center for Iranian purchasing agents. Their Logistics Support Center, with a staff of 320, was "the largest military mission in London after that of the United States."[12] It was located in the same building as the National Iranian Oil Company, which was "next to Britain's Department of Trade and Industry." Reportedly, as much as 70 percent of Iran's arms purchases were managed by the London office through private, offshore dealers and shipping brokers. However, "many of the so-called private arms dealers . . . [were] really agents for governments."[13]

Israel was a special case with a long history of arms sales to Iran dating back to the time of the shah. Following a brief hiatus after the shah fell, Israel resumed arms sales to Iran. President Carter attempted unsuccessfully to put a stop to them, which impacted negatively on his efforts to gain the freedom of the hostages. When Reagan took office, Secretary of State Haig had given his quiet approval for sales, as part of his strong support for Israel.[14]

In 1983, after Shultz had replaced Haig and Yitzhak Shamir had replaced Menachem Begin, Operation Staunch appears to have succeeded in curtailing Israeli arms sales, at least direct sales.[15] Ambassador Fairbanks acknowledged that he and his staff "leaned pretty heavily on Israel . . . . We told them they just

---

[9] John Fialka, "How Iranian Dealers Buy Arms of All Sorts through British Office," *Wall Street Journal*, January 30, 1987, 1.

[10] Kenneth Timmerman, *Fanning the Flames: Guns, Greed & Geopolitics in the Gulf War* (online), chap. 7, http://kentimmerman.com/krt/fanning_index.htm.

[11] Ibid.

[12] Amir Taheri, *Nest of Spies: America's Journey to Disaster in Iran* (New York: Pantheon, 1988), 159.

[13] Fialka, "How Iranian Dealers Buy Arms [. . .]."

[14] Seymour Hersh, "The Iran Pipeline: A Hidden Chapter/a Special Report; US Said to Have Allowed Iran to Sell Arms to Iran," *New York Times*, December 8, 1991, 1.

[15] Trita Parsi, *Treacherous Alliance: The Secret Dealings of Israel, Iran, and the US* (New Haven: Yale University Press, 2007), 113.

didn't want to be selling arms to Iran."[16] But Israel, like practically all of the others, continued to sell arms *indirectly*.[17] Before being pressured to curtail sales, according to the *Observer*, Israeli arms sales to Iran were "valued at between $500 million and $800 million a year."[18]

Crucial developments in 1984, especially the change in Soviet strategy toward Iran, produced a new calculation in Washington. The initial Soviet strategy toward Iran, the use of Iraq as defensive bulwark, as anvil, so to speak, against Iran's hammer, in a war of attrition against Iran, had failed and produced a fundamental change. By early 1984, it was clear to attentive observers throughout the region that the new Russian strategy was to turn Iraq into an offensive force capable of defeating Iran.

From late 1983 the Soviets had replaced "every piece of ground equipment Iraq had lost during the first two years of the war." Then, they began to provide Iraq with a major infusion of new weaponry. In March 1984, the Soviets offered Saddam a $4.5 billion package, "the biggest arms package the Soviets had ever proposed." Moscow prepared to "rush deliveries of additional MiG-21 and MiG-23 fighters, Mi-25 Hind helicopter gunships, and 350 Scud-B missiles." By the summer of 1984 Soviet cargo vessels were arriving at the Jordanian port of Aqaba, and "endless truck convoys traveled across the desert to Baghdad."[19]

It was this unheralded but ominous turn in the military balance that persuaded Iranian leaders to seek out and make contact with American representatives in the fall of 1984 and prompted President Reagan to prepare the grounds for a response. The Iranians attempted to make contact in a variety of ways, some not entirely positive on the face of it. Their agents in Beirut, the Hezbollah, in the context of a proclaimed campaign to drive the Americans from Lebanon, began attacking and kidnapping Americans and other foreign nationals. First, was the murder of Malcolm Kerr, president of the American University of Beirut on January 18, 1984. On February 11, an American, Frank Regier, and a Frenchman, Christian Joubert, were abducted. On March 7, CNN bureau chief Jeremy Levin was kidnapped. Regier was freed on April 15 when a rival group of Amal militiamen raided the Beirut hideout where he was being held. Levin escaped, or was allowed to escape, nearly a year later on February 14.

Identification of those responsible for these early incidents was muddied by the fact that Hezbollah was not the only terrorist organization operating in Lebanon. If the Iranians were employing terrorists to force contact with the United

---

[16] Kenneth Timmerman, *The Death Lobby: How the West Armed Iraq* (New York: Houghton-Mifflin, 1991), 141.

[17] Ari Ben-Menashe, *Profits of War: Inside the Secret US-Israeli Arms Network* (New York: Sheridan Square, 1992), claims that clandestine sales continued throughout.

[18] *The Observer*, September 29, 1985, cited by Bishara Bahbah, "Arms Sale: Israel's Link to the Khomeini Regime," *Washington Report on Middle East Affairs* (January 1987): 10.

[19] Timmerman, *Death Lobby*, 185.

States, the Soviets, through their minions, were attempting to use the same tactics to prevent it. Muammar Qaddafi, in particular, seems to have funded terrorists to take actions designed to block any Iranian American contacts. There ensued a period of competitive hostage-taking among rival terrorist organizations.

Qaddafi apparently backed the Lebanese terrorist, Imad Mughniyeh in the execution of several terrorist acts. Mughniyeh, operating a small cell within Hezbollah called Islamic Jihad, carried out several hostage seizures and airline hijackings in hopes of gaining release of prisoners held in Kuwait, called the Al-Dawa 17, one of whom was his brother-in-law, Mustafa Badreddine.[20]

Tripoli, Damascus, and Tehran all supported terrorist groups in Lebanon where they competed with each other as often as they cooperated and contended with the Israelis. It was difficult for Western intelligence to place terrorists with organizations and to differentiate between the isolated acts of terrorists and state-supported activities. Radio intercepts were a crucial means of tracking and sorting out the many groupings.

But the abduction of William Buckley on March 16 was a different matter. On-scene intelligence reports claimed that Buckley had been seized by an Iranian terrorist group and quickly transferred to Tehran.[21] These reports appeared, in retrospect, to have been only partially accurate. Buckley may have been transferred to Tehran, but he was soon returned to Lebanon. Later hostage accounts revealed that Buckley had been held in Beirut for most of his time of captivity, until his death in mid-1985.

Buckley was the CIA's Beirut station-chief, and one of the agency's top operatives in the Middle East. Iranian leaders correctly assumed that Washington's clandestine service would do everything in its power to gain the release of its valuable intelligence agent. Two other Americans were taken hostage in 1984, Benjamin Weir, on May 8 and Peter Kilburn on December 3.[22]

Iran also employed more "traditional" means of making contact. In early June 1984, parliamentary leader Ali Akbar Hashemi Rafsanjani declared that Iran wanted "talks and meetings" to avoid intervention by both the Soviet Union and the United States. As the United States posed no threat to intervene, this was, of course, but a thinly veiled expression of concern regarding the Soviet threat and an invitation to Washington.

Rafsanjani went on to indicate Iran's interest in contact by saying that "as far as is possible we will prevent such a disaster for humanity from happening

---

[20] David Martin and John Walcott, *Best Laid Plans: The Inside Story of America's War against Terrorism* (New York: Touchstone, 1988), 204-5.

[21] "Meeting with [Excised] Re: Beirut Kidnapping," March 17, 1984; and "Update on Contact with Iranian Terrorist Source," March 17, 1984, *Digital National Security Archive-ProQuest*, DNSA Collection: Iran-Contra Affair.

[22] It is frequently incorrectly asserted that Weir was kidnapped two months earlier, on March 8.

by diplomacy and by appropriate talks and meetings."[23] At a press conference in early July, Rafsanjani made a direct reference to the United States, albeit to praise the quality of American arms. He would not rule out the possibility of purchasing American arms "directly or indirectly," he said, because they were better than Soviet or French weapons.[24]

In late July, West German Foreign Minister Hans-Dietrich Genscher traveled to Tehran for a state visit. He was the first Western foreign minister to visit Iran since 1979. In addition to signing a long-term oil agreement, Rafsanjani used the occasion to urge "other countries" to help bring the war to an end.[25] After Genscher departed, a Kuwaiti newspaper reported that the West German foreign minister had passed on a US proposal for an "amelioration" of relations with Washington.[26] This report was probably planted by the Iranians to elicit a response from Washington. If it had been true, there would have been no reason for the convoluted sequence of events that followed.

There was also an unsuccessful attempt to establish contact through Canada. During a trip to Ottawa and Toronto in November, Ayatollah Mohammad-Reza Mahdavi Kani, a member of the ruling circle, sought to persuade the Canadian government to act as an intermediary with the United States.[27] No doubt the Canadian government passed on this message to the State Department, but no response was made, understandably, because Shultz opposed any opening.

At the same time that Iranian leaders were extending feelers to make contact with Washington, they were intensifying their efforts to acquire additional weaponry. Their purchasing agents scoured the international arms markets seeking weapons with which to counter the stepped-up Iraqi attacks. Since their weapons systems were US-based, as Rafsanjani stated, they were particularly interested in acquiring US anti-tank and anti-aircraft weapons to contend with the growing Iraqi advantage in tanks and strike aircraft.

Reagan Prepares a Response

President Reagan recognized that the failure of Soviet strategy toward Iran and the Iranian extension of feelers to the United States opened the possibility of a rapprochement with Tehran. The president saw the prospects unfolding of not only restoring relations with the Iranian regime, but of completing the containment structure around the Soviet Union and strengthening his drive for victory in the Cold War.

---

[23] Jonathan Randal, "Iraq Moves Tanks to Southern Front," *Washington Post*, June 3, 1984, A15.

[24] Samuel Segev, *The Iranian Triangle* (New York: Free Press, 1988), 130-31.

[25] "Iran Said to Seek New Ties to West," *New York Times*, July 23, 1984, A1.

[26] "Kuwaiti Paper Reports Genscher Carried US Proposal," *Foreign Broadcast Information Service (FBIS) Daily Report, South Asia*, July 27, 1984, I 2.

[27] Taheri, *Nest of Spies*, 164.

Secretary Shultz, anticipating the president's moves toward Iran, sought to preempt him. On January 20, 1984, he designated Iran a state sponsor of international terrorism, adding another argument to those used in advocating the cessation of arms sales to Iran under Operation Staunch initiated a month earlier, on December 15, 1983. At the same time, he insured that the State Department would turn away all Iranian attempts to make contact.

The president's response came in the immediate aftermath of the abduction of William Buckley. The numerous Iranian signals of a desire to make contact obviously did not go unnoticed, and the president set the wheels in motion to bring about an opening. He sought to do this in several ways: legislatively, by strengthening anti-terrorism law; administratively, by attempting to change current policy toward Iran; operationally, by assigning to CIA chief Bill Casey the task of attempting to rescue Buckley, a process that *inter alia* would involve making high-level contacts with Iranian leaders; and through extension of subtle policy signals.

On April 3, 1984 the president signed NSDD 138, defining the government's anti-terrorism policy. The directive authorized the conduct of "guerrilla warfare against guerrillas," and action against states supporting terrorism, singling out Iran, Libya, Syria, Cuba, Nicaragua, North Korea, and the USSR.[28]

On April 26, the White House sent four separate legislative bills to the Congress designed to strengthen the government's efforts to combat international terrorism. The first was to establish federal jurisdiction over any kidnapping whose purpose was to "compel third parties to do or to abstain from doing something." Second was the Aircraft Sabotage Act, designed to bring American law into conformity with international law. Third, was an act to authorize the government to pay rewards for information on terrorists. And fourth was a proposed act to prohibit the support or training of terrorists.[29]

There matters stood until the summer of 1984 when the change in Soviet policy toward Iraq had become apparent. As the first step, the president sought through the formal interagency policy process to reevaluate policy toward Iran. On August 31, McFarlane requested that the Department of State lead an interagency study of US relations with Iran after Khomeini. The study preempted and incorporated data from a Special National Intelligence Estimate (SNIE) the CIA was preparing. As Shultz controlled the interagency process, the result was fully predictable. On October 19, State circulated its study, concluding that any changes in American policy would have to await the death of Khomeini. The United States had "no influential contacts" in the Iranian government or with

---

[28] "NSDD 138, "Combatting Terrorism," April 3, 1984, https://fas.org/irp/offdocs/nsdd/nsdd-138.pdf.

[29] "President's Anti-Terrorist Legislation," April 26, 1984, in Christopher Simpson, *National Security Directives of the Reagan and Bush Administrations: The Declassified History of US Political and Military Policy, 1981-1991* (Boulder: Westview, 1995), 407.

influential political groups and there was "little that the United States could do to establish such contacts." Charles Hill, Shultz's aid, wrote the cover letter stating the secretary's belief that American "powerlessness . . . would continue indefinitely."[30]

In December, John McMahon, CIA Director of Operations, number two in the agency after Casey, but Shultz's ally, sent a letter to Admiral Poindexter, deputy director of the NSC, echoing the same view as the State Department of American "powerlessness." Regarding the utility of covert operations in Iran, McMahon thought that the People's Mujahedin (Mujahedin e Kalq) were "well organized, influenced by the Soviets, and likely to succeed Khomeini."[31] In short, there was nothing that the United States could do.

The State Department then "distilled these views into a draft National Security Decision Directive (NSDD) at the end of 1984." When approved by the president, an NSDD formalizes policy. This decision document would have directed the US government to be ready to "exploit opportunities that might arise in Iran," but reaffirmed existing policies. In its essence, the draft would have reinforced Operation Staunch, the policy of discouraging arms transfers to Iran.[32] In the rules-based policy maneuvering that characterized American politics, Shultz seemed to have gotten the better of the president, but Reagan simply declined to approve the NSDD, leaving the policy issue open.

On the other hand, the president had approved subtle measures to send signals of his own to Tehran. Early in 1984 he had authorized Commerce Secretary Malcolm Baldridge to allow some sales of dual use equipment to Iran. Through the first half of the year Commerce had authorized the sale of 100 jeeps and the release of two Boeing 707 jets the shah had purchased, but which were still in the US for refurbishing at the time of the hostage crisis. Both Weinberger and Shultz had opposed the actions, but Baldridge supported them as part of the president's aggressive export policy.[33]

Sales of military equipment went through intermediaries. International arms dealers routinely employed fake end user certificates to disguise the destination of weapons shipments. In July, for example, the *Christian Science Monitor* disclosed that 25 F-5 jets were being shipped to Iran, although their purported destination was Turkey. In this instance, Lloyds of London had been asked to insure delivery. Both Britain and Turkey were heavily involved in sales

---

[30] John G. Tower et al., *Report of the President's Special Review Board: February 26, 1987* (Washington, DC: US Government Printing Office, 1987). [Hereafter referred to as the *Tower Report*], III-3; B-2.

[31] Ibid, B-2.

[32] *Tower Report*, B-2-3.

[33] *The Chronology: The Documented Day-by-Day Account of the Secret Military Assistance to Iran and the Contras* (New York: Warner, 1987), 59-60. [Hereafter referred to as *The Chronology*.]

and services to both sides.[34] Indeed, the Turkish air corridor was the most direct way into Iran. Nothing came of these probes.

But what seemed to be the most promising avenue of contact was Casey's efforts to obtain the release of William Buckley based on the assumption that he was being held by Iran, or by Iran's surrogates. Casey had ordered "a major drive to recruit former members of SAVAK who had fled into exile in Western Europe and the United States."[35] He assumed that some of these men would have remained in touch with former colleagues in Tehran. At the same time, he asked retired former CIA deputy director of operations, Theodore (Ted) Shackley to quietly explore these contacts.[36]

From the group of SAVAK exiles, the CIA approached the shah's former head of counterespionage, General Manouchehr Hashemi, and arranged for him to meet Shackley. The result of their meeting was a plan for Hashemi to introduce Shackley to his Iranian contacts in Hamburg, West Germany, an enclave of Iranian exiles. In the latter part of November, Shackley traveled to Hamburg where he was introduced to Ayatollah Mehdi Karoubi, a close confidant of Khomeini's, and Manucher Ghorbanifar, an Iranian exile and self-styled dealmaker and entrepreneur. It would eventually turn out that Ghorbanifar would become Iran's designated interlocutor, but his role and status were unclear at the beginning and controversial thereafter. Nevertheless, in wide-ranging talks, November 19-21, the prospects seemed bright not only for ransoming Buckley, but also for establishing contact with high-level Iranian leaders.[37]

The Iranians wanted an answer from Washington by December 7 about Buckley, but Ghorbanifar, whose own path to the meeting with Shackley had been circuitous, warned him not to deal with the CIA, because, he said, the agents he had dealt with in the past had treated him deceitfully. Shackley accepted this position and immediately upon returning to Washington sent his report to his former colleague, Vernon Walters, instead of to Casey. Walters had been a deputy director of CIA but was now serving as an Ambassador at-large in the State Department.

Walters passed Shackley's report to Shultz's aides, Richard Murphy, head of the State Department's Bureau of Near Eastern Affairs, and Robert Oakley, head of counterterrorism. Both men regarded Ghorbanifar's proposals, particularly his plan to ransom Buckley, as a "scam," and deep-sixed the effort.[38] Their reply to Shackley was: "thank you but we will work this problem out via

---

[34] Ibid., 61, and "Britain Says It Is Training Troops from Both Sides," *Manchester Guardian*, April 2, 1984, 1.

[35] Taheri, *Nest of Spies*, 166.

[36] "Theodore (Ted) Shackley," *Spartacus Educational* (online at http://www. spartacus.schoolnet.co.uk/JFKshackley.htm). Shackley was a renowned clandestine agent, who had retired from the agency under a cloud.

[37] *Congressional Report on the Iran-Contra Affair*, 164.

[38] Ibid.

other channels."[39] In short, Shackley's effort was dismissed. Once again, Shultz had headed off an attempt to make contact with Iranian leaders.

Except for his close aides, Casey's views did not dominate the agency. Supporters of the new world order establishment dominated the upper ranks of the CIA, especially in the directorate of operations under John McMahon. That explains why Shackley agreed with Ghorbanifar not to go through the CIA, but it does not explain why he failed to report directly back to Casey. Sending his report to the State Department, even though it was through former CIA colleague Walters, guaranteed that the approach would fail.

Manucher Ghorbanifar's meeting with Shackley was his fifth attempt in 1984 to make contact with American leaders from his base in Western Europe. In January, he had sent a letter to Reagan that was never received. Later that month he sought to make contact through US Army intelligence that went nowhere. In March and June, he had contacted the CIA in Frankfurt, offering access to high Iranian leaders and a scheme to ransom Buckley. In attempting to determine his credibility, the CIA administered lie-detector tests on both occasions, which Ghorbanifar failed ignominiously. Deciding that he was a "nuisance," on June 25 the Frankfurt office declared him a "fabricator," and issued a "burn notice," which meant that agency officers could have nothing to do with him.[40]

Although the Frankfurt office issued the burn notice, McMahon had made the decision at Langley. On its surface, the decision to discredit Ghorbanifar appeared to have been an error. Expendable, deniable, private intermediaries were the common and principal means of brokering initial contacts between adversaries. As we shall see, Ghorbanifar was to Iran what Adnan Khashoggi was to Saudi Arabia, what Michael Ledeen was to the United States, and what Yaakov Nimrodi and Adolph Schwimmer were to Israel.[41] It is true that in the Iranian case there were several exiles who claimed influence in Tehran, and it was not easy to determine their bona fides. What seemed to be an error, however, was completely consistent with McMahon's and Shultz's efforts to close off any contact with Iranian interlocutors. Later, when the opportunity arose, Casey would choose to work with Ghorbanifar.

The Israeli Connection

American leaders were not the only ones to note the change in Soviet strategy and its implications for themselves. Israeli leaders, too, recognized the change and quickly realized both the negative implications for Israel in an Iraqi victory and the positive implications for a resumption of arms sales to Iran. For a variety of reasons, both domestic and foreign, Israel's leaders recognized that a change of its own leadership had become necessary. The Israeli economy was

---

[39] *Tower Report*, B-3.
[40] *Congressional Report on the Iran-Contra Affair*, 164.
[41] See Michael Ledeen, *Perilous Statecraft* (New York: Scribner, 1988), 100, 106, for a discussion of a nation's needs for "deniable intermediaries."

staggering badly under the burden of the Lebanon invasion and relations with Washington were still cool at best under Yitzhak Shamir, whose antipathy toward the United States was well known.

Consequently, in April 1984, the 10th Knesset was dissolved a year early, requiring a new election. Although a Labor Alignment victory was expected, the election of July 23 produced a surprising result; neither of the two main parties, Likud or the Labor Alignment, received a clear majority out of 120 seats. In fact, while remaining the dominant two parties, both lost seats compared to the previous election, Labor dropping from 47 to 44 and Likud dropping from 48 to 41.

The Labor-Alignment's Shimon Peres, the vote leader, was tasked with putting together a majority government, but after over a month of negotiations, failed to obtain the needed 61-seat plurality. Realizing that only Labor/Likud cooperation stood a chance a putting together a stable majority, it was decided to form a National Unity Government. However, as former Ambassador Samuel Lewis observed: "they joined forces in a coalition cabinet, but with great reluctance and only for lack of any alternative."[42]

They agreed that Peres would be prime minister for the first two years and Shamir foreign minister; then they would switch posts for the last two years. Yitzhak Rabin would be Minister of Defense and David Kimche would remain as Director of the Foreign Ministry. Peres's position appeared to be strong, but appearances were deceiving. Although he had appointed Amiram Nir as his counterintelligence adviser, replacing Likud's Rafi Eitan, Shamir and his allies held control of Mossad and the Finance Ministry. Rabin, a fellow Labor Party leader, was a rival of Peres. Kimche, whose patron was Ariel Sharon, was also from Likud, but his relations with Mossad, his former place of employment, were not good. Although Peres, Shamir, and Rabin were known as the "prime minister's club," the reference was ironic, for their interests obviously did not coincide in all matters.

Seven years of Likud rule had resulted in Likud men being sprinkled in important positions throughout the government bureaucracy, especially in the intelligence community. Under the terms of the unity government Peres was unable to replace Likud personnel with Labor personnel. With Shamir in control of the intelligence apparatus, Peres decided to construct his own parallel, but much smaller, organization, a job he entrusted to Nir. Strikingly, the Mossad played no apparent role in the events that followed.

A key decision was to restart the arms sales to Iran, an important strategic issue, which would also represent not only a strong source of revenue, but also a way of resuming the repatriation of Iranian Jews. Most importantly, however, the decision reflected the realization that the military balance was tipping against Iran. As Israel's main enemy in the region was Iraq, long-term strategy was to ally with Iran against Iraq, a strategy that had become more complicated but not invalidated

---

[42] Samuel Lewis, "Israel: The Peres Era and Its Legacy," *Foreign Affairs, America and the World*, 1986.

with the ascent of Khomeini. Weapons sales represented an important entrée to the Iranian leadership, despite public hostility.

Shamir, however, would not agree to turn over control of the operations of the Joint Committee on Israel-Iran relations, which was in charge of arms sales, to Peres, or permit Mossad to cooperate. The impasse prompted the prime minister to establish his own arms sales conduit to Iran, which involved two steps.[43] First, it was necessary to establish independent contact with Iranian leaders and, second, to get permission from Washington to resume sales.

Peres assigned David Kimche the task of overseeing the Iran project and directed two of his wealthy friends to explore the possibilities.[44] The two men were Al Schwimmer, an arms dealer and father of Israel's aircraft industry, and Yaakov Nimrodi, who had been Israeli military attaché to Iran in the 1960s and had opened the first arms channel under the shah. Both were experienced dealmakers with extensive international contacts, and deep knowledge of Iran, especially Nimrodi.

The major obstacle to resumption of arms sales was the United States. Operation Staunch had largely shut down overt sales of American and Israeli weapons and spare parts, although the Joint Committee had continued to broker covert sales through Poland and North Korea.[45] At a minimum, Peres sought to gain Washington's permission to resume sales of Israeli weapons. In discussions with President Reagan during his state visit on October 9, there can be no question that among the topics discussed, the issue of resumption of arms sales was one of them. Indeed, it appears that despite public denials, Reagan had agreed to permit the resumption of limited sales of Israeli arms to Iran. Later in October, Iraqi, Saudi, and no doubt American intelligence identified and began to track flights, presumably arms shipments, between Israel and Iran.[46]

On the second task of making contact with Iranian leaders, according to Kimche, sometime in mid-1984 he and his small group had made contact and begun discussions with disaffected Iranians in Hamburg, who were "both willing and able over time and with support to change the government."[47] Their principal interlocutor was none other than Manucher Ghorbanifar. And the person who had introduced them was Adnan Khashoggi.

---

[43] Ben-Menashe, *Profits of War*, 167-68.

[44] Ledeen, *Perilous Statecraft*, 117, erroneously claims "Kimche knew nothing of the [Iran] initiative until [July 1985]."

[45] Ben-Menashe, *Profits of War*, 143-44.

[46] Bishara Bahbah, "Arms Sale: Israel's Link to the Khomeini Regime," *Washington Report on Middle East Affairs*, January 1987, 10.

[47] Robert C. McFarlane, *Special Trust* (New York: Cadell & Davies, 1994), 19. David Kimche, *The Last Option: After Nasser, Arafat & Saddam Hussein* (London: Weidenfeld and Nicolson, 1991), 211, leaves the impression that his first involvement in the Iran initiative was his meeting with McFarlane on July 3, 1985.

Casey and the Saudi-Iranian Connection

Khashoggi's appearance was a function of King Fahd and Bill Casey's mutual interest. During Casey's visit to Riyadh in February 1984, the king had "suggested" that the United States approach the Iranians.[48] It seems that the Saudis, too, realized that the battlefield balance was on the verge of swinging to Iraq. Although the Saudis were financing Iraq, it was not unusual for them to play both sides in a conflict. Whoever won, they would be on the winning side. They were more than willing to pay insurance for their oil tankers moving through the gulf. And they wanted to insure against inflammation of Shiite minorities in the region, especially in their own country.[49]

Casey's response at the time was "muted," as the administration was only just in the early stages of internal deliberations over a change in Iranian policy. Within a month, however, with Buckley's abduction, Casey became intensely interested in seeking an approach to the Iranians, who, he believed, were holding Buckley. Thus, King Fahd's personal middleman, Adnan Khashoggi, became active "beginning in the summer of 1984," renewing acquaintances with old business partners Schwimmer and Nimrodi, making contact with Iranian exiles, and, as word got around, eventually encountering Ghorbanifar.[50]

Through mutual Iranian acquaintances Khashoggi met Ghorbanifar in the fall in Hamburg at a private sale of the former shah's Persian rugs. Their discussions ranged far and wide focusing on a change in Tehran's policy and also its need for US arms. Ghorbanifar, who, recall, was at this moment also engaging with Ted Schackley, offered information that Tehran would not seek to disrupt pilgrimages to the Grand Mosque the way Shiites had in 1979. This was enough for Khashoggi to invite him to Riyadh to meet with Saudi officials. While there, Ghorbanifar arranged for the Saudi foreign minister, Saud Al-Faisal, to visit Tehran and, as a sign of good faith, the Saudis financed a small arms deal to Iran through Khashoggi and Ghorbanifar.[51] Thus, by the end of 1984, a Saudi-Iranian connection had been established.

---

[48] Peter Schweizer, *Victory: The Reagan Administration's Secret Strategy That Hastened the Collapse of the Soviet Union* (New York: Atlantic Monthly Press, 1994), 181.

[49] Wolf Blitzer, "A Saudi Finger in Every Pie," *Jerusalem Post*, November 28, 1986, 5.

[50] *The Chronology*, 58.

[51] Segev, *Iranian Triangle*, 14. Later, Khashoggi was very careful to say that he was not acting on the explicit instructions of the king. He asked Fahd: "do you give me the freedom to discuss it with the Americans? With the Egyptians? With others? He said, 'I give you nothing. I know nothing. You are a free man.' So, I went to Egypt . . . " Later, he also went to see Peres. Deborah Hart Strober and Gerald S. Strober, *Reagan: The Man and His Presidency* (New York: Houghton-Mifflin, 1998), 400. Cf. Ledeen, *Perilous Statecraft*, 110-11, who offers a quite different chronology.

In early 1985 after the election, as noted in chapter one, the president resolved to implement the "Reagan Doctrine," intensify the offensive against the Soviets, and move forward with his Iran initiative. In this context, Shultz and the new world order faction stepped up their efforts to block the president's policies and implement their own. The first step, January 18, as noted above, was to constrict the president's power to authorize covert operations, which was accomplished with the signing of NSDD-159.

NSDD-159 diluted the president's authority by requiring all covert operations to be ratified by a ten-man committee, instead of the previous arrangement whereby the president and CIA director Casey possessed sole authority. Moreover, all "findings" were henceforth to be "in writing."[52] Now Shultz could theoretically block any attempt to change policy toward Iran formally, through the interagency process, as before, and now through the new authorization process for covert operations. The master bureaucrat had thwarted the president once again, or so it seemed.

Casey was also active in supporting the president and moving his agenda forward. Following the Shackley dead-end, in January 1985, the CIA director had a meeting in London with his old friend and fellow entrepreneur, Roy Furmark. Casey told Furmark that the United States "was secretly permitting arms sales to Iran."[53] Casey's intent was to encourage his friend to set up a private arms operation to Iran, perhaps along the lines of what he had already succeeded in doing in Central America. (Casey's revelation strengthens the view that the president had authorized the resumption of Israeli sales during the Peres visit, although Casey did not identify Israel by name.)

With information of this potential financial opportunity in hand Furmark approached Samuel Evans, former chief counsel to Adnan Khashoggi, and asked him to arrange an introduction. (One must assume that Casey had directed Furmark to contact Khashoggi, who had already established contact with the Iranians.) When they met a few weeks later, Furmark brought along an associate of his, Cyrus Hashemi, a naturalized American citizen of Iranian extraction, who was a banker and arms trader, operating out of London.[54] Hashemi also had a relationship with Casey, having been involved in the release of the American hostages from Iran in 1980-81. More importantly, the previous May, he had been caught in an FBI sting of a group attempting to sell arms to Iran. In seeking to obtain a dismissal of charges against him, Hashemi agreed to act as an informant.[55]

---

[52] "Covert Action Policy Approval and Coordination Procedures," in Simpson, *National Security Directives*, 493-97.

[53] James Traub, "Katzenjammer Falcon," *New York Magazine*, February 9, 1987, 38. See also William Rempel, "Casey Reportedly Knew of Iran Arms Deals in Early '85," *Los Angeles Times*, January 6, 1987, 12.

[54] Traub, "Katzenjammer Falcon," 39.

[55] Draper, *Very Thin Line*, 134.

Saudis, Iranians, and Israelis

On March 5, at a meeting in London, Khashoggi introduced Hashemi to Ghorbanifar, but also brought in Nimrodi and Schwimmer, assuring them that "King Fahd and Prince Sultan know about this meeting and gave me their blessing." Agreeing to cooperate, with Furmark's help, Khashoggi and Hashemi set up the World Trade Group as a shell company to sell arms to Iran, while Nimrodi and Schwimmer returned to Tel Aviv to report to Peres.[56]

Nimrodi and Schwimmer told Peres that Ghorbanifar proposed to broker the purchase of $2 billion in Israeli weapons, presumably through the World Trade Group. Peres undoubtedly was interested in such a major arms deal, but cautiously responded with a counteroffer to sell food, but no arms. Understanding that this was just the beginning of a negotiation, the prime minister appointed Schlomo Gazit, former head of military intelligence, to coordinate future contacts. The two Israelis flew to Geneva to pass on Peres's reply. Ghorbanifar was "disappointed." He had expected a positive response, especially as "King Fahd had given Khashoggi the go-ahead for the deal." Still hoping to go forward, explaining that the situation at the front was desperate and arms were vitally needed, he compiled a smaller list of weapons amounting to $33 million.[57]

At Schwimmer's suggestion, Peres agreed to bring Ghorbanifar and Hashemi to Israel to check them out. They arrived on April 9, staying for three days at Nimrodi's house in the suburbs of Tel Aviv. While they were there, Peres received a lengthy background report on the two men from the Mossad. The report recommended against any dealings with Hashemi on the grounds that he was unreliable, perhaps suspecting that he was an FBI informant. It suggested that if Ghorbanifar, an equally shady character, could provide proof of his contacts in Iran, the Israelis could work with him.[58] The Israelis quietly dropped Hashemi from their plans, as did Khashoggi; the World Trade Group would remain an unused and empty shell.

To prove his veracity, Ghorbanifar telephoned Mohsen Kangarlu, Iran's deputy prime minister, from Nimrodi's home with the Israelis listening in on the conversation. The call left no doubt that Ghorbanifar had contacts at the highest level in Tehran. Peres concluded that although Ghorbanifar was untrustworthy, he was Tehran's interlocutor. The top Israeli leadership—Peres, Shamir, and Rabin— debated the merits of doing business with Ghorbanifar over the next two weeks, bringing him back for another visit, without Hashemi.

---

[56] "Roy Furmark Deposition," *Congressional Report on the Iran-Contra Affair*, 164 and Segev, *Iranian Triangle*, 14-15, 18. From a comparison of their accounts, it is evident that both the congressional committees and Segev had access to, and cite, the Israeli government's historical chronology, which is not publicly available. The written chronology was supplied to the congressional Iran-Contra committees in lieu of live testimony.

[57] Segev, *Iranian Triangle*, 18-19.

[58] Ibid, 20.

The clincher came when Nimrodi went to Geneva to check out Ghorbanifar's finances. He found an account belonging to the Iranian National Oil Company, to which $100 million had recently been deposited and "Ghorbanifar's access to the account . . . authorized by Iran's prime minister and oil minister." Peres thereupon approved the plan to work with him, but to keep ties unofficial and to restrict the circle of those knowledgeable, he substituted Nimrodi for Gazit. Nimrodi now had the job of managing the relationship with Ghorbanifar.[59] In effect, Peres had cut Israeli intelligence out of the action, assigning the operation to trusted, private operators.

With funds available, Peres agreed to go forward with the small $33 million arms deal Ghorbanifar had proposed the previous month. Code-named Operation Cosmos, the plan called for Nimrodi to use his own funds in order to guarantee shipment and preserve deniability for the Israeli government. A freighter was loaded and ready to sail from Eilat on April 23 and, as agreed, an Iranian officer had flown to Israel to inspect the cargo and escort the ship to Bandar Abbas. Just before the ship set sail, however, Ghorbanifar called from Geneva and asked for a delay, due to "internal difficulties" in Tehran.[60]

A few days later, at the end of April, Ghorbanifar flew to Tel Aviv, his third trip, to apologize for the mishap and plead for a delay of a month or two in the Israeli weapons shipment. What Iran needed immediately, he said, was to purchase American-made anti-tank TOW missiles to counter the growing Iraqi superiority in tanks. Amid great consternation and name-calling, at what was now a costly venture for Nimrodi, Ghorbanifar swore that he was acting on the authority of the Iranian prime minister, that he would make up any losses suffered in the postponement, and that he would try to obtain the support of the Americans by offering to gain the release of Buckley.[61]

In retrospect it is clear that the Iranians cancelled the arms deal because there was no American involvement. However, having drawn the Israelis in, they now used them to gain access to the Americans. On the other hand, the Israelis, realizing that there would be no arms sales without American involvement, now had every incentive to approach Washington.

Ghorbanifar's request for American weapons created a new situation. If the issue were solely the sale of Israeli weapons, Peres would face no difficulty. He was not prepared to accede to an Iranian request to purchase American equipment from Israel without the president's approval, as required by United States law, and without amending the understanding he had reached with Reagan during his visit to Washington the past October.

When Khashoggi was informed of the new request, he sent a note to NSC head Robert McFarlane on May 2 "to ready Washington for Iran's request through the Israeli channel." He urged the administration to be receptive to Tehran because

---

[59] Ibid, 21-23.
[60] Ibid, 24.
[61] Ibid, 24-25.

"the succession struggle could begin in earnest even before Khomeini's death and that it was in America's interest to try to influence the choice of successor."[62]

Crisis and Opportunity in Washington

Khashoggi's memo reopened the issue of Iran policy in a new way, bringing to a head the worst fears of Shultz and the new world order faction. As Howard Teicher, the NSC officer charged with managing the interagency policy process for southwest Asia noted: by "the end of April . . . the interagency process on southwest Asia was deadlocked over the question of policy toward Iran."[63] In other words, up to this point, Shultz had successfully fended off all attempts to bring about a change in policy. The memo, the tortuous, long-range result of Casey's initiative of over a year earlier, had turned the Iran issue on its head by raising the question of what the United States should do *if the initiative came from Iran?*

Shultz, McFarlane and the new world order faction knew what the president's response would be. The cooperation of the Saudis, Israelis, and Iranians had produced the opening the president sought. Other recent events, they also knew, would only increase the pressure on him to act. From early in the year, Hezbollah had gone on a hostage-taking spree in Lebanon. Between January and mid-June militants had taken a dozen men hostage. Five were Americans: Father Lawrence Jenco, on January 8; Terry Anderson, on March 16; David Jacobson, on May 28; and George Sutherland, on June 9. As noted above Frank Regier and Jeremy Levin had been seized but escaped and three others, a Swiss and two Englishmen, had been taken and released after a short time. There were seven Americans in captivity and five Frenchmen.

The combination of circumstances left no doubt that Reagan would respond affirmatively to an Iranian request to effectuate an opening. Shultz and the new world order faction therefore decided that their only course of action was to seize control of the initiative and sink it. Fortunately, they had a man ideally placed to undertake this mission in Robert McFarlane, who, in policy discussions

---

[62] Ibid, 134-35. Draper, *Very Thin Line*, 626n45, basing his view on Dan Raviv and Yossi Melman, *Every Spy a Prince* (Boston: Houghton Mifflin, 1990), 334-35, claims that Segev confused Khashoggi's message with an analysis done by Ghorbanifar on the same date. But the authors and the content of their messages are completely different. Ghorbanifar analyzed the internal situation in Iran, while Khashoggi addressed Iran's request to Washington. Moreover, Segev, x, claims that he interviewed "most of the Israeli participants and . . . had access to government papers not yet declassified." Mention of "government papers" implies a reference to the classified historical and financial chronologies the Israeli government provided to the US House and Senate committees that prepared the *Iran-Contra Affair* study. A comparison of the references to the chronologies in their report with relevant passages in Segev's book makes it clear that he made use of them.

[63] Howard Teicher and Gayle Radley Teicher, *Twin Pillars to Desert Storm* (New York: William Morrow, 1993), 330-31.

espoused a pro-Iran stance. For the next six months, he would almost single-handedly and with considerable skill manage and orchestrate the Iran initiative from its inception to its apparent demise, and then promptly retire from government, mistakenly believing that he had accomplished his mission of sinking the initiative.

This was not the scheme of a former Kissinger aide attempting to duplicate the feats of his mentor. McFarlane was acting on behalf of the new world order faction desperate to prevent an opening to Iran, which would compromise their strategy of accommodation with the Soviet Union. Throughout, and afterward, McFarlane would claim that he was acting on the president's instructions but could never produce a scintilla of evidence to support his claim. In fact, he was acting on the instructions of Shultz, although their collusion was carefully masked. McFarlane was in an extremely delicate situation torn between his loyalty to the president and the demands of the new world order faction. The evidence indicates that the weight of this plan of deception created enormous psychological stress on the NSC chief. Ultimately, the pressure of this contradiction would lead McFarlane to attempt suicide.

Naturally following the unfolding events, McFarlane's first move was to confirm the Iranian request. To maintain secrecy, he, like Peres, would operate completely outside formal government channels and use a private emissary. His choice for this mission was Michael Ledeen, a journalist-scholar, who, whether unwittingly or not, was deeply entwined with the new world order faction. Haig had brought him in as a political adviser to the State Department in 1981 where McFarlane met him. In November 1984, McFarlane hired him on as a consultant to the NSC to work on terrorism issues and Iran.[64]

McFarlane would utilize Ledeen as his private interlocutor throughout the opening to Iran, despite strong objections from NSC colleagues. As Walsh observed, by using Ledeen as his private messenger, McFarlane "pretended not to have official NSC involvement in these overtures." Ledeen testified that he "had an understanding with Mr. McFarlane that neither of us would keep anything in writing regarding this initiative."[65]

Ledeen's main value was the personal relationships he had with several world leaders, including Italian Prime Minister Bettino Craxi and Israeli Prime Minister Shimon Peres. Craxi was an old friend of twenty years and Ledeen had met Peres when he was consultant in the State Department in the early 1980s and the prime minister was leader of the Labor opposition to Likud. These relationships would prove to be very useful when it was necessary to convey private messages by trusted emissaries. That was the case here.

---

[64] Ledeen, *Perilous Statecraft*, 100.
[65] Ledeen, Grand Jury testimony, September 18, 1987, 34, as cited in Lawrence E. Walsh, *Final Report of the Independent Counsel for Iran-Contra Matters*, vol. 1 (Washington, DC: United States Court of Appeals for the District of Columbia Circuit, August 4, 1993), 88.

In fact, McFarlane had planned to send Ledeen on a "mission of inquiry" to Western Europe in January and had instructed his deputy Admiral John Poindexter to write a letter of introduction for him. For one reason or another, that trip never came off. However, Ledeen did travel to Western Europe in March, where he reportedly was advised by an intelligence colleague to consult the Israelis for information about Iran. Accordingly, McFarlane agreed to send Ledeen to Israel in April, but objections arose from several senior members of the NSC staff.

National Security Council director of political-military affairs Don Fortier expressed these reservations in a note to McFarlane on April 9. Although he had no objection to him carrying messages, he "disapproved of using Ledeen as the government's 'primary channel for working the Iran issue with foreign governments.'"[66] Responding to Fortier the same day, McFarlane sought to allay his concerns. "I want to talk to Shultz so that he is not blindsided when Sam Lewis reports—as he will surely find out—about Mike's wanderings. So, for the moment let's hold on the Ledeen aspect. I will get back to you."[67]

Ledeen's Trip and Its Aftermath

That was where matters stood for the next three weeks until McFarlane received word of Iran's imminent weapons request from Khashoggi, whereupon he hurriedly sent Ledeen to meet with Peres to confirm it. In his haste, McFarlane did not confer with Shultz beforehand, or notify Ambassador Lewis that Ledeen was making the trip, even though he knew that Ledeen's presence could not be kept secret. On the other hand, he instructed Ledeen on precisely what to say to Peres. According to Ledeen's recollection, McFarlane "told me specifically what to say and what tone of voice I was to use when I said it to Peres." Ledeen was to say that the US was interested in an information exchange on Iran as a "research project" undertaken for the NSC and that Ledeen would report directly to McFarlane.[68] In other words, no one else in the US government would know.

Meeting Peres on May 4, the Israeli prime minister was cautious about sharing information. He allowed as how "it was possible that Israeli information about Iran was better than the American's, but it was still insufficient." After more information was developed, he said, then "there could be another discussion to examine to what extent it was possible to frame a new Iran policy." Ledeen claimed that Peres was "happy to work together to try to develop better information about Iran,"[69] and sent him to have a talk with Schlomo Gazit to arrange an information-sharing program. In fact, the "information program" was a code term for the incipient Iran initiative and Gazit would become its

---

[66] *Tower Report*, B-4 and Draper, *Very Thin Line*, 138.
[67] *Tower Report*, B-5.
[68] Draper, *Very Thin Line*, 138.
[69] *Tower Report*, B-5.

coordinator. The entire arrangement would be informal and outside government, as Gazit was then president of Ben Gurion University.[70]

Toward the end of their discussion, Peres broached the subject that McFarlane had actually sent Ledeen to confirm. He said that "Iran wanted to purchase artillery shells and other weapons and military equipment from Israel, but that Israel was not prepared to do so without American consent." Peres wanted Ledeen to "sound out McFarlane about the Iranian request."[71]

Peres' statement to Ledeen was curious, to say the least. Whatever his personal relationship with him, the Israeli prime minister was not prepared to divulge highly classified information to an unofficial envoy. Indeed, Ledeen notes that he himself "was not eager" to get involved and told Peres that he "preferred not to be the channel for this request." After some further discussion, however, he "agreed to pass the message."[72]

As noted above, if the question was merely one of selling Israeli weapons and equipment, not only could Peres decide that question himself, he had already done so. Israel was already selling its own weapons to Iran, with American assent, which he knew that McFarlane knew. Therefore, one must deduce that Peres's mention of "artillery shells and *other* weapons and military equipment from Israel," was a veiled reference to an Iranian request to purchase American weapons from Israel's inventory.

That McFarlane understood Peres's meaning was reflected in his next move. After Ledeen returned to Washington to report on May 13, the NSC adviser authorized him to tell Peres "it's okay, but just that and nothing else."[73] In other words, McFarlane, on his own authority and without reference to Reagan, or American law, authorized Peres to make a one-time shipment of Israeli-owned, American weapons to Iran, establishing the precedent for future sales.

Then, McFarlane ordered an update of the previous year's SNIE on Iran, which would reflect the gist of the message from Peres, that friendly states sell arms to Iran. This was a new notion, which, moreover, flew directly in the face of Operation Staunch. Graham Fuller, the CIA's national intelligence officer for Near East and South Asia, and Howard Teicher, of the NSC, worked together on the update, but the idea of friendly states selling arms appeared first in a memo Fuller sent to Casey four days later, on May 17.

Fuller argued that the Khomeini regime was "faltering," and a succession struggle would soon break out. Moscow held the advantage and the United States needed to develop a "broad spectrum of policy moves designed to give us some leverage." Without naming Secretary Shultz, Fuller attacked his policy of attempting to deny arms to Iran and being ready to use force against Iran, if Tehran

---

[70] Ledeen, *Perilous Statecraft*, 102.
[71] Segev, *Iranian Triangle*, 137.
[72] Ledeen, *Perilous Statecraft*, 103.
[73] *Tower Report*, B-6. Mayer and McManus, *Landslide*, 125, also note that "McFarlane told Ledeen to authorize a single small Israeli arms sale to Iran," but assume that it was "the mortar shells that Ghorbanifar had wanted."

was involved in a terrorist attack. This, he thought, was "no longer sensible," and "may now serve to facilitate *Soviet* interests more than our own." After discussing a variety of possible options, Fuller concluded: "the best course . . . was to have friendly states sell arms that would not affect the strategic balance as a means of showing Tehran that it had alternatives to the Soviet Union."[74]

Meanwhile, Fuller and Teicher were hard at work revising the previous fall's SNIE. Circulated for discussion on May 20, the revised estimate, *Iran: The Post-Khomeini Era,* included the carefully worded recommendation that the extent to which "European states and other friendly states—including Turkey, Pakistan, China, Japan, and even Israel—can . . . fill a military gap for Iran will be a critical measure of the West's ability to blunt Soviet influence." Even though this formulation also called for the reversal of Operation Staunch, it was sufficiently subdued that it passed through the interagency process without arousing controversy.[75]

The SNIE then became the basis for a new draft NSDD on Iran. On May 28, Don Fortier sent a memo to McFarlane to say that he and his colleagues, including Graham Fuller, with whom they "worked closely," would need a few more days before completing a final draft. He said: "the Israeli option is the one we have to pursue, even though we may have to pay a certain price for the help." Finally, Fortier continued to object to Ledeen as the "right interlocutor."[76]

McFarlane's answer to Fortier was to approve another trip by Ledeen to Israel, but he quickly postponed it when he received a cable from Shultz protesting Ledeen's earlier trip.[77] It seems that on May 30 Ambassador Lewis got wind of Ledeen's earlier trip, described as "a secret mission from the White House," and inquired at both Minister of Defense Rabin's and Prime Minister Peres' offices about its purpose. Peres's office declined to respond, but a spokesman at the Defense Ministry told Lewis that the subject was "too hot" to discuss with him and that Rabin would discuss it with the secretary upon his arrival in Washington. However, when Rabin met with Shultz on June 1 the subject did not come up; hence, Shultz's protest to McFarlane.[78]

Shultz's protest was made by cable from Lisbon on June 5, four days after his meeting with Rabin. If the issue was of importance to the secretary, he most certainly would have raised it immediately with McFarlane while in Washington, instead of waiting four days to send him a cable from Lisbon. Not

---

[74] Fuller to DCI/DDCI, "Toward a Policy on Iran," May 17, 1985, *Tower Report*, B-6-7.

[75] "Iran: The Post-Khomeini Era," SNIE, May 20, 1985, *Tower Report*, B-7-8.

[76] Fortier, "PROF Note to McFarlane," May 28, 1985, *Tower Report*, B-8.

[77] *Congressional Report on the Iran-Contra Affair*, 165.

[78] Segev, *Iranian Triangle*, 139, says Rabin met with Shultz on June 1, but Shultz, *Turmoil and Triumph*, 793, claims that he met with Rabin on June 3 and was in Lisbon the next day. If true, it would mean he probably had no time to discuss the issue with McFarlane personally, but neither meeting date affects the reason for sending the cable, as a response to Fuller's memo.

only the delay, but also the form of the protest suggested that something else was going on here besides Shultz's objection to Ledeen's trip to Tel Aviv.

That something was Fuller's memo on the need for a new Iran policy, a copy of which Casey had sent to Shultz on June 4.[79] Shultz's protest to McFarlane was in reality a response to Fuller's proposal. It allowed him to go on record opposing collaboration with Israel; and at the same time, to distance himself from the actions of the national security adviser in order to avoid what already was a spreading sense of their collusion. That might actually have been an equally important reason for the cable. As McFarlane himself noted, fears were running "rampant," especially in the Pentagon, that there was a "McFarlane-Shultz cabal" influencing the views of the president.[80] Thus, Shultz declared:

> Israel's agenda is not the same as ours. I consequently doubt whether an intelligence relationship such as what Ledeen apparently has in mind would be one which we could fully rely upon and it could seriously skew our own perception and analysis of the Iranian scene. We of course are interested to know what Israel thinks about Iran but we should treat it as having a bias built in.

Next, Shultz considered it "deleterious to encourage or even merely acquiesce in someone like Mr. Ledeen undertaking a mission such as this without our Ambassador in Israel being informed." It suggested that the White House had no confidence in its own representative. Finally, Shultz said that he only learned of Ledeen's mission from Lewis, not the defense minister himself when they met, which made him all the more "unhappy." "I would appreciate," the secretary concluded, "hearing from you what you know about it."[81]

McFarlane had no inkling of Shultz's motives, and was taken aback by the reprimand. Replying two days later, he expressed his "disappointment" at the secretary's "prejudgment." Clearly rattled, he told Shultz a string of falsehoods to exculpate his actions. He denied that he had sent Ledeen, who, he claimed, had gone "on his own hook." (McFarlane himself authorized his trip.) He excused his failure to notify the secretary because he had only heard from Ledeen "last week" and hadn't had time to speak with him. (Ledeen had reported to McFarlane on May 13, three weeks earlier.) He claimed that it was Israel that had posed the question of cooperation to Ledeen (when it had been the reverse).

---

[79] *Tower Report*, B-7. Martin and Walcott, *Best Laid Plans*, 223, claim that Casey "hand-delivered" Fuller's memo to Shultz.

[80] McFarlane, *Special Trust*, 316.

[81] *Iran Contra Investigations, Joint Hearings before the Senate Select Committee on Secret Military Assistance to Iran and the Nicaraguan Opposition and the House Select Committee to Investigate Covert Arms Transactions with Iran*, 100th Cong., 1st sess., 100-9, July 23, 24, 28 and 29, 1987 (Washington, DC: US Government Printing Office, 1988), Exhibit GPS-5, "Cable to McFarlane, Re: Ledeen Visit to Israel, Dated June 5, 1985," 494-495.

Then, McFarlane declared that he would send "unequivocal instructions" that the United States had "no interest at all." Although he thought that that might not be "wise," he said that he was "turning it off entirely and, of course, would never have turned it on without talking to you."[82] In fact, McFarlane did not turn off the initiative; quite the reverse. However, his final remark about not doing anything without first talking to the secretary reinforced suspicions of a "McFarlane-Shultz cabal."

A New Draft NSDD
and International Complications

On June 11, Fortier and Teicher submitted their draft NSDD to McFarlane, recommending that he provide copies only to Secretaries Shultz and Weinberger for their comments. Six days later, however, McFarlane sent copies not only to Shultz and Weinberger, but also to Casey, noting in his cover memo that the CIA's updated SNIE, which had also just been distributed, made plain that instability was accelerating in Iran and that it seemed "sensible to ask whether our current policy toward Iran is adequate to achieve our interests." If they agreed a policy change was warranted, then, McFarlane said, "I would refer the paper to the SIG(FP) in preparation for an NSPG meeting with the president."[83]

The draft described an Iranian regime facing increasingly adverse political, military and economic circumstances—growing indecision in the face of Khomeini's fragility, disillusionment over a seemingly endless war, and declining revenue from oil production. The authors saw Iran on the verge of a succession struggle whose course was "impossible to predict." Within the government there was division but no clear opposition leader. Opposition groups, however, were proliferating and were clearly demarcated into conservative, radical, and military factions, with the Revolutionary Guard portrayed as an additional instrument of state power. Although deeply fractured, "in any scenario," the guard would be at the center in any power struggle.

The authors believed that conservative groups within the government and leaders in the regular army were inclined to be more pro-Western, but radicals and the revolutionary guard undoubtedly would seek to move Iran in the opposite direction and reject cooperation with Washington. The shortcoming of the analysis, however, was its lack of specificity. The conservative-radical-military breakdown identified no one in particular. Indeed, the only name mentioned was Khomeini's.

The analysis of Iran's position between East and West was more straightforward. The Soviet Union was far better positioned to take advantage of

---

[82] Ibid., Exhibit GPS-6, "Cable from McFarlane, Re: Ledeen Visit to Israel, Dated June 7, 1985," 498.

[83] SIG(FP) stood for Senior Interagency Group (Foreign Policy). Peter Kornbluh and Malcolm Byrne, *The Iran-Contra Scandal: The Declassified History* (New York: New Press, 1993), 220.

a succession struggle than was the United States and would exert a maximum effort to prevent the restoration of a pro-Western government. "Without a major change in US policy," Washington's position would not improve. Toward that end, the United States must undertake a range of short and long-term initiatives "to enhance our leverage in Tehran," minimize that of Moscow, and ultimately bring about the normalization of relations with Iran.

First and foremost, the United States must "encourage Western allies and friends" to help Iran to meet its import requirements to diminish the attractiveness of Soviet trade and assistance. This included the "provision of selected military equipment" to Iran on a case-by-case basis. The authors also recommended that Washington establish contact with allies and "be ready to communicate through them to Iran." The US should be ready to establish links with receptive Iranian leaders but continue to oppose the regime itself and be ready to take action against the Iranian-supported terrorist infrastructure. Nothing in the draft NSDD, nor the SNIE which underlay it, mentioned the issue of hostages.[84]

The draft, its authors noted, was "provocative," in that it called for a dramatic reversal of policy toward Iran, without stating that it would mean the repudiation of the policy championed by Secretary of State Shultz. Reaction from the secretaries, however, was delayed by the intrusion of a major event on June 14, which, as Cannon notes, "plunged" the president into "one of the gravest crises of his presidency."[85] This was the seizure of an American airliner flying from Athens to Rome with 153 passengers and crew, including 135 US citizens. The event—due to extensive worldwide television coverage—would capture the attention of the Western world for 17 days and bring to a head the Reagan administration's policy deliberations on a range of issues.

---

[84] Ibid, "US Policy toward Iran," NSDD (draft) June 17, 1985, 221-26.
[85] Lou Cannon, *President Reagan: Role of a Lifetime* (New York: Simon & Shuster, 1991), 605.

Chapter 9

Crucible of Decision

The hijacking of TWA 847 created a crisis of the first order in the Reagan administration whose outcome moved the president to make three crucial decisions, two secret and one public. The first secret decision was to strike powerfully at Muammar al-Qaddafi, whose role as a Soviet surrogate in instigating the crisis was the proverbial last straw for the president. The second was to move forward with an opening to Iran, whose assistance in resolving the crisis indicated Tehran's interest in improving relations, despite the involvement of its sometimes uncontrollable agents in terrorist acts against Americans in Lebanon. The increasingly evident divisions within the Iranian leadership appeared to make an opening feasible. The public decision, announced as the crisis was being resolved, was the president's agreement to meet with Soviet leader Mikhail Gorbachev in November.

The president's decisions were not supported unanimously within the leadership. Secretary Shultz and the new world order faction, while supporting the president's decision to move forward with the Soviet Union, was lukewarm regarding the decision to strike at Qaddafi, and he continued vehemently to oppose opening relations with Iran.

The Strategy of Terror

The hijacking of TWA 847 was the first attack against an American airline since the early 1970s, but one of several airline hijacks in the Middle East within the past year.[1] The hijacks coincided with a general upsurge of terrorism in the region carried out by several armed, terrorist groups. These groups, all connected to national sponsors, at times acted in the name of their organizations and at times in the name of organizations with which they falsely claimed a connection. Falsely claimed or attributed attacks were a common way of providing self-protection.

---

[1] In July 1984, terrorists diverted an Air France jet to Tehran's Mehrabad airport. In December, four or five Arabs of Hezbollah commandeered a Kuwait Airways flight and diverted it to Mehrabad. Two days before the hijacking of TWA 847, a Royal Jordanian plane had been seized, flown to Beirut and blown up. See Barry Hillenbrand and Johanna McGeary, "The Gulf: Horror Aboard Flight 221," *Time*, December 17, 1984.

Lebanon was the chaotic scene of intense civil strife between Palestinians and Lebanese factions as they fought for control over Beirut. Arafat's PLO was holed up in the refugee camps, Sabra, Shatila, and Bourj el- Barajneh, encircled by Syria's Amal, Iran's Hezbollah, Israel's Maronites and the Druze. These were but the most visible of the armed, terrorist groups, whose relationships were constantly fluctuating according to the issue of the moment.

All but the Maronites and the Druze opposed Israel, which had withdrawn from Beirut, but maintained a position in southern Lebanon; and the United States, for supporting Israel. The Israelis had added insult to injury by imprisoning several thousand men, mostly Shiites, as they withdrew, releasing them sporadically afterward, in return for captured Israelis. Washington had strongly objected to what in effect was Israeli hostage-taking and demanded they be released.

Terrorist actions also occurred in an international context. To the extent that terrorist attacks weakened US and Israeli positions in the region, as well as forestalled any contacts between the US and Tehran, they served the strategic interests of the Soviet Union in its determination to drive the United States from the region and Iran into its orbit.

The Soviets, from the beginning in 1917, had constructed a global clandestine apparatus to serve their needs in the struggle against the West. As terrorism increased in value as a low-cost instrument of state policy, the Soviets devoted more resources to it. The Soviet role in support of international terrorism was well understood by American leaders, who chose, however, not to publicize it.[2]

By the 1980s, Moscow had established a mature, worldwide system of training camps located on Soviet territory and throughout the territories of client states where operations could be staffed, planned, and practiced.[3] They managed a complex apparatus that could recruit personnel, socialize them into terrorist "causes," and train them in required skills, like bomb making. Moscow's logistics network managed the travel and special needs of its operatives, including the provision of false documents, laundered money, safe houses, weapons, explosives, and secure communications. Finally, the Soviets advised and consulted their client states on how to develop their own systems.[4]

---

[2] See Chapter 5 above for a discussion of the Long Commission Report and the decision not to identify the Soviet Union as a state supporter of international terrorism.

[3] *Soviet Support for International Terrorism and Revolutionary Violence*, SNIE 11/2-81 (Washington, DC: Central Intelligence Agency, May 27, 1981). See also, *The Soviet Bloc Role and International Terrorism and Revolutionary Violence*, NIE 11/2-86W (Washington, DC: Central Intelligence Agency, August 1986); and Drew Middleton, "Soviets Seen Adopting 'Low-Intensity Warfare,'" *Air Force Times*, August 5, 1985, 69.

[4] As the authors of *The 9/11 Commission Report: Final Report of the National Commission on Terrorist Attacks upon the United States* (New York: Norton & Company, 2004), 365, put it: "A complex international terrorist operation aimed at

Indeed, in January 1985, the foreign ministers of Libya, Syria, and Iran met ostensibly to map out a new anti-American strategy, agreeing to "escalate terrorism against US interests and personnel on a world-wide scale." Reality seemed to be less grandiose than the headlines. Sources "close to the Syrian government" said that Damascus and Tripoli "spearheaded the drive" to develop coordination among the three countries. However, "at Iran's urging," the group avoided creation of a formal alliance that would appear to put the group on the side of the Soviet Union; "Iran doesn't want to appear to be on either side of the superpower struggle."[5]

The Syrian-Libyan effort was consistent with Moscow's interest in preventing Iran from shifting toward the United States and Tehran's refusal to be pigeonholed was consistent with Iran's interest in developing relations with the United States, while not burning bridges to Moscow. On the other hand, Hafez al-Assad was especially sensitive to Qaddafi's repeated attempts to make inroads into Lebanon, which he considered to be a Syrian preserve. Thus, the "cooperation" of the three countries was more apparent than real and, in essence, represented yet another of Qaddafi's many attempts to gain influence through organizational schemes.

TWA 847

On June 14, 1985, at 10:00 a.m. and an hour behind schedule, TWA 847 lifted off the runway at Eleftherios Venizelos airport in Athens, Greece, on its daily scheduled flight to Rome. On board the Boeing 727 were 145 passengers, mostly Americans, and eight crew members. Minutes after reaching cruising altitude, just after Captain John Testrake had turned off the fasten-seatbelt sign, two young Palestinian males, who had been seated in the last row, leapt from their seats brandishing guns and hand grenades and rushed to the cockpit.

Before the two hijackers could force their way into the cockpit, Captain Testrake pressed the 7500 number on the plane's transponder, signaling to monitoring air traffic controllers that there was a "hijack-in-progress." The seven-hour time difference between Athens and Washington, made it a few minutes before 4:00 a.m. when word reached Washington that the hijack of an American airliner was under way.[6]

---

launching a catastrophic attack cannot be mounted by just anyone in any place." See also, William Jasper, "No State Sponsors, No Terror," *New American*, August 18, 2009.

[5] "Libya, Syria and Iran Coordinate Schemes to Strike US Targets, Arab Sources Say," *Wall Street Journal*, June 19, 1985, 34. The *Journal* article said their meeting was held in Tehran, but Yossef Bodansky, *Target America: Terrorism in the US Today* (New York: S.P.I. Books, 1993), 44, claims the meeting took place in Hermel, in the Bekaa Valley, Lebanon, and was attended by senior intelligence officials, not foreign ministers, and accorded a much greater initiative to Iran.

[6] David Martin and John Walcott, *Best Laid Plans: The Inside Story of America's War against Terrorism* (New York: Touchstone, 1988), 163.

The hijackers demanded that Captain Testrake fly them to Algiers. Testrake, co-pilot Phil Maresca, and flight engineer Christian Zimmerman responded as best they could to make the two men understand—they spoke no English—that there was insufficient fuel to reach Algiers. It was common airline practice to fuel an aircraft for the scheduled distance to be flown. For the 655-mile flight to Rome the plane's tanks were just over a third full, 2,600 gallons (17,000 pounds), which was not nearly enough to fly the 1,120 miles to Algiers. (In retrospect, this indicated poor planning on the part of the hijackers.)

Fortunately, the language barrier was broken when chief flight attendant Uli Derickson explained that she was German, not American, and found that one of the hijackers spoke German—a completely chance occurrence. With Derickson interpreting, Testrake said they could reach Cairo, just less than 700 miles away; but the hijackers told him to fly to Beirut, 734 miles away, for "fuel only."[7]

There were originally three hijackers, but one had been bumped from the overbooked flight, another organizational glitch. Well after the fact the two on board would be identified as Mohammed Ali Hammadi and Hasan Izz-Al-Din. The bumped third member, Ali Atwa, although failing to get a seat on the flight, would subsequently participate in the hijack. All had flown to Athens from Beirut the previous day.

On the flight to Beirut the hijackers terrorized and cowed the passengers by running up and down the cabin aisle brandishing their weapons and randomly beating them with seat armrests used as clubs. They moved the men to the window seats and forced all to keep their heads down to prevent them from seeing anything or communicating with one another. With the help of the flight attendants the hijackers identified and dispersed among the passengers seven navy divers. They also sought unsuccessfully to find out if there were any Jews on the plane.

On approach to Beirut International airport, just before noon local time, tower control initially refused permission to land, but grudgingly relented when the hijackers threatened to crash-land and blow up the plane. Two days before, a Royal Jordanian Airways plane had been hijacked and blown up on the runway and its wreckage was still smoldering as TWA 847 taxied by.[8]

Over the radio the hijackers demanded fuel, threatening to "kill an American" unless their demands were met. To hasten a response, they began loudly beating one of the navy divers, Robert Stethem. As the plane was being refueled, they also demanded to speak with an official of Amal, the group that controlled southern Beirut and the airport. No Amal official was willing to talk to them, indicating serious differences and obviously no prior coordination between the hijackers, who apparently were part of Hezbollah, not Amal.[9]

---

[7] John Testrake, *Triumph over Terror, on Flight 847* (Eastbourne: Kingsway Publications, 1988), 70-71.

[8] "Journey of Flight 847: A Logbook of Terror," *New York Times*, June 17, 1985, A9.

[9] "Remembering the 1985 Hijacking of TWA Flight 847," *Securitas Magazine* (May-June 2005).

At the same time, the hijackers spewed out a series of demands over the radio in Arabic that no one aboard the plane understood. They demanded that governments across Europe and the Middle East release jailed Shiites everywhere. Specifically, they demanded the release of the Kuwait 17, seven hundred prisoners held by Israel, two held by Spain, and two held by Cyprus. They also demanded "world" condemnation of Israel and of the United States for its support for Israel.

With tanks full, passengers and cargo combined put the aircraft several thousand pounds overweight, a condition that enabled Captain Testrake and Uli Derickson to persuade the hijackers to release 17 women and two children to lighten the load. At that point, 1:30 in the afternoon, an hour and a half after arriving, the plane took off for Algiers 1,800 miles away.[10]

The initial early morning response from Washington was understandably disjointed based on fragmentary information. When the plane landed in Beirut, President Reagan sent the first of several cables to Syrian president Hafez al-Assad asking for assistance.[11] When the plane took off and it was understood to be headed for Algiers, the focus shifted there. US ambassador Michael Newlin was directed to request of the president of Algeria, Chadli Bendjedid, that the plane be permitted to land and then be detained. President Reagan also sent a personal message imploring him to attempt to convince the hijackers to surrender.

Meanwhile, at 3:30 in the afternoon, exclaiming that they were running out of fuel, Captain Testrake was given permission to land at Houari Boumediene International airport. Airport security surrounded the plane and officials arrived to talk, a process that dragged on for the better part of four hours. The hijackers' basic public demand was for the release of the 766 prisoners held by Israel in Atlit prison. For "humanitarian reasons" they released 21 more passengers, but threatened to kill others if an attempt was made to assault the plane.[12]

As they talked the hijackers demanded that the plane be refueled, but Algerian authorities stalled. To convince them to cooperate they began severely beating Stethem, but, as he was barely conscious and could not cry out, they took another American, army reservist Kurt Carlson, and began beating him and directing his shouts into the cockpit radio.[13] After several tense moments and the passage of three deadlines, a fuel truck arrived, but the driver demanded prepayment for the fuel. Once again, flight attendant Derickson saved the day, producing a Shell gas card for payment, whereupon the plane's fuel tanks were topped off at just over nine thousand gallons. Derickson was charged six thousand dollars, but the larger point was that the Algerians refused to cooperate with the hijackers, except minimally.[14]

---

[10] Testrake, *Triumph over Terror*, 76.
[11] Lou Cannon and John Goshko, "US Stands Firm against Demands of Jet's Hijackers," *Washington Post*, June 20, 1985, A1.
[12] Testrake, *Triumph over Terror*, 81.
[13] Martin and Walcott, *Best Laid Plans*, 172.
[14] Testrake, *Triumph over Terror*, 80-81.

Original Plan Gone Awry

At 8:15 in the evening, TWA 847 took off from Algiers, destination unknown. Once airborne, the hijackers told Captain Testrake to head back to Beirut. To him this meant "the hijackers didn't really have a game plan. They'd known what to do to get this far—but not what to do afterward."[15] Indeed, getting to Algiers was their objective, but, having failed to accomplish their unspecified purpose once they got there, they were now on the way back to Beirut to determine their next course of action.

Approaching a blacked-out Beirut International a few minutes past two in the morning, tower control again refused permission to land, informing Captain Testrake that barricades had been placed on the runway. Declaring his aircraft to be in distress and nearly out of fuel, the captain related the hijackers' threat to crash-land the plane. Relenting, the tower controller advised Testrake to circle the airport while he arranged to have the barriers removed. After circling the airport several times, the runway lights switched on, and Testrake was given permission to land.

Wary of a trap, the hijackers ordered Testrake to brake the plane in the middle of the runway while they began to converse with the control tower. In addition to demanding food and fuel, they evidently demanded that Amal join in the hijacking, which was refused. They also threatened to kill the eight Greek passengers on board, if the Greek government failed to release their accomplice, who had been apprehended at the airport.[16] As their argument intensified, one of the hijackers suddenly dragged the barely conscious seaman Stethem to the doorway, shot him in the head and dumped his body onto the tarmac, screaming that they meant business and that unless their demands were met in five minutes, they would kill another.

At this, the tower gave permission for Testrake to taxi over to the refueling area. When they got there and as the plane was being refueled a group of gunmen, variously estimated to number between five and a dozen, charged onto the plane. Although the hijackers had attempted to draw Amal into their action, those who boarded the plane were Hezbollah gunmen. Indeed, one of them was the leader of the group, Imad Mughniyeh, who identified himself simply as Jihad.

Apparently, it was Islamic Jihad, a radical cell within the Iran-sponsored Hezbollah group, that carried out the TWA 847 hijack. To reporters searching for information, some "people identifying themselves as spokesmen" for the group claimed that Islamic Jihad bore responsibility for the hijacking. Others, however,

---

[15] Ibid, 81.

[16] Shortly after the hijack was reported, Israel's intelligence representative in Athens went to the airport, discovered that one of the three hijackers' tickets had not been used, and concluded that the third hijacker, Ali Atwa, was still probably in the airport. With the support of the airport police, they paged Atwa, saying he had an important call, and when he appeared, he was arrested. See Ronen Bergman, *The Secret War with Iran* (New York: Free Press, 2007), 101.

denied the group's responsibility, vowing "retaliation against media that say Jihad was responsible."[17] The implication was that Imad Mughniyeh was a member of this cell, but had acted independently of Hezbollah, undertaking this particular operation supported by a different sponsor.

For the past two years Mughniyeh's Islamic Jihad had concentrated attacks mostly against American and French targets in Lebanon. Islamic Jihad's objectives, like every other group's, were proclaimed to be the removal of American and Israeli presence in the Middle East in general and Lebanon in particular. But Mughniyeh had additional motives that made him one of the most vicious and feared terrorists.

Mughniyeh pioneered the use of suicide bombers and was behind the bombings of several US or allied installations in 1983: the American embassy in Beirut in April, the Marine barracks and the French legation in October, and the US and French embassies in Kuwait in December. When Kuwaiti authorities captured, tried and sentenced a group of those behind the attacks, Mughniyeh obtained an additional rationale. One of the seventeen terrorists convicted and sentenced to death was reportedly his cousin and brother-in-law, Mustafa Badreddine. Thus, all subsequent attacks, including hostage seizures from the first months of 1984 in Lebanon, had included the demand for the release of the "Kuwait 17."

But there was more. According to Woodward, CIA director Casey, with the support of the Saudis, had arranged to take out Sheikh Mohammed Hussein Fadlallah, the spiritual leader of Hezbollah who had been deeply involved in the bombings of American and French facilities.[18] On March 8, 1985, a huge car bomb exploded outside his headquarters killing 80 people and wounding over 200. Fadlallah escaped unscathed, but among those who perished was Mughniyeh's younger brother, Jihad.

President Reagan denied responsibility, declaring that "never would I sign anything that would authorize an assassination . . . . I never have, and I never will, and I didn't."[19] McFarlane later agreed that Reagan had no involvement. He suggested that CIA-trained "rogue operatives" from Lebanese intelligence carried out the attack without CIA approval. The CIA, however, was widely believed to have been responsible.[20]

Mughniyeh, who spoke English, assumed control of the hijack operation from the moment he boarded the aircraft, making two decisions. The first was to go back to Algiers, to attempt to fulfill the original plan, and the second was to

---

[17] Christopher Dickey, "Hijackings: Tool of Terrorism," *Washington Post*, June 16, 1985, A18.

[18] Bob Woodward, *Veil: The Secret Wars of the CIA, 1981-1987* (New York: Simon & Shuster, 1987), 397.

[19] "Did a Dead Man Tell No Tales?" *Time*, October 12, 1987.

[20] "Target America: Terrorist Attacks on Americans, 1979-1988," *Frontline* video archive.

take out hostage insurance against any rescue attempt. (Word had already gotten out that the United States had dispatched a Delta Force team to the Middle East.)

For insurance, the hijackers selected out two groups of seven and five men from among the passengers, took them off the plane, and sequestered them in the slums of West Beirut. One group included five military men and two Greeks and the other included two Americans with Jewish-sounding names and three others selected at random. Mughniyeh would control one of these two groups until the very last minutes of the crisis.

Algiers Redux

A little over three hours after landing at Beirut, with the plane refueled and passengers fortified with sandwiches and soft drinks, TWA 847 took off at daybreak headed again for Algiers. While en route the hijackers radioed a demand for the release of their accomplice Ali Atwa, in return for which they would release the Greek passengers. If he were not released, they would begin to kill them. The Greek government immediately complied, flying Atwa to Algiers that afternoon where he was permitted to join the gunmen on the plane.

Upon learning that the plane was headed back to Algiers, Secretary Shultz instructed Ambassador Newlin to request that the Algerian government permit the plane to land and allow the United States to send in a rescue force. Newlin forcefully objected to the instruction about trying a rescue. He did not believe that the Algerians would "ever consent to have a foreign military force operate on their territory." Any attempt to try would provoke "armed opposition from the Algerians, and the terrorists would probably blow up the plane with everybody in it."[21]

The plane landed in Algiers at 7:45 a.m. Shultz thought the best option was to keep the plane in Algiers, where "the Algerians could try to bring the crisis to an end," although he still clung to the hope that, failing that, they would agree "at some point to let our shooters . . . take over the plane."[22]

But the Algerian government would have none of it. As Newlin had said, they flatly opposed any US military presence, let alone operations, on their soil. At the same time, Algerian foreign ministry officials persuaded the hijackers to release not only several Greek passengers, but also all of the women, children, and flight attendants, in exchange for Atwa. Left aboard the aircraft were 44 male passengers, the three-man flight crew, and about a dozen hijackers.[23]

Based on their discussions, the Algerians believed that "they could probably persuade the hijackers to release the passengers, if the United States

---

[21] David Wills, *The First War on Terrorism: Counter Terrorism Policy during the Reagan Administration* (New York: Rowman & Littlefield, 2003), 94.

[22] George Shultz, *Turmoil and Triumph* (New York: Scribner, 1993), 654-55.

[23] Stephen Labaton, "Aid Obstacles to Passenger List, Fate of 15 Unclear," *Washington Post*, June 17, 1985, 16.

could guarantee that Israel would release the Atlit prisoners" they held.[24] The release of the Atlit prisoners in exchange for the passengers seemed to offer the prospect of a prompt settlement. Although the president supported this idea, Shultz strongly opposed a "swap," insisting that American policy was not to make deals with terrorists and not encourage others to do so.[25]

Although President Reagan repeatedly in internal discussions proposed this idea, Shultz refused to agree to it. In the end, a swap is what would actually transpire, but two weeks would be spent attempting to work out staggered releases by Israel and the hijackers to avoid the appearance of a swap and maintain the façade of adhering to principle. This fooled no one. Shultz's opposition and the president's disinclination to override him meant the loss of an early opportunity to resolve the question in Algiers.

By early morning on Sunday, June 16, however, the hijackers already had been in one place too long and had become concerned about an attack on the plane. (They would spend over 24 hours on the ground in Algiers.) Waking early, Mughniyeh demanded that the plane be refueled. To overcome reticence by the tower to send the fuel truck, Mughniyeh said to the captain "we want to play a little game here." He opened the microphone and told the crew to yell loudly to pretend that they were being beaten. At the same time, he fired a few shots from his pistol through the open cockpit window. The fuel truck arrived in minutes.[26]

Discussing their destination as the plane was being refueled, Mughniyeh said, "we want to go to Aden." When the captain pointed out that South Yemen was well beyond the range of the aircraft and would require a refueling stop in Cairo, Mughniyeh replied: "Okay, we will fly back to Beirut for fuel. Then we will go somewhere else." As the hijackers talked among themselves, Testrake could make out the word "Tehran," a "somewhere else" he did not want to go. As he noted later: "It was obvious to all of us that the hijackers were fresh out of ideas and were just fumbling about without a real plan of attack."[27] Whatever their objective had been in returning to Algiers a second time, they had failed to achieve it.

At eight o'clock in the morning, Sunday, June 16, over the objections of Ambassador Newlin, TWA 847 took off from Algiers heading back to Beirut. When Newlin asked why, his Algerian interlocutors said that they had heard that Delta Force was on its way and assumed the hijackers probably heard about it, too, because they were threatening to blow up the plane.[28] It seems that the Algerian authorities, too, had been concerned about an American attack on the plane, and permitted it to depart before anything could happen.

---

[24] Wills, *First War on Terrorism*, 97.

[25] Shultz, *Turmoil and Triumph*, 656.

[26] Testrake, *Triumph over Terror*, 90-1,

[27] Ibid, 92.

[28] Martin and Walcott, *Best Laid Plans*, 182.

An Intelligence Discovery

While the plane was en route to Beirut, American intelligence produced surprising information that would have a bearing on the developing crisis. Reports based on "hard intelligence" concluded that "two senior officials of the Greek government of Andreas Papandreou [were] implicated, though perhaps indirectly, in the hijacking . . . " The two officials were Costas Laliotis, an aide to the prime minister, and Agamemnon Koutsogiorgas, Minister of Interior. Both reportedly were "supporters and protectors of international terrorism in Greece," who had been the "focus of administration criticism . . . for quite some time." [29] According to another account, the arms used in the hijacking were believed to have been smuggled aboard the aircraft by Palestinians working there illegally due to the intercession of the two Greek officials, an allegation vehemently denied by a Greek embassy spokesman.[30]

When Israel drove the Palestinians from Lebanon during the 1982 war, over two hundred were evacuated to Greece and Cyprus. The Greek government had helped some of these refugees obtain work permits and employment "on the ground crews at Athens International Airport." Indeed, the Director of Public Order, Athanassios Trouras, acknowledged that weapons "might have been hidden aboard the aircraft as it stood on the tarmac after arriving from Cairo." American intelligence thus concluded that "the weapons used by the Moslem Shi'ite terrorists—9mm Mauser handguns and grenades—were positioned aboard the TWA Boeing 727 while it was being serviced during its stopover in Athens, allowing the hijackers to bypass the airport's metal detectors and other security equipment."[31] A member of the service crew, probably one of the cleaning crew, evidently secreted the weapons package in one of the lavatories on the aircraft.

One of the passengers, Peter Hill, a tour operator from Chicago, offered corroboration. Hill was sitting in the back row of the plane next to the two hijackers. Before takeoff one of the Arabs pushed his way into the lavatory, refusing to keep seated as requested by the cabin attendant. Hill "next heard 'a tremendous crash, a smashing of glass . . . .' Shortly afterwards, the Arab returned to his seat . . . and began whispering to his companion."[32]

The reports also pointed to the instigator of the hijacking, although were mute on his purpose. It turned out that Muammar Qaddafi had contributed "large sums of money" to Andreas Papandreou's 1981 election and that "Libya and other Arab extremist groups therefore had a certain ability to collect favors from the

---

[29] Ted Agres, "Two Greek Officials Implicated in Hijack," *Washington Times*, June 20, 1985, A1.
[30] John P. Wallach, "US Expected Bombing, Not Hijack," *San Francisco Examiner*, June 21, 1985, A5.
[31] Agres, "Two Greek Officials Implicated in Hijack."
[32] Martin and Walcott, *Best Laid Plans*, 161-62.

Greek government." One of those "favors" was to look the other way on "terrorist operations occurring within Greece, but not directed against that country."[33]

Thus far, the evidence strongly suggested that Qaddafi had arranged to provide for the placement of weapons on board TWA 847 for an Imad Mughniyeh-led terrorist mission to hijack the plane, but said nothing about its purpose, except that their mission was to fly to Algiers. The purpose surely could not have been primarily to bargain for the release of prisoners held by Israel who were already in the process of being released. To accelerate the process may have been in the interests of Mughniyeh, but Qaddafi? Why had he instigated the hijacking?[34]

It was too soon to work through the larger reasons for Qaddafi's motives, but, for the moment, at least, the president could proceed with reasonable confidence that Hafez al-Assad was not a co-conspirator. This came through in the persistent refusal of his Lebanese surrogate, Amal, to become involved in the hijacking. Iran's role, too, was as yet unclear, but it seemed unlikely that the Iranians would sponsor an action that would undercut their concurrent attempt to establish an arms relationship with the United States, although it was possible that a faction opposed to such an attempt was involved.

Based on this information, it is reasonable to speculate on the contents of the president's June 16 letter to Assad, while TWA 847 was en route to Beirut for the third time. Shultz says that in the letter, "we asked him to work on Berri to try to end the crisis." The reference was to Nabih Berri, the leader of Amal, who, up to this point had determinedly stayed out of the incident, twice attempting to prevent the plane from landing in Beirut and refusing to talk to the hijackers.[35] But obviously there was more to the letter than that.

To encourage Assad's cooperation through Amal, the president most assuredly told him that he knew that Qaddafi was the perpetrator and that Assad had nothing to gain from supporting the Libyan dictator, who he knew was attempting to encroach on his turf in Beirut. (In the Shiite-PLO battle for control of Beirut, Qaddafi supported the Palestinians.) But it was most immediately important to safeguard the remaining passengers to prevent the hijack from exploding into a crisis that would engulf Syria itself. Thus, having Berri and Amal take control of the passengers from Hezbollah when the plane arrived was the most prudent course.

Shultz, however, persisted in an attempt to use force to take control of the plane, seeking to persuade Captain Testrake to fake engine failure and land at

---

[33] Agres, "Two Greek Officials Implicated in Hijack."

[34] It was in this immediate context that, on June 17, Secretary Weinberger initially responded to the draft NSDD on Iran with the comment that opening up to Iran would be similar to "asking Qaddafi over for a cozy lunch." He would send a fuller, more restrained, but still negative response a month later. Caspar W. Weinberger, *Fighting for Peace: Seven Critical Years in the Pentagon* (New York: Warner Books, 1990), 363.

[35] Shultz, *Turmoil and Triumph*, 656.

Larnaca, Cyprus, where a rescue could be attempted. Weinberger and the Joint Chiefs disagreed. JCS Chairman John Vessey noted "the prospect for a successful rescue mission was virtually nonexistent." In his view, the "only safe way is to talk them out."[36]

Captain Testrake had a larger concern, fearing that the hijackers wanted to go to Tehran.[37] When the hijackers were not in the cabin, he began to ask over the radio: would the passengers be safe in Tehran? Once there would they be permitted to leave? But the only answer that came back, from the tower at Athens, was the suggestion to divert to Larnaca. Testrake and his crewmembers wanted no part of a rescue attempt, which they recognized would only mean the probable deaths of many passengers, crew, and terrorists. He agreed with the idea of faking engine failure, but disregarded the suggestion of landing at Larnaca, and instead proceeded to Beirut.[38]

At just after 2:30 Sunday afternoon, June 16, Captain Testrake made his final approach as airport personnel removed fire trucks from the runway. Walid Jumblatt, leader of the Druze and also Transport Minister in the Lebanese government had first given the order to refuse permission to land, but controllers relented when Testrake told them he was running out of fuel.[39]

The captain and crew had decided to shut down the engines so the plane could not fly anywhere else. Thus, by the time the aircraft was rolling to a stop on the runway, the crew had faked engine failures on two of the three engines. Claiming that the engines were "way overdue for an overhaul" and that replacement engines would have to come from the United States, which would take "at least two to three weeks," Testrake had neatly put an end to any schemes Mughniyeh might have had that the plane could fly on from Beirut. The hijack problem, in short, would be resolved one way or another in Beirut.[40]

Assad and Berri Take Charge

As TWA 847 came rolling to a stop on the runway, American intelligence noted, "contingents from the Amal militia were arriving at the airport."[41] This, it would shortly become clear, was the first step in Assad's decision to take control of the hijacking away from Mughniyeh and Hezbollah, but it would not be clean-cut, or easy. Amal's leader, Nabih Berri, would be his

---

[36] Wills, *First War on Terrorism*, 102 and Martin and Walcott, *Best Laid Plans*, 185.
[37] Samuel Segev, *The Iranian Triangle: The Untold Story of Israel's Role in the Iran-Contra Affair* (New York: Free Press, 1988), 142, says that "the Iranian government announced that it would not allow the plane to land on its territory," indicating that the hijackers had contacted Tehran while en route.
[38] Testrake, *Triumph over Terror*, 93.
[39] Joseph Berger, "Gunmen Negotiate as Hostages Plead for Reagan to Act," *New York Times*, June 17, 1985, A1.
[40] Testrake, *Triumph over Terror*, 97-98.
[41] Wills, *First War on Terrorism*, 98.

agent in the effort. His objective was to surround the Hezbollah hijackers with his men, but also position them for a defense against a possible rescue attempt.

According to observers "several jeeps loaded with Amal militiamen pulled up to the plane." After some discussion the hijackers agreed to send a representative from the group "to meet with Mr. Berri, the Amal leader, at his home." The hijackers promised no harm would come to the passengers while the talks with Mr. Berri proceeded, but reiterated their threat to blow up the plane if their demand for the release of the Lebanese detainees was not met.[42]

While the negotiations were occurring in Beirut, back in Washington, the NSPG was meeting. They would meet sometimes several times a day throughout the crisis. Reagan attended most of the meetings and was in contact when he was elsewhere.[43] The NSPG membership consisted of Reagan, Bush, Shultz, Weinberger, McFarlane, Regan, Poindexter, and Vessey. Baker and Meese, also members, attended occasionally. Others would be invited as needed. In the absence of hard information about the situation among the Beirut factions, or on the plane itself, a trigger-happy Shultz repeatedly proposed ways to assault the plane, whether in Beirut, or in Jordan, even as he acknowledged the reservations of Weinberger and Vessey about the inevitability of "lots of casualties."

At the 1:00 p.m. meeting (eight o'clock in the evening in Beirut), Shultz informed the group that Assad had replied to the president's letter and confirmed that he had "stimulated" Berri to take control of the situation.[44] This was very important information, confirming that Assad was not one of the sponsors, which promised the way to a resolution.

The immediate problem, however, was how to respond to the Israelis, who seemed to want no part of the crisis. Against the backdrop of large-scale demonstrations in Tel Aviv in opposition to the recent decision by the government to swap 1,100 Lebanese for three Israeli soldiers, protestors demanded that the government hold on to the Atlit prisoners.

Government spokesmen gave contradictory accounts. One said that Israel would not agree to any "exchange" of prisoners for passengers. Defense Minister Rabin was quoted to the effect that while the government would meet with Red Cross representatives, "the Americans will have to crawl on all fours before we even discuss" releasing the Lebanese detainees. Another spokesman, however, said that Israel "would consider a formal US request to swap the prisoners for the passengers."[45]

Parsing these statements went to the heart of the coalition government then in power, the "marriage of inconvenience," as one commentator described

---

[42] Berger, "Gunmen Negotiate as Hostages Plead for Reagan to Act."

[43] Wills, *First War on Terrorism*, 214. While an invaluable account, Wills contradicts himself in the view that "there is little evidence of Reagan's involvement" in the crisis. He compounds his error by the observation, 218, that "most documents from that crisis remain classified," making his conclusion both wrong and a non sequitur.

[44] Ibid, 101.

[45] Ibid, 98.

it.[46] The author of the no exchange line was evidently deputy Prime Minister Yitzhak Shamir, whose visceral hatred for the United States was well known. Defense Minister Rabin, who was only slightly less antagonistic, was willing to discuss a swap, if the Americans crawled on all fours for it. And Prime Minister Peres was the apparent author of what became the initial official position: that the government would consider an exchange, if Washington requested it.

Secretary Shultz, assuming Peres's position to be the official one, interpreted, or perhaps, *mis*interpreted, his point. He considered the call for a "request" to be an invitation for "us to ask them to release all or nearly all of the many Lebanese Shiite prisoners they held in exchange for the release of TWA 847 and its remaining passengers. . . . putting the responsibility on us." In his view, this meant "if people were killed, we couldn't say it was because of Israel's refusal to swap prisoners for hostages."[47] In reality, the split in Israel's coalition and domestic opposition dictated a passive approach. The important point was that Peres had invited Washington to discuss it.

Finally, the secretary read a statement signed by 32 passengers aboard the plane, imploring the president "not to take any direct military action" and "negotiate quickly our immediate release by convincing the Israelis to release the 800 prisoners as requested. Now."[48] Perhaps reassured, the president and his advisers decided not to force Israel's hand and to go slow and not precipitate any unwanted action by those holding the passengers.

Meanwhile, Mughniyeh and his gunmen on the aircraft were surrounded by Amal gunmen on the tarmac, as they argued all Sunday afternoon and into the evening over the radio with Nabih Berri and his representatives in the control tower. Finally, late in the afternoon, Berri announced the outcome of their "negotiations." He would place the passengers under his "protection" and mediate for the hijackers. In fact, they divided control of passengers, plane and crew. After midnight his men removed all of the passengers from the plane and dispersed them in small groups throughout the squalid neighborhoods of West Beirut, while the flight crew remained on board the aircraft.[49]

The situation as of Monday morning, June 17, was the following: Berri had 43 passengers under guard in West Beirut (he sent one of the passengers, who was ill, to the local hospital), while Mughniyeh had the plane and its three-man crew. CIA informants had located and discovered that the two leaders also divided control of the two groups removed from the plane during the second stopover.[50] Finally, heavily armed Amal militiamen and Hezbollah gunmen surrounded the airport, which now made a rescue attempt out of the question.

---

[46] Joseph Kraft, "Marriage of Inconvenience," *Washington Post*, June 25, 1985, A15.
[47] Shultz, *Turmoil and Triumph*, 655-56.
[48] Berger, "Gunmen Negotiate as Hostages Plead for Reagan to Act."
[49] Andrew Borowiec, "Shi'ites Said Holding Hostages in West Beirut," *Washington Times*, June 18, 1985, A1.
[50] Wills, *First War on Terrorism*, 99.

Berri put a humane face in place of the murderous visage of the terrorists, turning the hijack into a quasi-diplomatic hostage negotiation. Berri's presence was somewhat comforting to the American people, who were treated to full television coverage of the event, because he had lived in America and frequently visited. His six children were educated there, his ex-wife lived there (in Detroit), and he still held a green card.[51]

Staking Out Negotiating Positions

That morning around nine o'clock (2:00 a.m. Washington time), Robert McFarlane, who had met Berri in 1983 when he was the president's envoy to the Middle East, spoke with him over the phone to reinforce Reagan's view that he held the key to resolution of the crisis. As McFarlane put it, it was now Berri's game to win or lose. White House spokesman Larry Speakes, emphasized that message, declaring that Berri "was the key to it, he has control over the situation."[52]

Berri wasn't buying that characterization, turning the tables. At a press conference later in the morning, he acknowledged that he was now "responsible" for the passengers, but it was still an "American problem." If Washington failed to press Israel to release the detainees, he would "wash his hands" of the passengers and return them to the Hezbollah "to do with them as they pleased."

Washington's response to that and to the Israeli government was a White House Statement read by Larry Speakes: "We do not make concessions and we don't encourage others to make concessions." The hijack situation, he said, had "effectively blocked Israel from proceeding with plans to release its Shiite prisoners." If it were cleared up, "it might be possible the Israelis would proceed on the schedule they'd previously announced." [53] To provide some incentive to Assad, it was announced that the aircraft carrier *Nimitz* and six other ships were proceeding to the Eastern Mediterranean.

Berri met with the British and Italian ambassadors, who warned him against underestimating Reagan. They pointed out that the United States and Jordan were just then beginning military exercises, which could be a cover for a rescue attempt. There were also reports of Israeli aircraft overflights. On Tuesday, June 18, to forestall hasty action, Berri announced that he was releasing the remaining six Greek passengers as a friendly gesture for the earlier Greek release of Ali Atwa. And he announced that his men were assuring the safety of the rest.[54]

---

[51] Jonathan Randal, "Crisis Go-Between: Berri, With Ties on Both Sides, Could Find Leadership Tested," *Washington Post*, June 18, 1985, A9.

[52] Bernard Weinraub, "Passengers Taken from Hijacked Jet, Lebanese Reports," *New York Times*, June 18, 1985, A1. US leaders understood that Assad controlled Beirut and that Berri was his agent. Thus, putting pressure on Berri made little sense.

[53] Ibid.

[54] Wills, *First War on Terrorism*, 107-8.

The important news was Assad's reply to Reagan's letter requesting his assistance. Assad wanted to know whether the president would "exert efforts" to gain the release of the Israeli detainees and "make public" the administration's view that holding them was a violation of the Geneva Convention? Reagan was receptive. White House spokesman Larry Speakes responded during the morning briefing that the United States "would like Israel" to "go ahead and make the release" of the detainees.

Shultz was apoplectic. While not saying so, he knew that Speakes had not spoken out on his own authority. It was Reagan who had authorized his remark, which was consistent with the position the president had been taking in the NSPG from the beginning. Furious, Shultz went to the president and demanded that he control the "action." All questions, he insisted, "were to be referred to the State Department."

The president relented, issuing a statement containing the "no concessions" line. Reagan also sent a message to Assad reiterating the no deals line and insisting that the hostage takers were the ones "blocking the release of the prisoners held by Israel."[55] On the other hand, the president decided to tell the Israelis "privately" that they could make the "exchange" of detainees for passengers.

The president's message seems to have been part of a plan to use the Red Cross as an intermediary. After visiting both groups, the "administration could cobble together an unspoken agreement in which each party's objectives were met, and the US and Israel could not be accused of conceding to the terrorists' demands." The Israelis rejected the ploy. The Red Cross "are not a party to it. We deal with the US," insisting on an American "request."[56]

Tuesday evening, the president held a news conference to reaffirm the policy. America, he said, will make no concessions, nor ask others to do so. He demanded the passengers be freed forthwith. In responding to a question, he made public, as Assad had requested, the US opposition to Israel's detention of prisoners "in violation of the Geneva accords," but he said, the United States would not "interfere" with Israel's decision on whether or not to release the prisoners. There was no "linkage" with the passengers.

Finally, when asked about his policy of "swift retribution," the president said that was so when it involved the actions of a government. In this case, there was "a problem identifying the perpetrators and their accomplices." Therefore, "I have to wait it out as long as . . . we have a possibility—I'll say a probability—of bringing them home."[57]

---

[55] Shultz, *Turmoil and Triumph*, 658.

[56] Edward Walsh, "Israel Agrees to Red Cross Meeting," *Washington Post*, June 19, 1985, A1 and Wills, *First War on Terrorism*, 109.

[57] Bernard Weinraub, "President Bars 'Concessions'; Orders Antihijacking Steps; 3 More T.W.A. Hostages Freed," *New York Times*, June 19, 1985, A1. See page A18 for transcript.

With the press conference statements, the president had reestablished the US "no concessions" negotiating position and declared that the ball was now in Berri's court. Whatever the hijackers' objectives had been, they had not achieved them. The "swap" of the Atlit detainees for the passengers was now the only issue on the table. The next several days witnessed a sustained attempt by those behind the hijackers to effect a change in public opinion, while negotiations continued by third parties.

On Wednesday June 19, Assad made an unannounced trip to Moscow to meet with Mikhail Gorbachev, who reportedly told him to make sure none of the passengers were harmed. It may be surmised that he also agreed that it was time to wrap up the crisis. On the same day, Iran sent a message "to the effect that Tehran wanted to do as much as it could to end the TWA crisis." The State Department sent a stiff reply, saying: "It is the view of the United States that the government of Iran cannot escape its responsibilities . . . to help secure the release of the hostages."[58] Finally, the Algerian government reported that Berri was willing to release the passengers if the United States could provide a "silent but firm guarantee" that the Israelis would release their prisoners by a "date certain."[59]

Reagan thought this was a promising step and wanted to call Berri and encourage him to release the hostages and then "work on the Israelis, but not as a quid pro quo." Shultz and McFarlane were concerned about an "unstructured call," and suggested a cable be sent first followed by a call. As for dealing with the Israelis, Shultz wanted nothing "in writing" that could be interpreted as collusion in brokering a deal.[60]

Meanwhile, this promising movement was obscured by what one of the passengers, Peter Hill, called a "bloody circus." First, on Wednesday, Hezbollah brought several reporters and TV cameramen to the plane for a "news conference" with the captain and crew. Responding to questions, they all assured the press that they were being treated fairly and warned against any rescue attempt.[61] The following evening there was a press conference with five of the passengers brought in from town, which, was terminated early when a scuffle broke out between some two hundred reporters and the gunmen. They also pleaded that no rescue attempt be made.[62]

On Thursday, the administration settled on its nothing-in-writing approach. *New York Times* reporter Bernard Gwertzman, quoting unidentified sources, said that Israel had agreed to release all Shiite prisoners to the Red Cross "within a few hours" of the release of the 40 passengers, but Berri reportedly was

[58] John G. Tower et al., *Report of the President's Special Review Board, February 26, 1987* (Washington, DC: US Government Printing Office, 1987), B-13.

[59] Wills, *First War on Terrorism*, 110.

[60] Ibid, 114.

[61] Testrake, *Triumph over Terror*, 131-33.

[62] "Hostages, at Beirut News Session Beseech US Not to Try a Rescue," *New York Times*, June 21, 1985, 1.

insisting that there be a "simultaneous" transfer.[63] Shultz was concerned that the Israelis would misread this report, which, he said, was untrue. Pleading innocence, he admitted they may have believed that "we had deliberately leaked this news . . . to send a signal to, or pressure, them."[64]

Whether it had been a deliberate leak, or not, the press report had the desired effect. The day before Shultz had put a question to Peres, asking what precisely Israel would do with the Atlit prisoners, if "there were no TWA 847 hostages being held?" This, of course, was merely a clumsy way of asking the Israelis what they would do *after* the TWA passengers had been released. Still in disarray, with Shamir objecting to any cooperation, the Israelis stalled.

After the Gwertzman article appeared, Shultz repeated the question. Peres answered early on June 21, his reply now endorsed by Shamir and Rabin. In the absence of the hijacking, he said, Israel would have proceeded with the release of the detainees depending on developments. In view of the hijacking, "we are not inclined to do this in a way that would appear to give in to the terrorists." In any case, detainees could appeal to a board headed by a district judge. One appeal already resulted in a decision to release 31 detainees the following week.[65]

Although Shultz interpreted this as a "complex and indefinite response," he had achieved the purpose of unifying the fractious Israeli government behind the position of releasing detainees piecemeal once the passengers had been released. Moreover, the question of who the detainees were came into focus. The Israeli defense ministry announced that "of the 766 detainees still in Atlit, 570 are Shiite Moslems, 147 are Palestinians and 49 others are Druze, Christians, and Sunni Moslems."[66] Algerian negotiators "could not imagine that the Shiites would knowingly seek to secure the release of Palestinians."[67]

Word came from Ambassador Reginald Bartholomew in Beirut that Berri was having some success in persuading the hijackers to give up, except for an "inner group of terrorists . . . not under anyone's control, not Iran's and not Hezbollah's." Shultz correctly surmised that they were "related by family to the Al-Dawa prisoners held by Kuwait," but did not know by whom they were led. Later, when the FBI examined the plane, Mughniyeh's fingerprint was found in the toilet, enabling analysts to establish that it had been Mughniyeh and his small band that was "not under anyone's control."[68] At least, not Iran's nor Hezbollah's.[69] The question was, who had leverage over the group? That very

---

[63] Bernard Gwertzman, "US Warns Shiites about Becoming Global 'Outcasts,'" *New York Times*, June 20, 1985, A1.

[64] Shultz, *Turmoil and Triumph*, 660.

[65] Shultz, *Turmoil and Triumph*, 661.

[66] Thomas Friedman, "Israel To Release 31 Prisoners Seized in Lebanon," *New York Times*, June 24, 1985, A1.

[67] Shultz, *Turmoil and Triumph*, 663.

[68] Bergman, *Secret War with Iran*, 101.

[69] Shultz, *Turmoil and Triumph*, 662. Actually, three days earlier, a US Navy source in the Middle East said, "there is also . . . some evidence that the identities of the

morning Mughniyeh, in a mask, had mobilized several hundred Hezbollah demonstrators at the airport shouting "death to America" and "death to Reagan," to demonstrate his defiance.[70]

Tension Increases—Worldwide

Two days after he had said he would "wait it out," the president reversed position, declaring, "our limits have been reached." The evening before, in San Salvador, two gunmen dressed in Salvadoran army uniforms had opened fire on a crowd at an outdoor cafe, killing thirteen people, including six US Marines, whom they apparently had "sought out." The gunmen were believed to be from the Farabundo Marti National Liberation Front that had been battling the government for the past five years. The president's shift seemed to be directed at "diminishing political fallout" from the Beirut hostage crisis as well as from the Salvadoran killings.[71]

Additional terrorist attacks occurring over the next couple of days suggested a global pattern. In Chile, terrorist bomb attacks on three electrical towers knocked out power in the grid feeding electricity to the capital, Santiago, a city of four million people. At Frankfurt International Airport, West Europe's busiest, unidentified terrorists set off a bomb near the ticket counters of Iranian, Spanish and Greek air carriers. Three people were killed and over 40 injured.[72]

Worst of all, on Sunday, June 23, two terrorist bombings of aircraft pushed the Reagan administration to its limit. An Air India flight from Toronto to New Delhi, after refueling in London, blew up over the Atlantic near Ireland, scattering debris over a five-mile radius of ocean. Three hundred and twenty-nine persons perished, with no survivors. At the same time a Canadian Pacific flight from Vancouver to Tokyo made a successful flight, but a bomb exploded in baggage from the plane after it landed at Tokyo International airport. Two baggage handlers were killed and four injured. Had the bomb detonated in flight the carnage would have resembled the Air India attack.

Baggage on the flights came from Toronto and Vancouver, cities with sizable Indian communities and "baggage originating in both those cities had been on both planes." The Canadian Pacific flight had left Vancouver after taking on

---

original pair of Lebanese Shiite hijackers . . . is now known to US authorities." Michael Getler, "Smaller Group Said to Include Military Persons," *Washington Post*, June 21, 1985, A1.

[70] Wills, *First War on Terrorism*, 116.

[71] Robert Merry, "Reagan Vows Determination on Terrorism," *Wall Street Journal*, June 21, 1985, 31; and Robert McCartney, "Gunmen Seen Singling Out US Marines," *Washington Post*, June 21, 1985, A1.

[72] "Chile: Bombings Leave Capital in the Dark," *USA Today*, June 21, 1985, 4; and "Frankfurt Terminal Bomb Kills 3, Leaves Dozens Hurt," *Washington Times*, June 20, 1985, A10.

connecting passengers from Toronto and passengers boarding the Air-India flight in Toronto included 29 connecting passengers from Vancouver.[73]

To those in the administration following these events it was difficult not to recall CIA deputy director Herb Meyer's warning months earlier that the "current outbreak of violence is more than coincidence . . . .I believe it signals the beginning of a new stage in the global struggle between the Free World and the Soviet Union . . . .What we are seeing now is a Soviet-led effort to fight back, in the same sense that the Mafia fights back when law enforcement agencies launch an effective crime-busting program."[74]

The Key Players Convene

Meanwhile, as the Israelis were releasing 31 of the Arab prisoners from Atlit, generating objections from Berri that it was not enough, American intelligence was tracking the movements of the relevant players in the TWA 847 crisis.[75] Hashemi Rafsanjani had traveled to Tripoli on June 21 for a three-day stay with Qaddafi; and Hafez Assad had returned from his visit to Gorbachev in Moscow in time to receive Rafsanjani in Damascus on June 24. There was a strong presumption that the conversations in Tripoli, Damascus, and Moscow would be decisive. Indeed, gathering in Damascus were not only Rafsanjani and Assad, but also Sheik Fadlallah and Nabih Berri.

While Rafsanjani was still in Tripoli, on June 22, Shultz sent a message to Assad. The US government, he said, understood the domestic constraints under which Berri operated and the limits of his influence with Hezbollah, but urged that Assad support him "in moving to release the passengers and crew." It was "the continued detention of passengers, crew and aircraft [that] constitutes a specific impediment to Israel's publicly-expressed policy to release the Atlit prisoners." Then, he said, disclosing his knowledge that Rafsanjani "may soon visit Damascus,"

> we believe that it would be useful . . . [to] urge your Iranian visitors to use their influence with those groups in Lebanon and which Iran is in contact to urge not only the release of the passengers and crew of TWA 847, but also the release of the American, British, and French kidnap victims—some of whom have now been in captivity for more than a year.[76]

---

[73] "Air-India Crash Kills 329," *Baltimore Sun*, June 24, 1985, A1.

[74] Herbert Meyer, "Why Is the World So Dangerous?" Memorandum to the Director of Central Intelligence, November 30, 1983, https://www.cia.gov/library/readingroom/docs/CIA-RDP88T00528R000100080009-5.pdf.

[75] Edward Walsh, "31 Arabs Are Freed by Israel," *Washington Post*, June 25, 1985, A1.

[76] As cited in Wills, *First War on Terrorism*, 118.

Assuming that Iran's influence with Hezbollah would be decisive in gaining the release of the passengers, the secretary also sought to enlist Assad's support in pressuring Iran to gain the release of the seven hostages it was holding in Lebanon. He only achieved part of his objective, because Hezbollah did not control the seven hostages; Mughniyeh's Islamic Jihad did.

When Rafsanjani ended his visit with Assad, he publicly denied Iran's responsibility for the hijacking in unmistakable terms but was silent on the seven hostages. Referring to the hijacking, Rafsanjani said: "had [Iran] known in advance about this kind of action, it would have acted to prevent it." The Iranian leader then met with Sheik Fadlallah, who was also in Damascus to take part in this meeting. It was, of course, Fadlallah who had influence with Mughniyeh, who not only controlled the seven hostages, but also four of the passengers. Berri controlled the rest. Sensing that the meeting of the main figures involved in this matter would be decisive, the Reagan administration imposed a news blackout in Washington, "a sure sign," according to Martin and Walcott, "that the posturing had ended, and the dealing had begun."[77]

Assad had hosted this meeting, no doubt on advice received from Gorbachev, with whom he had spent the previous few days. Assad had control over Beirut and northern Lebanon, by virtue of the extension of Syrian political/military presence and through his agent Nabih Berri; but under his umbrella operated other terrorist groups, such as Hezbollah and Islamic Jihad, that were not under his control. That was where Sheik Fadlallah and Rafsanjani came in. Rafsanjani held sway over Hezbollah, but not Islamic Jihad. If anyone held any influence over Islamic Jihad and its leader, Imad Mughniyeh, it was Sheik Fadlallah, which gave significance to Rafsanjani's meeting with the cleric.

Curiously, there was a major absence in the gathering. If American intelligence was correct in identifying Muammar Qaddafi as the facilitator, if not instigator, of the hijacking, his absence from the gathering in Damascus suggested that the others were not cooperating with him and were prepared to settle. The willingness of the hijackers to release the Greek passengers aboard the plane suggested the Qaddafi-Papandreou tie and added another point to the thesis that the Libyan dictator was the perpetrator.

Qaddafi himself appeared to throw a monkey wrench into the gathering in Damascus. After Rafsanjani left Tripoli, Libyan state radio declared that Libya and Iran had announced plans to "promote 'Islamic revolution' on a worldwide scale and to form an army to 'liberate Palestine.'" Qaddafi's number two, Abdel Salam Jalloud, appeared to level a direct challenge to Syria's dominance in Lebanon, saying "Libya and Iran have decided to work together in order to reunite the Moslem and Palestinian forces in Lebanon."[78]

This was clearly an attempt by Qaddafi to create bad blood between Rafsanjani and Assad. He knew, as did everyone else, that at this moment, in

---

[77] Martin and Walcott, *Best Laid Plans*, 196 and Wills, *First War on Terrorism*, 120.
[78] "Libya and Iran Pledge to 'Liberate Palestine,'" *Wall Street Journal*, June 25, 1985, 34.

Lebanon, Syrian-supported Shiites were attempting to destroy Arafat's PLO in the battle for control of Beirut. Their reconciliation was hardly imminent, or likely. Moreover, Assad had "given ample evidence" that he would not "tolerate intervention in Lebanon by any foreign state, be it Arab, or non-Arab."[79] Furthermore, Rafsanjani's public remark that Iran would have "prevented" the hijacking had Tehran known about it in advance made plain that neither he, nor Assad was working with Libya. Qaddafi's ploy had failed.

Endgames

The unfolding of events is much more clear-cut in retrospect than at the time. Still, the question is: did the Reagan leadership realize that Assad and Rafsanjani had combined to resolve the crisis, and decide to put on a display of its own fortitude to demonstrate to the public that it had determined the outcome? Or were they still uncertain that the crisis was coming to an end and decided to give it a push?

Whatever the truth of the matter, and the timing is unclear, after the NSPG meeting of June 25, the president divulged that he had decided on a series of ever-escalating steps that he hoped would force a resolution of the crisis.[80] White House spokesman Larry Speakes announced that if diplomatic efforts were not successful in freeing the passengers "within the next few days," the president was considering using military and economic means to shut down Beirut airport and blockade Lebanon.

The president, it was said, was hopeful the crisis would be resolved soon, but becoming concerned that the hijacking stalemate was beginning to resemble the Iranian hostage crisis. Although public opinion was still strongly behind the president, there was also growing sentiment that he should "do something." Thus, his decision seemed to be saying to Assad, in particular, "now is the time to act or be tagged with some of the blame and some of the consequences if you fail to do so."[81]

Raising the ante succeeded. The Israelis responded first through a back channel Shultz had set up with Benjamin Netanyahu, Israel's ambassador to the United Nations. Peres sent word to Reagan that a public request was no longer necessary. Israel would do "whatever the United States wanted." Peres's shift opened the door for an exchange of letters formalizing what had come to be known as the "no-deal deal," the agreement for Israel to release the Atlit detainees as soon as the TWA passengers were released.[82]

---

[79] Ibid.

[80] Don Oberdorfer, "Reagan's Shift Risks Forcing His Hand If Deadline Passes," *Washington Post*, June 26, 1985, A17.

[81] Ibid. See also Lou Cannon and John Goshko, "US Weighs Blockading Lebanon, Airport Boycott," *Washington Post*, June 26, 1985, A1.

[82] Martin and Walcott, *Best Laid Plans*, 197-98.

Berri responded the next day, June 26. After freeing one of the passengers for medical reasons, he offered to transfer the remaining 39 to either the French or Swiss embassies in Beirut, or to Damascus, to be held "in escrow" until the Atlit detainees were released. He also demanded that the United States remove all of its ships from the vicinity of Lebanon and pledge not to attack Lebanon once the passengers were released.[83] The president dismissed the escrow idea, as did the Swiss and French, who wanted no part of it. He also rejected the demand to remove US ships, which were in international waters, but felt that the State Department should be prepared to respond positively to the no-retaliation demand, which would not be inconsistent with declared policy toward Lebanon. Shultz, however, procrastinated in issuing a statement.

Assad also responded, sending a message to Reagan affirming that progress was being made. Attempting to insinuate himself into Israeli politics, positing an explicit *quid pro quo*, he asked: "what if the hijackers were informed that Syria would guarantee the release of the Lebanese prisoners after the TWA passengers were freed?" Shultz, in his response to Assad, insisted that there was no connection between the two: "Syria may be confident in expecting the release of the Lebanese prisoners after the freeing of the passengers of TWA 847, without any linkage between the two subjects."[84]

The secretary believed that this was the "moment" when a resolution of the crisis became "imminent." Indeed, he, the president, and vice-president, all sought to parlay the imminent resolution of the TWA crisis into the release of the seven hostages held by Mughniyeh and Islamic Jihad, demanding publicly that they be included with the passengers. It was a long shot, but it played well with the families of the hostages who throughout had pressed the president in public appearances and newspaper ads to take action on behalf of their loved ones.

It was also a long shot because American leaders were still uncertain "whether Islamic Jihad exist[ed] as a coherent organization or is merely a shadowy coalition of extremist Shiites loosely affiliated with Iran . . . . [whose] radicalism contrasts with the more moderate policies of Mr. Berri's Amal faction." They "assume that the captors of the seven, or of some of them, are at least tolerated by Syria, which also is loosely allied with Iran."[85] Nevertheless, the president was not willing to press this demand to the point of fouling resolution of the TWA crisis.

At this delicate moment, Muammar Qaddafi deftly tossed yet another political hand grenade into the mix, which held the potential to blow apart a solution to the crisis at the last moment, and at the very least, to undercut and embarrass Hafez al-Assad. The grenade was lobbed from an unexpected quarter—from Malta by Qaddafi's new ally, the Prime Minister of Malta, Karmenu Mifsud

---

[83] Bernard Gwertzman, "US Weighing Shiite Offer on Moving Hostages," *New York Times*, June 27, 1985, A1.

[84] Shultz, *Turmoil and Triumph*, 664.

[85] Henry Trewhitt, "US Says 7 Seized Earlier Must be Released as Well," *Baltimore Sun*, June 28, 1985, A1.

Bonnici. Qaddafi and Bonnici had signed a treaty of "friendship and cooperation" the previous November, effectively incorporating Malta into the Soviet-Libyan scheme.[86]

Thus, on June 28 an "unsolicited offer of assistance" came from a senior Maltese official to Ambassador James Rentschler. The Maltese official offered to contact and persuade Berri to send the passengers to Israel. Then, they could appeal to the Israelis for their release and the release of the detainees, an appeal which Israel could hardly refuse coming from Americans who had suffered 17 days of captivity.[87]

Rentschler had "no cause to question" the official's motive and thought the offer "well meaning, but greatly muddled." Unfortunately, it was more than that. If adopted, this "Maltese option" would have cut Assad out completely, required the unlikely cooperation between Amal and Israel, turned Berri against Assad, disrupted US cooperation with Syria, and Syrian cooperation with Iran. Coming at the very moment that Assad and Rafsanjani were putting the final touches on a settlement, switching to the Maltese option would have been a very bad mistake, and the US government wisely avoided this trap.[88]

By June 29, after Reagan had telephoned Assad to reiterate his previous assurance that Israel would release the Lebanon detainees once all of the hostages were released, everything seemed to be in order. Passengers were assembled for transport from Beirut to Damascus, while the Pentagon dispatched a C-141 transport plane to Damascus. At the last minute, however, it was discovered that the four hostages being held (we now know) by Mughniyeh as insurance, were not among the passengers.

Mughniyeh insisted that the United States issue to Syria a public guarantee that there would be no retaliation. Without it, the crisis would drag on indefinitely. McFarlane thought that this was more an attempt to make Berri look bad than a genuine fear of an American attack. In any case, it was agreed, "a restatement of the administration's formal policy concerning the sovereignty of Lebanon would be accepted by Hezbollah as a non-retaliation pledge."[89] A statement was promptly issued.

Assad, however, also sought to squeeze the lemon. He wanted Israel to transfer the Atlit detainees to Syria and not simply release them into Lebanon. Shultz maintained that the passengers and detainees were separate issues, and that the detainee matter would have to be discussed after the passengers were released. Assad's ploy may have been intended to disguise the fact that he could not

---

[86] "The Libyan-Maltese Alliance," Joseph Churba, ed., *Focus on Libya: February 1984 to June 1989* (Washington, DC: Pemcon, 1989), 89-92.

[87] Wills, *First War on Terrorism*, 130.

[88] Shultz, *Turmoil and Triumph*, 665, refers implicitly to this episode in noting that many "diplomatic volunteers," had suddenly "emerged from all over the landscape, offering to get involved in 'the release.'"

[89] Wills, *First War on Terrorism*, 132.

produce the four still being held by Mughniyeh and Shultz's response implied an absence of leverage over Israel.

At this point, McFarlane claimed he instructed NSC deputy director Oliver North to contact Rafsanjani—reportedly through Manucher Ghorbanifar—to obtain his assistance in the release of the last four passengers. Although Ledeen relates the story of Ghorbanifar's participation, the timing of North's involvement in the opening to Iran seems premature.[90] In any case, it is not clear that Rafsanjani was able to exert leverage on Mughniyeh, but Assad was.

Humiliated by the failure to finalize the arrangements to which he had agreed, Assad took action. After meeting with representatives from Iran and Hezbollah, he contacted the Iranian Revolutionary Guard Headquarters in Baalbek. To them he issued an ultimatum: "release the hostages or get out of Lebanon" and sent his chief intelligence officer for Lebanese affairs, Brigadier General Ghazi Kanaan, to ensure compliance.[91]

The four remaining passengers were released at just after noon on June 30 and the entire group set out in a Red Cross convoy for Damascus an hour later. Their ordeal was over. Reagan sent a cordial note of thanks to Rafsanjani, but what was to have been a similarly cordial telephone call to Assad turned out badly. The president harangued the Syrian leader mercilessly, repeatedly condemning Syrian policies and demanding that Assad bring the hijackers to justice and produce the seven hostages. Vice President Bush, appalled at Reagan's outburst, sent his own note of thanks to Assad in an attempt to repair the damage of the president's intemperate remarks.[92]

Aftermath

That evening, President Reagan addressed the American people on national television to announce that the 39 passengers were at last free. The president demanded justice and declared that the United States would not rest "until the world community meets its responsibility." And trying one last time to pry the seven hostages from Hezbollah's grip, he called upon "those who helped secure the release of these TWA passengers to show even greater energy and commitment to secure the release of all others held captive in Lebanon." Finally, he put the terrorists on notice, declaring "we will fight back against you in Lebanon and elsewhere."[93]

---

[90] Michael Ledeen, *Perilous Statecraft: An Insider's Account of the Iran Contra Affair* (New York: Scribner, 1988), 114.

[91] Wills, *First War on Terrorism*, 132, and 249-50, n155. Martin and Walcott, *Best Laid Plans*, 200, say the threat was to "get out of the Bekaa Valley."

[92] Ibid., 202, and Lou Cannon, *President Reagan: The Role of a Lifetime* (New York: Simon & Shuster, 1991), 607.

[93] David Hoffman, "39 US Hostages Freed After 17-Day Ordeal; Reagan Vows to 'Fight Back' at Terrorism," *Washington Post*, July 1, 1985, A1.

In remarks to reporters, White House officials then loudly, and brazenly, denied there had been any "deal" with the Israelis. "They had made no deals with Israel to free the Lebanese prisoners it holds." An administration official, evidently Secretary Shultz, declared "at no time, from the first day to the last, did we ever urge, cajole, suggest directly or indirectly by any US official to my knowledge, absolutely never any hint of it from the president, that [the Israelis] alter their policy about no concessions, or, in this case, no releases, at any point . . ."[94]

There could be only one reason administration officials adopted this patently false position. They must have obtained secure knowledge that Israel was not going to carry through on its commitment to release promptly the 766 detainees held in Atlit prison. Denying the existence of any deals meant that the United States could not be held responsible for, or forced to exert pressure on, Israel's subsequent actions.

On July 3, Israel released only 300 detainees from Atlit. As for the remaining 466, Defense Minister Rabin said they would be "released in accordance with developments in South Lebanon." No date was mentioned. In fact, it would not be until September 10, ten more weeks, that the remaining prisoners would finally be released.[95]

If Israel reneged on the promise to release all 766 detainees upon the release of the TWA passengers, the United States, too, reneged on its pledge not to retaliate against Lebanon. On July 2, President Reagan issued orders for the government to "put Beirut International Airport out of action." Washington terminated the once-a-week flight between Beirut and Washington by Lebanon's Middle East Airlines as well as flights by US and Lebanese cargo carriers to Beirut and attempted to influence other countries to do the same.[96]

There was an immediate outcry from Lebanon against the US government's actions. Lebanon's prime minister Rashid Karami lodged a formal protest. Finance Minister Camille Chamoun called upon Washington to "reconsider the measure and not carry it out." Amal leader Nabih Berri bemoaned the fact that the Americans had broken their promise that there would be no reprisals. Islamic Jihad issued a statement proclaiming a great victory over the United States, but also its intent to create a "nightmare" for America, striking at its interests "in the region and throughout the world."[97]

Behind the scenes at this time, the president made three key decisions. First, culminating four months of negotiations, was the press release issued on June 29 announcing that President Reagan and Mikhail Gorbachev had decided

---

[94] Ibid.

[95] Shultz, *Turmoil and Triumph*, 667; and "Release of Captives by Israel Set for Today in Border Zone," *New York Times*, July 3, 1985, A14. Some accounts put the number of detainees at 735.

[96] Nora Boustany, "Lebanese Criticize America," *Washington Post*, July 3, 1985, A14.

[97] Richard Beeston, "Shi'ites Warn More Anti-US Blows Coming," *Washington Times*, July 3, 1985, A1.

to meet in the fall.[98] A few days later it was disclosed that they would meet in Geneva, Switzerland, November 19-21. Their meeting would not be the "well-prepared summit" that Reagan had insisted upon during the first term, but the two leaders would "do more than just get acquainted and shake hands."[99] The timing of the announcement seemed to indicate some connection to the just concluded TWA crisis.

Officials declined to discuss an agenda, though likely topics were arms control and trade relations. Reagan was understood to be interested in "sitting down with the Soviet leader without pre-negotiated agreements to sign," although expectations for direct results were "quite low." The view from the State Department, however, was decidedly more upbeat. A spokesman said, "we believe we can and should solve all outstanding problems in the agenda before us."[100]

Despite his decision to meet with Gorbachev, however, the president took the opportunity of the TWA settlement to point once again to the "close relationship" the Soviets had to terrorist states. In a speech at the Annual Convention of the American Bar Association on July 8, he urged his audience to "look beyond" the spate of recent terrorist acts and "not allow them—as terrible as they are—to obscure an even larger and darker terrorist menace." We must avoid the temptation "to see the terrorist act as simply the erratic work of a small group of fanatics." The terrorist attacks of the past few years, he said, "form a pattern of terrorism that has strategic implications and political goals. And only by moving our focus from the tactical to the strategic perspective, only by identifying the pattern of terror and those behind it, can we hope to put into force a strategy to deal with it."

The president noted the alarming increasing trend of terrorist acts against the United States and its allies. From some five hundred in 1983, "to over 600" in 1984, and "at the current rate, as many as 1,000 acts of terrorism will occur in 1985." The Middle East has been one principal point of focus for these attacks; Western Europe and NATO another.

The president singled out Iran and Libya as supporting "state-approved assassination and terrorism," then added three more states—North Korea, Cuba, and Nicaragua—that were also "actively supporting a campaign of international terrorism against the United States, her allies, and moderate Third World states." These states were not the only ones that support international terrorism, "they are simply the ones that can be most directly implicated." This terrorism, he averred, was "part of a pattern, the work of a confederation of terrorist states." Those involved were being "trained, financed, and directly or indirectly controlled by a

---

[98] John Wallach, "Gorbachev and Reagan Agree on Fall Talks," *Baltimore Sun*, June 29, 1985, A1.
[99] Gary Lee, "Reagan-Gorbachev Meeting Set for Nov. 19-21 in Geneva," *Washington Post*, July 3, 1985, A1.
[100] Ibid.

core group of radical and totalitarian governments—a new, international version of Murder, Incorporated."

"We can be clear on one point," Reagan stated. "These terrorist states are now engaged in acts of war against the Government and people of the United States. And under international law, any state which is the victim of acts of war has the right to defend itself."

Then, toward the end of his speech, the president focused on the Soviet Union. "The question of the Soviet Union's close relationship with almost all of the terrorist states that I have mentioned and the implications of these Soviet ties on bilateral relations with the United States and other democratic nations must be recognized." During the recent hostage crisis, the Soviet government "suggested that the United States was not sincerely concerned about this crisis, but that we were, instead, in the grip of—and I use the Soviets' word here—'hysteria.'" The Soviets also charged that the United States was simply looking for a "pretext" to invade Lebanon. There was, he concluded, a non-Soviet word for "that kind of talk . . . an extremely useful, time-tested original American word, one with deep roots in our rich agricultural and farming tradition." [Laughter][101]

Press coverage of the president's speech noted the conspicuous absence of Syria from the president's list of state-supporters of terrorism, suggesting "Mr. Reagan seemed to be noting the role of Syrian President Hafez Assad in helping to free the TWA hostages." But two accounts, in particular, in the *Wall Street Journal* and the *New York Times*, also curiously omitted one of the president's most important points: the relationship of the Soviet Union to these terrorist states.[102]

Reconstruction of Events

At the outset of the crisis, the administration had assumed that Syria and Iran sponsored the hijack and Hezbollah carried it out. However, as evidence accumulated, it became clear that a quite different interpretation fitted the facts— one more consistent with the prevailing strategic context. It had been Moscow and Qaddafi, not Syria and Iran that were the sponsors of the hijacking, and Imad Mughniyeh, not Hezbollah, who was the perpetrator. In fact, Hafez al-Assad of Syria and Ayatollah Hashemi Rafsanjani of Iran had played critical roles in resolving the crisis both directly and through their surrogates in Lebanon, Amal and Hezbollah.

---

[101] Ronald Reagan, "Remarks at the Annual Convention of the American Bar Association, July 8, 1985," *Public Papers of the Presidents of the United States, Ronald Reagan, 1985*, bk. 2, *June 29 to December 31, 1985* (Washington, DC: US Government Printing Office, 1988), 894-400.

[102] See David Ignatius, "Reagan Warns 5 Nations of US Right to Defend Itself against Acts of Terror," *Wall Street Journal*, July 9, 1985; 3 and Bernard Weinraub, "President Accuses 5 'Outlaw States' Of World Terror," *New York Times*, July 9, 1985, A1.

The Soviets hoped to use the hijack to erect a barrier to US-Iran rapprochement. They enlisted Qaddafi in this scheme because it would also serve his interests. In NSDD-168, April 30, 1985, the Reagan administration had decided to contain Qaddafi by strengthening relations with Libya's neighbors. Improving relations with Algeria was the centerpiece of this strategy.[103] In flying the hijacked plane to Algiers, Qaddafi hoped to disrupt US efforts to improve relations with that country.

To execute the hijacking, Qaddafi enlisted arch terrorist Imad Mughniyeh, who also had an interest. Not only had Mughniyeh been on a terrorist rampage, his brother-in-law, Mustafa Badreddine, was one of the Al-Dawa 17 imprisoned by Kuwait for terrorist acts against American and French embassies in November 1983. Indeed, his younger brother had been killed in a US-sponsored, Lebanese government attempt to kill Sheik Fadlallah in March of 1985. So, for reasons of revenge and the possibility of gaining the freedom of his brother-in-law, Mughniyeh accepted this contract.[104]

Ironically, the hijacking had the opposite effect from that desired by the Russians and Qaddafi. Reagan had decided to strike at Qaddafi and proceed with an opening to Iran. The ongoing political struggle between the president and the new world order faction would greatly affect the way both of these decisions would be executed in the months ahead, but the president's general course had now been set. It is first to the question of the opening to Iran that we now turn.

---

[103] "US Policy Toward North Africa", NSDD 168, April 30, 1985, in Christopher Simpson, *National Security Directives of the Reagan and Bush Administrations: The Declassified History of US Political and Military Policy, 1981-1991* (Boulder: Westview, 1995), 528-32.

[104] See Bergman, *Secret War with Iran*, 72-74, for a full account of Mughniyeh's activities.

Chapter 10

Shultz and
McFarlane Seize Control

The TWA crisis in June 1985 offered a positive way forward toward an opening to Iran for the president. Reagan had made contact with and thanked Rafsanjani for his assistance in resolving the crisis, opening a direct channel of communication to Tehran. At the same time, during the crisis, CIA Director Casey had developed what appeared to be two direct channels of access to the Iranians. It was also increasingly clear that the Iranian leadership sought contact, as it was in desperate need to acquire American weapons to counter the growing strike power of Soviet-supplied Iraq.

The prospect of an imminent opening of direct contact with Iran caused alarm within the new world order faction, whose leaders, Secretary Shultz and National Security Adviser McFarlane, moved quickly to take control. This same prospect greatly concerned Israeli prime minister Shimon Peres, who feared that Israel would be cut out of the action and denied the opportunity of lucrative arms sales. The result was the evolution of a surprising, but temporary coincidence of interests between the new world order faction and Peres.

Shultz and McFarlane realized they could use Israel to preempt Reagan, based on the Israelis' desire for arms sales to Iran, cut out Casey in the process, seize control of the gambit themselves, and derail it. For the new world order faction, however, the cooperation with Peres would be a temporary expedient, lasting only until the objective of derailing the opening to Iran was accomplished.

The Israeli leadership understood fully that American and Israeli interests did not coincide in all respects and that their role in American policy was limited. The Israelis sensed the discord within the Reagan leadership and sought repeatedly to ascertain whether the decision to approve Israeli arms sales was an agreed position within the administration. As a matter of insurance, they sought to draw the United States government more deeply into the arms sales venture, which only added to the complexity and consequences for all concerned.

Cutting Casey Out

Shultz and McFarlane's first tasks were to close off the initiatives Casey had developed, which had reached a promising point by the middle of June coincident with the outbreak of the TWA crisis.[1] Casey's efforts had produced two avenues of direct contacts to Tehran. The first was through Cyrus Hashemi to Mohsen Kangarlu, and the second was through Adnan Khashoggi to Ayatollah Hassan Karoubi. Both contacts, ironically, involved the essential participation of Ghorbanifar; indeed, it was the case that all avenues to Tehran passed through him.

Shultz and his CIA allies quietly sank the Hashemi opening in a bureaucratic haze. After Khashoggi and the Israelis had dropped Hashemi in early April (see chap. 8), he sought to join up with Ghorbanifar and approach Casey on his own. Thus, in mid-June, acting through John Shaheen, a friend of Casey's, Hashemi offered to set up a meeting with "a high-ranking Iranian official" in Western Europe.

After bringing American and Iranian officials together, Hashemi hoped to arrange the purchase of TOW missiles for Iran, facilitate the release of the Al-Dawa prisoners in Kuwait, the hostages in Lebanon, and, in return for all this, obtain a nullification of the charges against him as a result of his entrapment in an FBI sting the previous year. Although Shaheen whittled down the proposal he sent to Casey to simply arranging a meeting with a high-ranking Iranian official, he obviously had informed the director of Hashemi's larger agenda because Casey's report of June 17 to the CIA's Near East Division Chief carried the subject heading: "release of the hostages."[2]

---

[1] George Shultz, *Turmoil and Triumph* (New York: Macmillan, 1993), 793, claims that his knowledge of the Iran affair "amounted to a series of isolated fleeting moments," information that was "fragmentary at best and perhaps was not even representative of what had in fact happened." However, Lawrence Walsh, the independent counsel, came to a much different conclusion. According to Walsh, *Final Report of the Independent Counsel for Iran-Contra Matters*, vol. 1 (Washington, DC: United States Court of Appeals for the District of Columbia Circuit, August 4, 1993), 325-26, contrary to their public testimonies, Shultz and McFarlane were in close contact throughout 1985 and 1986. Inside the State Department, Shultz and eight of his top aides had "significant contemporaneous knowledge" of the Iran initiative. Shultz, Deputy Secretary John Whitehead and Under Secretary Michael Armacost "met daily to keep each other informed." Executive Secretary Nicholas Platt and Shultz's assistant Charles Hill kept a "detailed handwritten record" of the secretary's activities. Assistant Secretary Richard Murphy, Deputy Assistant Secretary Arnold Raphel, and Ambassador Robert Oakley were referred to as the "floating directorate" that kept track of "US and Israeli contacts with Iranians and arms shipments to Iran during 1985 and 1986." Shultz misrepresented his "contemporaneous knowledge" of events to the Tower Board, the Senate-House investigators, and in his memoirs. It was only five years later that Walsh and his team unearthed the data of Shultz's and McFarlane's close monitoring of events.

[2] "Casey memo 6/17/85 to CIA Chief of the Near East Division, Subj: Release of the Hostages, C-8965-66," *Report of the Congressional Committees Investigating the Iran-Contra Affair* (Washington, DC: US Government Printing Office, 1987), 171 [Cited hereafter as *Congressional Report on the Iran-Contra Affair*.]

The Near East Chief passed on Casey's memo to Under Secretary Richard Murphy at the State Department on June 22 with the notation that Casey was "very anxious to move ahead" on a meeting with the Iranian official, with no mention of hostages, or arms sales. Murphy's memo to Under Secretary Michael Armacost carried the subject heading: "Possible Iranian Contact." Armacost approved a plan for a meeting two days later.[3]

In "early July," however, when Hashemi identified the participants in the proposed meeting as "Deputy Prime Minister" [Mohsen Kangarlu], referred to as the "Second Iranian," and Manucher Ghorbanifar, described as "ranking intelligence officer," the CIA balked. Willing to meet with Kangarlu, the agency refused to "do business" with Ghorbanifar, the deemed "fabricator." Although some effort was made to arrange a meeting with Kangarlu, it led nowhere.[4] It is apparent that, despite Casey's expressed desire to "move ahead" on this contact, highly placed leaders at the CIA and the State Department blocked a meeting with a deputy prime minister of Iran on the grounds that his interlocutor was an undesirable character.[5]

Meanwhile, at about the same time that the new world order faction was sinking the Hashemi approach, Shultz took on the task of torpedoing the draft NSDD on Iran. On June 29, just as the TWA crisis was being resolved with Rafsanjani's crucial and timely assistance, the secretary sent in his "comments" on the draft NSDD. Couched in a pseudo-academic, almost professorial tone, Shultz thought the draft constructive and perceptive, but disagreed "with one point in the analysis and one specific recommendation." The secretary then proceeded to attack the proposed new policy in its entirety. He objected to the central policy recommendation that "Western friends and allies" provide arms to Iran and insisted that the arms ban remain in force. Even if the draft were revised to reflect this concern, he wanted "to see the draft again before it is put in final form."[6]

He also disputed the interpretation that the Soviets were "better positioned" than the United States to take advantage of a succession struggle. He thought that the "limits" on the Iranian-Soviet relationship were "underplayed," although "hints of possible improvements in Iranian-Soviet relations [were] worrisome." In his view, the "Soviets, while conscious of the strategic prize Iran constitutes, have other important regional relations and interests." His formulation

---

[3] Ibid., "Richard Murphy memo, 6/22/85, to Armacost. Subj: Possible Iranian Contact, S-3812-13."

[4] CIA memos dated July 9, 15, and 23, on Shaheen, Hashemi, and a possible meeting with the "Second Iranian," indicate that the effort to arrange a meeting fizzled out by the end of July. *Congressional Report on the Iran-Contra Affair*, 171-72.

[5] William Rempel, "Iran Arms Dealers May Use Secret CIA Links as Defense," *Los Angeles Times*, August 4, 1988, C1.

[6] Shultz to McFarlane, "US Policy toward Iran: Comments on Draft NSDD," June 29, 1985 (declassified and released, July 21, 1987), John G. Tower et al., *Report of the President's Special Review Board: February 26, 1987* (Washington, DC: US Government Printing Office, 1987), B-9.

was vague, but the implication was that the Soviets had other interests that took priority over Iran:

> The draft NSDD appears to exaggerate current anti-regime sentiment and Soviet advantages over us in gaining influence. Most importantly, its proposal that we permit or encourage a flow of Western arms to Iran is contrary to our interest both in containing Khomeinism and in ending the excesses of this regime. We should not alter this aspect of our policy when groups with ties to Iran are holding US hostages in Lebanon. I therefore disagree with the suggestion that our efforts to reduce arms flows to Iran should be ended.[7]

In these "comments" Shultz, for the first time in all of the discussions regarding an opening to Iran, raised the issue of "groups with ties to Iran . . . holding US hostages in Lebanon." This was an obvious reference to the last-minute glitch in the TWA hijack that Rafsanjani had assisted in resolving, but which had had no impact on gaining the release of the other seven American hostages still in captivity. In other words, Shultz sought by this reference to dismiss prospects of an opening to Iran.

His view of "our fundamental policy goal," however, was crystal clear. While claiming that the goal was to "wind down" the Iran-Iraq war, which meant stalemate, all understood that the Soviets were rapidly arming Iraq and that there was "a steady decline in Iran's military capability." The inevitable outcome of these trends was obvious—an Iraqi victory, a policy result Shultz had been supporting for over two years.

Shultz also ignored the obvious consequence of blocking arms shipments to Iran—that a successful embargo would force the Iranians into Moscow's arms, if only for self-protection. In short, the essence of Shultz's "comments" was to insist on a policy course that would only result in Iran's defeat and slide into the Soviet sphere—the very outcome that the NSDD warned against. Once again, the issue was starkly strategic. Should the United States attempt to bring Iran back into the Western camp, as the president desired, or back Iraq against Iran, as the new world order establishment demanded?

Shultz's opposition stymied the formal attempt to enact a change of policy toward Iran. From the hindsight of over four decades, the judgment of history clearly is that this was a monumental strategic blunder; a blunder, moreover, based upon a terrible error in judgment that withdrawal from Iran (and other concessions) was a necessary condition for détente with the Soviet Union. Finally, it overlooked the fact that the Soviet Union was unable to match the qualitative surge in American military power then under way and was straining mightily to keep its very regime intact.

---

[7] Ibid.

Preempting Direct
Contact by Cutting the Israelis In

By the end of June, the Iranian regime was becoming increasingly desperate to acquire weapons from the United States to counter the growing Soviet-supplied Iraqi armed forces. The one-time, McFarlane authorized, Israeli shipment of American weapons in mid-May had led to nothing. Therefore, sometime in the third week of June, Ayatollah Khomeini agreed to a change in policy toward the United States, appointing a five-man committee to manage a new approach.[8]

Appointed to the committee were Rafsanjani, as chairman; members were Mir Hossein Mousavi, the prime minister; Mohsen Rafiq Doust, minister in charge of the revolutionary guards; Mohsen Rezai, commander of the revolutionary guards; and Ahmed Khomeini, the Ayatollah's son. Mohsen Kangarlu, deputy prime minister and chief of intelligence, would be added soon afterward.

The Iranian decision was to authorize Ghorbanifar to reach out to the Americans through their Israeli contacts, Kimche, Nimrodi and Schwimmer, and Saudi middleman Khashoggi. Within days, on June 19, Ghorbanifar met with them in Hamburg to propose the sale of 100 TOWs, claiming that the sale would be followed by release of the American hostages.[9] His timing, however, could not have been worse, as Shultz and President Reagan repeatedly declared during the TWA hijacking—under way at that moment—that the United States would make no deals with terrorists.

For Iran, the hostages had served the purpose of drawing US attention, but they were now an obvious impediment. (They would become useful leverage again once negotiations/discussions began.) Hostage-taking was not all done by pro-Iranian terrorists as Shultz incessantly maintained. As we have seen, some, if not most, were taken by Imad Mughniyeh, who did contract work for a number of state sponsors, including Qaddafi and the Russians. It is not at all clear that the American leadership, or analysts in the intelligence agencies, understood the distinction between Hezbollah and Islamic Jihad at this point, or that Imad Mughniyeh was the terrorist responsible for the recent hijackings.[10] The plain fact

---

[8] Samuel Segev, *The Iranian Triangle: The Untold Story of Israel's Role in the Iran-Contra Affair* (New York: Free Press, 1988), 147. See also, "The Ayatollah's Big Sting," US News and World Report, March 30, 1987, 18-28, which places this meeting in January 1985.

[9]*Report of the Congressional Committees Investigating the Iran-Contra Affair* (Washington, DC: US Government Printing Office, 1987), 166. [Cited hereafter as *"Congressional Report on the Iran-Contra Affair."*]

[10] According to Ronen Bergman, *The Secret War with Iran* (New York: Free Press, 2007), 96, Mughniyeh was an unfathomable mystery to Israeli intelligence, which could not determine where he "fit in," in the terrorist infrastructure of the Middle East.

was that Iran did not "control" Mughniyeh and therefore could not deliver the hostages.

In any case, the Iranians shifted their approach to get around the hostage impediment. As we have seen, Iranian parliament speaker Rafsanjani was instrumental in obtaining the release of the TWA passengers. Now, using the Ghorbanifar-Israeli-Saudi channel, they proposed direct contact with the American leadership. The Iranian *démarche* came on July 1 in the form of a 47-page analysis of the internal Iranian political situation passed by Adnan Khashoggi to key interested leaders, including King Fahd of Saudi Arabia, King Hussein of Jordan, President Mubarak of Egypt, Prime Minister Peres of Israel, and US national security adviser Robert McFarlane. In his cover letter to McFarlane, Khashoggi said the analysis had been written in part by "a single senior individual . . . in charge of Iranian intelligence in Western Europe."[11]

The detailed analysis described a leadership in turmoil, with three broad but fluid factions maneuvering to succeed Khomeini. None questioned the legitimacy of the regime or sought to reverse the Islamic revolution. However, there were differences with respect to external relations. "Moderates" led by Hassan Karoubi, and "pragmatists" led by Rafsanjani were willing to cooperate with the West against the Soviet Union, as opposed to "extremists" led by President Ali Khamenei and Prime Minister Mir Hossein Mousavi, who insisted on uncompromising domestic policies, the exportation of the Islamic revolution, and, presumably, cooperation with the Soviets.[12]

Khashoggi's cover letter was an invitation to the United States, through pursuit of a "wise and flexible" policy, to attempt to influence the outcome of the struggle. Sensing an opportunity, Prime Minister Peres moved quickly. Apparently alone among the four heads of state who received Khashoggi's packet, Peres immediately dispatched Kimche, who was traveling to Washington on foreign ministry business, to meet with McFarlane to offer a way forward.

Kimche met with McFarlane on July 3, and although McFarlane had the communication from Khashoggi in hand when they met, there is no suggestion in the record that it was discussed. Of course, it must have been discussed, as Iran was the purpose of Kimche's visit. Kimche said that "Israel had contacts with Iranians who had direct access to leading figures in Iran's political establishment and who had expressed a desire eventually to meet official American representatives on an unofficial basis." He claimed that McFarlane "enthusiastically encouraged us to continue these contacts," but warned that "in

---

[11] Theodore Draper, *A Very Thin Line: The Iran-Contra Affairs* (New York: Hill and Wang, 1991), 152, believes this "senior individual" to have been Ghorbanifar, but it is not clear who he was. Ghorbanifar was not, as Draper acknowledges, "in charge of Iranian intelligence in Western Europe." Moreover, Draper's source, Khashoggi, in a cover letter to McFarlane, *Congressional Report on the Iran-Contra Affair*, Appendix B, vol. 11, 190, does not identify the senior individual and says he is in contact with several Iranian officials.

[12] Segev, *Iranian Triangle*, 154-55.

all probability," there would come a point where "we would be faced with a request for some American arms."[13]

McFarlane, as is the case on almost every issue, has provided contradictory accounts. To the Tower Board he reinforced Kimche's view, but added a point that Kimche omitted, namely that the Iranians believed that "they could influence the Hizballah in Lebanon to release the hostages" and wanted to know where to deliver them.[14] In his memoir, published last among all of the publications of those involved in the events, he went further. He claimed that Kimche intimated that if the US agreed, the Israelis were willing to assassinate Khomeini and "accelerate matters" in the region. McFarlane claims to have rejected the suggestion out of hand. "We cannot engage with you in an enterprise in which anyone's purpose is to assassinate the Ayatollah."[15]

McFarlane recounts that he informed Reagan of his meeting with Kimche "a day or so" later and that the president was especially keen on the possibilities of opening up a dialogue with the Iranians. "Gosh, that's great news," he reportedly said. McFarlane claimed, however, there was "a precondition." In getting back to Kimche, McFarlane said that before "opening any dialogue . . . we would need evidence of their genuine power in the form of the release of all our hostages."[16] McFarlane's account thus connected an opening to Iran with release of the hostages, but not arms for hostages, and assumed that Iran could deliver the hostages.

There are reasons to doubt McFarlane's account of a conversation with Reagan "a day or so" after his meeting with Kimche, or at any time before he spoke to the president in the hospital on July 18 recovering from an operation on his colon. First, on July 8, in an address before the American Bar Association, the president pointedly singled out Iran and Libya as supporting "state-approved assassination and terrorism," which he considered to be "acts of war against the Government and people of the United States."[17] Surely, the possibility of a dialogue with Iran would have caused him to temper his statement, if McFarlane had just informed him of Iran's inquiry.

Second, Reagan, in his largely ghostwritten memoir, even though clearly designed to comport with the new world order rendition of this history, completely

---

[13] David Kimche, *The Last Option: After Nasser, Arafat & Saddam Hussein* (London: Weidenfeld and Nicolson, 1991), 211.

[14] John G. Tower et al., *Report of the President's Special Review Board: February 26, 1987* (Washington, DC: US Government Printing Office, 1987), B-14. [Hereafter cited as *Tower Report.*]

[15] Robert C. McFarlane, *Special Trust* (New York: Cadell & Davies, 1994), 20-21. Kimche denied that he discussed a plot to kill Khomeini. See Walter Pincus, "Reagan Ex-Aide Details Start of Iran-Contra in Book," *Washington Post*, September 11, 1994, A11.

[16] McFarlane, *Special Trust*, 23-24.

[17] David Ignatius, "Reagan Warns 5 Nations of US Right to Defend Itself against Acts of Terror," *Wall Street Journal*, July 9, 1985, 3.

ignored the episode. Instead, he says "during Bud McFarlane's visit to Bethesda Naval Hospital [on July 18] and in following meetings, he informed me that representatives of Israel had contacted him secretly to pass on information from a group of moderate, politically influential Iranians."[18] Reagan thus dated his introduction to the Iran story nearly two weeks after McFarlane indicates.

Third, Don Regan, chief of staff, also disputed McFarlane's claim to have told Reagan of his conversation with Kimche before he entered the hospital. Regan was present during McFarlane's daily briefings of the president and would have been privy to such a conversation, if it had taken place. After Reagan had entered the hospital, McFarlane demanded that he be permitted to see him immediately after his operation. According to Regan " . . . if he had [told the president earlier] I don't know why he would have felt such a sense of urgency ("I've just got to see the president") to tell him the same thing a second time."[19]

Greed, Politics, and the New World Order Faction

The chronology of events is particularly important here, as the period between Kimche's meeting with McFarlane and McFarlane's meeting with the president brackets the moment when the new world order faction saw an opportunity to seize control of the Iran initiative, divert it away from direct contact with the Iranians, and sink it with an arms-for-hostages deal. According to Segev, "Kimche left Washington empty-handed," but while in Paris on a stopover en route to Jerusalem "received a telegram from Peres instructing him to proceed to Geneva."[20]

In Geneva, July 7, Kimche met with Schwimmer, Nimrodi, Ghorbanifar, and Khashoggi and was informed that Ayatollah Hassan Karoubi would be in Hamburg the next day to dedicate a Muslim study house. They all proceeded to Hamburg the next day for a meeting with Karoubi at the *Vier Jahreszeiten* (Four Seasons) Hotel. The import of the Iranian cleric's view was that his people wanted "a free and independent Iran with good relations with all, but especially with the United States." Kimche averred that Israel "would like to serve as a bridge . . . between you and the West." Karoubi declared, "we must set a common goal and frame appropriate methods of action" and promised to "submit a detailed proposal in writing that can serve as a basis for discussion between us." [21]

After hearing the results of their meeting, Prime Minister Peres, acting in accordance with the channel set up by McFarlane, sent Schwimmer to Washington on July 11 to meet with Ledeen.[22] Schwimmer carried with him a

---

[18] Ronald Reagan, *An American Life* (New York: Simon & Shuster, 1990), 504. *Congressional Report on the Iran-Contra Affair*, 167, supports the president's view.

[19] Don Regan, *For the Record* (New York: Harcourt, Brace, Jovanovich, 1988), 20.

[20] Segev, *Iranian Triangle*, 155.

[21] Ibid., 157, 159.

[22] Michael Ledeen, *Perilous Statecraft: An Insider's Account of the Iran Contra Affair* (New York: Scribner, 1988), 119, notes that during Kimche's meeting with McFarlane

transcript of the meeting with Karoubi and urged Ledeen to meet with Karoubi himself through Ghorbanifar, their interlocutor.

Ledeen left a message for McFarlane regarding his meeting with Schwimmer, saying:

> It is indeed a message from [the] Prime Minister of Israel; it is a follow-on to the private conversation he had last week when David Kimche was here. It is extremely urgent and extremely sensitive and it regards the matter he told David he was going to raise with the President. The situation has fundamentally changed for the better . . . . This is the real thing and it is just wonderful news.[23]

McFarlane's desk calendar confirmed that he met with Ledeen two days later during which the latter undoubtedly passed on the transcript of the meeting with Karoubi.[24] As shown in the transcript, Karoubi asked for nothing but a high-level dialogue with the United States. He made no request to purchase arms, or reference to the hostages.[25]

But the Israelis, Ghorbanifar, and Khashoggi were not satisfied with merely establishing a high-level dialogue for the United States. Their interest was in making money, in the short run by selling arms, and, beyond that, to becoming major commercial brokers to benefit from the financial bonanza that would flow when Iran's contacts with the West had been reestablished. Thus, according to Ledeen, it was Ghorbanifar who put together the package that included not only the establishment of high-level contacts and development of a "dialogue," but also permission for "Israel to sell several hundred TOW antitank missiles to the Iranians," which would gain the release of the hostages.[26]

McFarlane, on the other hand, says that it was "the Israelis" who pressed for some "tangible show" of the Iranians' ability to deliver and the Iranians who said they could obtain the release of the seven hostages held in Lebanon, but would need to show "some gain," in the form "specifically" of "delivery from Israel of 100 TOW missiles."[27]

There is little doubt that McFarlane understood the distinction between opening a "dialogue" and trading arms for hostages and absolutely no doubt about who wanted what. He immediately sent a message to Shultz, who was traveling in Australia, combining all three elements—dialogue, arms sales, and hostage

---

on July 3, the Israeli "asked him whether the American government was truly interested in pursuing the matter [of an opening to Iran] and, if so, whether I was the proper channel. McFarlane had said yes to both questions, and Schwimmer had accordingly flown to the United States to brief me."

[23] *Tower Report*, B-16, n.10.

[24] Ibid.

[25] For the transcript, see Segev, *Iranian Triangle*, 157-59.

[26] Ledeen, *Perilous Statecraft, 118.*

[27] *Tower Report*, B-16-17.

release—into one package the way Ghorbanifar had, although stating that "the larger purpose would be the opening of the private dialogue with a high level American official and a sustained discussion of US Iranian relations."[28] The NSC adviser favored "going ahead," but would "abide fully by your [Shultz's] decisions."

Shultz replied immediately, instructing him "we should make a tentative show of interest without commitment." The secretary's immediate priorities, however, were the hostages, not a strategic opening. He did not "think we could justify turning our backs on the prospects of gaining the release of the other seven hostages and perhaps developing an ability to renew ties with Iran under a more sensible regime . . . " Finally, wanting to keep knowledge of this proposal secret from other members of the administration, especially Casey, the secretary told McFarlane to "manage this probe personally, but the two of us should discuss its sensitivity and the likelihood of disclosure after my return." He said to tell Schwimmer that "you and I are in close contact and full agreement every step of the way."[29]

Shultz closed his message to McFarlane with the startling observation that conveying their "full agreement" was "all the more important in view of the present lack of unity and full coordination on the Israeli side." Was this reference to the obvious discord among Peres, Rabin, and Shamir? If so, it was quite ironic considering the deep split between the president and the new world order faction. Discussing this message in his memoir, Shultz observed, "McFarlane could be deceived into unwise actions, I feared."[30] Shultz, in other words, would decide.

Shultz's reply to McFarlane was extraordinary, to say the least. Just two weeks before, in his comments on the draft NSDD on Iran, he had railed against changing policy to permit "Western friends and allies," which emphatically meant Israel, to sell arms to Iran as "contrary to our interests." Yet, here he was expressing his "full agreement" to this very proposal! Shultz's concern about McFarlane being deceived was misplaced. In fact, McFarlane was more the deceiver, than the deceived. Immediately upon receiving Shultz's reply, he began pressing Regan to arrange a meeting for him with the president.

The problem was that the president had entered Bethesda Naval Hospital on Friday, July 12, to have a small polyp removed from his colon. During the procedure doctors discovered a much larger, cancerous polyp, and the president decided to have it removed immediately. Therefore, the next day, Saturday July 13, the president underwent a second operation. This time because it was a more invasive procedure it was decided to invoke the 25th amendment designating George Bush acting president during the hours Reagan was incapacitated.

Following Reagan's successful surgery, and he reclaimed his presidential powers, Nancy Reagan decided to prohibit all visitors except for

---

[28] Ibid., B-17.
[29] Ibid.
[30] Shultz, *Turmoil and Triumph*, 795.

herself and chief of staff Don Regan, while the president recuperated. Thus, the president was incommunicado during the next four days, much to McFarlane's discomfiture as he importuned Regan daily with pleas that he had "just got to see the president."[31] His urgency increased with the arrival on July 16 of the memorandum promised earlier by Karoubi. The memo was quickly passed to Ledeen, who immediately turned it over to McFarlane.[32] Ledeen left for a trip to Israel the evening of July 16, which was partly a family vacation, but also partly another mission for McFarlane to meet with Ghorbanifar.[33]

Karoubi said that Iran faced two possible futures if current trends continued. Iran would either descend into a Lebanon-like chaos or become a Soviet "puppet state." To avert either of these outcomes, "we must immediately begin to bring together the moderate and patriotic forces of pro-Western sympathies who oppose the extremists and the anti-Western Left." Within a month he promised to "send you the final plans . . . and details of the things we need . . . ." For the moment, in anticipation of the coming presidential and Majlis elections, Karoubi sought "some financial aid," for distribution among the clergy in Qom, merchants in the bazaar, and in south Tehran. Finally, to demonstrate his credibility, he appended a list of "people who support our line."[34]

What was striking about the memo was the focus on political cooperation to the complete exclusion of any other matter, let alone request for arms, or any discussion of hostages. At this point, Karoubi only wanted American financial support for pro-Western candidates in the coming elections. Successful election of pro-Western candidates held the potential for a peaceful turn in Iran and McFarlane and Shultz knew that Reagan would respond to this plea with alacrity. Thus, it was vital for them to head this proposal off at all costs and as soon as possible.

Karoubi's memo gave McFarlane added incentive to pester Regan for an appointment to see the president. Finally, on the morning of July 18, Nancy Reagan relented, agreed that the president was sufficiently recovered to begin receiving visitors, and McFarlane was admitted. Only the president, McFarlane, and Regan were present. What was discussed is in dispute and for good reason, for the hospital meeting marked the beginning of the long road to scandal surrounding arms for hostages.

---

[31] It was during these days, too, that both Secretary of Defense Weinberger and CIA Director Casey sent in their responses to McFarlane regarding the NSDD Draft on Iran, Weinberger, on July 16, opposing and Casey, on July 18, supporting it.

[32] *Congressional Report on the Iran-Contra Affair*, 167.

[33] Segev, *Iranian Triangle*, 161-63. Ledeen, *Perilous Statecraft*, 119, obscures the memo transfer, not to mention its content, by claiming that McFarlane saw the president on July 16, a falsehood. As we will see below, it is clear that McFarlane lied to him.

[34] Segev, *Iranian Triangle*, 162-63.

McFarlane's Bait and Switch on Reagan

According to Don Regan's notes and recollection, during a conversation lasting no more than "ten or twelve minutes," McFarlane "asked the President if he was interested in talking to the Iranians." He reasoned "this was a good idea because the United States ought to be talking to the Iranians about the future so as to have established contacts if and when a new government came into being in Tehran." The hostages were "discussed in a general way," in the sense that "the Iranians, who had already been helpful in connection with the TWA hijacking might be disposed to be helpful in other situations if we were more friendly to them."[35]

But, insisted Regan, "there is nothing in my notes or in my memory to suggest that the idea of swapping arms for hostages was mentioned by either man on this occasion." Any mention of such a scheme, he continued, "would have made me prick up my ears."

> It hardly seems likely that an entirely new policy, involving a brusque departure from past practices and established principle—and bringing in a third country, Israel, as a middleman in a secret arms sale—could have been decided on in such a brief encounter.[36]

Thus, according to Regan, McFarlane asked the president if he was interested in a dialogue with the Iranians, not to authorize an Israeli arms sale, or a swap of arms for hostages. The president was, indeed, interested in "talking to the Iranians," and instructed McFarlane to "go ahead. Open it up."[37]

But that is not what McFarlane did. Here was the bait and switch. Although asking and receiving permission from the president to open up a "dialogue" with the Iranians, McFarlane immediately informed Kimche that, "in principle," the president had approved "the sale of TOWs by Israel."[38] In short, although the president had authorized only talks, McFarlane authorized Israeli arms sales, and he did so as part of the new world order scheme to prevent an opening to Iran.[39] Furthermore, he made no record of the decision because it would document his perfidy.

---

[35] Regan, *For the Record*, 20-21.

[36] Ibid., 21.

[37] *Tower Report*, citing Regan's testimony, B-16.

[38] *Congressional Report on the Iran-Contra Affair*, 167. Caspar W. Weinberger, *Fighting for Peace: Seven Critical Years in the Pentagon* (New York: Warner Books, 1990), 369, comes to the same conclusion, observing that McFarlane "took it upon himself to advise the Israelis it was all right for them to sell the weapons we had furnished them . . ."

[39] Ibid. Weeks after the scandal erupted, on November 21, 1986, McFarlane claimed that the president was "all for letting the Israelis do anything they wanted at the very

What is even more remarkable about this sequence is that McFarlane already had authorized Ledeen to convey this message to the Israelis *two days before* he met with the president in the hospital. The point centers on the confusion regarding when McFarlane actually saw the president. Although the fact is clearly established that McFarlane saw the president on the morning of July 18, several sources say that the meeting took place two days earlier, on the 16th, which is manifestly not the case, but essential to make the claim that McFarlane's instructions to Ledeen were based on authorization from the president. Ledeen recounts that he and his family

> Were scheduled to leave for Israel on the evening of July 16th . . . . The president was facing surgery at Bethesda Naval Hospital that very morning. McFarlane undertook to discuss this sensitive issue with Reagan prior to my departure, and did so on the morning of the 16th, after the president's surgery. *As McFarlane described it to me early that afternoon,* it was the first matter raised with Reagan after he emerged from anesthesia, and I suspect that this is one reason why the president's memory about the discussion has always been rather fuzzy.[40]

The dating conflict is best explained by yet another of McFarlane's unilateral actions, all part of the bait and switch. He informed Ledeen that he had seen the president when he obviously had not, in order to allow him to travel with the "authority" of the president to Israel. Ledeen had no means of verifying, and no reason to doubt, the word of his chief. McFarlane's need to "cover" this action with an actual conferral of presidential authority, however, was what undoubtedly lay behind his insistent demands to see the president.[41]

McFarlane's go-ahead message to Kimche for arms sales, along with Ledeen's arrival, no later than July 18, precipitated a flurry of activity over the next twelve days, and while the sequence of events is not completely clear, the substance is crystal clear. Ledeen reinforced McFarlane's authorization for arms sales and Kimche immediately alerted Peres's team, Khashoggi, and Ghorbanifar.

Toward the end of the month, Khashoggi set up a meeting in Hamburg, reportedly attended by "Ghorbanifar, Kimche, other Iranians and Israelis, and two Americans, possibly from the National Security Council." The Israelis were most likely Kimche and Nimrodi (Schwimmer was on a business trip in China), but the

---

first briefing in the hospital," but he was never able to produce a shred of evidence to substantiate this claim. Nor does the extant record support it.

[40] Ledeen, *Perilous Statecraft*, 119, emphasis added.

[41] Ledeen was not the only one to claim that McFarlane's meeting with the president occurred on the 16th. Draper, *Very Thin Line*, 156, also made this claim because it was the only way to connect the presumed chain of authority—from Reagan to McFarlane to Ledeen.

identities of the "other Iranians . . . and two Americans" is unknown.[42] Ledeen also mentions a Hamburg meeting, affirms that Kimche attended, but says that it occurred before he arrived in Israel.[43] One must question how he knew. Did the Israelis tell him, or was Ledeen one of the Americans at the meeting? Moreover, there was no reason to hold a meeting until "authorization" had been given by the president, and that did not happen until July 18.

The Israeli historical chronology says that unidentified "Israelis," presumably Kimche and Nimrodi, but not Ledeen, met with Ghorbanifar in Israel on July 25 where the essential *quid pro quo* of arms for hostages was worked out. They then briefed Ledeen separately on July 28.[44] Ledeen claims that he met with them all, including Schwimmer, on July 29.[45] Although Ledeen denies that he was sent to negotiate in any way and says that his "role was always . . . to attend meetings, listen, ask questions, find out as much as I could, and then report back," it is clear that he participated in a negotiation.[46]

According to Segev, during their meeting "Ghorbanifar made the link between supplying weapons and freeing the hostages explicit," describing it as "a necessary test to prove the sincerity of both sides." Kimche said "Israel would be ready to supply the missiles only if secrecy could be guaranteed and the hostages freed." Ghorbanifar said realistically that while some hostages would be released within "two or three weeks," the Iranians would keep some others as a "bargaining card."[47]

Having reached the fundamental decision that weapons would come before a dialogue, there was a tacit agreement to drop Ayatollah Hassan Karoubi, who wanted no arms, and deal with Mohsen Kangarlu, who did. Thus, Ghorbanifar called Kangarlu to brief him on the proposed arrangement. The Iranian official thought the release of Buckley would be a fair exchange for the weapons, but the Israeli side made it plain that the weapons would have to be paid for in advance.[48]

When Kimche reported back to Peres, Shamir, and Rabin on the proposed deal, Rabin objected to dealing with Ledeen, a messenger. He observed that from his experience as ambassador to the United States, "he knew that it was best to negotiate with the decision-makers and not with their occasional messengers." In short, Rabin insisted on a "more unequivocal US

---

[42] Scott Armstrong et al., *The Chronology: The Documented Day-by-Day Account of the Secret Military Assistance to Iran and the Contras* (New York: Warner Books, 1987), 137.

[43] Ledeen, *Perilous Statecraft*, 121.

[44] *Congressional Report on the Iran-Contra Affair*, 167.

[45] "Ledeen Deposition," *Congressional Report on the Iran-Contra Affair*, Appendix B, vol. 15, 978.

[46] Ibid., 974.

[47] Segev, *Iranian Triangle*, 164-65.

[48] Ibid., 165. Buckley, it was later learned, had died on June 3.

authorization."[49] When informed of Rabin's reaction, Ledeen replied, "the Israelis had already received sufficient authorization from the response that the president had given in the hospital." Nevertheless, "the Israelis were insistent on confirmation."[50]

According to Ledeen, afterward on July 30, he and the Israelis met and decided to report immediately to McFarlane. However, Ledeen explained that he did not want to cut short his vacation, and since Kimche was going to Washington anyway, it was agreed that Kimche would "report on these conversations to McFarlane."[51] Much of what Ledeen claims may be true, but its essence was not. As it was the Israeli leadership that insisted on direct confirmation from McFarlane, Kimche would have been assigned the task of obtaining it regardless of what Ledeen did. Thus, on August 2, Kimche flew to Washington "to meet with McFarlane and to obtain the specific US position on Israel's sale of the TOWs."[52]

Meanwhile, Ghorbanifar was also active. Following the meetings, he proceeded to Marbella, Spain, to meet with Khashoggi. Roy Furmark, New York oil consultant and Casey's "go-between" with Khashoggi, was present on Khashoggi's yacht moored off Marbella when Ghorbanifar arrived. No one else was there. The Iranian was excited about the prospect of an Israeli arms deal with Iran, but, given the mistrust of the two parties for each other, it would be necessary to provide outside "bridge financing" for the transaction. Khashoggi readily agreed to provide the money, offering to make a million-dollar prepayment.[53]

After their meeting, Furmark and Ghorbanifar flew to Tel Aviv to inform the Israelis of Khashoggi's willingness to provide the million-dollar bridge money. Attending this meeting were Nimrodi, Schwimmer, and, for the first time, Prime Minister Peres's counterterrorism adviser, Amiram Nir, but not Kimche, who was on his way to Washington to put the final piece of the proposal into place—approval of President Reagan.[54]

Kimche had traveled to Washington expressly to obtain approval for the proposal worked out over the previous few weeks, the proposal that McFarlane himself—through Ledeen—had initiated. Before they agreed to engage in the proposed arms sale, however, the Israeli leadership wanted several assurances. They wanted Washington's confirmation that the proposed plan was indeed strategic, that is, aimed at an opening with Iran, and not merely a tactical maneuver to gain the release of Buckley and the other hostages; that the plan had the "agreement of the president and his cabinet"; and that the president agreed to

---

[49] Segev, *Iranian Triangle*, 166.

[50] *Congressional Report on the Iran-Contra Affair*, 167.

[51] "Ledeen Deposition," *Congressional Report on the Iran-Contra Affair*, Appendix B, vol. 15, 986.

[52] *Congressional Report on the Iran-Contra Affair*, 167.

[53] "Furmark Deposition," *Congressional Report on the Iran-Contra Affair*, Appendix B, vol. 11, 73-76.

[54] *Tower Report*, B-18,

timely replenishment of the weapons the Israelis sold with "new and modern" models.[55]

Kimche put these questions to McFarlane during two days of meetings, August 2-3. Once again, attempting to avoid a paper trail, McFarlane violated standard procedure and "made no memorandum of the meetings," thus his view is based on his recollection, which changed over time. Based on McFarlane's testimony before the congressional committees, the initiative came from the Israelis. It was the Israelis, he claimed, who "asked for permission to sell 100 TOWs," and that he, McFarlane, had merely "agreed to present the issue to the President." [56] This, however, was the very opposite of the truth.

Based on Israeli classified data, the Kimche-McFarlane meetings explored the parameters of the arms sale proposal and Israeli concerns. On the strategic question of establishing ties to Tehran, Kimche gave McFarlane Karoubi's memo (which he already had), with its attached name list of Iranian supporters. He claimed that this "moderate" faction needed to acquire the weapons to demonstrate its superior contacts to the United States and ability to "deliver" over rival factions. In addition, the weapons would help "broaden its base of support in the army and the Revolutionary Guard."[57]

Then, Kimche put forward the proposed deal worked out with Ghorbanifar, Khashoggi, and Ledeen. In exchange for the delivery of 100 TOW missiles, Iran would arrange for the release of four hostages. Israel would be prepared to deliver 400 additional missiles, depending on the outcome of the first deal. Kimche wanted to know whether the United States would replenish the weapons within 30 days of delivery.

On the matter of the president's consent, McFarlane agreed to put the question before the president to establish whether arms shipments were "consistent with American policy and goals," but affirmed that on the question of replenishment, Israel "has bought weapons from the United States for years and always will, and so you don't need to ask whether you can buy more weapons."[58] McFarlane thus left the "general impression . . . that the US would reply favorably."[59]

Reagan Says No; McFarlane Says Yes

As the Tower Board put it, "what followed is quite murky," in large part because McFarlane continued his practice of making no record of any of the discussions between the president and his top aides. The Board concluded that there had been several meetings in early August with "one or more of the principals in attendance" at each one. At the same time "White House records . . .

---

[55] Segev, *Iranian Triangle, 166.*
[56] *Congressional Report on the Iran-Contra Affair*, 167.
[57] Segev, *Iranian Triangle*, 168.
[58] *Tower Report*, B-19.
[59] Segev, *Iranian Triangle*, 168-169, incl. n3.

show no meetings of the NSC principals in August scheduled for the purpose of discussing [Iran], although there were meetings at which "this issue could have been discussed." Worse, in another McFarlane "lapse," defying standard procedure, "no analytical paper was prepared for the August discussions and no formal minutes of any of the discussions were made."[60]

Most of the NSC principals recalled a meeting on August 6, during which the Israeli proposal was discussed. They agree that both Shultz and Weinberger expressed strong objections and that the president made no decision. But that is where agreement ends. Weinberger says that Shultz, McFarlane, Regan, and either Casey or his deputy John McMahon met with the president in the sitting room in his White House quarters. Weinberger omitted Vice President Bush and was unsure whether Casey attended or not.[61]

Secretary Shultz testified to the congressional committees that Reagan, Bush, Shultz, Weinberger, Regan, and McFarlane, but neither Casey nor McMahon, was present on August 6.[62] Yet, to the Tower Board and in his memoir, he recalled the meeting on that date as "one of my regular meetings with the president," during which "Bud McFarlane brought up the idea of talks with Iran." Thus, for Shultz, there were two meetings on August 6 where the Israeli proposal was discussed.[63]

In his memoir, McFarlane presents yet a third story, claiming that in attendance were the president, Bush, Weinberger, Regan, and General John Vessey. Moreover, he says that the Israeli proposal was piggybacked onto another matter, a briefing by Weinberger and Vessey to discuss "proposed changes to our nuclear targeting doctrine."[64] This would appear to explain why there was no White House record of a meeting to discuss Iran.

For this information, however, McFarlane relied upon the White House attendance log, which betrayed him. Vessey had been scheduled to brief the president, but the briefing had been canceled at the last minute. As described by Walsh, "Weinberger had first offered Vessey a ride to the White House meeting and then, after checking, had to tell Vessey that he was not invited. The next day, Weinberger told Vessey that he 'wouldn't believe what was being proposed,' namely negotiation with the Iranians."[65]

McFarlane says neither Shultz, nor Casey, attended the meeting, although he avers that he had spoken to Shultz "earlier, on the phone," when the secretary expressed his opposition to any arms deal. As McFarlane described it Bush and Regan were "mildly supportive of the plan, Shultz and Weinberger were opposed, while he, McFarlane, supported it. The president's response was to say,

---

[60] *Tower Report*, III-6.

[61] Weinberger, *Fighting for Peace*, 368.

[62] *Congressional Report on the Iran-Contra Affair*, 167.

[63] Shultz, *Turmoil and Triumph*, 796 and *Tower Report*, III-7.

[64] McFarlane, *Special Trust*, 32.

[65] Walsh, *Final Report of the Independent Counsel*, 1:406n10.

"I'll think about it."[66] (Tellingly, he omits any reaction by Vessey. He also omits Shultz's message to him of July 14 expressing his "full agreement" to proceed.)

Despite differences in recollection of who attended the crucial meeting of August 6, all agreed that the president made no decision to authorize an Israeli arms sale. According to Chief of Staff Regan, "the President told McFarlane to 'go slow' at the August meeting," so as to "make sure we know who we are dealing with before we get too far into this."[67] However, in his testimony, McFarlane said that he informed Kimche of the president's affirmative decision on that day, August 6.[68]

In an interview with Mayer and McManus, McFarlane claimed that the president's decision came "a day or so" after the August 6 meeting. The president called him at home from Camp David to say that he wanted to "go ahead with the Iranian matter we discussed." Thus, according to his second account, the president authorized the Israeli arms deal "a day or so" after the August 6 meeting.[69]

However, once again McFarlane's claim was exposed as a falsehood and he subsequently changed his story. If the president had authorized the Israeli sale, it would have been one of the major decisions of his presidency, requiring a formal record. Yet, as reporters Mayer and McManus discovered, not only was no directive issued, there was no White House record of the telephone call, nor did McFarlane make any note of a call from the president.

Worse, between Tuesday, August 6, and Saturday, August 10, the president had not traveled to Camp David. He remained at the White House where McFarlane saw him each of those days. On August 11, the president flew to his ranch in California and McFarlane accompanied him on Air Force One. As Mayer and McManus put it, "there was no obvious reason for Reagan to call his aide at home, something he rarely did in any case."[70] There was ample opportunity to convey his decision to McFarlane in person, if in fact he had done so.

The Tower Board and the congressional committees accepted McFarlane's account, despite its many and obvious contradictions, concluding that the president "most likely approved the Israeli sales before they occurred." It was their view that "McFarlane had no motive to approve a sale of missiles to Iran if the President had not authorized it."[71] But, as this account maintains, he had both motive and opportunity. In any case, after his story was exposed as false, he changed it once again in his memoir.

In his memoir, McFarlane placed the call from Camp David *before* his meeting with Kimche and said that it had come to his White House office on Saturday July 27, where he happened to be, not to his home. In the call, the

---

[66] McFarlane, *Special Trust*, 32-34.

[67] *Congressional Report on the Iran-Contra Affair*, 167.

[68] "McFarlane Testimony," *Iran-Contra Affair*, Hearings, 100-2, at 48-50.

[69] Jane Mayer and Doyle McManus, *Landslide: The Unmaking of the President* (Boston: Houghton Mifflin, 1988), 128.

[70] Ibid., 129.

[71] *Congressional Report on the Iran-Contra Affair*, 168 and *Tower Report*, III-8.

president was said to want to "find a way" to do the "Israeli thing." Then, *after* the meetings of August 6, McFarlane said that "a little after noon" the president called him into the Oval Office to tell him that he wanted to go ahead with the Israeli arms sale because "it's the right thing to do."[72] Again, no record was made of the decision, or of the telephone call, or of his visit to the Oval Office.

Compounding McFarlane's problems is Segev's assertion that McFarlane notified Kimche that the president had authorized the sale on August 6, the day of the meeting.[73] This assertion invalidates McFarlane's initial testimony that the president authorized the sale "a day or so" after August 6, but, at least, makes physically possible his revised story. Plainly, contrary to the Tower Board and congressional committees which accepted McFarlane's claim, not only does the evidence strongly indicate that the president gave no authorization for an Israeli arms shipment to Iran before it occurred, but also that McFarlane had a clear motive to undertake this action on his own.

McFarlane and the First Arms Shipment

As soon as McFarlane notified them the Israelis prepared the first shipment of TOW missiles for delivery to Iran, code-named "Operation Cappuccino." The way McFarlane had arranged the deal must have given the Israeli leadership some qualms, as it was apparent to those closely following the action that the American leadership remained sharply divided, and the Israelis politically at risk. "Rabin refused to allow Israel to ship the weapons without written authorization from the US." Reportedly, McFarlane provided authorization "after consulting with Reagan."[74] However, once again, there was no record of a prior presidential authorization.

Khashoggi wired the promised $1 million to Nimrodi's Credit Suisse bank account in Geneva on August 7 (which incidentally reinforces the view that McFarlane had notified the Israelis on the 6th). With funds in hand, Schwimmer took care of the logistics. McFarlane had arranged for a CIA proprietary in Miami, Florida, to ship the weapons, so Schwimmer flew to Miami where he chartered a DC-8 cargo jet from an American company, re-registered it in Belgium, and hired a three-man American crew. Plane and crew arrived in Tel Aviv on August 18, followed by the arrival of Ghorbanifar the next day.[75]

---

[72] McFarlane, *Special Trust*, 31, 34.

[73] Segev, *Iranian Triangle*, 169.

[74] Scott Armstrong et al., *The Chronology: The Documented Day-by-Day Account of the Secret Military Assistance to Iran and the Contras* (New York: Warner Books, 1987), 148.

[75] Segev, *Iranian Triangle*, 172-73. The company was International Airline Support Group, Inc, owned by Richard R. Wellman. The CIA's airline proprietary project officer later testified that this August flight "was not an Agency flight." Furthermore, the agency only "found out after the fact" that the proprietary had chartered the plane. "Airline Proprietary Project Officer Deposition," *Congressional Report on the Iran-Contra Affair*, Appendix B, vol. 1, 18. Furthermore, the authorization for the flight

In the meantime, McFarlane arranged a secure communications scheme with Kimche through Ledeen. Ledeen had returned to Washington from his vacation in Israel in the second week of August. In his report to McFarlane he said he had become "extremely suspicious" of Ghorbanifar because he was simply "too good to be true." McFarlane was noncommittal, but, "a couple of days later," having heard from Kimche that the operation was set to go, the national security adviser had another meeting with Ledeen and told him that "the president had approved this test." Ledeen was "to meet with Kimche as quickly as possible to assure [him] that the President had in fact made this decision and to arrange a way [to] . . . communicate with the Israelis securely without going through the normal communication systems in the Israeli embassy or the American Embassy in Tel Aviv."[76]

Ledeen flew to London on August 20. Meeting in a hotel room at Heathrow airport, Ledeen passed on an elementary code scheme that would enable them to establish secure telephone communications and Kimche handed Ledeen typed notes of their July conversations with Ghorbanifar.[77] Kimche cautioned him that the Iranians would not deliver everything they promised, but, even if they "delivered significantly less than what they had promised," it was still worth a try.[78]

Around midnight on that same evening of August 20, the DC-8 took off from Tel Aviv for Iran loaded with 96 TOW missiles, four short of the agreed 100. The missiles were packed in pallets of twelve missiles per pallet; thus, eight pallets were shipped.[79] In addition, according to Ledeen, the Israelis were determined to avoid a repeat of the April fiasco, and insisted that Ghorbanifar accompany the cargo, or the mission would be canceled.[80]

Taking off from Ben Gurion airport, the unmarked cargo plane flew west for a time before turning 180 degrees to enter Cyprus airspace where the pilot requested and was given overflight clearance across Turkey to Tehran. Nearing Tehran, however, the plane encountered two Iraqi fighter aircraft, which forced the pilot to take evasive action and divert to Tabriz. Mohsen Kangarlu and several aides met the plane. From Tabriz the plane flew on to Tehran where Ali Shamkhani, deputy commander of the Revolutionary Guards met the plane and

---

came from McFarlane, not the CIA. According to the CIA Air Branch chief, when asked about the cargo regarding the August flight, he replied: "you don't ask unnecessary questions when it comes out of the White House." "CIA Branch Chief Deposition," Ibid., vol. 4, 818.

[76] "Ledeen Deposition," *Congressional Report on the Iran-Contra Affair*, Appendix B, vol. 15, 988-89.

[77] Ibid., 993.

[78] *Tower Report*, B-25.

[79] Israeli historical chronology, as cited in *Congressional Report on the Iran-Contra Affair*, 172n93.

[80] Ledeen, *Perilous Statecraft*, 131.

took control of the missiles, after receiving the concurrence of Prime Minister Mousavi.[81]

When the first arms delivery occurred, McFarlane was in California with the president. The president had left Washington on August 11 and would remain at his ranch until September 2 as part of his recovery from cancer surgery. While at the ranch his only contact with White House business was through Regan and McFarlane, and Nancy Reagan limited that to "written communications and phone calls."[82] In other words, during the period of the first Israeli arms delivery, the president was at the ranch, out of the White House, and, it seems clear, out of touch.

Meanwhile, after his meeting with Kimche, Ledeen flew to Los Angeles. After delivering a scheduled speech, he traveled up the coast to the Biltmore Hotel Resort in Santa Barbara where the presidential party stayed. There he briefed McFarlane on his meeting with Kimche and turned over the typed report of the July meetings.[83]

When informed of the Israeli delivery McFarlane realized that the scheme to sink the opening to Iran had reached a critical point. Up to now, all of the action had involved McFarlane maneuvering the Israelis and Iranians into an arms-for-hostages transaction. The US government was completely uninvolved, save for his own assurances to the Israelis and Ghorbanifar that the president was committed to the operation. However, McFarlane knew that the Israelis would immediately place before Weinberger a request for prompt replenishment of the weapons and he had to get to the secretary before they did.

So, on August 22, McFarlane flew back to Washington. Aboard Air Force One, he called Weinberger to arrange a meeting, and, as soon as he landed that evening went directly to the Pentagon for a 40-minute conclave with the defense secretary, his aide Colin Powell, and General Charles Gabriel, Acting Chief of the General Staff.[84] McFarlane informed the secretary that the president had approved the Israeli missile transfer and also the decision to replenish Israeli stockpiles.[85] According to Powell's recollection:

> McFarlane described to the Secretary the so-called Iran Initiative and he gave to the Secretary a sort of a history of how we got where we were that particular day and some of the

---

[81] Segev, *Iranian Triangle*, 174.

[82] Mayer and McManus, *Landslide*, 132, observe that in addition the two aides were "locked in a debilitating rivalry and by the summer of 1985 their fighting had descended to . . . a mean and petty level."

[83] "Ledeen Deposition," *Congressional Report on the Iran-Contra Affair*, Appendix B, vol. 15, 993.

[84] Weinberger Diary, August 22, 1985, as cited in Walsh, *Final Report of the Independent Counsel*, 1:407nn15 and 16.

[85] Robert Parry, "Colin Powell: Failed Opportunist," *Consortiumnews*, November 26, 2004, www.consortiumnews.com/2004/112604.html

thinking that gave rise to the possibility of going forward with such an initiative and what the purposes of such an initiative would be . . .[86]

Powell recalled that the secretary's response was "negative," repeating his oft-stated opposition to the so-called "initiative." But, despite his suspicions that this was another instance of McFarlane acting in the president's name without authorization, Weinberger complied, failing to confirm with the president. In retrospect, he certainly should have. There was no record, no directive; nothing but McFarlane's say-so. Had Weinberger checked and called the president to confirm, the Iran-Contra debacle might never have occurred. But he didn't, although he did procrastinate on replenishing the TOWs.

Entangling Reagan in an Arms-for-Hostages Scheme

Arranging for replenishment was the necessary step in McFarlane and the new world order faction's derailment plan. From this point onward, McFarlane's efforts focused on drawing the president, the CIA, Defense Department, and the NSC into the arms-for-hostages scheme, while keeping Shultz and the State Department out, and extricating himself and Ledeen from it, as well. Indeed, he began to speak of retiring from government service.

The day after his meeting with Weinberger, August 23, McFarlane called the president at the ranch on what Reagan referred to as his "secret phone" to alert him to the possibility of a hostage release. His message was cryptic, saying only "a man high-up in the Iranian govt believes he can deliver all or part of the 7 kidnap victims."[87] McFarlane mentioned nothing else, making no reference to the Israeli arms shipment, or replenishment of arms, or that it was the result of the president's policy.

According to Regan, during a daily briefing after the president had returned from the ranch in early September, McFarlane informed him that the Israelis had shipped arms to Iran. Reagan became "quite upset" at the news because he had not known anything about it. McFarlane brazenly disclaimed any knowledge or connection to the Israelis, declaring that they "simply had taken it upon themselves to do this."[88]

However, it soon became apparent that something was wrong. Although the Israelis had delivered the TOWs, the Iranians failed to obtain the release of a single hostage. Extremely agitated, Nimrodi called Ghorbanifar, who was in

---

[86] "Colin Powell Deposition," *Congressional Report on the Iran-Contra Affair*, Appendix B, vol. 21, 228. Powell remembered the conversation with McFarlane but was vague as to the date.
[87] Ronald Reagan, "Diary," August 23, 1985, as cited in Walsh, *Final Report of the Independent Counsel*, 1:407n12.
[88] *Tower Report*, B-24 and Walsh, *Final Report of the Independent Counsel*, 1:518-19n89.

Tehran, and arranged to meet him in Nice. In a rancorous discussion on August 27, at first Ghorbanifar claimed that as the Revolutionary Guards had seized the missiles, the "moderates" felt no obligation to free hostages.[89] Of course, this argument effectively demolished the idea of a separate "faction," moderate or otherwise, that could be armed against the government because it was the government that was receiving the weapons.

Then, Ghorbanifar argued that the 100 missiles were really the first part of the "test" they had discussed and that the entire deal included the 400 remaining missiles, which would result in the release of at least one hostage. To indicate Iran's commitment, Ghorbanifar showed the Israelis that the Iranian government had transferred $1,217, 410 to his account to repay Khashoggi, plus expenses. He also disclosed the Saudi financier's agreement to provide additional bridge money, $4 million, for the rest of the shipment of four hundred TOWs.[90]

When informed of this meeting, McFarlane immediately sent Ledeen back to Europe to confirm it. During a "hard" meeting at the George V Hotel in Paris, on September 4, Ledeen and the Israelis—Kimche, Schwimmer, and Nimrodi—emphasized to Ghorbanifar Iran's need to honor its side of the bargain. Ghorbanifar, in order to demonstrate Tehran's commitment, called Kangarlu in Tehran, who reaffirmed the arrangement. To verify Ghorbanifar's claims, both the Israelis and the NSA listened in on the call.[91]

It was agreed that Israel would ship 400 TOWs and the Iranians would release a hostage. According to McFarlane, he was given the choice of which hostage to be released and asked for Buckley, but, when told that he was too ill to travel, he picked Benjamin Weir, the longest-held hostage. (Although unknown to the US side at that time, Buckley had already died in early June from harsh treatment and medical malpractice.)[92]

In his testimony to the Tower Board, however, McFarlane told a different story: that Kimche had called him in the second week of September just prior to the second delivery of the 400 TOWs to say that "a hostage would be released and that he expected all the hostages to be released soon." There was no reference to Buckley, or of offering the national security adviser a choice of whom to release.[93]

In fact, McFarlane acted weeks before Kimche's call, in late August, to begin the process of entangling the US government in his scheme. Assuming that a hostage would be released following the second Israeli arms shipment, McFarlane instructed NSC staff member Lt. Colonel Oliver North to prepare

---

[89] Segev, *Iranian Triangle*, 175. Ledeen, *Perilous Statecraft*, 132, thought that rather than a scam, "the Iranians themselves were surprised at what had happened."

[90] *Congressional Report on the Iran-Contra Affair*, 168.

[91] "Ledeen Deposition," *Congressional Report on the Iran-Contra Affair*, Appendix B, vol. 15, 995-96; and Segev, *Iranian Triangle*, 176.

[92] McFarlane, *Special Trust*, 38, acknowledges that he selected Weir after learning that the Iranians would not release Buckley.

[93] *Tower Report*, B-26.

"contingency plans for extracting hostages . . . from Lebanon."[94] North had not been involved in McFarlane's "Iran initiative" up to this point and now was tasked specifically with "extracting hostages . . . from Lebanon," not an opening to Iran.[95] McFarlane picked North because, in addition to his assignment to support the Contras, North was then the NSC coordinator of the Counterterrorism Task Force, a recently formed offshoot of the Terrorist Incident Working Group (TIWG) that had been set up the previous year.[96]

The Task Force had been created during the TWA 847 crisis and was primarily responsible for making the arrangements to bring the passengers home. Reagan had ordered the establishment of the Task Force in the White House because the TIWG, run by Secretary Shultz in the State Department, had proven to be bureaucratically cumbersome with over two dozen members and operationally inept during the crisis. The Task Force had fewer than a dozen members drawn from CIA, DOD, FBI, State, and JCS.[97]

As soon as he was directed to prepare contingency plans to extract hostages, on August 30 North obtained a passport from the State Department under the name of William P. Goode, for use in "a sensitive operation in Europe in connection with our hostages in Lebanon." The next day, Deputy NSC chief John Poindexter set up a "private method of interoffice computer communication" with him called "private blank check," which enabled North to bypass the normal screening of computer messages by the Executive Secretary of the NSC.[98]

A few days later, on September 12, North tasked Charles Allen, who was CIA National Intelligence Officer for Counterterrorism (and a member of the Counterterrorism Task Force that North coordinated) to "increase intelligence efforts against Iran and Lebanon." He assumed that the Iranian-sponsored Hezbollah had seized Buckley and "might" release him "in the next few hours or days."

Allen wanted to know who should receive the intelligence and, at McFarlane's instruction, North told him to send reports to Vice Admiral Moreau, of JCS; Casey, or McMahon, in CIA; McFarlane, and North. McFarlane said that he would brief Shultz directly, so nothing should be sent to State. The congressional committees' report exonerated Shultz and the State Department completely, concluding that:

---

[94] *Tower Report*, B-25.

[95] Oliver L. North and William Novak, *Under Fire: An American Story* (New York: Harper Collins, 1991), 26, claims his "operational involvement" in the Iran initiative began on November 17 when Israeli Defense Minister Rabin telephoned him.

[96] Ibid., 198-99.

[97] Ibid. Noel Koch and Richard Armitage from Defense, Dewey Clarridge and Charles Allen from CIA, Buck Revell and Wayne Gilbert from FBI, Robert Oakley from State, and Arthur Moreau and Jack Moellering from JCS, would all in one way or another be involved in the Iran-Contra affair.

[98] *Tower Report*, B-25.

denied access to the intelligence, the State Department was not told of the Israeli TOW shipment, was not advised of the linkage of Weir's release to arms shipments and was not informed of the President's decision or the US Government's involvement.[99]

As is now known, this was erroneous. Shultz and his close aides were kept completely informed of events, following them closely and daily, but McFarlane's instruction had provided political cover of deniability.[100] Originally, McFarlane had also omitted Weinberger from the list, which meant that he was unaware of the first two TOW shipments in advance. Later, however, when the secretary learned from his Assistant Colin Powell that he was being cut out of the intelligence, he demanded and was included in the dissemination list. [101]

The Second Israeli Arms Delivery

Authorized by Peres and Rabin on September 9, the second Israeli arms delivery proceeded along the lines of the first, but more smoothly and with a better result. Schwimmer chartered the same DC-8 transport and hired the same three-man crew that he had for the first trip. Nimrodi accompanied Khashoggi to Geneva to deposit bridge funds as he had in August, only this time the Saudi financier deposited $4 million to pay for the 408 TOW missiles to be shipped. On September 11, Kimche telephoned McFarlane to tell him that the arms would be shipped within the next few days and that the Iranians would release one hostage, but it would not be Buckley. When asked if he had a preference for the release of any particular hostage, "McFarlane answered in the negative."[102]

Late on the night of September 14, the DC-8 charter left Tel Aviv, arriving five hours later at Tabriz. A few hours after the delivery, the Rev. Benjamin Weir was released in Beirut near the US embassy. McFarlane ordered Ambassador Reginald Bartholomew to withhold any announcement of his release for a few days, expecting that the "other hostages would be released in three batches without publicity." But no others were released, prompting Shultz to conclude, "Weir had been freed by terrorists who wanted to publicize their demand for their Al-Dawa cohorts to be released from Kuwait."[103]

---

[99] *Congressional Report on the Iran-Contra Affair*, 169

[100] Walsh, *Final Report of the Independent Counsel*, 1:332-341; and n1, above.

[101] *Congressional Report on the Iran-Contra Affair*, 169; and *Tower Report*, B-25.

[102] Segev, *Iranian Triangle*, 177, thus offers yet a third explanation for the first hostage release. McFarlane, nn91 and 92 above, first claimed that he selected Weir when Buckley was unavailable, then said Kimche simply told him a hostage would be released without identifying anyone. Kimche himself, in *Last Option*, 212, says "it was Ghorbanifar who informed us of the imminent release of the Reverend Benjamin Weir after we had delivered 500 TOW anti-tank shells."

[103] Shultz, *Turmoil and Triumph*, 797.

Weir himself was a decidedly unpleasant surprise. North, who was sent to debrief him found him "openly hostile to the United States and to Israel." Worse, having been in captivity for 495 days, he was openly sympathetic with his captors—a classic instance of the Stockholm syndrome. Rejecting a letter from the president requesting his cooperation, he "emphatically refused to provide us with any information that might result in the use of military force to rescue his fellow hostages."[104]

Despite his uncooperative attitude, Weir inadvertently revealed some very important information. He said "he had reached an understanding with his captors about what he would and would not disclose publicly. To protect the other hostages, he would not identify his captors, say where he was held or provide details on his repatriation." He also disclosed that on the day of his release he had spoken with Rev. Lawrence Jenco, Terry Anderson, David Jacobson, and Thomas Sutherland, but had not seen either Peter Kilburn, or William Buckley.[105]

In a public speech he warned, as Shultz expected, "unless the Reagan administration pressures Kuwait to release 17 terrorists convicted of seven bombings in December 1983, the remaining Americans may be executed and more US citizens kidnapped."[106] Demanding the release of the Al-Dawa 17 was a clue to who had taken Weir and at least four of the other hostages. During the TWA crisis discussed in the previous chapter, intelligence analysts had determined that the sticking point to a resolution of the crisis had been an unidentified "inner group of terrorists . . . not under anyone's control, not Iran's and not Hezbollah's."[107]

By the time of Weir's release, the FBI, in examining the hijacked TWA aircraft, had found Imad Mughniyeh's fingerprints in the lavatory.[108] They were therefore able to conclude that he had been the leader of this "inner group." The fact that Weir had been prompted to make the same demand for the release of the Al-Dawa 17 as the TWA hijackers had meant that Mughniyeh was also the one holding the hostages.

If intelligence analysts had examined the personal backgrounds of the Al-Dawa prisoners they would undoubtedly have confirmed this deduction when they discovered that one of the prisoners was Mughniyeh's brother-in-law, Mustafa Badreddine. Shultz himself had concluded that members of this inner group "were related by family to the Al-Dawa prisoners held by Kuwait."[109]

But there was an even more disturbing deduction for the Shultz-McFarlane scheme to entangle the president. If Mughniyeh was not under the control of either Iran or Hezbollah, then neither could deliver the hostages and the new world order scheme for entangling the president in an arms-for-hostages

---

[104] North, *Under Fire*, 28.
[105] "Benjamin Weir's Secret Passage," *Time*, September 30, 1985.
[106] Ibid.
[107] Shultz, *Turmoil and Triumph*, 662.
[108] Bergman, *Secret War with Iran*, 101.
[109] Ibid.

scandal would not work. McFarlane and Shultz must have realized that the Israelis knew this and that they and the Iranians were entangling them in a pure and simple arms deal.[110]

Despite his own conclusions that the "inner group" of terrorists was holding the hostages and was not under the control of Iran or Hezbollah, Shultz continued to maintain that "Iran, not Syria, was in the position, if any country was, to call the shots when it came to the remaining American hostages."[111] This view, it is obvious, was contradicted by what Shultz already knew, but was consistent with his ideological predisposition to oppose any dealings with Iran.

The new world order derailment scheme had run into unexpected complexity with the discovery that Mughniyeh was the principal hostage-taker. Worse, if he was not under either Iran's or Hezbollah's control, then his connection to Qaddafi and ultimately to Moscow inevitably would come to light, no matter how well disguised his command links were. The prospect that Moscow could be found to be the deep sponsor of terrorist acts against Americans would be the very opposite of what the new world order faction sought.

It is impossible to know how far the new world order faction intended to take the derailment scheme, but there can be little doubt that the discovery Mughniyeh was the operational mastermind meant that the possibility of freeing the hostages was slimmer than thought. For McFarlane it was now more important than ever to move to the endgame, extricate himself from his gambit, and implicate the president more deeply.

---

[110] Bergman, *Secret War with Iran*, 96, says, however, that "for years, the Israelis could not fathom the hierarchical arrangements between Hizballah's various components and Syria and Iran . . . . Where, for example, did Mughniyeh himself fit in? There was a prolonged debate in the intelligence community over whether he was a member of Hizballah, or directly subordinate to Iranian intelligence." A third possibility, of course, was that he was an "independent contractor," loosely affiliated with several terrorist organizations.

[111] Shultz, *Turmoil and Triumph*, 662 and 667.

Chapter 11

The Attempt to Shut
Down the Iran Initiative

In the fall of 1985, the new world order faction moved to close off any possibility of an opening to Iran. Having cooperated with the Peres leadership to set the hook in the form of Israeli arms deliveries and the release of a hostage, McFarlane and Kimche now prepared for the next step, of entangling the United States government illicitly in the scheme. On this narrow objective the two men cooperated, but with full understanding that their interests were not entirely congruent.

The point of divergence lay in the expected outcomes of their scheme. For the new world order faction entangling the United States directly in the arms-for-hostages scheme was designed to close off any possible rapprochement with Iran, but the Israelis calculated it would ensure their continued access to the lucrative Iranian arms market. In 1985 alone, independent Israeli arms sales to Iran were reportedly valued conservatively at between $500 million and $1 billion.[1] (By way of comparison, in their entirety, US-Israeli arms sales to Iran in 1985 and 1986 that were part of the Iran initiative did not exceed $50 million.)

At the same time, all parties, including the United States, Syria, Iran, and Israel, were sending agents to scour the Lebanese countryside in a search for the hostages, who had become highly valuable commodities. In short, whoever could find the hostages would hold great leverage over Washington, unless, of course, US agents found them first.

Not only was a race going on to find the hostages. Perhaps most important were apparent changes at the global level. Here, two developments were paramount. First, preparations for a Reagan-Gorbachev summit held ominous implications for Iran. As the Iranian leadership saw it, a move to US-Soviet détente implicit in the summit would, as it had in the 1970s, consign Iran to the Soviet sphere and leave Tehran to the machinations of Moscow.

Second was the imminent collapse of oil prices, which would have a dramatic impact not only on Moscow's revenues, but on Iran's, as well. From early September rumors abounded about a coming price drop, which actually began in November. A sharp reduction in oil income would impact heavily upon

---

[1] Martin Sieff, "Former NSC Aide Says Iran Arms Worth Much More Than Reported," *Washington Times*, December 5, 1986, A8.

Iran's ability to finance its war with Iraq. These developments, combined with the growing Soviet supply of Saddam Hussein's forces with missiles, rockets, tanks, and aircraft, galvanized the Iranian leadership into a determined attempt to reach an accommodation with Washington.

The Iranian leadership was desperate. Not only were strategic trends increasingly adverse, the situation on the ground in the war with Iraq and with regard to the hostages was of great concern. Moscow's rearming of Saddam's forces portended serious losses, if not defeat, if compensating weaponry were not acquired. Worse, the Iranians knew and suspected that Washington also knew, or would soon realize, that they could not deliver all of the hostages on demand. Hence, the Iranian approach was to pretend that they could deliver the hostages and attempt to strike a large deal, to get as much as they could before the Americans realized the truth.

Each side had tricks to play to maneuver their counterparts into desired positions. The result was a period full of surprises. Deceit reigned, as all sides operated on the false assumptions that the United States genuinely sought rapprochement through arms-for-hostages and that Iran actually controlled the fate of the hostages.[2] The result was a series of unpredictable and explosive developments that reached a climax at the end of the year in what appeared to be the end of the initiative.

McFarlane's Hand-Off

Having started the arms-for-hostages initiative on his own without presidential authority, McFarlane now sought to implicate the president and draw others in the US government into the scheme, especially CIA and Defense, but not State. McFarlane also handed off the management of this initiative to his untutored deputy in the NSC, Oliver North, while he moved to a less prominent, but still controlling, position. The procedure was remarkably similar to the scheme his mentor Henry Kissinger had employed with regard to Angola in 1974, unilaterally and clandestinely initiating involvement, then later passing the project of supplying the FNLA and Holden Roberto off to the CIA.[3]

When McFarlane directed North to prepare to recover the hostages he thought would be released following Israel's September arms shipment, North went to Charles Allen, the CIA's NIO for counterterrorism to activate intelligence

---

[2] As John G. Tower et al., *Report of the President's Special Review Board: February 26, 1987* (Washington, DC: US Government Printing Office, 1987), IV-2, concluded: "if the US objective was a broader, strategic relationship, then the sale of arms should have been contingent upon first putting into place the elements of that relationship. An arms-for-hostages deal in this context could become counter-productive to achieving this broader strategic objective."

[3] See Richard C. Thornton, *The Nixon-Kissinger Years*, 2nd ed. (St. Paul: Paragon House, 2001), 360-69.

coverage of Iranian leaders and their contacts in the Beirut area.[4] Thus, the circle of those with knowledge of McFarlane's scheme immediately widened, as intelligence reports began to circulate within the upper echelons of government.

Immediately after the September 14 release of Rev. Benjamin Weir, and knowing that Casey was receiving the intelligence reports, McFarlane informed him for the first time of his "contacts with Iran."[5] Weinberger, too, hearing of "strange" reports about an arms-for-hostages swap, called Casey to compare notes. Casey was as "surprised" as Weinberger and suspected that "Bud [McFarlane] is not telling us all he knows or has promised."[6] Clearly, the exchange proves that neither Casey nor Weinberger, both of whom were the president's allies, was part of McFarlane's scheme.

The role of Shultz and the State Department in the Iran initiative has been almost completely overlooked because, when the scandal erupted, Shultz denied knowledge of conspiracy and congressional investigators were loath to probe his veracity. The Independent Counsel investigation, however, subsequently uncovered voluminous evidence of the State Department's involvement in the factional struggle. As Walsh notes,

> regarding the November Hawk shipment . . . Shultz and other
> senior department officials were informed contemporaneously
> of many of its details, including . . . the flight plan, the need for
> overflight clearances, the delay in the shipment and the reasons
> the Iranians eventually returned the missiles.[7]

In other words, Shultz and his cadre of aides also were independently following the events closely. Nick Platt saw the downside of Weir's release at once. Three days later Platt observed that the release of only one hostage meant that McFarlane's scheme "appears not going anywhere." He noted cryptically that the hostage-release process had turned into a "race between Syria [and Iran] to round up hostages so [country name redacted, but clearly the United States] can pay or the Israelis can pay Iranians with weapons sales."[8]

A few days later, Shultz and two of his aides, Michael Armacost and John Whitehead, discussed their concerns about the deal. Shultz was "not comfortable" with what he saw as "strange bargaining going on," but did not know what to do about it. McFarlane had "taken control" of the operation and was playing his cards close to the vest. When Armacost asked McFarlane's deputy, John Poindexter, about it, he replied that things were "very confused." (Armacost thought that Poindexter was "being cute" with him, but in fact McFarlane had not

---

[4] Lawrence E. Walsh, *Final Report of the Independent Counsel for Iran-Contra Matters*, vol. 1 (Washington, DC: United States Court of Appeals for the District of Columbia Circuit, August 4, 1993), 206.

[5] Ibid.

[6] "Weinberger Note," September 20, 1985, in Ibid., 207.

[7] Ibid., 337.

[8] "Platt Note," September 17, 1985, in Ibid., 335n73.

yet brought Poindexter into his scheme, either.)[9] Whitehead wondered whether they had told the president. Shultz thought they had but was concerned that Reagan didn't "appreciate the problems with arms sales to Iran."[10]

A week after Weir's release, McFarlane instructed North to assume the responsibilities held by Ledeen, but to do so in a circumspect manner. Deniability was the criterion. Accordingly, North informed Ledeen "McFarlane has told me I'm supposed to now handle all the operational aspects of this, and McFarlane has no knowledge . . . that Ledeen is doing anything, much less that North has taken over what he is doing."[11]

To assure a smooth transition from Ledeen to North with the Israelis, Schwimmer flew to Washington toward the end of September where, according to North's calendar, he met with him and Ledeen, on September 26.[12] Schwimmer returned two weeks later with Nimrodi and Ghorbanifar for further introductions, although the issue of hostage William Buckley's fate gave added urgency and dimension to their trip.

On October 1, the Israelis had carried out a major air raid on PLO headquarters in Tunis in retaliation for the PLO "Force 17" murder of three Israelis aboard a yacht off Cyprus.[13] Two days later Islamic Jihad, Mughniyeh's group, declared that it had executed William Buckley "because of US involvement in Tuesday's Israeli air raid on Yasser Arafat's PLO headquarters in Tunis."[14] There was a presumption, though no confirmation, that Buckley was dead, so North asked Ledeen to arrange for Ghorbanifar to come to Washington as soon as possible to discuss Buckley and the other hostages.[15]

Some, like North, held out a slim hope that Buckley was still alive, but others, like Charles Allen, thought that he was already dead.[16] (It would be at least another month before it would be confirmed that he died in June of harsh treatment and had not been executed by Mughniyeh.) The prospect of hostages being

---

[9] "Poindexter Deposition," *Report of the Congressional Committees Investigating the Iran-Contra Affair* (Washington, DC: US Government Printing Office, 1987), Appendix B, vol. 20, 1094. [Cited hereafter as *Congressional Report on the Iran-Contra Affair*.] In describing this period, Poindexter said, "In November of 1985 I was very confused as to what had been approved and what hadn't been approved and frankly thought it had been run in a very slipshod manner."

[10] "Hill Note," September 21, 1985, in Walsh, *Final Report of the Independent Counsel* 1:335n74.

[11] *Tower Report*, B-28n19.

[12] Ibid., B-29.

[13] "Israeli Jets' Raid Target Was Elite Arafat Unit," *Washington Times*, October 4, 1985, 6.

[14] "Terrorists Say They Executed US Hostage," *Washington Times*, October 4, 1985, 1.

[15] *Congressional Report on the Iran-Contra Affair*, 169.

[16] "Charles Allen Deposition," *Congressional Report on the Iran-Contra Affair*, Appendix B, vol. 1, 351.

systematically executed, however, raised the question of whether the United States could have any further dealings with Iran.

Schwimmer, Nimrodi, and Ghorbanifar met North briefly in his office in the Old Executive Office Building on October 8, but the seizure of the Italian cruise ship *Achille Lauro* the day before claimed all of North's attention and he left Ledeen in charge of their meeting.[17] Thus, although McFarlane had attempted to move Ledeen out of the picture, circumstances kept him directly involved for several more weeks. He would report directly to McFarlane on the results of their conversations.

The four men engaged in a wide-ranging discussion regarding the continuation of arms for hostages. Ghorbanifar assured them of the hostages' safety and that Tehran could deliver. He also put forth Tehran's desire to acquire a broader category of weapons, beyond the anti-tank TOW missile. They were especially interested in acquiring the latest versions of air-to-air weapons, Phoenix and Sidewinder, as well as the anti-ship and anti-air, Harpoon and Hawk.[18] "For each bundle of advanced weapons, they were offering one or more hostages," Ledeen observed.[19]

Ghorbanifar's request did not include a specific proposal; he was most interested in learning what the American reaction would be to a large arms-for-hostages deal. To pique Washington's interest, he also confided to Ledeen that "it had become possible for us to talk directly to spokesmen for the 'conservative line' . . . and we were promised meetings within the next month."[20]

During the course of their discussions Ledeen voiced his objections to continuing on the arms-for-hostages track and argued for a straight political dialogue. Schwimmer and Nimrodi immediately objected, ostensibly on the grounds that there were also Israeli Jews in Iran whom they hoped eventually to repatriate, but actually because of their concern to keep open the arms sales connection. A straight political dialogue would cut them, and Israel, out. When Ledeen asked Ghorbanifar for his view, the Iranian surprisingly agreed with Ledeen, declaring that developing a political relationship "should be the focus of their energies." Involvement in arms and hostage matters, he warned, posed the risk that "we shall become hostages to the hostages."[21]

---

[17] Samuel Segev, *The Iranian Triangle: The Untold Story of Israel's Role in the Iran-Contra Affair* (New York: Free Press, 1988), 182-3. Ghorbanifar traveled to Washington under the alias of Nicholas Kralis.

[18] The Phoenix was a long-range air-to-air missile carried exclusively by the F-14; the Sidewinder was a short-range air-to-air missile; Harpoon was an over-the-horizon anti-ship missile; and the Hawk was a medium-range surface-to-air missile.

[19] Michael Ledeen, *Perilous Statecraft: An Insider's Account of the Iran Contra Affair* (New York: Scribner, 1988), 137.

[20] Ibid.

[21] *Tower Report*, B-29 and "Ledeen Deposition," *Congressional Report on the Iran-Contra Affair*, Appendix B vol. 15, 1015.

In reporting on their discussion to McFarlane, Ledeen strongly expressed the view that not only should the United States get out of the hostage business, based on Ghorbanifar's promise of direct contacts with Iranian leaders, he wanted out of it, too. McFarlane agreed, declaring, "I have a bad feeling about this whole operation, and said his intention was to shut the whole thing down." This was not Ledeen's view. "I asked him not to shut the whole thing down, but to let the political thing go ahead." McFarlane said he would think about it. When Ledeen told him that Ghorbanifar had arranged a meeting with a senior Iranian official in Europe at the end of the month, McFarlane "approved the trip for me to go and meet with this person."[22]

Islamic Jihad's announcement that it had executed William Buckley had dramatically affected all concerned. Assuming Iran controlled the hostages, it raised the fundamental question of whether any relationship with Iran was possible. This was certainly the case for North, who apparently did not yet realize that the Iranians had precious little leverage or control over Mughniyeh's Islamic Jihad. As noted above, however, Shultz and McFarlane, if not Casey, were fully apprised that Mughniyeh was the wild-card terrorist not under anyone's control yet acted as if Iran could control the hostages.

Tehran did not control Mughniyeh and therefore could not deliver the hostages on demand, but only insofar as they could persuade or bribe him to part with them. The Iranians, desperate for weapons and realizing that the Americans were dubious about continuing, therefore, through Ghorbanifar, were at great pains to insist that they *could* deliver the hostages. Given the American interest in them, to claim otherwise would end their chances of acquiring weapons.

At the same time, they would repeatedly hint at the need to get beyond the hostage issue, as Ghorbanifar had just demonstrated in his talks with Ledeen. In any case, sensing that the Americans would realize at any moment that they could not deliver on the hostages the Iranians sought as large a deal as possible, as soon as possible, promising to release all of them in a grand bargain.

The Israelis were, perhaps, affected most by the claim of Buckley's execution. The arms-for-hostages deal was Peres's entrée into the Iranian arms market and if it collapsed the market would disappear. The Israeli answer to this conundrum was to inveigle the US government deeper into the game of supplying arms to Iran. Up to this point, the United States was effectively uninvolved; except for McFarlane's as yet unrealized promise to replenish the weapons the Israelis had sold to Iran. Israeli threats to stop further arms supply unless the United States promptly replenished weapons already delivered was in essence a bluff.

Israel's desire to involve the US government more directly dovetailed perfectly with the new world order faction's objective and was the basis for the collusion between McFarlane and David Kimche which would produce what became known as the Hawk deal.

---

[22] Ibid., 1019-20.

The Hawk Deal in International Context

Over two months passed between the September Israeli shipment and the November Hawk deal. McFarlane explained the lag in terms of the press of events and his preoccupation with the president's "crowded" schedule. First, was the *Achille Lauro* hijack in the second week of October, which resulted in tense standoffs with Egypt and Italy over the hijackers.[23] Then, in rapid succession came the president's visit to the United Nations in late October with its attendant speeches and meetings, including a meeting with Soviet foreign minister Eduard Shevardnadze, followed by preparations for the Reagan-Gorbachev Geneva summit, November 19-21. McFarlane continued, "I spent nearly all my time chairing meetings on our arms control positions and on four major addresses we wanted the president to deliver in support of our goals at the summit." Thus, he says, "I sent the Iran file to the back of my mind."[24]

Indeed, McFarlane was busy. The October-November time frame saw the national security adviser at the center of a major controversy over arms control, which was part of the Washington-Moscow maneuvering before the summit. In brief, although Gorbachev was a new face and had adopted a more open style compared to previous Soviet leaders, he sought to accomplish the same objectives as had Andropov and Brezhnev—strategic weapons dominance over the United States, intermediate-range nuclear missile domination over Western Europe and Japan, and control over Iran.

After six months of fruitless negotiations at Geneva, in September Gorbachev produced an arms control proposal that promised a 50 percent reduction in offensive forces, but only if the United States cancelled SDI, which, of course, would ensure Moscow's strategic weapons dominance. Also, having failed to prevent the US deployment of the Pershing II/Cruise Missile package to Western Europe, Gorbachev sought to define these weapons out of existence.

The Soviets sought to accomplish this by resurrecting their old definition of what constituted a strategic weapon: any weapon, including an aircraft, that could strike the Soviet Union. The SALT II treaty defined a strategic weapon as any ballistic missile with a range exceeding 3,200 miles. If the Soviet definition were accepted, it would mean that forward-based aircraft and the just-deployed Pershing II/Cruise Missile package to Western Europe would be counted as strategic weapons and be part of the fifty-percent reduction. No Russian intermediate-range weapons would be affected, thus insuring Moscow's nuclear domination of Western Europe and Japan.

As the Soviet Union had more missiles than the United States, a 50 percent reduction on both sides would still leave the Soviets with their existing advantage. There were other hedges in their proposal, but its gist would leave the

---

[23] See Michael Bohn, *The Achille Lauro Hijacking: Lessons in the Politics and Prejudice of Terrorism* (Dulles: Potomac Books, 2004). Bohn was director of the White House Situation Room during the events.

[24] Robert C. McFarlane, *Special Trust* (New York: Cadell & Davies, 1994), 40-41.

Soviet Union with strategic and intermediate-range weapons' advantages vis-a-vis the United States, Western Europe, and Japan. In truth, the Soviet proposal's one-sidedness was transparent and patently unacceptable, except as a propaganda and negotiating tactic.[25]

Conferring with his aides, President Reagan decided to "undermine their propaganda plan by offering a counter proposal which stresses our acceptance of some of their figures, such as a 50 percent cut in weapons and a total of 6,000 warheads, etc. Those are pretty much like what we've already proposed."[26] However, he did more than offer a counterproposal. Over the subsequent months the president took steps to clear the way for SDI testing and development to proceed beyond basic research and he raised fundamental geopolitical issues that would have to be discussed at the summit.

Reagan understood that the Soviets were engaging in a bidding game to see if there was a price at which he would give up SDI. It was an open secret that the administration was split between those, like Shultz, who wanted to use SDI as a "bargaining chip" to get an arms control agreement and those like the president and Weinberger, who saw strategic defense as essential to American strategy. The president was firm: "we would *not* trade away our program of research—SDI—for a promise of Soviet reduction in nuclear arms."[27]

The first step, in which McFarlane was centrally involved, was to strengthen the SDI program by reinterpreting the terms of the 1972 ABM Treaty to permit work to proceed beyond mere research to testing and development. Appearing on the television news program *Meet the Press* on Sunday, October 6, and in the course of criticizing the Soviet arms control proposal, McFarlane reaffirmed the president's determination to pursue a vigorous SDI program, which was clearly consistent with the ABM Treaty. Then, he said, "research, testing and development of new defensive weapons 'involving new physical concepts . . . are approved and authorized by the treaty. Only deployment is foreclosed . . . '"[28]

His assertion immediately created a storm of controversy. Up to this point, the United States had defined the treaty as permitting only a limited ground-based deployment and prohibiting anything beyond laboratory research on new missile defense components. The new "broad" interpretation would permit the United States to go beyond laboratory research to testing and development of systems based on new physical principles.

---

[25] Robert Toth, "US Criticizes Soviet Arms Plan, Warns of Allied Split," *Los Angeles Times*, October 9, 1985, 1 and Elizabeth Pond, "US Arms Expert Sees Pluses and Minuses in Soviet Proposal," *Christian Science Monitor*, October 11, 1985, 9.

[26] Ronald Reagan, *An American Life* (New York: Simon and Schuster, 1990), 629.

[27] Ibid., 628.

[28] Lou Cannon, "Reagan Aide Faults Soviet Arms Plan," *Washington Post*, October 7, 1985, A1. For the private bureaucratic discussions that preceded McFarlane's public statement, see Don Oberdorfer, *The Turn: From the Cold War to a New Era: The United States and the Soviet Union, 1983-1990* (New York: Poseidon, 1991), 123-26.

Critics howled, demanding that the United States adhere to the treaty as originally understood, but the new interpretation was straightforward.[29] "Agreed Statement D" of the treaty stipulated that "in the event ABM systems based on other physical principles and including components capable of substituting for ABM interceptor missiles, ABM launchers or ABM radars are created in the future, specific limitations on such systems and their components would be subject to discussion . . . ."[30]

The statement "in the event ABM systems based on other physical principles . . . are created in the future" implied clearly that for a "system" to have been created there would ipso facto have to have been research, testing, and development. As SDI was based on "other physical principles," it followed logically and legally that the program had to go beyond research to testing and development before it could be termed a "system" subject to discussion.

Nevertheless, of all the critics Secretary Shultz complained the loudest. In an "emotionally charged meeting," which one administration source described as a "knock-down, drag-out meeting," Shultz pulled out all the stops in an effort to force the president to back away from the broad interpretation, including another threat to resign. Citing "messages of concern" from London and Bonn and support of arms control negotiator, Paul Nitze, Shultz said that a change of such magnitude would cause a storm among US allies as well as in the congress.[31]

The president countered Shultz by citing the State Department's own legal counsel Abraham Sofaer, whose analysis supported the broad interpretation. Sofaer pointed out that the negotiating record showed Moscow's refusal to accept a total prohibition of ABM systems based on other physical principles.[32] He also showed that the illegal Krasnoyarsk radar was part of a very robust Russian missile defense system that flaunted the treaty's restrictions.[33] Nevertheless, the argument that carried the day was that, as it would be some time before the US program would be ready to go beyond the research stage, the broad interpretation was premature.

Thus, the outcome of the argument was Shultz's formulation that the United States would continue to conduct the SDI program "in accordance with a

---

[29] For one critique, see Alan Sherr, "Sound Legal Reasoning or Policy Expedient? The 'New Interpretation' of the ABM Treaty," *International Security* 2, no. 3 (Winter 1986-87): 71-93. See appendix A for State Department legal adviser Abraham Sofaer's statement before the House Foreign Affairs Committee.

[30] For the treaty and appendices, see Gerard Smith, *Doubletalk: The Story of SALT I* (New York: Doubleday, 1980), 487-502.

[31] Don Oberdorfer, "Shultz Was Key in ABM Policy Switch," *Washington Post*, October 17, 1985, A4. Nitze had actually changed his view to support of the broad interpretation.

[32] "Written Statement of Abraham D. Sofaer," October 22, 1985, Appendix A, in Sherr, "Sound Legal Reasoning or Policy Expedient?" 90.

[33] David Yost, "Soviet Ballistic Missile Defense and NATO," *Orbis* 29, no. 2 (Summer 1985): 281-93.

restrictive interpretation" of the ABM Treaty, even though "a broader interpretation of our authority was fully justified."[34] Although it seemed that Shultz had forced the president to back down, a White House spokesman later declared that the president's position remained that "research stops short of deployment [but] it encompasses research, testing and development."[35]

Although the president's position was clear, even if the administration's position was ambiguous, the fact was a major evolution of US strategy had taken place. The public argument had the effect of making it seem—especially to the Soviets—that the SDI program was further along than the administration admitted and ready to enter the "testing" stage.[36]

A few days later the president raised other matters for resolution before an improvement in relations with Moscow could occur. In a major address celebrating the 40th anniversary of the United Nations, the president laid out his agenda for the forthcoming summit. Calling for a "fresh start," the president offered to discuss America's "deep and abiding differences" with the Soviet Union on the basis of complete candor. He began by declaring that the United States, as a free society, "cannot accommodate ourselves to the use of force and subversion to consolidate and expand the reach of totalitarianism." [37]

He pointed to three areas of conflict: Soviet treaty violations, the strategic weapons balance, and regional conflicts. Focusing on the 1972 ban on biological and toxin weapons, the 1975 Helsinki Accords, and US-Soviet strategic weapons agreements, the president said that we feel it will be necessary to discuss "what we believe are violations of a number of the provisions in all of these agreements."

He went on to refer to the recent Soviet arms control proposal, which he said contained several "seeds" we could "nurture," but in discussing the "vital relationship between offensive and defensive systems," he wished to focus on "the possibility of moving toward a more stable and secure world in which defenses play a growing role." "If," he declared, we are "destined by history to compete, militarily, to keep the peace, then let us compete in systems that defend our societies rather than in weapons which can destroy us . . . "

---

[34] Don Oberdorfer and David Ottaway, "US Clarifies ABM Pact View," *Washington Post*, October 15, 1985, A1 and William Beecher, "White House Moved to Save Face on Interpretation of ABM Treaty," *Boston Globe*, October 16, 1985, 18. See also George Shultz, *Turmoil and Triumph* (New York: Scribner, 1993), 578-82.

[35] Charles Mohr, "US Keeps Options For 'Star Wars,'" *New York Times*, October 20, 1985, A7.

[36] John Fialka, "Reagan Team Justifies Star Wars Plan by Claiming Loophole in ABM Treaty," *Wall Street Journal*, October 22, 1985, 64.

[37] Ronald Reagan, "Address to the 40th Session of the United Nations General Assembly, New York, October 24, 1985," *Public Papers of the Presidents of the United States, Ronald Reagan, 1985*, bk. 2, *June 29 to December 31* (Washington, DC: US Government Printing Office, 1988), 1285-89.

Finally, he pointed to Soviet involvement in five regional conflicts: Afghanistan, Cambodia, Ethiopia, Angola, and Nicaragua, pledging that American support for "struggling democratic resistance forces must not and shall not cease." At the same time, he proposed a three-part negotiating framework for resolving them, involving discussions between the parties to end each conflict, negotiations between the United States and the Soviet Union on how best to assist in conflict termination, and American developmental assistance once conflicts ended.[38]

Having set the agenda for the coming summit, in early November, the president announced Washington's counterproposal to Moscow's arms control proposal on the eve of Secretary Shultz's trip to meet with Soviet foreign minister Eduard Shevardnadze. He characterized the proposal as "deep cuts, no first-strike advantage, defensive research—because defense is safer than offense—and no cheating."[39]

Reagan's proposal in essence took on Gorbachev's bidding game and went one further. Where Gorbachev proposed a reduction to 6,000 total warheads, Reagan proposed more than fifty percent cuts in offensive forces, to a limit of 4,500 total warheads, with 3,000 on heavy missiles. He would set a limit of no more than 350 long-range bombers and 1,500 cruise missiles. Reagan's proposal was unconditional, although it contained no offer on defensive arms, whereas Gorbachev conditioned his offer on the cancellation of SDI.[40] Nevertheless, as the November summit approached, the two sides appeared to have set the stage for a substantive discussion, if not for an actual agreement.

The Hawk Set-Up

The September-November period was filled with intense activity and McFarlane was deeply involved in a variety of policy-related moves. Yet, for all of that, he had by no means sent the "Iran file" to the back of his mind. Indeed, the weeks leading up to the Geneva summit were when he and David Kimche put in place the Hawk deal, which entangled the US government directly and illegally in the arms-for-hostages scheme.

In late October, on the 27th, McFarlane sent Ledeen to Geneva to meet with Hassan Karoubi, the senior Iranian leader in the meeting arranged by Ghorbanifar. Kimche, Schwimmer and Nimrodi also attended. It was Ledeen's

---

[38] Raymond Coffey, "Reagan Shows Fist, Open Hand to Soviet," *Chicago Tribune*, October 25, 1985, 1; Lou Cannon, "President Calls for 'Fresh Start' With Soviets," *Washington Post*, October 25, 1985, A1; "On to the Summit," *Wall Street Journal*, October 25, 1985, 18; and Lou Cannon and David Hoffman, "Arms Control, Regional Peace; Reagan Signaling Gorbachev That 2 Issues Are Linked, Officials Say," *Washington Post*, October 25, 1985, A31.

[39] Lou Cannon, "Reagan Announces Arms Plan; Shultz to Seek 2nd Summit," *Washington Post*, November 1, 1985, A1.

[40] William Chaze, "Back in the Game," *US News & World Report*, November 11, 1985, 28.

first face-to-face meeting with Karoubi, but not the others, who knew him well. Ledeen, of course, was familiar with Karoubi's earlier memo that had been passed to him by the Israelis and prodded McFarlane into action in July.

After professing his group's desire for an improvement in relations with the United States, Karoubi got to his point. He claimed that as a result of the mid-October elections "he and his men were now in key positions and that they could influence their country's policy and bring about the release of the five remaining American hostages." They could also apply pressure on Hezbollah in Lebanon "to refrain from further kidnapping."[41]

In return for getting the hostages out, Karoubi wanted a one-time "blanket order" of 150 Hawk missiles, 200 Sidewinder missiles, and 30-50 Phoenix missiles. There would be a staggered release of hostages in three groups interspersed with arms deliveries. Although surprised by the large number of weapons being asked for but encouraged by the prospect of the release of the rest of the hostages, Ledeen agreed to present this offer to his superiors in Washington.[42]

Before he left, in a separate conversation, Kimche told Ledeen that Rabin was "very upset about the US failure to "replenish the TOW missiles" and doubted that he would "agree to sending more arms to Iran until arrangements are made for supplying replacements."[43] Although Ledeen had reported previously about Rabin's concern to have the TOWs replenished, he promised to bring it up again upon his return.

Ledeen returned to Washington on October 30 to report to both McFarlane and North. Upon hearing what Ledeen had to say, McFarlane expressed skepticism about "the existence of moderate elements in Iran, let alone their ability to come to power." Nevertheless, he did not reject the offer, but instructed North and Ledeen that no weapons would be shipped without the release of "live Americans." Apparently, there was no discussion about the replenishment of the TOWs.[44]

The next day, October 31, and unbeknownst to Ledeen, McFarlane received word from Kimche that the Iranians had upped the ante. After the meeting with Ledeen, Ghorbanifar had flown to Dubai for a meeting with Kangarlu who was there on a weapons buying trip. After hearing Ghorbanifar's report and checking with Rafsanjani, Kangarlu drafted a formal proposal that added a written pledge of cooperation, while increasing Iran's demands for sophisticated American weapons worth hundreds of millions of dollars:

> From this moment onwards, Iran pledges not to engage in any hostile acts against the US—neither bombings, nor kidnappings, nor attacks on American interests in the Middle

---

[41] Segev, *Iranian Triangle*, 183.
[42] *Congressional Report on the Iran-Contra Affair*, 175.
[43] Segev, *Iranian Triangle*, 184.
[44] *Congressional Report on the Iran-Contra Affair*, 175.

East. Iran likewise pledges to aid the Afghan rebels in their struggle against the Soviet army of occupation and to transfer to them, any equipment made available to them by the US . . . .
As for the hostages, Iran is prepared to guarantee the release of only five of them. Iran has no authority or involvement regarding other hostages.[45]

Kangarlu proposed a five-step plan for weapons deliveries and hostage releases beginning on November 12 and ending on the 25th. Except for the first weapons shipment, when the sequence would be delivery first, hostage release second, Iran would release one hostage at 5:00 p.m. on the day of each subsequent delivery, which would arrive at midnight. The Rev. Martin Jenco would be released first, followed by Thomas Sutherland, Peter Kilburn, David Jacobson, and Terry Anderson.

Each delivery would include 35 Hawk, 50 Sidewinder, and 15 Phoenix missiles. These numbers were substantially higher than those specified by Karoubi. By comparison there were to be 175 total Hawks compared to 150 in Karoubi's proposal, 250 Sidewinders compared to 200, and 75 Phoenix missiles compared to 50. Once completed, Iran would host a visit by a senior US representative.[46] On the other hand, Iranian support for the anti-Soviet resistance in Afghanistan was an unanticipated bonus.

Ghorbanifar left Dubai for London on October 30 for a meeting with Kimche, Schwimmer, and Nimrodi.[47] When Kimche saw the Iranian offer he knew at once that it boded ill for Israel. If it went forward as proposed, the hostages would be freed, the United States and Iran would reestablish political relations, and Israel would be shut out of the Iranian arms market. Israel would undoubtedly be the main supplier for the five proposed arms deliveries, but after that, when US-Iranian relations were reestablished, Washington would become the main supplier of arms to Iran, and Israel would be relegated to the sidelines. Thus, Kimche could not allow the deal to stand as proposed.

As their discussion progressed, Kimche focused on three points, the number and types of weapons and the release sequence for the hostages. Within minutes, Kangarlu's original proposal lay in shreds. As the discussion continued, "the participants began calling Washington, Jerusalem, and Tehran" for guidance. As Segev notes, "during the following days the Hawk deal would come together in long telephone conversations between American and Israeli officials, and between them and the Israeli and Iranian middlemen." At the very least, this must be taken to mean that Kimche talked with McFarlane and Peres, and Ghorbanifar with Kangarlu, if not also Rafsanjani.[48]

---

[45] Segev, *Iranian Triangle*, 184-85. The reference to "only five" hostages evidently referred to the Americans and excluded the French hostages.
[46] Ibid., 185.
[47] Ibid., 194.
[48] Ibid., 194-95.

Kimche related McFarlane's view that hostages must be released first before any weapons were delivered. Ghorbanifar countered with the argument that weapons had to be delivered first, and then hostages would be released. Kimche declared that Israel could not deliver the amount and type of weapons specified "because of the American embargo." Initially, he said, Israel could only deliver the Hawk missile. After telephoning Kangarlu and receiving permission to negotiate for "Hawks only," Ghorbanifar proposed a way out of the impasse.[49]

Ghorbanifar declared that Iran desperately needed Hawk missiles to defend against "high flying Iraqi and Soviet planes."[50] He proposed that to break the impasse "Israel supply 80 missiles in a single shipment, with five American hostages and two Lebanese Jews, also captives, being released simultaneously." Afterward, "Kimche briefed McFarlane on his conversation with Ghorbanifar."[51] McFarlane must have agreed, for that is the deal that was supposed to constitute the first shipment. As it evolved, however, the Israelis would not be able to ship all 80 Hawk missiles in a single aircraft, which resulted in what was supposed to be three deliveries and a sequential release of the hostages. That, too, would not transpire, for the Hawk deal quickly turned into a fiasco. Operation Espresso, the Israeli code-name for the Hawk deal, would leave a bitter taste for all concerned.

The Hawk Entanglement

Both the Israelis and the new world order faction wanted to use the Hawk deal to entangle the United States government in arms sales, but for quite different reasons. To reiterate, the Israelis involved were Prime Minister Peres and his men, Kimche, Schwimmer, and Nimrodi; the principal figures for the new world order faction were Shultz and McFarlane, but not their aides, who were unaware of their collusion. Each group used the other to achieve its objectives, which were only partially congruent. And in each group the principals sacrificed their minions in the pursuit of success and to avoid blame.

Shultz and McFarlane wanted to employ the Israelis to entangle President Reagan in an arms-for-hostages deal that would torpedo his plan for rapprochement with Iran. Israel was the vehicle for this objective, but the coincidence of interest was only temporary. Once achieved, as we shall see, the new world order faction would attempt to severely cripple the US-Israeli relationship and close off the Israeli arms conduit.

---

[49] Ibid., 194.

[50] Ghorbanifar's technical unfamiliarity with weapons specifications—the Hawk missile was a low-altitude, not a high-altitude interceptor—would shortly become a major source of friction, although it is true that the Israelis did not correct his misunderstanding.

[51] Ibid., 194. McFarlane, *Congressional Report on the Iran-Contra Affair*, 175, testified to congressional investigators that he and Kimche had "a series of meetings . . . in the fall of 1985." However, the record indicates that there were none between the November 8 meeting and the one on December 8.

Peres, on the other hand, understood that Israel's interests were not the same as America's and feared that if the arms-for-hostages deal went through it would mark the end of Israeli arms sales to Iran. McFarlane was threatening to shut the operation down and resign and so to avoid being left hung out to dry Peres sought to go beyond McFarlane and draw the United States government directly into the arms sales business with Iran to ensure Israel's own continued access to what was a lucrative arms market.

The two groups colluded over the next two weeks, as McFarlane tried to draw Defense and the CIA into the Hawk deal, while the Israelis tried to involve the State Department. Shultz, who followed events very closely, and McFarlane ensured that the State Department was not implicated in the arms sales. Weinberger objected strenuously to the Hawk deal, and kept Defense out of it, but the CIA illegally became entangled.

The deal with the Iranians agreed in principle, the Israelis wanted face-to-face confirmation of US government participation. In the second week of November Peres sent Kimche, Rabin, and Amiram Nir, his counterterrorism expert, to Washington to talk to McFarlane and North. Kimche arrived on November 8, Nir on the 14th and Rabin on the 15th.

Although Ledeen says he asked Kimche to come to Washington to remonstrate with McFarlane, who was depressed (there were rumors about affairs with a reporter and a White House staffer) and on the verge of resigning his office because of an on-going battle with Chief of Staff Don Regan, Kimche had his own reasons for making the trip.[52] With North now about to become more deeply involved as McFarlane's surrogate, it was important for Kimche to meet him.

More important, however, was the Israelis' need to assess the United States commitment to the deal. Ironically, it appears that Ledeen did not know the true purpose of Kimche's trip and it was only later that he learned of the Hawk deal.[53] In any case, Kimche lunched with North and Ledeen on November 9, and the next day lunched with North and McFarlane, without Ledeen.[54] There can be little doubt that McFarlane and Kimche privately worked out the final details of the plan at this time during the "series of meetings" McFarlane testified that he had with Kimche "in the fall of 1985."[55] Moreover, Kimche was now also acquainted with North, who was being groomed to play a larger role.

Following Kimche's visit, that same day McFarlane moved to entangle the defense department. He met with Weinberger and disclosed that the "hostage

---

[52] Theodore Draper, *A Very Thin Line: The Iran-Contra Affairs* (New York: Hill and Wang, 1991), 181, thought it "odd" that a "part-time" consultant should "enlist an Israeli official to come all the way to Washington to strengthen the 'resolve' of an American superior." See also, Ledeen, *Perilous Statecraft*, 149-50.

[53] Ibid., 150-51.

[54] Scott Armstrong et al., *The Chronology: The Documented Day-by-Day Account of the Secret Military Assistance to Iran and the Contras* (New York: Warner Books, 1987), 173.

[55] *Congressional Report on the Iran-Contra Affair*, 175.

release efforts were tied to arms sales to Iran." As the defense secretary noted in his diary, McFarlane "wants to start 'negot.' [negotiations] Exploration with the Iranians (+ Israelis) to give Iranians weapons for our hostages." McFarlane presented the issue to Weinberger as if they were at the start of discussions, when, in fact, he had already worked out the deal.

Weinberger, of course, was viscerally opposed to any deals with Iran and their conversation was heated but inconclusive. The next day, however, in a follow-up discussion, Weinberger allowed as how "we might give them—thru Israelis—Hawks but no Phoenix."[56] In this way, Weinberger sought to avoid direct US involvement, while complying with what he thought was the president's policy.

Weinberger's shift of position may have been the result of a change of administration attitude toward "talking to terrorists." On November 8, a packet of letters from four of the hostages was tossed from a car onto the doorstep of the West Beirut Office of *Associated Press*. A cover letter signed by Jenco, Anderson, Jacobson, and Sutherland urged the president to negotiate with their captors. The result was the administration decided it would "talk directly with terrorists as long as concessions or blackmail are not involved."[57]

White House spokesman Edward Djerejian distinguished between "negotiations" and "talk." We do not negotiate with terrorists, he said, but are prepared to "talk to all parties . . . even the abductors of American hostages—in an effort to obtain their safe release." The *L.A. Times* reporter, Eleanor Clift, astutely observed that Islamic Jihad was thought to be holding the hostages and was demanding the release of the Kuwait-held Al-Dawa 17 in exchange for release of the hostages.[58]

In any case, within days, Secretary Shultz learned of McFarlane's meeting with Weinberger. The secretary's aides, Charles Hill and Nick Platt, each had made a record and, in a meeting, just before Shultz left for Geneva, the five of them, including Armacost and Whitehead, discussed what they had learned. According to Hill's note: "in last few days Bud asked Cap how to get 600 Hawks and 200 Phoenix to Iran. It's highly illegal. Cap won't do it I'm sure. Purpose not clear. Another sign of funny stuff on Iran issue."[59] Thus, contrary to Shultz's testimony to congressional investigators, he was well informed of the Hawk deal days before it occurred.

Amiram Nir arrived for a meeting with North on November 14. The two had worked together during the *Achille Lauro* crisis and North had been impressed and grateful for the help Nir had given in tracking down the terrorists. As it was apparent that Washington was attempting to locate those holding the hostages, Nir

---

[56] Walsh, *Final Report of the Independent Counsel* 1:91.

[57] Eleanor Clift, "US Revises Its Stances on Talking to Terrorists," *Los Angeles Times*, November 13, 1985, 1.

[58] Ibid.

[59] "Hill Note," November 14, 1985, as cited in Walsh, *Final Report of the Independent Counsel*, 1:91; and "Platt Note," November 14, 1985, in Ibid., 350.

offered to cooperate with North in a covert operation to find them. He would remain in Washington for the better part of a week and reach a tentative agreement on two plans, but not on how to fund their operation.[60] His true mission, however, may have been to keep in as close touch with North as possible over the next several days as the Hawk deal unraveled.

On the same day that Nir and North began their talks, McFarlane and Poindexter met with Casey and McMahon in the White House for their regular weekly briefing. During the briefing, McFarlane made it a point to tell them that, having heard rumors regarding Weir's release that the US was indirectly involved in shipping arms to Iran, "or at least to wink at some transferred from Israel," he "called David Kimche . . . on the open line to assure him that that was not the case and that no deal had been struck for the release of Weir." Calling on an "open line," rather than a secure line indicated that McFarlane wanted to establish for the record in the intercepts that he had not been involved in an arms-for-hostages arrangement.[61]

When the briefing was over and McMahon had left the room, McFarlane "casually" mentioned in an aside to Casey that the "Israelis plan to move arms to certain elements of the Iranian military who are prepared to overthrow the government."[62] This was an extraordinary remark and its purpose unclear. Israel providing arms for a military coup was never part of any discussion. Was it simply loose talk, or intended to prepare Casey to be supportive of Israel when the CIA was called upon to assist? McFarlane knew that Rabin was arriving the next day, so informing Casey of an imminent aggressive Israeli move would be certain to elicit his approval and support.

The following morning, November 15, Casey met with Rabin, who wanted to know whether the president still approved Israeli arms sales to Iran.[63] The CIA director may have reassured him based upon the information McFarlane had just given him the day before. Had McFarlane not informed Casey of the impending action, it is not at all clear that he would have known what Rabin was talking about. McFarlane had only briefed Casey once before on his "contacts with Iran," and that had been almost two months earlier on September 20, in the aftermath of Weir's release.[64] That had been Casey's first inkling of McFarlane's Iran initiative. Clearly, the CIA director was not "in the loop."

Following his meeting with Casey, Rabin met with his counterpart, Weinberger. His talking points included discussion of the supply of "American arms to Israel, including construction of new submarines for the Israeli navy."

---

[60] *Congressional Report on the Iran-Contra Affair*, 175-76.
[61] "John McMahon Deposition," *Congressional Report on the Iran-Contra Affair*, Appendix B, vol. 17, 84-87.
[62] McMahon, "Memorandum for the Record," November 15, 1985, in Walsh, *Final Report of the Independent Counsel*, 1:207; and *Congressional Report on the Iran-Contra Affair*, 176.
[63] Walsh, *Final Report of the Independent Counsel*, 1:207.
[64] See the section above on "McFarlane's Hand-Off."

Oddly, he does not seem to have discussed the subject of TOW replenishment with the defense secretary, or the impending arms shipment to Iran.[65] He reserved those topics for his discussion with McFarlane.

In his meeting with McFarlane, Rabin informed the national security adviser that Israel would be making another arms shipment within the next few days. He wanted reassurance that the president was behind the arms sales, that it was a "joint project" between the two countries, and that the United States would replenish the weapons Israel delivered. The answers he got, however, were anything but reassuring.

Rabin "wanted to reconfirm that the President of the United States still endorsed this concept of Israel negotiating these arms sales." Instead of a simple "yes," McFarlane replied in his typically vague and circuitous manner: "the president's authorization for Israel to sell arms to Iran subject to replenishment by the United States was still in effect." Then, he said, even more vaguely, that this authorization was based on "recent questions and reaffirmation by the president that I had received."[66]

If Rabin was unsettled by McFarlane's tangential reply as to whether Reagan "still endorsed this concept," he was further disturbed by McFarlane's answer to his next question. Rabin wanted "reassurance that the matter was indeed a joint project between the United States and Israel." McFarlane replied: "while the United States supported Israel's activities, it was going along with Israel on this matter." "Going along with Israel on this matter" was hardly the answer Rabin expected. The only reading of this reply was that it was not a "joint project."[67]

Finally, with respect to replenishment, McFarlane assured him that he would be assigning the task to North within the next two weeks "to find a technical means of achieving the replacement." Whatever McFarlane meant by "technical means," replacement of weapons Israel would deliver would not occur for months, if it would be two weeks before McFarlane assigned North the task to do it.[68]

McFarlane's vague and troubling answers to Rabin's very specific questions undoubtedly confirmed in his mind that Israel was about to get itself into a very dangerous position, unless the United States was brought directly into the "project." Thus, whatever his differences with the prime minister, he was prepared to cooperate in the Peres plan to do just that. The means of bringing the United States in would center on the flight logistics of the first Hawk missile shipment to Iran.

The plan was for Israel to botch the shipment and request American assistance in transporting the arms and for McFarlane to respond by facilitating the government's entanglement. Moreover, the president's national security adviser would orchestrate this maneuver from Geneva, Switzerland, where President Reagan and Mikhail Gorbachev were to meet.

---

[65] Segev, *Iranian Triangle*, 195.
[66] *Congressional Report on the Iran-Contra Affair*, 176.
[67] Ibid.
[68] Ibid.

The Geneva Summit

When Reagan and Gorbachev met November 19-21, the strategic situation had almost completely reversed since the Carter-Brezhnev meeting of 1979. Then, Moscow was on the offensive with a SALT II-codified strategic supremacy over the United States, dominance over Western Europe and Japan, and support for a worldwide network of revolutionary client regimes, which augured a transformation of the global order to the disadvantage of the United States.

President Reagan not only had defeated this Soviet strategy, but he had also reestablished American strategic and intermediate-range weapons advantage, rebuilt the western alliance, and was providing support for anti-Soviet resistance movements worldwide. He had codified his approach in a new strategic doctrine set forth in NSDD-75, based on strategic defense. The meeting in Geneva was thus the first act for him in a projected long play to create a new, re-designed global order.[69]

Reagan and Gorbachev had come to Geneva committed to a successful meeting, and by all accounts they got along amicably, but with their opposing positions well publicized in advance. In its essence, Reagan wanted to engage Gorbachev, and through him the Soviet leadership, to persuade them that agreeing with his strategy of shifting to the strategic defensive and arms reductions would not leave the Soviets worse off. Gorbachev, on the other hand, knew that he could count on the support of Shultz and most of the political establishment and hoped that the summit would be where he could convince the president to abandon SDI in return for substantial weapons reductions.

Reagan, therefore, needed to establish a negotiating baseline beyond which he would not go. That baseline was the annual report on Soviet treaty violations. On June 10, in NSDD 173, the president had instructed Weinberger to deliver the report by November 15 and to include recommendations of "appropriate and proportionate responses to these violations."[70] The defense secretary delivered his report on November 13.

In a letter accompanying the report, Weinberger addressed the president's Geneva meeting, cautioning him not to compromise on three issues: on continued observance of SALT II, restrictions on SDI research, and on a proposed communiqué.[71] Weinberger argued that continued adherence to SALT II would "sharply restrict the range of responses to past and current Soviet violations." Limiting the SDI program to research only "would diminish the

---

[69] See Arnold Horelick, "US-Soviet Relations: The Return of Arms Control," *Foreign Affairs* 63, no. 3 (1984): 511-537.

[70] Christopher Simpson, *National Security Directives of the Reagan and Bush Administrations: The Declassified History of US Political and Military Policy, 1981-1991* (Boulder: Westview, 1995), 549-55.

[71] "Weinberger Letter to Reagan on Arms Control," *New York Times*, November 16, 1985, A7.

prospects significantly that we will succeed in bringing our search for a strategic defense to fruition." Finally, agreement to a communiqué that allows "the Soviets to appear equally committed to full compliance . . . will make the difficult task of responding to . . . violations even more problematic."[72]

In the executive summary of the report, which, as in the previous report, found twenty-three Soviet treaty violations, Weinberger argued, "our original assumptions that the Soviets would not violate agreements . . . have been proved false." Consequently, the only path to improved US-Soviet relations was paradoxically through "a vigorous US defense program and forceful responses to all perceived Soviet violations." Otherwise, he said, "current and future Soviet violations pose real risks to our security and to the process of arms control itself."[73]

The report, summary, and cover letter were strictly in conformity with past practice and analysis of Soviet treaty violations. The problem arose when they were leaked to the press just before the summit. The resultant furor seemed to point to Weinberger as the culprit. McFarlane, when asked whether the release was intended to "sabotage the summit talks," responded, "sure it was."[74] Whoever leaked the material, and it was probably not Weinberger, it served the president's purpose of publicly setting the baseline for his discussions with Gorbachev.

Indeed, when asked bluntly whether he would fire Weinberger for "pressing his views too vigorously," the president barked to newsmen "hell no!"[75] Weinberger did not accompany the president to Geneva, but his chief aides, Fred Ikle and Richard Perle did. Perle took with him a secure communication device so that he could be in touch with the defense secretary should the need arise for his advice.[76]

In fact, the president hewed to Weinberger's advice, refusing to bend on SDI and insisted on the need to go beyond research to some testing to determine the validity of concepts. The president also refused to agree to Shultz's proposal for a communiqué, but late in the afternoon of the second day agreed to issue a joint statement. Communiqués are negotiated in advance and Reagan wanted to ensure that any summit statement accurately reflected what he and Gorbachev actually discussed; not what state department officials cooked up beforehand. The issue of continued adherence to SALT II did not arise.[77]

During the course of their talks the president hammered Gorbachev on the human rights issue, which the Soviet leader considered none of the outside

---

[72] Ibid.

[73] Walter Pincus, "Weinberger Urges Buildup Over Soviet 'Violations,'" *Washington Post*, November 18, 1985, A1.

[74] Bernard Weinraub, "Reagan Aides Upset by Disclosure of Weinberger's Letter on Arms," *New York Times*, November 17, 1985, A1.

[75] Barbara Rehm and Bruce Drake, "'Hell, no,' Cap Won't Go," *New York News*, November 18, 1985, A3.

[76] Jay Winik, *On the Brink* (New York: Simon & Schuster, 1996), 387-88.

[77] Jack Matlock, *Reagan and Gorbachev* (New York: Random House, 2004), 149-55.

world's business, but agreed to evaluate persons on a case-by-case basis.[78] The essence of the meeting from the president's point of view were three proposals he made to Gorbachev: for a transition to strategic defense, treaties on strategic and intermediate-range missiles, and a formula for the resolution of regional conflicts.

Reagan reiterated his concept of a transition from security based on offense to one based on defense, a sharp reduction of strategic missiles and the complete liquidation of intermediate-range weapons. He also offered a formula for the resolution of regional conflicts, calling for termination of military support, sponsorship of negotiations between the parties, and provision of developmental assistance afterward.

Gorbachev avoided any commitments but did reaffirm that the Soviet Union had altered its strategic conception from "equal security" to "reasonable sufficiency," a major change in their national security requirements. He also responded to Reagan's regional conflicts formula with a hint about withdrawing from Afghanistan, which Reagan ignored.[79]

In response to Gorbachev's demands to end SDI, Reagan declined, but surprised the Soviet leader by offering to "share the benefits" of any promising missile defense technology that might emerge from research *and* testing. After heated exchange, Gorbachev declared his disagreement, but acknowledged the president's belief in what he said. Reagan went further than his aides expected by also offering to invite Soviet scientists into US laboratories where SDI research was being conducted.[80]

The joint statement, hammered out during an all-night session, was a sober recapitulation of what the two leaders had discussed, and emphasized Reagan's oft-stated view that nuclear war cannot be won and must not be fought.[81] Also, as Reagan wanted, there was no "statement of principles," "guidelines," or "road map." Nor were SALT II, the ABM Treaty, and SDI mentioned in the statement, although the two leaders hoped for "early progress" on two issues on which they found common ground: the possibility of a fifty-percent reduction in strategic arms and an "interim agreement" on short-range weapons based in Europe.[82]

After it was over, the president reported to Congress that while the two sides remained "far apart," "we met, as we had to meet. I had called for a fresh start—and we made that start . . . . We understand each other better. That's the key to peace." The president reported that Gorbachev had agreed to an exchange

---

[78] Shultz, *Turmoil and Triumph*, 603 and Matlock, *Reagan and Gorbachev*, 161.

[79] Shultz, *Turmoil and Triumph*, 601 and "Soviet May Seek Afghan Pullout Plan, US Says," *New York Times*, November 25, 1985, A8. See also Oberdorfer, *The Turn*, 141-42.

[80] Matlock, *Reagan and Gorbachev*, 167.

[81] Ibid., 165 and Rowland Evans And Robert Novak, "Reagan's New Realism," *Washington Post*, November 22, 1985, A23.

[82] Walter Pincus, "Little Gained on Arms Reduction," *Washington Post*, November 22, 1985, A11.

of meetings over the next two years. The summit, he said, was a good start, but for now "our byword must be, steady as we go." [83]

The Arms-for-Hostages Trap

While Reagan was in Geneva, the Israelis carefully orchestrated the Hawk deal to entangle the United States government in arms sales to Iran. The August and September TOW shipments had been logistically straightforward. The Israelis shipped the missiles by DC-8 charter jets directly from Tel Aviv to Tabriz and Tehran, respectively, via the airspace of Cyprus and Turkey, a roughly four-hour trip of 1,500 miles.

The Hawk arrangement was quite different: more complex, longer, and open to mishap. Despite the presumed urgency in getting the weapons to Iran, Kimche and Schwimmer chose to ship the weapons first from Tel Aviv to Lisbon, Portugal, and then from Lisbon to Tabriz. The Lisbon route would add 5,000 miles to the trip and at least an additional day, counting turnaround time, if all went as planned.

Why not use the same route as before? According to the congressional report, the Israeli "planners chose this circuitous routing because direct flights from Israel to Iran would draw attention given [their] poor relations . . . "[84] When Poindexter asked North about it, he claimed that a direct flight would "compromise origins and risk eventual uncovering of many operational details."[85] Yet, none of this had concerned the Israelis just two months earlier, least of all their so-called "poor relations" with Iran.

Rabin, too, gave an inherently implausible explanation. He said to North that because of an incident over Turkish airspace "a few months earlier, the Israelis had concluded that direct flights were too dangerous. Instead, they had arranged to move the shipment through several other intermediate points, disguised . . . as oil-drilling equipment."[86] The implausibility of this explanation was that despite moving the shipment "through several other intermediate points," it was still routed over the same Turkish airspace as the August and September flights.[87]

It was common practice for Israel to move weapons through third countries and use neutral carriers to disguise origins, but why pick Lisbon, the furthest location in Western Europe from Iran? Was it because Portugal itself was a major arms shipper to Iran? By 1985, "43.8% of all Portuguese arms exports,"

---

[83] David Hoffman, "President Pushed for Missile Defense," *Washington Post*, November 22, 1985, A1.

[84] *Congressional Report on the Iran-Contra Affair*, 179.

[85] Ibid., 190n56.

[86] Oliver North and William Novak, *Under Fire: An American Story* (New York: Harper Collins, 1991), 29.

[87] The alternate route into Iran was down the Red Sea, around the Arabian Peninsula and into Bandar Abbas on the Persian Gulf.

$28 million, were going to Iran.[88] Or, was it because Lisbon International Airport was also a major transshipping point for arms exporters of all types? The Israelis themselves were using Lisbon as one of their intermediate points for arms exports. Soprofina was an Israeli front company used for this purpose and Israel Airline Industries had a major warehouse complex located at the airport where arms could be stored, laundered and sanitized, manifests created, and end-user certificates obtained. [89]

Or, did Kimche and Schwimmer pick Lisbon because Richard Secord, North's agent in the contra supply effort, also operated out of the same airport? Secord, the Israelis knew, was arranging weapons shipments for the Contras through DefEx, a Portuguese arms shipper that had a warehouse at the airport.[90] What would be more convenient when the Israelis professed to encounter complications in their shipment than to call on Secord for assistance?

For the moment, all seemed in order. On the morning the president departed for Geneva, November 16, in a brief conversation McFarlane had told him enigmatically "there was something up between Israel and Iran," which "might lead to our getting some of our hostages out, and we were hopeful . . . ." According to McFarlane, the president simply said, "cross your fingers or hope for the best, and keep me informed."[91] The national security adviser did not mention that it was an arms-for-hostages deal and simply left it to the president's imagination to decipher what he meant by "there was something up."

The very next day, however, the Israelis began to encounter "problems." In retrospect, it seems more than a coincidence that the Israelis chose to commence the Hawk mission when President Reagan (and McFarlane) were in Geneva. The day after they had arrived, Rabin called McFarlane to tell him "Israel was unwilling to commence the shipment without satisfactory arrangements for replenishment by the United States."[92] In other words, Rabin said that he was unwilling to wait for McFarlane to task North to make the arrangements in two weeks, after the delivery had occurred. He wanted action now, or Israel would not "commence the shipment."

McFarlane immediately called North, as did Rabin. Rabin informed North that Israel planned to move 80 Hawk missiles by November 20, but he

---

[88] Kenneth R. Timmerman, *Fanning the Flames: Guns, Greed and Geopolitics in the Gulf War* (1988), chap. 7. Online at http://www. kentimmerman.com/krt/fanning_index.htm).

[89] Segev, *Iranian Triangle*, 199 and Ronen Bergman, *The Secret War with Iran* (New York: Free Press, 2007), 118.

[90] Segev, *Iranian Triangle*, 198, claims to the contrary that "only afterward did the Israelis discover that Lisbon was an important logistic base for Secord . . . "

[91] *Congressional Report on the Iran-Contra Affair*, 176, misdates this conversation, placing it on November 17, but accurately notes that it occurred before the president left for Geneva, which he did on the morning of the 16th. See "Scheduled Events at the US-Soviet Summit," *Washington Post*, November 19, 1985, A20.

[92] *Congressional Report on the Iran-Contra Affair*, 177.

refused to act "without satisfactory arrangements for replenishment by the United States." After speaking to Rabin, North checked back with McFarlane, who confirmed, "the Israelis are trying to ship some Hawk missiles to Iran. The whole operation is being handled by a couple of private Israeli citizens. They've run into some logistical problems. Get back to Rabin and take care of it. Just fix it. Go up to New York and see Rabin."[93]

Rabin's phone calls to McFarlane and North were the first step in the Israeli plan to entangle the US government in the arms-for-hostages scheme. McFarlane's assignment of North to "just fix it" was the second. Up to this moment, North had not been involved in the scheme, except for intelligence monitoring of activity concerning the hostages. Nor had the United States government. As North put it: the calls "marked a major change in the US government's role in the arms sales to Iran." McFarlane "gave me the go ahead for direct US involvement, and assured me that the President had approved it."[94]

Thus was North "thrown into this on the night of November 17." [95] It is difficult to avoid the impression that McFarlane had carefully set North up to play the role he now assigned to him. North eventually would become a major player in the Iran initiative, as he already was in the Contra operation, but in the fall of 1985 when McFarlane assigned him the task of "fixing" the Israeli problem, he was an over exuberant, gung-ho, Marine who believed he could solve any problem, but who knew nothing about the history of the Iran initiative, or his boss's machinations.

North flew up to New York City the next day, the 18th, to meet with Rabin and Israel's Defense Procurement Mission Chief, Avraham Ben-Yosef. While there, North called Schwimmer in Tel Aviv, who told him that the plan was for Israel to ship 600 Hawks to Iran in groups of 100 over the next three or four days. Israel would ship the first 100 from its own stocks, after which all five hostages would be released. Other shipments would follow.

---

[93] North, *Under Fire*, 26-27 and McFarlane, *Special Trust*, 42-43. Both accounts telescope events, but in different ways. Later, when Walsh attempted to subpoena Kimche and Schwimmer, the Israeli government quashed the subpoena in US District Court on the grounds that "Kimche and Schwimmer were acting on behalf of the Israeli Government, not as private citizens, and that any cooperation Mr. Walsh desires from them should be handled on a Government-to-Government basis." See Thomas Friedman, "Iran-Contra Hearings; Israel Gives US Iran Role Report," *New York Times*, August 1, 1987, A1.

[94] North, *Under Fire*, 27. Kimche called McFarlane and Schwimmer called North on the same day, conveying the same message: no replenishment, no deal. See Segev, *Iranian Triangle*, 195-96.

[95] *Congressional Report on the Iran-Contra Affair*, 177. North testified "I didn't know the details of who [McFarlane] worked it out with, except the persons that he sent to me, first of all, in the case of Mr. Ledeen and second of all, in the case of those who came from overseas to meet with us." Draper, *Very Thin Line*, 186. The reference to Ledeen was to his October 30 meeting with him and McFarlane.

North agreed to authorize the Israeli purchase of 600 replenishment weapons, recording in his notebook: "Schwimmer to P/U [pick up] HAWKS in US"[96] He also passed on McFarlane's instruction that Ben-Yosef keep the purchases under $14 million per order. Any number higher than that would have to be reported to Congress. (In fact, Ben-Yosef wrote up the first purchase for $18 million, which immediately drew congressional scrutiny.)

Rabin then explained another predicament, saying, "at the last minute they had run into problems with landing rights and other clearances." He wanted North to "find us an acceptable airline that can move this stuff." North replied, "we don't have these kinds of assets sitting around." Rabin reassured him, "don't worry . . . . Our people will take care of the logistics. We just need an airline."[97]

From Schwimmer, North learned that he had arranged for an El Al 747 cargo jet to take 80 Hawks from Tel Aviv to Lisbon but had "neglected" to apply for landing approvals at Lisbon until the last minute. When he did, "he found that the Portuguese authorities were reluctant to grant them."[98] In retrospect, the landing clearances omission appeared to be a red herring, but North, unfamiliar with transport procedure and under the pressure of the moment, took Schwimmer's explanation at face value. In fact, landing clearances are routinely granted two to three days in advance, but in emergencies are granted within hours. It was true, however, that diplomatic authorization was required for flights carrying dangerous goods, but equally true that there were many firms that provided the service of arranging for necessary clearances.

Schwimmer had employed Israel's national airline, El Al, to ship the cargo. The airline ordinarily would have applied for landing clearance in Lisbon as routine procedure at the same time it filed a flight plan for the trip, arranged for flying time through appropriate air corridors, and set out alternative airports in case of emergencies, bad weather, etc. Schwimmer himself was perhaps the most experienced airman in Israel, which made it extremely unlikely that either he or the airline would have "neglected" a matter of critical importance that was moreover part of standard operating procedure.

To North, however, the solution seemed straightforward: if they could arrange for a landing clearance for the El Al jet there would be no need to find another airline. Checking with McFarlane, North decided to enlist Secord, whom he knew had extensive experience shipping arms out of Europe; indeed, out of Lisbon, and from the very airport in question.[99] With the decision to send Secord to arrange for landing clearance in Lisbon, Schwimmer "instantly" agreed to transfer $1 million to Secord's Lake Resources account in Geneva, to give him

[96] *Congressional Report on the Iran-Contra Affair*, 177.

[97] North, *Under Fire*, 30.

[98] Draper, *Very Thin Line*, 185.

[99] *Congressional Report on the Iran-Contra Affair*, 178. North, *Under Fire*, 30, says he picked Secord, while Secord, *Honored and Betrayed*, 219, says North told him McFarlane had recommended him.

sufficient funds to charter another aircraft, or bribe officials.[100] The money would, of course, implicate Secord in the scheme.

North arranged to meet with Secord the next day, the 19th, to brief him on the task and to hand him a letter of introduction to establish his bona fides if and when it became necessary. It described his mission as arranging for "the transfer of sensitive material being shipped from Israel," and enjoined him to exercise "great caution" and discretion to ensure that the activity not be disclosed. North signed the letter for McFarlane (who, later denied having authorized North to write it).[101] Secord quickly contacted his business agent in Lisbon, Thomas Clines, who happened to be in Washington, and the two of them flew to Lisbon that night.

Meanwhile, McFarlane was attending to two other tasks, which were to entangle the president and also Weinberger in the arms-for-hostages scheme, with mixed success. Late on the morning of the 19th, after the first Reagan-Gorbachev session, and before lunch, McFarlane briefed the president and Don Regan on the arms-for-hostages plan in Regan's small bedroom.[102] In a twenty-minute "difficult to follow" talk, including the cover story about shipping oil drilling equipment, McFarlane laid out the entire scheme:

> Intermediaries, timing, secret messages, transshipment and verification of weapons, guarantees that the hostages would in fact be released by their captors on the word of people in Tehran and Tabriz who ostensibly had no direct control over their action, only 'influence' and good offices.[103]

According to Regan's vivid recollection, "this was certainly the first time the president had heard the whole scenario," but McFarlane's timing "could not have been worse." The president had "just left Gorbachev; he had had no lunch; and many other items dealing with the summit, which was uppermost in his mind, remained to be discussed."[104] McFarlane did not seek the president's approval, "he simply told the president that the Israelis were about to act."[105]

---

[100] Draper, *Very Thin Line*, 184, thought that this "crossover" of funds "intermingled" the Iran and Contra operations for the first time, but it did not. There were separate accounts for each funding source. Richard Secord and Jay Wurts, *Honored and Betrayed: Irangate, Covert Affairs, and the Secret War in Laos* (New York: Wiley, 1992), 220, notes, "when Schwimmer was informed, he had the money instantly deposited to Lake Resources." The Lake Resources ledger, however, shows the deposit occurred on November 20. *Iran-Contra Affair*, 179.

[101] *Congressional Report on the Iran-Contra Affair*, 179.

[102] McFarlane, *Special Trust*, 43, says he briefed the president *before* the first session.

[103] Regan, *For the Record*, 320, claims Shultz was present when he was not. See Shultz, *Turmoil and Triumph*, 798n8. McFarlane clearly understood that the Iranians had "no direct control" over Mughniyeh.

[104] Don Regan, *For the Record* (New York: Harcourt, Brace, Jovanovich, 1988), 321.

[105] *Congressional Report on the Iran-Contra Affair*, 178.

The oddity about the briefing was that McFarlane knew that the Israelis were *not* about to act. They had been denied landing clearance in Lisbon and without it nothing would move. Why would McFarlane lay out in intimate detail an operation that had yet to be confirmed, let alone begun? A few hours later, he called Shultz at his suite and gave him the same briefing, except to say, "four hostages would be released on November 21." This was even more baffling than his briefing to the president because the number of hostages was five not four, and McFarlane had no way of knowing the exact date of release for an operation that had not yet begun, unless he were privy to Israeli planning.[106]

Shultz's reaction was "stony anger. I told McFarlane that I had been informed so late in the operation that I had no conceivable way to stop it."[107] But Shultz's aides had been following events very closely, keeping him informed at every step. Early on the morning of the 18th, Charles Hill had told Shultz that McFarlane had tried to see him the night before about the hostages. "He thinks something's coming down in the next week or so." Shultz responded: "it's a bad deal."[108] Ambassador Oakley also sent a memo to Shultz on the 18th, possibly based on telephone intercepts, noting the "expectation of a possible breakthrough on the hostages on November 20 or 21."[109] Thus, not only was Shultz being kept abreast of events as they occurred, but also, as we shall see, there was an opportunity for him to attempt to "stop" the operation.

McFarlane was also busy attempting to draw Weinberger into the scheme and retroactively cover North's previous "authorization" for Israel to purchase the missiles. The first day of the Geneva Summit, the 19th, he cabled the defense secretary and "asked him to sell 500 Hawks to Israel, which would transfer them to Iran in exchange for the release of five hostages on November 21."[110] But Weinberger was too crafty for McFarlane and gave him the bureaucratic runaround. He tasked Henry Gaffney, acting director of Defense Security Assistance Agency, to determine the availability of the Hawks and the legality of the sale. His report was negative. The Hawks could not be sold for re-transfer without congressional notification and intentionally packaging them under $14 million was "a clear violation."[111]

Weinberger promptly passed this message on to McFarlane. The next day, the second day of the summit, McFarlane told Weinberger that, "notwithstanding the legal problems, President Reagan has decided to send Hawk missiles to Iran through Israel." Israel, he said, would sell only 120 not 600 and

---

[106] Shultz, *Turmoil and Triumph*, 797.

[107] Ibid., 798.

[108] "Hill Note," November 18, 1985, in Walsh, *Final Report of the Independent Counsel*, 1:336.

[109] "Oakley Memorandum," November 18, 1985, Walsh, *Final Report of the Independent Counsel*, 1:336.

[110] "Weinberger Diary," November 19, 1985, Walsh, *Final Report of the Independent Counsel*, 1:408, 92.

[111] Ibid.

these would be "older models." He also informed the secretary that the hostages would be released on November 22, which indicated that he was keeping in touch with the Israelis and North about the clearance problem.[112] McFarlane had worked around Weinberger's block for the moment, but replenishment of Israeli weapons still needed to be addressed. Weinberger, on the other hand, managed to keep the defense department out of McFarlane's Iran scheme, but the CIA would not be as lucky.

The CIA is Caught

On Tuesday evening, the 19th, relieved at having arranged what he thought was the solution to the problem of obtaining a landing clearance, North stopped off on the way home for a drink and a chance to catch up with two of his former comrades, Dewey Clarridge and Vince Cannistraro. They had met and worked with each other the previous year when North had put together the Contra support network but had since been reassigned elsewhere.[113] Clarridge was now the CIA's European Division Chief and Cannistraro was working counterterrorism at the NSC.

They met at a favorite CIA watering hole in Mclean, VA, not far from agency headquarters, a restaurant and bar called Charley's Place. Their meeting was significant because, when the crisis broke a year later, Clarridge would be charged with denying he learned at this meeting that the US was involved in shipping weapons to Iran. Walsh would claim that he and the CIA had from that point illegally participated in a covert activity without presidential authorization. As a result, he would be forced into retirement in 1987 and given a formal reprimand for his brief, but critical role.

It is vital to understand the legal framework that established the basis for CIA activity because from this point forward all participants strove to act within its scope. Two edicts, the Hughes-Ryan Amendment of 1974 and NSDD 159, were the main elements in the framework. The Hughes-Ryan Amendment required the president to issue a written finding to authorize CIA or Defense Department involvement in any covert activity. The requirement that a finding had to be in writing was re-emphasized in NSDD-159, which the president had just signed in January 1985. Moreover, a president's finding could only anticipate future activity and not be retroactive. NSDD-159, in particular, had to be fresh in the minds of those for whom it mattered.

At Charley's Place, North undoubtedly recounted the story of the elementary Israeli screw-up in failing to obtain a landing clearance and how he had called on their mutual acquaintance, Richard Secord, to solve it. Clarridge claims that the subject of "Iran did not come up," and that he did not know Secord, but notes that they did discuss Lisbon's "clogged" pipeline, although only in the

---

[112] Ibid., "Weinberger Diary," November 20, 1985, 409 and 428.
[113] Clarridge had been Latin America Division Chief and Cannistraro Central American Task Force chief.

context of shipping arms to Central America.[114] North may or may not have given Clarridge a "heads-up" call to be ready to help out in case Secord was unsuccessful, but he had no reason to ask for help at this point.

Walsh's charge was based on the recollection of the third party at the meeting, Vince Cannistraro, who recalled that North said, "he needed Clarridge's help getting clearance to fly a shipment of military equipment to Iran." Unfortunately for Walsh, Cannistraro could not remember the date of their meeting, which undermined his case.[115]

However, Walsh's charge was dubious for several other reasons. The meeting at Charley's Place occurred while Secord and Clines were on the way to Lisbon where they would arrive the next morning. If, as Walsh also notes, Secord was "confident" that he could obtain landing clearance through his contacts, then there was no reason to ask Clarridge for assistance on a problem that had not yet arisen. Moreover, if North requested "help" on the 19th, why did Clarridge wait over two days until early in the morning of the 22nd to send his first cable to Lisbon? Furthermore, his first cable was simply to instruct the CIA chief of mission in Lisbon to provide assistance to Secord, who actually declined his help, at first.[116]

Finally, on the 20th, North sent Poindexter a detailed PROF message, which laid out the entire scheme, to commence on November 22, including the provision of "appropriate arrangements" with Lisbon air control, delivery of weapons to Tabriz, and the release of all five hostages in Beirut. He specifically noted, "all transfer arrangements have been made by Dick Secord, who deserves a medal for extraordinary short notice efforts."[117] As all of the parties to this mission were in virtually constant contact by secure communication means, North's message to Poindexter reflected Secord's expectations at that moment.

Secord's business colleague, Jose Garnel, one of the owners of DefEx, who had a brother-in-law in the foreign ministry, had contacted Portuguese authorities earlier that day, asking for landing clearance for two aircraft in transit to Iran. He had made his request on Secord's behalf, although Garnel simply identified Secord as a retired US general. (Secord was traveling under the name of "Copp.") Secord himself had spoken with the minister of defense, who assured

---

[114] Duane R. Clarridge, *A Spy for All Seasons: My Life in the CIA* (New York: Scribner, 1997), 309.

[115] Walsh, *Final Report of the Independent Counsel* 1:254, established the date of their meeting as November 19 based on North's calendar; Clarridge claims they met on November 20.

[116] Clarridge, *Spy for All Seasons*, 312. Walsh, *Final Report of the Independent Counsel*, 249, says he sent his first cable late on November 21, but acknowledges in note 16 that the cable is dated November 22.

[117] *Congressional Report on the Iran-Contra Affair*, 180. The PROF system was a secure email program that Poindexter designed for the NSC.

him that approval was forthcoming, and Secord had called Schwimmer to tell him things were in order.[118]

However, within the Portuguese foreign ministry things were decidedly not in order. When the clearance request was made, Portuguese ministry officials, fully conversant with declared US policy toward Iran, asked for an explanation from the US embassy. As the ambassador Frank Shakespeare was away, on the 21st, the chargé d'affaires, James Creagan, sent the political counselor to the ministry to explain. He told ministry officials that "the shipment was not authorized by the United States and was contrary to US Government policy strongly opposing arms sales to Iran."[119] Furthermore, he said, "he knew nothing that would justify the mission, because he had nothing in his channels."[120]

With a red flag from the US embassy, the Portuguese foreign ministry became increasingly reluctant to be a party to the affair and this attitude became more pronounced as the hours passed. What explains the Portuguese foreign ministry's attitude? It would seem that here is where Shultz found the opportunity to throw a monkey wrench into the operation and force the CIA into greater involvement. US embassy officials would not take it upon themselves to respond to the ministry's inquiry without first checking with Washington.[121] It is my conjecture that Shultz's aide, Ambassador Robert Oakley, replied to the chargé in the secretary's name with the instruction to restate US policy opposing arms sales to Iran.

Actually, it is more than conjecture because, when the chargé told the CIA's chief of mission what happened, he immediately sent a cable to Clarridge at CIA headquarters "to find out if the Secretary of State, Secretary of State Shultz, was aware of the mission and if he approved [US] involvement."[122] In other words, the CIA chief of mission had been told that Shultz opposed it.

Clarridge passed this message over to Poindexter at the NSC. His response, on the 22nd, which Clarridge forwarded to Lisbon, contradicted the instruction from State. Poindexter said, "the Secretary of State and Ambassador Oakley were the only two State officials who were aware of the mission, that they concurred . . ." However, because of the operation's "sensitivity," only CIA communications channels were to be used, not the State Department's.[123] Poindexter's attempt to get around Shultz' opposition would not work. By the time his cable reached Lisbon, events were already careening out of control, entangling the CIA in an apparent arms-for-hostages transaction.

---

[118] Segev, *Iranian Triangle*, 198, 200.

[119] *Congressional Report on the Iran-Contra Affair*, 180.

[120] "CIA Chief Deposition," *Congressional Report on the Iran-Contra Affair*, Appendix B, vol. 4, 1159; and "State Deputy Chief of Mission Deposition," vol. 8, 271-72.

[121] Ibid. See the embassy's reporting "Cable from American Embassy [Lisbon] to Department of State Headquarters," November 22, 1985, 180 and 190n82. Unfortunately, the content of the cable is unavailable.

[122] Ibid., "CIA Chief of Mission Deposition," volume 4, 1162.

[123] Ibid., and "Deputy Chief of Mission Deposition," volume. 8, 272-74

Chapter 12

Israel Entangles the CIA

On the evening of November 21, 1985, in Tel Aviv, Kimche, Schwimmer and Nimrodi's assistant, Yehuda Alboher, met to discuss their next steps. After calls to North in Washington, Ben-Yosef in New York, Secord in Lisbon, and Nimrodi in Geneva with Ghorbanifar, they assessed the situation.[1] There had still been no resolution of the weapons replenishment problem, only North's promise, but no decision by the Pentagon, which deeply concerned the Israelis. Worse, the US government still remained on the sidelines of the mission, as only Secord, a private citizen, had become directly involved. North had turned Rabin's initial ploy to have the US provide Israel with an airline into an effort to obtain landing clearance for Israel's own plane, which was promised but not confirmed.

There was another stunning, recent development that preoccupied them. It was the arrest of an American intelligence specialist spying for Israel that threatened to disrupt the entire US-Israeli relationship. On November 18, naval intelligence had detained Jonathan Jay Pollard for questioning. Pollard was an American Jew working as an intelligence analyst for the Naval Investigative Service. Offended that the United States was not sharing all of the intelligence that it should with its ally, Israel, Pollard volunteered his services to Tel Aviv as a "walk-in" spy.[2]

The Pollard Affair

For over a year Pollard had accessed "almost every document in the American intelligence network." He provided Israel with mountains of intelligence, including satellite reconnaissance photos, message traffic, targeting data on the Soviet Union, information on the Middle East, the identity of American agents, ultra-secret technology, and much more. He gave Israel an

---

[1] Samuel Segev, *The Iranian Triangle: The Untold Story of Israel's Role in the Iran-Contra Affair* (New York: Free Press, 1988), 198.

[2] Dan Raviv and Yossi Melman, *Every Spy a Prince* (New York: Houghton Mifflin, 1990), 306. See also "The Jonathan Pollard Spy Case: The CIA's 1987 Damage Assessment Declassified," National Security Archive, The George Washington University, https://nsarchive2.gwu.edu/NSAEBB/NSAEBB407/.

inside look at America's innermost secrets. Eventually, his actions aroused suspicion among his co-workers, who alerted naval authorities.[3]

Extensive surveillance of his activities led to a decision to call him in for questioning on November 18. Released after questioning, Pollard immediately contacted his handler at the Israeli embassy and demanded assistance to flee the country to Israel. He and his wife, Anne Henderson Pollard, attempted to seek sanctuary in the Israeli embassy three days later. Though gaining entry, they were turned over to the FBI who arrested them.[4]

As soon as Pollard called the embassy for help on the evening of the 18th it was clear that his cover had been blown and Pollard's handlers all quickly fled to Israel. Thus, even before he had been arrested on November 21, in Israel "intelligence officials and politicians there already knew" that Pollard's exposure "was bound to harm Israel's relations with the United States."[5]

There are multiple theories about the Pollard case, ranging from poor spy craft on his part, a general spy roundup by the FBI, an extension of internal Israeli politics to Washington, to an extension of internal American politics to Israel. Probably each of these is partially correct. Pollard had become careless in his work. His supervisor "noticed 'huge stacks' of top-secret material on Pollard's desk that were not related to his assigned tasks."[6] In this version, suspicion led to surveillance; surveillance to apprehension.

There was a heightened sense of insecurity within the American intelligence community as a result of a string of arrests during 1985 of several spies. Among these were the navy spy ring operated by John Walker, Arthur Walker, Michael Walker, and Jerry Whitworth; Samuel Morrison, a civilian intelligence analyst with Naval Intelligence Command; Ronald Pelton, an NSA communications specialist; Edward Howard, former CIA employee; Larry Wu-tai Chin, CIA analyst; Sharon Scranage, CIA clerk; and Richard Miller, an FBI veteran. The result was a massive government-wide campaign to tighten security throughout the intelligence community.[7]

There was also the view that Pollard had been a deliberate casualty of the ongoing conflict between Israel's Likud and Labor parties. Pollard was connected to a spy network in the United States run by Rafi Eitan called LAKAM, and his exposure severely damaged Yitzhak Shamir's Likud Party. The sensational charge associated with this theory was McFarlane's relationship with

---

[3] Gordon Thomas, *Gideon's Spies: The Secret History of the Mossad* (New York: Thomas Dunn, 2009), 85-86.

[4] Joe Picharallo, "Navy Employee Is Charged with Passing Defense Secrets," *Washington Post*, November 22, 1985, A1; and "Navy Employee Is Accused of Passing Secrets to Israel," *Wall Street Journal*, November 22, 1985, 6.

[5] Raviv and Melman, *Every Spy a Prince*, 317.

[6] Ibid., 315.

[7] "Pentagon Orders Security Crackdown on Code Experts," *Philadelphia Inquirer*, November 27, 1985, 12.

Eitan and his role in facilitating Pollard's work, which, it is claimed, was the real reason for the national security adviser's resignation.[8]

The theory in the current work, however, argues that Pollard's arrest was the result of the ongoing conflict between the Reagan and new world order factions. The new world order faction orchestrated the arrest of Pollard to cripple the US-Israeli relationship and shut down the Iran initiative. McFarlane, though a member of this faction, was a necessary casualty. Moreover, it was Peres, rather than Shamir, who had to bear the brunt of the ensuing spy scandal.[9] If McFarlane's resignation had any impact in Israel, it was on Peres's strategy to retain and enlarge access to the Iranian arms market.

Over the next several weeks Shultz led a "spy probe" in Israel to determine the scope and propriety of "activities" that "were inconsistent with official Israeli policy."[10] At the same time, what can only be called a witch-hunt took place, as nameless "sources" began to label Jewish-American officials in the US government as Israeli informants.[11] Pollard was tried and sentenced to life imprisonment, "having been found guilty of being the greatest traitor in the history of the United States."[12] But, if the purpose behind the anti-Israel campaign was to frighten Peres off from cooperating with Reagan, it backfired.

The Israelis Prod Washington

Kimche, Schwimmer, and Alboher, meeting on the evening of November 21, were undoubtedly alarmed by the news about Pollard. Coming on top of the persistent American reticence to replenish the weapons or failure to obtain landing clearances, they could not but assume that their worst fear of being hung out to dry by the Americans was about to come true. They were therefore more determined than ever to press forward with their plan to bring the United States government directly into the arms-for-hostages scheme.

Beginning that evening, they bombarded McFarlane, North, and Secord with phone calls demanding action. Rabin called McFarlane threatening to cancel the mission. "If the Iranian project were not viewed as a joint US-Israel operation, Israel would not undertake it alone."[13] Rabin and Kimche made calls to North

---

[8] Ari Ben-Menashe, *Profits of War* (New York: Sheridan Square Press, 1992), 174-76.

[9] "Peres Reported to Admit That Navy Man was Spy," *Philadelphia Inquirer*, November 26, 1985, 4.

[10] "US Widens Spy Probe in Israel," *Washington Times*, December 10, 1985, A2 and Joseph Harsch, "Spy Case Brings Sea Change in US-Israel Ties," *Christian Science Monitor*, December 20, 1985, 7.

[11] Howard Teicher and Gayle Radley Teicher, *Twin Pillars to Desert Storm* (New York: William Morrow, 1993), 380-84.

[12] Thomas, *Gideon's Spies*, 408.

[13] *Report of the Congressional Committees Investigating the Iran-Contra Affair* (Washington, DC: US Government Printing Office, 1987), 189n16. [Hereinafter cited as *Congressional Report on the Iran-Contra Affair*].

demanding that he "put White House pressure on the Pentagon to expedite the replenishment."[14] Ben-Yosef also called North to demand that the United States promptly sell the latest model Hawk missiles as replenishments. Privately, however, the Israelis had decided to send older ones to Iran.[15]

Their decisive act, however, was to send the El Al 747 cargo jet to Lisbon even though they knew that landing clearance had not been attained, thus forcing American involvement. There is confusion in the record surrounding this crucial decision, however. Segev says that Schwimmer called North and Secord on the evening of November 21 and they agreed that the plane would take off twenty-four hours later, on Friday evening, the 22nd.[16]

The joint congressional study contradicts this, noting "although the clearance for landing in [Lisbon] had not been authorized on the morning of November 22, the El Al 747 carrying the 80 Hawk missiles was ordered to take off . . . "[17] Draper also remarks on this decision, describing it as "one of the most peculiar episodes in this melodrama." He says "Schwimmer decided to send an El AL plane loaded with 80 Hawk missiles out of Tel Aviv toward Lisbon—without a clearance," but doesn't say when.[18] The behavior of American officials, however, establishes the plane's departure time as the morning of the 22nd.

Segev notes that "on Friday morning Secord called Schwimmer and asked for takeoff to be delayed by a few hours, since he had not yet been able to arrange the landing rights in Lisbon."[19] Asking to delay the takeoff indicates that the plane was about to depart. If the plane was not supposed to depart until evening, there does not seem to be any reason to ask for a delay in the morning. Nevertheless, against Secord's plea, but in accord with their own plan to prod the Americans into commitment, Schwimmer sent the plane out. The result predictably drove North and Secord into a frenzy.

---

[14] Segev, *Iranian Triangle*, 198.

[15] Ibid., 198-99.

[16] Ibid., 199, 201. Segev is at pains to pass the blame for the failure of this mission on the Americans, who he saw as "incompetent," and to protect Schwimmer, who he says was shocked by their actions.

[17] *Congressional Report on the Iran-Contra Affair*, 181.

[18] Theodore Draper, *A Very Thin Line: The Iran-Contra Affairs* (New York: Hill and Wang, 1991), 189

[19] Segev, *Iranian Triangle*, 199.

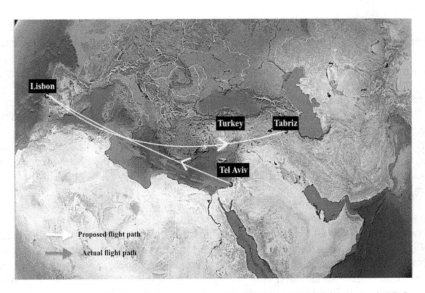

Ill-Fated Hawk Flight: On November 22, 1985, an El Al 747 cargo jet left Israel with 80 Hawk missiles for delivery to Iran, by way of Lisbon, Portugal. The flight was aborted for failure to obtain landing clearance in Lisbon. Involvement of US persons and assets in attempts to complete the mission contributed to President Reagan's entanglement in the Iran-Contra scandal.

When the Israelis began bombarding North with demands the previous evening of November 21, he became concerned that the United States was verging on the prospect of becoming directly involved and asked McFarlane if there were a covert action finding that would permit it. The answer he received, copying it down in his notebook, was "RR said he would support 'mental finding.'"[20]

Under the pressure of the moment, McFarlane had given North the only answer he could think of. Findings were highly secret, compartmented documents, not subject to verification by anyone without the "need to know." However, the entire notion of a "mental finding" was preposterous and absurd, requiring the skills of a mind reader. Moreover, it flew in the face of NSDD 159, which specifically required that all covert action findings be in written form. In the heat of the moment, McFarlane's answer satisfied North, and was the critical act that pushed the CIA into direct and illegal involvement (fortunately, North had the presence of mind to jot down McFarlane's authorization, which would come in handy later).[21]

---

[20] As quoted in Draper, *Very Thin Line*, 212.

[21] The Foreign Assistance Act, as amended, section 654, says of Presidential Findings: "In any case in which the President is required to make a report to the Congress . . . concerning any finding or determination under any provision of this Act . . . that finding or determination shall be reduced to writing and signed by the President."

North had no reason to question his boss, who, he assumed, was transmitting the view of the president.[22] With authorization in hand in the form of the "mental finding," North called Clarridge for help. Arranging to meet him at his office in Langley at just after 4:00 a.m. (which was 9:00 a.m. in Lisbon and 11:00 a.m. in Tel Aviv), North said that he faced an emergency and needed to obtain landing clearances in Lisbon for an El Al 747 that was "already airborne."

Explaining with the cover story that he needed to assist an Israeli shipment of oil drilling equipment to Iran, Clarridge replied "sending *anything* to Iran was a violation of the US embargo on Iran and in contravention of US policy of not negotiating with terrorists." North reassured him, based on McFarlane's "mental finding" remark, that "the president had approved both lifting the embargo and negotiating for the hostages."[23]

A skeptical Clarridge only became convinced "after hearing North on the phone with McFarlane in Switzerland and Poindexter at the White House." Aside from the fact that McFarlane was then in Rome, not Geneva, it was clear that North was following the orders of his superiors. It was, of course, axiomatic that the mission of the CIA is to support the policies of the executive branch. In any case, Clarridge also checked with Casey who approved. As far as Clarridge was concerned, "the decision had been made by the president."[24]

Clarridge sent "flash" cables to his Lisbon mission chief instructing him to "contact Secord . . . and offer him assistance" in the fulfillment of his mission. As noted above, however, at this point, Secord felt he had the clearance matter well in hand and declined assistance. However, a few hours later, around 1:00 p.m., Secord was hit with a double whammy that changed his mind. To his astonishment, he learned that not only had Schwimmer sent the plane against his instructions, but also that the Portuguese government had refused to issue the landing clearance. Worst of all, intensifying the pressure, the plane was nearing the point where, if there were no clearance, it would have to turn around to have enough fuel to get back to Tel Aviv.[25]

Secord in a panic called the CIA mission chief back and made an "urgent request for assistance."[26] He suggested that they bring in the embassy chargé to

---

[22] Oliver North in North and William Novak, *Under Fire: An American Story* (New York: Harper Collins, 1991), 34, says, "I don't know exactly what McFarlane told the President. I do know that he told me that the President had approved our involvement. 'Fix it,' McFarlane had said, and that's all I needed to hear. It was the kind of challenge I thrived on, and I jumped right in. I can do it, I thought. I'm a Marine. This whole deal is screwed up, but I can take care of it."

[23] Duane R. Clarridge, *A Spy for All Seasons: My Life in the CIA* (New York: Scribner, 1997), 310-11.

[24] Ibid.

[25] *Congressional Report on the Iran-Contra Affair*, 181.

[26] "CIA Cable," November 23, 1985, in Lawrence E. Walsh, *Final Report of the Independent Counsel for Iran-Contra Matters*, vol.1 (Washington, DC: United States Court of Appeals for the District of Columbia Circuit, August 4, 1993), 249.

make a formal request and cabled Clarridge requesting approval. Clarridge obtained approval from Poindexter and replied to his mission chief in Lisbon to say that the "NSC wanted the CIA senior field officer to bring the chargé into the operation and to 'pull out all the stops' because the El Al plane was only one hour from aborting."[27]

Complementing this action, North contacted Oakley in the State Department to obtain his agreement to authorize the Lisbon chargé to support the clearance request. (Here, one wonders whether North was unaware that the State Department was on the other side, or thought that he could personally persuade Oakley, with whom he worked on the Counterterrorism Task Force.) Oakley told North that he would help but did not. Instead, he called Clarridge and told him "the State Department was aware of the operation," but that "Clarridge should contact the foreign minister . . . for assistance."[28] In other words, Oakley was intent on keeping the State Department out of the action, but willing to push the CIA in deeper.

Secord, meanwhile, applied a second time for a landing clearance and frantically, if clumsily, attempted to gain personal access to both the prime minister and the foreign minister to plead his case. As they were returning from a trip, Secord tried to contact them at the airport, talking his way into the VIP lounge. When he realized he had gone to the wrong terminal, he made a scene and aroused the antipathies of Portuguese authorities, who became more averse than ever to granting a clearance.[29]

Next, the CIA mission chief sought to see the foreign minister, who was in a meeting, but was told that Portugal would need "a formal statement from the US Embassy."[30] The time spent waiting for the foreign minister, who showed no inclination to meet with US representatives, and in deliberating over whether or not to put their request in writing, took the El Al plane to the turnaround point and it was forced to abort and return to Tel Aviv. It would no longer be available.

That afternoon, hoping to reschedule the mission for the next day, North finally convinced McFarlane to call the Portuguese foreign minister to request approval for a landing clearance. At the same time, he formulated three options for continuing the mission. They could charter a new airline and pick up the materiel in Tel Aviv, fly to Lisbon and transfer the cargo to three DC-8 aircraft Schwimmer had chartered, and proceed to Iran; they could fly the three chartered aircraft to Tel Aviv, pick up cargo and fly back to Lisbon and thence to Iran; or

---

[27] "Director 625908," November 22, 1985, Ibid., 250. See also "Deputy Chief of Mission Deposition," *Congressional Report on the Iran-Contra Affair*, Appendix B, vol. 8, 272-74.

[28] Walsh, *Final Report of the Independent Counsel*, 1:255. *Congressional Report on the Iran-Contra Affair*, 181 errs in stating that Oakley told North that the Embassy "could request clearances."

[29] Draper, *Very Thin Line*, 191.

[30] "CIA Cable," November 22, 1985, in Walsh, *Final Report of the Independent Counsel*, 1:250.

they could fly the three aircraft to Tel Aviv, abandon the Lisbon route, and fly directly to Iran. North observed, "everybody involved '(including Kimche)' believed the first option to be the best."[31] In other words, the situation had now reverted to the very first proposal Rabin made to North, which was to "find us an acceptable airline that can move this stuff."[32]

McFarlane, contacted in Rome, promptly called the Portuguese foreign minister that afternoon at 5:30 and claimed to have received approval for a landing clearance to be granted the next morning. McFarlane also claimed that he had "persuaded [the foreign minister] to approve the flights without a diplomatic note." However, when the chargé contacted the ministry the next morning, neither the secretary-general, nor the chef de cabinet knew anything about any agreement and continued to insist on a diplomatic note. Indeed, the foreign minister himself went further, publicly insisting, not only on a diplomatic note, but also on one that said, "the purpose of the mission was to secure the release of the US hostages."[33]

The truth is that while McFarlane did place a call to the foreign minister, he had not persuaded him to grant a landing clearance but told North that he had.[34] But why? There were three reasons McFarlane lied to North. He did not want to involve the State Department, which sending a note would do (indeed, McFarlane decided not to send one); he wanted to buy some time for Clarridge to arrange for an alternate aircraft, which would bring the CIA into the operation illegally and irreversibly; and he wanted to ensure that all other options had been foreclosed.

McFarlane didn't want North to know there was no clearance yet because if he did, the solution would simply be to use the three DC-8s Schwimmer had already deployed to Lisbon, fly them to Tel Aviv, pick up the missiles, and fly them to Iran. This would not involve the CIA, or the US government. So, it was important to buy just enough time for Schwimmer to cancel his charter with the DC-8s, which would leave the operation with no aircraft and force the CIA to provide them.

Thus, North and Clarridge, operating on the assumption that a clearance would be granted the next morning, November 23, and assuming that all they needed was a replacement for the El Al 747, worked out a solution. Reporting to Poindexter at 6:00 in the evening, North said two CIA proprietary 707s from St. Lucia Airways would be made available to Secord to pick up the Hawks in Tel Aviv, deliver them to Lisbon where they would be transferred to Schwimmer's three chartered DC-8s, and flown to Tabriz.[35]

This solution lasted less than an hour. At 7:00 p.m. North reported to Poindexter that Schwimmer had "released their DC-8s in spite of my call to DK [David Kimche] instructing that they be put on hold until we could iron out the

---

[31] John G. Tower et al., *Report of the President's Special Review Board: February 26, 1987* (Washington, DC: US Government Printing Office, 1987), B-33.

[32] North, *Under Fire*, 30.

[33] Walsh, *Final Report of the Independent Counsel*, 1:250-52.

[34] Draper, *Very Thin Line*, 188.

[35] *Tower Report*, B-33.

clearance problem in [Lisbon]." North thought Schwimmer "released them to save
$ and now does not think they can be re-chartered before Monday."[36] Secord
suggested using one of the Lake Resources aircraft scheduled to transport
ammunition to the Contras. This would delay delivery to the Contras by a few
days but would "at least get this [Iran] thing moving." North concluded: "so help
me I have never seen anything so screwed up in my life."[37]

Saturday morning, the 23rd, North learned that the Portuguese
government would not issue landing clearances without a note and Secord's idea
also fell through, so he began to explore alternate routes, the most obvious being
the original route the Israelis had used in August and September, flying directly
from Israel to Iran.

These developments had a different impact on Clarridge. As it became
evident by afternoon that Lisbon was out and that the CIA was the only remaining
transport option, Clarridge "understood that we as an agency might be on the brink
of getting into this endeavor. We'd no longer be simply providing
communications; we could be perceived as participating in NSC activities. When
I realized that this might bring the CIA into North's operation, I called Ed
Juchniewicz for approval."[38] As Casey, McMahon, and Clair George were out of
Washington that weekend, Juchniewicz was acting director of operations.

The question was: could the CIA legally provide a proprietary aircraft
for this NSC mission? If the mission were construed as a covert activity, then the
president would need to issue a finding to authorize it. On the other hand, if it
were simply a commercial venture, a finding would not be necessary. Hearing that
North was requesting the use of the CIA's proprietary aircraft, Juchniewicz asked:
Is this a straight commercial deal? Clarridge replied that it was. North would lease
and pay for the use of the aircraft and pilots. On the grounds that it was a
commercial arrangement, the acting chief of operations gave his ok.

This entire exchange exposed McFarlane's claim of Reagan's "mental
finding" as false. Even though North had used it to gain Clarridge's assistance,
Clarridge did not use it to justify the CIA's involvement. He sought approval from
Juchniewicz on other, safer, grounds. The "mental finding" would never be
brought forward as a justification for anyone else's actions (until McFarlane tried
to talk Attorney General Edwin Meese into employing it after the crisis broke, but
it was immediately discarded).[39]

But, for Clarridge, it was "important to the Agency that North pay for
the use of the aircraft and pilots. That would confirm the commercial nature of the
operation. If the arrangement had not been a commercial one and no money

---

[36] *Congressional Report on the Iran-Contra Affair*, 182.

[37] Ibid.

[38] Clarridge, *Spy for All Seasons*, 313.

[39] Edwin Meese, *With Reagan: The Inside Story* (Washington, D.C.; Regnery, 1992),
266-68, did argue that Reagan had made an "oral" finding, which was also dubious,
but which put the president in a better legal position. See chap. 13.

changed hands, then it would have become a CIA covert operation in support of the National Security Council," and "require a presidential finding."[40]

Hook, Line, and Sinker

Authorized to support North in a "straight commercial deal," Clarridge sprang into action, assembling the required expertise, as North, Charles Allen, the Air Branch chief, and intelligence officers congregated in his office "command post" to provide support for the mission.[41] They all assumed, as Allen did, that, although "it was not the norm," it was "a White House request" and they "did not question it." They all further assumed, like the airline proprietary project officer, that they were operating under a finding, which, as was standard, "would be staffed all the way up to the DDO."[42]

Nobody believed the Israeli cover story about oil drilling equipment, yet all would later deny any certain knowledge that missiles were the cargo, even if they suspected otherwise, because of the legal exigencies under which they operated. When the crisis broke a year later, and it was learned that they had been tricked, that there had been no finding to authorize their actions, the participants sought to cover their activities by claiming they did *not* know missiles were the cargo, until later in January. In January, when the president did sign a finding, their actions became "legal."[43]

Clarridge contacted his field agents to arrange overflight clearances over Turkey, and landing and overflight clearances for Cyprus, as well. Once they decided to dispense with Lisbon and fly direct from Tel Aviv, to disguise the origins of the flight they decided to stop in Larnaca, Cyprus, before proceeding on through Turkey to Iran. All of this required coordination, not only with his agents in the field, but also with Schwimmer and Kimche in Tel Aviv.

Air Branch could not obtain the use of a proprietary 747 on short notice, so two St. Lucia Airways 707s were advanced and by the evening of November 23, one had flown in to Tel Aviv. It had been a remarkably quick response, but problems immediately surfaced. When loading the missiles onto the plane, the size of the missile containers restricted the number the plane could accommodate to eighteen, instead of eighty. This meant that five flights would have to be made to deliver the first tranche of eighty; and, after consultations with Ghorbanifar in Geneva, one hostage would now be released after each partial delivery, instead of all five at once.[44] The Iranians, *inter alia*, had re-established the principle of releasing one hostage for one shipment of arms.

---

[40] Clarridge, *Spy for All Seasons*, 313.

[41] *Congressional Report on the Iran-Contra Affair*, 182.

[42] "Charles Allen Deposition," Ibid., Appendix B, vol. 1, 410; and "Airline Proprietary Project Officer Deposition," 139-40.

[43] See Walsh, *Final Report of the Independent Counsel*, 1:260-62, especially n170, for the charges against Clarridge.

[44] Segev, *Iranian Triangle*, 202. See also Draper, *Very Thin Line*, 192-94.

Worse, as they were loading the missiles, it was discovered that the plane bore a US registry, while the other standing by did not. So, in the interests of maintaining some degree of plausible deniability, the non-US registered aircraft was substituted for the US registered plane—at a cost of some additional delay of unloading and re-loading the aircraft.[45] Schwimmer tried to talk the captain into using the US-registered plane, but disguising it by painting over the registry numbers, which seemed "crazy" to the airline proprietary officer, and he refused.[46]

There were also money problems. As it was absolutely essential that the Israelis pay for the aircraft to maintain the commercial nature of the flight, the proprietary's manager demanded a $30,000 down payment, which didn't sit well with Schwimmer, who claimed he had to scramble for funds.[47] The oddity here was that the Iranians had just deposited over $24 million in Nimrodi's account to cover the purchase and transport of 80 Hawk missiles.

The Israelis had additional tricks to play. When the plane finally took off for Iran via Cyprus, Schwimmer inexplicably neglected to include a manifest with the flight documents. When they landed in Larnaca, customs officials became suspicious and wanted to inspect the cargo. The pilot and crew managed to write out a manifest on the spot and talk themselves into the air without disclosing the cargo.[48] Had Cypriot customs inspected the cargo and discovered the missiles the subsequent brouhaha would have led to the probable confiscation of the cargo, if not the exposure of the American role. All of which raised the question of what the Israelis were up to. Would exposure be the next best thing to involvement?

In any case, once the plane was in the air over Turkey, Clarridge received a cable from his man in Ankara, who said that the Turkish foreign ministry wanted to know whether the plane was carrying weapons. Clarridge doubted the story he was told that Turkish air traffic controllers had learned about the cargo from querying the pilot and so reaffirmed the cover story that the plane was hauling oil drilling equipment. He believed that "someone in the Turkish Foreign Ministry decided to go on a fishing expedition and just threw out the question . . . to see what the response would be."[49] But the real question was: who suggested to the Turkish foreign ministry that there might be weapons on board? Could it have been someone in the US embassy?

Yet another change in the flight plan caused in-flight problems. At the last minute, the destination was changed from Tabriz to Tehran, requiring a

---

[45] "CIA Air Branch Chief Deposition," *Congressional Report on the Iran-Contra Affair*, Appendix B, vol. 4, 847-48.
[46] "Airline Proprietary Officer Deposition," *Congressional Report on the Iran-Contra Affair*, Appendix B, vol.1, 38-39.
[47] For discussion of these travails, and more, see Segev, *Iranian Triangle*, 202-04 and Draper, *Very Thin Line*, 193-94.
[48] "Airline Proprietary Officer Deposition," *Congressional Report on the Iran-Contra Affair*, vol. 1, 41-42.
[49] Clarridge, *Spy for All Seasons*, 314-15.

change of air corridors. The new route was inconsistent with the over flight clearance request, prompting additional probing questions. As the congressional study observes, "ironically, the pilot told the flight controllers the true nature of the cargo even while Clarridge was spreading the cover story to high level officials . . ."[50]

The plane arrived in Tehran's Mehrabad airport on the morning of November 25, to the surprise of the airport personnel. Having been diverted from Tabriz, word had not been forwarded to Tehran. Nevertheless, after some slight confusion, the unloading of the missiles was uneventful, and the plane departed later the same day. Fortunately for the crew, they had left before the missile crates were opened and inspected.

When Iranian technicians took one look at the contents, they were outraged, thinking initially that they had been the victims of yet another hoax. As Secord observed, during 1985 and 1986, "every con artist on the planet seemed out to make a buck at Iranian expense."[51] The 18 Hawk missiles were not what they had bargained for. Believing that they were ordering high-altitude anti-aircraft missiles to contend with Soviet and Iraqi reconnaissance aircraft penetrating their airspace, what they got were low-altitude anti-aircraft missiles, which could not serve that function. Prime Minister Mousavi was beside himself with rage, railing at Kangarlu in Geneva, "You idiot! They tricked you again. We can't depend on you!" Perhaps as bad, several of the missiles had Stars of David stamped on them.[52]

The Iranians refused to accept the missiles, which were eventually returned (in February 1986), and demanded their money back. Iran had deposited $44 million in Ghorbanifar's account on November 22 for 80 Hawks and future arms purchases. No bridge money from third parties was involved here, indicating the seriousness of the Iranian side. Ghorbanifar transferred $24 million to Nimrodi, who, in turn, paid $11.8 million to the Israeli Ministry of Defense for the planned first shipment of 80 Hawks. With the failure of the Hawk deal, the Iranians wanted the $24 million back.[53] Some of it, however, had already been spent and arguments swirled around every stage of the money's return.

The Israeli Defense Ministry refunded $8.1 million to Nimrodi, keeping back $3 million plus for the 18 Hawks not yet returned. Nimrodi refunded $18.6 million to Ghorbanifar for the 62 missiles not shipped. The remainder, minus "expenses," that is, money skimmed at each stage, kickbacks, and bribes, would be refunded to Ghorbanifar in February 1986, after 17 of the 18 Hawk missiles were returned (the Iranians had test-fired one missile).

---

[50] *Congressional Report on the Iran-Contra Affair*, 185.
[51] Richard Secord and Jay Wurts, *Honored and Betrayed: Irangate, Covert Affairs, and the Secret War in Laos* (New York: Wiley, 1992), 222.
[52] Segev, *Iranian Triangle*, 205.
[53] Segev, 206-07 and Draper, 196-97 offer similar accounts of these money movements.

Despite Clarridge's precautions, the CIA had become directly involved in the Hawk mission, not just by sending cables, but by providing communications support, using its influence in arranging overflight and landing clearances, and supplying planes and pilots. When the crisis broke a year later, the charge against Clarridge would be that he had known all along—from his first meeting with North at Charlie's Place on November 19—that North was arranging for the shipment of missiles to Tehran and thus not only he, but also the CIA, was engaged in illegal covert activity without the authority of a presidential finding. What was conveniently overlooked, however, was that the CIA's involvement was the direct result of McFarlane's transmission of the president's purported "mental finding" to North, who used it as the basis of his request to Clarridge.

Reagan Turns the Tables

The failure of the Hawk deal intensified the struggle between those who wanted to continue with the arms-for-hostages scheme and those who wanted to shut the operation down. The president, now fully apprised of the issues, decided, as he had time and again, to take what had been done and employ it for his own purpose—to attempt to establish a political relationship with Iran—but he did so without informing the leaders of the new world order faction, or Congress, of his decision.

The Hawk failure was the climax of McFarlane's scheme. He now moved to use it as the rationale for shutting down the initiative entirely, according to the new world order faction's plan, and pirouetted to side with Shultz and Weinberger in opposition to the program. The Israelis, however, immediately acted to keep the program going and Kimche began to cooperate with North and Secord in developing a new plan.

The president chose a third course, which was for the United States to take control of the arms-for-hostages scheme, subordinate the Israelis to it, and seek to parlay it into a diplomatic relationship with Iran. In a very real sense, the president turned the tables on the new world order faction, who had sought to use the arms-for-hostages scheme as their way of *preventing* the establishment of relations with Iran.

The Israelis, too, became victims of their own success. Their plan to draw the United States deeper into the scheme succeeded too well, as Reagan took control of the policy, relegating the Israeli role to logistical support. Of course, Reagan's action did not occur in a vacuum. His was but one successful move in a contest with moving parts; others—the Israelis, the new world order faction, even those who thought they were acting on behalf of the president—would make moves of their own.

As soon as John McMahon learned of Clarridge's actions on the morning of November 25, he recognized the CIA's need for legal authorization to justify "implementation of this mission." After angrily placing a hold on any further CIA involvement, he called the agency's general counsel, Stanley Sporkin, and told him that "I wanted a Finding and I wanted it retroactive to cover that flight." [54] Informed that a finding was being prepared, North called Schwimmer to tell him that there would be no more flights "until we tell you."[55]

McMahon should have been familiar with the law on presidential findings, which stipulated that a finding dealt with "anticipated future intelligence activity," not with what had already been done. Sporkin, however, did know the law, or quickly became informed of it, and told McMahon that there was no need for a finding to cover the proprietary flight. Upon reflection, however, he agreed that it "wouldn't hurt" to cover the CIA's effort in attempting to influence foreign governments to obtain landing clearances,[56] even though he knew it was, at the very least, unprecedented. Sporkin sought to lend some quasi-legal heft to the retroactive feature of the finding by describing it with the Latin phrase *nunc pro tunc* (literally "now for then").[57]

What Sporkin did, however, was to stretch the finding well beyond providing mere cover for the CIA into legal authorization to "facilitate the release of the American hostages." The finding authorized:

> assistance by the Central Intelligence Agency to private parties in their attempt to obtain the release of Americans held hostage in the Middle East. Such assistance is to include the provision of transportation, communications, and other necessary support. As part of these efforts certain foreign materiel and munitions may be shipped to the Government of Iran, which is taking steps to facilitate the release of the American hostages.
>
> All prior actions taken by US Government officials in furtherance of this effort are hereby ratified.[58]

This finding represented a serendipitous capstone of the new world order faction's plan to entangle the president in an arms-for-hostages scheme, their way of derailing an opening to Iran. It authorized future (and legalized past) CIA involvement in the scheme but failed to embed it in the larger strategic context of a diplomatic opening to Iran. Thus, while the finding's immediate effect was to sanction the CIA's involvement, the longer-term danger was that the unvarnished arms-for-hostages formula would pose a major political liability for the president—if it ever became public.

Sporkin had prepared this finding in less than 24 hours and the question is: from whom had he learned that the proprietary flight had been part of an

---

[54] *Congressional Report on the Iran-Contra Affair*, 185.

[55] Draper, *Very Thin Line*, 207.

[56] "John McMahon: Memorandum for the Record," December 5, 1985, *Congressional Report on the Iran-Contra Affair*, Appendix B, vol. 12, 166-67.

[57] "Edward Makowka Deposition," Ibid., vol. 17, 598-99.

[58] McMahon, "Memorandum for the Record," *Congressional Report on the Iran-Contra Affair*, 186.

exchange of arms for hostages? Sporkin told McMahon that he intended to speak to the White House counsel, Fred Fielding, and to the attorney general, Edwin Meese.[59] There is no record of a discussion with Fielding; Findings were routinely sent to the Justice Department to ensure "legal sufficiency." However, Meese denied that Sporkin had contacted him or the department.[60]

On the evening of November 25, McMahon sent two of the CIA technicians involved in the proprietary flight to brief Sporkin, the Air Branch deputy chief and the CIA group chief (oddly, neither Clarridge nor Allen, who knew the purpose of the flight).[61] Sporkin claimed that these "two guys from operations . . . told him the operation was, in essence, an arms-for-hostages trade."[62] However, both men contradicted Sporkin, and testified, "nothing was said to indicate that the proprietary's flight was related to an effort to free hostages." [63] If neither of these men told him of the flight's purpose, who did?

There are three possibilities. Sporkin must have spoken to McFarlane, Poindexter, or North. McFarlane was the obvious candidate because this had been his scheme from the beginning and the finding served his purpose. However, he was not in Washington (although location meant little, as these men were, or could be, in contact from anywhere). Poindexter was in Washington holding down the fort at the NSC, had not been privy to McFarlane's scheme, and was only just beginning to get a feel for what was going on.[64] North, on the other hand, was directly and continuously involved; thus, the probability is that Sporkin spoke to North, if not also to McFarlane. It seems that in the matter of the November finding, North became the unwitting agent for McFarlane and the new world order

---

[59] "John McMahon Deposition," *Congressional Report on the Iran-Contra Affair*, Appendix B, vol. 17, 296.

[60] "Edwin Meese Deposition," Ibid., vol. 18, 33-34.

[61] Allen had shown Clarridge "reports indicating that the flight was part of an operation aimed at the liberation of hostages, but the CIA was permitted to reveal only that the flight had a humanitarian purpose." Scott Armstrong et al., *The Chronology: The Documented Day-by-Day Account of the Secret Military Assistance to Iran and the Contras* (New York: Warner Books, 1987), 185.

[62] Walsh, *Final Report of the Independent Counsel*, 1:540. See also "Testimony of Stanley Sporkin," *Iran Contra Investigations, Joint Hearings before the Senate Select Committee on Secret Military Assistance to Iran and the Nicaraguan Opposition and the House Select Committee to Investigate Covert Arms Transactions with Iran*, 100th Cong., 1st sess., 100-6, June 23, 24 and 25, 1987 (Washington, DC: US Government Printing Office, 1988), 121, 130.

[63] *Congressional Report on the Iran-Contra Affair*, 185-86 contradicts the technicians and follows Sporkin's line.

[64] "John Poindexter Deposition," Ibid., Appendix B, vol. 20, 1094. "In November 1985, I was very confused as to what had been approved and what hadn't been approved and frankly thought [the Iran initiative] had been run in a very slipshod manner."

faction, although his immediate purpose was to provide legal cover for his own actions.[65]

When North heard that McMahon was demanding a finding, he realized that McFarlane had lied to him about the "mental finding." If the "mental finding" were valid there would have been no need for another one. North got in touch with Sporkin that evening to ensure that the finding he was preparing not only covered the CIA's role in the Hawk shipment, but also would legalize the mission itself (and his role in it). If Sporkin spoke to McFarlane, he received the same advice. However, from this point onward, McFarlane and North moved along opposing policy paths, although North's realization of McFarlane's opposition was slow in coming.

North had had "nothing to do" with the first draft and by the time he got in touch with Sporkin, one of the attorneys in the CIA general counsel's office, Bernard Makowka, had already typed up a first draft of the finding in response to Sporkin's directive.[66] It retroactively sanctioned the CIA's support for Israel's shipment of missiles to Iran, including a provision for notification of congressional intelligence committees, but said nothing about facilitating the release of the American hostages.

By the next morning, however, reflecting his conversation with North and probably also with McFarlane, Sporkin changed the draft finding entirely. He removed the provision for congressional notification, scratched out Israel and substituted "private parties," erased missiles and substituted "foreign material and munitions," and inserted the phrase "release of the American hostages," three times, to make its purpose unmistakable.[67]

After instructing Makowka to "keep no copies," Sporkin turned in the finding to Casey on Tuesday morning, November 26.[68] The director immediately called McFarlane and Don Regan to get their approval.[69] In a cover memo to Poindexter, Casey instructed, "it should go to the President for his signature and should not be passed around in any hands below our level."[70] Poindexter, however, kept the finding to himself because Reagan already had left for California that morning. Although the president returned to Washington on

---

[65] North's prominent role with Sporkin in formulating both the January 6 and 17 findings reinforces the argument that he was also involved with him on this one.

[66] "Sporkin Testimony," *Iran-Contra Investigations, Joint Hearings*, 100-6, 212.

[67] "Makowka Deposition," *Congressional Report on the Iran-Contra Affair*, Appendix B, vol. 17, 597-98. "Sporkin Testimony," *Iran-Contra Investigations, Joint Hearings*, 100-6, 127, denied that he had been "asked to alter the finding."

[68] "Makowka Deposition," *Congressional Report on the Iran-Contra Affair*, Appendix B, vol. 17, 604. Back-up copies were found later after a search of hard drives.

[69] "McMahon: Memorandum for the Record," December 5, 1985, *Congressional Report on the Iran-Contra Affair*, Appendix B, vol. 12, 166.

[70] "Memorandum from Casey to Poindexter," November 26, 1985, in Walsh, *Final Report of the Independent Counsel*, 1:208n52.

December 2, Poindexter did not present it to him for signature until three days later, on December 5.[71]

The Policy Scramble

Within a matter of 24 hours—indeed, the same 24-hour period surrounding the formulation of the finding—the Hawk mission had collapsed in failure. On the morning of November 25, in McFarlane's absence, "Poindexter told the president at his regular 9:30 a.m. briefing that a shipment of arms to Iran had just taken place."[72] All eagerly awaited the announcement that hostages had been released. They waited in vain; no hostages were freed.

Instead, a few hours later, Ghorbanifar, on the verge of hysteria, called Ledeen to describe the Hawk fiasco. Claiming that the Israelis and the Americans, indeed, Reagan himself, had "cheated" Iran, he conveyed a message from Prime Minister Mousavi that he wanted Ledeen to deliver to the White House. The message stated:

> We have fulfilled our every promise, and now you have cheated
> us. You must immediately remedy this terrible situation or else
> dire consequences will follow.[73]

Ledeen drove down to the West Wing "early in the evening," hoping to see McFarlane, but he was in California and "unavailable." Instead, he delivered the message to Poindexter, who, receiving it, told Ledeen that he was being "taken off the project," because, he said, "we need people with more technical expertise." Ledeen was stunned, thinking that Poindexter "knew nothing about the political contacts with Iran. Only McFarlane and North... were privy to this information."[74]

In fact, it was McFarlane who wanted to take Ledeen out of the line of fire to cover his own tracks. His intent, like Kissinger's maneuver over the Angolan affair, was to "bring this operation into the NSC," where he could hide his own responsibility and pin it on someone else, like Poindexter.[75]

---

[71] "Donald Regan Deposition," *Congressional Report on the Iran-Contra Affair*, Appendix B, vol. 22, 612. Regan claimed that he never saw the November finding. "I don't recall ever seeing nor hearing about the Sporkin finding in November of 1985."

[72] *Congressional Report on the Iran-Contra Affair*, 185. The president's daily brief (PDB) was a CIA-compiled account of the events of the previous 24 hours. In the Reagan administration, however, the CIA did not directly brief the president, but gave the briefing book to the national security adviser, who did. See John Helgerson, *CIA Briefings of Presidential Candidates* (Washington, DC: Central Intelligence Agency, 1996), chap. 6.

[73] Michael Ledeen, *Perilous Statecraft: An Insider's Account of the Iran Contra Affair* (New York: Scribner, 1988), 161-62.

[74] Ibid., 162.

[75] The next day, November 26, McFarlane wrote North that he was "inclined to think that we should bring this operation into the NSC and take Mike [Ledeen] out of it but

Thus, by the evening of November 25, Poindexter learned of the Hawk disaster. Did he tell McFarlane, or the president? Although McFarlane was out of town and although there were rumors of his imminent resignation, he was still the national security adviser and Poindexter most certainly spoke with him. In fact, McFarlane was deeply involved in and in frequent contact with the president regarding another airline hijacking that had begun two days before and had just ended very badly.

On November 23, EgyptAir flight 648 took off from Athens headed for Cairo. Within minutes of being airborne, three Palestinian members of Abu Nidal, led by Omar Rezaq, commandeered the aircraft. In what was another Qaddafi-sponsored terrorist plot,[76] they ordered the pilot to take the plane to Tripoli, but, as the hijackers began to check passengers' passports, an Egyptian Security Service agent pulled out his gun and killed one of the terrorists instantly. In the ensuing gunfight, the Egyptian agent was wounded along with two flight attendants, and the aircraft's fuselage was punctured, causing depressurization of the passenger cabin.[77]

As the pilot took the aircraft into an emergency descent to 14,000 feet to allow passengers to breathe without oxygen masks, the hijackers commanded him to land at Luqa airport in Malta. After an emergency landing, which airport controllers initially attempted to prevent, the hijackers demanded fuel for the aircraft, intending to fly on to Tripoli. As Maltese authorities refused to comply unless all passengers were released, the hijackers began shooting them, first two Israeli, then three Americans, to show they meant business. (Fortunately, three of the five survived.)

Maltese Prime Minister Karmenu Mifsud Bonnici, an ally of Qaddafi's, personally assumed control of the negotiations with the hijackers. Indeed, NSA intercepts convinced American leaders that Qaddafi was sending instructions to the hijackers and perhaps to Bonnici, who may have expected an outcome similar to the TWA 847 hijacking that ended without excessive violence.[78] But Mubarak had a more forceful response in mind, perhaps to make up for his gaffe in allowing the terrorists to escape in the Achille Lauro affair the previous month.

Bonnici was caught between the demands of the hijackers for fuel and free passage and the demands of the Egyptian and American governments to permit Egyptian Special Forces to storm the plane. Shultz declared publicly "terrorists deserve no quarter. Terrorists should have no place to hide. We must

---

will await John's [Poindexter] thoughts. No further communication with Mike on this until I have thought it through." Armstrong et al., *The Chronology*, 187.

[76] It was later learned that Libyan embassy personnel had smuggled the weapons into the boarding area in diplomatic pouches, which were not subject to security screening.

[77] J.A. Mizzi, *Massacre in Malta: The Hijack of Egyptair MS 648* (Valletta: Techonografia, 1989).

[78] David C. Wills, *The First War on Terrorism: Counter-Terrorism Policy during the Reagan Administration* (Lanham, MD: Rowman & Littlefield, 2003), 176.

stamp out this terrorist activity."[79] On *Meet the Press*, he said, "the way to get after these people is with both barrels," endorsing a military raid.[80] A state department spokesman said, "we were prepared to offer all appropriate assistance."[81]

Unlike the TWA instance, this time Shultz would get his wish. Under great pressure, Bonnici dragged out the negotiations with the hijackers for almost an entire day before finally agreeing to permit Egyptian Task Force 777 to attack the plane on the evening of November 25. US Delta Force had trained the Egyptian unit and, although the state department offered to send a special operations team to assist them, Bonnici rejected the offer.[82]

The plan was to attack the plane after nightfall under cover of delivering food to the passengers. Inexplicably, an hour and a half before the planned time of the raid, the Egyptian commandos stormed onto the plane after detonating explosives attached to the cabin doors and luggage compartment. The explosions ignited a fire that spread rapidly in the cabin, causing a suffocating, toxic smoke.

Realizing they were under attack the two hijackers tossed grenades into the cabin area, killing and wounding many. Casualties mounted as the commandos fired indiscriminately throughout the smoke-filled cabin. In all, 60 of the 91 passengers were killed, and many were wounded. The leader of the hijackers, Omar Rezaq, initially escaped by disguising himself as a wounded passenger, but was later caught. In short, the "rescue" resulted in one of the worst airline hijack tragedies in history, discrediting the feasibility of assaulting a passenger aircraft.[83]

President Reagan, Secretary Shultz, and McFarlane were heavily involved throughout the hijack as Egyptian president Hosni Mubarak asked for and received US assistance. McFarlane called the president early in the morning of November 24 to obtain permission to authorize US planes stationed at nearby Sigonella air base in Sicily to provide protective air cover against a possible interception by Qaddafi's planes as the Egyptians deployed forces to Malta. The next day, the 25th, there was extended discussion of the horrific outcome. Finally, on November 29, McFarlane passed on Mubarak's request for fighter escorts as he extracted his forces from Malta.[84]

The EgyptAir crisis thus bracketed the failure of the Hawk mission and may well have affected the president's response to it. It also shows McFarlane fully engaged with the president, who had left Washington at 9:00 a.m. Tuesday

---

[79] Bernard Gwertzman, "US Lauds Raid, Regrets Deaths," *New York Times*, November 25, 1985, A1.

[80] Terry Atlas, "US Stands Behind Jet Raid," *Chicago Tribune*, November 26, 1985, 1.

[81] "US Says It Was Prepared to Employ Force," *Philadelphia Inquirer*, November 25, 1985, 13.

[82] David C. Martin and John Walcott, *Best Laid Plans: The Inside Story of America's War Against Terrorism* (New York: Touchstone, 1988), 266.

[83] "Hijack Rescue Leaves Dozens Dead," *Washington Times*, November 25, 1985, A1.

[84] Douglas Brinkley, ed., *The Reagan Diaries* (New York: Harper Collins, 2007), 372.

November 26 for Los Angeles. McFarlane was already in San Francisco where he joined Shultz for his 65th birthday celebration at the Bohemian Grove, afterward going to Santa Barbara.[85] It is probable that McFarlane delivered the president his daily briefings on November 27 and 29, the days before and after Thanksgiving.

Detailing the movements of the key players is essential to establish the context for an apparent presidential decision on the morning of November 26. The congressional report asserts that Reagan "authorized continuing the arms-for-hostages transaction" on the morning of the 26th when Casey "sent the Finding to the White House." The report further claims, "North's notes indicate that he was so informed by Poindexter at an hour-long meeting." The note read:

> 0940-1050. Mtg w/JMP. RR directed op to proceed. If Israelis want to provide diff model, then we will replenish. We will exercise mgt over movmt if yr side cannot do. Must have one of our people in on all activities. [86]

The report supports this note by a citation from the Israeli historical chronology that "later that day, North related to an Israeli official that the Americans wanted to carry on even if the supply of additional arms was needed and even if the weapons had to come from the United States."[87] Draper says North had a second meeting with Poindexter on November 26, citing another North note, where North was instructed to have either Secord or Kimche tell the Iranians that the US was not at fault in the Hawk fiasco and was willing to commit to shipping 120 more Hawks, if the Iranians would secure the release of all of the hostages "on 1st delivery" and "reiterate" their commitment to no more terror against the US. Finally, Washington would arrange a "change of team" to ensure success.[88]

However, there are multiple problems with the assertion that Reagan directed the operation to proceed at this moment, beginning with the question of who told Poindexter that the president had authorized the operation to proceed? The best estimate is that, as the president was on his way to California and not informed of the need for a decision on the morning of November 26, it was McFarlane who told Poindexter to proceed, and he promptly relayed that information to North.

These multiple problems further entail the reliability of North's notebook entries, the substance of policy, and its timing. North frequently misdated entries in his notebooks. Indeed, both Draper and the congressional report identify some of North's misdated entries, casting suspicion on their reliability.[89] The widely

---

[85] Robert C. McFarlane, *Special Trust* (New York: Cadell & Davies, 1994), 330, makes no mention of the hijack.

[86] *Congressional Report on the Iran-Contra Affair*, 186-87.

[87] Ibid., 187.

[88] Draper, *Very Thin Line*, 200.

[89] Ibid., 632n101. Draper says North misdated his entry regarding the second meeting of November 26, as October 26, while the congressional report dated it on November 27. *Congressional Report on the Iran Contra Affair*, 210n1, says the November 27

quoted Israeli historical chronology was and remains a classified document, and thus also unverifiable.

Policy substance is another issue. As it evolved, the president's policy would look only vaguely like that described in North's purported notes of November 26 and it would take over a month of internal wrangling before a decision to proceed with arms sales would be made. Clearly, the decision to assume control of the arms-for-hostages program, whatever its larger rationale, was not a matter to be decided lightly—especially as the entire approach of trading arms for hostages had not been Reagan's policy in the first place.

The shipment of 120 Hawks would never be a part of any plan. The "change of team" formulation was obviously incorrect because at that very moment Kimche, Schwimmer, and Nimrodi were conferring with North and Secord about a new plan. The Israeli team would not be removed from the action until a month later. The replenishment question was yet another matter that would not be resolved for several months and McMahon had stopped CIA support for the proprietary flights, pending the signing of a finding. Thus, literally nothing in the North notes of November 26 was true, or actual policy, at that moment.

Finally, there is the timing issue. Poindexter had not learned of the Hawk fiasco until the evening of November 25 and the president left for Los Angeles the next morning at 9:00 a.m. The finding was sent over to the White House on the morning of November 26, but not until after the president had gone. It seems unlikely, therefore, that the president would have made a decision to proceed based upon a document he had not yet seen. In fact, the operation did not proceed because in the absence of a signed finding, the CIA continued planning but stood down.

More importantly, there was not much time to make a decision on the morning of the 26th and while it is possible that Poindexter, and the president, if not also Casey, had conferred the evening before, it is unlikely that a decision was made then. The congressional report removes even this narrow decision window by stating that it was not until "after midnight on November 26," that is, early morning of the 27th, that "Allen learned [from radio intercepts] that officials in Iran were upset that the wrong model Hawks had been delivered" and, therefore, only sometime after that a decision to proceed was made.[90] Thus, it seems, advancing the decision date obscures the argument that then ensued over whether or not to proceed.

The Issue Is Joined

Two policy arguments collided at this time. While McFarlane and Shultz were attempting to use the failed Hawk delivery as the reason to shut down the Iran initiative entirely, North, Secord, and Poindexter were actively working out

---

entry was misdated October 27. At the very least, there is confusion as to whether the second meeting occurred on November 26, or 27.

[90] *Congressional Report on the Iran-Contra Affair*, 187.

a new arms-for-hostages plan with Kimche, Ghorbanifar et al, to keep it alive. There is nothing in this record to suggest a foregone conclusion that the president had made the decision to take control of the initiative at this point.

There can be little doubt that when McFarlane joined Secretary Shultz for his birthday celebration at the Bohemian Grove outside of San Francisco the two men discussed McFarlane's plan to resign as well as the best way to utilize the act in furthering their larger objective. McFarlane decided to "inform" the president of his "thinking" during his daily briefing on the 29th. Determined to "turn off the Iran arms deals," he told Reagan "this is not working."

> Our hopes at the beginning of this were to be talking to Iranian politicians and to have a political agenda. It has ended up that we are talking to Iranian arms merchants, with no apparent prospect of establishing a political agenda.[91]

According to McFarlane, the president agreed, saying: "OK . . . Get the guys together," by which he meant to convene an NSPG meeting when he returned to Washington. McFarlane immediately called Poindexter, but told him to set up two meetings, not one. The first, as instructed, was of the NSPG for December 7; the second was with Ghorbanifar in London the next day.[92] McFarlane's plan was straightforward. At the NSPG meeting, he would side with Shultz and Weinberger to shut down the initiative. Then, he would fly to London to inform Ghorbanifar that the deal was off.

McFarlane's next step was to hand in his resignation, of which there are two versions. Mayer and McManus say that on Saturday November 30, McFarlane drove up to the ranch and handed the president's military aide his letter of resignation, prompted by word from his secretary that *Newsweek* was about to publish a rumor about it.[93] McFarlane, however, claims that four days later, "on December 4, I wrote my resignation letter and slipped it into the binder I gave the president every morning during the daily briefing . . . "[94] The president's diary entry, however, settles it, stating that on Saturday, the 30th, the president received an "eyes only" resignation letter from McFarlane.[95]

The next day, Sunday December 1, according to the president's diary, Reagan saw McFarlane in Los Angeles at his Century Plaza hotel headquarters "for a few minutes" to make sure that he truly wanted to leave government.[96] McFarlane confirms that it was during his meeting with the president at the Century Plaza that he discussed his resignation with him.[97] However, as the

---

[91] McFarlane, *Special Trust*, 46.

[92] *Tower Report*, B-44.

[93] Jane Mayer and Doyle McManus, *Landslide: The Unmaking of the President* (Boston: Houghton Mifflin, 1988), 169-70.

[94] McFarlane, *Special Trust*, 330-31.

[95] Brinkley, *Reagan Diaries*, 373.

[96] Ibid.

[97] McFarlane, *Special Trust*, 331-32.

president had left Los Angeles for Washington, via Seattle, on the 2nd, it was patently impossible for McFarlane to have slipped his resignation letter into the briefing book on December 4 and then discussed his resignation with the president the next day at the Century Plaza hotel in Los Angeles.

There was more to McFarlane's resignation than meets the eye. He may not have intended to resign, but to use a threat to resign as part of his and Shultz's plan to shut down the Iran initiative. Both he and Shultz had used the threat to resign as a tactic before.[98] But, if this was the tactic, he was in for a surprise. By this time Reagan was fully apprised of the Hawk fiasco as well as McFarlane's role in it. As Mayer and McManus observe, "unlike a year earlier when Reagan had refused to accept McFarlane's resignation, this time he accepted it on the spot—to what others said was McFarlane's great disappointment." Indeed, McFarlane "regretted his resignation almost instantly," but it was too late. He had gambled and lost.[99]

By accepting McFarlane's resignation, the president regained control of the NSC with the appointment of Poindexter, which would also strengthen the president's voting position in the NSPG. Once again, the president had turned the tables on the new world order faction, but not completely. In a move reminiscent of the ousting of Alexander Haig, McFarlane retained computer access to the NSC from his home and was allowed to keep his White House pass but was no longer a regular member of the decision-making process.[100]

In the meantime, North had sent Secord to Tel Aviv as soon as he learned of the botched Hawk shipment to find out what had happened. As Secord told it, North had sent him "to Tel Aviv ASAP to get the full story from David Kimche," so he "flew to Israel via chartered Lear jet," arriving by November 28, at the latest.[101] Secord, a retired American general, operating under an assumed name (Copp), cut an impressive figure, with a Lear jet at his disposal to "shuffle people" around the capitals of Europe.[102]

In Tel Aviv, Secord discussed the Hawk mission with Kimche, assuring him that "I was not in town on a fault-finding mission, but to prevent any problems from recurring."[103] Kimche simply professed to be "puzzled" by the Iranian rejection of the missiles, but eager to work out a new plan. The perennial issue of replenishment for the first 504 TOWs Israel had delivered came up in discussion with Menachem (Mendy) Meron, Director General of the Israeli Ministry of Defense. Secord observed laconically that the US could not "just ship weapons"

---

[98] See Draper, *Very Thin Line*, 260, for a list of Shultz's resignation threats.

[99] Mayer and McManus, *Landslide*, 170.

[100] See the author's *Ronald Reagan: Revolution Ascendant*, chap.11, for Haig's unusual resignation.

[101] Segev, *Iranian Triangle*, 209, claims Secord went to Paris first, on November 29.

[102] Secord, *Honored and Betrayed*, 221-22, said he was using "the Lear jet . . . to shuffle people between Tel Aviv, Lisbon [sic] and Paris." He undoubtedly meant London, not Lisbon, as Portugal was not on his itinerary this trip, but London was.

[103] Ibid., 220-21.

without congressional approval, indicating that some other means would have to be devised to compensate Israel for these missiles.[104]

Secord's meeting with Schwimmer was quite different. The Israeli was "very defensive" about his handling of the affair claiming that he was simply following the orders of his friend Shimon Peres. He claimed that they had "assumed the "I" in I-HAWK meant that the "improved" Hawk missile had high-altitude capability, "which it did not." Schwimmer was plainly "embarrassed" by what he had been asked to do. The bill for the two proprietary 707s Clarridge had arranged and the Lear jet Secord was using came to $200,000, which had been paid for out of the $1 million Schwimmer had advanced earlier. He told Secord to keep the remaining $800,000 for future needs. [105]

Secord and Kimche decided to set up a meeting in London for all of the principals to meet and "sort through the issues." At North's direction, however, Secord's next stop was Paris and the Georges V Hotel, where, on November 29, he and Kimche met Ghorbanifar and Nimrodi. After a lengthy negotiation, in which Ghorbanifar initially sought to place a large order of advanced weapons, including the Maverick, Dragon, and the Phoenix missile, as well as more Hawks, and 4,000 TOWs, he eventually agreed to a smaller weapons purchase in return for which all five American hostages and one French hostage would be released. Fifty Hawks and 3,200 TOWs were divided into five packages that would be delivered in the course of a single day, December 12, at phased intervals, with each plane delivery followed by release of a hostage. To Secord, this was "a ransom deal if I ever heard one," but that was what was agreed.[106]

Secord, Kimche and Ghorbanifar agreed to consult their principals, after which they would meet North in London on December 8 to finalize arrangements for the December 12 delivery. Throughout, Secord was in contact with North, using a special "brevity code" that enabled them to communicate over commercial phone lines. Kimche, receiving approval from Peres, proceeded to Geneva with Ghorbanifar on December 4 to meet with Karoubi. The Iranian leader attempted unsuccessfully to raise the price back to 4,000 TOWs but agreed to 3,300.[107]

Secord's negotiation trip and McFarlane's resignation ploy set the stage for what was expected to be the decisive NSPG meeting of December 7. To prepare for it, North put together a long memorandum for Poindexter based on Secord's meetings with Kimche and Ghorbanifar and their colleagues. The memo was equal parts policy review, strategic assessment, operational plan, and emotional plea.

North reviewed the Hawk mission, noting that it had "created an atmosphere of extraordinary mistrust on the part of the Iranians," as Ghorbanifar

---

[104] Ibid., 223.

[105] Ibid., 221. Segev, *Iranian Triangle*, 210, attempting to protect Schwimmer, accused Secord of "exploiting the failure of Operation Espresso to get himself involved in the Iranian dealings, in place of Schwimmer and Nimrodi."

[106] Secord, *Honored and Betrayed*, 227 and Segev, *Iranian Triangle*, 210.

[107] Segev, *Iranian Triangle*, 210-11.

charged the Israelis with playing a "cheating game." Nevertheless, Secord and
Kimche had managed to renew the dialogue promising hope for "achieving our
three objectives." North saw these as providing support for a "pragmatic" army
faction, return of the hostages, and the end of terrorism.[108]

Reflecting Kimche's input, North saw Israel's objectives as wanting to
perpetuate a stalemate in the Iran-Iraq war, promoting the emergence of a more
moderate government, and effecting through arms sales and/or barter
arrangements the recovery of Iranian Jews. In view of this, North thought,

> we should probably be seeing the return of the AMCIT hostages
> as a subsidiary benefit—not the primary objective, though it
> may be a part of the necessary first steps in achieving the
> broader objectives.[109]

Injecting a note of urgency and alarm, North noted that all agreed that
time was running out and to stop now would incur the risk of "never being able
to establish a foothold for longer-term goals" and raise the greater likelihood of
reprisals in the form of seizures of more hostages and even executions of those
still being held.

However, North's description of the hostage situation was oddly
misinformed, saying curiously that "the hostages . . . may be killed or
captured/released [sic] by the Syrians, Druze, Phalange or Amal in the near
future."[110] If anything, these groups were attempting to locate and free the
hostages. Worse, there was no discussion of Hezbollah, or the group that actually
was holding the hostages, Imad Mughniyeh's Islamic Jihad.

North enumerated the details of the deal negotiated by Secord and
Kimche with Ghorbanifar. The 3,300 TOWs and 50 Hawks would be broken
down into five packages and delivered on December 12 with release of one
hostage per delivery. He noted that the Iranians had demonstrated their sincerity
by depositing $41 million for purchase of the weapons and had prepared the 17
Hawks (minus the one test-fired) delivered in November for return shipment.

Although the hostages were not to be released until after deliveries had
begun to guard against a possible double-cross, North said that if the first two
deliveries of 300 TOWs each "do not produce the desired outcomes, all else
stops." Besides, he said, we had their money: "all $ are now under our control."
Then, he said contradictorily, that the hostages must be released "before the A/C
actually crosses into Iranian airspace." It was not clear whether a hostage was to
be released after the first delivery, or while the plane was still in the air.

Again, reflecting Kimche's input, North folded into the plan's "opsec,"
or operational security concerns, replenishment for the missiles and other
weapons Israel would deliver, including the 504 TOWs sent in August and

---

[108] *Tower Report*, B-34.
[109] Ibid., B-35.
[110] Ibid., B-34-35.

September. As a sweetener, it would be a cash deal. The Israelis would pay cash for replenishment weapons and not use Foreign Military Sales credits, as was normally the case, which would not draw congressional scrutiny.

As to procedure, North said that Secord, Kimche, Schwimmer and he were to meet on Saturday morning, December 7 in London to go over the deal and if everything was in order, then Kimche and Schwimmer would meet Ghorbanifar and his Iranian superior "at another hotel . . . to formalize the plan." If all agreed, North would transmit the deal to Poindexter and, if the president approved, Kimche and Schwimmer would meet again with Ghorbanifar and his Iranian chief on Sunday morning to finalize the agreement.[111]

In his closing paragraphs, North claimed that he and Clarridge had "been through the whole concept twice looking for holes and can find little that can be done to improve it," but, though Clarridge knew a great deal, "the only parties fully aware of all dimensions of what we are about are you and RCM [McFarlane]." Finally, he pleaded, "if we do not at least make one more try . . . we stand a good chance of condemning some or all [of the hostages] to death and a renewed wave of Islamic Jihad terrorism."[112]

---

[111] Ibid., B-36-37.

[112] Ibid., 37. Clarridge, *Congressional Report on the Iran-Contra Affair*, 195, denied discussing this plan with North, saying that he had a "tendency to use [his] name with McFarlane and Poindexter because if [he] said it was a good idea, then they tended to think it was a good idea."

Part IV

Betrayal of Ronald Reagan

Chapter 13

Reagan's Iran Initiative

From early December of 1985, the Reagan and new world order factions contended over the Iran initiative and the president would resurrect it from the depths to which McFarlane and the new world order faction believed they had consigned it. In a covert action finding in January, he authorized a new and legal approach involving the CIA, the NSC, and third parties, relegating the Israelis to a supporting role. The president's objective was to bring about a political rapprochement with Iran, which *inter alia* would result in the release of the five American hostages being held in Beirut.

It would take the better part of a month for the president and his aides to devise a policy that was substantially in compliance with American laws and to marshal majority support within the NSPG. Reagan was unable to gain the support of new world order faction leader George Shultz, but obtained the reluctant, yet crucial, assistance of Casper Weinberger, the secretary of defense, even though he continued to object to the policy.

The plan was for a limited delivery of munitions to Iran to result in the release of the hostages, after which a high-level meeting would inaugurate a full-blown rapprochement. Unfortunately, while accepting American weapons, the Iranians stalled on bringing about the release of the hostages, fundamentally because they exercised only limited influence over Imad Mughniyeh, who held them.

The Two Factions Collide

North's memo to Poindexter came just as the latter and McFarlane were engaged in "several lengthy meetings," on December 3 and 4, following the outgoing national security adviser's return to Washington.[1] There can be little doubt that McFarlane told Poindexter of his intent to shut the initiative down. Shultz, speaking to him the next day, gave him the same opinion.[2] Poindexter, of course, was firmly committed to the opposite course, having authorized the

---

[1] *Report of the Congressional Committees Investigating the Iran-Contra Affair* (Washington, DC: US Government Printing Office, GPO, 1987), 195. [hereinafter cited as *Congressional Report on the Iran-Contra Affair*]

[2] John G. Tower et al., *Report of the President's Special Review Board: February 26, 1987* (Washington, DC: US Government Printing Office, 1987), B-40.

formulation of a new plan, which Secord, Kimche, North, and Ghorbanifar had just worked out.

When Poindexter realized that McFarlane and Shultz were intent on shutting the initiative down, he decided not to bring up the existence of the unsigned finding he had received from Casey a week earlier authorizing CIA involvement.[3] He also realized that he would have to remove McFarlane from an operational role, so he instructed North to rewrite the new plan, taking McFarlane out of it and shifting his participation into the future.

The next day, December 5, North dutifully rewrote his memo, retitling it "Special Project Re Iran," summarizing its main points, but tweaking it in three areas. He inserted a flat "guarantee" that Iran would release the hostages, added a brief description of Hezbollah in Lebanon, and removed McFarlane from direct participation in the deal.

Their Iranian interlocutors, North said, will "guarantee" the release of the five American and one French hostages in return for delivery of 3,300 TOWs and 50 Hawks and also that "no further acts [of] Shia fundamentalist terrorism" will occur.[4] They "are cognizant of the pressure being placed on the Hizballah [sic] surrogates in Lebanon and that the leverage they now exercise "may no longer be available in the near future." What he meant by "Hizballah surrogates" was left to the reader's imagination.

With regard to McFarlane's role, North neatly took him out of the current operation and shifted his participation to the future. Thus, where in the December 4 memo North had suggested a McFarlane "meeting with the Iranians to obtain release of the hostages" *before* delivery, in the December 5 memo, he said that "McFarlane would step in to supervise achieving the longer-range goals" *after* the hostages were released.[5]

On Thursday morning, December 5, Poindexter delivered the president's daily brief, at which he claimed to have "presented" Sporkin's November 26 finding to the president, who, he says, "signed it." But had he? The evidence for his assertion is flimsy in the extreme. Reagan himself later said flatly "I do not recall signing a Finding relating to Iranian arms transactions in November or December 1985. I am aware that an unsigned version of such a Finding exists . . . although I am told that a signed version has not been found."[6]

---

[3] *Congressional Report on the Iran-Contra Affair*, 195. 197. McFarlane "does not recall any discussion of the status of the covert action finding . . ." and "Poindexter did not even mention the finding" in his call to Shultz.

[4] *Tower Report*, B-41.

[5] Ibid., B-37, 42. See also Theodore Draper, *A Very Thin Line: The Iran-Contra Affairs* (New York: Hill and Wang, 1991), 224.

[6] Reagan, "Response to Grand Jury Interrogatories," cited in Lawrence E. Walsh, *Final Report of the Independent Counsel for Iran-Contra Matters*, vol. 1 (Washington, DC: United States Court of Appeals for the District of Columbia Circuit, August 4, 1993), 470. Arthur Liman, lead congressional investigator, in "Hostile Witness,"

Don Regan, who attended the briefing, said that neither he, nor any members of his staff "can remember seeing that document." McFarlane, too, did "not recall any discussion of the status of the covert action finding." Poindexter says that he gave the finding to legal counsel Paul Thompson for deposit in his safe at the NSC.[7] That was the only copy, which was contrary to procedure. Copies should have been passed to the CIA and other involved department heads.

While Poindexter insists that the president signed the finding, he could not recall the "precise date" he signed it.[8] The December 5 date seems to have stemmed from McMahon's "memorandum for the record," in which he noted "someone told him on December 5 that the president had signed [it]." No one, it seems, except Poindexter, admits even to seeing the finding. Thompson, who was supposed to have put it in his safe, never saw it, only the folder in which it had been placed.[9] North claimed that the finding had been signed but admitted that he "never saw" the draft, either.[10] There is additional circumstantial evidence that the finding was not signed on December 5, or earlier. That day, Poindexter called Shultz to brief him about the planned operation and the meeting for the 7th, but made no mention of the finding.[11]

Why did Poindexter maintain that Reagan signed a finding on December 5? Given the preparation for the delivery/swap of the 12th, Poindexter may have wanted to ensure that the CIA continued planning to carry out its presumed role. Hence, Poindexter let McMahon know that the president had signed the finding, even though he was "never happy with it" and "wanted to get a broader finding."[12] Nor did he let anyone else know it existed, which, in fact, defeated its purpose. Finally, the main reason that Reagan would not have signed the finding was that to do so would have acknowledged his attempt to cover up an illegal action he had never authorized.

North left for London via New York on December 6, to meet with his Israeli and Iranian colleagues, as planned. In New York City, he met with Israeli procurement chief Ben-Yosef about the replenishment of the 504 TOWs Israel had shipped in August and September. Based on what actually transpired later, North's advice was simply to add the 504 replacement missiles onto a future weapons sale to Iran.

However, the sole source for North's discussion with Ben-Yosef, the Israeli historical chronology, presents an entirely different, and incredible picture.

Washington Post, Sunday Magazine, August 16, 1998, said that he did not believe Poindexter.

[7] *Congressional Report on the Iran-Contra Affair*, 195-97. See also, "Excerpts: Hold Body and Soul Together," *Los Angeles Times*, May 12, 1987, 15.

[8] "John Poindexter Deposition," *Congressional Report on the Iran-Contra Affair*, Appendix B, vol. 20, 1101.

[9] "Paul Thompson Deposition," Ibid., vol. 26, 998-99.

[10] *Tower Report*, B-40.

[11] *Congressional Report on the Iran-Contra Affair*, 197.

[12] "John Poindexter Deposition," Ibid., 1025, 1104.

Three Israeli officials were privy to the discussions. One, unidentified, "made handwritten notes of their meeting on December 12, 1985." The other two "did not recall the remarks of North." They should have, for North allegedly told Ben-Yosef that the "US did not have the money to pay for the 504 missiles already supplied to Iran." If Israel wanted to be repaid, he said, "it should get the money from the two Israeli arms dealers," Nimrodi and Schwimmer.[13] The problem with this account, however, is that their discussion was not about repayment, but replenishment.

The unidentified Israeli also claimed that North told them "he intended to divert part of the profits [from arms sales] to the Contras." Both Segev and the congressional report repeat this claim, which also lacks credibility, particularly as the notes of the meeting were reportedly written six days after the event and two of the three persons present could not substantiate the conversation.[14]

The explanation lies, perhaps, in what transpired between North's visit and the cancellation of the December 12 delivery. The Israelis simply concocted the notes when it became clear that there would be no deal in order to plant the seeds of later controversy and divert blame from themselves. Certainly, North, properly sensitive to security, had no reason whatsoever to discuss with the Israelis what he planned to do with "profits" from Iran arms sales and every reason not to. They had no need to know.

In any case, North flew from New York City to London, arriving on December 7 to meet with Kimche, Ghorbanifar, Nimrodi, Schwimmer, and Secord, to iron out the final details of the deal for 3,300 TOWs and 50 Hawks.[15] Ghorbanifar, seeking to stress the urgency of the moment confided that "nine Hizbollah leaders had been summoned to Tehran on Friday [December 6] and that, given the pressure inside Lebanon, all it would take for the hostages to be killed would be for Tehran to 'stop saying no.'"[16] This was not an entirely empty threat, but, as the hostages had been taken to obtain policy leverage, to have killed them would have been self-defeating.

On the same day, however, Iran made a move that greatly heartened these men. Iran's foreign minister, Ali Akbar Velayati, began a three-day visit to Saudi Arabia—the first such visit by an Iranian official since the 1979 revolution. The meeting with King Fahd was read as a signal "Iran really was abandoning its ambition of exporting its Islamic revolution."[17] It was in this "atmosphere of

---

[13] Samuel Segev, *The Iranian Triangle: The Untold Story of Israel's Role in the Iran-Contra Affair* (New York: Free Press, 1988), 213.

[14] Ibid., and *Congressional Report on the Iran-Contra Affair*, 197.

[15] Segev, *Iranian Triangle*, 214-15, claims that North met first with Kimche and then with the others.

[16] Scott Armstrong et al., *The Chronology: The Documented Day-by-Day Account of the Secret Military Assistance to Iran and the Contras* (New York: Warner Books, 1987), 207

[17] Segev, *Iranian Triangle*, 215.

expectation," then, that the Americans, Israelis, and Iranians awaited the arrival of Robert McFarlane.

The New World Order Faction Blocks Action

Just as North was arriving in London on Saturday morning, the president was meeting with his top aides in the White House family residence. Present for this informal NSPG meeting, the first full discussion by the American leadership of a specific plan for the Iran initiative, were Shultz, Weinberger, Regan, McFarlane, Poindexter, and McMahon, standing in for Casey, who was traveling abroad. Vice-President Bush, to avoid taking sides, decided to attend the Army-Navy football game.

Discussion swirled around the Secord-Kimche-Ghorbanifar plan to sell 3,300/50 missiles for the hostages. Shultz repeated his now all-too-familiar refrain objecting to any deals with Iran or terrorists. Weinberger supported him, adding that any arms shipments would violate the Arms Export Control Act. McMahon declared that there were no moderates in Iran to support. McFarlane, who was the initiator of the deals, swung to support Shultz and Weinberger in "recommending an end to them."[18] Regan's position surprised the president most when he said that the best solution to a losing proposition was to "cut your losses."[19]

The president, "fully engaged," wanted to proceed, claiming "the American people will never forgive me if I fail to get these hostages out," because of legal technicalities. Interestingly, the Sporkin finding, supposedly signed just two days before, which the president could have produced as a *fait accompli* to legalize the deal, did not come up. Furthermore, even though Poindexter had Casey's proxy vote in favor,[20] the balance of voting opinion at the meeting was at best four against four, or five to three against the president, depending on where Regan stood. Bush's vote would have been crucial, but he was not there to cast it.

In the face of the deadlock (Weinberger thought the deal was "finished"; Shultz wasn't so sure), the president cancelled the 3,300/50 plan. Instead, he decided that McFarlane should go to London and propose to Ghorbanifar an alternative. If the Iranians released the hostages, then the United States would be prepared to provide weapons in the context of a political dialogue. Otherwise, the United States would not sell weapons to Iran, or permit others, which meant Israel, to do so.[21] Shultz "did not object" to this approach, although he thought, "the prospects for success were minimal."[22]

---

[18] Armstrong et al., *The Chronology*, 207-08. *Iran-Contra Affair*, 198, incorrectly claims that McFarlane "spoke in favor of continuing the initiative."

[19] "Donald Regan Deposition," *Congressional Report on the Iran-Contra Affair*, Appendix B, vol. 22, 583. In his testimony to the Tower Board, B-45, however, Regan claimed that that he "favored keeping the channel open; if necessary, selling a modest amount of arms."

[20] Walsh, *Final Report of the Independent Counsel*, 1:206.

[21] *Ibid.*, 199 and *Tower Report*, B-44-45.

[22] George Shultz, *Turmoil and Triumph* (New York: Macmillan, 1993), 799.

McFarlane left Washington that evening of the 7th, arriving in London the next morning. After breakfast with North and Secord at the Hilton Intercontinental, McFarlane met privately with Kimche to give him advance notice of the policy change. Kimche was understandably "upset," believing that the United States was "missing a big opportunity." There was a need for "patience," he argued. However, McFarlane responded, "well, we just don't see that; and further, we think it is being skewed off in the wrong direction."[23] With that, they went off separately to the meeting with Ghorbanifar.

McFarlane, North, and Secord arrived at Nimrodi's duplex off Hyde Park around one in the afternoon. There to meet them were Kimche, Schwimmer, Nimrodi, and an Israeli general representing Rabin. Ghorbanifar was alone. The Iranian started the conversation by immediately doubling the price of the agreed package of 3,300 TOWs and 50 Hawks for the five American and one French hostage to 6,000 TOWs, plus Hawks and Phoenix missiles. He declared that the new price was "one box for one thousand TOWs," referring to the hostages as "boxes." And, he went on, "if you ship another thousand immediately, I can guarantee two boxes." He could also deliver "one box for some Phoenix missiles, if you deliver them immediately."[24]

McFarlane's response, however, stunned the Iranian. Without haggling about price, as Ghorbanifar undoubtedly expected, McFarlane simply informed him "under instructions" that the arms sale deal was off. Instead, McFarlane put forward the proposal that the Iranians free the hostages first, after which the United States would enter into a political relationship that would include the subsequent provision of weapons.[25]

Ghorbanifar, thunderstruck, thought McFarlane was "crazy." He claimed that the Iranians were "desperate," and "too weak for political talk." A political relationship must wait, he said, until his clients "get strong and take power." That meant weapons sales had to come first. He shrieked "if I take this news back to my colleagues, they will go mad! They might say, to hell with the hostages! Let the Hezbollah kill them!"[26]

Ghorbanifar was not the only one who had been stunned by McFarlane's performance. Both North and Secord, who flew back to Washington with McFarlane aboard the Gulfstream III jet, were also dumbfounded. Instead of coming to *sanction* the deal they had painstakingly put together with the Israelis and Iranians, McFarlane had shut the entire project down. However, although the new world order faction appeared to have won the battle, the war continued. Before the three men had landed at Andrews Air Force Base outside Washington, the next battle was already underway.

---

[23] *Tower Report*, B-45.

[24] Richard Secord and Jay Wurts, *Honored and Betrayed: Irangate, Covert Affairs, and the Secret War in Laos* (New York: Wiley, 1992), 231.

[25] Robert C. McFarlane, *Special Trust* (New York: Cadell & Davies, 1994), 48.

[26] Ibid., 49.

Iran: The End and the Beginning

On the plane back from London, December 8, while McFarlane was preparing his report for the president about shutting down the initiative, North, on the same plane, was preparing a memorandum entitled "Next Steps." Addressed to McFarlane and Poindexter, North presented an entirely different interpretation of what had happened in the meeting with Ghorbanifar. Where McFarlane described Ghorbanifar as the most "despicable" man he had ever met, with whom the United States could not do business, North and the Israelis saw him as "genuine," and "the deepest penetration we have yet achieved into the current Iranian government."[27]

While acknowledging, "information is incomplete," motivation "uncertain," and "our operational control tenuous," North argued, "much of our ability to influence the course of events . . . depends on the validity of what Ghorbanifar has told us." However, "while it is possible that Ghorbanifar is doubling us or simply lining his own pockets, we have relatively little to lose in meeting his proposal." The worst case would be if the Israelis delivered a small number of TOWs and no hostages were released. On the other hand, "a supply operation now could very well trigger the results he claims."

"Our greatest liability throughout has been lack of operational control over transactions with Ghorbanifar." North pinned the blame for the Hawk fiasco on Schwimmer, who arranged for weapons "not requested by Ghorbanifar" and negotiated terms "disadvantageous to the IDF," making it difficult for us to replenish the Israelis. His latest proposal would have swapped 3,300 TOWs for three hostages, but "at a price which would not allow the IDF to recoup expenses, thus complicating our ability to replenish IDF stores."

"The question which now must be asked is should we take a relatively small risk by allowing . . . a small Israeli-originated delivery of TOWs and hope for the best, or should we do nothing?" Raising the specter of hostage executions, North said there appeared to be four options available: go forward with the Ghorbanifar/Schwimmer 3,300 plan; carry out a rescue raid with its attendant risks; allow the Israelis to deliver only 400-500 TOWs, maybe get a hostage out, and pick up the Hawks still in Iran as a "show of good faith"; or "do nothing."

Then, he added, as if in afterthought, "there is a fifth option which has not yet been discussed." "We could, with an appropriate covert action Finding commence deliveries ourselves, using Secord as our conduit to control Ghorbanifar and delivery operations." North thought this option had "considerable merit," in that it would make it easier to replenish Israelis stocks, and provide weapons that the Iranians want, and Israelis do not have, like the advanced Hawk (PIP II).

---

[27] "Next Steps," North to McFarlane/Poindexter, December 9, 1985, *Tower Report*, B-48-49.

On December 10, McFarlane reported to the president on his trip. Present also were Weinberger, Casey, Regan, Poindexter, and possibly Bush and North.[28] Shultz was en route to a NATO ministerial meeting in Brussels. McFarlane "recommended that we not pursue the proposed relationship with [Ghorbanifar]." But, in discussion of the options in North's memo, the president, concerned about reprisals against the hostages, asked if we couldn't continue to "let Israel manage this program" without any commitments from us.[29]

The president "felt that any ongoing contact would be justified and any charges that might be made later [about trading arms for hostages] could be met and justified as an effort to influence future events in Iran." The president made no decision at this briefing, although Weinberger thought the initiative had been "strangled" and Armacost reported to Shultz that it had been agreed to drop it. Casey, however, "had the idea that the president had not entirely given up on encouraging the Israelis to carry on with the Iranians."[30] Regan and Poindexter thought the same. They were right.

After the briefing, Poindexter instructed North to "keep the Iran initiative moving forward," but contrary to the congressional report, the president's immediate decision was not to authorize either a resumption of Israeli arms shipments, or a raid.[31] Instead, he decided to pursue a diplomatic approach and sent Ambassador Dick Walters to Damascus with a message asking President Assad for his assistance. As Weinberger noted in his diary "President still wants to try to get hostages released—but forcible storming would mean many deaths—decided to send Dick Walters to Damascus."[32] Unfortunately, the approach to Assad yielded nothing because the Syrian leader had even less influence over Mughniyeh than the Iranians, at least at this point in time.

---

[28] Ibid., B-49. *Congressional Report on the Iran-Contra Affair*, 199-200, says that North was there, and Weinberger was not. McFarlane gave two versions. In one he thought Bush was there and Casey was not, and in the other he recalled that Casey and Weinberger were there, and Shultz was not. See *Tower Report*, B-50.

[29] Ibid. and *Congressional Report on the Iran-Contra Affair*, 200.

[30] "Casey to DDCI," December 10, 1985, in *Tower Report*, B-50-52 and *Congressional Report on the Iran-Contra Affair*, 200.

[31] *Congressional Report on the Iran-Contra Affair*, 200, says "following the briefing" Poindexter told North to prepare a new finding, change the Israeli team, and find a legal way to sell arms to Iran. In fact, these steps would not be taken until early January.

[32] "Weinberger Diary," December 10, 1985, in Walsh, *Final Report of the Independent Counsel*, 1:410 n64. In his memoir *Fighting for Peace: Seven Critical Years in the Pentagon* (New York: Warner, 1990), 373, Weinberger says of McFarlane's trip and subsequent report "to the best of my knowledge, McFarlane had no instructions, nor do we know what he actually had told the Iranians. He 'debriefed' some of the December 7 attendees on December 10, but I always felt that McFarlane's 'debriefings' were imaginary reports on what he wanted his auditors to hear."

Draper says that North went to see Sporkin about a new finding on December 9, the day *before* the briefing. This could only have been a heads-up call based on his 5th option in the Next Steps memo, because it obviously was not a result of decisions yet to be taken at the December 10 meeting. Draper does acknowledge, however, that "actual work" on the new finding "did not start until January 2, 1986," twenty-four days later.[33]

The decision to resume discussions with the Israelis came after a series of emotional meetings the president had with the families of the hostages a few days later, in mid-December, to "tell them that attempts to free the hostages by Christmas [had] failed." After these very emotional meetings, the president ordered Poindexter and Regan to "redouble efforts to gain their release." Poindexter immediately directed North to contact Amiram Nir.[34]

After communicating with North, Nir persuaded Prime Minister Peres to add him to the Kimche/Schwimmer/Nimrodi team, and Peres agreed. In a meeting with Schwimmer on December 25, the prime minister explained that "given McFarlane's resignation and Nir's close ties to Poindexter and North, it was worth bringing Nir onto the Israeli team." Schwimmer "had no objections."[35] At this point, it was not yet a case of changing the team, just adding to it. Besides, Nir had some new ideas about recovering the hostages and obtaining American weapons.

Drawing on past Israeli experience, Nir's idea involved Israel selling 4,000 TOWs to Iran from its own stocks, and the United States pre-positioning a like amount of US TOWs in Israel. "In case of an emergency" with Syria, Israel would purchase these weapons from proceeds obtained in the sale to Iran. Then, as in the TWA 847 crisis, he proposed the swap of twenty or thirty Israeli-held Shiite prisoners in Al Haim prison in Southern Lebanon for the five American hostages held in Beirut. In this concept, Israel would bear all the responsibility and the United States could deny any involvement.[36]

Before Nir's ideas could be formulated into a concrete proposal to Washington, however, there occurred two terrorist attacks at airports in Rome and Vienna, in which over a hundred people were either killed or wounded. These events intensified the administration's focus on the problem of terrorism and Qaddafi, who had been implicated. Indeed, the problems of Qaddafi, international terrorism, and the Iran Initiative intertwined within Reagan's inner circle over the next several weeks.

Qaddafi and State-Supported Terrorism

The administration had been singularly unsuccessful in its efforts at combating terrorism in general and at confronting Qaddafi in particular since

---

[33] Draper, *Very Thin Line*, 240.
[34] Armstrong et al., *The Chronology*, 225.
[35] Segev, *Iranian Triangle*, 222-23.
[36] Ibid.

taking office. Although Reagan had signed NSDD 138 in April 1984 authorizing a "proactive" approach to terrorism, its main effect had been to precipitate a public debate between Shultz and Weinberger over the best way to combat terrorism. Shultz pressed for the proactive use of American military power against terrorists, while Weinberger sought to narrow the circumstances under which it could be used. The result was, as Noel Koch, Assistant Secretary of Defense for International Security Affairs observed: "no part of it was ever implemented."[37] It was all talk and no action, but the administration began to focus on Qaddafi in 1985.

In March, the CIA released a Special National Intelligence Estimate that concluded that Qaddafi was sponsoring a worldwide campaign against American interests and supporting a phalanx of terrorists groups of all stripes, including the PLO, Abu Nidal, and Imad Mughniyeh.[38] On April 30, the president signed NSDD 168, "US Policy Toward North Africa," which was designed to contain and isolate Qaddafi by improving relations with his neighbors. An interagency group was authorized to review US policy toward Libya and "prepare policy options to contain Qaddafi's subversive activities." [39]

What emerged from the review was a two-pronged policy proposal, code-named Flower, whose components were Tulip and Rose. Tulip was a covert operation to support anti-Qaddafi groups that sought to overthrow the dictator. Rose was a US-supported attack by Egypt against Libya. However, neither policy proposal fared well in inner councils. Both Shultz and Weinberger opposed Rose, as did Mubarak of Egypt, and the Senate Intelligence Committee vetoed Tulip.[40]

After the TWA crisis, with pressure mounting on the president to take action, on July 20, he signed NSDD-179, creating a government-wide task force on combating terrorism and placing Vice President Bush in charge. Bush was tasked with devising plans for "preemptive or retaliatory actions to combat terrorism" and accorded the authority to call on virtually all sectors of the US government for assistance in his task.[41]

The administration did not initially connect Qaddafi to the spate of American hostage seizures in the first half of the year. Eventually, he was identified as a supporter of Imad Mughniyeh, whose men had hijacked TWA 847 in June, and Mughniyeh was determined to have masterminded the seizure of the hostages. Qaddafi was also identified as the supporter of Abu Nidal, whose men had seized the *Achille Lauro* in October and hijacked EgyptAir 648 in November.

---

[37] Joseph Stanik, *El Dorado Canyon: Reagan's Undeclared War with Qaddafi* (Annapolis: Naval Institute Press, 2003), 95-97.

[38] *Libya's Qadhafi: The Challenge to US and Western Interests*, SNIE 36.5-85 (Washington, DC: Central Intelligence Agency, March 1985).

[39] Stanik, *El Dorado Canyon*, 100; and Christopher Simpson, *National Security Directives of the Reagan and Bush Administrations: The Declassified History of US Political and Military Policy, 1981-1991* (Boulder: Westview, 1995), 448, 528-32.

[40] Stanik, *El Dorado Canyon*, 102-3.

[41] Ibid., 101; and Simpson, *National Security Directives*, 454, 576-77.

Although Qaddafi denied involvement in all of these events the evidence was more than circumstantial. However, most of it was classified and publicly unusable, leaving the president frustrated and hamstrung.

The massacres at the Rome and Vienna airports changed that. Two days after Christmas, at just after nine in the morning, four young men, high on amphetamines, mingled in with the crowd in front of the ticket counters at the Leonardo da Vinci airport outside Rome. In their bags they carried thirteen grenades and four AK-47 automatic rifles. Without warning they began rolling grenades across the floor and raking the terminal with bullets, hitting people in line at the El Al, TWA, and Pan Am ticket counters. The shooting rampage went on for five minutes. Eventually, airport police killed three of the four terrorists, but the cost was high—a dozen dead and 74 wounded, including several Americans.[42]

At about the same time, three young men rushed into the second-floor departure area at Vienna's Schwechat airport, opening fire with AK-47 rifles and rolling grenades at passengers waiting to check in for an El Al flight to Tel Aviv. After two minutes, the gunmen fled the terminal, commandeered a car and tried to escape. In a running gun battle with the police the assailants were captured two miles from the airport. The toll was three dead, including one of the terrorists, and forty-seven wounded.[43]

Qaddafi publicly hailed the terrorists as "heroic," and acknowledged that he had provided Abu Nidal shelter in Tripoli. Indeed, his fingerprints were soon found figuratively all over these massacres, although the terrorists attempted to implicate Assad of Syria, as, for their own reasons, did the Israelis.[44] The grenades used by the assailants were traced to Libyan munitions stocks, the forged travel documents traced to passports confiscated from Tunisian guest workers, and communications intercepts linked Qaddafi to Abu Nidal.[45]

President Reagan was stunned and, while he declared the evidence against Qaddafi "irrefutable," the United States' public response was muted.[46] Behind the scenes, however, within hours of the massacres, planners had begun work on contingency measures, identifying political, military, and economic

---

[42] Ed Magnuson, "Terrorism: Ten Minutes of Horror," *Time*, June 21, 2005.

[43] Ibid.

[44] The Soviets were redeploying surface-to-air missiles (SAMs), including mobile missiles, to the Bekaa along the Syrian-Lebanon border to replace those that the Israelis had knocked out during the 1982 war. Thus, Peres was seeking reasons to strike at Syria. See William Smith, "Middle East: An Eye for an Eye," *Time*, June 21, 2005.

[45] Daniel Bolger, *Americans At War, 1975-1986* (San Francisco: Presidio, 1988), 386, Stanik, *El Dorado Canyon*, 106, and David C. Wills, *The First War on Terrorism: Counter-Terrorism Policy during the Reagan Administration* (Lanham: Rowman & Littlefield, 2003), 177.

[46] George Wilson, "Reagan Denounces Warning by Qaddafi on Retaliation," *Washington Post*, January 3, 1986, A1.

options against Libya. After almost ten days of discussions at upper levels of the bureaucracy key meetings were held on January 6 and 7 to decide on the course of action to take.[47] Coincidentally, these would be the same two days when key decisions were made regarding the Iran initiative.

A Decision on Israel and Iran

Both Peres and Rabin had approved Nir's ideas and authorized him to go first to London to meet with Nimrodi and Ghorbanifar to obtain the approval of the Iranians and then to Washington to present the proposal to the Americans. In London, on December 30, Nimrodi introduced Nir to Ghorbanifar and briefed him on the previous deals. Nir was supposed to meet Schwimmer in New York before going to Washington, but instead went directly to Washington to meet with North and Poindexter, on January 2. This marked the beginning of a serious rift among the Israelis, as Schwimmer believed that he had been "tricked" and complained to Peres that Nir was attempting to cut him and the others out.[48]

In Washington, Nir's proposal to North and Poindexter was for Israel to undertake unilaterally the sale of 4,000 TOW missiles to Iran and with the proceeds, purchase replacement missiles from Washington. At the same time, Israel would release twenty or thirty Shiite prisoners from the Al Haim prison in southern Lebanon and Iran would release the five American hostages. To "test Iran's intentions," Israel would make an initial delivery of 500 TOWs. If the hostages were freed, Israel would deliver the remaining 3,500; if not, Israel would bear the cost of the 500 and the operation would be terminated.[49]

Poindexter said the United States would not preposition missiles in Israel, but would either sell them, or in an emergency, fly them in. To Nir's stand that replenishment of missiles was "a precondition for any further Israeli sales to Iran," North responded that Israel just couldn't buy missiles from the Pentagon. "There was a legal process, including congressional approval." But he reassured Nir that "the price tag would be within Israel's means." North agreed that Israel would sell weapons to Iran at an "inflated price" and use the proceeds "to buy replacements for Israel and to fund joint, covert activities, mostly in the area of counterterrorism."[50]

The congressional report claims that during these discussions with Nir in early January, North's mention of "joint covert operations" also referred to the "finance [of] US activities in Nicaragua," or what would later become known as the "diversion." This seems unlikely. Later in the same account, the report quotes North himself saying that "other operations" did *not* refer to the Contras. "I do not believe [Nir] mentioned contras at that meeting, but my recollection is we began to talk in early January about other joint US-Israeli, and in some cases unilateral

---

[47] Wills, *First War on Terrorism*, 177-81.
[48] Segev, *Iranian Triangle*, 223-24.
[49] Ibid., 224-25. Cf. *Congressional Report on the Iran-Contra Affair*, 201.
[50] Segev, *Iranian Triangle, 224-25.*

Israeli operations of a certain kind."[51] By "operations of a certain kind," North meant the possibility of an Israeli rescue of the hostages.

After contacting Casey, who liked Nir's plan, Poindexter instructed North to go see Judge Sporkin to draft a new finding. Over the next few days, and after several re-writes, North and Sporkin produced a finding. The objective was threefold: to bring about the establishment of a moderate government in Iran; to acquire intelligence from Iran unavailable elsewhere; and to further the release of the five American hostages held in Lebanon.

The third point, release of the hostages, was not inserted until the final draft. North had wanted to keep it out, but Sporkin, with Casey's assent, reinserted it. To achieve these ends the United States was prepared to provide various forms of assistance, including arms, to friendly selected liaison services and third countries. Because of the project's "sensitivity," the president elected to "limit prior notice" to Congress until otherwise directed.[52]

During the president's daily briefing on the morning of January 6, attended by the vice-president, Deputy NSC Adviser, Don Fortier, and Regan, Poindexter raised the subject of the Israeli proposal. According to Regan, "the president decided that we should pursue this line, that we should be prepared to sell arms, and that we should make a Finding that would authorize and justify [it] . . . " Poindexter then handed the draft finding to the president, saying that this was the proposal to be discussed the following day, and the president mistakenly signed it.[53]

Later that day, Sporkin realized that the wording of the finding was inconsistent and confusing regarding whom the United States was to assist. In one place it said the United States was prepared to assist "selected friendly liaison services and third countries" and in another place said "third parties and third countries." So, to be consistent, Sporkin inserted the following language "selected friendly liaison services, third countries, and third parties . . . ." The change was prescient. Sporkin thought at the time that the term "third parties" referred to Ghorbanifar and the Iranians, but it would come to refer crucially to Secord, instead.[54] Sporkin's emendation meant that the draft would have to be retyped and, of course, signed again.[55]

However, between the time that the finding was retyped and signed by the president on January 17, the entire initiative would be restructured in almost every aspect, requiring yet a new finding. On January 7, after a full NSPG meeting that dealt with Qaddafi, which will be discussed below, the president gathered his top aides for a principals only meeting in the Oval Office.[56] In attendance were

---

[51] *Congressional Report on the Iran-Contra Affair*, 201-202

[52] *Tower Report*, B-58-60.

[53] Ibid., B-60-61.

[54] *Congressional Report on the Iran-Contra Affair*, 208.

[55] *Tower Report*, B-61.

[56] "Recollection of Attorney General Edwin Meese," in *Tower Report*, B-61.

the president, vice-president, Shultz, Weinberger, Casey, Meese, Regan, and Poindexter.

In contrast to the meeting a month earlier, on December 7, where McFarlane, McMahon, Shultz, Weinberger, and Regan had all voiced opposition to the initiative, at this meeting the president had almost unanimous support. Casey was there instead of McMahon, Poindexter was there instead of McFarlane, Meese was there for the first time, Bush was also there, and Regan had changed his mind.

Although Weinberger claimed that the discussion of Nir's proposal was "very much a re-run" of the December 7 meeting, the very opposite was true.[57] Nir's plan was substantially different from the Schwimmer/Ghorbanifar plan discussed in December; there was no American role. After a vigorous discussion in which everyone had his say, the president had overwhelming support for going forward with Nir's plan. As Shultz noted "it was clear to me by the time we went out that the President, the Vice-President, the Director of Central Intelligence, the Attorney General, the Chief of Staff, the National Security Adviser all had one opinion and I had a different one, and Cap shared it."[58] The voting margin was six to two, but even that understated the president's support and Shultz's isolation.

It was true that Weinberger shared Shultz's opinion, but unlike Shultz accepted the president's decision, even though reluctantly. Aside from his visceral objections to dealing with the Iranians, the defense secretary's main substantive objections had been to their legality. Israeli sales of US weapons to Iran would violate the Arms Export Control Act, as would US sales to replace those arms Israel sold to Iran. Moreover, such sales would have to be reported to Congress.

But Reagan had brought Attorney General Meese to the meeting specifically to provide a ruling on this matter. Meese produced the 1981 opinion by his predecessor, William French Smith, which ruled that the CIA, obtaining weapons from the Defense Department under the Economy Act, could legally sell them to third countries. The Economy Act permitted intra-governmental transfers, which meant weapons could be sold at or below cost.

Furthermore, reporting requirements under the Economy Act were less stringent. Meese's ruling meant that the finding would have to be rewritten to include reference to the authority contained in the Economy Act, which was not in the January 6 draft.[59] Weinberger reluctantly accepted the ruling.[60] "We would carry out the Commander-in-Chief's orders to do this, and obviously hold it as closely as possible because that was not only the direction [directive] but the obvious thing to do."[61]

---

[57] *Congressional Report on the Iran-Contra Affair*, 203.

[58] *Tower Report*, B-63-64.

[59] For Poindexter's memo accompanying the January 6 finding, see *Tower Report*, B-58-60.

[60] *Congressional Report on the Iran-Contra Affair*, 203.

[61] *Tower Report*, B-65.

North immediately sent Nir a message in rudimentary code (whose meaning, unfortunately, even a beginner code-breaker could decipher, not to mention the Soviets, who undoubtedly intercepted it). The message read:

> Joshua has approved proceeding as we had hoped. Joshua and Samuel have also agreed on method one. Following additional conditions apply to Albert. (A) Resupply should be as routine as possible to prevent disclosure on our side. May take longer than two months. However, Albert says if crisis arises, Joshua promises that we will deliver all required by Galaxie in less than eighteen hours. (B) Joshua also wants both your govt and ours to stay with no comment if operation is disclosed. If these conditions are acceptable to the Banana then Oranges are ready to proceed.[62]

Aside from confusing Joshua with Albert in the sixth sentence, it was self-evident that Joshua was the president and Samuel, connected to resupply, was the secretary of defense. The only indecipherable term was "method one," which referred to direct sale of weapons to Israel, instead of Nir's idea of prepositioning. The rest of the message was straightforward, except for the silly but transparent references to Banana and Oranges.

North obviously wanted to respond positively to the Israeli proposal, but his message was premature. The US government was not "ready to proceed." The reason Reagan had not produced the finding he had signed the day before was because when Meese ruled that the Economy Act could be the legal authority for selling weapons the president realized that the finding would need to be revised to include it. In addition, he had not decided how weapons would be sold, or at what cost. Although Poindexter later noted the finding had not been fully staffed, in fact it had not included the legal authority justifying the president's decision.

A Decision on Libya

Meanwhile, these same two days saw the president preoccupied with the issue of what to do about Qaddafi. These meetings were the culmination of arguments that had swirled throughout the bureaucracy and the leadership for the previous ten days. On January 6, after his daily brief the president went into an NSPG meeting where Shultz argued for an immediate air strike against Libya. He buttressed his proposal with a legal opinion from Abe Sofaer, State Department legal counsel, that Qaddafi's support for terrorist acts against the United States justified armed retaliation.[63]

Weinberger objected that all diplomatic and economic options had not been exhausted. Furthermore, air attacks would strike civilians and many of the one thousand-plus Americans working in Libya could become hostages. This

---

[62] *Congressional Report on the Iran-Contra Affair*, 204.
[63] Wills, *First War on Terrorism*, 181.

argument, in particular, persuaded the president against hasty action, and he postponed a decision. Instead, he instructed Casey to move forward on Tulip, the covert operation to support anti-Qaddafi dissidents, and Weinberger to intensify efforts on Rose, the plan to support an Egyptian invasion of Libya.[64]

By the next day, January 7, at a follow-on NSPG meeting, the president had decided on a strategy. Rather than act precipitously, as Shultz demanded, or avoid military action altogether, as Weinberger cautioned, the president decided upon a several months-long, diplomatic, economic, and military plan that would clear the decks for action. The gradual build-up of pressure on Qaddafi would either cause him to discontinue support for terrorist acts, or, if he continued, the United States would carry out attacks against him.[65]

The strategy of pressure would involve a public information campaign, economic sanctions, diplomatic suasion of allies, and increasing naval pressure in the Gulf of Sidra. President Reagan established the basis for the new strategy with the issuance of Executive Order 12543, which declared Libya to constitute "an unusual and extraordinary threat to the national security and foreign policy of the United States." The order banned the import or export of "any" Libyan goods or services, denied entry into the United States of any ships or aircraft, and generally prohibited provision of any credit, services, travel, or trade with Libya.

That evening, in a nationally televised press conference, the president announced the terms of the executive order. Declaring a "national emergency," he said that there was "irrefutable evidence" of Qaddafi's involvement in the Rome and Vienna massacres and denounced him as a "pariah" for his "longstanding involvement in terrorism," and castigated Libya as an "outlaw regime." [66]

Acknowledging that earlier steps taken against Qaddafi had "not been sufficient," the president promised that if the steps he was now introducing "do not end Qaddafi's terrorism, I promise you that further steps will be taken." Concerned for the safety of the 1,000 to 1,500 Americans working in Libya, he warned them "to leave immediately." Those who refused, "will be subject to appropriate penalties upon their return" to the United States.

One commentator viewed Reagan's action as "anticlimactical" because he had already banned oil imports from Libya in 1982 and total trade had already dropped from its high of $7.6 billion in 1980 to $300 million. Furthermore, Libya's assets in the United States were left undisturbed. The small print made it even worse because the sanctions did not apply to subsidiaries of American

---

[64] Stanik, *El Dorado Canyon*, 109 and Wills, *First War on Terrorism*, 177-81

[65] Douglas Brinkley, ed., *The Reagan Diaries* (New York: Harper Collins, 2007), 381. As Reagan put it in his diary entry for this day: "If Mr. Q decides not to push another terrorist act—O.K. we've been successful with our implied threat. If on the other hand he takes this for weakness & does loose another one, we will have targets in mind & instantly respond with a h—l of a punch."

[66] Bernard Weinraub, "President Breaks All Economic Ties with The Libyans," *New York Times*, January 8, 1986, A1.

companies, which further muted their effect. That provision was said to have been insisted upon by Secretary Shultz, who was concerned that the Europeans would refuse to cooperate.[67]

The next day, January 8, Reagan issued NSDD-205, which set in motion the strategy against Qaddafi.[68] Although all future decisions would be shrouded in secrecy, the early stages were featured in the press. The press campaign focused on the many and varied means by which the United States could deal with Libya. Economic sanctions were activated, now including the freezing of all Libyan assets in the United States.[69] Shultz sent his aides, Whitehead and Oakley to Europe to gain allied support. And Weinberger ordered the fleet in the Mediterranean to begin freedom of navigation exercises in the Gulf of Sidra.

From the outset the president's policy encountered bumps in the road. Whitehead's and Oakley's European trip was singularly unsuccessful. Leaders in West Germany, Britain, France, Italy, Holland, Spain, and Belgium all expressed skepticism about the "effectiveness" of economic sanctions. French Prime Minister Laurent Fabius captured the sentiment of the European leaders when he said "there is no point beating the air with a sword. If sanctions are going to be ineffective, they have no interest."[70]

Qaddafi immediately reinforced the European attitude, calling in envoys from France, Italy, Belgium, the Netherlands, Spain, and Greece to assert their "common interests." He noted that there were 45,000 Europeans working in Libya in 230 companies. This represented, he said, $13 billion in contracts, with $36 billion more planned for those who cooperate. Raising the specter of war, Qaddafi declared that if the United States attacked Libya from European bases, then "we will close our eyes and ears and hit indiscriminately." He threatened to react with suicide squads to hit ports, towns and more. "If it comes to war, we will drag Europe into it."[71]

In short, the Qaddafi problem essentially would be Reagan's. But, even within the administration, there was criticism. Vice-President Bush's secret report on terrorism, leaked to the press, recommended that the president "stop making warlike threats of retaliation unless he intends to take military action."[72] Then, an unnamed State Department official claimed that the United States had "only circumstantial evidence linking Libya to the Abu Nidal terrorist group." The

---

[67] Bernard Gwertzman, "Why Reagan Shuns Force," *New York Times*, January 8, 1986, A1.

[68] Simpson, *National Security Directives*, 654-55.

[69] Robert Greenberger, "Libya's US Assets Frozen by Reagan in Retaliatory Step," *Wall Street Journal*, January 9, 1986, 25.

[70] "Allies Spurn US Call for Libya Sanctions," *Washington Post*, January 9, 1986, A18.

[71] Christopher Dickey, "Libya Seeks to Divide US, Allies," *Washington Post*, January 10, 1986, A1.

[72] James McCartney, "Reagan Draws Fire on Terror Threats," *Philadelphia Inquirer*, January 8, 1986, 1.

official said, "there isn't any smoking gun."[73] Shultz himself disagreed, declaring that Qaddafi was not only "harboring terrorists . . . he is a terrorist" and the United States "could use military force" against him.[74]

Over the next several weeks, both the Soviets and the Americans moved pieces around the Mediterranean. The Russians moved their Mediterranean flagship, a submarine tender, to Tripoli and deployed a new SA-5 ground to air missile battery to Sirte to provide anti-aircraft coverage over the Gulf of Sidra. The Russians realized, however, that there was little they could do to protect Qaddafi and would not go to war with the United States over Libya. At the same time, Qaddafi crowed "Reagan has backtracked from war," but, "if it comes, I believe it will be in the sea hundreds of miles away from land."[75]

At the same time, the United States initially sent a second carrier, the *Saratoga*, to the Mediterranean to join the *Coral Sea* already on station. In March, Weinberger ordered a third carrier, *America*, to join the other two. By mid-March, the United States would have deployed three carrier task groups comprising 26 combatants, with 250 aircraft.[76] Qaddafi had drawn a line across the northern Gulf of Sidra, which he called the "line of death." By mid-March, the US Navy was preparing to cross it.

Taking Control of the Iran Initiative

Pursuant to President Reagan's decision to proceed with Nir's plan, between January 9 and 13, Assistant Secretary of Defense Noel Koch and head of the Israeli Procurement Mission, Ben-Yosef, were designated to work out the details of the "replenishment sales." At this point, the plan was still for Israel to sell 4,000 TOW missiles to Iran and use the proceeds to purchase replacement missiles from the United States. After a few days of intense haggling, however, in which Nir and North also played major roles, the negotiations collapsed.

At the outset, Nir informed North that the proceeds Israel derived from the August-September 1985 sales "had been used for other purposes" and were "not available" now. Koch informed Ben-Yosef that the lowest price the basic TOW had ever been sold for was $6,800. Nir responded by insisting that Israel "could pay only $5,000-$5,500 per missile." The two sides were at an impasse.

To narrow the difference, North postulated that if Israel charged Iran $10,000 per missile, then, they would receive ten million for the first one thousand missiles and forty million for four thousand. After deducting administrative costs, commissions to Ghorbanifar and Schwimmer, and a contribution to their covert operations fund, Israel would be able to purchase 4,000 replacement TOWs at

---

[73] Greenberger, "Libya's US Assets Frozen [. . .]."

[74] James Morrison, "Shultz Warns Force Remains an Option to Stop Terrorism," *Washington Times*, January 10, 1986, A1.

[75] "Qaddafi Says Reagan 'Has Backtracked,'" *Washington Post*, January 15, 1986, A5.

[76] Stanik, *El Dorado Canyon*, 130.

$6,000 each, or 4,500 TOWs at $5,333 each, the latter number including the 500 TOWs from August-September 1985.[77]

When North explained this formula to Koch, the latter said that the sale of 4,000 TOWs would immediately signal to interested observers, like the Russians, that they exceeded Israel's needs and therefore were for a third party, which would raise questions. Secondly, the dollar amount would greatly exceed the $14 million level requiring congressional notification. The solution was to "go black," have the president issue a finding and conduct the sales covertly under the Economy Act, which would allow them to set a lower price.[78] (Ironically, without knowing it, Koch and his aides at DOD had come to the same approach that Meese had proposed at the January 7 NSPG meeting.)

When Koch talked to Weinberger about the negotiations the secretary was greatly agitated, exclaiming that the president's initiative "was a very foolish undertaking." Referring implicitly to their common background experience of Watergate, Koch asked: "was there a legal problem with this? Is somebody going to go to jail?" Weinberger replied: "yes," but Koch did not think the secretary "intended it seriously," and he therefore "did not take that seriously." He had "assumed if there was any prospect of its being illegal, that [Weinberger] would have stopped it. Since he didn't . . . I assumed it was legal.[79] Weinberger, although reluctantly following orders, nonetheless remained adamantly against involvement.

At the same time, however, CIA lawyers raised more fundamental concerns. An internal memorandum for Sporkin outlined the difficulty. Arms previously obtained by Israel under the Arms Export Control Act, or the Foreign Assistance Act, "could not be sold to Iran" without US consent, notice to Congress, and determination of the eligibility of the third country recipient. As there was to be no prior notice and Iran had been designated a "terrorist state," the proposed approach of Israeli sales, not to mention replenishment of weapons already sold, "was not feasible." However, hitting upon the same solution as DOD and Meese, the lawyers also suggested that it would be legal under a presidential covert action finding to use the Economy Act, whereby the DOD could sell to the CIA, which, in turn, could sell to either Israel or Iran.[80]

Another issue was the role of Ghorbanifar, whom the Israelis still viewed as a necessary interlocutor with Iran. So did the new world order faction. When word got around in early December that Reagan was going to press forward with the initiative, McFarlane had contacted Ledeen and told him to put Ghorbanifar in touch with Casey.[81] Astoundingly, after only a few days before calling

---

[77] *Congressional Report on the Iran-Contra Affair*, 204.
[78] Ibid.
[79] Walsh, *Final Report of the Independent Counsel*, 1:411n68 and *Congressional Report on the Iran-Contra Affair*, 205.
[80] Ibid., 205.
[81] *Tower Report*, B-52.

Ghorbanifar the most "despicable" person he had ever met and refusing to deal with him, McFarlane was putting him back into the game.

The new world order faction's vacillating attitude toward Ghorbanifar made it abundantly clear that he was simply an instrument in their scheme. At the earliest stage of the opening to Iran, the new world order faction turned off Casey's initiative on the grounds that Ghorbanifar was a "fabricator." McFarlane, however, deliberately included Ghorbanifar in his arms-for-hostages scheme with the Israelis. Then, in December, McFarlane turned off the scheme on the grounds that Ghorbanifar was a "despicable" character. Now, here was McFarlane bringing Ghorbanifar back into the game. Clearly, the on-again, off-again use of Ghorbanifar had nothing to do with his character, but with his utility at any particular moment. In this case, it seems, McFarlane hoped Ghorbanifar would do what he could not—bring down the initiative.

Ledeen met with Charles Allen and Clarridge, telling them that he "had McFarlane's approval" and mentioned that Kimche was also still involved.[82] The ostensible reason for bringing Ghorbanifar back in was his "important intelligence about Iranian-backed terrorism in Western Europe." Casey met Ledeen on December 19 and arranged for the head of the CIA's Iranian desk to meet with Ghorbanifar. After meeting with him, however, they still didn't like him, describing Ghorbanifar as "a guy who lies with zest."[83]

Despite the reservations of his people, Casey sent a memorandum to the president on December 23, saying that while we had "to be careful talking to Ghorbanifar," he agreed to take another polygraph test, which Casey felt was "worth doing for what we might learn." Ghorbanifar took the test on January 11 and "showed deception on almost all questions." Tellingly, the test revealed that Ghorbanifar "knew ahead of time that the hostages would not be released [in November] and deliberately tried to deceive us . . . "[84] The recommendation was that "the Agency have no dealing whatsoever with Ghorbanifar."[85]

Unwilling to accept the polygraph results, Casey sent Allen to meet with Ghorbanifar and provide a personal assessment. After a five-hour session, on January 14, Allen told the director that the Iranian was "hard to pin down" and was "very clever." Allen called him "a con man," to which Casey replied jokingly that he himself was "a con man's con man." In short, Casey decided that Ghorbanifar would continue to play a role in the initiative.[86]

Casey, and perhaps others, had begun to realize that the United States should structure the initiative the same way that the Israelis and Iranians had by using private cut outs. Peres had used private individuals, Kimche, Schwimmer,

---

[82] *Tower Report*, B-52. Michael Ledeen, *Perilous Statecraft: An Insider's Account of the Iran Contra Affair* (New York: Scribner, 1988), 201, says that it was his idea to approach Casey, which North approved.

[83] *Tower Report*, B-53.

[84] Ibid., B-54-55.

[85] *Congressional Report on the Iran-Contra Affair*, 205.

[86] Ibid., 206.

Nimrodi, and now Nir to deal with both Iran and the United States. Iran was using Ghorbanifar in the same role. Moreover, it became increasingly clear that Ghorbanifar was eager to bypass Israel and deal directly with the United States. Thus, was conceived the idea of using Secord as an "agent" for the United States to deal directly with Iran.

On January 14, the issue of Secord's role crystallized. At first, North proposed that the DOD sell directly to Secord, bypassing the CIA. In this scheme, Secord would deliver the TOWs to the Israelis, who would transfer them to Iran under arrangements made by Ghorbanifar. When apprised of this idea, Koch declared that Weinberger, who objected to Secord's involvement, "will blanch," forcing a change. Casey had wanted to avoid agency involvement, too, but, with Weinberger's objection, agreed that Secord could be an "agent for the CIA," with the agency otherwise uninvolved. Under this scheme, DOD would sell to Secord as the CIA's agent; he would then sell and ship to the Israelis, who would transfer to Iran through Ghorbanifar.[87]

However, the CIA's lawyers objected to the use of an agent, who would have "no connection with CIA other than to act as a 'middleman.'" George Clarke, one of Sporkin's staff lawyers, insisted that he "would feel more comfortable if the CIA were directly involved in the activity and that it would be essential that we act in furtherance of a traditional covert action objective." There was, in short, "no way" to structure the deal "without the CIA's getting involved."[88] The CIA had become involved, marginally, to be sure, but now legally for the first time in the Iran initiative.

The persistent problem was how to replace the TOWs Israel had sold to Iran in August-September 1985. Israel had acquired these weapons under the AECA and therefore retransfers, or sales, would require "US consent, notice to Congress, and [consideration of] the eligibility of the third country recipient for US aid."[89] As Poindexter had not been privy to any of McFarlane's dealings with the Israelis, he directed North to contact him and "find out what the understanding had been on replenishment of the first 504 TOWs."

McFarlane, of course, had no choice but to continue the lie and falsely said that the "United States had undertaken to sell, over time, 'requisite TOWs to replace the TOWs'" that Israel had sold to Iran for Weir.[90] The truth was the president had undertaken no such commitment, which was why, some six months later, nothing had yet been done. There had been no consent, no notice to Congress, and Iran was ineligible for aid. Finally, as was the case in *all* of McFarlane's machinations on this issue, there was no paper trail. The best he could ever come up with was a "mental" finding.

---

[87] *Congressional Report on the Iran-Contra Affair*, 206.

[88] Ibid., 207.

[89] *Congressional Report on the Iran-Contra Affair*, 205.

[90] Ibid., 207. Cf. *Tower Report*, B-68, which cites North's PROF note to Poindexter of January 15, 1986, reporting his conversation with McFarlane.

On the morning of January 16, North devised a solution to the problem of replenishment of the 1985 sales. He proposed that for the first 1,000 TOWs, they cut out the commissions for Schwimmer and the Iranians, which would mean that Secord would receive a larger share. With that larger sum, he "could purchase 504 TOWs from the United States and ship them to Israel as replenishment for the 1985 transactions."[91] North's proposal was under consideration that afternoon as Poindexter convened key participants to resolve outstanding issues.

Meeting in Poindexter's office were Weinberger, Casey, Meese, Sporkin, and possibly North. Shultz was not present, nor, unusually, it seems, was Regan. After mulling over the legal impediments, Attorney General Meese made a momentous decision. "Israel should not ship weapons out of its stocks." Instead, he recommended "the United States . . . sell directly to the Iranians." Direct sales, under the authority of the Economy Act, he said, "would avoid the restrictions of the Arms Export Control Act, including Congressional reporting requirements." Weinberger was stunned, declaring that he wanted to have his lawyers "look at it and see that the analysis is correct."

By the next morning, Friday, January 17, Weinberger sent word that his lawyers "agree with the analysis and . . . have signed off on the project."[92] After the president had returned from a "brief talk" to the American Legislative Exchange Council, he met with the vice-president and Regan. They were joined by Poindexter and Don Fortier, who went over the details of the hastily rewritten memorandum. After discussing it for a few minutes, the president "gave the go-ahead" and signed the finding.[93]

There is confusion in the record over the January 17 finding. The Tower report and the congressional report both state, respectively, that the January 17 finding was "identical to the January 6 document with Sporkin's revision . . . " and that the two documents were "almost identical." Draper follows this interpretation, describing the two findings as "almost identical" and "virtually the same."[94] The implication is that the policy authorized by the two findings was also the same, which it decidedly was not.

All findings come in two parts, a memorandum describing the policy and the finding authorizing it. While the authorizations in the January 6 and 17 findings were "almost identical," the policies being authorized were completely different. The January 6 finding authorized an Israeli plan to "unilaterally commence selling military material to western-oriented Iranian factions." Israel

---

[91] *Congressional Report on the Iran-Contra Affair* says, 207, their commissions should be cut by 25% and 15%, respectively, and 208, "cut out" completely. Cf. Draper, *Very Thin Line*, 254.

[92] *Congressional Report on the Iran-Contra Affair*, 208.

[93] *Tower Report*, B-65-67 and Brinkley, *Reagan Diaries*, 384. The oft-repeated phrase, "I agreed to sell TOWS to Iran," does not appear in the president's diary entry for January 17.

[94] *Tower Report*, B-65, *Congressional Report on the Iran-Contra Affair*, 208, and Draper, *Very Thin Line*, 256-57.

would also release Shiite prisoners from jail and Iran would affect the release of the five American hostages. In this plan the "only requirement the Israelis have is an assurance that they will be allowed to purchase US replenishments for the stocks that they sell to Iran."

The January 17 finding specifically rejected the Israeli plan but supported the objective of promoting a "more moderate Iranian government." The memorandum stated, "the objectives of the Israeli plan could be met if the CIA, using an authorized agent as necessary, purchased arms from the Department of Defense under the Economy Act and then transferred them to Iran directly after receiving appropriate payment from Iran."

Israel's role under the new plan, as Segev notes, was changed from being an arms seller to serving solely as a "liaison with Ghorbanifar and his contacts in Tehran."[95] The Israelis would "make the necessary arrangements for the sale of 4,000 TOW weapons to Iran" and insure that "sufficient funds to cover the sale would be transferred to an agent of the CIA." Left unstated in the memo was the identity of the CIA's "agent," who was Richard Secord, and the transshipping point to Iran, which would be Israel.[96] Secord would take delivery of weapons in the United States; ship them to Israel, and from there forward them to Iran.

The memorandum closed with a test for success and a loophole. "If all of the hostages were not released after the first shipment of 1,000 weapons, further transfers would cease." This test suggested that the main purpose was to gain the release of the hostages, but the next sentence altered that perception entirely. It stated, "on the other hand, since hostage release is in some respects a byproduct of a larger effort to develop ties to potentially moderate forces in Iran, you may wish to redirect such transfers to other groups within the government at a later time."[97]

Also included in the memorandum, but not in the finding itself, was the recommendation that the president exercise his "statutory prerogative to withhold notification of the finding to the Congressional oversight committees until such time that you deem it to be appropriate." This was not an attempt to circumvent the Congress, as was later claimed, because the assumption was the hostages would be released after the first delivery of TOW missiles. Thus, the time frame envisaged by the recommendation was, at most, a few days. Unfortunately, this was not how it turned out.

To avoid the charge that the administration was dealing with the Khomeini regime, the justification given for direct arms sales was to support "moderates," who could change Iranian policy. The fact was that the concept of Iranian moderates was that of the Iranians themselves, who passed it on to Washington. American analysts perceived no "moderates" in the Iranian leadership. American leaders, however, adopted it for its obvious political utility, or "cover."

---

[95] Segev, *Iranian Triangle*, 231.
[96] *Tower Report*, B-66.
[97] Ibid.

There was another potentially explosive issue, which was that Reagan had decided to cut the Israelis out. Meese had justified direct US sales, instead of indirect sales through Israel, on the grounds that it would avoid violating the Arms Export and Control Act. However, the United States did not employ that law; it legalized arms sales under the Economy Act, which just as easily could have justified sales through Israel. Thus, it seems, the January 17 finding was the first step in a series designed to cut Israel out of the initiative. It would be easier said than done.

After two weeks of discussions and intense legal scrutiny the president's advisers had formulated a covert action finding that would allow the United States to sell arms directly and legally to Iran. The objective was to reestablish political relations severed seven years earlier and, in the process, gain the release of the five American hostages being held in Lebanon. "Operation Recovery" was under way. The assumption was that the Iranians, too, wished to reestablish political relations. It was an assumption that would be put to the test in coming days.

Chapter 14

Moscow Enters the Game

President Reagan's decision to proceed in secret with a now fully legal Iran initiative did not occur in a vacuum. It was part of a larger set of decisions to implement NSDD-75, the strategy toward the Soviet Union adopted in early 1983.[1] Having defeated Soviet strategy in 1983-84, Reagan sought to deal from a position of "greater relative strength" to begin the process of putting his own strategic construct in place.[2]

Thus, in early 1986, to increase pressure on the Soviets, the president decided to include provision of Stinger anti-aircraft missiles and other military aid to resistance forces in Angola and Afghanistan and communications equipment for the Contras in Nicaragua. More would be sent once Congress appropriated requested funds for the Contras. Similarly, increased financial support was funneled into Eastern Europe to support dissidents in Poland and Czechoslovakia, into Africa for anti-Soviet forces in Mozambique, and into Southeast Asia for anti-Vietnamese forces in Cambodia.

The president's strategy was designed to vanquish the Soviet Union in the Cold War and bring about a new global balance based on American hegemony. The president and his close aides fully understood that the policies enacted in early 1986, if successfully implemented, would very likely take a major step toward achieving this general objective because they calculated that the Soviets were overextended geopolitically, and the Soviet economy was visibly faltering and moving toward a crisis of the regime. The Russians, in short, were going broke and could no longer compete with the United States in the global arena.

In the course of the year the president guided the nation onto an active course against the Soviet Union and its allies. In addition to funneling increased military support to anti-Soviet forces, he authorized a major strike against

---

[1] For NSDD-75, see Christopher Simpson, *National Security Directives of the Reagan and Bush Administrations: The Declassified History of US Political and Military Policy, 1981-1991* (Boulder: Westview, 1995), 255-63.

[2] In his *Annual Report to the Congress*, Fiscal Year 1987, 3-4, Secretary Weinberger openly declared the change. "Rather than dealing from weakness . . . the United States is now beginning to deal from strength and the promise of greater relative strength . . . . Nothing could so enhance the prospects for long-term peace as Soviet acceptance of the proposition that they can achieve no significant exploitable military advantage over us."

Moscow's Libyan ally, Muammar Qaddafi, in an attempt to dissuade the Libyan dictator from further support for international terrorist activities. He supported clandestine sabotage by Afghan rebels against targets inside the Soviet Union itself. Then, he dismissed Gorbachev's arms control gambit at Reykjavik designed to maintain the status quo, and instead put forth a new strategy.

Gorbachev, though promoting détente and arms control, responded to the president's challenge with a significant change in Soviet strategy. The core objectives of the Soviet Union under Brezhnev, Andropov, and Chernenko had been to perpetuate strategic weapons superiority over the United States; maintain military dominance across the Eurasian landmass; and draw Iran into Moscow's political orbit. Gorbachev had recognized that this core strategy had failed and so revised each element of it in an attempt to retain some advantage.

An outgrowth of his "new thinking," Gorbachev abandoned the long-term Soviet strategy of seeking change and advantage through nuclear coercion and shifted to one of seeking détente with the United States and mutual cooperation with other states and clients. As I have argued elsewhere, only a dramatic reduction in security costs would enable Gorbachev to modernize his failing economy.[3] The shift from a zero-sum to mini-max approach would be codified at the 27th Party Congress at the end of February 1986, but several of its policy parts would be put into practice beforehand.

The centerpiece of Gorbachev's strategy was détente with the United States, and he made politically extravagant proposals to dissuade American leaders, especially the new world order faction, from pursuing Reagan's strategy. After digesting the results of the Geneva Summit, Gorbachev offered détente to the United States and in a January 1986 letter to Reagan proposed the complete abolition of "all nuclear weapons" by the end of the century.[4] The proposal, like all Soviet proposals, had a catch: Reagan would have to agree to cancel the Strategic Defense Initiative. That dulled some of the luster from Gorbachev's supposedly transformational idea, which was best understood as pie in the sky instead of SDI.

On the Eurasian balance, Gorbachev renounced the aim of nuclear superiority, while offering détente with both European and Asian states. During a visit to Paris in October 1985, he offered Soviet inclusion in a common European "home," another remarkable idea, and said that Moscow now sought "reasonable sufficiency,"[5] rather than nuclear superiority. He offered dramatic improvements in relations with both Japan and China, as well. In fact, Gorbachev's proposals would have considerable appeal among the political left in all of these countries but would have uneven results.

---

[3] Richard C. Thornton, "Mikhail Gorbachev: A Preliminary Strategic Assessment," *World and I* (January 1993), 583-93.

[4] Don Oberdorfer, *The Turn: From the Cold War to a New Era: The United States and the Soviet Union, 1983-1990* (New York: Poseidon Press, 1991), 156-58.

[5] Ibid., 141.

Gorbachev also sought to take up Reagan's earlier proposal of a zero option for Europe in an attempt to reverse the failure to prevent the deployment of the Pershing II/cruise missile package to Western Europe. In this proposal the United States would remove the Pershing II and cruise missiles and the Soviet Union would scrap its SS-20 force. If accepted, this quite transparent plan would eliminate American missiles from Western Europe and reestablish Soviet ballistic missile advantages over Eurasia once again, because the Russians would simply replace the SS-20 with other missiles, particularly the SS-25. At the stroke of a pen, the situation would revert to what had existed prior to the deployment of the Pershing II and cruise missiles.

Gorbachev's proposals, however, contrasted sharply with Soviet policy behavior. Although professing a desire for regional political solutions, Gorbachev continued to supply heavy weapons to Afghanistan, Angola, and Nicaragua, and supported police crackdowns against dissidents in Eastern Europe.[6] In this context, Gorbachev's most skillful gambit came in Southwest Asia, where it went virtually unrecognized by American leaders and was designed to keep alive Moscow's Iranian strategy by frustrating Reagan's attempt to reestablish relations with Tehran.

Moscow's Shift on Iran

The essence of Moscow's Iranian strategy since 1979 had been twofold. First, it was to create a geopolitical pincer against Iran, with Iraq on the western flank and the Soviet Union—from its position in Afghanistan—on the eastern flank. Second, it was to weaken Iran in a war of attrition against Iraq, leaving it vulnerable to an internal takeover. Saddam's role, after the first weeks of the conflict, had been to play anvil to Iran's hammer.

When Reagan foiled Moscow's Iran strategy in early 1984, the Soviets abandoned it and began to rearm Saddam's forces for a war of conquest. The Iranian response had been to intensify ongoing worldwide efforts to obtain weapons to counter the Iraqi buildup. In that context, they extended feelers for reestablishment of relations with the United States, their hated enemy, as the only means of counterbalancing Soviet support for Iraq.

Those were the circumstances that had offered President Reagan the opportunity to develop a political relationship with Iran and fulfill the objective of reconstituting the containment structure around the Soviet Union. As demonstrated in previous chapters, the president sought to respond positively to the Iran opening, but by the end of 1985 his internal foes, the new world order faction, had thwarted this opportunity with the arms-for-hostages deal, turned fiasco.

Nevertheless, for Moscow, the fiasco raised alarm at the prospect of an American-Iranian rapprochement, which had to be prevented at all costs, or it

---

[6] Peter Rodman, *More Precious than Peace: The Cold War and the Struggle for the Third World* (New York: Scribner, 1994).

would completely defeat Soviet strategy. This prospect prompted Gorbachev to make another policy shift, in hopes of avoiding the dreaded outcome. The overriding problem was how to avert the worst case of US-Iran rapprochement and keep Iran isolated. Moscow's pincer strategy had failed and arming Saddam for a war of conquest had backfired, driving the Iranians into Washington's arms.

Gorbachev decided to reverse course—dismantle the pincer put in place in 1979-80, relax Iraqi military pressure against Iran, and withdraw from Afghanistan. As a plan of strategic deception, Gorbachev adopted an even-handed approach toward Iran in the conflict with Iraq, offering to improve relations, and to provide additional weapons from Soviet clients.[7] The objective was to dissuade the Iranian leadership from taking the fateful step of reestablishing relations with the United States and renewing Iran's anti-Soviet posture in the US containment structure.

The Soviets hoped that as a result of their commencement of withdrawal from Afghanistan, holding back the Iraqis, relaxing military pressure on Iran, and offering improved relations, the Iranians would believe that they were in no danger of defeat and would refrain from taking an irrevocable step toward the United States. The Soviets hoped that with less concern about military defeat, the Iranians' basic antagonism toward the United States would resurface and they would decline the reestablishment of diplomatic relations—Moscow's worst case—and maintain an independent stance. Only this would keep open the possibility of drawing Iran into Moscow's orbit later on.

The first step was to gain Saddam Hussein's agreement, which would be no easy task. The Soviets had built up Saddam's forces and were putting Iraq in position to achieve victory in the long war. He would have to be dissuaded from such a course and apprised of its dangers at the present moment. Therefore, the Soviets invited Saddam for a state visit on December 16-17, 1985, his first visit in seven years. It was also Saddam's first trip outside Iraq since the war began. Upon arrival, he and Iraqi Foreign Minister Tariq Aziz met with Gorbachev and Soviet Foreign Minister Shevardnadze for a two-hour discussion, reportedly on "the Iran-Iraq war and bilateral relations."[8]

It was clear from the press accounts of both countries that the discussion had been difficult. *Al Thawra* said that the two men agreed on "most" of the issues discussed, while *Pravda* described the meeting as "businesslike, frank, and friendly."[9] The code words "most," "businesslike" and "frank" all implied that the atmosphere was "cool" and that there had been disagreements. Furthermore, in an unprecedented omission, no communiqué was issued after the visit.

Andrei Gromyko, in his new role as president of the USSR, also met with Saddam, Aziz, and key Iraqi generals. In a statement after their talks, in addition

---

[7] "Moscow Shift: Animosity to US Doesn't Make Mideast Pro-Soviet," *Economist*, February 12, 1986.

[8] Haim Shemesh, *Soviet-Iraqi Relations, 1968-1988: In the Shadow of the Iraq-Iran Conflict* (Boulder: Lynne Rienner, 1992), 198.

[9] Ibid.

to announcing the provision of "new types of weapons" at current levels, Gromyko complained about the Iraqi attitude in a way that indicated what the Russians had asked of Saddam:

> Those who contrary to any reason are calling for the war to be continued 'to a victorious end,' considering it as a means to settle accounts with the adversary and impose their will upon him, are behaving irrationally. [10]

In his own speech after their meeting, Saddam hinted his agreement as he called upon "friendly states, among them the Soviet Union, to increase urgent efforts either in the Security Council or at other levels to establish a just and comprehensive peace."

Pravda's report on the talks after his departure noted that both sides "vigorously opposed any attempts to impose from outside . . . regimes which are alien to them."[11] Parsing these hints, it seems that the Russians were asking Saddam, at least for the time being, to postpone a continuation of the war "to a victorious end" and he had, no doubt reluctantly, agreed. What else he agreed to would shortly become clear on the battlefield.

On Afghanistan, according to Gorbachev, the decision to withdraw was "adopted in October 1985." He maintained that "a clear goal ha[d] been set—to speed up the process in order to have a friendly country and leave."[12] Recall, at the Geneva Summit, he had hinted to Reagan a willingness to withdraw with appropriate guarantees and afterward Washington had "expressed its willingness in principle to guarantee an Afghan accord."[13]

While Saddam was still in Moscow, and no doubt with his agreement, the Soviets sent a message to Tehran promising to pursue a "neutral policy" in the war.[14] At the same time, they reinforced the change in Afghan policy by having their Afghan client Najibullah reiterate to Pakistani authorities that the Soviets had decided on a withdrawal timetable.[15] Afghan negotiators passed this information to UN mediator Diego Cordovez during the sixth round of the UN-sponsored proximity talks with Pakistan, in December 16-19, 1985; again, while Saddam was still in Moscow. [16]

---

[10] Ibid.

[11] Ibid., 198-99.

[12] "Notes from Politburo Meeting, 13 November 1986," in *Cold War International History Project (CWIP) Bulletin*, no. 14/15 (Winter/Spring, 2003-2004): 144.

[13] John W. Parker, *Kremlin in Transition*, vol. 2, *Gorbachev, 1985 to 1989* (Boston: Unwin Hyman, 1991), 85.

[14] Shemesh, *Soviet-Iraqi Relations*, 201.

[15] According to Rodman, *More Precious than Peace*, 326, the Soviets had begun informing UN interlocutors of their intent to withdraw according to a timetable from mid-1985.

[16] Parker, *Kremlin in Transition* 2: 85.

(Gorbachev's position would become unmistakable a few weeks later when in his speech to the 27th Party Congress in late February 1986 he described Afghanistan as a "running sore," and declared that a "step by step withdrawal [plan] has been worked out with the Afghan side.") [17]

Thus, by the end of 1985, Gorbachev had put in place the new policy structure toward the region. To ensure that Iranian leaders fully understood the new shift, on February 2, he sent first deputy foreign minister Georgi Kornienko to Tehran—the highest official to visit Tehran since the establishment of the Islamic Republic. In talks with the top Iranian leadership, Kornienko discussed, and evidently resolved to Iran's satisfaction, the entire gamut of issues outstanding between the two countries.

Two public irritants were resolved. First, was the continuing fallout from the defection to the West of Soviet resident KGB chief Vladimir Kuzichkin. Second, was the wholesale expulsions of Soviet personnel from Iran the following year. [18] Indicating improved relations, Iran's foreign minister Ali Akbar Velayati accepted an invitation to visit Moscow and the two sides agreed to resume airline service between their countries.

Although there is no record of other topics discussed, Majlis leader Rafsanjani's remarks at a news conference suggested that matters relating to the ongoing war with Iraq were discussed. Kornienko's visit, he said,

> will have a great effect on our relations with the Soviet Union and the Eastern World. One can be optimistic in fields such as technical military, economic, and possibly political relations. [19]

Kornienko's visit was followed a week later by the beginning of an Iranian offensive against Iraq, which resulted in a victory at the Al Faw peninsula. By all accounts it was a "stunning victory that . . . sent a psychological shock throughout the region." [20] The near-unanimous view also claimed that the occupation of Al Faw put Iran into position to attack Basra from the south, cut off access to Kuwait and strongly affect Iraq's naval access to the gulf. A closer look, however, belied these claims on every count but one—that it had been a psychological victory.

Throughout the previous fall both Iraq and Iran had strengthened their respective positions in anticipation of renewed fighting. Iran had deployed some 200,000 men to the southern sector of the front from north of Basra to the mouth of the Shatt al-Arab on the gulf and an assault on Basra was widely anticipated.

---

[17] Ibid.

[18] John W. Parker, *Persian Dreams: Moscow and Tehran Since the Fall of the Shah* (Washington: Potomac Books, 2009), 21.

[19] *Middle East Contemporary Survey*, ed. Itamar Rabinovitch and Haim Shaked, vol. 10, *1986* (Boulder: Westview, 1988), 45-46.

[20] Mohiaddin Mesbahi, "The USSR and the Iran-Iraq War: From Brezhnev to Gorbachev," in Farhang Rajaee, ed., *The Iran-Iraq War: The Politics of Aggression* (Gainesville: University of Florida Press, 1993), 82.

To strengthen defensive positions, Iraqi forces struck first on January 6, recapturing most of the Majnoon oil complex north of Basra, but the Iranians managed to hold on to a small position on the island.[21]

On February 9, Iran commenced a series of attacks in two broad thrusts, north of Basra and against Al Faw. The first was a two-pronged amphibious attack under cover of heavy rains and darkness across the 300-yard-wide Shatt al-Arab, toward Al Faw. One Iranian division of 10,000 men took the island group of Umm al-Rasas and another the town of Siba. Iraqi forces quickly engaged and retook Umm al-Rasas, but on the 11th, the force at Siba pressed southward to take an abandoned oil depot on Al Faw at the very tip of Iraq and held it.[22]

At the same time, Iranian forces struck north of Basra at Qurna and Amara in the area of the Hawizeh Marshes—the scene of several small-scale skirmishes the previous year.[23] After three days of heavy fighting, Iraqi firepower drove back the invaders with heavy losses. Iraqi commanding general, Maher Abd al-Rashid told journalists visiting the front that he had requested permission from Saddam Hussein "to launch a counterattack into Iranian territory," which would have encircled and cut off Iranian forces from support, but Saddam had "refused" his request.[24]

By the middle of February, Iranian forces had consolidated a position of some 150 square miles on the southern half of the Al Faw peninsula. As Pelletier notes, Iraqi forces had quickly "set up blocking lines to the west and north of the occupied area." In fact, Al Faw occupied a "dead space in the Gulf and up to this point in the war had been of no military significance." The peninsula was honeycombed with defense works, which enabled the Iranians to fend off Iraqi attacks, but they could not utilize the peninsula as a springboard for an attack north toward Basra, or to cut off access to Kuwait. "Penned up there, their military effectiveness would be nil. Indeed, they could be left there for the duration of the conflict."[25]

The victory at Al Faw had a much greater impact politically than militarily. While the Iranians were never able to exploit their position to break out of the peninsula, the political significance of their success had an immediate impact on Iran's response to the United States. Indeed, it would seem that the victory at Al Faw related to what Gorbachev and Saddam Hussein had agreed to in their meetings in December.

The Iraqis had been slow to respond to the Iranian move to Al Faw, which they considered to be a diversionary attack. The dilatory response gave Iran

[21] Edgar O'Ballance, *The Gulf War* (London: Brassey's, 1988), 173.

[22] Anthony Cordesman and Abraham Wagner, *The Lessons of Modern War*, vol. 2, *The Iran-Iraq War* (Boulder: Westview, 1990), 219-20.

[23] Anthony Cordesman, *The Iran-Iraq War and Western Security, 1984-1987* (London: Jane's, 1987), 92.

[24] O'Ballance, *Gulf War*, 179.

[25] Stephen Pelletiere, Douglas Jonson, and Leif Rosenberger, *Iraqi Power and US Security in the Middle East* (Carlisle: US Army War College, 1990), 9.

the chance to secure a bridgehead on the peninsula. The heavy rains explain the failure to provide timely air support. Moreover, Iraq had positioned only a small, 1,000-man force of reservists to guard the port town, which had been rapidly overrun.

Cordesman thought "Iraqi planners [did] not seem to have fully considered the possibility of an Iranian amphibious assault in this area" and criticized the area commander, who "[did] not seem to have realized the need to destroy an enemy landing force before it can secure a bridgehead."[26] Yet, he also noted that Iraqi intelligence for months had observed the Iranian stockpiling of small craft and pontoon bridging equipment south of Abadan, the training of amphibious commando units, and their infiltration to the southern front in the latter half of 1985.[27]

Given the many months during which Iraqi intelligence observed Iranian preparations for amphibious operations, it is highly unlikely that Iraqi commanders failed to "realize" what the Iranians were planning and take contingency measures. Iraqi counter deployments along the southern front confirm their understanding of Iranian options. Moreover, Iraq held an overwhelming five-to-one advantage in firepower over Iran.

Rather, as argued here, the delayed Iraqi response was deliberate. The delay could be explained on the grounds that Basra was Iran's actual objective, not the relatively insignificant target of Al Faw, or because bad weather hindered a rapid response. I believe Saddam decided to allow the Iranians a small victory to encourage them in the belief they could still succeed without making an irrevocable political commitment to the United States.

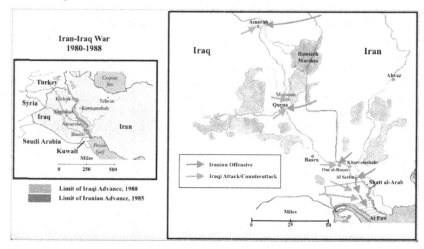

Iran-Iraq Battleground and Al Faw Campaign

---

[26] Cordesman, *Iran-Iraq War and Western Security*, 93.
[27] Ibid., 89.

The Iranian Response to Washington

President Reagan had informed Secretaries Shultz and Weinberger of his decision to proceed with the Iran initiative at a family group meeting in the White House after he had signed the finding on the morning of January 17.[28] However, he apparently had not shown either man the actual finding. Shultz would later testify that he had not known of the president's decision until after the crisis broke in November.[29] Weinberger would also claim that "neither Secretary Shultz, nor I, nor even Don Regan, saw the final, January 17 finding (until it was revealed publicly)."[30] Weinberger was wrong about Regan, whom Poindexter had briefed along with the president and Bush, on January 17, but it was true that Regan was uninvolved in the project thereafter.

Both Weinberger and Shultz had been disingenuous about their knowledge of the initiative. Not only had Weinberger learned of the president's decision on the day it was made, the next day Poindexter informed him that he should prepare 4,000 TOWs for sale to Iran. Although briefly considering resignation, the secretary decided to stay on, follow orders, and hope to be able to reverse the policy later on.[31] Indeed, no weapons could have been sold without the secretary's authorization. Thus, he knew about the initiative, even if he had not seen the finding.

Shultz was an altogether different matter. Claiming minimal knowledge throughout, in fact, as Walsh reveals, "the notes of Hill, Platt, and others . . . reflect Shultz's awareness of ongoing arms-for-hostages negotiations during nearly this entire period [between December 1985 and May 1986]."[32] He had also placed an ally, Peter Rodman, into the NSC, who kept him informed. Indeed, Poindexter, North, and Fortier briefed Rodman on the January 17 finding in February, and he thought the policy was "crazy."[33] As will be noted below, Shultz

---

[28] Lawrence E. Walsh, *Firewall: The Iran-Contra Conspiracy and Cover-Up* (New York: Norton, 1997), 328.

[29] *Report of the Congressional Committees Investigating the Iran-Contra Affair* (Washington, DC: US Government Printing Office, 1987), 209 [hereafter cited as *Congressional Report on the Iran-Contra Affair*]; and George Shultz, *Turmoil and Triumph* (New York: Scribner, 1993), 812.

[30] Caspar W. Weinberger, *Fighting for Peace: Seven Critical Years in the Pentagon* (New York: Warner Books, 1990), 376.

[31] Ibid. 83-84.

[32] Lawrence E. Walsh, *Final Report of the Independent Counsel for Iran-Contra Matters*, vol. 1 (Washington, DC: United States Court of Appeals for the District of Columbia Circuit, August 4, 1993), 337-38. In *Firewall*, 328-30, Walsh also details Shultz's knowledge throughout.

[33] Rodman, *More Precious than Peace*, 421. On May 22, Rodman wrote a critical memo to Poindexter "warning that the policy seemed to be degenerating into an arms-for-hostages deal. He did not include me in important deliberations after that point." The memo is reprinted in John G. Tower et al., *Report of the President's Special Review Board: February 26, 1987* (Washington, DC: 1987), B-100.

on at least two occasions would attempt to place bureaucratic roadblocks into the path of the initiative in an attempt to stop it.

Meanwhile, North immediately contacted selected CIA and DOD personnel to arrange for the agency's acquisition of the TOWs to be shipped. The decision to keep the process secret even within those organizations led, according to the congressional report, to a "significant pricing error" for the TOWs, which "North exploited to the advantage of the Enterprise."[34] The price the DOD charged the CIA was $3,469, instead of $8,435, which resulted in a significantly larger profit for the CIA "agent" Secord. However, there was no pricing error. Under the Economy Act, as an intra-governmental transfer, the DOD "sold" weapons at cost, not at the price it would charge to an outside buyer, or at replacement cost, both of which would have been much higher.

Within a few days the pricing and transportation arrangements were settled and North and Secord flew to London to meet Nir. At the same time, Nir had arranged to cut out Kimche, Schwimmer and Nimrodi in what was a messy, unpleasant series of exchanges filled with recriminations. Nir had argued that those involved in the initiative had changed on the American side, and North was now the lead player. Since he knew North well, Nir suggested that Kimche, Schwimmer and Nimrodi should stand aside. Objecting, the trio appealed to Peres, who upheld Nir.[35]

In London, January 22, North and Secord met with Nir to work out the details of the Israeli role. The next day the three of them met with Ghorbanifar to reach agreement with the Iranian side. As North laid it out in a 50-step "notional timeline" for Poindexter after his return, the United States would sell and ship 4,000 TOW missiles to Iran in four tranches, pick up and return the rejected Hawks to Israel, and also furnish an "intelligence sample" to Iran. Israel would repay Iran $5.4 million for the returned Hawks and release 100 Shiite prisoners held by the Southern Lebanon Army (part of Nir's original proposal). Iran would pay for the weapons and arrange for the release of the five hostages.[36]

North had tape-recorded the session with Ghorbanifar, establishing for the record that they had discussed using the profits from the arms sales, or "residuals," for other purposes. Ghorbanifar waxed ecstatic, claiming that the profits would enable the United States to resolve the hostage problem, the terrorist problem, and support for the Contras, all "free of charge. . . . Everything free." North later acknowledged, "using the Ayatollah's money to support the Nicaraguan resistance was the right idea."[37]

The entire series of shipments and exchanges were to take place between January 24 and February 25 and set the stage for a meeting soon after between high American and Iranian officials to begin the process of reestablishing relations

---

[34] *Congressional Report on the Iran-Contra Affair*, 215.
[35] Samuel Segev, The *Iranian Triangle: The Untold Story of Israel's Role in the Iran-Contra Affair* (New York: Free Press, 1988), 236-38.
[36] *Tower Report*, B-71-73.
[37] *Congressional Report on the Iran-Contra Affair*, 216.

between the two countries. The crucial phase, however, was the first. According to North's notes, the Iranian Government was to deposit $40 million in Ghorbanifar's Swiss account. He would deposit $10 million to Secord's account for the first 1,000 TOWs. Secord would transfer $3.5 million to the CIA, which would confirm to DOD that funds had been transferred. Defense would then make the weapons available for pickup by Secord. The CIA would furnish an intelligence package, Secord would ship the missiles, Israel would release Shiite prisoners, and Iran would arrange for the release of the hostages. All this would be accomplished by February 9, an ambitious schedule to say the least.[38]

North's notional timeline was an impressive feat of logistical planning, which, however, immediately became obsolete, except as a baseline schedule to be repeatedly adjusted. It also included the fantastic prediction, which Ghorbanifar proclaimed would come true, that on February 11, the Ayatollah Khomeini would step down as supreme leader of Iran.[39] When North returned to Washington, he informed Poindexter that he had "found a way that we can provide some funds to the democratic resistance through funds that will accrue from the sale of arms to the Iranians." After thinking it over for a few minutes, Poindexter agreed.[40]

According to North's timeline, Ghorbanifar was to transfer $10 million to Secord's account on January 29 to pay for the first 1,000 TOWs, which would be delivered on February 8. The Defense Department, on Weinberger's orders, would do nothing until it had money in hand. Once Secord transferred funds, the department would move weapons from the storage depot in Anniston, Alabama, to Kelly Air Force Base, Texas, where Secord would pick them up and fly them to Israel.

When Ghorbanifar failed to deposit the $10 million on January 29, a concerned North called him and was reassured that the money would be deposited on February 4. North then got together with Secord and the CIA's Near East Division Chief, Thomas Twetten, to "develop another schedule based on an anticipated bank transfer to the CIA account on February 4."[41] Yet, that schedule slipped too, as North jotted in his notes "Gorba going to bank to make transaction tomorrow." However, there was no deposit on February 5, either.

During the January 22 meeting, the four men had agreed to meet again in London, on February 6, to authorize the final go ahead. Ghorbanifar's failure to transfer funds on January 29, February 4, or 5, lent great urgency to the scheduled meeting of February 6. When North, Secord, and Nir arrived in London for the meeting, however, Ghorbanifar failed to appear. As Secord recounted it,

---

[38] *Congressional Report on the Iran-Contra Affair*, 215-16 and *Tower Report*, B-71-73.

[39] Ibid., B-73.

[40] *Congressional Report on the Iran-Contra Affair*, 216.

[41] *Congressional Report on the Iran-Contra Affair*, 217; and Theodore Draper, *A Very Thin Line: The Iran-Contra Affairs* (New York: Hill and Wang, 1991), 282, who identifies DC/NE and C/NE as Twetten.

"We tried to track him down on the phone using a dozen numbers Nir carried for that purpose—Gorba's contacts and relatives in Nice, Paris, Frankfurt, and Bonn—but with 'no joy,' as military pilots say when their target is not sighted."[42] Needless to say, without Ghorbanifar, the entire scheme was dead in the water.

What had happened? Although many on the American side impugned Ghorbanifar for his failure to perform according to agreement, it seems obvious that Ghorbanifar, as interlocutor, was responding to the decisions of those higher up. It was the leaders in Tehran that had decided to hold off on the transaction with Washington. The Russians had gotten to the Iranians just before they accepted the American offer. Kornienko had arrived on February 2, as noted above, and persuaded the Iranians to hold off taking any irrevocable steps until they could evaluate the result of the imminent battle, which began on February 9. The Soviet leader's extraordinarily well-timed visit raises the question of Moscow's knowledge of American policy.[43]

The Iranian decision to stall created a major crisis for Ghorbanifar. As interlocutor he bore the brunt of the American ire and if the "stall" became a permanent decision against establishing a relationship he faced irrelevance. The fact is the Iranian government, having decided to hold off regarding the US, had not transferred $40 million into Ghorbanifar's account and therefore there were no funds for him to transfer to Secord. Unless and until he could find a way to find the funds to keep the project alive, the deal would be off, so he stayed away.

Scrambling for funds, Ghorbanifar appealed to Adnan Khashoggi. As Ghorbanifar told it, Khashoggi lent him $10 million on February 7, depositing it "directly" into Secord's Lake Resources account at the Swiss bank, Compagnie de Services Fiduciaire (CSF).[44] It would take a few days for the funds to clear and not be until February 10 and 11 that funds were transferred from the Lake Resources account to the CIA accounts, which were in the same bank, two deposits of $1.85 million each, totaling $3.7 million.[45]

This sequence also implies that Ghorbanifar must also have appealed successfully to Tehran to let him keep the Americans in play. Tehran, of course, still wanted weapons, but now no political commitment. So, they agreed to Ghorbanifar's weapons' purchase scheme on condition that he arrange for outside financing. As this was now, strictly speaking, Ghorbanifar's deal and not

---

[42] Richard Secord and Jay Wurts, *Honored and Betrayed: Irangate, Covert Affairs, and the Secret War in Laos* (New York: Wiley, 1992), 245.

[43] We now know that Aldrich Ames, the mole in the CIA, was providing Moscow with a great deal of information. Were White House policy decisions among them? Were knowledgeable Iranian, or even Israeli opposition leaders passing information to Moscow?

[44] *Tower Report*, B-74. Willard Zucker, an American tax lawyer, controlled the bank. See Walsh, *Final Report of the Independent Counsel*, 1, chap. 8, "The Enterprise and Its Finances," 79-104.

[45] *Congressional Report on the Iran-Contra Affair*, 217.

Tehran's, there could have been no commitment regarding the hostages simply because Ghorbanifar had no influence whatsoever over Mughniyeh.

Indeed, as Ghorbanifar recounted the Khashoggi loan: "there was no talk of release of hostage. There was no hostage. So, it is proof to you that there is no deal on hostage. There is no deal for hostage, tit for tat—give me, take this."[46] Moreover, the Iranian government now saw the hostages as insurance *against* any political commitment in the same way that hostages had been used before in 1979 and 1980.

Ghorbanifar had "resurfaced" with funds in hand on February 7, as Secord noted, giving "some improbable explanation for his disappearance." Did the president realize what had happened? As I will recount in the next chapter, it appears that Reagan began to prepare for a tactical shift in his approach at this time. But, for the moment, he decided to press on. Indeed, he had little choice, but to see how events would play out. Thus, North and Secord rescheduled delivery of the first 500 missiles for February 17 and also set up the meeting with an Iranian leader in Frankfurt for February 19.[47]

Ignoring Tehran's failure to deposit the funds on time and despite numerous adjustments in schedule, it seemed the president had decided to risk the sale of a relative handful of weapons to establish official contact with Iran, the main objective of his policy. It was now a transaction with Ghorbanifar, not with Tehran, but did Reagan know that? The evidence is that he did. Although Secord claimed he did not discover that Khashoggi was bankrolling Ghorbanifar, not the Iranian government, until August 1986, North knew by early May, but apparently not in February.[48] One must presume others in the government were also fully aware of the change in procedure. Ghorbanifar underestimated the capabilities of US intelligence, for, as the Tower Report notes, he "went to . . . much trouble to keep [this secret] from us."[49]

North's PROF note to Poindexter of February 13 following his return to Washington laid out the new timetable. The first 500 missiles would now be delivered to Bandar Abbas on Monday February 17, instead of February 8, and "the meeting we had wanted to pass the second set of intel [had] now been slipped to Weds [February 19] by Gorba." The second 500 missiles were to be delivered on Friday, the 21st and 25 Hezbollah prisoners would be released "shortly after." Then, and only then, "if all goes according to plan," the hostages would be released on Sunday, the 23rd, two weeks after the original date of February 9.

This was not simply a new schedule, but a new deal. There would be no release of the hostages after the first 500 TOWs had been delivered, but only after the first thousand. And the hostages would be released only after the Hezbollah

---

[46] *Tower Report*, B-74.

[47] Ibid. and Secord *Honored and Betrayed*, 252.

[48] In a PROF note to Poindexter on May 5, North said "we know that Khashoggi is the principal fund raiser for Gorba and that only after Gorba delivers a cargo does he get paid by the Iranians." *Tower Report*, B 93-94.

[49] Ibid., 283.

prisoners were released. In other words, Ghorbanifar's insistence that there had been no arms-for-hostages deal was literally true. It was to be a trade of prisoners for hostages, preceded by a separate sale of weapons. In any case, the president decided to gamble that a demonstration of American good faith with delivery of the weapons, would gain both the release of the hostages and a meeting with the Iranians.

An Opening to Iran?

According to the new timetable, Secord delivered the first 500 TOWs to Bandar Abbas, on February 17. The aircraft then flew to Tehran, picked up the 17 previously rejected Hawks, and returned early the next day to Ben Gurion airport in Israel. That morning, Ghorbanifar called Secord to arrange for the promised meeting at the Iranian embassy in Frankfurt on February 19. He said that Kangarlu would head a six-man delegation and wanted to exchange names and titles with the American participants.[50]

Reporting on this call, Secord said that Ghorbanifar also wanted to confirm the delivery of the second 500 TOWs scheduled for Friday morning, February 21. He promised that "they will release all the hostages, if repeat, if intelligence is good," either Friday, or Saturday. He also promised to arrange the long-sought future meeting with Iranian leaders, while the US was delivering the remaining 3,000 TOWs. Ghorbanifar "repeatedly stressed need for good current intelligence." Secord ended his message, saying that he had rejected the Iranian embassy in Frankfurt as a venue and they had agreed to meet at a hotel, instead.

North immediately asked Casey for another intelligence package and tasked Clarridge with arranging fake identification documents for himself, Secord, and Albert Hakim, Secord's partner in the Enterprise. Ghorbanifar knew North and Secord, so it made no sense to assume different identities. It would only cast suspicion on US motives when he pointed out that they were not who they said they were. Hakim was another matter. As a prominent former member of the shah's regime, he was considered an enemy of the state, who could not afford to be recognized. He donned a disguise (a wig and glasses) and participated as a DIA official under the name of Ibrahim Ibrahimian.[51]

The problem was that the Iranian side as represented by Ghorbanifar had once again changed the nature of the arrangement by interjecting the value of the intelligence as a pre-condition for the release of the hostages. As the value of the intelligence lay in the eye of the beholder, this raised the distinctly unpleasant prospect that the release of the hostages could be delayed indefinitely.

---

[50] *Tower Report*, B-75.
[51] *Congressional Report on the Iran-Contra Affair*, 218. "Albert Hakim Deposition," Appendix B, vol. 13, 599, says the alias was "Ebrahim Ebrahimian." Draper, *Very Thin Line*, 282, notes Hakim's false job description (but appears unaware of his name change) and says North traveled as Mr. Goode and Secord as Major Gen Adams. Draper saw this as "youthful playacting" on North's part.

Nevertheless, the ever-optimistic North concluded, "we appear to be much closer to a solution than earlier believed. Kangarlu's attendance at the [coming] Frankfurt meeting tends to support our hope that this whole endeavor can succeed this week, if we *appear* to be forthcoming."[52]

When North, Nir, Twetten, and Hakim arrived in Frankfurt on February 19 (Secord was in Tel Aviv supervising the weapons delivery to Iran), Ghorbanifar was there but Kangarlu failed to show. Placing a call to Tehran, Kangarlu told Ghorbanifar "his bosses would not release him and had given him other assignments." Exasperated, North angrily rejected Ghorbanifar's pleas to wait and decided to return to Washington until Kangarlu actually came to Frankfurt. More importantly, he also canceled delivery of the second 500 TOWs, scheduled for February 21, which produced a prompt Iranian agreement to meet on the 24th.[53]

The day before the scheduled meeting, Ghorbanifar telephoned Allen, a call that the latter recorded. When Casey decided to work with Ghorbanifar, he assigned Allen the task of keeping in contact with him, ostensibly for his value with regard to counterintelligence matters, but, in fact, also as a way the CIA could monitor the evolving relationship with the Iranians.

Obviously intending to encourage the American side, Ghorbanifar declared that the Iranians had finally "made up their minds." It was, he said, "a real breakthrough." Exuding more than his usual confidence, he said, "these people . . . are ready to make a real firm response and [agree to] collective cooperation for the future." Concluding, he observed, "I think this time with all the strings I have pulled now it is going to work out."[54]

Thus, when North, Secord, Nir, Hakim, and Twetten arrived at the Frankfurt Sheraton hotel on the evening of February 24 for the first meeting between American and Iranian officials in over six years, expectations could not have been higher. Ghorbanifar introduced them to Mohsen Kangarlu, a deputy prime minister, who was accompanied by three intelligence officials. As they began their discussion, however, it soon became apparent that each side had come to the meeting with radically different expectations of the other, courtesy of Ghorbanifar.

Ghorbanifar had enticed Kangarlu to Frankfurt based on his assurance that the Americans were willing to sell the most advanced weapons to the Iranians. He had told the Americans that Iran was going to release the hostages and prepare for a high-level meeting with President Khamenei, Prime Minister Mousavi, and Majlis Speaker Rafsanjani. Thus, Kangarlu wanted to talk about weapons, while North sought to arrange the high-level meeting. Ghorbanifar, as interpreter, attempted to reconcile these irreconcilable expectations, intentionally

---

[52] *Tower Report*, B-76, emphasis in original.
[53] Secord, *Honored and Betrayed*, 253.
[54] Draper, *Very Thin Line*, 283.

mistranslating what was being said, until Hakim, after repeatedly correcting him, was asked to take over the job.[55] The first meeting, in short, was a disaster.

The next day, however, once Kangarlu was disabused of the notion of acquiring the highly sophisticated *Phoenix* air-to-air missile and other advanced weapons, discussion centered on the American agenda: delivery of the second 500 TOWs, release of the hostages, and a high-level meeting. They agreed that delivery of the second shipment of TOWs would result in the release of "a couple of hostages," presumably two. The rest would be released "after a meeting among high-level officials at Kish Island off the coast of Iran." When all the hostages were released, the United States would deliver the remaining 3,000 TOWs.[56]

North departed Frankfurt on February 26, having assured Kangarlu that the second 500 TOWs would be shipped the next day. Secord and Hakim stayed overnight, meeting with both Nir and Ghorbanifar the next morning, and then with Kangarlu later to confirm delivery of the second shipment. In a message to North on the 27th, Secord reported that Kangarlu emphasized the need for strict secrecy and "a quick meeting at Kish." He intimated that he could "possibly surprise us by getting some hostages released before the meeting."[57]

Immediately upon his return to Washington, North conferred with Casey, Poindexter, Twetten, and George to go over the results of the meeting. They agreed, "we are indeed headed in the right direction."[58] Overlooking the "money problem" and despite all the "adjustments in schedule," after a remarkably brief period of time, just six weeks from signing the finding, the American side seemed to think that the president's initiative was on the verge of success.[59]

A word about the decision-making process. Although the president does not appear in the record as the main decision-maker, and Casey, Poindexter, North, and Secord appear prominently in apparent decision-making roles, it is obvious that the president was in overall command. Poindexter briefed him every morning and there is no doubt whatsoever that the president guided the process from the Oval Office.[60] The idea that Poindexter, North, or even Casey would make crucial decisions affecting the fate of the president's policy without his input is, frankly, preposterous, their willingness to take responsibility for failure after-the-fact notwithstanding. The axiom of politics is that the president takes credit for successes; his staff takes responsibility for failures.

---

[55] "C/NE Deposition," (Twetten), *Congressional Report on the Iran-Contra Affair*, Appendix B, vol. 5, 936-37; and *Tower Report*, B-77.
[56] *Congressional Report on the Iran-Contra Affair*, 219.
[57] *Tower Report*, B-78.
[58] Ibid.
[59] The congressional report interprets this moment as reflective of just "another promise" by the Iranians, rather than the point of possible breakthrough. See *Congressional Report on the Iran-Contra Affair*, 221.
[60] Walsh, *Firewall*, 155, says that in his deposition, Vice-President Bush artfully "acknowledged that the Iranian initiative had been discussed in the president's intelligence briefings more often than once a month but less often than once a week."

At this critical moment, when it appeared that an opening to Iran was imminent, the president decided to move forward with a unified leadership and so offered the new world order faction an opportunity to close ranks. Thus, as preparations for the meeting on Kish Island began, the president through Poindexter offered McFarlane the opportunity to lead the US delegation, an offer that he accepted without hesitation. North elaborated on the events leading up to this point in an exchange of PROF messages with him, advising him to "pack your bags and be ready to go in about a week or so."[61]

At the same time, the president instructed Poindexter to brief Secretary Shultz on the upcoming meeting and solicit his support. According to the secretary, Poindexter said to him the hostages would be released, but

> the Iranians wanted a high-level dialogue, covering issues other than hostages. He said the White House had chosen McFarlane for the mission, and that he would go to Frankfurt . . . to meet with a deputy of Rafsanjani . . . . The Iranians had asked for help on intelligence as to what the Soviets were doing on the Iranian border and in Afghanistan. [Poindexter] saw a path to reemerging relations.[62]

Shultz was shown McFarlane's negotiating instructions and approved them but thought it "unlikely" he would succeed. Nevertheless, he said, "well, if you've got that arrangement, that's great."[63]

The situation was not clear-cut. No hostages had been released since Weir the past September and the United States had delivered one thousand missiles. Moreover, the atmosphere surrounding the meetings had reeked with suspicion, deception, and mistrust. Kangarlu hinted that the US and Iran should have direct talks, which alarmed Nir and Ghorbanifar, who, fearing they would be cut out, repeatedly stressed their relevance to the proceedings. North and Hakim also tried to convince Kangarlu that Ghorbanifar was no longer necessary as a conduit and Hakim began regular contact with Kangarlu, bypassing Ghorbanifar. Word of this reached Peres, who, also concerned about being cut out, immediately sent a letter to Reagan promising continued Israeli assistance.[64]

Backbiting intensified among the Americans, too. The CIA, perhaps sensing a historical moment approaching, wanted to be a part of it and tried to cut out Secord and Hakim on the grounds that they were "outsiders." But North would not have it, insisting that both remain on the team. Finally, at Claire George's and Tom Twetten's insistence, North agreed to bring George Cave, a retired CIA

---

[61] For the exchange, see *Tower Report*, B-78-80.

[62] Ibid., B-79.

[63] Ibid.

[64] Segev, *Iranian Triangle*, 247-49 and Draper, *Very Thin Line*, 286.

agent who spoke fluent Farsi, into their operation.[65] Counterintelligence chief Charles Allen, also became increasingly involved.

The situation facing the President Reagan on Iran was directly analogous to the situation Nixon faced with China fifteen years earlier. Although McFarlane would be denigrated for attempting to duplicate the feat of his mentor, Henry Kissinger, by embarking on the secret mission to Iran, the relevant analogy was not McFarlane and Kissinger, but Reagan and Nixon.

Then, Nixon had sought to present a unified leadership in the opening to China and so sent Kissinger, of the new world order faction, to lead the secret trip to Beijing. Now, Reagan sought to do the same and unify the American leadership in the opening to Iran. In both cases, incidentally, the new world order faction would attempt to sabotage these respective openings.[66] So much for bipartisanship in strategic matters but including the opposition in a great if obviously risky matter of state is an unspoken rule of politics. The intent was to ensure that, depending on the outcome, neither side could blame the other for failure, but both could claim credit for success.

In the China instance, Mao was determined to establish relations with the United States and so Kissinger's efforts failed until later when he became secretary of state. After Nixon resigned, the US-China relationship would founder until President Carter resuscitated it in 1978.[67] McFarlane would be more "successful" because the Iranian leadership was not sufficiently convinced that an opening to the Great Satan was then in its interest.

Tehran Plays a Delaying Game

The Iranian leadership had shifted to a delaying game, based on their mistaken beliefs that they were achieving success on the battlefield against Iraq and that Moscow would end support for Saddam Hussein. A series of incremental successes, beginning with the taking of the Al Faw peninsula and followed up with battlefield advances along the front, including seizure of a strip of Iraqi territory at Sulaymaniyah in the Kurdish north, fed these beliefs.[68] In fact, none of these "victories" was in any way decisive, although the propaganda campaign accompanying them claimed otherwise.

It was against the backdrop of these battles that the turn in Tehran's position occurred, prompting a reciprocal turn by the president. A few days after North returned to Washington, in early March, he received word, apparently

---

[65] *Congressional Report on the Iran-Contra Affair*, 222 and *Tower Report*, B-80.
[66] For Nixon's approach, see Richard C. Thornton, The *Nixon-Kissinger Years: The Reshaping of American Foreign Policy*, 2nd ed. (St. Paul: Paragon House, 2001), chaps. 1, 3, and 9.
[67] For the history on these developments, see Richard C. Thornton, *China: A Political History, 1917-1980* (Boulder: Westview, 1982) and *The Carter Years: Toward a New Global Order* (New York: Paragon House, 1991).
[68] Cordesman and Wagner, *Lessons of Modern War* 2: 217-24.

separately from both Hakim and Nir, that the Iranians had changed their mind about both the Kish Island meeting and the weapons they wanted.[69] Hakim reported that Kangarlu had reverted to his earlier position and wanted to buy the Phoenix and Harpoon missiles before any hostages would be released and Ghorbanifar passed word that Iran wanted a preparatory meeting in Paris before setting up the Kish meeting.[70] These "messages" raised doubts among agency officials that Ghorbanifar could deliver the hostages, and concern that the Iranians were attempting to use "salami" tactics simply to obtain more weapons.

Ghorbanifar was also becoming uneasy as Washington became increasingly suspicious of his ability to deliver. North had told Nir about Kangarlu's conversation with Hakim, intensifying both Nir's and Ghorbanifar's fears that they were being cut out. Ghorbanifar called Allen in Washington in an attempt to establish his own direct channel through the CIA.[71] Although there was growing dissatisfaction with Ghorbanifar's performance and pressure grew to seek another means of access to the Iranian leadership, the fact was that it was Tehran's position that was changing.

Nevertheless, North, Twetten, and Cave went to Paris to meet with Ghorbanifar and Nir on March 8. Ghorbanifar launched into what had become a common refrain about how essential he was to the initiative and how with the sale of a few more weapons the hostage problem could be cleared up and profits could be used for the Contras. Specifically, he reiterated Kangarlu's demand for Phoenix and Harpoon missiles, in addition to the pending order of *3,000 TOWs*. He also said that the Iranian military needed spare parts for its mostly inoperative Hawk missile system and submitted a request for 240 items.[72] Finally, he said that the leadership had decided that Kish Island was unacceptable; the high-level meeting would have to take place in Tehran.[73]

Despite Nir's exhortation to the Americans that these sales would result in the release of all of the hostages, North smelled a rat. They had clearly taken a step backward. Changing the site of the meeting meant further delays. Aside from reiterating to Ghorbanifar Washington's willingness to meet, he made clear that the United States would not sell anything before all of the hostages were released. During this exchange, however, North disclosed US intelligence regarding the decrepit state of Iran's weapons' capability. Responding to the demand for advanced weapons, he observed that even if the United States sold them, the Hawk

---

[69] *Congressional Report on the Iran-Contra Affair*, 222, says that Kangarlu called Hakim, who told him; but Secord, *Honored and Betrayed*, 254, says Nir called North, to pass on Ghorbanifar's message.

[70] See North memo to Poindexter, "Terms of Reference US-Iran Dialogue," April 4, 1986, *Tower Report*, B-86-90, the so-called "diversion" memo. *Congressional Report on the Iran-Contra Affair*, 225, titles this memo "Release of American Hostages in Beirut."

[71] Segev, *Iranian Triangle*, 254.

[72] *Tower Report*, B-87. The list would not be received until March 28.

[73] Segev, *Iranian Triangle*, 254 and *Iran-Contra Affair*, 223.

"launchers for these missiles were in such disrepair that the missiles could not be launched."[74]

The real tipoff to Tehran's stall was the spare parts list itself. Secord, who had "crafted, installed, and verified" Iran's Hawk missile system a decade earlier, saw the list as "meaningless." "From the first time I eyed the list, I knew the Iranians were in deep yogurt militarily—through a lack of technical competence and knowledgeable leadership." They asked for "high value" electrical generators, which "could be obtained easily from their own internal market." They also asked for "printed circuit boards, simple cable connectors . . . and an oscilloscope—Radio Shack stuff that had little or nothing to do with the HAWK's mission peculiar systems."[75]

When North reported to Poindexter upon his return, the national security adviser reacted very negatively, recognizing the stall. No doubt conveying the president's instructions, he said that he was "fed up and wanted to just cut it off entirely." He turned to North and said, "forget it. It wasn't going anywhere."[76] Accordingly, over the next three weeks, until the end of the month, North made no further effort to contact Ghorbanifar, or Nir. Nor would he take their calls. At this point, it appeared as if the initiative was dead, but it wasn't. In fact, it was during this time that the president decided to change tack, as will be discussed in the next chapter.

Unable to reach North, Ghorbanifar and Nir tried to keep up contact through Allen, calling him every few days. On March 9, Ghorbanifar assured him that the Paris meeting had been "successful, although additional effort remained."[77] Ghorbanifar went to Tehran on March 13 to consult on the next steps forward. Upon his return, on the 17th, he immediately called Allen to claim that he had been in discussions with the top Iranian leadership and that they wanted to move forward with another meeting.[78]

Nir also called Allen, passing on news that Ghorbanifar was "under pressure in Tehran," and was in "financial difficulty," although the "Israelis were helping him." Later in March, Ghorbanifar called Allen again, upset because the FBI was seeking information about him. His "California girlfriend's house had been entered, as had Furmark's office in New York." He blamed the CIA, but ever suspicious, believed he was being cut out.[79]

---

[74] *Tower Report*, B-87.

[75] Secord, *Honored and Betrayed, 258.*

[76] *Tower Report*, B-82.

[77] C. Allen, "Conversation with Subject," March 11, 1986, *Tower Report*, B-83.

[78] Draper, *Very Thin Line*, 294.

[79] C. Allen, "Memoranda for the Record," *Tower Report*, B- 85nn61,63.

Point at the Mulberry
Bush to Curse the Locust Tree[80]

There were other reasons for Poindexter, and the president, too, to be "fed up" with the Iranians besides their dilatory tactics. Larger issues occurring at this time were consuming most of their attention. The United States was about to enter the third phase of the plan decided upon in early January (see chapter 13) to gradually increase pressure on Qaddafi, isolate him, and reduce his value as a Soviet strategic asset. The means to this end, as in 1981, was the right to navigate freely in the international waters of the Gulf of Sidra.[81]

During the first two phases, January 26-30 and February 12-16, Task Force 60 commanded by Admiral Frank Kelso had sent the carrier groups *Coral Sea* and *Saratoga* on freedom of navigation exercises just north of 32 degrees, 30 minutes north latitude. This placed his carrier group outside the Gulf of Sidra but sent his combat air patrols into the Tripoli FIR, or flight information zone, over the Gulf of Sidra. Qaddafi had claimed the international waters south of thirty-two thirty as Libyan waters and declared the latitude the "line of death," vowing to destroy all intruders.

The day before the first exercise, Qaddafi boarded the missile patrol boat *Waheed* at the port of Misrata and declared that he would sail to Benghazi to demonstrate that the Gulf of Sidra belonged to Libya. Dressed in a yellow silk flight suit and wearing a navy cap, he declared "I am going out to the parallel 32.5 which is the line of death, where we will stand and fight with our backs against the wall . . . "[82] Rough seas forced the *Waheed* to return ignominiously back to port in Misrata in less than an hour.

During the first two exercises, however, there was no fighting. No Libyan ships ventured out to sea, although 150 Libyan aircraft were intercepted without incident, encounters that provided American airmen with a wealth of tactical combat information about Libyan procedures and tendencies.[83] These essentially routine and peaceful interactions would all change in phase three.

On March 14, at an NSPG meeting, President Reagan authorized the execution of phase three, code-named Prairie Fire. The third exercise would commence on March 23 and be far different from the first two. A third carrier, *America*, had joined the task force, bringing the American force complement to three carriers, 26 ships, and 250 planes. Kelso positioned the three carriers 150

---

[80] Ancient Chinese stratagem *zhi sang ma huai* is interpreted here to denote striking at an adversary's smaller ally in order to send a signal to the adversary.

[81] Howard Teicher and Gayle Radley Teicher, *Twin Pillars to Desert Storm* (New York: William Morrow, 1993), 340-343.

[82] Michael Goldsmith, "Qaddafi Sails Near US Exercises," *Washington Post*, January 26, 1986, A21.

[83] Joseph Stanik, *El Dorado Canyon: Reagan's Undeclared War with Qaddafi* (Annapolis: Naval Institute Press, 2003), 123-126. The account of Prairie Fire generally follows Stanik.

miles north of latitude 32° 30′, while the Aegis cruiser *Ticonderoga*, and destroyers *Scott* and *Caron* were poised to sail south past the "line of death" into the international waters of the Gulf of Sidra, under the cover of carrier aircraft flying combat air patrols.

At noon on March 24 the *Ticonderoga* and the two destroyers pushed across 32° 30′ latitude over 30 miles into the gulf, commencing four days of action carried out almost entirely under cover of darkness. Qaddafi's forces fired first, launching a salvo of SA-5 surface-to-air missiles at US fighters and then attempted to penetrate the battle group with several anti-ship missile boats. It was a futile effort.

US air and naval units, demonstrating the use of the latest weapons systems, like the Aegis radar, Harpoon anti-ship missile, HARM anti-radiation missile, and Rockeye cluster bomb, sank two and probably three missile boats, and put the Soviet-manned, SA-5 missile battery at Sirte out of action.[84] The Libyan air force, which had flown over 150 sorties during phases I and II, stayed in their hangars because the majority lacked night-fighting capability.[85]

Anticipating the humiliation his forces were about to suffer at the hands of the American navy, on the second day of Prairie Fire, March 25, Qaddafi sent cables to the People's Bureaus in East Berlin, Paris, Rome, Madrid, Geneva, and Belgrade, ordering terror attacks against American military and civilian targets. The cables, intercepted by American intelligence, which was on special alert, expressly called for execution of the "plan" that would "cause maximum and indiscriminate casualties."[86] Three days later he issued a formal public call for "all Arab people to attack anything American."[87] Apparently, he also had contacted his agents Abu Nidal and Yasser Arafat by personal courier, as it was one of these two whose men struck first.

A week later, on April 2, Flight TWA 840, on its daily run from Rome to Athens, suffered a mid-air explosion as it was descending into Athens, but managed to land safely. Four American passengers of the 115 on board were sucked through the hole in the fuselage created by the explosion, falling to their deaths 15,000 feet below. The prime suspect was a known Lebanese terrorist who went by the name of May Elias Mansur; and the pressure-timed explosive was a

---

[84] "Soviet Advisers Reported in Libya," *Washington Post*, January 1, 1986, A26. Reporting on a leak to the Egyptian newspaper, *Al Ahram*, it was revealed that "the Soviet experts who run these missiles receive their orders directly from Moscow . . . . Libyans are banned from entering those bases."

[85] Stanik, *El Dorado Canyon*, 131-139; and Daniel Bolger, *Americans at War, 1975-1986* (San Francisco: Presidio, 1988), 292-400.

[86] Stanik, *El Dorado Canyon*, 142-143. Seymour Hersh, "Target Qaddafi," *New York Times*, Sunday Magazine, February 22, 1987, says that NSA moved a satellite to a new position over the Mediterranean to improve coverage.

[87] Weinberger, *Fighting for Peace*, 182.

signature trademark of Abu Ibrahim, a master bomb-builder of the Palestinian group called May 15.[88]

Under the circumstances, it was easy to indict Qaddafi, who applauded the terrorist act, but there was no direct tie-in. However, there were clearly ties between him and Abu Nidal and Yasser Arafat, both of whom also had connections to the May 15 group. The Arab Revolutionary Cell, an Abu Nidal front group, claimed responsibility, saying it was retribution for US attacks on Libya in the Gulf of Sidra.[89] As one Western diplomat observed, "the renegade Palestinians are an obvious source of men and know-how. They don't cost very much to finance, and it is very difficult to trace any links back to Libya."[90]

If the connection between Qaddafi and the terrorist attack on TWA was murky, the next series of events was more clear-cut. Two days later, British intelligence intercepted a message from the Libyan People's Bureau in East Berlin to Tripoli saying, "we have something planned that will make you happy." At just before two o'clock in the morning of April 5 a bomb exploded in the restroom of La Belle Discotheque, a popular nightclub in West Berlin. The bomb injured 229 people, including 78 American servicemen, and killed two. Literally, minutes afterward, a second message to Tripoli was intercepted saying, "an event occurred. You will be pleased with the result."[91]

The shock of the West Berlin attack dominated the headlines, overshadowing the wave of Qaddafi-inspired terror attacks that accompanied it. On the same day the French government expelled two Libyan diplomats for "plotting an attack with hand grenades and machine guns on the American visa office in Paris." The next day, Libyan agents attempted to fire rocket-propelled grenades into the American embassy in Beirut and sought to buy the hostages being held by terrorists in Beirut. They also attempted to kidnap the American ambassador to Rwanda.[92]

Over the next few days, intelligence came in reporting that Qaddafi was planning "about three dozen operations against American diplomatic missions, military installations, and commercial interests overseas." The CIA specifically identified "nine Libyan operations either ordered by Qaddafi or already

---

[88] Stanik, *El Dorado Canyon*, 143. May 15 commemorates the displacement of Palestinians from Israel after the 1948 war.

[89] David C. Martin and John Walcott, *Best Laid Plans: The Inside Story of America's War against Terrorism* (New York: Touchstone, 1988), 285, say that "later, intelligence officials concluded the bombing was probably the work of a close associate of Yasser Arafat who called himself Colonel Hawari and who had recruited two expert bomb makers trained by Abu Ibrahim."

[90] William Smith, "Terrorism Explosion on Flight 840," *Time*, April 14, 1986.

[91] Hersh, "Target Qaddafi," and Leslie Gelb, "How Libya Messages Informed US," *New York Times*, April 23, 1986, A6.

[92] Martin and Walcott, *Best Laid Plans*, 289; and Keith Richburg, "US Had Word of More Plots," *Washington Post*, April 15, 1986, A1.

underway," creating a powerful sense of urgency in the White House.[93] But there was an even larger concern.

For over two months, the CIA had been reporting from its agents that the KGB was planning a terror campaign in West Germany against Americans and American interests. The Soviets were looking for "restaurants near US military bases where it could hide "mini bombs." The KGB planned on exploding these bombs when the restaurants were busy, and then blaming the carnage on German terrorists."[94] Were the Soviets planning on using Qaddafi's terror campaign as the cover for their own? Was this Gorbachev's work, or that of his internal adversaries?

Reagan's decision was to strike hard at Qaddafi, authorizing a much larger attack than had been planned. Certainly, the larger attack was intended to ensure the infliction of maximum damage, but it was also designed to dissuade Qaddafi and Moscow from taking any further terrorist action. If the Soviets were deterred, it would send a clear signal that the correlation of forces had changed in America's favor. If they failed to protect Qaddafi, all of Moscow's clients would be forced to reconsider the value of Moscow as an ally. If they carried out their planned wave of terror, they would have to reckon with a no-longer passive America and the end of their push for détente.

On April 9, with the "smoking gun" of the intelligence intercepts in hand, the president met with his chief advisers to decide on a final target list. Five targets were selected, three in Tripoli and two in Benghazi. UK-based F-111 bombers would strike targets in Tripoli: the military airfield, where Qaddafi's IL-76 transports were located; the Murat Sidi Bilal terrorist training camp; and the Bab al Aziziya barracks, a walled, 200-acre compound housing his East German security forces, residence, and headquarters.

Carrier-based aircraft would attack the two targets in Benghazi: the Benina airfield, where a squadron of MiG-23 Floggers (Qaddafi's only night-flying aircraft) were based; and the Jamahiriya Guard Barracks, his eastern command center. Contrary to some later commentary, there was no attempt to target Qaddafi himself, which was against American law.[95] For security purposes, Qaddafi never slept in the same bed two nights in a row, making it virtually impossible to target him. However, it was the consensus that if he happened to perish in the attacks, no one would shed any tears.

The decision to carry out a large raid instead of a surgical strike was passed to Air Force planners on April 12. Since January, when contingency planning began at Lakenheath Air Base in the UK, they "had been planning for a small, surgical raid by no more than six jets. Now, however, with very little time left to adjust, the size of the mission had been tripled." The planners were stunned by what they believed was a serious tactical error that "major changes to the

---

[93] Stanik, *El Dorado Canyon*, 147.

[94] Pete Early, *Confessions of a Spy: The Real Story of Aldrich Ames* (New York: Putnam, 1997), 194.

[95] Hersh, "Target Qadaffi."

targets . . . and especially to the raid's size were all being made within forty-eight hours of the planned takeoff time."[96]

Then came worse news, the most direct route would not be available. The president had sent UN Ambassador Vernon Walters to Western Europe over the weekend of April 11-13, to confirm allied support for the coming strike. Except for Prime Minister Thatcher, the results were disappointing. Thatcher agreed to permit US aircraft to employ British bases for the mission, which she saw as a matter of self-defense. She had her own reasons for striking back at Qaddafi. The Libyan leader had supported the IRA attempt to assassinate her in October 1984 and a Libyan diplomat had shot and killed a British policewoman performing crowd control duties in front of the People's Bureau in London earlier in April of that year.

Aside from Thatcher, however, no other West European leader supported the US plan. François Mitterrand and Jacques Chirac stunned Walters by refusing permission for US aircraft to overfly French territory. The recent French election had installed Chirac in a co-leadership role with Mitterrand and he rejected the US request "out of hand," taking what was described as a "traditional Gaullist line" of non-intervention.[97] He also claimed incorrectly that the United States had not given France sufficient advance notice. The fact was that since early February, US and French officials had been engaged in "joint military planning" for the raid.[98] Spanish Prime Minister Felipe González, following the French lead, also refused overflight permission.

The West Germans and the Italians, as Libya's largest trade partners, also refused to offer support. West German foreign minister Hans-Dietrich Genscher, warning against hasty action, "rejected economic sanctions as too ineffectual and military force as too reckless in dealing with Qaddafi."[99] According to Shultz, Prime Minister Craxi told associates "he hoped the United States would . . . take out Libya's military infrastructure and bring about Qaddafi's downfall." Of course, he admitted, "public opinion in Italy meant that he could not openly support such an effort, indeed, he would have to oppose it."[100]

Craxi did more than oppose US action, he tipped off Qaddafi. According to a report by Abdel-Rahman Shalgham, then Libya's ambassador to Italy, that was confirmed by Italy's foreign minister Giulio Andreotti, Craxi secretly sent

---

[96] Robert Venkus, *Raid on Qaddafi* (New York: St. Martin's, 1993), 86.

[97] Jeremiah O'Leary, "Mitterrand Favored Raid to Oust Qaddafi," *Washington Times*, April 21, 1986, A1.

[98] Teicher and Teicher, *Twin Pillars*, 345. Howard Teicher and Walters had arranged for the cooperation during a visit to Paris in early February. Chirac may not have been briefed about this arrangement.

[99] William Drozdiak, "Walters Discusses Terrorism with European Leaders," *Washington Post*, April 14, 1986, A15.

[100] Shultz, *Turmoil and Triumph*, 682 and Bernard Weinraub, "US Says Allies Asked for More in Libya Attack," *New York Times*, April 22, 1986, A1.

word to Qaddafi that there would be "an American raid against Libya."[101] Craxi's message came immediately after his meeting with Walters, giving Qaddafi time to prepare his defenses several days in advance.

Although the Russians adopted a very low profile in Libya, in anticipation of the American attack, it would appear that Moscow got word to Qaddafi just before the planes arrived over Tripoli, enabling the Libyan leader to escape harm. American intelligence had pinpointed Qaddafi "at work in his tent" just before midnight Tripoli time, which was "the last fix" obtained on him.[102] That was just over two hours before the bombs began to fall.

When the mission was "well underway," Secretary Shultz called in the Soviet chargé d'affaires and "informed him of the operation."[103] Perhaps, Shultz did not wait long enough, for Qaddafi was warned and fled to safety minutes before the attack. There can be no doubt that the chargé immediately sent word back to Moscow. The question is: Did Moscow have sufficient time to warn Qaddafi? Certainly, his ally Bonnici of Malta did, telling him that the raid was under way as American planes were sighted streaking over Maltese airspace.[104]

Eighteen F-111 Aardvarks forced to fly 2,800 miles over the Atlantic and around the Iberian Peninsula because of the French refusal to grant overflight permission, pummeled targets in Tripoli, while 15 carrier-based A-6E Intruders struck targets in Benghazi. One F-111 bomber was lost. Over 80 aircraft, from refueling tankers, to defense suppression FA-18 Hornets and A-7 Corsairs, electronic countermeasure EF-111 Ravens, and SR-71 Blackbird reconnaissance planes, supported the mission. It was the "longest fighter combat mission . . . in the history of military aviation."[105]

The raid on Tripoli not only crippled Libya's terrorist infrastructure, but also more importantly marked a "turning point" in the use of American power against international terrorism.[106] In eleven minutes over target, 30 aircraft dropped over 90 mostly laser-guided 2,000-pound bombs on the five selected targets in Tripoli and Benghazi. Two bombs went off target, causing some collateral damage, including to the French embassy. Qaddafi claimed that his adopted 15-month old daughter, Hana, was killed in the attack, a claim that

---

[101] Nick Squires, "Italy 'tipped off' Libya about 1986 US raid," *The Telegraph*, October 30, 2008, 1.

[102] Hersh, "Target Qaddafi."

[103] Stanik, *El Dorado Canyon*, 180.

[104] Kennedy Hickman, "International Terrorism: Bombing of Libya (Operation El Dorado Canyon)," *About.com.*

[105] Robert E. Venkus, *Raid on Qaddafi: The Untold Story of History's Longest Fighter Mission by the Pilot Who Directed It* (New York: St. Martins, 1992), xi.

[106] Lou Cannon and Bob Woodward, "Reagan's Use of Force Marks Turning Point; More Terror and Retaliation Seen," *Washington Post*, April 16, 1986, A1.

lingered for years, but was false. Hana grew up to become a medical professional in Libya.[107]

Qaddafi escaped harm, although he was badly shaken by the near miss and went into seclusion for several months to plot his revenge. Some authors, like Hersh, claimed that the US had sought to assassinate Qaddafi, which was false. The most obvious target for such an attempt was the Libyan leader's tent. As Venkus notes, "the tent should have been targeted if that was the mission's goal."[108] It was not. Most important, the American strike had made Libya's vulnerability and isolation starkly obvious to all.

Moscow had declined to enter into even the standard friendship treaty with Libya, as it had done with South Yemen, for example, and, in the current crisis, had failed to provide anything but lukewarm diplomatic support and replenishment of Libya's weapons.[109] Seeking some minimal protection from the communist camp, at the end of April, Qaddafi secretly applied for membership to the Warsaw Pact. Even here, "the Soviet Union insisted on certain conditions before the application [was] processed."[110] It was not granted.

President Reagan addressed the nation after the raid had ended. "Today, we have done what we had to do. If necessary, we shall do it again." Administration officials hastily declared that future actions would be on a case-by-case basis, not the beginning of a long war. They declared that the bombing was designed "to show the Libyan military that there was little it could do to combat American power and little that the Soviet Union would do to protect Libya."[111]

Privately, Poindexter focused on the raid's impact on Moscow. The attack, he said, had "helped to demonstrate to the Soviet Union and others throughout the world that we were not going to be stepped on, that if provoked we were going to respond with deadly force. I don't think that lesson was lost on the Soviets."[112] It was not lost on the Iranians, either. Even as the United States was preparing to confront Qaddafi in the Gulf of Sidra, the Iranians were backing away from improving relations, but trying to keep open the door to weapons sales from Washington.

---

[107] Martin Evans, "Libya: Hana Gaddafi 'Alive and Well,'" *The Telegraph*, August 26, 2011. See also Colin Freeman and Robert Mendick, "Emails Show British Government Knew Hana Gaddafi Was Still Alive," *The Telegraph*, September 24, 2011.

[108] Venkus, *Raid on Qaddafi*, 154.

[109] "Gorbachev's Condolence Message to Qaddafi," *New York City Tribune*, April 29, 1986, 11.

[110] "Libya Is Said to Apply to Warsaw Pact," *Baltimore News American*, April 26, 1986, 2.

[111] Leslie Gelb, "US Aides Deny Attack Is Start of an Escalation," *New York Times*, April 16, 1986, A15.

[112] Robert Timberg, *The Nightingale's Song* (New York: Touchstone, 1995), 379.

Chapter 15

The President Stands Tough

By the middle of March 1986, President Reagan had managed to bring Shultz and the new world order faction into agreement on the need to adopt tougher measures against the Soviet Union and its allies. He had also offered McFarlane an opportunity to make a secret trip to Tehran in a renewed effort to reestablish relations with Iran. The president knew that the new world order faction would attempt to kill an opening to Iran again as they had in the past, so, this time, he added a twist in an attempt to foil his adversaries.

At the same time, Reagan continued to spar with Gorbachev over the next steps in arms control and a formula for the resolution of third-world conflicts. Over the past year, Gorbachev, while professing interest in better relations with the United States, had continued to resupply Soviet clients in Angola and Nicaragua, as well as Soviet forces in Afghanistan, with sufficient military strength to enable them to maintain the advantage against the resistance fighters.

Gorbachev's blatant hypocrisy enabled the president to convince the Congress and Secretary Shultz of the need for tougher measures against the Soviet Union and its clients. Even so, throughout 1985, there had occurred a bruising bureaucratic struggle over the implementation of the Reagan Doctrine. The indecision over whether or not to apply pressure on Qaddafi, and to adopt a more aggressive policy against international terrorism, discussed above, had been part of that struggle, as had battles over whether or not to increase support for the anti-Soviet resistance movements in Afghanistan, Angola, and Nicaragua.

There is a substantial record detailing each facet of this struggle, which, taken together reflected the conflict over grand strategy.[1] Secretary Shultz and others in the bureaucracy, like John McMahon, Deputy Director of the CIA, had argued persistently that a strategy of "bleeding the Russians" would eventually

---

[1] On Afghanistan, George Crile, *Charlie Wilson's War* (New York: Grove, 2003), Steve Coll, *Ghost Wars* (New York: Penguin, 2004), Mohammad Yousaf and Mark Adkin, *The Bear Trap* (London: Leo Coper, 1992), Kirsten Lundberg, *Politics of a Covert Action: The US, the Mujahideen, and the Stinger Missile* (Boston: Harvard, 1999). On Angola, Chester Crocker, *High Noon in Southern Africa* (New York: Norton, 1992), J.E. Davies, *Constructive Engagement?* (Oxford: James Curry, 2007). On Nicaragua, Roy Gutman, *Banana Diplomacy* (New York: Simon & Shuster, 1988), Peter Rodman, *More Precious than Peace* (New York: Scribner, 1994), James M. Scott, *Deciding to Intervene* (Durham: Duke University Press, 1996).

lead to negotiated solutions. This was, of course, the fundamental thrust of the new world order faction's détente strategy.

The Russians did not cooperate. They reinforced their allies, delivering powerful Mi-24 Hind armored helicopters and special operations forces (*Spetsnaz*) to their clients (in Nicaragua, Cubans were the functional equivalent), enabling them to dominate their adversaries. Even though the United States allocated more funds and weapons to the resistance forces during the year, it had become increasingly obvious that the strategy of bleeding the Soviets had failed to elicit an interest in negotiating outcomes anywhere.

Soon after the Soviet introduction of armored helicopters the idea of providing Stingers, the very effective infra-red-guided, anti-aircraft missile, to counter them was advanced and debated for most of 1985. The new world order faction opposed the provision of Stingers, based on the notion of "plausible deniability," and sought to disguise the US role by purchasing communist-bloc weapons for the resistance fighters. This scheme was not only ineffective, but also naive. The Soviets understood full well that the United States was buying weapons from its clients to support the resistance movements, and to the extent possible, sabotaged communist bloc weapons purchased by the US.[2]

By early in 1986, it was clear that Reagan had won the Stinger battle for Angola and Afghanistan, but not for Nicaragua. Jonas Savimbi, leader of the National Union for the Total Independence of Angola (UNITA) and President Zia of Pakistan had expressed their wishes for the Stinger. The Contras had to be satisfied with the Redeye, the much less effective precursor of the Stinger, and would not receive it until much later. Nevertheless, it was clear that the notions of "bleeding the Russians" and "plausible deniability" had been repudiated. The CIA's chief proponent of "bleeding the Russians," McMahon, resigned at the end of February and Shultz reluctantly agreed that more pressure was needed, although he "continued to have reservations" about the visibility of American arms.[3]

Finally, the long-sought meeting with the Iranians was arranged for late May and the president offered McFarlane the opportunity to head the mission. He did this fully aware that the new world order faction opposed an opening to Iran, but offered the opportunity, nonetheless. Reagan was less concerned about achieving immediate success with Iran than laying the foundation for future relations, but he did anticipate solving an immediate funding need for the Contras.

Funding the Contras

The problem of how to deal with Nicaragua and its communist government seemed intractable. Since 1982, Congress, led by the powerful

---

[2] John Walcott and Tim Carrington, "Role Reversal: CIA Resisted Proposal to Give Afghan Rebels US Stinger Missiles," *Wall Street Journal*, February 16, 1988.
[3] Peter Samuel, "Decision to Give Stingers to Rebels Is Hailed," *New York City Tribune*, March 31, 1986, 1. See also Lundberg, *Politics of a Covert Action.*

Democratic majority in the House of Representatives had systematically squeezed off the president's ability to support the Nicaraguan resistance forces by refusing to authorize lethal aid and restricting government involvement through amendments to annual appropriations bills. These were collectively known as "Boland Amendments" reflecting principal sponsor Rep. Edward Boland (D-MA), chairman of the House Permanent Select Committee on Intelligence.

A critical moment occurred in the spring of 1984 when press reports revealed the CIA's involvement in mining Nicaraguan harbors. The resulting flap prompted the House and the Senate to pass nonbinding resolutions prohibiting the use of US funds to support mining. Worse, the flap placed in jeopardy all funding for the Contras. The president had responded by arranging for temporary funding by third countries and parties and by directing the NSC to establish a logistics support system for the Contras. The plan was to use private funds until the House could be persuaded to restore full government funding and involvement. The Senate, with a Republican majority, supported the president's proposals.[4]

Shultz and McFarlane attempted to prevent the president from soliciting funds from third countries, postulating that it might be an impeachable offense, but the attorney general ascertained that such funding was legal as long as there was no reimbursement by the United States.[5] Cleared to proceed, within months the president had raised over $10 million for the Contras. The private fund-raising effort was entirely legal and public, although donor identities were not disclosed.

On Casey's recommendation, in mid-1984, North tapped Richard Secord to set up a logistical network to funnel weapons and supplies to the Contras.[6] By September, press reports were quoting administration officials and rebel leaders that the administration had already raised over $10 million.[7] (A major donor was King Fahd of Saudi Arabia, who secretly agreed to provide $1 million per month through the end of the year. Fahd also was secretly providing matching funds for the Afghan rebels.)

Attempting to thwart the president's effort, Congress enacted the most restrictive amendment—Boland II—in October 1984 as part of a continuing appropriations bill for FY 1985. The amendment mandated that no funds appropriated to the CIA, Defense Department, or "any other agency or entity . . .

---

[4] Gutman, *Banana Diplomacy*, 199-203.

[5] Lawrence E. Walsh, *Final Report of the Independent Counsel for Iran-Contra Matters*, vol. 1 (Washington, DC: United States Court of Appeals for the District of Columbia Circuit, August 4, 1993), 2 and n4. See also Peter Kornbluh and Malcom Byrne, *The Iran-Contra Scandal: The Declassified History* (New York: New Press, 1993), 77.

[6] Oliver North and William Novak, *Under Fire: An American Story* (New York: Harper Collins, 1991), 251.

[7] Walsh, *Final Report of the Independent Counsel*, 1:161-63 and Philip Taubman, "Nicaragua Rebels Reported to Raise Millions in Gifts," *New York Times*, September 9, 1984, A1. Taubman named Israel, Argentina, Venezuela, and Guatemala, in addition to Taiwan, but made no mention of Saudi Arabia.

involved in intelligence activities" could be spent on or in support of military or paramilitary operations in Nicaragua. The President's Intelligence Oversight Board found a loophole, reasoning that the NSC fell outside the definition of an entity involved in intelligence activities, as it was part of the president's office.[8] An additional loophole enabled the president to pay involved NSC personnel out of his own office contingency fund.

By the spring of 1985, the arrangement by which donations went to Contra leader Adolfo Calero, who paid Secord and others to acquire arms, was viewed as unsatisfactory. There was concern that Contra leaders were refusing to coordinate their efforts and were skimming funds from the donations. Accordingly, the decision was made to unify the resistance leadership and to centralize the finances.

At a meeting in Miami in June 1985, North brought together the three main Contra leaders, Calero, Arturo Cruz, and Alfonso Robelo and renamed the resistance as the United Nicaraguan Opposition (UNO). At the same time, North removed Calero from control over donated funds. He decreed that all future donations would go to Secord's Enterprise, specifically to the Lake Resources account, although Calero could retain for his use whatever funds still remained from earlier donations.

Referring to the Lake Resources account, North later testified, "when private money was raised for the Contras, this was where it was sent."[9] The decision to shift control of funds from Calero to Secord had an unintended consequence. When Secord later became involved in Iran arms sales, it established the presumptive basis for the explosive charge that he had diverted profits from Iran arms sales to the Contras.[10]

The charge, however, was difficult to substantiate. In his exhaustive analysis of money transfers, Walsh notes, from mid-1985, "the money originally used to purchase weapons [for the Contras] came from commingled funds in Enterprise accounts—including US funds generated by the sale of arms to Iran and funds donated to the Contras" from the Saudis, Taiwanese, and private sources.[11] By commingled funds, he meant that the money from various sources

---

[8] For the Democratic and Republican interpretations of the amendments, see *Report of the Congressional Committees Investigating the Iran-Contra Affair* (Washington, DC: US Government Printing Office, 1987), 395-407 and 489-499 [hereafter cited as *Congressional Report on the Iran-Contra Affair*]. The Boland amendments were included in appropriations bills for fiscal years 1983-1986.

[9] North, *Under Fire*, 268.

[10] See John Singlaub and Malcolm McConnell, *Hazardous Duty: An American Soldier in the Twentieth Century* (New York: Summit, 1991), 451ff, for an unflattering treatment of Secord and North. Singlaub competed with Secord for the role of main Contra supplier.

[11] Walsh, *Final Report of the Independent Counsel*, 1:164. Walsh claimed that profits from Iranian arms sales belonged to the US government, a claim that was disputed and which will be dealt with below.

had become so entangled in Secord's books that it was impossible to determine which funds went to purchase what.

For example, although Walsh claimed that the $1 million the Israelis delivered to Secord in November 1985 derived from Iranian arms sales, he acknowledged (in a footnote) that "because of the commingling of funds in the Lake Resources account it is not possible to directly tie the Israeli deposit to an expenditure of funds on the Contras."[12] Indeed, he also acknowledged that this was true for all of the funds in Secord's possession. "Because of the commingling of Enterprise funds, it was not possible to determine precisely how much money was diverted."[13]

In this judgment, Walsh echoed Secord, who said, "lax financial controls . . . allowed funds from various sources and intended for certain projects—Contra or Iranian—to become commingled."[14] Nevertheless, Walsh insisted, despite his own lack of evidence, that a diversion had occurred and estimated that a minimum of $3.6 million surplus Iranian funds had been spent on the Contras.

In any case, from mid-1985 Secord used his newly acquired pool of funds to establish an air supply network. He purchased seven old aircraft of various types, hired crews, set up a full-service repair and refurbishment facility in Miami, an arms warehouse in Lisbon, Portugal, and also purchased a cargo ship.[15] Operating from airbases in Ilopango, El Salvador, Aguacate, Honduras and later Santa Elena, Costa Rica, Secord began supply operations in early 1986. The trials and tribulations of setting up and running this network have been well-documented, but the best that can be said for it is that it sustained the Contra forces at a bare bones level but was not sufficient to make them a threat to the Nicaraguan regime.[16]

Meanwhile, the Soviets had taken advantage of the opportunity afforded by the cutoff of Contra funds to strengthen the Sandinistas. By November 1984, in addition to other military supplies, they had deployed Mi-24 Hind helicopter gunships to Nicaragua, just as they had to Angola and Afghanistan.[17] The results

---

[12] Walsh, *Final Report of the Independent Counsel*, 1:168n32.

[13] Ibid., 171.

[14] Richard Secord and Jay Wurts, *Honored and Betrayed: Irangate, Covert Affairs, and the Secret War in Laos* (New York: Wiley, 1992), 254-55.

[15] Ibid., 262, claims that he "never saw" funds from Saudi Arabia or Taiwan, but the probable explanation is that when the funds were transferred from Calero, they were not identified as to source. Walsh, *Final Report of the Independent Counsel*, 1:160, for example, lists the source of $11.3 million transferred to Secord's account simply as coming from the "Contras."

[16] See Secord, *Honored and Betrayed*; Robert Kagan, *A Twilight Struggle: American Power in Nicaragua* (New York: Free Press, 1996); Gutman, *Banana Diplomacy*; Rodman, *More Precious than Peace*.

[17] "Official: Nicaragua Has Soviet Helicopters," *Evening Herald* (South Carolina), November 16, 1984, 10. The helicopter deployment revealed a US intelligence flub.

were the same in all three countries, as their clients wreaked havoc among the resistance forces, who had no defense against the "flying tanks." Over the next year, Moscow had built the Nicaraguan army into a force 100,000 strong, the largest armed force in Central America. By comparison, although the Contras had also grown, their forces had not yet reached 15,000.[18]

Given their superior forces, the Sandinistas were disinclined to negotiate with the Contras, most of whom had withdrawn from Nicaragua to Honduras.[19] Even the Democratic Left in the House conceded that the balance had skewed. Secretary Shultz, who had pressed hard for adoption of a political solution in Nicaragua, was also forced to concede that the Contadora process was at a dead end. The Reagan leadership had moved into rare agreement on the need to strengthen the Contras. If there were to be any chance of reinvigorating the negotiating process, the Contras would have to be strengthened.

Opinion in the House and Senate also seemed to have reached the tipping point. In December 1985, while reapproving the Boland amendment, the Congress also agreed to provide some funding to the CIA to assist the Contras in "communications" and to provide "advice" on logistics. However, Senate and House Intelligence Committee chairmen disagreed on how the funds could be used. Senate Intelligence Committee Chairman David Durenberger (R-MN) believed that the CIA could provide advice on logistical matters but House Intelligence Committee Chairman Lee Hamilton (D-IN) emphatically declared that such advice was "not appropriate."[20]

Believing that opinion in the Congress and, indeed, in the nation was swinging in favor of aid to the Contras, the president determined to give it a push.[21] In private, Reagan signed a finding on January 9, 1986, positively interpreting the congressional authorization. Thirteen million dollars were designated to provide communications assistance and logistical advice, although

---

Intelligence reports identified a dozen crates aboard a Soviet freighter headed for the port of Corinto; the supposition was that the crates contained MiG-21 jet fighters and the United States duly filed a public protest. However, as Shultz described it, "the Soviets and the Nicaraguans . . . lured us into visible protests in opposition to MiG-21s and then supplied the kind of aircraft [MI-24] that, ironically, would do far greater damage to the Contras in the field than would jet fighters." George Shultz, *Turmoil and Triumph* (New York: Scribner, 1993), 424-25.

[18] James LeMoyne, "Most Contras Reported to Pull Out of Nicaragua," *New York Times*, January 30, 1986, 10.

[19] Ibid.

[20] John G. Tower et al., *Report of the President's Special Review Board: February 26, 1987* (Washington, DC: US Government Printing Office, 1987), C-6n5.

[21] Robert Merry, "Congress Shifts toward Reagan on Aid for Contras in Nicaragua," *Wall Street Journal*, January 13, 1986, 30.

Hamilton continued to assert that CIA "participation in planning or execution of military activities, or acting as military advisors, is prohibited."[22]

Publicly, the president requested that the Congress authorize $100 million in support for the Contras. In this "first major test of the 'Reagan Doctrine,'" the president's advisers calculated that "if the president can present the request as part of a strategy for forcing the Nicaraguan government to negotiate seriously with the opposition, Congress might support him."[23] A major public relations campaign accompanied the request.

Secretary Shultz also lent his support for aid. In congressional hearings in February, the secretary declared that the "Sandinista game plan was . . . to persuade people not to help the Contras for long enough so that, with this big Soviet buildup of advanced weapons, they will wipe them out before we wake up." For any negotiations to occur, let alone succeed, he said, Congress had to approve Contra aid first. Only if the Sandinistas realize that they cannot win will they agree to negotiate. In short, "if you do not have any cards to play," he argued, "you cannot get into the card game."[24]

Believing that the ground was prepared, the president, on February 25, formally requested that Congress authorize $100 million in aid for the Contras. The bulk of it, $70 million would be for military assistance, the rest for humanitarian aid. No new money would be involved. The request was to permit the president to reprogram, that is, to transfer, funds from one account to another in the existing defense budget. The $27 million in humanitarian aid the Congress authorized the previous year would run out at the end of March and the Contras were sorely in need of weapons. "You cannot fight Soviet helicopter gunships flown by Cubans with food and boots and bandages," Shultz said.[25]

In an unexpected response, however, the House balked. Four House committees quickly voted to bar any aid to the Contras. Voting mainly along party lines, the Committee on Intelligence, the Sub-Committee on Western Hemispheric Affairs, the Appropriations Committee, and the Foreign Affairs Committee all voted against. Only the Armed Services Committee recommended approval. Even some Senate Republicans supported the Democrats. Sen. Nancy Kassebaum (R-KS) complained that the administration's approach was based on "simplistic reasoning," was filled with gross "distortions," and was "highly offensive."[26]

---

[22] Bob Woodward, "CIA Provided Contras $13 Million in Assistance under Reagan 'Finding,'" *Washington Post*, January 14, 1987, A1.

[23] Robert Parry, "Swing Votes Could Deliver Contra Aid," *Washington Post*, January 27, 1986, A4.

[24] Kagan, *Twilight Struggle*, 423.

[25] David Shipler, "Reagan Asks $100 Million for Contras," *New York Times*, February 26, 1986, A3.

[26] Milton Coleman and Edward Walsh, "2 More House Panels Bar Contra Aid," *Washington Post*, March 7, 1986, A4; and Steven Roberts, "House Panels Bar Help for Contras," *New York Times*, March 6, 1986, A9.

The sharp congressional rebuke prompted efforts to work out a compromise, but, after a few days, the president himself ruled it out. "In the last few days here in Washington there has been talk of compromise on this issue: smaller amounts of aid, delay in providing it, restrictions on the uses to which it could be put, all the usual temporizing and quibbles," Reagan said. The reason for hardening against compromise was the belief that it was undermining the effort to gain passage of the president's request.[27]

Reagan decided to make a direct appeal to the American people to bring pressure to bear on the Congress. In a television address on March 16, the president condemned Nicaragua as a "cancer" that "poses a direct threat to the United States." Posing a challenge to the House Democrats, he said, "stopping Communism and international terrorism there would serve as a historic test of his presidency." He appealed to the American people to "demand that Congress endorse the Administration's $100 million aid package."[28]

Three days later, the Democrat-controlled House voted to reject the president's aid package for the Contras. Sixteen Republicans joined 206 Democrats to defeat the proposal 222 to 210. In a statement issued after the vote, Reagan predicted ultimate victory, vowing "to come back again and again until this battle is won, until freedom is given the chance it deserves in Nicaragua."[29] There was general sentiment on both sides of the aisle that the president would eventually win passage for aid, as it would require only six Republicans to change their votes, but it would be at least a month, or more, before another vote would be taken. The problem was what to do in the meantime.

Reagan Rips Off the Ayatollah

The president was clearly stung by the congressional rebuff and hurt by his failure to generate popular pressure on the House. Sixteen Republicans had deserted him, and his aides had failed to do their homework. They had encouraged the president to climb out onto a limb, which the Democrats gleefully sawed off. Allowing the president to suffer such an embarrassing defeat was unprecedented. One author, Gutman, characterized the Contra aid plan as an amateurish "caricature of a legislative strategy."[30]

If there was a moment when what would later be termed the "diversion" of funds to the Contras began to be considered seriously, it was when the House rejected President Reagan's proposal for a $100 million support package for the

---

[27] Edward Walsh and Milton Coleman, "Idea of Compromise on Contra Aid Fades," *Washington Post*, March 12, 1986, A7 and Bernard Gwertzman, "Reagan Aides Open Compromise Talks on Aiding Contras," *New York Times*, March 9, 1986, 1.

[28] Bernard Weinraub, "Reagan Condemns Nicaragua in Plea for Aid to Rebels," *New York Times*, March 17, 1986, A1.

[29] Edward Walsh, "House Defeats Reagan Request for Contra Aid," *Washington Post*, March 21, 1986, A1.

[30] Gutman, *Banana Diplomacy*, 322-23.

Contras on March 20, 1986. However, the term "diversion" is a misnomer, and both the term and the concept need definition. The term to divert is defined as to cause something to change course, as to divert water from a channel. As such the concept is of a flow, which is changed from one direction to another. Neither the term nor the concept correctly describes what occurred, for there was no flow and no change of direction.

There was no flow of funds. In fact, there were only three instances when profits from arms sales to Iran were recorded in Lake Resources books and could have been "diverted": February, May, and October 1986. Secord acknowledged a $5 million surplus from the February sale, but showed that $2 million had been set aside for aircraft insurance, $1.7 million to purchase and retrofit the cargo ship, *Erria*, and $300,000 for miscellaneous expenses. This left approximately $1 million for the Enterprise. It is unknown how much, if any, of the $1 million was expended on direct purchase of weapons or supplies for the Contras, but it was obviously not much.[31] More to the point, at this time there was no pressing need to fill a gap in funding as the president was at that moment in late February just making his request for funds to the Congress, and he expected prompt passage.

If the February shipment was too early for the diversion, the October shipment was too late. Congress authorized the $100 million for the Contras in late June and funds had begun to flow in mid-October. This leaves the May sale, which occurred during the period when the Congress had rejected the president's request and bridging funds were most needed. In fact, the May arms shipment of Hawk missile spare parts recorded the largest sale, of $15 million.

According to Secord, after all payments were made to the CIA for the cost of the parts, shipping, and insurance, there was an estimated surplus of somewhere around $3 million. This was not far off from Walsh's estimate of $3.6 million and appears to be the likely point when funds were "diverted" to support for the Contras.[32] At the time, however, North mistakenly thought there would be a surplus of $12 million, enough to sustain the Contras in the field for five or six months and bridge the gap until Congress would vote to resume funding.

As to a change of direction, there could only be a diversion if there was a specific purpose from which funds could have been diverted. The profits from arms sales were expressly dedicated to build up Secord's private company, the Enterprise, and support its activities, central to which was support for the Contras. The use of money for any activity that strengthened the Enterprise was wholly appropriate and therefore not a diversion.

Surplus funds from the May Iran arms sale were indeed used to support the Contras in their time of dire need, but it was not a diversion and was entirely legal. Secord, in effect a private person, was free to use his funds in any way he wished. Secord had no contractual relationship with the US government, was not even named in the January 17 finding, and operated on a handshake agreement. However, this would not be the view of congressional Democrats who rushed to

---

[31] Secord, *Honored and Betrayed*, 254.
[32] Ibid., 260.

the attack when the initiative was exposed and insisted that all surplus funds from arms sales belonged to the government. No court ever validated that claim.

In March of 1986, determined to sustain the Contras, Reagan hit on the idea of using surplus monies from Iran arms sales. The idea of using surplus funds for other purposes had been floating around the NSC for a couple of months. So, it was no surprise that it came up for consideration as Congress voted down the president's request, and conveniently just at the moment that the Iranian government proposed a new arms deal for Iran.

As recounted in the previous chapter, Poindexter had told North to break off contact with the Iranians and so from March 9 he had refused to accept any calls from either Ghorbanifar or Kangarlu. In the interim, Ghorbanifar had traveled to Tehran and returned with another idea, which he asked Nir to pass on to North.[33] Before North could respond, Kangarlu also communicated with him via the "phone-drop in Maryland which we had established for this purpose." He asked, "why we had not been in contact" and urged that we proceed expeditiously because conditions in Beirut were "deteriorating rapidly." A subsequent call led to the president's decision to resume negotiations on the Hawk spare parts package worked out earlier.[34] North then contacted Ghorbanifar and arranged for him to come to Washington to negotiate a deal.

After meeting with Nir in London on April 2, Ghorbanifar took the three-and-a-half-hour supersonic *Concord* flight to Washington, arriving the next day. Upon arrival Ghorbanifar joined North, Cave, Twetten, and Allen for an all-night session at a hotel in Herndon, Virginia, not far from CIA headquarters.[35] The US team was composed of three CIA officers (although Cave was retired) and North. During their deliberations Ghorbanifar called Kangarlu in Tehran several times to clarify various points.[36] The result was an agreement that would involve the sale of 240 Hawk spare parts, a high-level meeting of US and Iranian leaders, and release of *all* of the remaining hostages "as soon as the US delegation arrived in Tehran."[37]

Immediately afterward, North sent a memo to Poindexter "to forward to the President," detailing the terms of the agreement and how the profits from the sale would be distributed.[38] On April 7, the Iranian government was to deposit $17 million in the Israeli account in Geneva. The Israelis would retain $2 million for themselves and transfer $15 million to Lake Resources. Secord would transfer

---

[33] "North PROF Note to McFarlane," March 20, 1986, *Tower Report*, B-85.

[34] Ibid., B-87.

[35] The *Iran-Contra Affair*, 224, omits Allen, while *Tower Report*, B-86, includes him as part of the negotiating team.

[36] Samuel Segev, *The Iranian Triangle: The Untold Story of Israel's Role in the Iran-Contra Affair* (New York: Free Press, 1988), 256.

[37] *Iran-Contra Affair*, 224.

[38] *Tower Report*, B-86.

$3.65 million of it to the CIA account for the Hawk spare parts. Once paid for, the Defense Department would assemble the parts for transport.[39]

Kangarlu confirmed that when McFarlane and his team arrived in Tehran on April 20, Rafsanjani and his delegation would meet them. In a matter of hours, the hostages would be released in Beirut and an Israeli cargo jet would deliver the Hawk spare parts to Bandar Abbas. With the hostage obstacle out of the way, the two teams would begin the process of reestablishing relations.

As for the surplus from the arms sale, North's memo continued, the $2 million withheld by the Israelis would be used to replace the 508 TOWs Israel sold to Iran in the fall of 1985. Twelve million dollars would be used

> to purchase critically needed supplies for the Nicaraguan Democratic Resistance Forces. This material is essential to cover shortages in resistance inventories resulting from their current offensives and Sandinista counterattacks and to "bridge" the period between now and when Congressionally approved lethal assistance . . . can be delivered.[40]

(When the scandal erupted, and investigators showed North this memo he "remembered that Poindexter requested drafting of the April memorandum about diversion." What Poindexter clearly meant by diversion was how much of a surplus there would be from the arms sale that could be used to support the Contras. Poindexter, however, denied directing North to prepare such a memorandum, insisting that he "directed North to put nothing in writing about the diversion." North, in turn, denied receiving this direction.

In a further twist, Poindexter went on to say that while he "admitted leading North to believe that the President had approved the plan . . . he [Poindexter] denied ever discussing it with the President." Parsing this dispute, it is North's account that rings true. Poindexter did in fact instruct North to draft a memorandum specifically "for Poindexter to forward to the president." Furthermore, the PROF computer system was the primary means by which these men communicated with each other between meetings, which meant that almost everything was in writing. North's voluminous memo output was proof enough to reject Poindexter's denial, which amounts to a classical instance of a subordinate falling on his sword for his superior.)[41]

Curiously, North's arithmetic was slightly off: $3.65 million from $15 million was not $12 million, but $11.35 million. Immediately, however, there was a larger problem. The Iranian government failed to deposit funds on April 7, as agreed, but Ghorbanifar called Allen the next day, the 8th, to tell him that he had "good news . . . an agreement had been reached in accordance with Washington's

---

[39] *Iran-Contra Affair*, 225.
[40] *Tower Report*, B-88.
[41] *Congressional Report on the Iran-Contra Affair*, 226.

wishes."[42] The implication was that Kangarlu had sold the deal to the Iranian leadership after some difficulty and that the money would be forthcoming momentarily. Yet, another week passed with no deposit, a week in which momentous events occurred.

If the Iranian leadership was balking at handing over $17 million before the middle of the month, the American air strike on Libya, on April 14-15, positively spooked them. The Iranians immediately sought to put some distance between themselves and the United States by raising new demands. Within hours of the attack, Ghorbanifar called Allen to pass on new terms from Kangarlu. He now wanted a meeting in Frankfurt before a meeting in Tehran, insisted on a sequential release of the hostages instead of their release all at once, and then said Iran would only begin the release process after all the spare parts had been delivered.[43] "If the US did not deliver all the Hawk spares with the arrival of the US delegation, only one hostage would be released." This was, Ghorbanifar said, a "take it or leave it" proposition.[44]

After a series of frantic phone calls involving North, Nir, Ghorbanifar, Kangarlu and Allen, North proposed to Poindexter that he make a quick trip to Frankfurt to meet with the Iranian interlocutors. Poindexter, clearly angered by the delays, replied:

> You may go ahead and go, but I want several points made clear to them. There are not to be any parts delivered until all the hostages are free in accordance with the plan that you laid out for me before. None of this half shipment before all are released crap. It is either all or nothing. Also, you may tell them that the President is getting very annoyed at their continual stalling. He will not agree to any more changes in the plan. Either they agree finally on the arrangements that have been discussed or we are going to permanently cut off all contact.[45]

Consequences of the Air Strike on Libya

Reagan and his aides apparently had not anticipated the impact the air strike on Libya would have on Iranian sensibilities, although Cave would come close to it later. In the immediate aftermath of the strike Ghorbanifar put off the proposed meeting with Kangarlu in Frankfurt. As Allen and Nir attempted to get into contact with him to reschedule the meeting, other disturbing news arrived.

On April 18, the dead bodies of American hostage Peter Kilburn and British hostages Leigh Douglas and Philip Padfield were found outside Beirut. Qaddafi had "bought" them from their captors and had them killed as a reprisal

---

[42] C. Allen, "Conversation with [Ghorbanifar]," April 8, 1986, *Tower Report*, B-90.
[43] C. Allen, "Conversation with Subject [Ghorbanifar]," April 16, 1986, *Congressional Report on the Iran-Contra Affair*, 227n125.
[44] "North PROF Note to Poindexter," April 16, 1986, *Tower Report*, B-91n65.
[45] "Poindexter PROF Note to North," April 16, 1986, *Tower Report*, B-91.

for the raid. A different group from the one that held the other American hostages had held Peter Kilburn. Nevertheless, reports about Qaddafi trying to buy the other hostages were unsettling.[46] Kilburn's case was especially galling, as North had attempted to cooperate with the CIA in freeing him in a ransom deal that had gone wrong just before the raid.[47] Had the Iranians been involved? If the Iranians controlled Hezbollah and could influence the hostage-takers, had they been involved in, or responsible for, the killing? These were unsettling questions that could jeopardize everything.

After several days of intermittent contact and cancellation of another Frankfurt meeting because Kangarlu would not appear, Cave attempted to reconstruct what was happening. Kangarlu, he believed,

> had probably received some kind of authority to cause the release of the hostages prior to our Libyan action and that the current delays and efforts to force new concessions are a consequence of internal disputes over what the Iranians should do about this matter in the wake of the US action in Libya.[48]

Cave's interpretation was insightful and plausible, but crucially incorrect. His assumption that Tehran possessed some sort of "authority" that could bring about the release of the hostages had little or no foundation.[49] It was increasingly understood that Imad Mughniyeh held the hostages, but the flawed assumption was that Hezbollah controlled and directed his actions, which was not the case, as we have seen. This assumption was the big disconnect in the American leadership's understanding of the dynamic interconnectivity of the terrorist network.

Cave's surmise that the Libyan strike had triggered "internal disputes" about how to deal with the hostages was closer to the mark but confused the issue. The question of how Tehran could position itself between the United States and the Soviet Union was an ongoing issue within the Iranian leadership since the beginning of the year and not the result of the Libyan strike. It had become increasingly apparent that Iranian strategy had shifted from seeking to reestablish relations with the United States to taking an equidistant position between the two superpowers.

In fact, the Tehran stall pre-dated the Libyan strike by two months, although the attack had clearly strengthened the Iranian leadership's resolve. The reason for the stall was the Iranian government's decision to maintain a middle

---

[46] David C. Wills, *The First War on Terrorism: Counter-Terrorism Policy during the Reagan Administration* (Lanham: Rowman & Littlefield, 2003), 212.
[47] David C. Martin and John Walcott, *Best Laid Plans: The Inside Story of America's War against Terrorism* (New York: Touchstone, 1988), 345-46.
[48] "North PROF Note to McFarlane," April 21, 1986, *Tower Report*, B-91.
[49] "George Cave Deposition," *Congressional Report on the Iran-Contra Affair*, Appendix B, vol. 3, 844. In fact, he would shortly change his view to say that Tehran had influence but no control over the hostages.

position and also began before Cave himself became involved. Thus, Iranian officials would not meet with the Americans and the government would not advance its own funds for weapons. Instead, Tehran forced Ghorbanifar to scramble to find the money to pay for the weapons.

Indeed, during April two deals blew up in his face. The first was a US Customs sting involving Cyrus Hashemi. Hashemi, working as an informant, cooperated in the arrest of six Israelis, including an Israeli general, and several others ostensibly attempting to purchase arms for Iran. Ghorbanifar, implicated as a financial backer for the arms dealers, was arrested briefly by the Swiss police, but released.[50]

Ghorbanifar's second operation involved an attempt to involve British business magnate Roland "Tiny" Rowland in a large sale of arms and other goods to Iran. Ghorbanifar, Khashoggi, and Nir approached the British entrepreneur in early April with a proposal to use his company, Lonrho, as an umbrella organization for the transaction. The trio claimed that the White House had secretly approved the sales, had cut out the State Department, and that the point man was Poindexter.[51]

Dubious, Rowland checked out the story with the embassy and Ambassador Charles Price passed word back to the State Department. Shultz, as might be expected, "expressed strong opposition on legal and moral grounds as well as concern for the President." Rowland was advised "to stay out of the plan" to sell arms to Iran. Shultz, feigning ignorance of the president's arms sale plan, confronted Poindexter, who acknowledged there was "a shred of truth" to the assertion of White House involvement with Ghorbanifar and the others, but denied that the approach to Rowland was "our deal."[52]

Shultz was in Tokyo with the president for an economic summit in early May. When informed of the approach to Rowland, and although claiming that he sought out the president, Shultz never spoke to him about it. However, he did express his anger and frustration to Don Regan, demanding "he should go to the president and get him to end this matter once and for all."[53] Regan, blindsided, "expressed alarm and promised to raise the matter with the President."[54] In truth, as Walsh noted, Shultz and his aides were monitoring every move made by North and Poindexter in the Iran arms plan, looking for opportunities to derail it.[55]

By the time the Rowland episode broke, North had finally arranged to meet Ghorbanifar in London, even though Kangarlu still refused to leave Tehran. (Poindexter told North to travel *incognito* to London and stay away from the

---

[50] *Congressional Report on the Iran-Contra Affair*, 226. See also, Michael Fredericks, *The Octopus Eagle* (Tallahassee: Loiry Publishing, 1987) and Ari Ben-Menashe, *Profits of War* (New York: Sheridan Square, 1992), 177-84.

[51] *Congressional Report on the Iran-Contra Affair*, 229.

[52] Ibid.

[53] *Tower Report*, B-93.

[54] *Congressional Report on the Iran-Contra Affair*, 229.

[55] Walsh, *Final Report of the Independent Counsel*, 1:340-41.

embassy so as not to inflame Shultz.)[56] North noted to Poindexter that he and Cave "intend to tell [Ghorbanifar] that unless a deposit is made by the end of the week, the whole operation is off."[57]

When they met the next day, May 6, at the Churchill Hotel, Ghorbanifar confidently assured them that "financing had been arranged," but, he said, he would deposit the funds in an account controlled by Nir, not Secord.[58] Again, this seemed to be a way for Iran to keep distance from direct contact with the Americans and disguise the fact that the money was coming from Khashoggi, not the Iranian government. Their discussion of the arms package was now expanded to include two radars, to sweeten the pot, which pushed the CIA's cost up to $12.6 million. Secord's markup raised the price to $15 million and Ghorbanifar's much higher to $23.6 million, $8.6 million over Secord's.[59]

North emphasized that the procedure must follow Poindexter's sequencing: a high-level meeting, release of hostages, and then delivery of the 240 spare parts. He also expected the Iranians to have sent a delegation to Beirut by the time the Americans arrived in Tehran. Thus, the Iranians would arrange for the release of the hostages in Beirut at the same time that the Americans were negotiating with them in Tehran. If all went as planned, the parts would be delivered.

Ghorbanifar confirmed Kangarlu's earlier offer that top Iranian officials would meet with the Americans, but now he also sweetened the pot. Not only would Rafsanjani lead the Iranian delegation, he said, but it would also include Prime Minister Mousavi, President Khamenei, and possibly also Khomeini's son, Ahmed, and conservative leader, Ayatollah Farsi.[60] These arrangements were even better than those negotiated during the February meetings and should have raised eyebrows. Even heads of state would not be afforded as high-level a meeting as was being promised.

When Cave got on the phone with Kangarlu to confirm the terms of the deal, however, a "major snag" immediately arose. Kangarlu demanded delivery of spare parts first, followed by a meeting, and then release of the hostages—the exact reverse of the American position. Indeed, Kangarlu wanted the Americans to bring the entire parts package with them. When that was rejected, after much haggling, they agreed the delegation would bring as many parts as the plane could

---

[56] "Poindexter PROF Note to North," May 5, 1986, *Tower Report*, B-94. It was, of course, not true as the *Congressional Report on the Iran-Contra Affair*, 229, claims that "Shultz would remain in the dark." Walsh, *Final Report of the Independent Counsel*, 1:340-43, shows definitively that Shultz was kept continuously informed of the initiative's progress, or lack thereof.

[57] "North PROF Note to Poindexter," May 5, 1986, in *Tower Report*, B-94.

[58] Ibid.

[59] *Congressional Report on the Iran-Contra Affair*, 230.

[60] "George Cave Deposition," *Congressional Report on the Iran-Contra Affair*, Appendix B, vol. 3, 627-28. Cave was quite "skeptical" that they would actually meet with Iran's highest leaders.

hold. Only then would the Iranians send a delegation to Beirut "to barter for the release of the hostages," which clearly implied that there was no guarantee that all would be released and probably none while the Americans were in Tehran.[61]

Given this impasse, North's PROF note to Poindexter when he returned to Washington was either a blatant breach of discipline, or something else, which will be discussed below. He wrote, "we have succeeded. Deposit being made tomorrow . . . . Release of hostages set . . . in sequence you have specified . . . . Thank God—he answers prayers."[62] North claimed success where there had been no success. The Iranians had not agreed to Poindexter's sequence, yet North's erroneous report asserting otherwise would be the basis for McFarlane's negotiating instructions in Iran.[63]

North expected Ghorbanifar to deposit $17 million on May 8, but no money arrived for nearly a week, and when it did there was only $15 million, and that was deposited on May 14 by Khashoggi, not the Iranian government. One of the checks for $5 million bounced, delaying confirmed receipt of the funds until May 16. The Israelis deposited $1.6 million for the replacement TOWs on the 15th.[64]

The "rubber check" precipitated a blunt exchange between Secord and Ghorbanifar, with the general declaring that he could no longer "tolerate" Ghorbanifar's deceitful tactics and would recommend that he be "terminated." Ghorbanifar misunderstood the remark to mean that Secord wanted him killed, which amused the general, who later explained that he only wanted to end all dealings with the Iranian.[65]

Secord's angry response had been based on the assumption that the Iranian government was providing the funds and Ghorbanifar was skimming off the top. It was only later, *after* McFarlane's failed mission to Tehran that he discovered Adnan Khashoggi had provided the funding for Ghorbanifar, not the Iranian government—"a bit of information that, all by itself, would've caused me to slam on the brakes and stop the transaction for security reasons, making the debate over McFarlane's trip academic."[66]

North, however, did know beforehand that Khashoggi was financing the arms transaction, but did not disclose this information to Secord. As he reported to Poindexter in early May before the meeting with Ghorbanifar in London: "We

---

[61] *Congressional Report on the Iran-Contra Affair*, 230.

[62] "North PROF Note to Poindexter," May 8, 1986, *Tower Report*, B-94 and *Congressional Report on the Iran-Contra Affair*, 231.

[63] Jane Mayer and Doyle McManus, *Landslide: The Unmaking of the President* (Boston: Houghton Mifflin, 1988), 226, come to the same conclusion, observing, "as North knew, the Iranians had not committed themselves specifically to release all the hostages. But North told Poindexter they had, and Poindexter so briefed McFarlane—which would lead to one of the major misunderstandings of the Tehran visit."

[64] Walsh, *Final Report of the Independent Counsel*, 1:169.

[65] Secord, *Honored and Betrayed*, 261.

[66] Ibid., 283.

know that Khashoggi is the principal fund raiser for Gorba and that only after Gorba delivers a cargo does he get paid by the Iranians."[67] Of course, the only way for North to "know" how the funding worked was from information provided by US government agencies, particularly the CIA and Treasury, which were tracking the money flows.

In any case, unaware of the origin of Ghorbanifar's funds, Secord deposited $6.5 million into the CIA's Geneva account on May 16, an amount that covered the cost of the spare parts ($4.3 million) and the 508 TOWs, but not the radar purchase, which was set aside for the time being.[68] That left roughly $10 million available in Lake Resources accounts. Secord, later attempting to account for the funds, explained that transportation, crew, and miscellaneous expenditures came to $1.2 million; and $900,000 was set aside to repay Israel for the original $1 million given the previous November, which, according to Secord, left between $8.1 million and $7.9 million. Then, after setting aside $4 million for self-insurance for the planes, the remaining $3.9 million was "surplus."[69]

In attempting to explain away this surplus, Secord had to do some financial juggling. He double-counted the transportation, crew, and miscellaneous expenses, which were actually built into the CIA price and his claim of a $900,000 repayment to the Israelis was made up out of whole cloth. Schwimmer had told him months earlier that the funds were his to use as he saw fit and need not be repaid. As we shall see, at this moment there was actually over $6 million in surplus funds available for the Contras.

There was yet another aspect to this shell game: the radars. The CIA price of $12.6 million included the cost of the radars, as well as the spare parts and the TOWs, but the explanation for setting aside the radar purchase was because "Iranian funds were never sent for the radars."[70] It was literally true that *Iranian* funds were not sent, but $15 million had been deposited in Lake Resources accounts, sufficient to cover the cost of the radars. But, as noted, Secord only deposited $6.5 million in the CIA account. A second explanation was that the Department of Defense refused to sell the radars because the request "came only from the CIA," not from the White House.[71] Both "explanations" were specious and suggest an effort to explain away missing "surplus" funds spent on the Contras.

On May 16, just as Secord was depositing the funds in the CIA Swiss account activating the arms sale to Iran, the president was calling an NSPG meeting to address the issue of soliciting funds for the Contras. The meeting included not only principals, but also note takers. Thus, North, Alan Fiers, Raymond Burghardt, Edward Djerejian, Craig Fuller and several other aides were

---

[67] "North PROF Note to Poindexter," May 5, 1986, *Tower Report*, B-93-94.

[68] *Congressional Report on the Iran-Contra Affair*, 231 and *Tower Report*, B-94 n66.

[69] Secord, *Honored and Betrayed*, 260.

[70] *Congressional Report on the Iran-Contra Affair*, 231 and 235n157.

[71] Ibid., 236n185.

sitting along the wall behind the principals.[72] When Shultz said he thought Congress would procrastinate on authorizing the $100 million, he was asked to "prepare a list" of countries to approach for assistance. The secretary suggested that the Saudis should be asked to help, unaware of the fact that the president already had solicited $32 million from King Fahd.[73] Shultz's suggestion was quietly shelved. (McFarlane would tell him later.)

As the discussion progressed, Walsh reveals, the president "startled the group in the situation room by asking, 'can't Ollie find funds until we get the hundred million dollars?'"[74] The president's outburst stunned those in attendance, especially the note takers. Although Don Regan immediately changed the subject and ensured that the president's question did not appear in the minutes of the meeting, it was clear especially to the note takers in attendance that the president had let slip the fact that he was deeply involved in the search for funds. Furthermore, he not only knew who North was, but also, he was fully aware of North's efforts to obtain funds for the Contras.

North, having just received word from Secord of the deposit of funds into Lake Resources before the meeting, was about to respond to the president's question when Poindexter hushed him up.[75] Afterward, North sent Poindexter a PROF note stating that the Nicaraguan resistance "now has more than $6M available for immediate disbursement [which] reduces the need to go to third countries for help."[76] In his reply, the national security adviser explained that he had hushed him up because "I just didn't want you to bring it up at NSPG. I guessed at what you were going to say."[77]

Incredibly, in yet another instance of protecting the president, Poindexter later claimed "he did not tell the president of the sudden availability of 'bridge funds.'"[78] Since the House rebuff of the president's $100 million request in late March, Reagan had been desperately searching the world for funds. Indeed, the very purpose of the May 16 meeting was to brainstorm fundraising possibilities, in part, because as far as the president then knew Iranian funds had yet to come in. It strains credulity to believe that Poindexter, having just learned of the answer to the president's prayers, would not have informed him of it, obviating any need for the meeting.

---

[72] Scott Armstrong et al., *The Chronology: The Documented Day-by-Day Account of the Secret Military Assistance to Iran and the Contras* (New York: Warner Books, 1987), 368.

[73] *Congressional Report on the Iran-Contra Affair*, 231.

[74] Lawrence Walsh, *Firewall: The Iran-Contra Conspiracy and Cover-Up* (New York: Norton, 1997), 286.

[75] Mayer and McManus, *Landslide*, 227.

[76] "North PROF Note to Poindexter," May 16, 1986, *Tower Report*, B-96. *Congressional Report on the Iran-Contra Affair*, 231, puts it slightly differently, having North say: "there is now 6M available for the resistance forces."

[77] "Poindexter PROF Note to North," May 17, 1986, *Tower Report*, B-96.

[78] *Congressional Report on the Iran-Contra Affair*, 231.

The Tehran Set-Up

The secret mission to Tehran, May 25-28, was originally designed to bring about the immediate release of the remaining hostages and establish the beginning of a new relationship with Iran, but by the time it occurred the president had dramatically altered its purpose. It had been clear to the president since the end of January that the Iranians were stalling, trying to shift to an equidistant position between Washington and Moscow, while still seeking weapons from the United States.[79] He also understood that Tehran had little or no control over Imad Mughniyeh, and therefore could not obtain the release of the hostages, except as a result of a negotiation with him. Thus, he knew that the stated objectives of the January 17 finding were beyond realization at this time. Only a change in Iranian policy would reopen the possibility of success.

Therefore, sometime during this period the president decided to change tack. Reagan had faced similar problems on three occasions in the first term when Helmut Schmidt, Zenko Suzuki, and Deng Xiaoping had all sought to maintain a middle position between the United States and the Soviet Union. In each case, Reagan shifted tactics after initial policy had failed and brought those nations into closer alignment with the United States.[80] Admittedly, the broken Iranian American relationship represented an added level of difficulty, but the structural problem was the same.

Also similar was the vehement opposition of the new world order faction to any improvement in relations with Iran. To deal with his internal opposition, Reagan drew the same play from the playbook he used against Haig, when he sent the former secretary of state to Beijing in 1981.[81] After the secretary quashed the proposed plan to develop a strategic partnership with Beijing, the president then excluded him from the action, taking control of the China issue to negotiate the August 17 communiqué that established the basis for future US-China relations.

The president used the same play now by naming McFarlane to head the mission to Tehran. In doing so, the president understood that it put him into position to ensure its failure, which, however, would then justify exclusion of the new world order faction from any future involvement. Indeed, McFarlane's 'all or nothing' negotiating instructions, and what he was told to expect from his counterparts, guaranteed a deadlock in Tehran.

The president's decision explains the curiously erroneous note North sent to Poindexter after the May 6 meeting with Ghorbanifar in London, when the impasse with Tehran had become glaringly evident. North's false PROF note to Poindexter that the Iranians had agreed with the president's terms, when they had not, was part of the plan to set up the new world order faction into believing that a deal was possible. The mission would, however, also serve to demonstrate

---

[79] Chap. 8, passim.
[80] See the author's *Ronald Reagan: Revolution Ascendant*, chaps. 9, 10, and 13.
[81] Ibid., chap. 9.

American *bona fides*, if and when Tehran decided to seek better relations at a later date; and also *inter alia* provide the necessary bridge funds for the Contras.

North's note to Poindexter was not sent immediately following the London meeting, but only after he had returned to Washington on May 8. North thus had ample time to discuss with Poindexter what the content of his note should be before he sent it. It was vital to show that the meeting had been a success because his note would be part of the negotiating record Poindexter would show to McFarlane when he briefed him before he left for Tehran. The president also met with him prior to his trip.[82] It is obvious that only the prospect of success would persuade McFarlane to agree to undertake what was a very risky mission.

The irony was that both Reagan and McFarlane thought the odds were small that the meeting could succeed but diverged on the reason for having it. Reagan saw it as earnest money for the future, while McFarlane thought that there was an 80 percent chance that this was "just another elaborate con" by the Iranians and hoped that by going he could convince the president to terminate the initiative, this time "once and for all."[83] In other words, McFarlane's intent was to kill the initiative.

Reagan agreed to permit the newly appointed head of NSC political-military affairs, Howard Teicher, to be a part of the group, because of his "past relationship with McFarlane . . . ," but excluded him from any role in preparation for the trip, because, as North told him, he "did not have a need to know." [84] Both McFarlane and Teicher opposed the participation of Amiram Nir, but acquiesced in deference to Prime Minister Peres, who pointed out that the Israelis were after all providing planes, warehouse space, and a forward base for the operation.[85] The group that flew to Tehran from Tel Aviv included McFarlane, North, Cave, Teicher, Nir, a CIA communications specialist, and two pilots. A second communications specialist would man a comm-link in Tel Aviv to permit secure, real time contact between Tehran and the White House.

McFarlane was not informed that his plane would also be carrying one pallet of spare parts and there is a discrepancy in the record regarding the total spare parts package. The congressional report states that a total of 13 pallets were shipped to Israel. The McFarlane aircraft carried one to Tehran and a second plane was to deliver the remaining twelve, pending release of the hostages.[86] Cave, however, said that there were only four pallets in total, the McFarlane aircraft

---

[82] Armstrong et al., *The Chronology*, 375.

[83] Robert C. McFarlane, *Special Trust* (New York: Cadell & Davies, 1994), 54.

[84] Howard Teicher and Gayle Radley Teicher, *Twin Pillars to Desert Storm* (New York: William Morrow, 1993), 363-364. Howard Teicher was the newly appointed NSC director of political-military affairs. When the crisis broke in November of 1986, a "senior White House official" would describe him as the "mastermind" of the whole affair! (see p. 372).

[85] Ibid., 365.

[86] *Congressional Report on the Iran-Contra Affair*, 232.

carrying one.[87] Depending on which is correct, McFarlane either brought with him one fourth of the total package, or one thirteenth.

Iran's complex agenda, however, disrupted the proceedings from the start. The Iranians wanted no strategic relationship with Washington but did want to keep the channels open to procure weapons. The Iranians also knew they could not deliver the hostages as the Americans demanded, but claimed they could because it guaranteed Washington's continued interest. Both sides' objectives were diametrically opposite. The Iranians demanded delivery of weapons before anything else, while McFarlane demanded release of the hostages before delivery of weapons.

Thus, from the first moments after arrival, the American group became the object of a carefully contrived Iranian negotiating approach. This meant, in the first instance, repudiating any prior agreement and eventually renegotiating another, which they also could not, or would not, honor. The procedure was intentionally intimidating and humiliating to the Americans, who were taken aback by their treatment, but it was designed to browbeat them into submitting to Iranian demands for weapons.

As the Iranians wanted no strategic relationship, they denied they had agreed to ministerial meetings and would not permit their leaders to meet with the Americans, sending only bureaucratic functionaries to deal with them. As they could not deliver all of the hostages, they denied they had agreed to do so. Finally, as their objective was to obtain the spare parts, they demanded that they be delivered before any steps were taken to gain the release of the hostages.

Ghorbanifar had preceded the McFarlane team to Tehran by three days, in more than enough time to be instructed in the role he was to play. He would be the greedy messenger, who deceived both sides in the interest of his own profit; and he would be condemned by both sides for his deception. Although this characterization fit Ghorbanifar perfectly, Iranian negotiating tactics should not be ascribed to him. Ghorbanifar's role was to be the convenient scapegoat, blamed by both sides.

There was no question about the arrival time of the aircraft, or the agreement upon which the trip had been arranged. In the aftermath of the failed mission, on July 8 Ghorbanifar wrote a letter to his superiors attempting to repair the damage and reminding them of what had happened in Tehran. He revealed that the Iranian negotiating strategy had, indeed, in McFarlane's words, been "just another elaborate con." Ghorbanifar declared:

> Prior to the arrival of the US team and myself in Tehran on 25 May 1986, there was full agreement that upon arrival of the high-ranking US delegation in Tehran, bringing some of the

---

[87] "George Cave Deposition," *Congressional Report on the Iran Contra Affair*, Appendix B, vol. 3, 629. Ghorbanifar, in a July 8 letter to his Iranian chief, said that the Americans "brought more than one fifth of the requested spare parts." *Tower Report*, B-133.

requested items, the Iranian authorities would begin
immediately mediating for the release of all American hostages
in Beirut, all together, and collectively. And that after this, the
remaining items requested by Iran would arrive in Tehran.[88]

Into Tehran

The Iranian ploy commenced the moment the unmarked Israeli 707
touched down at Mehrabad airport outside Tehran. There was no one to receive
them and they were forced to languish in the formerly resplendent, but now
shabby VIP lounge for over an hour and a half before Ghorbanifar arrived with
Kangarlu and a crew of revolutionary guards, claiming that the plane had arrived
early. McFarlane, according to one account, had expected to be met at the airport
by Rafsanjani himself and transported to the meeting place in a motorcade.[89]

After taking their passports (all of the group traveled with fake Irish
passports), confiscating a cake that North brought for Ghorbanifar's mother, and
decorative pistols intended as gifts for the Iranian leadership, the hosts bundled
the Americans into cars for a quick ride downtown to the Independence Hotel, the
former Tehran Hilton. This took the Americans aback, as the agreement had called
for them to be housed in private lodging outside the city.[90]

At the hotel came another unpleasant surprise. Just as the Americans
were settling in on the top (15th) floor of the hotel, a scuffle broke out in the
parking lot. One group of revolutionary guards got into a shoving match with
another and word filtered up to the Americans that their guards had foiled an
attempt to arrest them.[91] In all likelihood, this was a staged event designed to raise
the anxiety level among the Americans, emphasize their isolation, and soften them
up for the hard line the Iranians were about to take.

But not immediately. Although Ghorbanifar kept reassuring McFarlane
that everything was progressing smoothly and release of the hostages was
imminent, no Iranian interlocutor appeared at the hotel until 5:00 p.m., nine hours
after their arrival. Worse, the Iranian official who arrived was not Rafsanjani, or
some other high official; it was a deputy prime minister, introduced to them as Ali
Najavi. His name was probably a pseudonym like those of other persons who
drifted in and out of the hotel—and the Irish names used by the Americans. The
Iranians, however, knew the identities of the Americans and Nir; Ghorbanifar had
told them.

Although disappointed, McFarlane went through his brief, emphasizing
US willingness to assist Iran, warning of Soviet designs on Iran, and the extreme
unlikelihood that Moscow would permit Iraq's defeat in the war. He also put

---

[88] *Tower Report*, B-133.
[89] Theodore Draper, *A Very Thin Line: The Iran-Contra Affairs* (New York: Hill and
Wang, 1991), 315.
[90] Segev, *Iranian Triangle*, 272.
[91] Draper, *Very Thin Line*, 315.

forward the US understanding of the sequence to be followed involving release of the hostages before anything else. "We are pleased that informal talks resulted in agreement on release of American hostages. Once that is completed, we can begin serious talks." [92]

The Iranian official responded by asserting Iran's core position "we don't want to ally with East or West, but that doesn't mean we don't want relations." He then surprised McFarlane by disclosing they had already off-loaded the pallet from the plane without authorization and declared, "we expected more than what came on the aircraft." McFarlane's startled reply was that "we could not bring it all on the plane. But the rest can be brought forward."[93]

The Iranian tossed two more surprises. First, regarding the hostages, he said that Iran "will send a delegation to Beirut to solve that problem." This, too, startled McFarlane, who had been led to believe that the Iranians had *already* sent people to Beirut for that purpose. This meant that gaining their release while he was still in Tehran would be extremely unlikely.

Then, Najavi said the Iranian military was suspicious of the individual remaining aboard the aircraft because the plane was on the military side of the airfield and suggested that he come to the hotel. McFarlane immediately objected, saying "we can't do that . . . . He performs communications functions."[94] To acquiesce would have meant that they would be completely cut off from contact with the outside world.

McFarlane did not take the exchange well, exploding repeatedly, venting his frustrations. Regarding the hostages, he exclaimed, "I have come. There should be an act of goodwill by Iran." Then again, regarding the single pallet, "I have come from USA . . . . I did not have to bring anything. We can leave now!" Najavi merely responded that he was not a decision maker. "We just give you a message and take your message."[95] In his reporting memo to Poindexter, McFarlane said, "the incompetence of the Iranian government to do business requires a rethinking on our part . . . "[96]

The next day, at 3:30 p.m., Najavi arrived again and McFarlane decided to force the issue. He asserted:

> There are crucial matters related to the Soviet Union, Afghanistan and Iraq that we should discuss. But we cannot begin to address these matters until preliminary problems are

---

[92] Howard Teicher, "Memorandum of Conversation," May 25, 1986, *Tower Report*, B-103.

[93] Ibid., B-104. George Cave, "Deposition," *Congressional Report on the Iran-Contra Affair*, Appendix B, vol.3, 837-38. Cave noted that the pilots had told them that while the Iranians had unloaded the pallet, they had not opened it, so he was at a loss to explain how Najavi could have determined what was inside the crate, or its condition.

[94] *Tower Report*, B-105.

[95] Ibid.

[96] Ibid., B-101.

solved. Perhaps your government is not ready to deal with these larger issues. Maybe we should wait for another day. But I must depart tomorrow night. I would like to meet with your Ministers. But I cannot if preliminary problems have not been solved. I have no more to say.

McFarlane closed the meeting by insisting that he wished to meet with ministers. "No other meetings are necessary." To Najavi's reply that an "important authority" would be arriving shortly, McFarlane said, "he would not meet the person. He came to meet with Ministers. The staff can meet this other person."[97]

This "other person" was Ali Najafabadi, chairman of the Majlis Foreign Affairs Committee and a senior adviser to Speaker Rafsanjani. Although scheduled to arrive at four he did not appear until after nine that evening. There can be no doubt McFarlane's adamant refusal to meet with anyone but a "minister" had an impact on his delay.

McFarlane's decision to stay in his room left the floor to North, who, along with Cave, Teicher, and Nir engaged in a lengthy discussion with Najafabadi, a fluent English speaker who exuded confidence and a sense of power. In McFarlane's absence, North laid out the internal US political situation, being careful not to be too explicit because Teicher was present taking notes.

Immediately after exchanging pleasantries, North warned "there are factions in our governments that don't want something like this to succeed." His next words were "that is why McFarlane grew angry when things didn't take place as I suggested they would." If North seemed to be suggesting that he and McFarlane were on opposite sides, Najafabadi certainly understood it that way. After his meeting with McFarlane the next day, he proposed that he and North work out terms of agreement without McFarlane.[98]

North followed up his warning about an opposing faction in the US government with an offer to provide a secure communications system to fool the Soviets, who were "trying to find out" what we were doing and "will make a major effort to expose us." Then, North offered to sweeten the spare parts package by including the radars back into the mix. "If your government can cause the release of the Americans held in Beirut, 10 hours after they are released, aircraft will arrive with the Hawk missile parts. Within 10 days of deposit [of funds], two radars will be delivered."[99]

As their discussion continued, Najafabadi said, "we have the same problem that you have. Some here oppose relations with the US." Moreover, "we see the Russian danger much more than you . . . . We feel it, touch it, see it. It is not easy to sleep next to an elephant you have wounded."

---

[97] Ibid., B-106.
[98] Howard Teicher, "Memorandum of Conversation," May 26, 1986, in Ibid., B-107.
[99] Ibid., B-108.

In his next breath, Najafabadi demolished the twin assumptions on which the trip had been based. Claiming a "misunderstanding," he said when we agreed to the meeting "it did not mean a direct dialogue would occur on the spot. It is too early at this stage." Furthermore, "there was no agreement that when McFarlane led the team it would lead to Ministerial meetings. Let us turn the key in a way that will work." Then, dropping a bombshell, he said "We don't see the release of hostages as the key."[100]

North said nothing about the hostages but protested that he "was told" there would be ministerial meetings. When Najafabadi questioned his source, North said that Ghorbanifar "had stated that the US team would meet with the senior leadership." But Najafabadi's retort was "the last phone call did not mention Ministerial meetings. We did not agree to such meetings for McFarlane. We keep our word."[101]

Najafabadi's reference to the "last phone call" was undoubtedly reference to the May 6 meeting, where the final arrangements for the trip had been confirmed. Recall, that was the meeting that produced North's false memo declaring that both sides had reached full agreement on the terms of the meeting. Here was further confirmation that such was not the case, and that the memo was part of the set-up of McFarlane.

Najafabadi had an inducement of his own, declaring that Rafsanjani had said officially that Iran was willing to purchase weapons from the United States and that Khomeini had said Iran was "ready to establish relations with all the world except Israel." There was a "$2.5 billion" deal on the table, "but you have to remove the obstacles." North asked whether a "secret meeting" could be arranged with Rafsanjani, but Najafabadi said no, it was too soon. McFarlane "would have to wait or come back" after some period of time, "after the hostages are free and the deliveries are completed." The Iranian ended their conversation, saying "we sent a man to Lebanon" and hope to have "news" by tomorrow. [102] (It was a two-and-a-half-hour flight between the two cities.)

The next morning, Tuesday May 27, Najafabadi arrived at ten with news from Beirut. It was not good. Mughniyeh (we now know) demanded that before any hostages were released, Israel must withdraw from both the Golan Heights and Southern Lebanon; Shiite prisoners taken by Colonel Lahad, commander of Israel's Southern Lebanon Army, must be returned to Beirut; and the Al-Dawa 17 prisoners in Kuwait must be freed. Finally, all expenses incurred by the hostage taking must be paid.[103]

The Iranian immediately tried to soften these clearly impossible demands, declaring, "we told them these conditions must be reduced. We can't make this work . . . . We are negotiating other conditions [and] we are hopeful . . . ." However, he then attempted to couple the spare parts issue to it by complaining

---

[100] Ibid., B-109.
[101] Ibid., B-110.
[102] Ibid., B-110-11.
[103] Howard Teicher, "Memorandum of Conversation," May 27, 1986, Ibid., B-112.

that Washington "should" deliver the rest. The implication was that delivery of the spare parts package would lead to a reduction of terrorist demands. What it really meant, however, was that there was now a third negotiating partner, Mughniyeh, a negotiating trap that promised indefinite delay.[104]

At this point, McFarlane, who was listening to the exchange, called down to invite Najafabadi to his suite. In a session lasting almost three hours he reiterated his brief about the Soviet threat and the agreement they had, stressing the sequence of hostage release first, followed by delivery of the spare parts. Najafabadi demanded to know "just who had agreed to these terms?" When McFarlane named Ghorbanifar and Kangarlu, Najafabadi declared "these were not the terms as he understood them," insisting "all deliveries [were] to occur before any release took place."[105]

When Najafabadi produced a letter from Ghorbanifar purporting to support his interpretation, McFarlane brought in Cave, who pointed out that the letter was entirely in Ghorbanifar's handwriting and bore no mark of American input. His bluff called, Najafabadi "asked for a break to confer with his colleagues." McFarlane agreed, but "hoping to build a little fire under them," reiterated that they had to leave that night. McFarlane's "judgment [was] that they are in a state of great upset, schizophrenic over their wish to get more from the deal but sobered to the fact that their interlocutors may have misled them." [106]

In retrospect, Najafabadi's request for a break to consult with his colleagues marked a turning point in the negotiation. Now faced with a deadline, with their bluff called, from the resumption of the talks that afternoon Najafabadi became much more conciliatory. Before the talks resumed, however, Ghorbanifar, who "did not seem concerned that his duplicity had been unmasked," arranged for his mother to prepare a sumptuous lunch for the visitors, "their only good meal of the trip."[107] During the meal, Ghorbanifar took Cave aside to ask him to confirm to the Iranians, if they asked, that the $24.5 million price tag for the weapons was correct. Cave asked North about it and the two of them questioned Nir. The Israeli reassured them that the price was correct, involving "other deals" and "enormous expenses."[108]

When Najafabadi returned at 5:00 p.m. to resume their negotiations, he tried one last time to obtain agreement on the delivery-first scheme. "If the plane arrives before tomorrow morning, the hostages will be free by noon," he said. McFarlane wouldn't budge, responding " . . . release the hostages, advise us, and [we] will deliver the weapons." The Iranian simply said "OK," and then asked for the "staff to work out an agreement." He wondered, "perhaps if we can reach agreement on this the staff can stay and complete the work?" McFarlane's response to this request was to say, "I will seek the president's decision, [but] I

---

[104] Ibid.
[105] Ibid., B-113-14.
[106] Ibid., B-114.
[107] Mayer and McManus, *Landslide*, 240-41.
[108] Ibid.

cannot know what he will say."[109] The meeting ended at 6:00 p.m. (In fact, McFarlane did not seek the president's decision.)

When Najafabadi returned at 9:30 p.m. North presented a 6-point draft proposal for their consideration. It was a restatement of the American position, stipulating that the plane carrying the spare parts would depart Tel Aviv at 0100, May 28, to arrive in Tehran at 0900. The Iranians were to "cause the release" of the hostages "not later than 0400." If the hostages were not safely in the hands of US authorities by 0400 the plane would be "turned around." If the hostages were released the US government would deliver two radar sets within ten days of receiving payment for same.[110]

The final two points committed the two governments to continuation of a "secret" political dialogue on the Soviet threat, Afghanistan, Nicaragua and other agreed topics "until such time as both sides agree to make such a dialogue public." To facilitate this dialogue, the US government would "provide a secure channel of communications between our two governments."[111]

After reading it, the Iranians talked animatedly among themselves, until Najafabadi asked plaintively, "how are we supposed to free the hostages by 0400?" When North reminded them that they had offered to gain their release by noon, Najafabadi agreed that he had said that, but protested, "it is now late," and switched topics to ask about the Al-Dawa 17. North said that the US could issue a statement about making every effort to insure "just and fair treatment" for the Shiite prisoners but could not interfere in the internal affairs of Kuwait.[112]

At around 11:00 p.m., McFarlane took Najafabadi aside for a private discussion. Half an hour later, he emerged looking grim. "Let's pack up and go," he said, "they're just stringing us along."[113] But North replied that they could not depart because the plane had not yet been refueled. Semi-stranded, with a failed negotiation, the Americans fumed as they began to pack up.

At 2:00 a.m. the next day, May 28, Najafabadi returned again, pleading for a few more hours until 6:00 a.m., indicating that they should be able to "get an answer on the hostages by then." McFarlane said, OK, we'll give you until six-thirty and, if "you give us a time we will launch the aircraft so that it will land

---

[109] Howard Teicher, "Memorandum of Conversation," May 27, 1986, in *Tower Report*, B-115.

[110] George Cave, "Record of Meetings," in Ibid., B-118-19.

[111] Ibid.

[112] Howard Teicher, "Memorandum of Conversation," May 27, 1986, B-116. Teicher also claims that North offered to "achieve the release" of the prisoners, but Cave emphatically disputed it. According to Cave, North did not "say anything about the release of . . . prisoners." See "George Cave Deposition," *Congressional Report on the Iran-Contra Affair*, Appendix B, vol. 3, 869.

[113] Mayer and McManus, *Landslide*, 242.

here two hours after the hostages are in US custody."[114] Najafabadi said he would be back in touch before six.

What happened next is mired in controversy. McFarlane accused North of launching the plane from Tel Aviv without his authorization; North claimed he sent a message to launch the plane to Dick Secord "with McFarlane's permission."[115] It is Secord, however, who reconciles these otherwise irreconcilable claims, and in the process exposes McFarlane's attempt to blame North and Ghorbanifar for the failure of the mission.

Secord says, "shortly after midnight on the 28th I received a message to launch . . . the second aircraft . . . but to be ready to turn it around on command."[116] The flight from Tel Aviv to Tehran would take about eight hours along a route that went over the Red Sea, around the Arabian Peninsula, and then north to Tehran.

McFarlane claimed that North sent the message to launch while he was asleep, but the time difference of one-and-a-half hours between Tel Aviv and Tehran makes this highly unlikely.[117] Two o'clock in the morning in Tehran was 12:30 a.m. in Tel Aviv. As noted, Najafabadi had returned at 2:00 a.m. to plead for more time. Thus, McFarlane could not have been asleep when the message to launch was sent at "shortly after midnight" Tel Aviv time, lending support to North's account.

Secord then notes that "four hours into the flight," he received instructions to turn the plane around. Unfortunately, he was unable to contact the plane, which was then at the southern end of the Red Sea. There were anxious moments until they restored contact, but "since the pilot had not received confirmation to continue, he followed his instructions and returned to Tel Aviv, where he landed without incident."[118]

McFarlane claims that when awakened at six and told that the plane had launched, he "angrily countermanded" North and turned the plane back just before it had reached the mid-point in the flight. The implication is that had he not countermanded North's order the plane would have flown on to Tehran.

The former national security adviser, however, bases this argument on a surprisingly faulty understanding of flight operations. All air missions have a planned fail-safe point requiring final confirmation to proceed. Failing receipt of confirmation at the fail-safe point, the mission is automatically scrubbed, and the plane returns to base. That is in fact what occurred in this case when Secord was unable to communicate with the plane.

---

[114] Howard Teicher, "Memorandum of Conversation," May 28, 1986, in *Tower Report*, B-117.

[115] McFarlane, *Special Trust*, 63 and North, *Under Fire*, 58.

[116] Secord, *Honored and Betrayed*, 267.

[117] McFarlane, *Special Trust*, 63. In his testimony, as recounted in *Congressional Report on the Iran-Contra Affair*, 241, McFarlane said that while he was "asleep," North "violated" his orders and "directed Secord to send the plane . . . "

[118] Secord, *Honored and Betrayed*, 267-68.

Secord believed that McFarlane had decided to launch the plane as a "negotiating ploy" to "create a tangible deadline." It failed because he did not realize that the Iranians did not control the hostages. In short, "Bud's demands for an 'instant' hostage release to match the transit schedule of the second plane was simply unrealistic." In other words, McFarlane had set conditions that were highly unlikely, if not impossible, to meet.

But not according to McFarlane. For him, North "had been deceiving Poindexter and the President, and now me." Indeed, "the collapse of the entire mission was due to lies and deceptions on the part of both North and Ghorbanifar."[119] But McFarlane's claim of innocence was simply designed to divert attention from his own actions in scuttling the mission. Iranian inability to gain the release of the hostages and disinclination to enter into a strategic relationship with the United States were decisive. For McFarlane and the new world order faction, rapprochement with Iran was to be prevented at all costs, even if this required the creation impossible conditions.

It was at ten minutes to eight o'clock in the morning, several hours *after* the plane had turned back to Tel Aviv, that Najavi arrived to offer a compromise on the hostages. "They think two can get out now but it will require 'joint action' on the other two." Ten minutes later, Najafabadi arrived to reaffirm the offer. McFarlane replied: "It's too late." "You are not keeping the agreement." "We are leaving."[120]

Teicher's notes left out the dispute that then ensued between McFarlane and North. The Iranian offer was to obtain the release of two hostages before delivery of weapons and possibly the remaining two after delivery. North thought this a deal worth taking and wanted McFarlane to call Poindexter and ask for guidance, but McFarlane would not consider it. At the same time, all the way to the airport and literally up to the plane's stairway the Iranians pleaded with McFarlane to reconsider, but he remained obdurate.[121]

The intelligence evidence surrounding the trip was ambiguous. On the one hand, NSA radio surveillance of Beirut indicated "no evidence that 'the hostages were about to be released or that anything unusual was taking place.'"[122] On the other hand, North reported that the CIA had informed them "Rafiq Dust, Iran's deputy foreign minister, had left Tehran for Damascus, as he had in previous cases when Western hostages were actually released."[123] The implication was that Iran had to coordinate with Syria on hostage matters and that the offer to release two might have worked.

The following day, in reporting to the president that the mission had failed, McFarlane, according to Mayer and McManus, said "the Iranians had

[119] McFarlane, *Special Trust*, 57-58.
[120] Howard Teicher, "Memorandum of Conversation," May 28, 1986, *Tower Report*, B-117.
[121] North, *Under Fire*, 59-61.
[122] *Tower Report*, B-118.
[123] North, *Under Fire*, 60.

insisted on the delivery of all the Hawk parts before releasing any of the hostages."[124] That, as the above account demonstrates, was not true. McFarlane had declined to tell the president of the compromise offer at the end and, indeed, urged that he discontinue the initiative.

The mission to Tehran had two very important consequences, one immediate and the other longer-term. In the immediate sense, it was a success for the new world order faction. The mission had failed to obtain the release of the hostages and reestablish relations with Iran. However, in the long term, its failure enabled the president to proceed with his plans to develop relations with Tehran without further participation of the new world order faction, although Shultz and McFarlane continued to play roles from off-stage, as it were, and would ultimately be successful in killing the initiative.

---

[124] Mayer and McManus, *Landslide*, 245-46.

Chapter 16

On the Verge of "Victory"

By the summer of 1986, President Reagan's general strategy of rebuilding the Western Alliance and defeating Soviet strategy seemed to be succeeding, or on the verge of succeeding, on all major fronts. In arms control, the president had reclaimed command of the negotiations from Shultz and set a high bar for Soviet compliance in his quest for a shift to the strategic defensive based on SDI. He had marshaled congressional and cabinet support for greater arms assistance to anti-Soviet resistance forces, especially in Angola, Afghanistan, and Nicaragua. Most importantly, he had secretly cleared the way for direct interchange with the Iranian leadership.

Secretary Shultz and the new world order faction opposed the president's strategy, favoring détente with the Soviet Union and accommodation to Soviet interests around the world. Shultz sought through arms control to establish détente based on mutual assured destruction, albeit at lower levels of weapons, and was willing to sacrifice SDI to get it. His objective in third world conflicts was to negotiate settlements rather than defeat Soviet client regimes. His agreement to support increased arms to Angola, Afghanistan, and Nicaragua stemmed from the fact that the Soviets were increasing the supply of arms to their clients, who were winning and not interested in negotiations. On the issue of Iran, Shultz was totally opposed to reestablishing relations, insisting that the United States support Iraq, instead. Despite Shultz's objections, by the summer of 1986, President Reagan appeared poised to take decisive steps toward the realization of his policy objectives.

Reagan in Command

The most highly visible aspect of President Reagan's strategy was the Victory Program of supporting anti-Soviet resistance forces, especially in Angola, Afghanistan, and Nicaragua. By mid-year, the decision to supply the Stinger missile to counter the Soviet deployment of helicopter gunships to Angola and Afghanistan was being implemented. Stingers were already in use with Savimbi's forces in Angola and the CIA was training Afghans in the United States on use of the weapon.[1] The appearance of Stingers on the Afghan battlefield would come in September. In both places they would turn the tide of battle.

---

[1] "Rebels Get First Load of Stinger Missiles," *Washington Times*, April 21, 1986, A5. See also Milt Bearden and James Risen, *Main Enemy: The Inside Story of the CIA's*

Another success was the House vote at the end of June to approve the president's $100 million program for the Contras. The vote reversed five years of continuous opposition by the House expressed in the Boland Amendments. Even so, Speaker Tip O'Neill's skillful legislative tactics delayed the beginning of money flows until the coming fiscal year, in October, but the CIA began active planning to resume its role in full support of the Contra forces as soon as the vote was cast.

In retrospect, however, the issues that would decide the struggle between Reagan and Shultz and the new world order faction occurred largely outside the public view. These were the arms control negotiations with the Soviet Union and the Iran initiative, which unfolded in secret over the second half of 1986. Shultz and the new world order faction were determined to achieve détente with Moscow through the arms control negotiations, while Reagan sought to strengthen the containment structure around the Soviet Union through the reestablishment of a strategic relationship with Iran.

Shultz and the new world order faction sought an accommodation with Moscow based on existing strategic doctrine, mutual assured destruction, while Reagan sought to dispense with MAD and persuade the Soviets to agree to a transition to strategic defense, based on sharp reduction of nuclear weapons and emphasis on missile defense. Both sides agreed on weapons reductions and SDI but disagreed on their purpose.

After the Geneva Summit in November 1985 (and McFarlane's resignation and replacement by John Poindexter in December) the president decided that he would become directly involved in the arms control process and "negotiate the key elements personally" with Gorbachev.[2] Recall, in early 1985, Secretary Shultz had demanded and obtained control of the negotiations. Taking this responsibility away from Shultz, even though he would obviously still have a major input into the process, may have been the reason the secretary made another of his offers to resign.

When he made it, the president's reaction startled him. Reagan said that "he wanted him to stay, but wouldn't try to talk him out of leaving."[3] Shultz's resignation threat was a bluff to regain control of the negotiations. His bluff called, he decided to stay, for the obvious reason that there was no guarantee that his successor would come from the ranks of the new world order faction, which would effectively kill arms control as the path to détente.

From early in the year, paralleling the negotiations under way in Geneva, Stockholm, and Vienna, Reagan and Gorbachev exchanged a series of letters, in which each leader made clear his respective position.[4] The letter format put the

---

Final Showdown with the KGB (New York: Random House, 2003), 215; and Mohammad Yousaf and Mark Adkin, *The Bear Trap* (London: Leo Cooper, 1992), 182.

[2] Jack Matlock, *Reagan and Gorbachev* (New York: Random House, 2004), 175.

[3] Ronald Reagan, *An American Life* (New York: Simon and Schuster, 1990), 642.

[4] In addition to the arms control negotiations taking place in Geneva, the Conference on Security and Cooperation in Europe occurred in Stockholm; and in Vienna,

president in charge of the process. In essence, Reagan sought to gain Gorbachev's agreement to reduce nuclear weapons and make a transition to strategic defense based on missile defense, while the Soviet leader offered to reduce strategic and intermediate-range weapons, but only if Reagan would renounce SDI. Reagan's agenda included formulas for the resolution of regional disputes, treaty violations, and human rights issues, while Gorbachev focused almost entirely on the US-Soviet weapons balance.

Gorbachev sought to set the agenda with his letter of January 15, 1986. The core of his proposal was an offer to eliminate all nuclear weapons by 1999, including all intermediate-range weapons from Europe, but *only* if Reagan were willing to renounce the "development, testing, and deployment" of SDI. In letters of February 6 and 22, just before the opening of the Soviet Union's 27th Party Congress, Reagan replied, agreeing in principle with the ideas of the zero option for intermediate-range missiles in Europe and a 50 percent reduction in US-Soviet "nuclear arms," but wanting no limits on "strategic defense research."[5] In short, "by late March," as Oberdorfer notes, "almost everything seemed bogged down in the usual suspicions and discord."[6]

Two events in April only served to harden these positions. The first was the strike against Qaddafi on April 14, a punch that Reagan subtly telegraphed in his letter of February 6. Discussing regional conflicts, the president sent a rather clear signal, which, in combination with other intelligence Moscow was receiving, indicated that the United States was preparing to strike Qaddafi. "What are we to make," he asked, "of your sharply increased military support of a local dictator who has declared a war of terrorism against much of the rest of the world and against the United States in particular?" And further, he asked, was the Soviet Union "so recklessly seeking to extend its influence in the world that it will place its prestige . . . at the mercy of a mentally unbalanced local despot?"[7]

When the attack came, Moscow's unwillingness to protect Libya, or do more than supply another SA-5 missile unit, was a major demonstration of ineffectualness. The Soviets bitterly criticized the United States, cancelling a scheduled meeting between Soviet Foreign Minister Shevardnadze and Shultz, which suggested that an improvement in relations was not imminent. Then, ten days later came the shocking nuclear incident at Chernobyl. Moscow's, indeed, Gorbachev's, inept handling of the crisis, failing even to acknowledge there had been one until Western European nations began to identify nuclear fallout over their countries, clearly cast a pall on Soviet efforts to demonstrate that the Soviet Union under Gorbachev was changing for the better.

---

representatives from NATO and the Warsaw Pact were negotiating reductions in conventional weapons.

[5] Reagan, *American Life*, 650-58.

[6] Don Oberdorfer, *The Turn: From the Cold War to a New Era: The United States and the Soviet Union, 1983-1990* (New York: Poseidon Press, 1991), 166.

[7] Reagan, *American Life*, 655.

At Geneva, Gorbachev had agreed to an exchange of visits, with the first to take place in Washington. US representatives repeatedly pressed their Soviet counterparts to set a date and the president extended an invitation for a late June visit, but the Soviets declined. Reagan's reaction was to continue to raise the issue, but also to increase the price Gorbachev would have to pay for a visit. Reagan wanted no arms control agreement without "substantial progress in other areas," like a Soviet withdrawal from Afghanistan, progress on treaty violations, and human rights, while Gorbachev would not agree to a visit without the certainty of an arms control agreement beforehand.[8]

Content to increase the pressure, on May 27 the president announced that the United States would no longer be bound by the SALT II treaty. After a "fierce argument" in which Shultz opposed denouncing the treaty, the president compromised, announcing that while the United States would no longer be bound by the unratified treaty, it would remain in compliance for the time being by dismantling two 20-year-old Poseidon-class submarines to make way for a new Trident sub, the USS *Nevada*, just beginning sea trials.[9] The immediate outcry from Congress, including some on the Republican side, and of course from the Soviets, prompted a clarification. Arms control adviser Paul Nitze explained that the president was committed "to take another look," if the Soviets "should take the initiative . . . to satisfy US concern on arms issues."[10]

The Soviet response came almost immediately, no doubt prepared earlier by knowledge of the argument that was riling the administration. In Geneva, on May 29, Soviet negotiators put forth the defense part of an offense-defense package. Their proposal called for "strengthening" the ABM Treaty with "limits on testing and a ban on deployment of antimissile systems" of all kinds. They wanted US commitment to adhere to the treaty for "fifteen to twenty years" and to stricter definitions of treaty terms. Their proposal, as Nitze observed, "would tighten the ABM Treaty even more than the so-called narrow interpretation."[11]

On June 11, the Soviets presented the offense part of the package. Moscow would be willing to negotiate an INF agreement separately from START, with zero missiles for the US and the Soviet Union and leaving undisturbed British and French systems. He also agreed to freeze Soviet missile forces in Asia. US forward-based systems in Europe, including the Pershing II and cruise missile bases, would be removed, as would Soviet SS-20s.

The Soviets proposed to reduce "strategic arms" by 30 percent, instead of their earlier proposal of 50 percent, but to increase the number of nuclear warheads and bombs by 25 percent, from 6,000 to 8,000. They also spoke only of

---

[8] Matlock, *Reagan and Gorbachev*, 176.

[9] Oberdorfer, *The Turn*, 168; and Lou Cannon and Walter Pincus, "Compliance with Salt Continued," *Washington Post*, May 28, 1986, A1.

[10] Don Oberdorfer, "US Is 'No Longer Bound' by SALT II, Weinberger Says," *Washington Post*, May 29, 1986, A1.

[11] Paul Nitze et al., *From Hiroshima to Glasnost* (New York: G. Weidenfeld, 1989), 416.

"significant reductions" in throw-weight, a retreat from an earlier willingness to reduce throw-weight by 50 percent.[12] The Russians seemed to be signaling a preference for negotiating an INF agreement over a START accord.

Gorbachev would include these proposals in a letter to Reagan on June 15, but the president began to formulate a response as soon as he received word from Geneva. On June 12, in a principals-only meeting of the president, Shultz, Weinberger, Casey, and Poindexter, a lengthy debate began on what would culminate in the president's July 25 letter to Gorbachev. These discussions would not circulate below the principals level and the information was not circulated to the Joint Chiefs for comment, or to the arms control bureaucracy.[13]

Shultz advocated as he had before that "we propose a trade-off of fifty percent reductions in nuclear arms for a willingness to forgo deployment of a strategic defense for the period during which reductions would take place."[14] Shultz also questioned whether "development and testing of SDI was permissible under the 1972 ABM Treaty." Weinberger argued that both were fully allowed under the "broad" interpretation of the treaty. Reagan "sided with Cap." He was "committed to the search for an alternative to the MAD policy." SDI, he maintained, was "not a bargaining chip."[15]

Weinberger departed completely from his past, persistent opposition to any agreement by offering the surprise proposal to "eliminate all ballistic missiles." The idea had bubbled around the Defense Department for some time. Its essential thrust was that since the Soviet nuclear arsenal relied almost exclusively on ballistic missiles, while the US was more diverse, including bombs and cruise missiles, the elimination of all ballistic missiles would work to US advantage.[16]

The president's letter, as it finally evolved, built on Gorbachev's proposal for offensive reductions and offered a compromise on SDI, consistent with his goal of a transition to the strategic defensive. The letter remained classified until 2009.[17] Thus, most of the works that discussed it presented only partial accounts. The only contemporaneous information about the letter came from newspaper leaks and later memoir references.[18]

---

[12] Ibid., 417.

[13] Admiral William J. Crowe, *The Line of Fire* (New York: Simon & Shuster, 1993), 265-66.

[14] George Shultz, *Turmoil and Triumph* (New York: Scribner, 1993), 722.

[15] Reagan, *American Life*, 666.

[16] Oberdorfer, *The Turn*, 170-74.

[17] Martin Anderson and Annelise Graebner Anderson, *Reagan's Secret War* (New York: Crown, 2009), 282-83, provide a lengthy excerpt. The full text can be found online at The Reagan Files, https://www.thereaganfiles.com/19860725.pdf.

[18] Walter Pincus and Lou Cannon, "Star Wars Compromise Discussed," *Washington Post*, July 10, 1986, A1, Leslie Gelb, "Reagan Reported to Stay Insistent on 'Star War' Test," *New York Times*, July 24, 1986, 1, and Leslie Gelb, "Reagan Seeks Soviet Agreement on the Deployment of 'Star Wars,'" *New York Times*, July 25, 1986, A1,

Without exception, the leaks focused on Reagan's proposals for SDI and said little or nothing about his proposals for offensive force reductions. In their memoirs, Weinberger says nothing, while Reagan hints that he sent Gorbachev a "sweeping new arms reductions proposal.[19] Shultz provides more, but badly distorts Reagan's proposal on missile reductions, saying: "A letter finally emerged that covered much familiar ground, including reductions by 50 percent in strategic weapons."[20] In fact, it was a "sweeping new . . . proposal." Reagan called for 50 percent reductions in ballistic missiles, which meant the heavy SS-18, not simply strategic weapons, and sought to move toward the "total elimination of nuclear weapons."[21]

Shultz's distortion of the July 25 letter stemmed from the fact that he opposed the proposal as well as the strategy of the transition to the strategic defensive. However, the letter itself casts new light on the arms control negotiations, including and especially on the Reykjavik meeting later in October and the events leading up to it.

On the defense side, the president proposed a five-year "program of research, development and testing, which is permitted by the ABM Treaty," to determine whether a system was feasible. If after this period either side decided to deploy missile defense, it would be obligated to "share the benefits of such a system," provided "there is mutual agreement to eliminate the offensive ballistic missiles of both sides":

> Once a plan is offered to this end, the details of the sharing arrangement and the elimination of offensive ballistic missiles would be the subject of negotiations for a period of no more than two years.[22]

If there were no agreement after two years "either side will be free to deploy unilaterally after [giving] six months' notice . . ." The seven-and-a-half-year testing/negotiation period was in part a response to Moscow's proposal that both sides adhere to the ABM Treaty for fifteen-to-twenty years. It was also partly a response to Shultz's proposal to "give up those deployment rights that we could not exercise anyway."[23] And it included a modified version of Weinberger's proposal to eliminate all offensive ballistic missiles.

There was also an offense side to the president's proposal that went far beyond that suggested in the memoirs of Reagan and Shultz. The president proposed that the two countries "begin moving toward our common goal of the

---

and Don Oberdorfer, "Reagan Called Ready to Make Deal on Defensive Arms," *Washington Post*, August 4, 1986, A1.

[19] Reagan, *American Life*, 665-66.

[20] Shultz, *Turmoil and Triumph*, 723.

[21] "Reagan to Gorbachev, July 25, 1986," online at The Reagan Files, https://www.thereaganfiles.com/19860725.pdf.

[22] Ibid.

[23] Shultz, *Turmoil and Triumph*, 718.

total elimination of nuclear weapons," by first implementing the principle of a fifty percent reduction of "strategic ballistic missiles warheads." The president said he was also prepared to limit long-range cruise missiles "below our current plan," and to limit the total number of ICBMs, SLBMs, and heavy bombers "to a level in the range suggested by the Soviet side."

Reagan next proposed to take immediate steps to eliminate the "entire class" of intermediate-range missiles worldwide, "which is consistent with the total elimination of all nuclear weapons." He thought an immediate agreement "would be the best outcome," but he wrote, "an interim approach, on a global basis, may prove the most promising way to achieve early reductions." On the question of Gorbachev's proposal for a complete ban on nuclear testing, the president demurred. While a complete ban was a long-term US objective, "we believe a safe, reliable and effective nuclear deterrent requires testing." [24]

With the July 25 letter Reagan had taken the high ground from Gorbachev by offering a concrete plan to rid the world of all nuclear weapons, but, contrary to Gorbachev's proposals, as part of a shift to the strategic defensive. It was a bold proposal that would heavily impact the Soviet Union's superpower status, which was based almost solely on possession of nuclear weapons. Indeed, Gorbachev's response to Reagan's letter was—silence. It would be almost three months, mid-October, before he would reply and then circumstances would have changed dramatically.

In Washington, meanwhile, a significant turn of events on the Iran/hostage front made clear that the president had not shut down the Iran initiative, but was continuing it. That news, combined with the president's dominance of the arms control process, not to mention his successes in supporting anti-Soviet resistance forces, created a major crisis for the new world order faction.

Secret Contact with Iran

During the Tehran meeting, although no immediate breakthrough had occurred in US-Iranian relations, unbeknownst to McFarlane there had been a major development. When North disclosed to Najafabadi in McFarlane's absence that there existed a government faction opposed to opening relations with Iran, the Iranians understood that a direct approach to the president would be necessary. Thus, they offered to dispense with Ghorbanifar as an intermediary and establish direct contact. As Cave reported:

> In Tehran, the Iranians talked about the undesirability of the Ghorbanifar [Kangarlu] channel. So . . . they agreed to look for a new channel and we were to consider the new channel.[25]

---

[24] "Reagan to Gorbachev, July 25, 1986."
[25] "George Cave Deposition," *Report of the Congressional Committees Investigating the Iran-Contra Affair* (Washington, DC: US Government Printing Office, 1987),

When we were in Iran, the Iranians told us that they were not happy with the Ghorbanifar [Kangarlu] channel. But, they said, if you guys insist on using it, it's all right with us. We, of course, had the problem with the Israelis on Ghorbanifar, even after Tehran. The Israelis were insisting . . . that Ghorbanifar had to be used. We decided to look for a second channel.[26]

This was, of course, precisely what the president had hoped to accomplish with the mission. He wanted direct contact unfettered by intermediaries and allies and without the knowledge of his factional adversaries. For two reasons, however, the president decided to keep Ghorbanifar in play, but at arm's length. One, there was some concern that, if cut off entirely, Ghorbanifar would blow the whistle on the operation and ruin the opening. Two, keeping him in play served to divert attention away from the secret effort to establish direct contact through a second channel.

From June, then, Secord and Hakim were tasked with searching for the new channel, while North, Allen, and Cave were charged with fending off Ghorbanifar and Nir, although Cave would become involved with the second channel after contact was made. Indeed, it seemed that the Iranian leadership, too, as intimated during the Tehran meeting, was attempting to distance itself from Ghorbanifar.

Shortly after the Tehran meeting, Ghorbanifar, Kangarlu and Nir sought to contact North, proposing a new arms deal they insisted would produce the hostages. For Ghorbanifar, in particular, there was urgency. Khashoggi had arranged to provide the $15 million financing for the TOWs, spare parts, and radars that were supposed to be a part of the Tehran mission. With only one pallet of arms delivered, the Iranians refused to make any payments—and Khashoggi wanted to be paid, with interest. The only way for Ghorbanifar to clear his debt to Khashoggi was for the United States to ship the rest of the spare parts order to Iran.[27]

However, when Ghorbanifar tried to get in touch with the American side through Nir, and Kangarlu contacted Cave by telephone, both found that the Americans stood firmly on their demand that the hostages had to be released before the rest of the spare parts shipment would be delivered. As before, Kangarlu demanded shipment before any more hostages would be released.

Ghorbanifar found himself locked in the middle and made extravagant promises to each side in an effort to break the logjam. To the Iranians he promised without authorization from the Americans that the United States would deliver additional missiles with the spare parts, if a hostage were released. To the

---

Appendix B, vol. 3, 690. [*Cited hereafter as Congressional Report on the Iran-Contra Affair.*]

[26] Ibid., 849.

[27] *Congressional Report on the Iran-Contra Affair*, 245.

Americans he claimed that the Iranians were preparing to release a hostage as a "gesture" for the fourth of July.

At the same time, the Iranians produced a price list for American weapons showing that they were being overcharged by six hundred percent. In discussions with Cave, Kangarlu attempted to place the blame on the Americans for the overcharge and to protect Ghorbanifar, but it was clear that the Iranian leadership blamed Ghorbanifar for the price gouge.[28] The arms merchant claimed "he had increased the price of the spare parts by only 41 percent," implying that it was the Americans who were at fault.[29] The effect of Iranian complaints about over-pricing was simply to stiffen American disinclination to resume any dealings with the Ghorbanifar-Kangarlu channel.

Indeed, that may have been its actual purpose. Cave thought that the Iranians were not at all surprised that Ghorbanifar was overcharging them.[30] As to the "price list," it was a Defense Logistics Agency list, which was not really a price list, but a list designed "to get the serial numbers and descriptions correct for ordering [weapons]." All pricing was based on replacement cost, in any case, which was much higher than the DLA list.[31] The Iranians knew all this, which, in Cave's view, meant that they were simply using it as a "device."

At the end of June, Ghorbanifar heard from Kangarlu that the Iranians would release a hostage as a humanitarian gesture in connection with the fourth of July. Ghorbanifar told Nir, who called North. North immediately sent a recovery team to Wiesbaden, West Germany, to receive the hostage. But the holiday came and went without the release of a hostage. The fiasco prompted North to refuse to take any more calls from Nir. Thus, by the end of June, North had put distance between himself and Ghorbanifar as well as the Israelis.

Meanwhile, the search for the new channel had begun and was showing promise. Secord and Hakim were placed in charge of the search, but it was actually Hakim who got in touch with friends and former colleagues, particularly in London, at the Iranian Purchasing Mission, to determine who among them might be informed that a new channel would be coming out of Iran. Recall that the Iranian Purchasing Mission was Iran's largest weapons acquisition organization outside of Iran.

By mid-June, Hakim had contacted an old colleague, Sadegh Tabatabai, who had worked for him years earlier and was reputed to be "well connected" to the Iranian leadership, including Rafsanjani. Hakim's enticement was the promise of commissions from the expected lucrative business with Iran. Before long, Tabatabai had assembled half a dozen contacts from among the exile group in Frankfurt and Iranians working in the Purchasing Commission in London. Tabatabai met with North in Washington on June 27. To assess his reliability, he

---

[28] Theodore Draper, *A Very Thin Line: The Iran-Contra Affairs* (New York: Hill and Wang, 1991), 378.

[29] Ibid., 379.

[30] "George Cave Deposition," 638-39.

[31] Ibid., 670-71.

was subjected to a polygraph.[32] The "vetting" of Tabatabai was underway around the same time that Ghorbanifar, Kangarlu, and Nir were promising the release of a hostage on July 4, that failed to occur.

There was considerable interest, then, in early July, when Tabatabai "reported to Albert [Hakim] that the Relative had come out and asked for an American contact." It was not clear who the Relative was, in this instance. Later, the term was used to refer to the second channel, who was then identified as Ali Hashemi Bahramani, Rafsanjani's nephew.[33] As Cave recalled, "we assumed that this was the Iranian effort also to set up a second channel."[34] North brought Tabatabai back to Washington again for more meetings. Hakim and Cave met with him on July 10 and 11, as did North, separately, on the same days.[35] Undoubtedly, North gave Tabatabai instructions on how to proceed when the Relative came out again.[36]

Two days earlier, Ghorbanifar, now in a panic over his debt to Khashoggi, had sent a letter to Kangarlu proposing three options to settle the spare parts issue and his own debt problem. Two options were for what was termed a "sequential delivery" whereby the Iranians would release one or two hostages, reimburse Ghorbanifar $4 million, and the United States would deliver the spare parts. Then, they would release another one or two hostages and the United States would deliver additional equipment, radars and TOWs, after which there would occur a high-level meeting. His third option was for Iran to return the initial pallet of weapons, close the case, and "pretend nothing happened."[37] Alternating delivery of weapons with the release of hostages would now become the norm in dealing with the Ghorbanifar-Kangarlu-Nir channel.

Jenco's Release and the New World Order Faction

Contrary to Shultz's later testimony that "from May 4, 1986 . . . until . . . November 3, 1986 . . . I received no information indicating that an arms transfer to Iran had occurred," Walsh demonstrates conclusively that his testimony was false. Shultz and his top aides closely monitored the president's Iran Initiative throughout.[38] They were fully informed about McFarlane's trip to Tehran, knew

---

[32] Draper, *Very Thin Line*, 398-399.

[33] See Draper, *Very Thin Line*, 400, for a discussion of the Relative, who might have been Rafsanjani's nephew, Ali Hashemi Bahramani; or his eldest son, Mehdi Bahremani.

[34] "George Cave Deposition," 851.

[35] Ibid., 675-76.

[36] *Congressional Report on the Iran-Contra Affair*, 249, states that the second channel had not been identified until "late July."

[37] "Ghorbanifar, July 8, 1986 Letter," John G. Tower et al., *Report of the President's Special Review Board: February 26, 1987* (Washington, DC: US Government Printing Office, 1987), B-134-35.

[38] Lawrence E. Walsh, *Final Report of the Independent Counsel for Iran-Contra Matters*, vol. 1 (Washington, DC: United States Court of Appeals for the District of

that negotiations had resumed with Ghorbanifar and Nir afterward, and were apprised of the proposed hostage release timed for the fourth of July. None of that was cause for alarm as far as the new world order faction was concerned, for there appeared to be no prospect for success. However, that would change with the events surrounding the release of hostage Father Lawrence Jenco.

Shultz's aides were initially unaware of the president's secret search for a second channel, but by the end of July began to suspect that something was up. They were unable to keep track of Secord and Hakim, who, as private citizens were off the new world order faction's radar, but they were able to monitor Cave's movements. Indeed, it may have been through keeping track of Cave that they stumbled onto the early contacts with the new channel. The discovery occurred in the context of the release of hostage Father Lawrence Jenco.

On July 21, North reported to Poindexter that Nir told him the Iranians had decided to release a hostage. To "preclude a repeat of July 4," he decided not to alert a recovery team, but did notify assets on the ground in Beirut. Then, on what he termed a "related subject," North informed him that "George Cave will proceed to Frankfurt to meet w/ Tabatabai, the cousin of the man I met with here" to determine his "real access" and whether he could "act as an interlocutor" to the Iranians.[39] (North erred here—as will become clear in a later message on July 25 to Poindexter cited below, Cave was to meet with Tabatabai and Speaker Rafsanjani's brother.)

There had been a recent flurry of activity, as foreign diplomats interacted with Iranian leaders. An unnamed Turkish official had engaged in a discussion with Iran's Deputy Foreign Minister, Ali Larijani, who expressed Iran's interest in an "easing of relations" with Washington. His memorandum of conversation was passed to Secretary Shultz and to the NSC. Upon receiving it, North proposed sending a positive reply to Tehran through this emissary, pending Shultz's approval. Shultz's reaction, however, revealed that he had learned of Cave's trip to Frankfurt, although not its purpose.

In a note to Poindexter, Shultz agreed to send a message through the emissary, but then asked "about a Cave meeting in the next few days." He explained his interest by saying that "he just wanted to be sure that we did not have any disconnect between what the [emissary] will be telling them and what Cave tells them."[40] Shultz was clearly fishing for information about Cave's trip and its purpose. Poindexter was noncommittal but told North.

North replied to Poindexter later that same day to say, "Cave is meeting w/ [a relation of a powerful Iranian official] and Tabatabai to determine level of

---

Columbia Circuit, August 4, 1993), 341. Walsh's conclusions were based on new data from Shultz's aides that had not been made available to the Tower Commission, or to congressional investigators. He restates his view in *Firewall: The Iran-Contra Conspiracy and Cover-Up* (New York: Norton, 1997), 320-335.
[39] "North to Poindexter," July 21, 1986, *Tower Report*, B-138.
[40] "Poindexter PROF Note to North," July 25, 1986, Ibid.

access and current political sentiments toward the present regime."[41] In other words, Cave was to meet with Tabatabai, who would introduce him to "a relation of a powerful Iranian official." According to Taheri, the man Cave met on July 27 was Mahmoud Rafsanjani, the brother of the Iranian Speaker.[42]

In any case, the amount of activity regarding Iran had suddenly intensified and what happened next seems to have alarmed the secretary and the new world order faction. The release of Jenco on July 26 came at the moment that Cave was making the first substantive contact with the relative of a key member of Iran's leadership, Rafsanjani. Looking at it from Tehran's point of view, the timing of Jenco's release must be considered as a diversion to distract attention from the imminent, high-level meeting with the president's representatives.

We now know that the notion of three competing Iranian factions was only partly true and that most if not all of the top leaders were involved, or at least informed, of the opening to the United States. It seems likely therefore that the Iranian leadership's decision to release Jenco at this moment was intended to create a diversion from Cave's meeting with Mahmoud Rafsanjani.

The president's men also were bent on diverting attention from Cave's meeting and pointed to Ghorbanifar. Poindexter claimed Ghorbanifar "convinced" Kangarlu to release Jenco, but all knew that Kangarlu was a manager, not a decision-maker.[43] The decision to release Jenco had been taken at a higher level and Kangarlu was ordered to execute it. Similarly, the decision to pay Ghorbanifar $4 million suggests that the Iranian leadership sought to put into effect one of Ghorbanifar's July 8 options, as a step toward settling with him and prompting delivery of the rest of the spare parts ordered earlier.[44]

Cave, meanwhile, had been very busy. Not only had he met with Rafsanjani's brother, Mahmoud, on July 27, but also later that same day he joined North, who had traveled to Frankfurt, for a meeting with Ghorbanifar and Nir. Kangarlu participated in their meeting by telephone. Both Ghorbanifar and Kangarlu claimed credit for the release of Jenco and insisted that now the United States must deliver the remainder of the spare parts package.[45] North agreed.

On the day Jenco was released, McFarlane probed Poindexter to find out how it happened. The president's men, Poindexter, North, and Director Casey as well, all wrote memos claiming that Jenco's release had been "directly related" to McFarlane's trip. Casey insisted that the Ghorbanifar-Kangarlu channel had "worked for the second time" and that it should be continued because they and Nir had every incentive to work for "further release of our hostages." He also

---

[41] "North PROF Note to Poindexter," July 25, 1986, Ibid., B-138-39.

[42] Amir Taheri, *Nest of Spies: America's Journey to Disaster in Iran* (New York: Pantheon, 1988), 217.

[43] "Poindexter PROF Note to McFarlane," July 26, 1986, *Tower Report*, B-139.

[44] "What We Know of the Jenco Release," North to Poindexter, July 26, 1986, Ibid., B-139-40.

[45] Ibid., B-142.

agreed that the United States should deliver the remaining spare parts, if only to avoid the loss of face for those involved, including Peres and Rabin.[46]

Casey's memo, and North's and Poindexter's messages to McFarlane had all been sent the day of Jenco's release, making it highly doubtful that they, or anyone, knew the reasons for it. It seems that this, too, was a pattern of internal disinformation designed to achieve the same objective from the American side that Jenco's release had been designed to do from the Iranian side. It was in the paramount interest of both sides to keep the second channel secret as it was being established. Indeed, once the relationship had been firmly established in the third week of September, the United States would peremptorily shut down the Ghorbanifar-Kangarlu channel and Casey would inform Shultz that they had opened a new channel.

But if the president's men were attempting to deceive the new world order faction about its developing clandestine relationship with Tehran, they failed. The very fact of Jenco's release was a shock to them. On the day he was released, several of Shultz's top aides sent memos arguing that the hostage release "was part of an arms deal," which they expected would continue.[47] Coming the day after the president's July 25 letter to Gorbachev, the situation looked bleak from their point of view.

Then, a few days later, on August 4, their suspicions were confirmed when the United States delivered the remainder of the spare parts package. The events meant to them that the president had boxed in the Soviets on arms control and was succeeding in his efforts to establish relations with Iran.

Shultz's immediate reaction was to submit his resignation once again. So, the next day, August 5, he went to the president and said he wanted to resign. As the president put it, "although he had never stopped letting me know that he didn't approve of the Iranian policy, that wasn't his reason. He thought that Cap Weinberger, Bill Casey, and John Poindexter were ganging up on him and pushing foreign policy issues that he opposed behind his back. He felt that I'd lost faith in him."[48]

According to Shultz, "I didn't want to abandon [the president], but I felt that he must correct the indecisiveness and backbiting involved in the current NSC and White House processes. I also knew that when it came to anti-Communist dictators, he and I were just not on the same wavelength. And I was sick and tired of fighting the same battles on Soviet matters over and over again."[49]

Unlike Reagan's ambiguous response to Shultz's resignation gesture in January (a response that suggested a willingness to allow the secretary to depart), the president refused to accept his resignation this time. The reasons were clear. In January, after Geneva, the president's policy had not been formulated and

---

[46] "American Hostages," memorandum from Casey, attached to "North PROF Note to Poindexter," July 26, 1986, *Tower Report*, B-140-41.

[47] Walsh, *Final Report of the Independent Counsel*, 1:343.

[48] Reagan, *American Life*, 523.

[49] Shultz, *Turmoil and Triumph*, 725.

Shultz's departure would not have had an adverse impact. Now, in August, the president's policies toward the Soviet Union and Iran were in place and Shultz's resignation would signal to Americans and non-Americans alike that there was major dissension in the president's ranks. So, the president remonstrated with his secretary, telling him to take some time off.

Shultz spent the next few days at his home in Palo Alto, California, and when he got back, he gave Don Regan his demands. He demanded greater control over the foreign policy process. Couched in terms of complaints about "the way the White House operates," Shultz wanted the right to form his own "team to deal with the Soviets," wanted the right to place his own people in important positions, demanded that the leaks from the White House and Defense Department stop, wanted a single channel (his) "going out to foreign governments," and he wanted to put an end to the CIA's "politically motivated distortion of intelligence."[50] This was nothing less than a repeat of Al Haig's demand to be the vicar of American foreign policy. Reagan, of course, wanted Shultz on board, just not in control.

In Shultz's view, the "White House and NSC staffs . . . were operating on the fringes of loyalty to the president and of common sense." In truth, however, Shultz's complaints about the White House, NSC, defense, and the CIA were indirect attacks on the president himself and were a clear expression of the differences between them.

At the end of the month, the president was in Santa Barbara at the ranch and Shultz had gone to his farm in Massachusetts. The secretary was "mulling over how best to persuade [the president] to change his White House and NSC decision-making process."[51] "Just then," he recalled, "a fresh Soviet-American crisis flashed onto my screen," which offered him the opportunity to do exactly that.

Crises and Opportunity
for the New World Order Faction

Shultz and his new world order cohorts did more than mull over how best to persuade the president. Marginalized in the administration and desperate to gain a dominant voice and change the president's strategy, they implemented three actions that they hoped would enable them to turn things around.

The first was enactment of an amendment to the Arms Export Control Act (AECA) on August 27 that augmented the secretary of state's counter-terrorism authority. The bill included a prohibition on weapons sales to countries designated by the secretary to be supporters of terrorism.[52] The amendment to the

---

[50] Ibid., 726.

[51] Ibid., 727.

[52] The Omnibus Diplomatic Security and Anti-terrorism Act of 1986, P.L. 99-399, Title V, Section 509, amended the Arms Export Control Act to preclude the export of items on the US Munitions List to any country determined by the Secretary of State to have repeatedly provided support for acts of international terrorism. The president

AECA would have established a clear impediment to arms sales to Iran, if the president's policy had been based on it; but unbeknownst to Shultz, the president had used the Economy Act, instead.

Second was a plan to precipitate an espionage crisis, which would enable the secretary to engage in direct negotiations with his Soviet counterpart. The crisis would be triggered by the arrest of a KGB agent for spying in New York City, with the full understanding that the Russians would retaliate in Moscow. Shultz would parlay the espionage crisis into the Reykjavik Summit.

Third was a scheme to utilize American intelligence to leak information to a Lebanese journal exposing the Iran Initiative. The Lebanese leak triggered a crisis of the president's foreign policy. Although the AECA impediment amounted to nothing and the president was able to weather the Reykjavik meeting without giving up his arms control strategy based on SDI, he would be less successful in managing what became the Iran-Contra crisis.

As part of a government-wide crackdown on espionage in the United States, the large Soviet spy presence in New York City was an obvious target. The Soviet UN Mission had 275 "diplomats," and over 800 Soviets worked in the UN Secretariat and other organizations where it was estimated that at least a fourth of them were spies. The personnel at the Mission held diplomatic immunity and if caught spying could only be expelled from the United States. Employees at other UN organizations, like the Secretariat, however, had no immunity and, if caught, could be tried and sent to jail.

Nevertheless, the Soviets were brazenly using many of their employees in the Secretariat to "run agents" and the FBI had been closely monitoring one such employee, Gennady Zakharov, a physicist by training, for over three years. In August, the bureau had planned a "sting" operation to catch Zakharov in the act of receiving classified information from one of his contacts, a Guyanese employee, who was a double agent.

As was standard practice, on August 21, the bureau circulated to the CIA, Department of State and other relevant agencies a request to authorize the arrest of Zakharov. When the form arrived at the desk of Jack Matlock, NSC coordinator for Soviet Affairs, he was "surprised . . . that the State Department made no objection to the arrest since retaliation against an American was likely to follow." Indeed, he thought "we could expect the KGB to arrest an American without diplomatic immunity in the hope of forcing a trade."[53]

Given Shultz's well-known antipathy to any actions that could impinge negatively on US-Soviet relations, Matlock was at a loss to explain State's approval. Oberdorfer claims that Shultz and the top officials concerned with Soviet affairs "were all on vacation" and that a lower level official signed off on

---

could waive the prohibition of a particular export if he determined it to be in the national interest and submitted a report to Congress justifying the determination. The waiver would expire after 90 days, unless Congress passed a law to extend it.

[53] Matlock, *Reagan and Gorbachev*, 198.

it.[54] Whether Shultz was on vacation when the request arrived, or not, the secretary always traveled with secure communication equipment, and so certainly would have been apprised of it. In short, one must conclude that Shultz approved of the FBI sting.

Why approve of an action that would assuredly lead to a crisis as soon as Moscow retaliated? Under any other conceivable circumstance, as Oberdorfer notes, the State Department's response would have been to "tell the Soviets quietly to send Zakharov home to avoid an all-but-certain crisis."[55] That State declined to take this approach speaks to the stalemate in US-Soviet relations that had developed over the summer. Even though delegations from the two countries continued to meet on arms control and other matters, there had been no progress at any level. What was needed was a way to move the relationship forward, and the proposed arrest of Zakharov offered Shultz that opportunity.

The FBI arrested Zakharov on August 23, an event not highly publicized; the KGB responded a week later with the arrest of Nicholas Daniloff, an American journalist of Russian descent, who had been working for *US News and World Report* in Moscow for the previous five years. His arrest exploded in the US media. The Russians insured that their sting mirrored the FBI's. Both men were set up by acquaintances, handed some classified material, and arrested. Neither had diplomatic immunity and both were charged with spying. The fundamental difference was that Zakharov was a spy, and Daniloff was not. Nevertheless, as in previous cases, Moscow wanted a trade.

Anticipating the arrest of an American, Shultz hoped to negotiate a resolution of the crisis and open the way to a summit meeting between Reagan and Gorbachev. It would be a classic case of not allowing a crisis to go to waste. Shultz would be creating a problem in order to solve it and parlay the outcome into better relations. And he would be in the driver's seat, not the president or the NSC, working out a solution with his opposite number, Eduard Shevardnadze, whom he was scheduled to meet in Washington on September 19.

The most recent precedent for the Zakharov-Daniloff arrests had occurred eight years earlier. On May 20, 1978, the FBI arrested two Soviets, Rudolf Chernyayev and Valdik Enger, on espionage charges. Both were working for the UN Secretariat and thus did not have diplomatic immunity. On June 12, the Soviets arrested an American businessman, Jay Crawford, who also had no diplomatic immunity, on currency violations. Two weeks later all three were remanded to the custody of their respective ambassadors. The Soviets convicted Crawford of black-market currency dealings and then deported him. The two Soviet UN employees were tried, convicted, and sentenced, but then traded for five imprisoned Soviet dissidents.[56]

---

[54] Oberdorfer, *The Turn*, 176.

[55] Ibid.

[56] The precedent was discussed widely in the press. See Bernard Gwertzman, "Soviet Is Given New US Offer in Daniloff Case," *New York Times*, September 11, 1986, 1. Neither Shultz, nor Oberdorfer, mentions this precedent in their accounts.

Shultz would attempt to follow this precedent closely, and the outcome would be identical in structure, but he had to struggle against the president who demanded that there be no trade because the two cases were not equivalent. In his view, Zakharov was a spy and Daniloff a hostage. Matlock agreed, advising that the president demand Daniloff's release before proceeding on any other matters and begin "periodic expulsions" of KGB agents until Daniloff was released.[57]

When Matlock attempted to coordinate policy with the State Department, however, the director of Soviet affairs told him bluntly: "the secretary wants to negotiate this . . . . We mustn't do anything precipitous." He "wants to work it out himself and he wants you guys to stay out of it. He'll talk directly to the president on this."[58]

Before Reagan returned to Washington to meet with Shultz, however, he and Gorbachev engaged in a game of tit for tat. The president first tried to obtain Daniloff's release, sending a letter to Gorbachev informing him that the journalist was not a spy. Moscow responded by charging him with espionage.[59] Reagan then warned Gorbachev that unless Daniloff was freed, "there is no way to prevent this incident from becoming a major obstacle in our relations."[60]

It was in a highly charged atmosphere, then, that Shultz and the president met the morning of September 9, with the president's warning headlined in the press. Shultz presented him with his recommendation, which was designed to bridge the difference between the president, who did not want a trade, and the Soviets, who did. Shultz's solution was based on the 1978 precedent. He proposed that the two men be remanded to their respective ambassadors. Zakharov would be held for trial and Daniloff expelled. If Zakharov were convicted the administration "would seek to trade him for Soviet refuseniks." Reagan authorized him "to make it work" as long as it was not an obvious trade.[61]

For his scheme to work, therefore, Shultz had to show "how to keep a trade from being obvious."[62] If Daniloff could legitimately be considered a spy under Soviet law that would at least superficially make the two cases equivalent. Casting doubt on Daniloff's innocence outraged the president and his men, but in Shultz's view was the path to a solution acceptable by both sides. Fortunately for Shultz, Soviet law was so ambiguous as to cover almost any eventuality. Article 65 on spying held that any foreigner in possession of information that could be used "to the detriment of the USSR." could be punished by several years in prison, exile, or even death.[63]

---

[57] Matlock, *Reagan and Gorbachev*, 199.
[58] Ibid., 199-200.
[59] Felicity Barringer, "Jailed American Charged in Soviet with Being a Spy," *New York Times*, September 8, 1986, A1.
[60] Gerald Boyd, "Reagan Sees Peril to US-Soviet Ties in Reporter Case," *New York Times*, September 9, 1986, A1.
[61] Shultz, *Turmoil and Triumph*, 735.
[62] Matlock, *Reagan and Gorbachev*, 202.
[63] "The Soviet Law on Spying," *New York Times*, September 8, 1986, A14.

Daniloff unwittingly had become entangled in CIA operations in Moscow as a transmitter of information. A CIA official also identified him during a telephone call the Russians had taped. Thus, even though Daniloff was not spying, he had been caught up in a clandestine web. Worse, Shultz strengthened Moscow's hand by passing a message on to Oleg Sokolov, the Soviet chargé d'affaires in Washington, "about the way the CIA station in Moscow had implicated Daniloff" without his knowledge.[64] Blaming poor CIA spycraft not only tended to alleviate Daniloff's predicament, it also cast Casey in a poor light, something Shultz seemed always eager to do.

On September 12, it was agreed to remand Zakharov and Daniloff to their respective ambassadors, completing the first step in Shultz's plan. Still, even though the stage was set for a resolution of the crisis along the lines of the 1978 precedent, several days passed without any movement. Soviet foreign minister Shevardnadze would be meeting with Shultz on September 19 and to give the Soviets a nudge, the day before he arrived, the administration announced that the United States was expelling twenty-five Russian "spies" from the Soviet UN Mission.

The administration had informed the Soviets in February of the decision to reduce their mission by 25, to a total of 218 by October 1, but had not identified by name those who would have to leave. Now this moment was chosen to do so, partly based upon information gleaned from Zakharov after his arrest. Reportedly, under interrogation "he sang like a tweetie bird," revealing the names of the KGB and GRU station chiefs, who were placed on the list.[65] Shevardnadze immediately howled, warning that "years of 'confrontation and dangerous contention' might be ahead" if the issue was not promptly resolved.[66]

Shevardnadze's visit with Shultz and the president marked the beginning of a ten-day process that not only resolved the Zakharov-Daniloff affair, but also reached agreement for the Reagan-Gorbachev summit that followed. It was clear from that first meeting when the Soviet foreign minister handed the president a letter from Gorbachev that the way was being cleared for a summit.

In the letter, after complaining that the Zakharov-Daniloff affair had been "exaggerated out of all proportion" and noting that the arms control negotiations "will not get anywhere if you and I do not involve ourselves personally," Gorbachev proposed:

> We meet one on one close by . . . in Iceland or in London,
> maybe just for a day, for a completely confidential, closed,

---

[64] Matlock, *Reagan and Gorbachev*, 210. Shultz, *Turmoil and Triumph*, 739, only includes part of this message.

[65] "Admitted Spy Zakharov Named Two High Soviet Agents, US Official Says," *Los Angeles Times*, October 17, 1986, 2.

[66] Bernard Gwertzman, "High Soviet Official Warns US on Ties," *New York Times*, September 19, 1986, A8 and Celestine Bohlen, "Parallel Seen in Response on Daniloff, KAL," *Washington Post*, September 22, 1986, A20.

frank conversation (possibly only in the presence of our ministers of foreign affairs). The result ... would be instructions to our appropriate departments for draft agreements on two or three questions that you and I could sign during my visit to the United States.[67]

Reagan agreed to this proposal, but only on condition that Daniloff be released without trial beforehand. The letter made clear that the Soviet leader was prepared to settle the Zakharov-Daniloff affair on Reagan's terms in order to obtain agreement for a "one on one" meeting. Shultz's reaction, however, was odd. As he saw it, it was only on September 20 that the president and his aides began to realize that the US case on Daniloff was "weak." Paradoxically, he then said, contradicting himself, "that was the day when I finally felt sure that we would resolve the problem on our terms and that we were headed for a summit."[68]

Shultz and Shevardnadze spent the next week meeting in Washington and New York hammering out an agreement whose purpose was to clear the way for a summit meeting. The agreement bore a strong resemblance to the 1978 outcome, but with two added twists. The Soviet Union would permit Daniloff to leave without trial. Zakharov would stand trial, plead no contest, and be expelled. The Soviet Union would permit dissidents Yuri Orlov and his wife to emigrate. That much was quite close to the 1978 precedent.

In this sense, strictly speaking, Daniloff's release was an independent act and Zakharov was traded for the Orlovs. Virtually everyone, however, considered the solution nothing more than a thinly disguised trade. The added twists were that the Soviet Union would accept a reduction in their UN Mission to 218 and the two countries would announce that Reagan and Gorbachev would meet in Reykjavik, Iceland, October 10-12.[69]

Shultz had negotiated through a complicated diplomatic and political thicket in more ways than one. Unnamed administration officials said "key decisions . . . had been made by a small group of senior officials, which did not include Secretary of Defense Casper W. Weinberger, a skeptic on arms control." They said that "all this was done in the closet by three men," the president, Shultz, and Poindexter.[70]

But, while the president and his secretary of state were cooperating in the matter of relations with Moscow, which the president was eager to do, the new world order faction and the president were in sharp conflict at this very same time

---

[67] Matlock, *Reagan and Gorbachev*, 208.

[68] Shultz, *Turmoil and Triumph*, 744.

[69] Ibid., 747. See also Lou Cannon, "Daniloff Freed by Soviets; US to Release Zakharov," *Washington Post*, September 30, 1986, A1; and Gerald Boyd, "Reagan and Gorbachev Agree to Meet Next Week in Iceland; Zakharov, Freed by U.S, Leaves," *New York Times*, October 1, 1986, A1.

[70] Michael Gordon, "US Hopes to Use Meeting in Iceland to Spur Arms Pact," *New York Times*, October 2, 1986, A1.

over the president's initiative toward Iran. At the critical moment, when a breakthrough with Iran appeared imminent, the new world order faction executed a behind-the-scenes move that exposed the president's secret initiative.

Contact with the Second Channel and its Repercussions

Once again, as in late July, the president's men, Poindexter and North, used a meeting with Ghorbanifar and Nir as a cover for meetings with Mahmoud Rafsanjani in early August. North requested travel orders for a trip to Frankfurt on August 6, but got off at Heathrow for meetings in London, instead.[71] There he joined Hakim and Mahmoud Rafsanjani for a meeting on August 7 and met the next day with Cave, Nir and Ghorbanifar. Hakim, meanwhile, went on to Madrid for another meeting with Iranian contacts on the 10th.[72]

North's meeting with Ghorbanifar and Nir (Kangarlu participated again by telephone) produced another sequential delivery plan to gain the release of hostages with an arms deal. Kangarlu complained that numerous items in the spare parts package were deficient, missing, or inoperable. North advised that they hold onto them pending another shipment. In fact, there would be no additional shipments through the Ghorbanifar-Kangarlu channel, as the Second Channel materialized.[73]

Hakim's meetings with representatives of the Second Channel on the other hand brought results. On August 19, Hakim informed North that he had arranged for a meeting with the Second Channel, identified as Ali Bahramani or Mehdi Bahramani, Rafsanjani's eldest son (or nephew, depending on the source). They were to meet in Brussels on August 25. Bahramani said "he had come with instructions to act as an intermediary, and that he was even willing to come to the United States."[74]

Secord and Hakim met with Bahramani for eight hours of discussions that constituted a comprehensive survey of issues, including the Soviet threat, Iran-Iraq war, weapons requirements, and Iran's postwar economic development needs. Secord made it clear that all things were negotiable once the hostage issue was settled and Bahramani expressed confidence that it would be resolved. He also revealed that he knew all about the efforts of Ghorbanifar and Kangarlu, the Israeli connection, and the McFarlane mission, characterizing Ghorbanifar as a "crook." When it was over, Secord reported, "we have opened up a new and probably much better channel into Iran."[75]

---

[71] *Tower Report*, B-148n86.

[72] Samuel Segev, *The Iranian Triangle: The Untold Story of Israel's Role in the Iran-Contra Affair* (New York: Free Press, 1988), 294, 298.

[73] "Next Steps with Iran," North PROF note to Poindexter, September 2, 1986, *Tower Report*, B-150.

[74] Draper, *Very Thin Line*, 399.

[75] "Secord (Copp) to North," August 26, 1986, *Tower Report*, B-149.

While North, Cave, Hakim, and Secord were working clandestinely to establish a Second Channel, it seems that the new world order faction was a step ahead in attempting to preempt them. During the meeting with Bahramani, the Iranian divulged that two groups, led by Alexander Haig and Senator Edward Kennedy, had attempted to meet with him, but he declined, preferring to deal with the president's representatives.[76] This meant that the new world order faction, too, knew the identity of the man code-named the Relative, were tracking his movements, and were trying to prevent a connection to the president.

Thwarted in their efforts at contacting the Iranian leadership, the new world order faction turned to a plan to expose the initiative. The plan was to utilize the DIA's agent and courier network in the Middle East to leak information about McFarlane's secret mission to Tehran. The information included "details of money transfers and bank accounts, with dates and places, most of it based on incidents and conversations that could only have been known to the Iranian or American negotiators."[77]

In Beirut, DIA's Tony Asmar ran an agent network whose main task was to keep track of the whereabouts of the hostages. Lester Coleman was the agent/courier who was tasked with passing him the damning material. To ensure security, the data was incorporated into an electronic chip in a Mattel *Speak'n'Spell* children's toy, which could only be accessed when Coleman and Asmar both typed in special code words.

Coleman, under cover as a TV news cameraman, flew from Washington-Dulles airport on September 4, bound for Heathrow, thence to Larnaca, Cyprus. From Larnaca, he took the ferry to Jounieh, Lebanon, where he met Tony Asmar on Monday, September 8, at his office in Karantina. His instructions were to "sit down with Tony, punch in your code word, he'll punch in his, and you'll retrieve the data we've loaded in. He'll know what to do with it." When they did,

> out poured a detailed account of visits made by Robert
> McFarlane and Lt. Colonel Oliver North to Iran, traveling on
> Irish passports, to organize the sale of TOW missiles and
> launchers to the Iranian government in exchange for the release
> of American hostages.[78]

One of Asmar's men "delivered the *Speak'n'Spell* material to a relative who worked for *Al Shiraa*, Beirut's pro-Syrian, Arabic-language news magazine."[79] The editor of the magazine, Hassan Sabra, a supporter of Iran's deputy supreme leader Ayatollah Hussein Ali Montazeri, sought confirmation of

---

[76] Ibid.

[77] Donald Goddard with Lester Coleman, *Trail of the Octopus* (New York: Signet, 1994), 191.

[78] Ibid., 190-91.

[79] Ibid., 192.

the story from his sources in Tehran.[80] It would take the better part of a month before the new world order faction's time bomb exploded in Tehran and in Lebanon, but by the first week in September, it was ticking. By then, too, every interested party had taken note of and reacted to the opening of the Second Channel.

In fact, Reagan's attempt at secrecy was more honored in the breach than in the observance. Ghorbanifar, Kangarlu, Nir, Prime Minister Peres, and the Russians all responded to the now genuine prospect of Washington's reestablishment of relations with Iran. At the end of the month, a few days after Secord's meeting with Bahramani, Kangarlu passed word to Ghorbanifar that the Americans had opened up a separate channel and that at least one meeting had already been held.[81]

This was devastating news for Ghorbanifar because with no further arms deals, he would have no means of paying off his considerable debt to Khashoggi and other creditors. In fact, Reagan had decided to cut him off unless there was no other alternative. Ghorbanifar would begin to work out a scheme to blackmail the Americans by threatening to expose the initiative. Over the next several weeks he would demand payment of various large sums, ranging from $4 million to $10 million, but for the moment, his immediate reaction was to inform Nir.

Nir, up to this point working on the assumption that the deal sketched out in London in early August was still in the works, quickly arranged to travel to Washington to plead his case. The implication of the new channel was that Israel, too, would be cut out of the operation. This prospect also prompted Prime Minister Peres and Defense Minister Rabin to include the issue as part of their agenda during visits to Washington, September 10 and 15, respectively. Peres would be making his final visit as Prime Minister before handing off the position to Yitzhak Shamir, as per their arrangement two years earlier.

The Russians, of course, had the most to lose. Reestablishment of US-Iran relations would completely defeat the Soviet strategy of drawing Iran into their orbit. Their choice was to promote the taking of another hostage in hopes of driving a wedge between Washington and Tehran. On September 8, a small group of toughs seized Frank Reed, Director of the Lebanese International School, an American institution. Word was put out that Mughniyeh's Islamic Jihad was responsible, but Bahramani quickly called Hakim to convey that "Reed was not, repeat not, held by Islamic Jihad, that no Iranian 'influenced' groups were responsible, and that Iran will do whatever they could [sic] to find him and either

---

[80] Segev, *Iranian Triangle*, 283-86. Segev explains that Montazeri was a bitter opponent of Rafsanjani within the religious establishment, and thus would have an interest in frustrating Rafsanjani's initiatives, including his outreach to the United States. Segev says Montazeri loyalists passed the information about McFarlane's visit to their ally, Hassan Sabra. Coleman, in *Trail of the Octopus*, 192, insists that it was neither the Iranians nor the Russians but he, with his *Speak 'n' Spell,* who, at the behest of the DIA, "blew the whistle on North, McFarlane, and Poindexter."

[81] *Congressional Report on the Iran-Contra Affair*, 251.

return him or tell us where he is being held."[82] American intelligence shortly confirmed that Reed "was taken by elements other than Hizballah—although they may have him in their hands now."[83]

Ironically, Kangarlu also decided to authorize the taking of a hostage, but for the opposite reason. He thought that it would make the Americans more cooperative. On September 12, three men seized Joseph Cicippio, controller of the American University of Beirut, as he walked to work. The group that seized him called itself the Revolutionary Justice Organization. North thought that both Reed and Cicippio were "probably in the hands of Libyan controlled group which earlier bought/killed Kilburn."[84]

American intelligence, monitoring Kangarlu's communication channels, learned that he had authorized the seizure of at least one of the hostages. Contrary to Kangarlu's assumption however, the seizure of new hostages gave the Americans another reason for not dealing with the Ghorbanifar-Kangarlu channel. When Ghorbanifar and Nir called their American contacts, North let them know that "new kidnappings had forced the United States to cut off any new arms shipments." North also hinted that he had "proof" that Kangarlu had been behind at least one of the hostage takings.[85]

As Peres, Rabin, and Nir would be coming to Washington in the second week of September, the president decided on September 8 on "new guidance." He would pursue the Second Channel and cut out Ghorbanifar except as a fallback and provide a full briefing to the Israelis. They remained indispensable as a forward logistical base. Therefore, the president instructed Poindexter and North to express appreciation for their assistance to date, but, given the Iranian antipathy to Israel, the United States would be establishing the relationship directly.[86]

Indeed, while Peres was still in Washington, the president authorized the very bold act of bringing Bahramani to the Capitol on September 19-20. In discussing preparations for the Iranian's trip, the question arose as to when or whether to inform Shultz and the new world order faction. North was still peddling the line to McFarlane that the United States was attempting with difficulty to work out the August 8 deal with the Ghorbanifar-Kangarlu channel.[87]

Casey said that he "planned to tell Shultz in general terms that we were talking to another high level Iranian and that we would fill him in after the interview." North protested, saying that "experience showed that Shultz would

---

[82] "North PROF Note to Poindexter," September 11, 1986, *Tower Report*, B-155. Reed would languish in captivity for three and a half years before being released in May 1990.

[83] Ibid., B-163.

[84] "North PROF Note to Poindexter," October 10, 1986, Ibid., B-167. The Revolutionary Justice Organization also seized the American book salesman Edward Tracy on October 21. They sometimes referred to themselves as Islamic Dawn.

[85] Segev, *Iranian Triangle*, 305-6.

[86] For the "talking points" for Nir, Peres, and Rabin, see *Tower Report*, B-154-56.

[87] "North PROF Note to McFarlane," September 3, 1986, Ibid., B-151.

talk," and eventually word would leak to the press, but Casey was determined. The director may have realized that the secret was already out and failing to inform the new world order faction would only work to their disadvantage.[88]

Washington and Frankfurt

Meanwhile, Secord flew Bahramani and his party from Istanbul to Washington, DC for two days of high-level talks designed to demonstrate sincerity of purpose. Their meetings took place in North's office in the Executive Office Building and Secord's office in Tysons Corner. Cave and Allen also participated. After the conclusion of talks on the first evening, North gave the Iranians a tour of the White House, including the Oval Office, Cabinet Room, and Roosevelt Room. The president was out of town, spending the weekend at Camp David.

Bahramani explained that the majority of Iran's top leadership had agreed to improve relations. The names he mentioned were: Rafsanjani, Rafiq-Dust, Jalali, Mousavi, and Khamenei. Khomeini's son, Ahmed, briefed his father on the progress of the initiative. He did not mention Ayatollah Montazeri, who was known to be viscerally opposed to reopening relations with the United States. Nevertheless, it was significant that the majority of the top Iranian leadership supported this effort.

The talks focused on the establishment of a strategic relationship, but also explored their differences. The two sides disagreed on the Soviet threat. The increase in Soviet aid flowing to Saddam Hussein was the driving force behind Iran's search for a counterweight and the United States sought to parlay Iran's search for weapons into an anti-Soviet stance. The Iranians, however, while seeking weapons, also intended to maintain a middle course, seeing the Russians as neither enemies nor friends.

Similarly, on the Iran-Iraq war, the US side sought neither victory nor defeat for either side; the Iranians wanted "some kind of victory" and the downfall of Saddam. The Americans made no commitment about Saddam, but were willing to meet Iran's practical weapons needs, such as ammunition and replacement barrels for artillery.[89] The Iranians, of course, were playing both sides. While the talks were occurring with Washington, Tehran was engaging in similar high-level discussions with the Russians. Nevertheless, the Americans were impressed with Bahramani's political acumen and sincerity.[90]

Both sides downplayed the hostage obstacle. Bahramani believed that it could be resolved quickly, although he admitted that Iran did not have complete control over the hostage takers. North expressed US willingness to expedite the process with additional arms sales. On Ghorbanifar, North advised that "Iran

---

[88] "North PROF Note to Poindexter," September 17, 1986, Ibid., B-156-57.

[89] Richard Secord and Jay Wurts, *Honored and Betrayed: Irangate, Covert Affairs, and the Secret War in Laos* (New York: Wiley, 1992), 290-91.

[90] Taheri, *Nest of Spies*, 227-28.

should pay him whatever they owe him so he will be quiet," but Bahramani replied "he had received all his money." This surprising reply raised the suspicion, never far from the surface as far as Ghorbanifar was concerned, that he might be attempting to blackmail the United States.[91] He also discouraged further contact with Ghorbanifar on the grounds that they had discovered a KGB agent on Kangarlu's staff.[92]

While no specific agreements were reached, Bahramani had presented an eight-point list of weapons needs and proposed the creation of a commission that would meet secretly in Lisbon or Istanbul to address issues of concern.[93] The main accomplishment had been to establish direct contact and the decision to continue meeting to work out a detailed plan for the development of relations. The American side was unanimous in believing that relations were headed in a very positive direction.

On September 26, as a show of good faith and a down payment on future arms purchases, Bahramani deposited $7 million into the Lake Resources account. North instructed Secord to deposit payment for 500 TOWs and Hawk parts into the CIA's account. No shipment would be made until after another meeting with Bahramani, which would have to include a resolution of the hostage obstacle.[94]

On October 2, Bahramani called Secord requesting that they meet in Frankfurt on the 6th. He claimed there was "now an internal consensus on how to proceed with regard to the hostages 'obstacle.'" Bahramani also indicated that he would be bringing along an official who had been involved in the previous negotiations and a Koran for the president. He asked that North bring a definitive sample of intelligence.[95]

North, Cave, Secord, Dewey Clarridge and Tom Twetten brainstormed a memo titled, "next steps for Iran," in which they devised their negotiating strategy for the Frankfurt meeting and a scheme to pacify the Israelis, i.e., Nir, while still keeping him out of the action. They decided that the intelligence they would provide would be "a mix of factual and bogus information" in hopes of enticing the Iranians to accept a communications team in Tehran that could provide real-time intelligence.[96]

---

[91] Draper, *Very Thin Line*, 410-12. In attempting to reconstruct payments to Ghorbanifar, Casey believed that Iran had paid him $4 million at the end of July, $6 million in early August, and $8 million on August 21. These payments supposedly squared accounts by mutual agreement. See "Casey Memorandum to Poindexter," regarding Roy Furmark's Comments on the Hostage Situation, no date, but probably written on October 23, 1986. *Congressional Report on the Iran-Contra Affair*, Appendix B, vol. 3, 1062-64.

[92] "North PROF Note to Poindexter," September 22, 1986, *Tower Report*, B-158-59.

[93] Secord, *Honored and Betrayed*, 290-91.

[94] "North PROF Note to Poindexter," September 26, 1986, *Tower Report*, B-160.

[95] *Congressional Report on the Iran-Contra Affair*, 253.

[96] "Next Steps for Iran," October 2, 1986, *Tower Report*, B-160-64.

As Bahramani said he was bringing a Koran, North's team decided to reciprocate with a Bible, inscribed by the president. As for Nir, the objective was to relegate him to a supporting role without affecting Israel's important political and operational role. Toward this end, Secord would go to Tel Aviv on the way to the Frankfurt meeting to brief Nir about the second channel but not include him at this stage. He would carry a letter from the president reaffirming the "joint effort" of the two countries.[97]

North, Cave, Secord, and Hakim met Bahramani in Frankfurt on October 6. The first surprise was the official who accompanied him. It was Ali Samii, the Iranian equivalent of a political commissar, who had actually been present in the background of both the February meetings with Ghorbanifar and the Tehran meeting with McFarlane. They had nicknamed him the "Monster," the "Engine," and the "General," because he clearly possessed the authority to make decisions.[98] The two Iranians would adopt the good cop/bad cop approach in negotiations with the Americans.

The second surprise was the admission that despite the so-called "internal consensus" on how to resolve the hostage obstacle, they had no solution. They admitted that they did not in fact control, nor could "100 percent" influence, Mughniyeh, who held Jacobson, Anderson, and Sutherland. They noted that these men were being held in two locations and they could gain the release of one, Jacobson, but not the other two. Furthermore, they had no idea where the two most recent hostages, Reed and Ciccipio, were being held, but it was not by any of their men, or Mughniyeh.

North presented a seven-point proposal, which, although laden with promises of weapons, intelligence, and technical support, had as its initial step the release of all three hostages upon delivery of the first 500 TOWs. It fell like a thud as soon as he put it forth. The evaporation of any prospect for gaining the release of all three hostages may have accounted for North's uncharacteristically grandiose, even shrill, representation of himself as the president's personal aide and confidential adviser as he strove to persuade the Iranians to reconsider.[99]

Instead, Samii proposed his own plan of nine points, which offered the release of one hostage after delivery of the TOWs, but sought to put the United States in the position of negotiating the release of the remaining two hostages by interceding with the Kuwaiti government for the release of the seventeen Al-Dawa prisoners. Three, including Mughniyeh's brother-in-law, Mustafa Badreddine, had been condemned to death. Five had been given four-year sentences, and nine were sentenced to longer terms. Cave claimed that the Iranians were told that the US could do nothing about the three condemned to death, could attempt to ensure that the five with four-year terms were in fact freed on time (sometime in 1987), and perhaps influence the release of two others.[100]

---

[97] Ibid.
[98] Draper, *Very Thin Line,* 420-21.
[99] Ibid., 421ff.
[100] "Cave Deposition," 951-52.

That was difficult enough, but the deal breaker was Samii's demand that the United States and Iran "work within the framework of the Hague settlement process to provide Iran with military items . . . that Iran had paid for . . . but had been embargoed after the Embassy seizure."[101] The "Hague settlement process" was a euphemism for the $12 billion in Iranian assets, including all weapons contracts that the United States had frozen after the embassy seizure in 1979. Implicit in the Iranian proposal was the request that the United States change policy and support Iran against Iraq and reopen the arms spigot full force.

This demand went well beyond North's brief and he pointed out that his seven-point proposal was the president's list. "That's all he authorized . . . . That is everything he authorized me to talk about."[102] North saw the two countries passing each other "like two ships in the night" and was afraid that he had "failed in my mission."[103]

North faced a quandary. He could not agree to negotiate a commitment on behalf of the United States to interfere in the legal processes of an ally, especially to seek the release of convicted terrorists responsible for the deaths of many Americans. Nor did he have any authority to negotiate about Iran's frozen assets or discuss a major change in policy. There can be no doubt that he called Poindexter for advice.

The decision was that discussion about frozen assets and a change of policy were simply ruled out. In order to prevent the negotiation from falling apart entirely, North, a representative of the US government, would extricate himself and permit Hakim and Secord, private citizens, to attempt to find a solution to the Iranian demand that the United States negotiate with the Kuwaiti government.

North's abrupt decision to take himself out of the negotiation and return to Washington has received various explanations. North himself implies that he left because of the controversy that had arisen over the shootdown of a Contra supply plane on October 5, in which the Sandinistas captured the lone survivor, Eugene Hasenfus.[104] He also claims that Secord also departed "to deal with the firestorm."[105] Draper follows this line of argument.[106] Segev says simply that the decision was "hard to explain."[107]

---

[101] *Congressional Report on the Iran-Contra Affair*, 256.

[102] Draper, *Very Thin Line*, 426.

[103] Ibid.

[104] The Hasenfus shootdown is an unresolved mystery. Walsh, *Firewall*, 79, says even after "it was learned from the CIA that the Nicaraguans had anti-aircraft weapons ready for a C-123 flight, William Cooper and Wallace Sawyer were nonetheless ordered to fly the C-123 mission in which they had died and Eugene Hasenfus had been captured." The implication is that they were deliberately sent into harm's way.

[105] Oliver North and William Novak, *Under Fire: An American Story* (New York: Harper Collins, 1991), 296.

[106] Draper, *Very Thin Line*, 427.

[107] Segev, *Iranian Triangle*, 308.

The congressional study states that "North had to return to Washington," without explanation, but does note that he "suggested to the group, 'why don't you guys hold this discussion after I'm gone, O.K.?'"[108] Another curiosity is that all accounts, save one, claim that North, Cave and Secord all left Hakim to continue the negotiations alone, much to the consternation of the Iranians, who did not know how to interpret what had happened.

Secord is the exception, who repudiates all of these accounts. He says that he learned of the shootdown on October 6 and informed North of it as soon as he arrived in Frankfurt that day. "There was nothing either of us could do about it now, especially with a critical meeting coming up, except to stay informed and pray that our local people could keep the thing contained."[109] Thus, North knew of the Hasenfus shootdown before the meeting with the Iranians began and it was unlikely that it was the reason for his abrupt departure a day later.

Secord also states unequivocally that while he did excuse himself briefly to change plane reservations, he returned to join Hakim in the negotiation. He also addresses the Al-Dawa 17 issue, stating that instead of the US government becoming directly involved, the solution was for the United States to offer a plan for the phased release of the prisoners, which Iran would take as their own and present to Kuwait. The United States would mediate, but not be directly involved. The Iranians "accepted" this plan.[110]

Hakim, Secord, Samii and Bahramani worked out a 9-point plan that was sent to North just as he was arriving in Washington. Known as "Hakim's plan," North obtained approval of it from Poindexter, Casey, and Twetten. The president, too, approved those parts of the plan "that applied to the US government," that is, *excluding* the plan to influence the Kuwaiti government.[111] As reworked by North, the plan provided for the following:

The Iranians would pay $3.6 million for 500 TOWs, which the US would deliver nine days after payment. Secord and Hakim would "help prepare a plan for approaching the Kuwaitis to guarantee no more terrorism against the Amir and by which the Amir will use a religious occasion to release some of the Al-Dawa. They will take this plan to the Hizballah as their idea (face saving gesture with the Hizb)." One and possibly two hostages would be released within four days of TOW delivery. If only one "whole process stops and we meet again." If two, then deliveries of additional TOWs, technical support, intelligence, etc., would commence.[112]

The plan as reworked left out any mention of the Hague settlement process, identified only TOWs for delivery and possibly Hawk spare parts, but made no reference to Bahramani's eight-point weapons list. It also identified

---

[108] *Congressional Report on the Iran-Contra Affair*, 256.

[109] Secord, *Honored and Betrayed*, 295.

[110] Ibid., 300-01.

[111] *Congressional Report on the Iran-Contra Affair*, 258 and Draper, *Very Thin Line*, 434-35.

[112] *Congressional Report on the Iran-Contra Affair*, 257-58.

Hakim and Secord—not the United States government—as being responsible for the plan for addressing the Al-Dawa 17 problem with Kuwait.[113] Finally, the plan called for the release of "some" of the Al-Dawa prisoners, not all of them.

The Iranians apparently privately insisted that the United States become involved directly with the Kuwaiti government over the Al-Dawa 17 issue. However, the United States made clear its position in "press guidance" issued from the White House on October 14, ostensibly in response to a *Newsweek* magazine article speculating about a trade of Al-Dawa prisoners for American hostages. "We will not negotiate the exchange of innocent Americans for . . . convicted murderers held in a third country, nor will we pressure other nations to do so."[114]

Although appearing definitive, this formula was quite close to that used to resolve the TWA 847 hostage incident that became known as the "no-deal deal," in which the United States in fact looked the other way as Israel released prisoners and Mughniyeh released passengers. Implicit was the prospect of another no-deal deal, but that was not to be.

What was also omitted was a response to the Iranian request that the United States change policy. The decision to focus narrowly on arms and hostages would have a predictable result. In less than a month the president's Iran initiative would come crashing down, the result of an exposure of its secret negotiations. In the meantime, the president was off to Reykjavik, Iceland for what was supposed to be a tête-à-tête preparatory meeting with Gorbachev, but what turned out to be potentially the most far-reaching deal in the history of US-Soviet relations.

---

[113] When the crisis broke in November, North blamed Hakim for the Al-Dawa arrangement, while Poindexter blamed Secord. See Draper, *Very Thin Line*, 434.
[114] Ibid.

Chapter 17

The Collapse of Reagan's Strategy

From the first week in October 1986 through the end of the month, in the context of a heated mid-term congressional election campaign, the president's strategy began to collapse like a slow-motion train wreck. The downing of the Contra supply plane and the subsequent claim of the lone survivor, Eugene Hasenfus, that the aircraft was part of an illegal, CIA-run operation began a slowly building crisis, led by congressional Democrats. The crisis was first muted by the focus on the Reykjavik summit, which seemed to offer promise, but then produced no agreement. Negotiations with the Iranians in late October also seemed at first to show promise but led nowhere. By the end of the month the administration seemed to be in a state of suspended animation.

The No-Summit Summit at Reykjavik

There was a deeper significance to the meeting at Reykjavik than met the eye. In remarks before the meeting, the president said that it was to be a "planning session" to prepare for Gorbachev's visit to Washington, either later in 1986, or in 1987, "a base camp before the summit," Reagan called it. He played down expectations for an arms control agreement and, instead, said he would "press" Gorbachev on human rights issues and regional conflicts, like Afghanistan.[1] In fact, however, the president planned a major démarche that would focus almost exclusively on arms control, and involve a proposed fundamental change of strategy. In short, the president sought to surprise Gorbachev with a proposal to bring about the end of the Cold War on his terms.

The meeting at Reykjavik was the culmination of a two-year-long negotiation that resembled a high-stakes card game, in which each leader attempted to outbid and/or bluff the other into submission. But in this game, Gorbachev was running out of chips. Reagan's strategy of promoting low energy costs had jump-started the American economy as well as those of Western Europe, Japan, and also China, while continuing to depress earnings for the Soviet Union, which depended heavily upon oil and gas exports for revenue. The costs to Moscow of maintaining its very large military infrastructure, its alliances, and far-

---

[1] Lou Cannon, "Reagan Vows to Pursue Human Rights, Regional Issues with Gorbachev," *Washington Post*, October 7, 1986, A1.

flung commitments around the globe were escalating beyond the Soviet Union's ability to pay.

In his July 25 letter proposing a shift to the strategic defensive, Reagan had offered Gorbachev a fundamental way out of the cul-de-sac into which the Soviet Union was heading. As Gorbachev well understood, the Reagan military modernization program had effectively neutralized Moscow's leverage against the United States and the Pershing II deployment eliminated it in Europe. Even though the actual numbers of weapons still favored the Soviet Union, the momentum clearly was with the United States.

Reagan's proposed abandonment of the doctrine of mutual assured destruction and adoption of a new strategy based on strategic defense offered Gorbachev the opportunity to eliminate the crippling costs of maintaining its massive, yet increasingly dysfunctional, strategic weapons arsenal designed to exert leverage on the United States and its European and Asian neighbors. Adoption of a defensive strategy would allow Gorbachev to shift scarce resources to needed modernization and developmental ends.

It was, therefore, with a high degree of anticipation that the president awaited Gorbachev's response to his proposal. The key questions were: did the Soviet leader have the wit, courage, and political power to make a truly historic decision to accept Reagan's proposed change of strategy? When his answer came, during their very first session at Reykjavik, it was clear that Gorbachev would not accept the president's offer. He strove to maintain the Soviet Union's strategic weapons advantage, regain lost leverage over Europe, retain it in Asia, and prevent the United States from moving onto the path of strategic defense.

Once it was clear that Gorbachev was bent upon maximizing Soviet advantage within the existing strategy of mutual assured destruction, Reagan shifted his approach, attempting to get what he could with respect to weapons reductions while keeping open the prospect of moving onto his preferred strategy based on strategic defense, with or without the Soviet Union.

Despite all the hoopla about reducing and even eliminating nuclear weapons as a threat to world peace, Gorbachev came to Reykjavik with the objective of maintaining the Soviet Union's advantages at the strategic and intermediate levels. His scheme was to offer even greater reductions than before in return for Reagan's abandonment or neutering of SDI. His intentions became obvious at their very first session, where Gorbachev presented a package of proposals that amounted to a response to Reagan's July 25 letter.[2]

In the July letter Reagan had reiterated the agreement reached at Geneva for a 50 percent reduction in strategic arsenals, but with a new twist, now specifically focusing on reducing "strategic ballistic missile warheads." He also offered to limit air-launched cruise missiles below current plans and reduce the total number of inter-continental ballistic missiles, submarine-launched ballistic

---

[2] For a brilliant synthesis of the Reykjavik meeting, see Walter Pincus, "Reagan's 'Dream' Was to Eliminate Ballistic Missiles," *Washington Post*, October 14, 1986, A1.

missiles, and heavy bombers "to a level on the range suggested by the Soviet side." Gorbachev's response was to agree to a minimum of 50 percent reduction in strategic offensive forces, especially the Soviet Union's heavy missiles and the United States' submarine-launched ballistic missiles.[3]

On Intermediate-range forces, Reagan had proposed to begin immediate reductions with the goal of the total elimination of intermediate-range nuclear missiles "worldwide," also referred to as a "global solution," by which he meant Europe and Asia. Gorbachev proposed the "complete elimination" of intermediate-range missiles from Europe, but not in Asia. In what he said was a major concession, he announced that the Soviet Union would disregard the missile forces of Britain and France and in return asked that the United States "withdraw the question of Soviet medium-range missiles in Asia," about which he was prepared to begin negotiations as reductions in Europe commenced.

Reagan had proposed that once the two countries had "achieved a 50% reduction in . . . strategic nuclear missiles" and "[were making] progress in eliminating long-range INF missiles, we would continue to pursue negotiations for further stabilizing reductions. The overall aim should be the elimination of all nuclear weapons." Gorbachev was silent about future negotiations for "further stabilizing reductions," and the goal of total "elimination of all nuclear weapons," but offered to freeze and begin negotiations on missiles "with a range of less than 1,000 km," a category of weapons Reagan had not mentioned in his letter.

Reagan's proposal had not included a time period for the reduction of offensive missiles but did for missile defense. He had proposed a five-year period in which both sides could carry out research, development, and testing, as permitted by the ABM Treaty, to determine feasibility of concept. If feasible, they would negotiate for an additional two years a treaty to share the developed technology, provided "there is mutual agreement to eliminate the offensive ballistic missiles of both sides." If that failed, then either side could give six months' notice and be free to deploy missile defense.

Gorbachev's counterproposal to Reagan's seven-and-a-half-year program was to "strengthen" the ABM Treaty and make it "timeless." He wanted adherence to the Treaty for ten years, with no right of withdrawal, after which the two sides would commence a negotiation for three to five more years when both sides would "decide what to do," in effect giving the Soviet Union a permanent veto.

Development and testing of SDI components would be confined to laboratories with "prohibition of outside-of-laboratory testing of means intended

---

[3]"Reagan to Gorbachev, July 25, 1986," online at The Reagan Files, https://www.thereaganfiles.com/19860725.pdf.
Gorbachev's response is taken from Document 10, "Russian Transcript of Reagan-Gorbachev Summit in Reykjavik, October 11, 1986 (Morning)," *The Reykjavik File*, The National Security Archive, George Washington University, https://nsarchive2.gwu.edu/NSAEBB/NSAEBB203/index.htm. [Hereafter cited as *Reykjavik File*.]

for space-based destruction of objects in space and on earth." There would, however, be no prohibition on "testing permitted under the ABM Treaty, i.e., testing of stationary ground-based systems and their components." It would also be necessary, Gorbachev said, to "prohibit anti-satellite means" because "if this were not done, then in the course of creating anti-satellite means it would be possible to develop antimissile weapons."

Gorbachev's determination to constrain or neuter SDI was actually a desperate attempt to close two growing loopholes in the ABM Treaty that had emerged since 1972 contained in Article IV and Agreed Statement D. Agreed Statement D stated that "in the event ABM systems based on other physical principles . . . are created in the future, specific limitations on such systems and their components would be subject for discussion." Article IV stipulated that the treaty's limitations "shall not apply to ABM systems or their components used for development or testing . . . within current or additionally agreed test ranges."[4]

The "future" mentioned in Agreed Statement D had arrived. The two loopholes meant that the United States (and also the Soviet Union) could develop and test current or future ABM systems at test ranges. There was, however, no definition of what constituted a test range. Moreover, there was no requirement to discuss limitations on "systems based on other physical principles" until a "system" had been created. As the United States had not yet developed and tested a "system," as Gorbachev acknowledged, there was nothing yet to discuss. This explained Gorbachev's determination to prevent testing "means," i.e. components, in space and confine testing to laboratories. His fixation on SDI was implicit recognition that the Soviets believed the United States was developing a missile defense in space based on "other physical principles."[5]

Reagan commented briefly on Gorbachev's package of proposals at the end of the morning session, but his full response would come only after he had consulted with his aides. Immediately after the morning session, when Shultz and the president gathered with their advisers in the secure bubble set up to prevent eavesdropping, the usually taciturn Shultz giddily described Gorbachev's proposals as laying "gifts at our feet." The president, however, was less sanguine, saying that Gorbachev had "brought a whole lot of proposals, but I'm afraid he's going after SDI."[6]

---

[4] Gerard Smith, *Doubletalk: The Story of SALT I* (New York: Doubleday, 1980), 489, 495.

[5] Many, if not most, US arms control specialists, including Paul Nitze, tended to argue that most SDI technology did come under the category of "other physical principles." See Paul Nitze et al., *From Hiroshima to Glasnost* (New York: G. Weidenfeld, 1989), 472-73.

[6] Jay Winik, *On the Brink* (New York: Simon & Schuster, 1996), 505. George Shultz, *Turmoil and Triumph* (New York: Scribner, 1993), 760-61, also describes this scene, but leaves out the president's remark about SDI.

The Second Meeting

Reagan decided to obtain agreement on arms reductions first and then try to persuade Gorbachev that his strategy of a transition to defense was in both countries' interest. When the afternoon session began, Reagan immediately declared, "reductions are the highest priority" and the "heart of the matter is reducing ballistic missile warheads." For its part, he continued, the United States was "prepared for appropriate corresponding reductions in all ballistic missile systems," as well as air-launched cruise missiles (ALCMs) and bombers.[7]

He was, however, disappointed by Gorbachev's INF proposal, which by failing to include zero for Asia, represented a "step backward" from his September letter. Indeed, the president "had thought we had agreed to pursue an interim global agreement" and insisted that the "issue must be dealt with on a global basis." After some discussion, the president said, "so let's agree to have 100 units [missiles] each in Europe and Asia, and then we will be making some headway."[8]

Reagan welcomed the fact that Gorbachev raised the issue of shorter-range missiles and the readiness to freeze them. "You and I can agree to instruct our diplomats to coordinate on the matter of limiting lesser-range missiles within the framework of an interim agreement." We can also agree on verification measures, including exchange of data and on-site inspections. Finally, he proposed to instruct our diplomats to formulate a "legally binding" INF treaty, which will limit these systems while negotiators reach agreement on further reductions of them.

Having expressed his interest in reaching agreement on missile reductions, the president turned to SDI. Saying that he had taken Gorbachev's concerns into account in his July 25 letter, Reagan "proposed a mechanism by which we could move toward a regime based on high reliance upon defense." This would not replace the ABM Treaty, although as a result of our negotiations "new provisions . . . would replace some provisions of the ABM Treaty." His proposal envisaged a stable, verifiable "transition . . . to a new balance of offensive and defensive weapons, and later on, to elimination of offensive ballistic missiles."[9] In other words, the president was proposing a new relationship in which neither power could attack the other with ballistic missiles.

He forcefully denied the notion that "space-based weapons could be used to destroy targets on the ground," noting "we already have an agreement prohibiting deployment of mass destruction weapons in space." Besides, the ICBM was the most effective and reliable weapon to strike targets on earth. He also denied that the United States could carry out a first strike and use its defense

---

[7] *Reykjavik File*, Document 11, "US Memorandum of Conversation, Second Reykjavik meeting, October 11, 1986."

[8] *Reykjavik File*, Document 12, "Russian Transcript of Reagan-Gorbachev Summit in Reykjavik, October 11, 1986 (Afternoon)." The US translation is less precise than the Russian here, failing to mention the September letter, or the phrase "step backward."

[9] Ibid., 2.

to prevent retaliation. "We do not have the capability for carrying out a first strike," he said.[10]

However, Reagan continued, Gorbachev's concerns had led him to "propose a treaty now which would lead to the elimination of all offensive ballistic missiles. Once we do that, the issue of a combination of offensive and defensive forces giving one side or the other an advantage would not arise."[11] With this formulation the president had subtly reversed the position he had taken in their morning session. Then, he had argued that SDI would make missile reductions possible. Now, he said that the elimination of ballistic missiles would make SDI possible.

Missile defense, the president said, would reinforce stability at lower cost, "protect each of us against cheating," and against the missiles of third countries. We were even prepared to "share the benefits of strategic defense" and were willing to "agree now to a Treaty committing to do so in conjunction with the elimination of ballistic missiles." But, he concluded, Gorbachev's proposal for a test ban was a non-starter. "Neither a test moratorium nor a comprehensive test ban is in the cards for the foreseeable future," although he was prepared to fix the defects in the verification protocols of the Threshold Test Ban Treaty and the Peaceful Nuclear Explosions Treaty signed, but not ratified, a decade earlier.

Then, it was Gorbachev's turn and he tried to pin the president down to specific commitments. First, he attempted to obtain Reagan's agreement to the transparently unfair 50% cut of nuclear weapons "across the board," acknowledging that "the structure will remain the same, but the level would be lower." Reagan at first said "this should be taken up by the experts," but then observed that although he himself "did not have all the numbers . . . he did know that the Soviets outnumber us by a lot. If we cut 50%, they would still have more than we do."

Gorbachev pressed the president to make a commitment on the spot, saying "this is not a matter for the experts." He handed the president a sheet of weapons data and said, "here is the data, let us cut this in half." Reagan said, "the idea was interesting," but he would have to "give the US side a chance," meaning to give the experts a chance to review it. Shultz chimed in on Gorbachev's side to say, "it was a bold idea, and we need bold ideas." "Gorbachev agreed that this was what we need." By this time, Reagan had recovered and asked Gorbachev again "if he agreed to his proposal for a meeting of experts" and Gorbachev, realizing that he had failed to bulldoze the president into an unwise decision, agreed.[12]

On INF, Gorbachev asked the president three times whether he accepted the zero option for Europe and Reagan replied "yes" each time but insisted that any solution had to be "global" to include Europe and Asia. Finally, Gorbachev

---

[10] Ibid.

[11] *Reykjavik File*, Document 11, "US Memorandum of Conversation, Reagan-Gorbachev, Second Meeting, October 11, 1986."

[12] Ibid.

asked: "if we find a solution on Asian missiles, do you accept zero in Europe?" Reagan's affirmative response sent this issue, too, off to the experts for resolution.

It was obvious that Gorbachev's primary objective on INF was the removal of the Pershing II missiles from West Germany, but his newfound reticence on zero for Asia was somewhat puzzling. It was equally obvious that the SS-20s were mobile missiles, which could be moved from Asia to threaten Europe in the future after the Pershing IIs had been withdrawn; but their presence also complicated Soviet prospects for any improvement of relations with China and Japan.

Gorbachev argued that they should work toward a total ban on nuclear testing, but in stages. "In the first stage," they could consider reducing yields, the number of tests, and the future of the treaties. "It would be clear movement had begun toward a total ban, at some stage." Reagan thought this proposal "interesting" and said that "their people should take it up."

Coming to his main argument, Gorbachev said that if we were going to "reduce strategic missiles and eliminate medium-range missiles," how could we abandon the ABM Treaty? It was "only logical" to strengthen the treaty by agreeing not to withdraw from it while "large-scale reductions would be taking place." "Otherwise, one side could believe that the other was doing something behind its back." Furthermore, his proposal to confine research to the laboratory was really "accommodating to the US side." It would enable the US "to see whether it wanted a full-scope three-echelon strategic defense or something else."

At this point, Reagan dropped a bombshell, saying that "with the progress we are making we do not need 10 years. He could not have said that a few years ago . . . [but] we do not think it will take that long. Progress is being made." Gorbachev was taken aback. After declaring that the Soviets were "not going to proceed with strategic defense themselves," an astounding remark given the extensive work the US knew the Russians were conducting on defense, including the phased-array radar at Krasnoyarsk, he then said he "took note of the president's statement that less than 10 years would be needed." He quickly moved to end the session. "Let us turn our experts loose to work . . . . The two of us have said a lot. Let them go to work now."

But Reagan wasn't quite ready to stop. Noting that they had been "so wrapped up" in arms matters that "they had not touched on regional, or bi-lateral, or human-rights issues," he proposed they set up a separate expert group for these issues. Gorbachev readily agreed. As they were finishing, Reagan noted that Gorbachev had said the Soviets would not develop strategic defense. If the Soviets come up with a better solution than SDI, "maybe they can give us theirs."

Gorbachev replied that their solution "would not be better, but different." Evading an answer to the question about sharing their solution with the United States, Gorbachev declared that he could not take Reagan's proposal about sharing SDI technology "seriously." As the United States was unwilling to share even the simplest technology, including milk factories, with the Soviet Union, he thought it would require "a second American revolution" to share missile defense technology, which "would not happen." [13]

The Experts' All-Nighter

If the Americans did not realize what Soviet strategy was after the first day—and Shultz's remark about Gorbachev "laying gifts at our feet" and Reagan's about his "going after" SDI suggest that they did not—the all-night session by the "experts" made it abundantly clear. They were now, as Shultz notes, in a full-fledged negotiation. [14] The experts were divided into two groups, one devoted to the arms control issues discussed thus far, and another to discuss regional, bilateral, and human rights issues. Paul Nitze and Sergei Akhromeyev led the former group; Rozanne Ridgway and Alexander Bessmertnykh the latter. [15] The appearance of Akhromeyev, chief of the Soviet general staff, surprised the Americans, who had not expected a military man to be there, let alone be involved in the negotiations. In fact, he was the chief negotiator. [16] The two groups met at eight o'clock that evening. The arms control group wrestled all night with the main issues Reagan and Gorbachev had discussed, not ending their discussions until six o'clock in the morning. The Ridgway-Bessmertnykh group wrapped up their discussions shortly after midnight. As Matlock, a participant in the Ridgway group saw it, they made "little progress" beyond compiling a "list of cooperative projects that might be undertaken." [17] Although neither group made breakthroughs, the Soviets made plain their determination to continue with the strategy laid out by Gorbachev.

Akhromeyev followed Gorbachev's lead in attempting to gain acceptance of the 50 percent cut, category by category. In any percentage arms reduction scheme, the Soviets, as Reagan observed, would emerge with the advantage because of the larger overall numbers of weapons in its arsenal. The Russians held a 9,000 to 7,000 advantage in overall weapons. Nitze countered by proposing "equal numerical end levels." Eventually, Akhromeyev accepted the

---

[13] Ibid.

[14] Shultz, *Turmoil and Triumph*, 762.

[15] In Nitze's group were Richard Perle, Max Kampelman, Mike Glitman, Ronald Lehman, Henry Cooper, Bob Linhard, Adm. Jonathan Howe, General Ed Rowny, and Ken Adelman. In Akhromeyev's group were: Victor Karpov, Valentin Fallin, Evgeni Velikhov, Georgi Arbatov, and Yuli Dubinin.

[16] Both Rowny and Shultz claim that Akhromeyev told them the identical story about being the "last of the Mohicans," a reference to James Fennimore Cooper's book. Either Akhromeyev told them the same story, or one of the authors is mistaken. As Rowny spoke Russian and Shultz did not, the likelihood is that Akhromeyev told Rowny the story during an off moment, as he claims. See Edward L. Rowny, *It Takes One to Tango* (Washington: Brassey's, 1992), 184, and Shultz, *Turmoil and Triumph*, 763.

[17] Jack Matlock, *Reagan and Gorbachev* (New York: Random House, 2004), 223.

equal end levels formula of 6,000 weapons and 1,600 delivery systems, but he had a fallback plan.[18]

While an arms reduction formula calling for equal numerical end levels would benefit the Russians less, they would still benefit because of the throw weight superiority of their heavy weapons and the sheer reduction in the number of US targets. To counter this, Nitze proposed sub-limits on categories to prevent a preponderance of weapons in a given category, but Akhromeyev refused to consider sub-limits. It was obvious that the Russians were determined to maintain strategic weapons advantage at whatever level of weapons was decided upon. As with all areas of disagreement, Nitze reserved the right to raise the issue again at the Geneva negotiations.

On INF, Akhromeyev also followed Gorbachev's lead, proposing zero for Europe and refusing even to discuss reductions in Asia. As Rowny noted, the Soviet general used an American expression to make clear he was not authorized to discuss Asian limits, saying "that decision can only be made by someone above my pay grade."[19] It would be up to Gorbachev to make that call. The Soviet objective was to obtain the complete removal of the Pershing IIs, while retaining some mobile SS-20s in Asia.

On SDI, Akhromeyev reiterated Gorbachev's pitch that research and testing be confined to the "laboratory." Nitze proposed that they compose a memorandum, laying out their areas of disagreement: specifically, on the length of the non-withdrawal period from the ABM Treaty and what was permitted during and after withdrawal. However, Akhromeyev refused even to agree on "how we disagreed."[20]

Nitze raised the subject of nuclear testing and presented a proposal that tied "step by step limitations on nuclear testing" to "reduction and elimination of nuclear weapons." Akhromeyev responded by proposing a "full ban on nuclear testing," without a link to weapons reductions. Soviet skepticism was evident in Georgi Arbatov's reaction to Nitze's expressed interest in the "complete liquidation of nuclear testing," when he said it would happen "in 100 years."[21] On the matter of a nuclear test ban, it seemed, both sides were bluffing. Everyone knew that to end testing meant the certain atrophy of nuclear weapons.

On INF it was the same. Zero for Europe meant the elimination of *Pershing II* and SS-20s positioned against each other, but the refusal to consider reductions in Asia meant that the Soviet Union would still have SS-20s deployed

---

[18] *Reykjavik File*, Document 17, "Russian Transcript of Negotiations in the Working Group on Military Issues, October 11-12, 1986." See also Nitze, *From Hiroshima to Glasnost*, 430. Edward Rowny, *It Takes One to Tango* (Washington, D.C.: Brassey's, 1992), 182, says Akhromeyev proposed the formula.

[19] Rowny, *It Takes One to Tango*, 185.

[20] Nitze, *From Hiroshima to Glasnost*, 432.

[21] *Reykjavik File*, Document 17, "Russian Transcript of Negotiations in the Working Group on Military Issues [. . .]."

and the United States would have no countervailing weapon, if the mobile SS-20s were subsequently moved within range of Western Europe.

The Soviet approach to SDI was double-barreled. Not only did Gorbachev demand an indefinite veto over an American decision to deploy missile defense years in the future, he also wanted to prevent any possibility of testing SDI components in space, which the ABM Treaty permitted. Here, on the pretext of "strengthening" the treaty, he was in fact demanding that it be rewritten to Soviet advantage.

Day Two, the Games Begin

When the two leaders reconvened Sunday morning for what was scheduled to be their final meeting it was apparent that Reagan had decided on a subtle shift in his negotiating strategy, perhaps recognizing that Gorbachev was not going to budge. When briefed before the meeting about the all-night negotiations, according to Rowny, the president was "delighted that progress had been made on START and was particularly pleased with the Soviet INF offer."[22]

When he began the meeting with Gorbachev, however, he professed dissatisfaction with the negotiators' efforts. It was part of the act. In fact, Reagan put a positive spin on their work, even though there had been no positive result. He hoped that by agreeing to nearly everything Gorbachev wanted he would persuade him to relent on his demands on SDI. Ironically, Gorbachev had decided to adopt the same strategy, but hoped for the opposite outcome, that Reagan would agree to constraints on SDI.

Reviewing the night's work of the arms control team the president said he was "disappointed with what had been achieved." However, it was his "understanding that the working group had been able to agree on a formulation for the outlines of a 50% reduction of strategic arsenals that should move the negotiations substantially ahead." On INF, after lecturing Gorbachev at length on the long-held US position, which Gorbachev knew well, of the need for a global solution, the president said that "in the right context we could accept 100 in Europe and 100 in Asia" and offered to "settle now" on that formula "and instruct our negotiators to work out details."[23]

On defense and space, Reagan acknowledged that they were at an impasse, but suggested that "to move our positions closer together," they should relegate the topic to their negotiators and instruct them to focus on three issues: first, to "synchronize" an investigation of strategic defense with their "shared goals of eliminating ballistic missiles"; second, to examine the timeframe for a transition to strategic defense; and third, to determine what "common understandings might be reached" for testing of advanced strategic defenses under the ABM Treaty. Reagan's proposal was to direct their negotiators to do what he

---

[22] Rowny, *It Takes One to Tango*, 186.
[23] *Reykjavik File*, Document 15, "US Memorandum of Conversation, Reagan-Gorbachev Final Meeting, October 12, 1986," 1-2.

and Gorbachev would not—determine how and when and under what conditions the two powers could shift to strategic defense.[24]

On the question of nuclear testing, Reagan made a 180-degree reversal of position, although carefully camouflaging the change by criticizing the negotiators' "lack of imagination." Where he had earlier declared to Gorbachev that any test ban was "not in the cards," he now agreed to begin "immediate negotiation on testing issues." When an undoubtedly privately alarmed Gorbachev asked, "what [do] you have in mind," Reagan read from the paper Nitze presented the night before:[25]

> The US and Soviet Union will begin negotiations on nuclear testing. The agenda will be . . . first to resolve remaining verification issues associated with existing treaties. With this resolved, the US and USSR will immediately proceed, in parallel with the reduction and elimination of nuclear weapons, to address further step-by-step limitations on testing, leading ultimately to the elimination of nuclear testing.[26]

To say Gorbachev was taken aback would be an understatement. Reagan had not only called his bluff; he raised the ante. By formally proposing to tie the end of nuclear testing to reductions in weapons inventories he was laying out a plan for the early end to their programs. This was anathema to Gorbachev. Therefore, the Soviet leader did not reply directly to the president's new proposal, but, instead, began a lengthy review of where things stood, emphasizing the "major concessions" he had made and demanding that the president reciprocate. It was a "dangerous mistake," he averred, to think that the Soviets needed nuclear disarmament more than the United States does; that "if you put a little pressure on the Soviet Union it will raise its hand and surrender . . . . It is not going to happen."[27]

---

[24] Ibid., 3.

[25] Ibid., and Document 14, "Russian Transcript of Reagan-Gorbachev Summit in Reykjavik, October 12, 1986 (Morning)," 2.

[26] *Reykjavik File*, Document 15, "US memorandum of Conversation, Reagan-Gorbachev, Final Meeting, October 12, 1986," 4. The Russian transcript (Document 16) is significantly different. "The United States and the USSR begin negotiations on questions of nuclear testing. Their agenda will include all aspects of nuclear testing, including the unresolved questions, existing treaties, monitoring, limits on the power of explosives, and others. These talks could occur together with stage-by-stage elimination of nuclear weapons and would ultimately lead to stopping nuclear testing." In the US version, limiting testing was to proceed "in parallel" with weapons reductions. In the Soviet version, testing limitation "could occur together with stage-by-stage elimination of nuclear weapons."

[27] *Reykjavik File*, Document 14, "Russian Transcript of Reagan-Gorbachev Summit in Reykjavik, October 12, 1986 (Morning)."

We took US concerns into consideration, he said, when we agreed that the "principle of 50% reductions should apply to all components of strategic forces, both platforms and warheads."[28] On INF, he probed again for the elimination of the Pershing II from Europe, asking," if we could find a concrete solution to the problem of intermediate-range missiles in Asia . . . you would agree to complete elimination of Soviet and American missiles, to a zero-level solution in Europe?"

Reagan would not agree to remove all of the Pershing II missiles in Europe as long as SS-20s remained in Asia. He asserted that with zero in Europe "it is not hard for you to move [SS-20s] from one place to another." You would have, he said, "an absolute advantage because we would have no deterrent in Europe." Trying to browbeat Reagan, Gorbachev said, "you appear to have forgotten the existence of English and French nuclear forces . . . . When we talk about a zero level for Europe, we are in fact talking about a zero level for ourselves."

As for moving Asian SS-20s, he said disparagingly, "I actually find it a little awkward to hear that in a conversation on our level." We could include treaty text that says, "the transfer of just one missile from Asia to Europe would be grounds for abrogation of the treaty." This was a semantic evasion. He knew that it was not necessary to transfer SS-20s "to Europe" for them to be in range of Europe, but he thought he could shame Reagan into buying his argument.

On the ABM Treaty, Gorbachev wanted to strengthen the treaty to ensure that while "unprecedented" reductions in strategic and intermediate missiles were occurring neither side would be "doing anything behind the back" of the other. Thus, he reiterated his insistence that both sides agree to a ten-year non-withdrawal commitment from the treaty and that the United States agree to confine all SDI testing to the "laboratory." Gorbachev wanted to have it both ways. While implying that the United States might do something "behind the back" of the Soviet Union to gain an advantage, he was offended by any suggestion that Moscow might do the same.

Reagan could not understand Gorbachev's objection to missile defense after the two sides had eliminated their missiles. They would obviously not need a defense against each other, but only against third parties, unless, of course the Russians cheated. He explained again that he was committed to the full exploration of missile defense but was willing to commit to a treaty obligation to share the technology with the Soviet Union, if it proved fruitful. All this could be made part of the ABM Treaty, strengthening it.

After going around and around with no give on either side, Gorbachev finally replied to Reagan's proposal about nuclear testing, but claimed that the president's proposal was one-sided. "You suggest talking about the problem of testing, but not about conducting negotiations on a complete end to testing." In fact, Reagan had proposed "the elimination of nuclear testing," but Gorbachev

---

[28] Ibid.

was intent upon separating the testing question from reduction of weapons. Gorbachev invited the president to comment, employing an American saying that "it takes two to tango."

Recalling the historical record when "the Soviet side used the period of the moratorium to prepare to create new types of nuclear weapons," Reagan insisted that "proper control" was necessary. "Only after finishing the development of controls will we be ready to stop testing." There was a good American saying that reflected this caution, he said, "once burned twice shy." At this, Reagan repeated his proposal tying testing stoppage with weapons reductions, but Gorbachev peremptorily declared, "that wording does not suit us" and proposed to set it aside by "having our experts sit down and work out a formula."

After this exchange, which clearly demonstrated Gorbachev's disinclination to accept the president's formula, their discussion became disorganized, seeming to move randomly from obscure topic to obscure topic. They discussed their respective national political systems, philosophies, political parties, movies, trade, and human rights, in a desultory fashion. In response to Gorbachev's claim that "the possibilities of agreement are exhausted," Reagan replied, "it seems to me that we have agreement on nuclear testing." But Shevardnadze immediately spoke up to turn the discussion away from testing. "I would still like to return to the question of the ABM Treaty," he said, and Gorbachev immediately seized on that idea.

Gorbachev declared that his proposals were "a definite package and would ask you to consider it as such." Reagan's plea that there need not be a "link" between offensive reductions and the ABM Treaty fell on deaf ears. Finally, observing that "X-hour is approaching," Gorbachev said "maybe, if the president does not object, we will declare a break for 1-2 hours" and let our ministers try to propose something. Thus, ended the morning session.[29]

The Focal Point Is SDI

Secretary Shultz and Foreign Minister Shevardnadze and selected aides met to try to "propose something." Shultz attempted to raise the issue of nuclear testing, remarkably claiming that he thought it was a "solvable drafting problem," but Shevardnadze promptly cut him off. "Almost taunting" Shultz, he asserted that "the Soviets had made all the concessions . . . . Now, it was our turn." Everything, he said, depended on "how to handle SDI."[30]

Bob Linhard and Richard Perle, sitting at the other end of the table, were prepared, having spent part of the previous evening discussing with Poindexter and Shultz a possible compromise based on President Reagan's July 25 letter.[31] They hurriedly put together a proposal that included the Soviet demand for a ten-

---

[29] Ibid.

[30] Shultz, *Turmoil and Triumph*, 768.

[31] Winik, *On the Brink*, 513 and Nitze, *From Hiroshima to Glasnost*, 433n6.

year non-withdrawal from the ABM Treaty; a 50 percent reduction of strategic nuclear arsenals during the first five-year period; elimination of all offensive ballistic missiles during the second; and the right to do research, development, and testing permitted by the treaty. After ten years, either side would be free to deploy defenses. Shultz handed the proposal to Shevardnadze, who thought it was "worth considering," but he believed Gorbachev would not agree with the right to deploy defenses after ten years.[32]

As soon as they broke up, the two sides briefed their leaders on the new proposal. Reagan liked it, observing, "he gets his precious ABM Treaty, and we get all his ballistic missiles. And after that we can deploy SDI in space. Then it's a whole new ballgame."[33] Gorbachev, as Shevardnadze predicted, did object to the right to deploy after ten years, but he took the proposal and used it as the basis for a counterproposal, which he offered to the president as soon as they reconvened.

Gorbachev's counterproposal contained two changes and one omission. He insisted that "testing of all space components of ABM defense in space shall be prohibited except for laboratory research and testing." His formulation used the term "strategic offensive weapons" compared to the US use of two terms, "strategic nuclear arsenals" in the first five-year period and "offensive ballistic missiles" in the second. Finally, Gorbachev omitted the sentence about the two sides being free to deploy defenses after the ten years were up.[34]

Their ensuing discussion revolved around the issues of testing and what could be done after ten years. Reagan insisted that testing permitted by the ABM Treaty be allowed, and that after ten years, each side could have the right to deploy defenses. Conversely, Gorbachev insisted that testing be confined to laboratories and stipulated against a unilateral right to deploy defenses after the ten-year period. He claimed that laboratory research would enable the US to determine whether defense was feasible. After the ten years were up, the two sides would continue discussions and "negotiate a mutually acceptable solution concerning their future course of action." In other words, Gorbachev reinserted the Soviet right to veto an American decision to deploy missile defense.[35]

At an impasse, they decided to take another break to "sort out the differences between the two texts." During the break, Reagan asked his aides whether the US "could carry out research under the restraints the Soviets [were] proposing?" Perle responded with an "unequivocal" no, but Shultz and Nitze "counseled him to accept the language proposed by Gorbachev," arguing that

---

[32] Winik, *On the Brink*, 513.

[33] Ibid., 514.

[34] *Reykjavik File*, Document 16, "Russian Transcript of Reagan-Gorbachev Summit in Reykjavik, October 12, 1986 (Afternoon)."

[35] *Reykjavik File*, Document 15, "US Memorandum of Conversation, Reagan-Gorbachev, Final Meeting, October 12, 1986," 4.

"they could worry about whether research could be conducted in the laboratory later." [36]

When they returned for their final session that evening at 5:30 p.m. it was clear that Reagan had sided with Perle. He presented his proposal again, altered slightly to reflect Gorbachev's objections, but it still contained the permission to conduct "research, development, and testing, as permitted in the ABM Treaty." He also included the right to deploy after ten years. Slightly amended, it now read: "At the end of the ten-year period, either side could deploy defenses if it so chose, unless the parties agreed otherwise."

Gorbachev dropped the issue of what would happen after ten years and shifted to two other issues. He wanted to know why Reagan had left the word "laboratory" out of his proposal. Reagan replied that, as the two sides had different views on testing, "their people in Geneva must decide what is permitted." Why had he employed two different terms for the weapons to be eliminated? Reagan's somewhat confused reply was that he thought "the Russians were mainly interested in ballistic missiles." Gorbachev repeated that they were interested in reducing "strategic offensive weapons."[37]

At this point the discussion veered wildly as each leader offered more in terms of weapons to be eliminated to convince the other, until Reagan asked:

> Do we have in mind—and I think it would be very good—that
> by the end of the two five-year periods all nuclear explosive
> devices would be eliminated, including bombs, battlefield
> systems, cruise missiles, submarine weapons, intermediate-
> range systems, and so on?[38]

Gorbachev replied: "we could say that, list all those weapons. Shultz chimed in: "then, let's do it." Reagan replied: "If we agree that by the end of the 10-year period all nuclear weapons are to be eliminated, we can turn this agreement over to our delegations in Geneva so that they can prepare a treaty which you can sign during your visit to the US." Gorbachev then said: "Well, all right. Here we have a chance for an agreement."[39]

Then, Gorbachev threw what Reagan would later call a "curve."[40] The term "laboratory" as a restriction on SDI testing had to be included as part of the overall package. Without it, there was no deal. Reagan was dumbfounded and said, "he could not confine work to the laboratory." Each man tried to convince the other "as a personal favor" to give in, to no avail. Gorbachev insisted that it

[36] Winik, *On the Brink*, 515.
[37] *Reykjavik File*, Document 15, "US Memorandum of Conversation, Reagan-Gorbachev, Final Meeting, October 12, 1986," 8-9.
[38] *Reykjavik File*, Document 16, "Russian Transcript of Reagan-Gorbachev Summit in Reykjavik, October 12, 1986 (Afternoon)," 8.
[39] Ibid.
[40] Ronald Reagan, *An American Life* (New York: Simon and Schuster, 1990), 677.

was a matter of "principle." Reagan replied that Gorbachev was "asking him to give up the thing he'd promised not to give up."

After a few minutes, it was over. They had come close to an historic agreement, but in the end could not bridge the strategic differences that separated them. Reagan had offered an opportunity to shift away from strategic offense to strategic defense and bring an end to the Cold War, but Gorbachev was not prepared to do away with the weapons that underpinned the very essence of the Soviet global position.

The outcome, however, was actually favorable to the United States. With no restrictions on the Strategic Defense Initiative the way was clear to proceed with testing, development, and deployment. The strategic weapons balance and the European missile balance were both more than acceptable positions. Indeed, the outcome at Reykjavik left the United States and its European allies in the best possible position. It was inevitable, as Reagan understood, that the Russians would come back to the negotiating table to attempt to redress these outcomes.

After Reykjavik

The meeting at Reykjavik had occurred at the climax of the congressional election campaign and the Democrats seized on the president's presumed failure to reach an agreement to further their own cause. Democrats (as well as Shultz and the new world order faction) saw SDI as a bargaining chip to be used to obtain an arms control agreement. But the president stood his ground. In his national broadcast to the American people after his return from Iceland, Reagan declared that as it was the SDI program that had brought the Soviet Union back to the arms control talks in the first place, he was not going to accept Gorbachev's attempt to "kill SDI" as the price for an agreement. SDI, he maintained, was America's "insurance policy" that the Russians would keep the commitments made at Reykjavik.[41]

As details began to filter out about the negotiations, troubles mounted for the president from within his own administration as well as from allies. The president had neither consulted nor informed the Joint Chiefs of his proposal to eliminate all nuclear weapons in ten years and news of this proposal caused great consternation within military circles.[42] Many believed that the forfeiture of nuclear weapons would open up the United States and the Western Alliance to Soviet blackmail because of Moscow's conventional force advantage.[43]

---

[41] Gerald Boyd, "President Won't Give Up 'Star Wars' but Says Pacts Are Possible," *New York Times*, October 14, 1986, 1.

[42] George Wilson, "Reagan's Offer Baffles Military, Hill Specialists," *Washington Post*, October 14, 1986, A17. See also Admiral William J. Crowe, *The Line of Fire* (New York: Simon & Shuster, 1993), 268-69.

[43] Mark Thompson, "US Offer at Odds with Pentagon," *Philadelphia Inquirer*, October 15, 1986, 11; Michael Gordon, "Reagan's Missile Offer Sets Off a Shifting Debate," *New York Times*, October 24, 1986, A14.

NATO allies also sought reassurance from Washington that any arms deal with Moscow would not de-couple Western Europe.[44] Before Reykjavik, it was thought that the United States would seek a "phased withdrawal" of intermediate-range missiles. "They were taken by surprise when the superpowers suddenly agreed to go directly to zero."[45] Thatcher was astounded.[46] West German chancellor Kohl and French president Mitterrand issued a joint statement declaring that any elimination of missiles must also "be accompanied by cuts in superior Soviet conventional forces."[47]

In Washington, Democrats were intent upon demonstrating that the administration was violating the Boland amendment in Central America, hoping to forestall the activation of the $100 million in aid the Congress had passed for Contra assistance earlier in June. Hasenfus had claimed that the CIA was directly involved in running the program, a charge not easily rebutted.[48] Eleven House Democrats sent a letter to the Justice Department demanding that Attorney General Meese assign a special prosecutor to determine the extent to which the government was complying with, or deviating from the Boland restrictions.[49]

At the same time, Senate Foreign Relations Committee "staff members said they would begin taking sworn depositions from persons willing to give testimony on additional allegations that . . . the Contras have been involved in gunrunning, drug trafficking, and money laundering." However, in a close 50-47 vote, the Senate rejected a demand that the president report to Congress on the aid program.[50]

Exposure of the Contra supply network strained ties with El Salvador and Honduras, whose airfields were being used for the operation.[51] Stories

---

[44] Gary Verkey, "Nervous NATO Allies Seek US Assurance on Superpower Arms Deal," *Christian Science Monitor*, October 23, 1986, 9.

[45] Don Cook, "Europeans, Buffeted by Missile Foes and Superpower Seesaw, Wait and Worry," *Los Angeles Times*, October 26, 1986, Part IV:2.

[46] Richard Beeston, "Thatcher to Warn Reagan on Arms," *Washington Times*, November 12, 1986, A7.

[47] "Soviets' Conventional Forces Worry West Germany, France," *Baltimore Sun*, October 29, 1986, A2; and Steven Erlanger, "For British, Germans, Arms Failure May Hurt," *Boston Globe*, October 21, 1986, 16.

[48] Lydia Chavez, "Salvadoran Air Base Is Called Center for C.I.A. Operations," *New York Times*, October 15, 1986, A1.

[49] Joanne Omang, "Democrats Demand a Contra-Aid Special Prosecutor," *Washington Post*, October 18, 1986, A15.

[50] Christopher Simpson, "Senate Won't Demand Report on Contra Aid," *Washington Times*, October 17, 1986, A4.

[51] Julia Preston, "Clandestine Missions Described," *Washington Post*, October 17, 1986, A1; Stephen Engleberg, "US-Salvadoran Ties Called Strained," *New York Times*, October 21, 1986, A3.

circulated about the "vast" private supply network supplying the Contras.[52] An earthquake in San Salvador offered an opportunity to provide economic assistance and the president moved quickly to sign the necessary orders to start the aid to the Contras flowing from US government coffers.[53]

Relations with Moscow were also strained. On Sunday, October 19, the Soviet Union expelled five American diplomats in retaliation for the expulsion of 25 Russian members of the Soviet mission to the UN on September 17. On October 21, the Reagan administration ordered the expulsion of 55 Soviets from the United States, the largest number of diplomats ever expelled from the country at one time.[54] Moscow responded immediately by barring 260 local Russian employees from working at the US embassy in Moscow and the consulate in Leningrad.[55] The Soviet action placed embassy personnel in "a stressful" situation for several months until the State Department could recruit and train replacements, but it brought an end to the "tit for tat" expulsions.[56] President Reagan managed to weather these relatively minor storms, but his main focus at the time was on the Iranian initiative, which had reached a critical point.

Forebodings of Failure

Following the October 6 meeting in Frankfurt, Cave and Hakim were in periodic, secure telephone contact with Bahramani and Samii in Tehran, awaiting a response to the 9-point plan. While they waited, however, a threat to the initiative appeared from an entirely different quarter. Adnan Khashoggi, concerned that Ghorbanifar had been cut out and that he would not recoup his investment, conjured up a threat to the initiative that he communicated through an associate of his, who was also a friend of Casey's.

To recapitulate, moving to the second channel left Ghorbanifar with no means of generating income to repay himself and co-investors. The Iranians had not produced the hostages; the Americans had not delivered the remaining spare

[52] "Private Pipeline to the Contras: A Vast Network," *New York Times*, October 22, 1986, A1; Robert Reinhold, "Ex-General hints at Big Role as US Champion of Contras," *New York Times*, October 14, 1986, A6.

[53] Stephen Engleberg, "Shultz Tours Salvadoran Rubble and Promises More American Aid," *New York Times*, October 17, 1986, A15; James Morrison, "Regan Order Could Get Aid for Contras Flowing Today," *Washington Times*, October 22, 1986, A1; Joanne Omang, "Reagan Restarts Contra Aid," *Washington Post*, October 25, 1986, A17.

[54] Bernard Gwertzman, "US Is Expelling 55 in Latest Reprisal on Soviet Envoys," *New York Times*, October 22, 1986, A1.

[55] Celestine Bohlen, "Soviets Retaliate, Limit US Embassy," *Washington Post*, October 23, 1986, A1.

[56] Matlock, *Reagan and Gorbachev*, 242; David Ottaway and John Goshko, "US Seeks to Halt Round of Expulsions, Act on 'Larger Issues,' " *Washington Post*, October 24, 1986, A1.

parts and radars; and the Iranians refused to pay Ghorbanifar, who, in turn, could not repay Khashoggi.

Hoping to prod the Americans into action, Khashoggi sent his "sometime partner," Roy Furmark, to see CIA Director Casey, an old friend.[57] Visiting Casey on October 7, Furmark laid out the finances of the May arms deal, Khashoggi's $15 million investment, and the $10 million shortfall. Furmark disclosed that Khashoggi had involved two Canadian investors in the deal, who, if they did not receive their funds back, would divulge the initiative to Democratic members of the Senate Intelligence Committee.[58] Casey was non-committal, perhaps realizing that such an action would ensure that they would lose their investment, but told Furmark to give all the details to one of his "guys."

A few days before, on October 1, Allen, reading the intelligence traffic, had grown concerned that too many people were knowledgeable of the Iran initiative and took his concerns to deputy director Robert Gates. Gates, recently promoted following McMahon's resignation in February, was only dimly aware of what was going on and was surprised by what he was told.[59] Allen was worried about operational security because North had comingled the Iran and Contra operations by using Secord in both. He feared that both operations were "spinning out of control."[60]

Gates agreed and took Allen to see Casey; as it happened, shortly after the director had met with Furmark on October 7. Responding to their uneasiness about North's actions, Casey expressed his admiration for North as "a man who gets things done," but shared their concerns about "opsec" and promised to look into it. In the meantime, Casey instructed Allen to put his views in writing.[61] Two reports in the same day detailing difficulty with the initiative clearly got Casey's attention. He quickly wrote a memorandum for the record of his conversation with Furmark and called Poindexter to inform him of the gist of his meetings.[62]

---

[57] Samuel Segev, *The Iranian Triangle: The Untold Story of Israel's Role in the Iran-Contra Affair* (New York: Free Press, 1988), 308-309.

[58] As Theodore Draper, *A Very Thin Line: The Iran-Contra Affairs* (New York: Hill and Wang, 1991), 450, notes, the Canadians, Donald Fraser and Ernest Miller, "were real enough, but their roles in Khashoggi's scheme had been invented." The actual investors behind Khashoggi were Saudis, but in order to lend political heft to his threat to disclose the initiative, Khashoggi enlisted his old Canadian acquaintances in the scheme.

[59] "Charles Allen Deposition," *Report of the Congressional Committees Investigating the Iran-Contra Affair*, Appendix B, vol. 1 (Washington, DC: US Government Printing Office, 1988), 824. [Cited hereafter as *Congressional Report on the Iran-Contra Affair*, Appendix B.]

[60] "Robert Gates Deposition," *Congressional Report on the Iran-Contra Affair*, Appendix B, vol. 11, 973.

[61] Draper, *Very Thin Line*, 441.

[62] "Allen Deposition," 829-30.

Two days later, on October 9, Casey included Gates for lunch in his office with North to get a status report on the Iran operation. After being briefed on the state of play there and the anticipated breakthrough with the second channel, Gates says he asked North about Hasenfus's charge about the Contra supply effort being a CIA operation. North replied bluntly that there was "absolutely" no CIA involvement.[63]

North, however, tells a different story about the meeting. He claimed he said, "sooner or later the real story [about the supply effort] was going to come out." Although Gates says that Casey mildly admonished North to "get this straightened out," North claims that Casey told him that Project Democracy was "over" and that he was to "shut it down and clean it up." Now that Congress had passed the aid legislation, Casey said, the agency "was going back in." North also said "Nicaragua wasn't the only thing on Casey's mind." He was "unhappy to hear that Furmark, an outsider, had detailed knowledge about Lake Resources, the use of the residuals, and my own involvement in all of this." [64]

Contrary to Gates, North says that "Casey's admonition to 'clean it up' meant more than just bringing back the pilots and others who had worked for Secord [in Central America]. Between the Hasenfus problem and Furmark we were facing the strong possibility of the imminent exposure of all our operations, including the hostage recovery effort." It was from this point, North claims, that he "tried to destroy all documents that mentioned the 'diversion,' or the names of people who might conceivably be at risk." This included the "ledger" that Casey had given him to keep track of the money and the names of individuals and organizations "whose public exposure would have been a disaster."[65]

On that same day, October 9, as Allen was preparing to write his memorandum, Nir telephoned him to emphasize that Ghorbanifar was at wits' end and would somehow "take his revenge" if he were not paid.[66] Nir's alarmist tone reinforced Allen's misgivings. His memo of the 14th described the ongoing initiative as a "disaster of major proportions" that is "likely to be exposed soon unless remedial action is taken."[67]

---

[63] "Gates Deposition," 988.

[64] "Gates Deposition," 988 and Oliver North and William Novak, *Under Fire: An American Story* (New York: Harper Collins, 1991), 297-98.

[65] North, *Under Fire*, 298-99. Draper, *Very Thin Line*, 443, says "the impression left by Gates's account is that Casey and North were remarkably unperturbed at this meeting" and suggests that Casey told North "privately" to clean things up. However, he concludes that "Casey had been holding out on his deputy, Gates." Jane Mayer and Doyle McManus, *Landslide: The Unmaking of the President* (Boston: Houghton Mifflin, 1988), 287, also say that Casey called North later "that week" to tell him to "clean things up."

[66] Draper, *Very Thin Line*, 443.

[67] Charles Allen, "Memorandum for Casey," October 14, 1986, *Congressional Report on the Iran-Contra Affair*, Appendix B, vol. 11, 1049-57.

Allen recommended an "orderly, damage-limiting shutdown" of the Ghorbanifar-Kangarlu channel, preparation of "press guidance" in the event of exposure, and the establishment of a high-level "planning cell" in the White House headed by "two or three" outside experts of high stature, like Henry Kissinger, or former CIA Director Dick Helms.[68] Allen's recommendations assumed that the White House had no "plan to deal with the potential disclosure" and his recommendation to bring in someone like Kissinger betrayed ignorance of the strategic conflict raging within the administration. Nevertheless, he had put down on paper the essence of the president's Iran Initiative and predicted "disaster."

On October 15, Allen turned his memo in to Gates, who immediately gave it to Casey. The two men went that same day to see Poindexter. The National Security Adviser read the memo, showing no sense of anxiety.[69] Casey suggested that perhaps it was time to go public and advised Poindexter to consult the White House counsel, Peter Wallison, to ensure that they were on firm legal ground. However, the national security adviser disagreed and said, "I don't know that I can trust the White House counsel." Casey subsequently decided, on the advice of Gates, to talk to the CIA's own counsel to review the case. The counsel, David Doherty, "did not believe there were any concerns from a legal or proprietary standpoint for CIA."[70]

Casey sent Allen to see Furmark, who turned the screw further, telling him that the "Canadians" were about to talk to Democratic Senators Leahy, Moynihan and Cranston. They intended to tell them that the government had been engaging in a back-channel arms deal with Iran and had swindled them out of their investment. They also intended to sue Khashoggi, who, in turn, would reveal US government involvement.[71] But Furmark thought the way out of the mess was for the administration to make at least a partial shipment of the remaining spare parts, so Tehran could pay off Ghorbanifar.[72]

Although their meeting was brief, Furmark having to return to New York, Allen was stunned by his depth of knowledge of the affair. Furmark had been present from the beginning in January 1985 and described its subsequent twists and turns, which meant he knew more about it, especially its origins, than even Poindexter, North, and Secord, who had only become involved themselves months later. It was also evident that he was closely associated with Khashoggi, Ghorbanifar, and the Israeli officials involved. Allen's view was that the risk of exposure was "growing daily" and recommended that a "group be formed" that

---

[68] Ibid., 1055-56.

[69] "Gates Deposition," 981-82.

[70] Draper, *Very Thin Line*, 442, 446.

[71] "Roy Furmark Deposition," *Congressional Report on the Iran-Contra Affair*, Appendix B, vol. 11, 133.

[72] "Allen Memorandum to Casey and Gates," October 16, 1986, *Congressional Report on the Iran-Contra Affair*, Appendix B, vol. 1, 1180-82.

was knowledgeable of the Ghorbanifar channel to "consider how to cope with this burgeoning problem."[73]

Casey immediately called Furmark and offered him a ride back to New York in his plane, as he was going there, too, for a public function. On the plane, Furmark gave him the same story he had given Allen, urging that the administration "try to send a small shipment so that Ghorbanifar may be able to take another 5 million to take the pressure off Khashoggi." Casey's reaction was that he would look into it and told Furmark to "just sit tight."[74]

Casey next arranged for Allen to go to New York to finish his debrief of Furmark and sent Cave along with him. No doubt, Casey wanted Cave's reaction to Furmark. On the evening of October 22, they met for dinner at the Chrysalis restaurant where they went over the details yet again. Cave revealed his direct involvement in the affair as a "logistician," and observed that it took 60 days for the financing of the previous deal to be concluded. The implication was that the Canadian investors were still within a reasonable time frame for concluding the deal and should not panic.

Furmark argued that the US had simply not completed its contract and completing it would lead to a "perfect result." Otherwise, Khashoggi also stood to lose the collateral he had put up for the loan, an astounding $30 million to $35 million, he claimed. Then, turning the screw further, for the first time Furmark revealed, "Ghorbanifar believed that . . . $15 million had gone to Nicaragua."[75] Allen had suspected for some time that profits from the arms sales had been used for the Contras and now his suspicions were confirmed. It is curious, to say the least, that the CIA, having labeled Ghorbanifar a "fabricator" and a liar throughout this process, was eager to believe him now.

Nevertheless, Cave wrote up a memorandum of conversation combining his and Allen's notes of the meeting with Furmark and the two of them briefed Casey on it the next morning of October 23.[76] Casey was "deeply disturbed" and immediately talked to Poindexter on the secure phone. Although Casey said he would send the memo over to Poindexter, he did not, because, as Allen told it to the Tower Commission afterward, "it fell into the wrong out box."[77]

We may be profoundly skeptical that the Cave-Allen memo got lost in the shuffle. At the same time, we may agree wholeheartedly with Chairman John Tower's observation that "anything that critical . . . he [Casey] would have

---

[73] Ibid., 1182.

[74] "Roy Furmark Deposition," 135.

[75] Ibid., 140-41.

[76] "Allen Deposition," 843-45.

[77] "Charles Allen Interview," John G. Tower et al., *Report of the President's Special Review Board: February 26, 1987* (Washington, DC: US Government Printing Office, 1987), B-169.

discussed with Admiral Poindexter" (and not put it in writing).[78] Time was of the essence. Casey wanted nothing more than to deep-six the Allen-Cave memo because it had laid out the covert operations on paper just at the moment of the expected breakthrough with the Iranians.

Iran's Calculus Changes

When Bahramani presented the 9-point plan to the Iranian leadership, they immediately realized that North had pulled the wool over his eyes. (As they would tell the Americans when they next met, they considered North's 7-point plan the "official position" of the US government and "the 9-point plan as simply a private agreement between Hakim and [Bahramani].")[79] Indeed, Bahramani was chastised and initially prevented from continuing as a negotiator.

Worse, what he had brought back was a change in US policy. The Iranians had sought to take the middle position between the United States and the Soviet Union, having relations with both, but an alliance with neither. They had sought to maneuver both powers to provide them with a maximum opportunity to defeat Iraq in the war and overthrow Saddam Hussein. The 9-point plan represented a failure of the American part of their strategy.

Iran had spent some ten months attempting to bring about a change in United States policy from neutrality (of sorts) to full support of Iran against Iraq, with all of its attendant weapons benefits. They had held out the prospect of parlaying arms-for-hostages into reestablishment of full diplomatic relations, although they wanted no alliance. They had changed interlocutors, offering direct contact with Rafsanjani, to increase their credibility, even as they grudgingly acknowledged only limited influence with the hostages' captors.

Having failed to draw the United States into full support against Iraq forced a change in Iranian calculations. Iran had sought full-scale weapons support, but no political alliance. Reagan had declined this bargain, shifting to a simple and limited exchange of weapons for the remaining hostages. The 9-point plan reflected that position.

The Iranians, of course, could not deliver the hostages without satisfying Mughniyeh's demands that the United States assist in obtaining the freedom of the Al-Dawa 17. In the 9-point plan, Hakim had offered a "plan" to mediate between Iran and Kuwait over these prisoners, but not a commitment to intervene in internal Kuwaiti politics. To accept this plan would mean that the best that

---

[78] Ibid. Draper, *Very Thin Line*, 446, says of Casey here that he was "either playacting, or already so weakened by illness that he was incapable of facing 'a disaster of major proportions.'"

[79] "Mainz Transcript, October 29, 1986," *Iran-Contra Investigation: Joint Hearings before the Senate Select Committee on Secret Military Assistance to Iran and the Nicaraguan Opposition and the House Select Committee to Investigate Covert Arms Transactions with Iran,* 100th Cong., 1st sess., 100-7, pt. 3, Appendix A, vol. 1 (Washington, DC : US Government Printing Office, 1988), 1647.

could be hoped for was limited US weapons support for Iran, and then only if the hostages were released.

On the other hand, there was the Soviet factor in the equation. They had offered to normalize relations and on October 9, Iran had declared that it was "ready to consolidate its good neighborly relations with the USSR."[80] Russian intelligence had obviously been following the negotiations with the Americans closely and timed their offer accordingly.

The Soviet agreement to "consolidate" relations implied a Soviet willingness to reduce support for Saddam again, as they had done in February. No doubt, the Soviets pointed out that although Saddam continued air attacks, he was reinforcing his defenses by constructing strengthened barriers, minefields, and dug-in tanks, rather than preparing his forces for offensive operations.[81] There can also be little doubt that Soviet restraint of Saddam would be contingent upon Tehran stepping away from Washington.

Thus, with full US support for Iran not possible, the choice before the Iranian leaders appeared to be at best limited US support for Iran against full Soviet support for Saddam, unless consolidation of relations with Moscow would be accompanied by reduced support for Saddam. One bright spot was the large increase in arms from China, spare US parts from Greece, and arms from Soviet client Czechoslovakia, which offered some hope that Iran could satisfactorily prosecute the war.[82]

As the Iranian leadership struggled over these options, Rafsanjani advocated making another attempt to draw the United States in, to which Ayatollah Montazeri violently objected. Montazeri, the designated successor to Khomeini, opposed the deal with the Great Satan and so directed his top lieutenant, Mehdi Hashemi to distribute "five million" leaflets throughout Tehran to expose Rafsanjani's secret negotiations with the United States. Presumably advocating the Soviet option, publicizing the negotiations was an attempt to prevent the continuation of efforts to draw the United States into support of Iran.[83] The timely arrival of information confirming McFarlane's trip to Tehran added fuel to the struggle.[84]

But Khomeini himself censured Montazeri, authorized the arrest of Hashemi and some 200 of his men, and ordered an investigation of his

---

[80] "Middle East and South Asia Review," *FBIS Daily Report, South Asia*, October 10, 1986, 1.

[81] Anthony Cordesman, *The Iran-Iraq War and Western Security, 1984-1987* (London: Jane's, 1987), 111.

[82] Ibid., 109.

[83] *Report of the Congressional Committees Investigating the Iran-Contra Affair* (Washington, DC: US Government Printing Office, 1987), 259. [Hereafter cited as *Congressional Report on the Iran-Contra Affair*.]

[84] Segev, *Iranian Triangle*, 283-86. The editor of *Al Shiraa* was Hassan Sabra, who was also a supporter of Montazeri. Segev discusses Sabra's role in attempting to confirm McFarlane's trip to Tehran in October.

"underground operations."[85] The fact that Montazeri continued to be referred to as the "appointed next leader" indicated that their differences had been over policy and was not the beginning of a succession crisis, as some Americans believed.[86]

In short, Khomeini overruled the objections of Montazeri, and authorized another meeting with the Americans, but sent only Ali Samii and kept Rafsanjani's man, Bahramani, in Tehran. This was no doubt punishment for his earlier failed negotiation of the 9-point plan. Thus, on October 19, the Iranians confirmed their acceptance of the 9-point plan and agreed to another meeting in Frankfurt to discuss its implementation. Their intent, however, was to change its terms.

On October 21, North and Secord flew to Geneva to conclude a complicated arrangement with Nir.[87] The US had agreed to sell 500 TOWs to Iran as part of the 9-point plan. Earlier, in May, the US had finally replaced the missiles Israel had sent to Iran in August 1985. The Israelis had rejected them as outmoded but kept them in storage. The deal with Nir was that Israel would send these outmoded models to Iran and receive new models from the United States. [88]

Part of their discussion involved Ghorbanifar, as Nir recounted the Iranian's payment demands. Secord was struck by North's passive, even phlegmatic reaction, not realizing that North had heard all of these details two weeks earlier from Casey. Secord thought of North that "maybe he was just tired." The two Americans also informed Nir that they were on their way to a meeting with Bahramani, but, as the Iranians had objected to an Israeli presence, he would not be invited.[89] Thus, part of the reason for the missile switch was to keep the Israelis on board.

On October 24, North and Secord flew to Frankfurt, joining Hakim, who had preceded them. They were to meet Bahramani and Samii at the Steigenburger Hotel. The first inkling that all was not well came when Hakim told them that Bahramani would not be coming. It immediately became obvious when they met that Samii, the "monster," had been sent to take a hard line. The Iranian began the meeting by telling them that he could only obtain the freedom of one hostage for

---

[85] Cordesman, *Iran-Iraq War and Western Security*, 123. See also "Clandestine Radio Reports 'Verbal Clash,'" *FBIS Daily Report, South Asia*, October 22, 1986, I 1; "Khomeyni Answers Reyshahri on Arrest of Hashemi," *FBIS Daily Report, South Asia*, October 28, 1986, I 1.

[86] "AFP Told Montazeri 'Still' Khomeyni Successor," *FBIS Daily Report, South Asia*, October 28, 1986, I 1. On the succession interpretation, see "Teicher Prof Note to Poindexter, November 4, 1986," *Tower Report*, B-171-72.

[87] *Tower Report*, B-171, says that North's calendar showed him departing for Frankfurt on October 26, but, in fact, as noted above, North and his team departed for Europe five days earlier, soon after hearing from the Iranians.

[88] Segev, *Iranian Triangle*, 309.

[89] Richard Secord and Jay Wurts, *Honored and Betrayed: Irangate, Covert Affairs, and the Secret War in Laos* (New York: Wiley, 1992), 303-04.

the 500 TOWs. He had "tried hard for a second 'box,' but could only guarantee one."[90]

This news upset North, who felt "the Iranians already seemed to be welching on the deal." (In fact, according to the 9-point plan, the Iranians had promised to obtain the release of "one [hostage] definitely and the second with all effective possible effort.")[91] Next, Samii claimed "with a straight face" that the "US had promised to intercede with the Kuwaitis" regarding the Al-Dawa 17. Secord immediately said that this was "a step backward and a bald-faced lie."[92] He was correct, the 9-point plan specified only that "Albert [Hakim] will provide the plan" for their release and it was understood that Washington would "mediate," not "intercede."[93]

Exasperated, North and Secord "demanded that the Relative [Bahramani] fly up for the meeting, or they could forget about the TOW delivery." Samii countered with the argument that to call Bahramani now would be "an insult" to him. In response, North said that as Bahramani had been "presented as the representative of Speaker Rafsanjani," he insisted that he be present. "After numerous phone calls [to Tehran], the Relative agreed the next day to join us."[94]

Cave arrived on the morning of October 26. Joining North, Secord, and Hakim, at noon they "picked up the Relative [Bahramani] at the Frankfurt airport and drove directly to Mainz about thirty minutes away." They went to Mainz ostensibly because no rooms were available in Frankfurt due to the International Book Fair then going on. Whether this was true or not, the fact was the CIA had bugged their rooms at the Mainz Hilton.[95]

Reviewing the 9-point plan, Bahramani confirmed that "only one release was feasible" in the next few days before the election. After lengthy discussion about the irrelevance of the coming election and the importance of obtaining the release of at least one more hostage, North closed the meeting with a threat to terminate their negotiations:

> Unless we could get the 9-point plan in motion to our mutual benefit without these acrimonious after-the-fact lapses of faith, it would be best for both sides to table the program—at least until more meaningful talks could be held between our two governments.[96]

---

[90] Ibid., 305.

[91] *Congressional Report on the Iran-Contra Affair*, 257.

[92] Ibid.

[93] Ibid.

[94] Secord, *Honored and Betrayed*, 305, notes "Ollie considered going back to Washington," but "after discussions with Poindexter, he agreed to wait while Cave flew over to join us." Reagan's instructions, conveyed through Poindexter, were to focus on the 9-point plan, get the hostages out, and press for more later.

[95] Ibid., 306.

[96] Ibid., 307.

North's threat, relayed immediately back to Tehran, seemed to have an effect. When they resumed talks the next morning, October 27, Bahramani and Samii both became much more forthcoming. Bahramani revealed they were unsuccessful in their endeavors to locate hostages Reed and Cicippio. He also revealed that the reason behind the attempt to obtain US intercession with Kuwait was because the 9-point plan "required ambassadorial-level communication" between Iran and Kuwait that they did not have. "Eventually," however, Bahramani "agreed that the Kuwait plan was acceptable as written."[97]

North also offered a major concession, reducing the price for the TOW missiles. Where, earlier, the unit price had been $13,000, North lowered it to $7,200, making the total for 500 $3.6 million. The Iranians seemed grateful for this concession and offered to demonstrate their bona fides. After the meeting, Hakim accompanied Bahramani and Samii to the Frankfurt branch of Credit Suisse to confirm deposit of the $3.6 million to the Lake Resources account. When it was confirmed, they offered to deposit a remarkable $40 million more to demonstrate their "good faith." On Secord's advice Hakim wisely declined this offer because "it might be construed as committing the US government," which, of course, was its purpose.[98] The deposit immediately triggered the delivery of the 500 TOWs from Israel the next day, October 28, and set the stage for the climactic meeting between the two sides.

Meeting in Mainz, October 29

From the US point of view, the meeting of the 29th was intended to reach agreements on implementing the 9-point plan. For the Iranians, however, it was designed to make another attempt to range the US firmly on the side of Iran as a major weapons supplier. Bahramani began the meeting, divulging the news that there was "dissension in Iran over the initiative"[99] and recounted the story of the leaflets spread around Tehran by "Montazeri's loyalists."[100] He reported that Montazeri's chief lieutenant, Mehdi Hashemi, had been arrested and the situation had been "brought . . . under control," but the crisis had "almost prevented" the two of them from coming to the meeting.[101]

This was both an adroit attempt to explain away the fact of Bahramani's own initial absence and turn it to advantage. He thought that the revelations "would hasten the exposure of the entire affair," and that, therefore, they should "expedite" the 9-point plan.[102] North agreed. He "immediately sent a KL-43 message to Admiral Poindexter telling him the news and recommending that we press on to do everything possible to get out more hostages before the Iran

---

[97] Ibid.
[98] Ibid., 309.
[99] *Congressional Report on the Iran-Contra Affair*, 259.
[100] Segev, *Iranian Triangle*, 310.
[101] Draper, *Very Thin Line*, 452.
[102] Segev, *Iranian Triangle*, 310.

initiative met the same end as Project Democracy. In his reply, the Admiral okayed what would be our final transaction."[103]

North's "message to Admiral Poindexter" was somewhat disingenuous. He was in constant contact with Poindexter and presumably was being briefed on current developments in Tehran essential to his mission. There can be little doubt, therefore, that North was fully apprised of the "dissension" in Iran before Bahramani recounted it to him because news of Montazeri's opposition was all over the Iranian press, which American intelligence assiduously monitored.[104]

Talk of dissension in Tehran led naturally to the state of play in Washington. Bahramani asked who supported the initiative besides the president and Poindexter? North replied that in addition to the two of them, the Vice President, Casey, and Regan supported the initiative, while Shultz and Weinberger opposed. "After that," he said, "nobody else counts . . . . Nobody in our Congress knows about it. And we're not going to tell them until we get all the hostages out."[105]

In return, Bahramani revealed that there were three groups in Iran, which he described as a "shareholding company," participating in this "venture." There was Rafsanjani's group, a right-wing group (whose leader was not named, but was probably either Ayatollah Khamenei's, or Ayatollah Farsi's group) and Montazeri's. Montazeri, however, "had lost ground . . . and been forced to withdraw from public activity."[106] Although Montazeri's objection had been public and therefore known to the Americans, the fact that Rafsanjani had included all three groups in the opening to the United States had stunned them.

Bahramani's revelation meant that Reagan had not been supporting a moderate faction against hard-liners after all, but dealing with what had been, up until then, a united leadership. The entire effort of shifting from Ghorbanifar to a second channel had been a charade, cleverly managed by the Iranians to give the Americans the impression that they were moving closer to developing a political relationship.

The unity of the Iranian leadership was further reinforced when, in naming the Iranian members to the proposed joint Iranian-American commission, Bahramani named none other than Kangarlu, who was Montazeri's man, and Najafabadi, the Majlis member who had participated in the McFarlane talks in Tehran.[107] Bahramani and Samii were apparently the other two.[108] The inclusion of Kangarlu meant that Ghorbanifar was also part of the scheme.

---

[103] North, *Under Fire*, 299.

[104] See notes 83 and 84 above.

[105] "Mainz Transcript, October 29, 1986," *Iran-Contra Investigation, Joint Hearings*, 100-7, Appendix A, vol. 1, 1592.

[106] Ibid., 1573-4. In another place, 1588-90, Montazeri was said to have "closed himself in."

[107] Segev, *Iranian Triangle*, 310.

[108] Draper, *Very Thin Line*, 657, n.20.

Much of the discussion revolved around arms and hostages. Going beyond the 9-point plan, Bahramani asked, "in Rafsanjani's name," that the US send technicians to repair the inoperative Phoenix missiles in their inventory. He also wanted helicopters, which were embargoed, and reconnaissance cameras for their Phantom jets.[109] Finally, he raised again the question of the funds that had been frozen years earlier.

North recognized that in asking for the Phoenix assistance "they are making a change—step six is the Hawk," referring to point six of the 9-point plan. He then countered by demanding that they obtain the release of all three of the hostages, not just two.[110] North said, "we have known for over a year that you need technical help, and we have offered to send it." North affirmed that he was prepared to stick by the proposal he had given the Iranians in May: "all the hostages [out] All terrorism stops." [111] But nothing could go forward until the hostages were freed. If they were freed, then everything was possible. Their meeting ended with Bahramani's promise that Jacobson would be released in a few days, and perhaps Sutherland.[112]

Afterward, the Americans discussed among themselves the prospects of actually freeing the hostages. North thought that "the only thing that was necessary [was] for the Imam to make very clear to people" his wishes. Hakim thought that they "do not want to use Khomeini . . . they don't want to use the big gun." Secord thought they could simply "send an order to the revolutionary guard to get them," but thought they didn't know where they were. North and Cave disagreed, arguing that they know "exactly where they are."[113]

There were several conclusions that emerged from this meeting. Despite all the hints and even outright admissions the Iranian interlocutors had given— especially Bahramani—the Americans still persisted in the erroneous belief that Khomeini's influence would govern Mughniyeh's decisions. Even though it was clear that the Americans knew Mughniyeh held the hostages, they believed that Khomeini's will would prevail.

---

[109] "Mainz Transcript, October 29, 1986," *Iran-Contra Investigation, Joint Hearings*, 100-7, Appendix A, vol. 1, 1604-5; and Segev, *Iranian Triangle*, 310.

[110] "Mainz Transcript, October 29, 1986," *Iran-Contra Investigation, Joint Hearings*, 100-7, Appendix A, vol. 1, 1604-5.

[111] Ibid., 1607-08.

[112] If Iranian intelligence was monitoring US publications, an item in *Newsweek*, October 20, 1986 would certainly have removed doubts about the US understanding of the hostage situation. The news item declared that Imad Mughniyeh was holding Jacobson, Anderson, and Sutherland. Islamic Jihad "had snatched their victims to trade for seventeen confreres in terror jailed in Kuwait. But intelligence sources believe they might settle for springing just three Lebanese Shiites among them, who have been sentenced to death."

[113] "Mainz Transcript, October 29, 1986," *Iran-Contra Investigation, Joint Hearings*, 100-7, Appendix A, vol. 1, 1618.

The revelation that the Iranian leadership had been manipulating the Reagan team, not the other way around, raised even more fundamental questions. It was impossible to avoid the conclusion that the hostages were simply being dangled as bait for weapons and that the prospects for a full-blown political rapprochement were nil. Before any of these points could sink in, however, the president's initiative came crashing down, the result of the new world order faction's time bomb planted months earlier.

Chapter 18

The Struggle for Power

The irony of President Reagan's Iran initiative was that his policy was failing even as it was being exposed by the new world order faction. Exposure of the initiative led immediately to a sustained effort by Secretary Shultz to seize control of foreign policy under the guise of a demand to end what he charged was an arms-for-hostages policy.

Reagan's response was first to attempt to sustain the initiative. When it became clear that the Iranians had rejected rapprochement, he attempted to end the initiative but retain control of policy. Finally, Shultz unveiled the entrapment of the president in the November 1985 Hawk shipment and its subsequent cover-up. The entrapment combined with the promise of additional revelations through a congressional investigation, with its threat of a Watergate-style outcome—that is, the possibility of impeachment by Democrats in control of both houses of Congress—led Reagan to give up the struggle for power with Shultz and focus on salvaging his presidency.

Exposure of the Iran Initiative

At the end of the Mainz meeting, Bahramani had assured North that he could arrange for two of the remaining three hostages, Jacobson and Sutherland, to be released. Samii had sought to extract 500 more TOWs as the price for a second hostage, but this didn't go over well with Secord and the matter was dropped.[1] Nevertheless, assuming that two hostages would be released, North made preparations to pick them up. Seeking to disguise Washington's role, he arranged for Terry Waite, a well-known British humanitarian and Anglican Church envoy, to travel to Beirut to receive them. Waite arrived in Beirut on October 31, with the story that he was expecting the imminent release of two hostages.[2]

---

[1] *Report of the Congressional Committees Investigating the Iran-Contra Affair* (Washington, DC: US Government Printing Office, 1987), 261. [Cited hereafter as *Congressional Report on the Iran-Contra Affair*.]

[2] Bernard Gwertzman, "US Looks for Sign in Captors' Move," *New York Times*, November 4, 1986, A11, and Jane Mayer and Doyle McManus, *Landslide: The Unmaking of the President* (Boston: Houghton Mifflin, 1988), 290.

At 7:00 a.m. on Sunday morning, November 2, David Jacobson was dropped off near the site of the old American embassy compound in west Beirut. According to Jacobson, Terry Anderson was also supposed to have been released later that day. He had been in contact with Anderson, as both men were being held in the same building, but in different cells. The third hostage, Sutherland was being held in a different place.[3] In a statement announcing Jacobson's release, Islamic Jihad—that is, Imad Mughniyeh—urged the US government to proceed with unspecified "current approaches that could lead, if continued, to a solution of the hostage issue," a veiled reference to the Al-Dawa prisoners in Kuwait mentioned in the nine-point agreement.[4]

Everything seemed to be going according to plan, but two hours after Jacobson was released, at 9:00 a.m., the newspaper *Al Shiraa* "hit the streets" with its weekend edition. In it was an article describing the ongoing Byzantine policy struggle in Tehran, including a jumbled account of McFarlane's trip to Tehran tacked on at the end.[5] The article apparently spooked Imad Mughniyeh, if not also Rafsanjani, and Anderson's release was canceled.[6]

Hoping that the second hostage's release was being delayed, not canceled, President Reagan decided to refuse comment to reporters' increasingly insistent questions about the *Al Shiraa* article, saying that it had no foundation.[7] Not so, Shultz. On his way to Vienna for a meeting with Shevardnadze, he cabled Poindexter from the plane with contrary advice to "get everything out in the open, and fast."[8] Seeing an opportunity to put an end to the president's initiative, Shultz continued: "we could make clear that this was a special, one-time operation based on humanitarian grounds . . . [but] that our policies toward terrorism and the Iran-Iraq war stand."[9]

The president disregarded Shultz's advice and decided to wait. Asked on the campaign trail in Las Vegas about his efforts to secure the release of the hostages, Reagan simply said that the government was working through channels that he couldn't "discuss."[10] Poindexter, in a reply to Shultz, said that the vice president, Weinberger, and Casey had all agreed with the president to decline comment for the time being, but Shultz refused "to go along." In remarks to his

---

[3] Deborah H. Strober and Gerald S. Strober, *The Reagan Presidency: An Oral History of the Era* (Washington: Brassey's, 2003), 472.

[4] Ihsan A. Hijazi, "Hostage's Release is Linked to Shift in Iranian Policy," *New York Times*, November 4, 1986, A1.

[5] Mayer and McManus, *Landslide*, 293.

[6] Strober and Strober, *The Reagan Presidency*, 472. Most sources state that the newspaper appeared the following day, November 3, but the *New York Times* articles cited above establish the date as November 2.

[7] Mayer and McManus, *Landslide*, 295-96.

[8] George Shultz, *Turmoil and Triumph* (New York: Scribner, 1993), 786.

[9] *Iran-Contra Affair*, 293. Shultz omitted this portion of his message to Poindexter from his memoir.

[10] Gwertzman, "US Looks for Sign in Captors' Move."

staff, he was already saying the president was stonewalling, which to him meant, "it was somewhat like Watergate."[11]

To say that Shultz was panicking or jumping to conclusions at this early date would be a misinterpretation. The exposure of the initiative was his opportunity to make yet another attempt to shut it down and take control of policy. Shultz's exchange with Poindexter marked the beginning of a fierce policy struggle between the president and the new world order faction.

The president immediately instructed Poindexter to gather together the relevant facts "to determine how the policy initiative had been conducted, conceived, approved, and so forth."[12] The problem was there was no record, no paper trail detailing the origins of the initiative. Recall, as part of the new world order faction's entrapment scheme, McFarlane had authorized Israeli action in the president's name and had made no record of his actions.

Unable to document the origins of the initiative, Poindexter had no choice but to ask the former national security adviser for his "help," and he readily acceded. In his PROF note reply to Poindexter, on November 7, McFarlane complained that he had "heard" Regan was "indicating to one and all that the whole Iran business had been my idea" and wanted to set out "just what the truth is." It was only years later, in his memoir, that McFarlane divulged the source of his information. It had come from none other than Brent Scowcroft, who called to tell him that "Regan is hanging you out to dry." Scowcroft's call should properly be understood as a signal for McFarlane to go into action.[13] Scowcroft, one of the leaders of the new world order faction, would be part of the later "investigation" of the president's policies.

If Regan had been attempting to pin "the whole Iran business" on McFarlane at this time it was not evident in press reports, as Scowcroft claimed. Quite the contrary. A *Los Angeles Times* report of November 6 cited Regan on the hostage issue, but he refused to discuss "how we negotiated." Nor was there any hint of recrimination or casting of blame, just an expressed concern to protect the hostages.[14] However, Mayer and McManus say that Regan, speaking on background as a "senior administration official" to reporters for weekly newsmagazines such as *Newsweek* and *Time*, said that the Iran initiative was "all McFarlane's idea."

As the scandal unfolded, the effort to indict the president would hinge upon the changing, self-serving, muddled, contradictory, and unprovable claims of McFarlane, crucially assisted by Shultz's open opposition to the Iran outreach. The narrative was amplified with almost daily well-informed leaks to the press,

---

[11] Shultz, *Turmoil and Triumph*, 787.

[12] "McFarlane Testimony, February 21, 1987," in John G. Tower et al., *Report of the President's Special Review Board: February 26, 1987* (Washington, DC: US Government Printing Office, 1987), D-3.

[13] Robert C. McFarlane, *Special Trust* (New York: Cadell & Davies, 1994), 91.

[14] Doyle McManus, "US Offer to Iran Seen as Subtle Policy Shift," *Los Angeles Times*, November 6, 1986, 13. Mayer and McManus, *Landslide*, 296.

asserting that President Reagan had been engaged in an illegal arms-for-hostages scheme.

In his PROF note to Poindexter, McFarlane said that the "Israelis approached us in June 1985" and the president "approved" of "engaging in a dialogue," with "no mention at all of any arms exchange." Then, "we heard nothing until August when the Israelis introduced the requirement for TOWs. I told Kimche no." The Israelis "went ahead on their own, but then asked that we replace the TOWs and after checking with the president, we agreed." Benjamin Weir was released "as a consequence of their action."

In this carefully hedged statement, McFarlane truthfully said the president had approved *only* of a "dialogue" with the Iranians, not an "arms exchange." Nor did he claim that the president had authorized the Israeli shipment of arms but said the Israelis had shipped arms "on their own." Finally, there was no charge of arms for hostages, as McFarlane assigned responsibility for the initiative to the Israelis.

However, McFarlane omitted the crucial facts that it had been he, not the president, who had given the Israelis the go ahead to ship arms and "agreed" to replace the TOWs the Israelis had shipped. Indeed, much of the new world order entrapment scheme had occurred while the president was recuperating at his ranch in Santa Barbara.[15] McFarlane also omitted any mention of the November Hawk fiasco and concluded with a discussion of his trip to London in December, turning off the initiative, and resigning from government.[16] This memo would constitute the first of several versions of the initiative by McFarlane that either ignored or carefully obfuscated his own role.

McFarlane's first story contained some truth but omitted crucial facts. However, in the absence of any written record, there was no one in the US government who could contradict him except the president himself, and he said nothing for the moment. Neither Poindexter, nor North, nor Casey, nor Weinberger, had been involved in the summer of 1985, as McFarlane played his cards close to his vest. His liaison to the Israelis had been Michael Ledeen, a private citizen. McFarlane had made an "explicit arrangement" with Ledeen that "we would not put anything on paper."[17] But, Ledeen, too, acted on the assumption that McFarlane had been carrying out the orders of the president.

The Iranians Say No to Rapprochement

Meanwhile, a burst of commentary from Iranian leaders not only fed the press frenzy surrounding the president, but it also signaled that the president's

---

[15] See Chapter 10.

[16] "McFarlane PROF Note to Poindexter," November 7, 1986, *Tower Report*, D-4. See also *Congressional Report on the Iran Contra Affair*, 299.

[17] Michael Ledeen, *Perilous Statecraft: An Insider's Account of the Iran Contra Affair* (New York: Scribner, 1988), 255, "took notes at the meetings I attended at McFarlane's instructions, but once I had briefed him, I destroyed the notes."

initiative had failed. On November 4, at a rally marking the seventh anniversary of the seizure of the American embassy, Rafsanjani and Prime Minister Mousavi spoke before a large crowd. Acknowledging the McFarlane trip, Rafsanjani said, "the Americans' immediate aim was to secure Iranian mediation in Lebanon, though their distant goal was to create amicable relations with Iran." Although "we have left the door open . . . Iranian action on the hostages is conditional on the United States proving that it is not engaging in 'senseless hostility' against Iran." However, he said, Iran's friends in Lebanon "do not owe us anything" and "have not pledged themselves to follow our orders."[18]

If Rafsanjani suggested that the door was still open, if only a crack, Mousavi immediately declared it was closed shut. He stressed that there was "no possibility at all of holding talks with the United States" outside of the framework of existing negotiations taking place at The Hague. He claimed that the reason for President Reagan's denials of the McFarlane mission were because "such news could create disgrace inside America."[19] To make his position clear he declared, "America's relations with us, because of its crimes against the Islamic Revolution, are the same as relations between a wolf and a lamb."[20]

The thrust of Iranian leaders' remarks was difficult to gauge because, immediately after the rally, Bahramani called North to arrange another meeting in Geneva on the November 8.[21] The president decided to stay his course, at least through the meeting, even though the questions and criticisms from the press about trading arms for hostages were reaching a crescendo. Indeed, a cascade of well-informed press stories began to appear based on official but unnamed sources.[22]

Under this growing cloud, North, Secord, Hakim, and Cave headed off to Geneva for what they thought would be a meeting with Bahramani and Samii, their usual interlocutors. However, upon arriving, they learned that only Samii and Bahramani's aide, but not Bahramani himself, were there. According to Samii, Bahramani was "lying low because the *Al-Shiraa* piece had raised his profile a little too high." Although the absence of Bahramani was a bad sign, Samii assured the Americans that both Bahramani and Rafsanjani "were anxious to

---

[18] "Middle East and South Asia Review," *Foreign Broadcast Information Service (FBIS) Daily Report, South Asia*, November 5, 1986, i.

[19] Ibid.

[20] "Musavi Views Remarks," *FBIS Daily Report, South Asia*, November 5, 1986, I 7.

[21] *Congressional Report on the Iran-Contra Affair*, 261.

[22] William Drozdiak and Walter Pincus, "Iran Says McFarlane Carried Out Secret Mission to Tehran," *Washington Post*, November 5, 1986, A1; John Walcott and Youssef Ibrahim, "US Suggests It Would Allow Weapons For Iran in Return for Hostages' Release," *Wall Street Journal*, November 5, 1986, 3; Walter Pincus, "Secret Talks With Iran Described," *Washington Post*, November 6, 1986, A1; Michael Dobbs, "Tehran Visit May Hurt US-Iraqi Ties," *Washington Post*, November 6, 1986, A38; Walter Pincus, "Shultz Protested Iran Deal," *Washington Post*, November 6, 1986, A1.

continue with the plan although we should expect to hear some anti-American propagandizing to appease the opposition."[23]

If the American team was being kept up to date on current developments in Tehran, as one would expect, this was a transparent attempt by Samii to deny what had been Rafsanjani's public repudiation of the "plan" the day before. At Friday Prayers on November 7, Rafsanjani carefully acknowledged that he had lost the policy struggle over whether or not to establish relations with the United States.

As the loser in the policy struggle, he was required to repudiate his own policy. He now claimed that McFarlane had come without "permission" and denied any purchase of arms from Israel, our "main enemy." Indeed, "as long as the United States backs Israel, we will consider the United States as the arch Satan. We will never be friendly with a country that financially supports Israel . . . "

Then, he said that Khomeini, the grand imam, had "commanded that as long as the United States is not chastised, we will not establish relations with it. This declaration by the imam of the Islamic nation has clarified our foreign policy course. Grand Ayatollah Montazeri also elucidated this issue in his recent speech." Finally, he concluded, "we have no responsibility whatsoever" for the US hostages in Lebanon. Indeed, in view of all the crimes the US has committed there, "what could the wronged people of Lebanon do if not take hostages?"[24]

For North, if not for his companions, the meeting in Geneva was a last-gasp attempt to get Anderson and Sutherland out, not to continue with the initiative, which was dead. In fact, neither the establishment of political relations, nor the subject of arms sales came up. The two sides first traded charges about the *Al Shiraa* article. Samii wanted the Americans to know that it had not been their doing and claimed that the newspaper was "under Syrian control." This, he said, "had led some in Tehran to conclude that the US might have had a hand in the exposé."

Cave replied that the US had "considerable information which clearly indicates that Hizbollah [was] involved with the newspaper . . . [and that] Mehdi Hashemi may have used it as a means of channeling his leak."[25] Cave certainly knew that Mehdi Hashemi was already in jail and that Samii's suspicions were

---

[23] Richard Secord and Jay Wurts, *Honored and Betrayed: Irangate, Covert Affairs, and the Secret War in Laos* (New York: Wiley, 1992), 320. Oliver North and William Novak, *Under Fire: An American Story* (New York: Harper Collins, 1991), 306, claims that the "Nephew" was present in Geneva, but, while North may have had a conversation with him, it could only have been over the phone.

[24] "Majlis Speaker: 'No Responsibility' for Hostages," *FBIS Daily Report, South Asia*, November 7, 1986, I 1.

[25] "George Cave Briefing of HPSCI Staffers," *Iran-Contra Investigation: Joint Hearings before the Senate Select Committee on Secret Military Assistance to Iran and the Nicaraguan Opposition and the House Select Committee to Investigate Covert Arms Transactions with Iran*, 100th Cong., 1st sess., 100-7, pt. 3, Appendix A, vol. 1 (Washington, DC : US Government Printing Office, 1988), 1762.

correct. The Iranians had sent a "high level" delegation to Damascus to look into the matter of Syrian involvement and evidently had been satisfied that Assad had played no role. Thus, their suspicion of an American "hand."[26]

North said how "keenly disappointed" the Americans were "about getting only Jacobson out." Samii "made it clear that the freeing of the Al-Dawa prisoners was a prerequisite to the release of the 'other two hostages.'" He conceded that even if only "some" prisoners were released "something" might be possible. North said that "we had done all that was humanly possible by talking directly to the Kuwaitis" and recommended that the Iranians send a delegation to Kuwait, promising that it would be "warmly received."[27] Samii replied that there had to be a deal before any senior Iranian officials would go to Kuwait.[28]

Samii also went to some lengths to cut ties to Ghorbanifar, claiming that the Iranians now "suspected" him of being an Israeli agent. This was a clear signal that he was out of favor in Tehran. However, in his next breath, Samii wanted the Americans to "appease" him to forestall any "trouble." Interestingly, the next day, when North and his team met with Nir, who had also come to Geneva, the Israeli disclosed that Ghorbanifar was spreading the word that "the United States was spending Iranian money in Nicaragua." The double irony here was that North informed Nir that the Lake Resources account had been closed because "some of the Iranian funds had become "mixed" with funds for Nicaragua."[29]

They had reached the end of the line. Both sides were shutting down the operation. As North concluded, "the Iran initiative was finally over."[30] But if he thought that the initiative would fade quietly into the background, he was in for a rude shock. When he returned to Washington the next day, he found the administration embroiled in a full-blown crisis.

Battle Lines Are Drawn

In view of the pummeling the administration was receiving in the press and on the Sunday talk shows, the president called a meeting of the National Security Planning Group on Monday morning, November 10. He decided that it was now necessary to put out a public defense of his policy and hoped to present a united administration to the public. He was under no illusions about Shultz's opposition of his policy. An additional purpose of the meeting, it seems, was to learn how much the secretary knew and what kind of attack to expect from him.

Shultz saw the burgeoning crisis as the moment "to get policy on Iran and on antiterrorism back on track, into my hands and away from the NSC staff."[31]

---

[26] "Teicher PROF Note to Poindexter, November 4, 1986," *Tower Report*, B-171-72.

[27] *Iran-Contra Affair*, 262.

[28] Theodore Draper, *A Very Thin Line: The Iran-Contra Affairs* (New York: Hill and Wang, 1991), 460.

[29] *Congressional Report on the Iran-Contra Affair*, 262.

[30] North, *Under Fire*, 306.

[31] Shultz, *Turmoil and Triumph*, 808.

It would be, he said, a "battle royal." To do it, he would need the support of key members of the NSPG. He believed he could count on Weinberger, who had opposed the policy, and sought to persuade the vice president and later Regan to support him, against the president.

In a telephone conversation with Bush's close friend and adviser Nick Brady on Saturday, Shultz warned that "the vice president could get drawn into a web of lies. If he blows his integrity, he's finished. He should be very careful how he plays the 'loyal lieutenant' role now." On Sunday, Shultz visited Bush at his home and "reminded him that he had been present at a meeting where arms for Iran and hostage releases had been proposed and that he had made no objection despite the objection of both Cap and me."[32] This was a signal that Bush should support Shultz in the coming arguments, at the risk of his political future.

Meeting in the Situation Room, Monday morning, were the president, Bush, Shultz, Casey, Weinberger, Meese, Regan, Poindexter, and Alton Keel, Poindexter's deputy. Reagan opened the meeting, stating that what we were doing regarding the Iran initiative was "right, and legal, and justifiable." We were trying to "turn around the strategic situation in the Persian Gulf, to move Iran to a constructive role, to help the Iranians with their problem with the Soviets. And, of course . . . we wanted the hostages back."[33] In this regard, he said, "we have not dealt directly with terrorists, no bargaining, no ransom."[34]

Poindexter next gave a history of the initiative, which, was based on McFarlane's memo, North's inputs, and his own analysis. It was filled with errors, half-truths, and misstatements because both North and McFarlane were determined to protect themselves and thus gave contradictory information and Poindexter could not sort out truth from fiction. In fact, Poindexter's history was so blatantly wrong as to guarantee a negative response from Shultz. Indeed, as the discussion proceeded, it was plain to all around the table that the argument was between Shultz and the president, with Meese attempting to support the president.

Poindexter stated that the origins of the initiative came earlier the previous year when North "stumbled onto an Israeli warehouse in Portugal." The Israelis claimed they were selling arms to Iran to get Jews out of the country and shipped five hundred missiles to Iran in August and September 1985 "without the knowledge of the United States. We were told after the fact."[35] Poindexter omitted any reference to the November Hawk shipment, just as McFarlane had.

In January, the president had signed a finding authorizing the initiative and instructing Casey to defer notification to the Congress. This led, Poindexter said, to the Ghorbanifar-Kangarlu channel, which culminated in McFarlane's trip to Tehran. This channel never "achieved anything," and was closed. Subsequently, a second channel was opened with Rafsanjani's "nephew," which

---

[32] Ibid., 808-9.

[33] Ibid., 812.

[34] Draper, *Very Thin Line*, 464.

[35] Mayer and McManus, *Landslide*, 297.

was much more productive. The United States sold a thousand TOWs and some Hawk missile battery parts; and three hostages were released.[36]

Poindexter concluded by claiming that "we have achieved . . . solid contact with Rafsanjani," a middle of the road politician opposed to Khomeini, who had the support of the Revolutionary Guards. The radical elements were for "war, terrorism, revolution . . . . They were the ones who were linked to Hezbollah in Lebanon and who were responsible for the last three hostage takings [Frank Reed, Joseph Cicippio, and Edward Tracy]." Montazeri, Khomeini's heir apparent, was "an independent player." We have convinced them that they can't win the war, that the hostages have to be released, and that the Soviets are a threat. The political situation, in short, "was fluid and susceptible to influence in a way that would be positive for us."[37]

Poindexter's rendition of the initiative's history was so uninformed that it bore little relationship to reality, especially the tale about the discovery of the Israeli warehouse in Portugal, one of North's concoctions, and the long and tangled relationship with Ghorbanifar. Ironically, the Israelis had a warehouse in Portugal, though its discovery had not marked the start of the initiative. It was Poindexter's analysis of the Iranian leadership dynamic and the assertion of a "solid contact" with Rafsanjani that jarred. He knew the initiative had failed, and that Rafsanjani had publicly repudiated it just three days earlier, but admitting it would be acknowledging the failure of the president's policy.

Shultz predictably "exploded" at what he said was a "ludicrous" tale riddled with "preposterous assertions." Reacting to the revelation of the January 17 finding, he claimed, "this is the first I ever heard of such a finding."[38] In fact, Reagan and Shultz had engaged in a "long discussion" of the initiative at lunch on the very same day that the president had signed the finding, although he had not shown him the actual document.[39] Shultz, therefore, had never known of the crucial, legal basis for proceeding with the initiative, which was the Economy Act and not the Arms Export and Control Act. His explosion related to his realization that Reagan had outmaneuvered him.

Shultz would claim falsely that he had known little to nothing of what had happened in 1986 to avoid even a taint of complicity in the initiative. Nevertheless, as Walsh documents in great detail, Shultz and his aides were fully

---

[36] Shultz, *Turmoil and Triumph*, 812.

[37] Ibid., 813.

[38] Shultz, *Turmoil and Triumph*, 812-13.

[39] Lawrence E. Walsh, *Final Report of the Independent Counsel for Iran-Contra Matters*, vol. 1 (Washington, DC: United States Court of Appeals for the District of Columbia Circuit, August 4, 1993), 338. "On January 17, 1986 there was another meeting at the White House to discuss the initiative. [Nick] Platt noted Shultz's report of that meeting as follows: 'long discussion of Polecat [the Iran initiative] at lunch. [Shultz] . . . want it to be recorded as: A, unwise, B, illegal.'"

knowledgeable about the president's policy, followed it closely from the outset, and carefully prepared a false story for the secretary after the crisis erupted.[40]

Poindexter's revelation of the January 17 finding meant that the president's policy had been entirely legal from that point. Shultz could and would criticize the advisability of the policy, but not its legality. He was left with McFarlane's entrapment schemes of 1985. There were few grounds on which to attack the president about the initial Israeli shipments of TOWs because it was essentially his word against McFarlane's. Shultz's only leverage was the November Hawk shipment, in which the CIA had become entangled, and that would be his main line of attack against the president.

Shultz charged that the president was paying ransom for the hostages, that it was "an arms-for-hostages deal." Reagan said, "it's not linked" and Meese interjected to say that "we didn't sell; Israel sold."[41] The president was literally correct, but disingenuous. The January 17, 1986 finding had authorized the sale of weapons to an authorized cut-out, who then re-sold them to Iran; the Iranians then attempted to exercise their influence over the hostage-taker, Imad Mughniyeh, in Lebanon. The linkage was indirect, but it was clear enough. It appeared to be a distinction without a difference.

Israel's role was to facilitate meetings with the Iranians, provide warehouse space for weapons, and to transport them as needed. Shultz charged that "conspiring with the Israelis . . . gave Israel a clear field, and they would then supply Iran with equipment that really mattered." Meese sought to distinguish between "trading directly with those who held the hostages and doing it through Iran," but Shultz warned against saying "something that's technically correct but not exactly representative of what we've done." In his view, the Iranians and the Israelis were "playing us for suckers."[42]

The president said he would "appreciate people saying you support policy" and Meese suggested the release of a public statement. Shultz, however, balked, saying, "I support you, Mr. President, but I am concerned about policy." Casey then "produced a draft statement to be released to the press," but signing such a statement was something Shultz "was not prepared to do." The tension in the room was palpable, as everyone, even Weinberger, who Shultz thought would unreservedly support him, wanted to rally around the president. Shultz left the meeting feeling that he was now "the most unpopular man in town."[43]

The meeting ended without agreement, as Shultz hurried off to a previously scheduled flight to Guatemala for an OAS meeting. While in flight, Poindexter contacted the secretary with a press release regarding the American

---

[40] Ibid., 325-74.

[41] Shultz, *Turmoil and Triumph*, 813; and Draper, *Very Thin Line*, 465.

[42] Shultz, *Turmoil and Triumph*, 814; and Draper, *Very Thin Line*, 466.

[43] Draper, *Very Thin Line*, 468; and Shultz, *Turmoil and Triumph*, 814. See also, Frank Morring, "Weinberger Defends Iran Arms Shipments," *Washington Times*, November 14, 1986, A9; and Molly Moore, "Weinberger Backs Policy Toward Iran," *Washington Post*, November 20, 1986, A24.

hostages in Lebanon whose main thrust was that "there was unanimous support for the President's decisions." The national security adviser said that the vice president, Weinberger, Casey, and Meese "had already cleared it."[44]

Again, Shultz balked, declaring that "I did not support this operation and I would not join in lying about it." It was "a lie . . . . It's Watergate all over again," he complained to his aides. He argued with Poindexter, demanding that the key sentence be revised to say simply "there was unanimous support for the President," omitting any reference to "decisions." Even with this change, Shultz "was uncomfortable."[45]

Democrats Attack; Reagan Defends

While Shultz was bolting on Iran policy, the newly elected Congress, with both houses now under Democratic control, planned investigations to determine "whether the National Security Council has been used to circumvent Congress, the Pentagon and the State Department in arranging for arms to be shipped to Iran in exchange for American hostages." The inquiries were expected "to go beyond the Iranian operation to the role of the NSC in supplying arms to the rebels in Nicaragua." In short, congressional Democrats were already connecting the president's Iran and Contra policies two weeks before the so-called diversion would be acknowledged. The House planned to hold hearings as early as December, with Senate hearings delayed until January when Democrats would assume control.[46]

Of course, aside from the merits of the case, which had generated a congressional uproar, investigations to determine whether the NSC was being used to circumvent Congress were a transparent and time-honored means whereby an opposition-controlled Congress could attack a president. To Reagan, it meant that he had to get out front, brief Congress and attempt to counter by obtaining the support of the people. He assembled his NSPG principals in the Situation Room on November 12 to brief key members of Congress: Senate leaders Robert Dole (R-KS) and Robert Byrd (D-WV); and House leaders Jim Wright (D-TX) and Dick Cheney (R-WY).

Reagan opened the meeting by defending his policy, affirming that no laws were broken, that there was no trade of arms for hostages, and that no officials were bypassed. The president reportedly argued "we would be at fault if Khomeini died and we had not made any preparations for contacts with a future regime . . . . The arms were necessary for that." However, an unnamed "official"

---

[44] Shultz, *Turmoil and Triumph*, 814. Draper, *Very Thin Line*, 469, says Poindexter "obtained the approval of Reagan, Weinberger, Meese, and Casey," omitting the vice president, which, if true, meant that Shultz's warning to him had made an impact.
[45] Shultz, *Turmoil and Triumph*, 814-15.
[46] Walter Pincus, "Hill Probes of NSC Planned," *Washington Post*, November 10, 1986, A1.

who attended the meeting "conceded that the supply of arms was 'intertwined' with the release of the hostages."[47]

Poindexter also gave a briefing, which focused on the policy after the January finding, intimating that the Israeli shipments of 1985 had occurred without authorization, and that the United States delivered only 1,000 TOWs and 240 Hawk spare parts, a relatively small outlay for a potentially significant outcome.[48] He did acknowledge, however, that the White House may have "made a miscalculation on who it could trust in Iran." [49]

Congressional leaders, especially the Democrats, reacted with great skepticism. Senator Byrd declared, "Iran is a terrorist state. You are selling arms. You want others *not* to sell arms. It's selling arms for hostages . . . and it's a bad mistake."[50] Representative Wright issued a statement after the meeting, characterizing the discussions as "frank and candid," and noting that he had "expressed certain convictions regarding the direction of our foreign affairs and how to improve future relations between the executive and legislative branches."[51] Sen. Dole thought the entire operation "a little inept," and Sen. Barry Goldwater (R-AZ) charged, "laws had been broken."[52]

Immediately afterward, as word leaked that the United States had sold arms for hostages, Shultz sought out Regan. He wanted him "to help me get Ronald Reagan out of the line of fire and turn this mess over to me to clean it up." He wanted the president to include a statement in his major speech the next day, that he would publicly transfer "Iran policy and terrorist policy back in my hands."[53] But Reagan was not ready to relinquish control, or to give up on his policy.

The next evening, November 13, the president addressed the nation. The Iran initiative was in the national interest, he maintained. He sought to reestablish relations with Tehran, bring an honorable end to the Iran-Iraq war, eliminate state-sponsored terrorism, and bring about the safe return of all hostages. The United States, he said, had not "swapped" arms for hostages. "I authorized the transfer of small amounts of defensive weapons and spare parts . . . to send a signal that the United States was prepared to replace the animosity between us with a new relationship." At the same time, we insisted as a condition of progress, that Tehran "oppose all forms of international terrorism" and "the most significant step which

---

[47] Bernard Weinraub, "Reagan Confirms Iran Got Arms Aid; Calls Deals Vital," *New York Times*, November 13, 1986, A1.
[48] *Congressional Report on the Iran-Contra Affair*, 295-96. The actual number of TOWs was later corrected to be 2,008.
[49] Walter Pincus and David Hoffman, "White House Briefs Hill on Iran Contacts," *Washington Post*, November 11, 1986, A1.
[50] Shultz, *Turmoil and Triumph*, 818.
[51] Weinraub, "Reagan Confirms Iran Got Arms [. . .]."
[52] Joseph Harsch, "The Iran Operation—a Little Inept," *Christian Science Monitor*, November 18, 1986, 21.
[53] Shultz, *Turmoil and Triumph*, 818.

Iran could take, we indicated, would be to use its influence in Lebanon to secure the release of all hostages held there."[54]

Despite making what appeared to be a defensible, if not compelling case, an *L.A. Times* poll taken afterwards showed that the American people did not believe the president was telling the truth. Only 14 percent believed Reagan's statement that he did not trade arms for hostages. Asked whether they thought the United States had upheld its policy of not negotiating with terrorists, 44 percent believed it was only "technically true," while 29 percent believed it "essentially false." Only 20 percent of those polled believed that the US government was in "full compliance with federal law." Forty-six percent believed that the statement was "essentially true," while 24 percent believed it was "essentially false."[55]

Shultz went to see the president the next day and said that he intended to resign but was willing to stay on for the next few weeks "to get him through the crisis." Reagan did not want him to resign, but the two men "argued" over Iran inconclusively, as the president insisted that his policy was correct. The secretary also pursued Regan again, importuning him to attempt to convince the president to "transfer the President's policy . . . to me." Regan "seemed to agree," he recalled, and urged that Shultz go on one of the Sunday talk shows. Shultz agreed.[56]

British prime minister Margaret Thatcher met with President Reagan at Camp David on Saturday, November 15. Shultz hoped to be able to find time to discuss with the president what he would say on television the next day, "with the aim of getting control of the policy shifted away from Poindexter and back to State." As there was no opportunity for a private discussion, Shultz handed to Regan the memo he had crafted authorizing the transfer of power to State. Looking at it, Regan sided with the president, saying: "we are not in a position to do what you're asking for."[57]

The next day, on *Face the Nation*, Shultz threw down the "gauntlet," declaring his total opposition to the president's policy. "It is clearly wrong to trade arms for hostages," he said, "because it encourages taking more." Will there be any more arms shipments? he was asked. "Under the circumstances of Iran's war with Iraq, its pursuit of terrorism, its association with those holding our hostages,

---

[54] Ronald Reagan, "Address to the Nation on the Iran Arms and Contra Aid Controversy, November 13, 1986," *The Public Papers of President Ronald W. Reagan*, Ronald Reagan Presidential Library, https://www.reaganlibrary.gov/archives/speech/address-nation-iran-arms-and-contra-aid-controversy-november-13-1986. See also Walter Pincus, "Reagan Told Deal Key to Iran's Help," *Washington Post*, November 14, 1986, A1.

[55] "Poll Shows Americans Doubt Reagan on Iran," *Washington Post*, November 18, 1986, A14.

[56] Shultz, *Turmoil and Triumph*, 819-20.

[57] Ibid., 821.

I would certainly say, as far as I'm concerned, no." Asked whether he had "authority to speak for the administration," Shultz responded, "no."[58]

Reagan Engages, Loses, and Switches

Not only had the president's Iran initiative failed, his defense of the Iran initiative had failed.[59] The many holes in the story had generated a profound skepticism. He had defended his decision as a matter of "national interest," claimed "progress continues to be made," and asked the American people for their support.[60] The response was overwhelmingly negative: from the political establishment, with Shultz's open rebellion; from the Democrat-controlled Congress, which was in an uproar; from the Republican leadership, which would not back him; from the media, which spewed an outpouring of critical articles cataloguing arms shipments in minute detail; and in public opinion, which demonstrated that the president's prize asset, his credibility, had been seriously impaired. He was condemned without trial for secretly trading arms for hostages, ignoring Congress, and violating his own policy.

So, Reagan decided to do what he had done before, in 1983 after the KAL 007 crisis. He would relinquish policy control to Shultz temporarily, but retain ultimate decision-making authority over strategy. In the meantime, the president would defend his policy against Shultz's charge that he had ransomed arms for hostages, which necessitated a convincing history of events, and prepare to defend himself against the attack on his presidency that was clearly building.

His immediate public reaction was to assert that he and Shultz were united. The day after Shultz's appearance on *Face the Nation*, the White House issued a statement declaring that the secretary "did speak for the administration," that "the President has no plans to send further arms to Iran," and that both were in "complete accord on this."[61] The president was asked at a picture-taking ceremony whether he would fire Shultz. "I'm not firing anyone," he replied.

At separate briefings, White House and State Department spokesmen sparred over who controlled what, differing "in their description of administration decision-making processes." White House spokesman Larry Speakes declared "the president makes the decisions," while State Department spokesman Charles

---

[58] Ibid.

[59] Perhaps the final nail in the president's Iran initiative was news on November 15, that Bahramani had fled Iran for Toronto, Canada, with an "investigator" hard on his heels. See Scott Armstrong et al., *The Chronology: The Documented Day-by-Day Account of the Secret Military Assistance to Iran and the Contras* (New York: Warner Books, 1987), 558.

[60] Ronald Reagan, "Address to the Nation on the Iran Arms Controversy," November 13, 1986.

[61] Shultz, *Turmoil and Triumph*, 823.

Redman said "this building, the State Department, is the focal point of foreign policy. That includes Iran, as well as all other areas of the world."[62]

Regarding the incipient challenge to the presidency, Reagan sought advice from former President Nixon and instructed Pat Buchanan, a White House speechwriter who had worked for him, to contact the ex-president. Nixon advised Reagan to admit that he had made a mistake, get the truth out, and avoid even the appearance of a cover-up.[63] Reagan agreed that it was vital to get the truth out and avoid a cover-up, but rejected the idea of admitting a mistake. Reagan believed that his policy of reestablishing relations with Iran was the right one and would adhere to it firmly.

Nixon's advice was not as valuable as his example. The lesson Reagan took from Nixon was that to fight the new world order establishment the way Nixon had would lead to the same outcome, the threat of impeachment and loss of the presidency. Reagan decided that it was more important to retain the presidency than it was to contend over a policy that had already failed. His plan would be to distance himself from the implementation of policy and place the blame on his aides for its improper execution.

Meanwhile, pursuant to Poindexter's direction, North prepared a sanitized "maximum chronology" of the arms shipments, based in part on McFarlane's memo of November 7, which dealt with the Israeli arms shipments of 1985, conversations with other government personnel, and his own records of the events. A chronology of events would establish the basic "party line" officials could rely on in testimony to Congress and in remarks to the public. It would contain the essential information on which the president's upcoming press conference would be based.

Only McFarlane had known of the genesis of the 1985 Israeli arms sales. North and Poindexter had become involved only in November with the Hawk fiasco. Thus, North's November 17 chronology accurately described the three arms shipments of 1986 but followed McFarlane's memo for the events of 1985, stating that the US Government was "not aware" of the Israeli TOW deliveries of August-September until afterward; and referencing the November Hawk shipment but keeping "silent on the question of US knowledge and approval." [64] North and McFarlane both had an interest in avoiding discussion of the November shipment.

When the crisis broke, Meese assigned his aide Charles Cooper the task of determining the legality of the arms deals and he had no difficulty determining

---

[62] Lou Cannon and Walter Pincus, "Reagan Has 'No Plans' to Ship Iran More Arms, but Order Still in Effect," *Washington Post*, November 18, 1986, A1.

[63] Mayer and McManus, *Landslide*, 307.

[64] *Congressional Report on the Iran Contra Affair*, 299. Mayer and McManus, *Landslide*, 308, say that this chronology stated that "Israel had delivered the HAWK missiles over the objections of the United States."

that the policy authorized by the January 17 finding was legal.[65] When he looked
at North's November 17 chronology, however, and saw that Israel had shipped
weapons in 1985, he realized that this information was a potential time bomb. The
shipments violated the Arms Export Control Act (AECA) and there had been no
congressional notification.

Cooper called Meese and Paul Thompson, Poindexter's counsel.
Poindexter then called McFarlane in to review North's chronology and directed
Thompson to call a meeting of the government's national security lawyers. The
next day, November 18, Cooper, Thompson, Peter Wallison of the White House,
Dave Doherty of CIA, Lawrence Garrett of DOD, and Abe Sofaer of State
gathered in Wallison's office. The meeting was designed for Cooper and
Thompson to brief the others, to test whether or not their story would pass muster.

Sofaer, State's counsel, thought Cooper's justification of the 1986 arms
sales, based on the January 17 finding, was acceptable, but "it was unclear . . .
whether [his] legal theory could be applied to the September 1985 shipment or to
other pre-1986 shipments." Referring to North's chronology, Cooper stated that
the "United States had no knowledge of the [1985] transaction until after the sale
had occurred."[66] Cooper, too, made no mention of the November Hawk shipment.

Sofaer "asked them what they had and whether we could be given
copies," but Thompson "refused to let us see it or to provide any additional
information." We had "no need to know," he said, shocking those "who had been
excluded." Sofaer thought it "ridiculous" that the very people "supposed to help
their clients satisfy legal obligations" were being denied the information needed
to do so. Sofaer became convinced that "Poindexter was blocking access to
information that could undermine the story he was attempting to develop."[67]

Later that same day, Poindexter briefed Sofaer and Armacost, but still
not Wallison, providing more information than Thompson had, but "still not all
of the facts." He "claimed that the United States had not sanctioned the September
1985 shipment of TOWs," but he, too, "did not mention the shipment of
HAWKs." Sofaer and Armacost left the meeting "certain that Poindexter was
making things up as he went along."[68]

They were only partly correct. Poindexter and North were scrambling to
string together the basic facts of the initiative. Their chronology obviously could
not be comprehensive, but they hoped that it would be sufficiently accurate to be
plausible and defensible. Potentially, it seemed, Reagan could be legally

---

[65] See *Congressional Report on the Iran-Contra Affair*, 380-81, for a discussion of the
legality of presidential findings.

[66] Abraham Sofaer, "Iran-Contra: Ethical Conduct and Public Policy," *Houston Law
Review* (December 2003): 1090-91. Peter J. Wallison, *Ronald Reagan: The Power of
Conviction and the Success of His Presidency* (Boulder: Westview, 2003), 188-89,
claimed that the purpose of the meeting was to "share [their] knowledge," but omits
the fact that Cooper and Thompson were briefing from the NSC chronology.

[67] Sofaer, "Iran-Contra: Ethical Conduct and Public Policy," 1091.

[68] Ibid., 1092.

vulnerable in terms of the Arms Export Control Act for the 1985 Israeli TOW and Hawk shipments, but the November Hawk deal presented the more serious problem of the CIA's entanglement. Both, recall, had been the result of the new world order's entrapment scheme.

On the TOW shipments, in his earlier memo to Poindexter, McFarlane had accurately related that the president had not authorized the Israeli shipment of arms (even though, in fact, McFarlane had led the Israelis to believe that the president had authorized their action). Thus, the administration's position consistently would be that the president had not authorized the August-September shipments.

On the Hawk affair, McFarlane again acted without presidential authorization and the Israelis had, for their own protection, entangled the CIA peripherally in the delivery to ensure US government commitment in what the Israelis considered to be a joint venture. McFarlane had informed the president of Israel's action in November just before it commenced, but in no sense was approval requested, or given. In both cases, as McFarlane knew, the Arms Export Control Act required congressional notification in advance.[69]

There were three findings in question, which provided presidential authorization for policy, the January 17, 1986 finding, the December 5, 1985 finding, and also the mistakenly signed finding of January 6, 1986. Poindexter argued that the January 17 finding, which formally authorized the initiative, superseded the previous two. The relevant laws governing the initiative in 1986 were the Economy Act and the Foreign Assistance Act, not the AECA. Congressional reporting requirements were less stringent for these and the president had specifically instructed Casey to defer notification to Congress until a later time.[70]

More serious was the December 5, 1985 finding that sought retroactively to ratify the CIA's involvement and expressly described an arms-for-hostages trade. The finding was almost literally the only direct evidence of what seemed to be the president's authorization of Israel's November Hawk shipment, and that had come after the fact. Thus, it could be construed as a cover-up. There was only one signed copy of this finding, which was in Poindexter's possession. The existence of the December finding appeared to explain why neither North nor Poindexter wanted to mention the November Hawk deal.

---

[69] A new section had been added to the AECA on August 27, 1986, prohibiting the export of arms to countries the Secretary of State determined were supporters of international terrorism, but it did not apply in the case of the January 17, 1986 finding, which was based on a different law—the Economy Act.

[70] Bob Woodward, "Reagan Ordered Casey to Keep Iran Mission from Congress," *Washington Post*, November 15, 1986, A1. "The president issued [a] written order to Casey in an attempt to protect his intelligence chief from the anticipated wrath of Congress." See also, *Iran Arms Sales: DOD's Transfer of Arms to the Central Intelligence Agency*, GAO Report, no. 132738, March 1987.

When McFarlane arrived at North's office on the evening of November 18, he changed North's chronology and the president's opening statement for his news conference the next day. In the process, he exonerated himself from any responsibility for the November 1985 Hawk shipment, but cleverly left the president open to a charge of a cover-up. North's chronology, as it had evolved to this point, simply stated that the November Hawk shipment was "not an authorized exception to [US] policy."

McFarlane deleted that sentence and inserted the following in its place: "Later in the fall, other transfers of equipment were made between Israel and Iran although some of the items were returned to Israel."[71]McFarlane had pinned the operation on Israel, removed all references to any US involvement, or even that a shipment of arms had occurred, and, according to Mayer and McManus, he inserted into the chronology that he, himself, "had actually objected to the sale."[72]

North confirmed that McFarlane "totally altered the facts about the [Hawk] delivery and our role in facilitating it, and made it appear that we didn't even know about it at the time." North had his own reasons for going along with McFarlane's decision not "to reveal our connection with that 1985 shipment." It not only could have led to disclosure of the December 5 finding, which "would have been enormously embarrassing for the administration,"[73] but also could have led to revelation of his own involvement in its formulation. Of course, in the fall of 1985 North could not have anticipated what would lie ahead for the initiative a year later.

Shultz Marshals His Forces

Shultz realized that the crisis was fast approaching a critical point and mobilized his forces for action. Aside from confronting the president directly, with support from his State Department team he sent legal counsel Sofaer into action with the charge that the president had lied about the November Hawk fiasco. Charging the president with an illegal action, however, also was a decision to sacrifice his ally, McFarlane, who would be exposed as lying about the Hawk shipment. Shultz's attack splintered the upper ranks of the administration as everyone took cover. As will be discussed in the next chapter, as soon as McFarlane learned that Shultz had sacrificed him, he began to claim that the president had authorized "everything" the Israelis did. Reagan, too, would move to protect his position by sacrificing his top aides.

Shultz saw the president alone in the early afternoon of November 19 before his press conference that evening, trying again to persuade him to

---

[71] *Congressional Report on the Iran-Contra Affair*, 300.

[72] Mayer and McManus, *Landslide*, 310-11, seeing a multiple cover-up, say "McFarlane wanted to obscure the circumstances under which he approved the first Israeli shipment in August 1985, which was almost certainly illegal under the Arms Export Control Act" and to deny his role in the November Hawk deal.

[73] North, *Under Fire*, 313.

relinquish control of Iran policy. After asserting that "terrible mistakes had been made," he "read to the president a statement that I wanted him to make on television declaring that there would be no more arms sales and that our Iran policy would be managed by the secretary of state." Reagan refused to turn over control to Shultz, insisting that the "operation was a good one and argued, furthermore, that Iran had "tempered its support for terrorism." Shultz strongly disagreed, insisting that even if it were true it was a "terrible deal to make."[74]

Shultz maintained that "terrorism is an international problem and we must treat it that way," but did not elaborate. Instead, he showed Reagan a report by his aide Jerry Bremer, which said "Lebanese groups associated with Iran" had taken the three recent hostages, Reed, Cicippio, and Tracy. (Bremer's argument was misleading and simplistic, but Shultz's main concern was its political utility, not the truth. The hostage takers were Lebanese, all right, and all may have had ties to Iran, but some, at least, also had ties to Qaddafi and the Russians, which he did not note.)[75]

Reagan did not know the details, and responded, "this is news to me." Shultz immediately said, "you are not fully informed. You must not continue to say we made no deals for hostages. You have been deceived and lied to. I plead with you . . . *don't* say that Iran has let up on terrorism." Reagan again responded, "you're telling me things I don't know." Shultz replied, "if I'm telling you something you don't know—I don't know much—then something is terribly wrong here!"[76]

Either wittingly or unwittingly this exchange between Reagan and Shultz would provide the president with his exit strategy. His defense would be that he had been "not fully informed" and "deceived and lied to" by his subordinates. At the time, however, Shultz had no inkling that Reagan was on the verge of a major decision. Returning to his office he thought he had failed to make an impression. "The president's staff was continuing to deceive him," he thought, but "he was allowing himself to be deceived."

Receiving the White House text of what the president would say at his press conference, Shultz became alarmed, fearing that the president would continue to run Iran policy out of the NSC. So, he called Regan, seeking his help once again. He "went over . . . the same points I had made to the president": the structure of the deals was clearly arms for hostages; Iran was still involved in terrorism; it was "disastrous" to intermingle intelligence and operations; running operations out of the White House was "idiocy," depriving the president of any

---

[74] Shultz, *Turmoil and Triumph*, 828.
[75] The so-called Revolutionary Justice Organization, a Libyan-controlled group that also did work for other clients, had taken all three. Indeed, Kangarlu had evidently sanctioned the taking of Cicippio. See "North PROF Note to Poindexter," October 10, 1986, *Tower Report*, B-167 and Samuel Segev, *The Iranian Triangle: The Untold Story of Israel's Role in the Iran-Contra Affair* (New York: Free Press, 1988), 305-6.
[76] Shultz, *Turmoil and Triumph*, 828.

insulation. Shultz felt that Regan "was increasingly awake to the fact that he, too, had been misled."[77]

During his press conference that evening, Reagan threw several curves, hoping to placate Shultz, while justifying his policy. In his opening statement, which was not the one McFarlane had prepared for him,[78] the president reiterated his purposes: to improve relations with Tehran, negotiate an end to the Iran-Iraq war, end terrorism, and effect release of the hostages.

Finessing Shultz's objections, the president said, "these policy objectives were never in dispute." The differences were in "how best to proceed." Several top advisers, he said, opposed making a limited exception of our arms embargo "as a signal of our serious intent." Others felt that "no progress could be made without this sale." Weighing their views, and the risks as well as the rewards, the president declared, "I decided to proceed."[79]

Shultz had demanded that the president announce that he would end the initiative and hand over control of Iran policy to the State Department. Instead, the president said:

> To eliminate the widespread but mistaken perception that we have been exchanging arms for hostages, I have directed that no further sales of arms of any kind be sent to Iran. I have further directed that all information relating to our initiative be provided to the appropriate members of Congress.[80]

Reagan had terminated arms sales, as Shultz demanded, but retained control of the policy reins. In a tense exchange with reporters involving 41 questions, the president maintained that the policy was not a "mistake," but a "high-risk gamble" that the circumstances warranted. He said, "we still have those contacts. We still have made some ground," with the recovery of three hostages. "What we did was right, and we're going to continue on this path." His answer referred to continuing efforts to recover the remaining hostages, but Shultz chose to interpret his answer as meaning the continuation of arms-for-hostages, ignoring the opening statement in which the president had said specifically he had ended them.

Four of the questions directly asked whether the United States had "condoned shipments by Israel." The president, not wanting to identify Israel by

---

[77] Ibid., 829. Shultz's charge that running operations out of the White House was "idiocy," was simply gamesmanship. Every president in the modern era has directed foreign policy, or policies, from the Oval Office. The president originates policies based on his strategy and the Department of State executes.

[78] McFarlane, *Special Trust*, 98, says "he didn't use the opening statement I had prepared."

[79] Ronald Reagan, "The President's News Conference, November 19, 1986," *The Public Papers of President Ronald W. Reagan*, Ronald Reagan Presidential Library, https://www.reaganlibrary.gov/archives/speech/presidents-news-conference-22.

[80] Ibid.

name, but continuing to maintain that he had not authorized any third country arms shipments, replied each time that "we did not condone and do not condone the shipment of arms from other countries." Twice reporters said erroneously that chief of staff Regan had acknowledged Israel's arms shipments to Iran and the president disputed their claim.[81]

As Regan saw it, the president had "carried off a difficult news conference better than his enemies wished to concede," although Shultz and his aides thought the president's performance disastrous.[82] Weinberger publicly backed the president, defending the initiative as "well justified," and backing away from any association with Shultz's criticisms. "It is certainly understandable that the president would want to do what he could to try to change [Iran's] policies . . . . Now if that doesn't succeed, why then, obviously, we'll not pursue it."[83]

The article on Weinberger was stuffed in the back pages of the *Washington Post*, but an interview with McFarlane made front-page headlines. The former national security adviser, associating himself with Shultz, claimed in an interview "the administration made a 'mistake' in providing arms to Iran as part of an arrangement that included release of US hostages."[84] Senior White House officials immediately pronounced themselves "flabbergasted" at McFarlane's comments.[85]

Don Regan, siding with the president and against Shultz, lashed out at McFarlane for his remarks. In a report leaked from a senior staff meeting, Regan declared, "let's not forget whose idea this was. It was Bud's [McFarlane's] idea. When you give lousy advice, you get lousy results." Other leaks noted, "second-guessing and increasingly bitter criticism . . . [had] swept the White House . . . . Everybody is running from this thing."[86]

Meanwhile, as soon as the press conference had ended, Shultz called the president and claimed that he had made "a great many factual errors," which he

---

[81] Immediately after the press conference, the White House issued a clarification in the president's name, acknowledging that "a third country [was] involved in our secret project with Iran," but still did not name Israel, and said that "all of the shipments . . . I have authorized or condoned taken in total could be placed aboard a single cargo aircraft." See Mayer and McManus, *Landslide*, 314.

[82] Don Regan, *For the Record* (New York: Harcourt, Brace, Jovanovich, 1988), 36. Shultz, *Turmoil and Triumph*, 830. Lou Cannon, "Reagan Defends Iran Arms Deal, Says It Freed 3 Hostages," *Washington Post*, November 20, 1986, A1.

[83] Molly Moore, "Weinberger Backs Policy toward Iran," *Washington Post*, November 20, 1986, A24.

[84] Lou Cannon, "McFarlane Calls Sending Arms to Iran a 'Mistake,'" *Washington Post*, November 20, 1986, 1.

[85] Bernard Weinraub, "White House 'Flabbergasted' at McFarlane's Comments That Iran Deal Was Mistake," *New York Times*, November 21, 1986, 6.

[86] David Hoffman, "Reagan Aides Cast Blame for Dealings with Iran," *Washington Times*, November 21, 1986, 1.

wanted to point out to him. Reagan agreed to see him the next morning, leading Shultz to believe that he "now had a shot at turning this fiasco around." Shultz's plan was to force Poindexter out and take his place. "I would be willing," Shultz said, "to turn State over to my deputy, John Whitehead, and become acting NSC adviser for a month. I would clean house and then turn the job over to whoever would be permanently appointed."[87]

When Shultz arrived at the White House, the president would not see him, so he spoke to Regan, instead. The secretary went through all of the president's mistakes and "put this idea" of taking control of the NSC to Regan. The chief of staff told him that the president had told Bush and Poindexter of the charge that he had been factually misled. Reagan, he said, wanted to "think it over at the ranch" over the weekend and convene a meeting of the NSPG on Monday "to go over what everybody knows and get it all together."[88]

At this, Shultz flew into a rage, exclaiming "that's a formula for catastrophe! . . . We have to make decisions. Here they are. Make them! The longer you wait, the worse it gets. It's not a matter of getting our lines straight! Think of the future!" Regan was "uncharacteristically subdued" and made no response. The president was not available. Shultz insisted on seeing him and said he would call Regan that afternoon and "push him on this again."[89]

Returning to his office, Shultz decided to apply greater pressure on the White House and use his trump card. He would bring in legal adviser Sofaer as his unwitting attack dog. As Sofaer recounted it, Shultz "decided to give me and Armacost access to some of the notes that Charlie Hill had kept of meetings and calls from the time Shultz became Secretary of State." One of Hill's notes was of McFarlane's meeting with Shultz in Geneva in November 1985 during which he "told Shultz that a shipment of Hawks was being made to Iran that month by Israel with US approval for the purpose of securing the release of hostages."[90]

Sofaer jumped or was led to conclude, "this single note established beyond any doubt that the White House knew of and had approved that shipment."[91] Sofaer assumed incorrectly, but not unreasonably based on what he was being told, that McFarlane knew what the president knew, and thus took Hill's use of the term "with US approval" to mean Reagan had approved the Hawk shipment as part of an arms-for-hostages deal, when he had not.

As it happened, that Thursday morning of November 20 Poindexter's office was a scene of hectic activity, as aides prepared statements for both the

---

[87] Shultz, *Turmoil and Triumph*, 831.

[88] Ibid.

[89] Ibid.

[90] Sofaer, "Iran-Contra: Ethical Conduct and Public Policy," 1094. Shultz, *Turmoil and Triumph*, 831, turns it around, claiming that "Abe Sofaer asked me to authorize him to tell White House counsel Wallison and Attorney General Ed Meese of the evidence that we had that administration officials knew of arms shipments that had been made before the January 17, 1986, finding."

[91] Sofaer, "Iran-Contra: Ethical Conduct and Public Policy," 1094.

national security adviser and Casey, who were scheduled to testify before the House and Senate Intelligence Committees the next morning. Shultz had just received an early draft of Casey's testimony and handed it to Sofaer just "after [he] had obtained the readout from Hill." Sofaer "immediately noticed" the statement that no one "at the CIA" had known that the November shipment had been an arms shipment. He then concluded "McFarlane's statement to Shultz did not establish that the CIA also knew that the shipment was arms, not oil-drilling equipment, but it made the truthfulness of the draft testimony statement highly unlikely."[92]

Mike Armacost jumped in to say that the CIA "had used its own airline, Southern Air Transport, to handle the work." (Armacost was incorrect—St. Lucia airlines was used, but saying it had been Southern Air Transport allowed him to make a connection with the Contras.)[93] He then surmised, "the testimony was false and possibly reflected some sort of conspiracy involving Central America as well. We agreed to demand that the CIA make the necessary changes in Casey's testimony."[94]

Shultz and his aides were building the case for arguing there was a conspiracy involving both Iran and the Contras. Carefully primed, Sofaer immediately placed calls to Meese and Wallison "to report the information [he] had learned from Hill's note . . . that the US government undoubtedly was aware that the November 1985 shipment was of Hawk missiles and that Casey's testimony was probably false in claiming that the CIA had no knowledge of that fact." Meese was not there but called back later to reassure Sofaer that he "knew of certain facts that explained all these matters," but Sofaer "refused to accept that response as adequate reassurance." [95]

In his call to Wallison, Sofaer claimed that the president's lawyer did not know about the Hawk shipment and implied that he was being deceived by "the people around him at the White House."[96] Wallison, however, said that he had a "vague recollection of having been told by Poindexter" earlier of the Hawk shipment. While he was on the phone, Cooper and Thompson had come into his office having finished working on the testimony for Poindexter and Casey. Sofaer claims that when Wallison asked if they knew about the shipment, they "admitted that they knew about it but had not told him." But Wallison denies this charge, too, saying that when he asked if they were aware of it, "they said they were not."[97]

By the time Sofaer had called about Casey's testimony, the draft had undergone several revisions, particularly about the November Israeli arms

---

[92] Ibid.
[93] See Bob Woodward, *Veil: The Secret Wars of the CIA, 1981-1987* (New York: Simon and Schuster, 1987), 420-21
[94] Sofaer, "Iran-Contra: Ethical Conduct and Public Policy," 1095.
[95] Ibid.
[96] Ibid., 1096.
[97] Wallison, *Ronald Reagan*, 194.

shipment. North, seeking to protect the NSC and himself, had insisted that Casey's testimony be broadened from "we in CIA" to "no one in the US Government" knew that the agency's proprietary airline had hauled missiles to Iran until mid-January of the following year.[98]

All in the meeting, including Poindexter, Casey, Meese, Gates, Thompson, Cooper and North knew that this was untrue, but agreed to it. Meese penciled in the change, which conveniently placed their knowledge of the event *after* the January 17 finding, legalizing it.[99] After Sofaer's blast, Casey's testimony was changed again, eliminating all reference to the shipment, which satisfied Sofaer. It wasn't the whole truth, he said, but "at least there wasn't a lie out there."[100]

Shultz's revelation of Hill's note, through Sofaer documenting McFarlane's call to him about the November Hawk shipment, was the straw that broke the camel's back. He had raised the ante, not only charging Reagan with an illegal act, but also with a cover-up. McFarlane had entangled the CIA in the Hawk shipment, but Reagan had attempted to cover it up with a clearly illegal, after-the-fact finding, the so-called December 5 finding. Worst of all, the finding justified a purely arms-for-hostages policy, which the president had consistently denied authorizing. The new world order entrapment had succeeded.[101]

That afternoon of November 20, Shultz arrived at the White House family quarters armed for a battle with the president. Reagan claims he had agreed to the meeting because Shultz had issued an "ultimatum," threatening to quit unless the president fired Poindexter.[102] Reagan also may have wanted to hear directly from Shultz about the November Hawk shipment.

Shultz had hoped Nancy would be there, but she stayed away; Regan was the only other person present. In an hour-long "tirade," Shultz went over prepared talking points denouncing every aspect of the president's policy. In a "hot and heavy" argument Shultz declared that Iran still supported terrorism and was the "main banker, patron, arms supplier, and adviser" of Hezbollah; the Iranians we had dealt with were "unscrupulous and untrustworthy"; we had traded arms for hostages; there was a serious question about the president's "right to defer for so long reporting to Congress."[103] When he raised the subject of McFarlane's November 1985 call to him about the Hawk shipment, Reagan disarmingly said

---

[98] James McCullough, "Personal Reflections on Bill Casey's Last Month at CIA," *Studies in Intelligence* 39, no. 5 (1996); and Draper, *Very Thin Line*, 488.

[99] "Meese Testimony," *Iran-Contra Investigation: Joint Hearings*, 100-9, 218-19.

[100] Mayer and McManus, *Landslide*, 321.

[101] But at the cost of sacrificing McFarlane, which did not sit well with Shultz's aide, Charles Hill. Hill was upset because Sofaer's disclosure could "be read as GPS [Shultz] fingering McF [McFarlane] on something that could get him prison." See "Hill Note," November 24, 1986, Walsh, *Final Report of the Independent Counsel*, 1:353n225.

[102] Ronald Reagan, *An American Life* (New York: Simon and Schuster, 1990), 529.

[103] Draper, *Very Thin Line*, 484.

that he "knew about that," but "that wasn't arms-for-hostages."[104] (In fact, no hostages had been released as a result of that shipment.)

Shultz's approach had been to say that he "agreed with the president's objective but parted company with the way it had been carried out." Placing the blame squarely on the national security adviser, he said that he had been "a victim of Poindexter's misinformation."[105] Shultz demanded that Reagan fire Poindexter on the spot, but the president demurred. "He still wanted to have a meeting on Monday at which everyone could exchange information." Reagan had heard him out without rancor and Shultz seemed surprised that he "didn't seem to resent my efforts, but I didn't shake him one bit."[106]

Shultz didn't realize it, but he was like a bull charging through an open door into the china shop. The president had already decided on a carefully choreographed preemptive maneuver to extricate himself from any danger to his presidency. Reagan knew that Shultz had one more bomb to throw. The secretary had attended the May 16 NSPG meeting at which the president had exclaimed, "Can't Ollie find funds" for the Contras, so he knew of the president's direct involvement in the search for funds.[107]

Shultz had raised the issue of the use of Iran surplus funds for the Contras among his aides. As Armacost had put it to Sofaer earlier that very day, they thought there was "some sort of conspiracy involving Central America [and Iran]."[108] Recall, congressional leaders in both houses had planned probes of both the Iran and Contra policies, already suggesting that connection.[109] Rumors were also flying around the administration of the use of Iran funds to support the Contras. Ghorbanifar had made the same charge and so had Furmark. If Shultz charged the president with illegal actions in regard to both Iran and the Contras, it would put him squarely on the road to impeachment.

Reagan and his close aides concluded that the game was up. The president had lost the struggle for power and it was time to insulate himself from all complicity, especially with regard to the November Hawk affair. It was important to move as quickly as possible, for time was now a factor. With a Democrat-controlled Congress set to convene and begin investigations, it was imperative to take preemptive action to establish the president's innocence immediately.

---

[104] Shultz, *Turmoil and Triumph*, 832.

[105] Draper, *Very Thin Line*, 485.

[106] Shultz, *Turmoil and Triumph*, 833.

[107] See Chapter 10.

[108] Sofaer, "Iran-Contra: Ethical Conduct and Public Policy," 1095.

[109] Walter Pincus, "Hill Probes of NSC Planned," *Washington Post*, November 10, 1986, A1.

Chapter 19

The Defeat and Survival of Ronald Reagan

President Reagan had lost the struggle for power to his Secretary of State. Worse, the prospect of the exposure of his cover up of the CIA's involvement in the November 1985 Hawk shipment threatened a major scandal. The issue was no longer Iran policy, which had in any case failed, but his own position, which had to be protected at all costs. So, he reluctantly relinquished control of policy to Shultz, employing a variation on a tactic he had used twice earlier in his presidency when a policy conflict had reached a tipping point. Each time the issue was control over the NSC and each time the president triggered an incident to disguise what had happened.

In two previous instances involving a change of control at the NSC, Richard Allen in 1981 and William Clark in 1983, the president employed a minor, domestic incident to divert attention away from a change at NSC.[1] In 1981, he had authorized a Justice Department investigation into Allen's alleged mismanagement of a $1,000 gratuity he had accepted on behalf of Nancy Reagan for an interview the first lady had given to a Japanese magazine. Allen had taken the money, placed it in his office safe, and forgotten about it.

Although the investigation uncovered no wrongdoing, the president used the incident to justify moving Allen out of his NSC post and replacing him with Judge Clark. Politically, Clark gave the president greater control over foreign policy, as the shift in personnel also marked a change in the structure of the policy-making process. Allen, as part of the president's compact with the new world order establishment, had had no policy role during his tenure, while Clark would play a major role in managing the president's foreign policy against the policy preferences of Secretary of State Haig and his successor Shultz.

A similar incident surrounded Judge Clark's removal from his NSC post in October 1983. As a result of the KAL 007 crisis, Shultz had demanded Clark's removal and the president had acquiesced but took the opportunity of the resignation of his Secretary of Interior, James Watt, to disguise this political defeat by shifting Clark from NSC to Interior. Although the maneuver kept Clark in the cabinet for another year, the NSC post went to Shultz's ally, Robert McFarlane. From that position, as recounted in this volume, the new world order faction engineered the entrapment of the president that led to the current crisis.

---

[1] See the author's *Ronald Reagan: Revolution Ascendant*, chap. 1, for Allen's removal; and above, chap. 4, for Clark's.

Reagan's Action Plan

The struggle with Shultz over Iran policy was the most serious crisis of Reagan's presidency, but his response was the same in principle as in the Allen and Clark instances. The difference was that this time the president had not merely suffered a setback but had lost power. Therefore, stakes were higher, and so the incident disguising the defeat was larger. To mask his defeat, the president would "discover" that his aides had diverted funds from Iran arms sales to the Contras without his knowledge. Taking command, he would dismiss those deemed responsible, then initiate measures to investigate and make public all of the information about it, including full disclosure to Congress, ensuring that there would be no possibility of a cover-up. [2]

In reality, the president decided to drape a political scandal over his policy failure and political defeat, the so-called "Iran-Contra diversion"; claim that he was "uninformed," place the blame on his aides, and turn over policy control to the secretary.[3] Poindexter and North were prepared to shoulder the burden of blame for their chief, and would do so, but were not apprised of the true nature and extent of their sacrifice. It would involve criminal and not merely political liability and would stretch out over several years after the president had left office.

Connecting the Contra program to the Iran initiative was also Reagan's subtle threat to the new world order establishment because it could implicate Vice President Bush, who was a strong supporter of the Contra program. If Bush were drawn into the scandal it would compromise his own prospects as Reagan's successor. The message was that if Reagan went down, Bush would go down with him and the new world order establishment would lose control of the presidency.

Attorney General Meese, Reagan's long-time fixer from the days of his California governorship, acting, he said, as the president's "legal adviser," not as Attorney General, would manage the exit strategy. [4] It must be emphasized,

---

[2] Lou Cannon, *Reagan* (New York: Putnam, 1982), 132-38, relates a lesson well learned from his California governorship. Reagan's staff had discovered a homosexual ring operating in the governor's office. Reagan forced those identified to resign but tried to keep the mess quiet. The cover-up failed, however, and the resultant scandal had a negative effect on his presidential candidacy. The lesson was that it was eminently preferable to divert attention away from a crisis than to cover it up.

[3] Stephen Engelberg, "Iran Defense for Reagan," *New York Times*, January 8, 1987, A1. "Senior White House aides have apparently decided it was better to suggest that Mr. Reagan was unaware of or misinformed about key decisions than to allow continued speculation about his involvement."

[4] "Meese Testimony," *Iran-Contra Investigation: Joint Hearings before the Senate Select Committee on Secret Military Assistance to Iran and the Nicaraguan Opposition and the House Select Committee to Investigate Covert Arms Transactions with Iran*, 100th Cong., 1st sess., 100-9 (Washington, DC: US Government Printing Office, 1988), 224 25.

however, as this account demonstrates, that the president was not a passive player in the drama. He was deeply involved in his own defense strategy and decided, if not directed, the policy that Meese executed.

The process actually commenced with Casey's testimony before the House and Senate Intelligence Committees on Friday morning, November 21, 1986. During his remarks, Casey three times volunteered that North had been responsible for "problems at the NSC." He had been "active operationally to help the Nicaraguan resistance" and "active in the private provision of weapons to the contras." [5] Casey had "kept away from the details because [he] was barred from doing anything . . . [but, he] knew that others were doing it." [6] Casey's remarks foreshadowed the decision to place the blame on North.

While Casey was giving his testimony, Meese called Poindexter to arrange a meeting with the president, Regan and himself for later that morning. Poindexter immediately called North to tell him that an investigation was beginning, and that Meese would be sending over his aides to look at documents, clearly a "heads up" call. North reassured his boss not to worry, that "it's all taken care of," obviously meaning that he had *already* disposed of all incriminating documents. [7]

At that moment, North was more worried about something else. It was Michael Ledeen, the one man besides McFarlane who knew the details about the events of 1985. Ledeen "wanted to speak publicly" about his role and North wanted to make sure he knew what to say, especially about the Hawk shipment. [8] North jumped into a taxi and sped off to Ledeen's home in Bethesda, Maryland, arriving at 11:00 a.m.

In what was a most unusual, indeed, startling coincidence, when North arrived at Ledeen's home, he found McFarlane already there. McFarlane wanted Ledeen to deny that he had "gone to Israel originally to carry out a specific mission for him at his request." Ledeen thought that McFarlane was trying to "protect" him, while in fact he was attempting to protect himself. North was concerned with "not what happened but what are you [Ledeen] going to say

---

[5] Oliver North and William Novak, *Under Fire: An American Story* (New York: Harper Collins, 1991), 325.

[6] Jane Mayer and Doyle McManus, *Landslide: The Unmaking of the President* (Boston: Houghton Mifflin, 1988), 323.

[7] Ibid., 325. Mayer and McManus say "Poindexter's warning to North touched off a frenzied weekend of destroying documents and warning confederates . . . sometimes only steps ahead of Meese's investigators," but North had been shredding documents for weeks.

[8] "Michael Ledeen Deposition," *Report of the Congressional Committees Investigating the Iran-Contra Affair*, Appendix B, vol. 15 (Washington, DC : 1988), 1472-73. [Hereafter cited as *Congressional Report on the Iran-Contra Affair*, Appendix B.]

happened." Ledeen reassured both men that his "role" had been "nothing more than being a person who listened at meetings and reported what I heard."[9]

North declined to get into the Hawk issue in depth in McFarlane's presence, but arranging for Ledeen to come to his office later that afternoon, accepted a lift from McFarlane back to Washington. North then returned to his office where he, his aide Robert Earl and secretary Fawn Hall proceeded to shred or otherwise dispose of every remaining document, PROF note and KL-43 message that could conceivably be incriminating.

When Ledeen arrived that afternoon, North asked him: "what would you say if you are asked about a shipment of HAWK missiles in November 1985?" Ledeen responded: "I would tell the truth which was that I was aware of it, that I knew that it had happened, but that I was not aware or could not recall who had made the decision to do it or when that decision had been made." North answered: "fine."[10]

Earlier that morning at 11:30, Meese had gone over to the White House for his meeting with the president, Poindexter, and Regan. His purpose was ostensibly to obtain the president's "approval" to interview those involved, review documents, "and pull together a coherent account."[11] Meese's true purpose, however, as Walsh concludes, was to build "a case of deniability for his client-in-fact, President Reagan."[12] Draper also argues that his purpose was to ensure that the president could not be implicated in any illegal act, particularly in regard to the November Hawk shipment.[13] Reagan told Meese to wrap things up over the weekend and be prepared to report back on Monday, November 24, to an NSPG meeting.

Meese returned to the Justice Department to select trusted aides to assist him in reviewing documents and accompany him in interviews with key individuals. Meese picked Charles Cooper, his own counsel, who had been

---

[9] Lawrence E. Walsh, *Final Report of the Independent Counsel for Iran-Contra Matters*, vol. 1 (Washington, DC: United States Court of Appeals for the District of Columbia Circuit, August 4, 1993), 98-99. See also the exchange between Ledeen and McFarlane in the *Wall Street Journal*: Michael Ledeen, "How the Iran Initiative Went Wrong," August 10, 1987, 26; Robert McFarlane, "Retreat, Then Rewrite," August 14, 1987, 15; and Michael Ledeen, "Reread, Then Reconsider," August 21, 1987, 15.

[10] "Michael Ledeen Grand Jury Testimony," in Walsh, *Final Report of the Independent Counsel*, 1:99n175.

[11] Ibid.

[12] Walsh, *Final Report of the Independent Counsel*, 1:525.

[13] Theodore Draper, *A Very Thin Line: The Iran-Contra Affairs* (New York: Hill and Wang, 1991), 499. See also *Report of the Congressional Committees Investigating the Iran-Contra Affair, with Supplemental, Minority and Additional Views*, 100th Cong., 1st sess. (Washington, DC: 1987), 644-47, for the skeptical observations of Congressmen Peter Rodino (D-NJ), Dante Fascell (D-FL), Jack Brooks (D-TX), and Louis Stokes (D-OH) regarding Meese's investigation. [Hereafter cited as *Congressional Report on the Iran-Contra Affair*.]

working on the problem since the crisis had broken, along with two of his deputies, William Bradford Reynolds and John Richardson. All three were loyal political appointees and competent lawyers, but with no investigative experience. The focus of their inquiry was supposed to be the November 1985 Hawk shipment but would turn out to be something very different.

Meese's men drew up a list of witnesses to be interviewed. They were: Bush, McFarlane, Shultz, Weinberger, North, Sporkin, McMahon, Thompson, Allen, the CIA's counsel and "operations officers." Curiously, there were no plans to interview the president, Poindexter, or Casey, although they would be "contacted" for assistance.[14] Nor was Secord or Hakim or anyone else identified as a person of interest. In fact, Meese would only "interview" McFarlane, Shultz, Sporkin, and North in his effort to establish an alibi for the president.

Meanwhile, Poindexter, too, had been busy shredding and deleting documents and memos about the initiative. In fact, Poindexter had been far more "productive" by himself than North had been with his entire team. According to Walsh, Poindexter had deleted 5,012 messages from his computer to North's 736.[15] More important, that afternoon Poindexter calmly tore up the one piece of hard evidence that documented the president's after-the-fact authorization for the Hawk arms-for-hostages deal, the only signed copy of the December 5 finding.[16]

The signed finding was a double-edged sword. While it seemed to show that the president had attempted to authorize an arms-for-hostages deal, it actually proved that he had not authorized the November Hawk shipment. If he had there would have been no need to sign an after-the-fact finding to justify it. Unfortunately, the president decided that the risks attending to the arms-for-hostages charge were greater than the benefit of using the finding to demonstrate that he had not authorized the November shipment, and so it was destroyed.

Poindexter, a computer expert, surely understood that there were backups in the computer system that could not be destroyed, and copies of other documents distributed throughout government offices, so his and North's deletion and shredding operations were only delaying tactics to buy time. A more devious interpretation would be that they anticipated that investigators subsequently would view their efforts as attempts to destroy evidence. (Indeed, Poindexter would be indicted on one charge of destroying evidence.)

Twice that afternoon North went over to the White House to see Poindexter, at 1:30 and 2:25.[17] The first time was with his "spiral notebook," which detailed his involvement in the November shipment. North read out his

---

[14] *Congressional Report on the Iran-Contra Affair*, 306.

[15] Walsh, *Final Report of the Independent Counsel*, 1:124.

[16] Ibid., 142; "Paul Thompson Deposition," *Congressional Report on the Iran-Contra Affair*, Appendix B, vol. 26, 1067; and Draper, *Very Thin Line*, 500. Mayer and McManus, *Landslide*, 329, say that Poindexter "simply" considered the document a "C.Y.A." finding to protect the CIA, and tore it up.

[17] *Congressional Report on the Iran-Contra Affair*, 306.

note of November 26, 1985, which said that Poindexter had told him that Reagan had "directed the operation to proceed." When North expressed his intention to destroy the notebook, Poindexter "did not object."[18] (As discussed in Chapter 11, Poindexter had merely passed on to North what McFarlane had told him.)

The second time North saw Poindexter, Meese was with him. According to North's aide, Robert Earl, when North came back from that meeting, he told him that "It's time for North to be the scapegoat, Ollie has been designated the scapegoat." North reportedly asked Meese if he could have twenty-four or forty-eight hours to finish cleaning up the document trail, but Meese replied that "he did not know whether he could have that much time."[19] (Both Meese and North later denied Earl's account, but there was no reason for Earl to have prevaricated.)[20]

Meese's "Investigation"

While Poindexter and North were tending to their records tasks, Meese put his plan into action. He declined to bring in the criminal division of the Justice Department because, he said, it was a political not a criminal problem, which left him in control. He also declined to seal the offices of the NSC, which gave North and Poindexter continued access to NSC files. North's office would not be sealed until November 25. Meese began his weekend "interviews" that afternoon of the 21st.

First on his list was McFarlane, who came to his office in the Justice Department at 3:30 p.m. Cooper, the only other person present, took notes. Meese asked McFarlane for his views "without distortion," and the former national security adviser generally went over the interpretation he had written in the November 7 memo to Poindexter and the November 18 rewrite of North's chronology, but, abjuring Meese's admonition, further distanced himself from responsibility.[21]

The Israelis, McFarlane said, through David Kimche had suggested arms sales in July 1985. Reagan had not authorized arms sales but was interested in a political opening. McFarlane emphasized that "no one in [the] US government . . . had contact with Israel" on the August-September TOW shipments. In this version, McFarlane sought to airbrush himself entirely out of the picture. The Israelis were the initiators and McFarlane simply a passive recipient of

---

[18] Ibid., 307.

[19] "Robert Earl Testimony," *Congressional Report on the Iran-Contra Affair*, Appendix B, vol. 9, 624-26. See also Mayer and McManus, *Landslide*, 327.

[20] "Meese Testimony," *Iran-Contra Investigation: Joint Hearings*, 100-9, 335-36; and "North Testimony," *Iran-Contra Investigation: Joint Hearings* 100-7, 144.

[21] "Charles Cooper Deposition," *Congressional Report on the Iran-Contra Affair*, Appendix B, vol. 7, 142.

information. He had "learned of the 1985 shipment of TOWs from Ledeen," his *non-governmental* go-between with the Israelis.[22]

When he got to the November Hawk shipment, he diverged even further from his earlier position. He now claimed that in November 1985 "he learned that Israel had shipped oil equipment," remembering "no mention . . . of arms." It was not until the following May, when he was preparing to go to Tehran, that he "learned" that the Israeli shipment had been Hawk missiles. At this, Meese surprised him with the revelation that Shultz had contemporaneous notes that said while in Geneva McFarlane had told him that the Israelis were shipping Hawk missiles in a planned arms-for-hostages swap.[23]

McFarlane, stunned at the realization that Shultz was sacrificing him in his battle with Reagan and flustered at being caught in a flagrant lie, mumbled that he "doesn't remember a chat with [George Shultz], but probably had one."[24] In his typical fashion, McFarlane responded elliptically to Meese's charge that he had contemporaneous proof of McFarlane's knowledge of the Hawk shipment, by admitting only that he had "probably" had a "chat" with Shultz. Of course, the issue was not whether he had engaged in a "chat" with Shultz, but what he had said.

When the interview ended and Cooper left the room, McFarlane asked Meese if he could talk to him for a moment. Thinking fast, he said he wanted the attorney general to know that the "president was 'four square behind' the arms sales from the beginning." According to McFarlane, "Meese expressed relief at this because the president's approval in advance of sales would constitute a finding." In Meese's view, the president's "legal position [was] far better the earlier he made the decision."[25] But, he said, there must be no suggestion of a cover-up.

Discussing McFarlane's performance afterward, both Meese and Cooper thought that he had been flustered and "not entirely forthcoming."[26] Indeed, from this point onward, McFarlane would change his story further to claim that the president had authorized Israeli arms sales from the beginning, even asserting that he had done so from the first briefing at the hospital. He would make this assertion even though he could provide no evidence to support it. Meese also would back this notion for its legal value to the president, not because it was the truth.[27] Then,

---

[22] Ibid. Walsh, *Final Report of the Independent Counsel*, 1:100; Robert C. McFarlane, *Special Trust* (New York: Cadell & Davies, 1994), 99; Mayer and McManus, *Landslide*, 329.

[23] *Congressional Report on the Iran-Contra Affair*, 308.

[24] "Cooper Deposition," 142.

[25] Walsh, *Final Report of the Independent Counsel*, 1:100.

[26] "Cooper Deposition," 142.

[27] Edwin Meese, *With Reagan: The Inside Story* (Washington, DC: Regnery, 1992), 266-67, claimed that the Hughes-Ryan Amendment did not require a *written* finding and that "approval was given orally by the president," based on McFarlane's say so. This is sheer sophistry, as only the most literal reading would permit this

when the story would not hold up, Meese would deny that the president knew anything.

Precisely because there was no evidence for his claim, McFarlane fell back on his construct of a "mental finding," which he had first sold to North during the Hawk shipment a year earlier. In a panic, as soon as he left the Justice Department, McFarlane attempted to cover his tracks. His first call was to North, from a telephone booth on the street (which, conveniently, could not be traced). According to North's note of the call, McFarlane recounted his interview with Meese and said, "RR said he [would] support 'mental finding,'" the exact phrase he had used in his call to North a year earlier.[28]

Twisting Meese's words, McFarlane told North that Meese "was relieved to learn" the president had approved the Iran initiative, which subsequently justified their actions. Of course, Meese had said nothing of the kind. He had said Reagan's legal position *would* be better the earlier he approved of the initiative—a conditional that McFarlane turned into a "fact." (Meese later testified that he never used, or would have used, the phrase, "mental finding," which, of course, had no legitimacy except in McFarlane's imagination.)[29]

McFarlane's next step was to call Shultz at the State Department "to try to obtain a copy of the Charles Hill note."[30] On the advice of Sofaer not to speak to anyone "likely to be under investigation," Shultz refused to take his call. McFarlane then called Sofaer, asking "to see the Hill note." Sofaer refused to let him see it, but "read the note to him." Sofaer did this for two reasons. He "wanted him to know that the effort to cook the facts about the November shipment was untenable and should be abandoned" and also to give him "information that could lead him to avoid committing perjury."[31]

---

interpretation. Hughes-Ryan required that the president provide a finding to the appropriate committees of Congress. Even if the president made an oral finding, he would have to deliver it to appropriate committees of Congress, not to his national security adviser; this would involve a written document. See Hughes-Ryan Amendment to the Foreign Assistance Act, Pub. L. 87–195, pt. III, §662, as added Pub. L. 93–559, § 32, Dec. 30, 1974, 88 Stat. 1804, codified at 22 USC. 2422 (repealed in 1991). Meese also overlooked NSDD 159, January 18, 1985, which explicitly required a written finding for all covert operations. Meese's memoir was published in 1992, before NSDD 159 was declassified, but he knew of its existence. The directive specifically included the attorney general in all NSPG meetings dealing with covert operations. See Christopher Simpson, *National Security Directives of the Reagan and Bush Administrations: The Declassified History of US Political and Military Policy, 1981-1991* (Boulder: Westview, 1995), 493-95.

[28] "North Notebook Entry," November 21, 1986, in Walsh, *Final Report of the Independent Counsel*, 1:100n187.

[29] "Meese Testimony," *Iran-Contra Investigation: Joint Hearings*, 100-9, 231.

[30] Walsh, *Final Report of the Independent Counsel*, 1:101.

[31] Sofaer, "Iran-Contra: Ethical Conduct and Public Policy," *Houston Law Review* (December 2003): 1099. In "Abraham Sofaer Deposition," *Congressional Report on*

That night an increasingly worried McFarlane sent a PROF note to Poindexter in which he doubled down on the "mental finding" notion. Referring to the November Hawk shipment as his "only blind spot," he said that "the matter . . . can be covered if the President made a 'mental finding' before the transfer took place." Then, he said, "on that score we ought to be ok because he was all for letting the Israelis do anything they wanted at the very first briefing in the hospital."[32] McFarlane seemed to believe that if he repeated his falsehood enough times to enough people it would become true. Actually, McFarlane was caught in a double lie: regarding the Hawk shipment and about Reagan's briefing at the hospital and his only way out was to claim that Reagan had authorized everything from the beginning.

The president, meanwhile, was playing his part. While North and Poindexter were working late destroying documents and McFarlane was attempting to puzzle out a plausible defense for himself, Reagan was attending a post-election Capitol Hill dinner for Senate Republicans. Unfortunately, there were more losers than winners—seven had lost and three retired—making the proceedings less than festive.[33] Indeed, in a major defeat, the Republicans had lost control of the Senate, which they had held since 1980.

Meese, however, was busy. He spoke with Shultz to arrange an interview for the next morning, and called Poindexter, Weinberger and Casey to alert them to the investigation. The content of their conversations is unknown. He also arranged for one of his attorneys, John McGinnis, to go over to the CIA that night to review intelligence reports relating to Iran arms sales. Briefing Meese early the next morning, McGinnis confirmed that the US government had been involved in the November Hawk shipment and determined that "excess profits" had accrued from the arms sales.[34]

McGinnis's information was intriguing but vague. CIA entanglement in the Hawk shipment was clear enough, based on an incomplete but sufficiently conclusive message trail, but the only way he could have determined that "excess profits" existed was by examining the bank account of Lake Resources, Secord and Hakim's vehicle for managing Iran arms sales. The CIA had an account at Compagnie de Services Fiduciaires (CSF) in Geneva where the Lake Resources account also was. Did the agency have access to Secord's account, as McGinnis implied? At that time, CSF reportedly was being "operated by former CIA officials," so that possibility cannot be discounted.[35]

---

the Iran-Contra Affair, Appendix B, vol. 26, 288-89, Sofaer appears to suggest that the call to him came first.

[32] Walsh, Final Report of the Independent Counsel, 1:101.

[33] Mayer and McManus, Landslide, 331.

[34] Congressional Report on the Iran-Contra Affair, 309.

[35] Scott Armstrong et al., The Chronology: The Documented Day-by-Day Account of the Secret Military Assistance to Iran and the Contras (New York: Warner Books, 1987), 598-99.

According to Richardson, however, McGinnis's "excess profits" determination had been based on "rumors at CIA [that Iran arms sales] money was funneled through Southern Air Transport" to the Contras, not facts. Undermining this "rumor" was his discovery that "the CIA did not use Southern Air Transport" for the November Hawk shipment, although it had been used later.[36] A different proprietary, St. Lucia Airlines, had been used in November. McGinnis's findings occurred before discovery of North's diversion memo the next day, but it is obvious that the existence of "excess profits" was a necessary precondition to any charge of a diversion of funds.

The next morning, Saturday, November 22, at 8:00, Meese and Cooper met with Shultz and Hill in the secretary's office at the State Department. Meese focused on the November Hawk shipment, stating that he wanted to "get the facts…and no cover-up." Shultz recounted his statement to the president two days before of "Bud's phone call to me on November 19, 1985, in Geneva" and Reagan's reply that he "knew all about that, but that wasn't arms for hostages." Shultz maintained, "no one looking at the record would believe that."[37]

Meese's concern was to insulate Reagan from any knowledge of the Hawk shipment. So, referring to Hill's note of the McFarlane conversation, Meese said, "the president had no notes and had trouble remembering meetings." Signaling the line he intended to take, he said, "certain things could be a violation of the law," but "the president didn't know about the HAWKS in November 1985. If it happened and the president didn't report to Congress, it's a violation." Hill "thought Meese was trying to get Shultz to back off of his claim that the President had admitted knowing about the HAWK shipment." [38]

Meese wanted to know specifically whether there was "any contact that I knew of between Bud and the president on this topic then?" Shultz replied, "not to my knowledge, though I don't know." That, apparently, was all Meese needed to assert definitively, standing over Shultz in what Hill interpreted as an intimidating "back on your heels" manner, "the president had not known of the

---

[36] "John Richardson Deposition," *Congressional Report on the Iran-Contra Affair*, Appendix B, vol. 23, 312-15. See Michael Tackett, "Air Carrier in Thick of Iran Tangle," *Chicago Tribune*, December 21, 1986, 1. Tackett notes that Southern Air Transport flew one mission from Kelly AFB to Tel Aviv in May 1986.

[37] George Shultz, *Turmoil and Triumph* (New York: Scribner, 1993), 835. According to Cooper's notes, Shultz said that McFarlane had come to his hotel, instead of making a phone call. See Draper, *Very Thin Line*, 503. In Shultz's testimony before Congress, he said "McFarlane had told him on November 18, 1985, in Geneva, that four hostages would be released . . . " The correct date was the 19th, not the 18th, and the number of hostages was five not four. See John G. Tower et al., *Report of the President's Special Review Board: February 26, 1987* (Washington, DC: US Government Printing Office, 1987), B-31. See also chap. 5 above.

[38] Walsh, *Final Report of the Independent Counsel*, 1:539, 544, citing Hill's note.

[HAWK] shipment that might be illegal, and that the shipments he did know of were not illegal."[39]

Shultz thought this was a weak position, saying "I would not want to be the president arguing it in public." Then, he offered up the very argument Meese and Reagan had decided to use in the president's defense, when he said, "another angle worries me. This could get mixed in with help for the freedom fighters in Nicaragua. One thing may be overlapping with another. There may be a connection." Meese "did not reply to this suggestion."[40]

Shultz claimed that Mike Armacost was the inspiration for his assertion of an Iran-Contra "connection," based on his view "that a contractor in the Iran arms deliveries, Southern Air Transport, had also been used in support of the Contras." He speculated "they may have shifted funds between the two trades."[41]

Behind their speculation lay a Justice Department investigation of Southern Air Transport, which had begun after the Hasenfus shootdown in early October. The department had begun to conduct "field interviews" of SAT crewmembers. Poindexter, responding to North's concerns that these interviews would interfere with ongoing hostage rescue operations, called Meese, who requested a postponement of the investigation. The Justice Department put off further interviews for over three weeks, although their investigation continued.[42]

Meese had remained silent about Shultz's suggestion of an Iran-Contra connection because it was a bombshell. If Shultz leaked that news to the press before Reagan could make it public himself, the disclosure would immediately sound the tocsin of a Watergate-style cover up. It meant that there was no time to lose. It was imperative for Reagan to make that revelation before Shultz did, in order to retain the initiative and not be forced onto the defensive.

Meese had planned on sending some of his men to review NSC files, but now it was urgent to get them over to North's office as soon as possible. Thus, immediately following his interview with Shultz, at 10:30 a.m. Meese told Cooper to call Thompson to tell him that two of his men, William Bradford Reynolds and John Richardson, were heading to North's office right away. They arrived at the Old Executive Office Building a little after 11:00 a.m.

"Discovery" of the Diversion Memorandum

In the entire history of the Iran-Contra Affair, the so-called "chance" discovery of North's memorandum proposing the use of Iran arms sales surplus

---

[39] Ibid. and Shultz, *Turmoil and Triumph*, 836.
[40] Ibid. Indeed, Meese would later deny that Shultz had made such a connection, but Hill's notes corroborated Shultz's account. See *Congressional Report on the Iran-Contra Affair*, 309.
[41] Shultz, *Turmoil and Triumph*, 836.
[42] Ronald Ostrow, "Said It Could Blow Lid off Arms Deal: North Warning to FBI on Probe of Airline Alleged," *Los Angeles Times*, January 14, 1987, A12; and Walsh, *Final Report of the Independent Counsel*, 1:551-52.

funds for the Contras, stands out as what Reagan called a "smoking gun."[43] On the face of it, however, given the immense significance of the memo, its discovery fit Meese's plan to protect the president far too perfectly for it to have been a chance occurrence.[44]

In short, when Meese sent Reynolds and Richardson to North's office, he was confident of what they would find. North and his colleagues, including Poindexter, had for weeks, since the Hasenfus shootdown, been carefully pruning their files of potentially damaging information. North had confidently told Poindexter just the day before that he had "taken care of" everything in his files. It therefore seems highly unlikely that North would have overlooked an obviously incriminating memo.

The high probability is that the memo was planted in North's files. If so, the question is: by whom? There are two persons who had means, motive, and opportunity: Reynolds and Poindexter. Reynolds, Meese's long-time confidant, who "discovered" the memo, could have brought it with him when he went to North's office and inserted it into North's files during an unobserved moment. There were several stretches of time during which he and Richardson were alone at their table and the only other person present, Colonel Earl, was in an adjacent room.

More likely, however, it was Poindexter who would have planted the memo. He was committed to taking responsibility for the diversion. He had full access to NSC offices and had a copy of North's memo. (North had sent five memos to Poindexter discussing use of residuals.[45]) The national security adviser could have pulled a copy from his files and simply walked over to the EOB and inserted it into North's files.

On Saturday morning, when Reynolds and Richardson arrived at the EOB, NSC counsel Paul Thompson let them into the building and showed them to North's office. Earl was the only one in the office at that time and he had laid out on a table numerous accordion-style file folders. Richardson thought they were there to look into the 1985 events, to determine whether the US government had "authorized or acquiesced in" the Israeli arms shipments.[46] After looking at the material laid out on the desk, Reynolds "suggested it would be easier if he just

---

[43] Ronald Reagan, *An American Life* (New York: Simon and Schuster, 1990), 530.

[44] As Draper, *Very Thin Line*, 507, notes: "It was . . . pure chance that enabled Reynolds to hit on the one paragraph that North had been most determined to conceal. One wonders what might have happened if North had successfully destroyed the telltale document and had obliged the two lawyers to come back without their revelation."

[45] "William Bradford Reynolds Deposition," *Congressional Report on the Iran-Contra Affair*, Appendix B, Vol. 22, 1128.

[46] "John Richardson Deposition," *Congressional Report on the Iran-Contra Affair*, Appendix B, vol. 25, 260-61.

took all this [the files] over to Justice," but Richardson advised against it, saying they could be "open to attack if we take custody out of the NSC . . . "[47]

"Sometime during the first hour of their review" of the files, the congressional report notes, Reynolds suddenly "found an item that seemed out of place." Standing out among the files contained in the reddish-brown accordion folders was a "white folder stamped with a red White House label."[48] According to Reynolds, Earl "was not in the room" when he discovered the memo.[49] Indeed, Thompson said that "no one at the NSC" saw Reynolds and Richardson find the memo, or even knew that it had been found.[50]

Inside the folder was a longer version of a memo Reynolds had come across earlier, but this one included a paragraph discussing how "residual funds" from arms sales to Iran would be used. It stated "$12 million will be used to purchase critically needed supplies for the Nicaraguan Democratic Resistance Forces." These funds would "bridge the period between now and when congressionally approved lethal assistance . . . can be delivered."[51]

The two men, even though realizing the importance of what they had found, decided nonchalantly to place the document with other documents they had selected for copying later in the day. Then, around 1:45 p.m. they broke for lunch and walked over to the Old Ebbitt Grill to join the attorney general and Cooper. As they were leaving, North arrived. They exchanged pleasantries and asked if there were any additional files for the 1985 period. North said he would check his files.

Meanwhile, Meese and Cooper had been interviewing Judge Sporkin and also been surprised by what they had learned. Sporkin told them about his drafting of the December 5 finding, when he learned about the CIA's role in the November Hawk shipment.[52] He knew that arms were involved, not oil drilling equipment, and that the purpose of the finding was to justify an after-the-fact CIA role in an arms-for-hostages transaction. Whether Meese already knew that Poindexter had destroyed the December 5 finding, or not, learning of the December 5 finding

---

[47] Ibid., 282.

[48] *Congressional Report on the Iran-Contra Affair*, 310. Mayer and McManus, *Landslide*, 333, described it as a "white manila folder with the letter W.H. in red." Reynolds's deposition in *Congressional Report on the Iran-Contra Affair*, Appendix B, Vol. 22, 1132, said the memo "was in a discrete manila folder that was readily identifiable."

[49] Ibid., 1129.

[50] "Paul Thompson Deposition," *Congressional Report on the Iran-Contra Affair*, Appendix B, vol. 26, 924.

[51] Draper, *Very Thin Line*, 505. See also chap. 9 above.

[52] *Congressional Report on the Iran-Contra Affair*, 309.

made it all the more imperative to act promptly to deflect attention from the entire affair with the "diversion."[53]

At lunch in the Old Ebbitt Grill, the four men discussed their discoveries. Reynolds disclosed the contents of North's memo but noted that there was no indication that any money transfer had actually occurred. It was, Reynolds said, an "aspiration," not a fact.[54] Meese said it would be necessary to query North directly about it. In this analysis, Meese now had his evidence; what was necessary was to obtain North's admission that he had written the memo, but also to ensure that it had never reached the president.

While Meese and his team were having lunch at the Old Ebbitt Grill, Casey, Poindexter and North were meeting in Poindexter's office in the White House. Afterward, Casey called Meese and arranged for him to visit him that evening at his home. At the same time, Meese called North and scheduled him to be interviewed the next afternoon at the Justice Department.

That evening, Meese went alone to Casey's home. He later claimed that Casey told him about the visit from Furmark over six weeks earlier. Reportedly, this involved the threat by Ghorbanifar and the Canadian financiers to go public with the charge that money had been diverted to the Contras.[55] Meese denied that he discussed the discovery of North's diversion memo, which seems highly improbable, given the fact that the reason Casey called him was to discuss that very subject, even if in a different context.

At the very least, Meese would most certainly have taken the opportunity to alert Casey to the imminent break in the crisis. Meese took no notes of their discussion, nor did Casey; but immediately after Meese left, Casey composed and sent a letter to the president urging him to fire Shultz. It read, in part:

> The public pouting of George Shultz and the failure of the State Department to support what we did [in Iran] inflated the uproar on this matter. If we all stand together and speak out I believe we can put this behind us quickly. Mr. President, you need a new pitcher.[56]

On Sunday, November 23, before going to his interview at the Justice Department, North went to see McFarlane at his office in downtown Washington. The main topic of their conversation was the diversion. Unless North was already informed and was attempting to prepare the ground for his defense, he had

---

[53] "William Bradford Reynolds Deposition," 1141. Reynolds, at least, learned for the first time that there had been such a finding, which was, he said, "a new revelation for him."

[54] Ibid., 1143.

[55] *Congressional Report on the Iran-Contra Affair*, 311 and "Meese Testimony," *Iran-Contra Investigation: Joint Hearings*, 100-9, 236-38.

[56] Mayer and McManus, *Landslide*, 336.

uncannily homed in on the issue that was about to explode in his face.[57] Yet, when it happened, not three hours later, he seemed oddly unprepared.

North arrived at the attorney general's office at 2:15 Sunday afternoon. With Meese were Cooper, Reynolds, and Richardson. Meese wanted North to go through the early history of the initiative, admonishing him to tell it straight to avoid any implication of a cover-up. But North had his own idea. Clearly assuming that he was to be the fall guy, North spun Meese a tall tale that put the Israelis at the center of the arms deals, the president interested solely in getting the hostages out, and the NSC and CIA as uninvolved in anything more than peripheral roles.

After about an hour discussing the 1985 events, in which North "dissembled" about the Hawk missiles and the retroactive finding of December 5,[58] Meese pulled out the nine-page, unsigned "diversion memo" and asked North if he had prepared it. North said yes. Looking at it he thought that it was "precisely the kind of document I had shredded. Or so I thought." North asked, "where did this come from?" But Meese merely replied, "that's not important." North asked if there had been a "cover memo," which he knew would indicate where the memo had been routed and who had received it. Reynolds answered that there had been no cover memo. [59]

As the memo was unsigned and had no cover letter it meant that there was no proof that it had ever reached Poindexter, let alone the president. Meese then pointed to the paragraph describing the diversion. When North saw it, he was startled and "visibly surprised." Meese asked if the transaction proposed in the memo had occurred and North answered that it had not. Meese then probed further: "did anything like this ever take place," and North answered, "yes."[60]

Meese asked whether the president had authorized the diversion and North said, "he didn't think so." At least, it had never been discussed at any meeting in his presence. Was there any government involvement, he was asked? North replied: "our involvement was none.... The CIA, NSC, none." Only three people knew, he said: himself, Poindexter, and McFarlane. The diversion was the Israelis' idea. Wanting to be "helpful," they offered to share some of the profits from the arms sales with the Contras.[61]

When Meese asked him how the diversion worked, North told another false story, omitting Secord and Lake Resources entirely, and asserting that the Israelis, specifically Amiram Nir, decided how much money would go to the Contras and deposited funds directly into accounts set up by Adolfo Calero in Switzerland. North's only role had been to advise Calero to set up the accounts

---

[57] *Congressional Report on the Iran-Contra Affair*, 312.

[58] Walsh, *Final Report of the Independent Counsel*, 1:540-41.

[59] North, *Under Fire*, 327-28.

[60] Ibid. See also Draper, *Very Thin Line*, 511-18, for a discussion of the interview, based on comparison of the accounts of North, Cooper, Reynolds, and Richardson.

[61] "John Richardson Notes," *Iran-Contra Investigation: Joint Hearings*, 100-9, 1413-15.

and give the account numbers to the Israelis.[62] The truth was that North could not say, as Secord notes, "that Contra-related payouts from Iranian profits ever *had* taken place.... Only Secord, Hakim, and Zucker [the Swiss banker who handled the Lake Resources account] had definitive knowledge in this area."[63]

Despite North's efforts at what he undoubtedly believed would be helpful prevarication, Meese got what he needed. North had told a false story that exonerated the president, the NSC, and the CIA, while taking the blame on himself. He admitted writing the diversion memo, yet assured Meese that it had not reached the president. The attorney general thus had the main ingredients for the president's defense, which he could present at any time.

Last Chance

But Reagan wasn't ready to accept defeat just yet. He decided to make one last attempt to obtain Shultz's agreement before throwing in the towel. This would come at the NSPG meeting, Monday afternoon, November 24. The plan was to present Shultz with a united front in support of the president in hopes that he would back down from his challenge. To prepare for it, the president had stories threatening Shultz's removal placed in the *Washington Post* and *Wall Street Journal* that morning divulging news of an imminent "shake up" in the administration. Shultz himself thought, "everything in [these stories] was likely to be a message dropped into the hands of reporters in the hope of influencing decisions and events."[64]

The *Wall Street Journal* article had Meese and former national security adviser William Clark "quietly...looking for candidates to replace" Regan, Shultz, and Poindexter. Former Transportation Secretary Drew Lewis, retiring Senator Paul Laxalt (R-NV), and Clark "have been rumored as possible choices." Forecasting the exact outcome, the story went on to say that, as Reagan had "long been reluctant to fire people," Regan and Shultz might stay, while Poindexter and North would go. Nancy Reagan reportedly was "furious" that "former advisers first backed the arms sales and now are trying to blame others." Regan, according to the article, "already has assigned considerable blame to...McFarlane, who initiated the Iran policy."[65]

The *Washington Post* reported that California "friends of Ronald Reagan," the name of the influential group that had supported the president at the outset of his political career, were urging him to replace Shultz, Regan, and Poindexter with Weinberger, Lewis, and Jeane Kirkpatrick, former US

---

[62] *Congressional Report on the Iran-Contra Affair*, 312-13 and Draper, *Very Thin Line*, 515-16.

[63] Richard Secord and Jay Wurts, *Honored and Betrayed: Irangate, Covert Affairs, and the Secret War in Laos* (New York: Wiley, 1992), 331.

[64] Shultz, *Turmoil and Triumph*, 837.

[65] Ellen Hume and Jane Mayer, "Reagan Faces Political Crisis in Choosing Whether to Oust Top Aides in Iran Flap," *Wall Street Journal*, November 24, 1986, 64.

representative to the UN. According to one member of the group, "the concern is that too many members of the present team are more interested in protecting their own hindsight than in protecting the president."[66]

The *Wall Street Journal* also carried an op-ed by Poindexter justifying the president's Iran policy and its continuation but admitting "a pro-US leadership that invites us back into Iran is not in the cards." It was nevertheless important to pursue a policy that seeks "an Iran that lives at peace with its neighbors" and that "no longer supports terror as an instrument of policy." The United States accepted the Iranian revolution and sought a nation at peace and "a force for stability in the region."[67]

The news stories set the stage for the NSPG meeting that afternoon, but it was testimony by Shultz's deputy John Whitehead before the House Foreign Affairs Committee that morning that ratcheted up the level of tension. Whitehead, testifying in place of Shultz, openly defended his chief, "denounced arms for hostages, said Iran supported terrorism, and pointed out the impossibility of coping with operations run clandestinely by the NSC staff." His testimony, regarded as a declaration of "open warfare on the White House basement," sent shock waves around Washington, igniting talk of another Watergate crisis.[68]

Meanwhile, Meese spent that morning touching base with all of the members of the NSPG, except Shultz. He also spoke with McFarlane to determine whether he did in fact know about the diversion, as North said, and whether he had told anyone else about it. McFarlane's answers were that North had told him about it in passing after the Tehran trip, but he had not talked to anyone else about it. No notes were taken at any of these meetings and Meese conveniently could not recall that anything of substance had been discussed.[69]

Meese went to the White House later that morning, at eleven o'clock, to speak to Regan. The president's chief of staff had been largely uninvolved in the initiative, but Meese needed him to take the lead from this point and also, later, to take some of the blame.[70] As Regan recalled, Meese said that "he had to see the

---

[66] David Hoffman and Lou Cannon, "White House Shake-Up Plotted," *Washington Post*, November 23, 1986, A1. In a later article by Walter Pincus and George Lardner based on documents released by the Independent Counsel, it was reported that Weinberger wrote in his diary on November 21, 1986, that William Clark wanted him to replace Shultz at State; and if so, Clark would return to the NSC to replace Poindexter. Pincus and Lardner, "Shultz Sought Nancy Reagan as Iran-Contra Ally," *Washington Post*, February 20, 1993, A1.

[67] John Poindexter, "The Prudent Option in Iran," *Wall Street Journal*, November 24, 1986, 30.

[68] Shultz, *Turmoil and Triumph*, 837.

[69] *Congressional Report on the Iran-Contra Affair*, 314.

[70] The *Tower Report*, IV-11, would reach the astounding conclusion that Regan "must bear *primary responsibility* for the chaos that descended upon the White House" when the crisis broke. Emphasis added.

president at once: his investigation had discovered…'things the president did not know'—including a possible diversion of funds from the Iran arms sale."[71]

Regan was horrified, but misunderstood what Meese was saying. He thought, "Meese meant money had been siphoned directly from the US Treasury," which truly would have been a disaster.[72] In any case, Regan immediately ushered Meese in to see the president, who was riffling through his three-by-five cards preparing for his meeting with South African Zulu nation chief Mangosuthu Buthelezi.

Oddly, despite telling Regan that he "had to see the president at once" about a "possible diversion," when he entered the Oval Office, he did not tell the president about the diversion. He said simply that he "wanted to forewarn him that something was very wrong in regard to the arms transaction." What he had found was "a terrible mess." Meese said he still had "a few things to button up" before giving a full report, but it was "going to be bad news." So, they agreed to meet after the NSPG meeting that afternoon.[73]

The NSPG meeting was the president's last attempt to obtain Shultz's support. They were all there: the president, Bush, Meese, Shultz, Casey, Regan, Weinberger, Poindexter, and also Cave. Shultz thought the purpose of the meeting was to hear Meese "present the results of his quick probe."[74] In fact, it was to put out the president's line on the November Hawk shipment to see if Shultz would buy it. The diversion was not discussed. (It was only five years later, in 1991, when Walsh discovered Regan's and Weinberger's mutually reinforcing notes, that it became possible to present an accurate portrayal of what happened at this meeting.)[75]

Poindexter, Shultz recounts, ran the meeting and reviewed the Iran initiative, as if nothing had happened. Cave gave the CIA's assessment on Iran, and then was excused from the meeting. Casey described the government's improved intelligence on Iran and Weinberger discussed the Iran-Iraq conflict, but "did not take [Shultz's] side of the argument with the vigor he had in such sessions long ago." Poindexter informed the group "we would proceed without

---

[71] Don Regan, *For the Record* (New York: Harcourt, Brace, Jovanovich, 1988), 37.

[72] Mayer and McManus, *Landslide*, 341.

[73] Regan, *For the Record*, 38. Meese claimed that he told the president the whole story of the discovery of the North memorandum, as well as North and McFarlane's "confirmation" of the diversion. See *Congressional Report on the Iran-Contra Affair*, 314.

[74] Shultz, *Turmoil and Triumph*, 838.

[75] Walsh, *Final Report of the Independent Counsel*, 1:542-43. Draper, *Very Thin Line*, 525, calls it a "peculiarly uninformative" meeting; Mayer and McManus, *Landslide*, 342, describe a "stilted discussion"; *Congressional Report on the Iran-Contra Affair*, 315, mentions Meese's notes, but not what he said.

changing the project or the policy." When Shultz strongly objected, Poindexter "ignored what [he] said."[76]

At this point, Regan raised the November Hawk issue and whether we objected to the Israeli shipment? [77] Poindexter responded first, saying "from July '85 to Dec. 7 McFarlane handled this all alone—no documentation." Meese then took the floor to discuss at length the position that the president would take, placing all the blame on McFarlane.

McFarlane, he said, had told Shultz about the delivery and possible hostage release, and noted that Shultz "didn't approve." The president was "only told maybe hostages out in short order." He gave "no specific OK for HAWKs." McFarlane told Shultz that the hostages were to come out first before arms were sent, but "that did not take place." Meese noted that it could be a violation of the law if arms were shipped without a finding, but "the president did not know."[78]

Although all understood that Meese was incorrect as to what the president knew, they all supported the president, except Shultz. The secretary declared that he "knew something of what [McFarlane] did." It seemed to him that "once again...they were rearranging the record."[79] As Shultz had suspected, they were trying to "lay all this off on Bud [McFarlane]. That won't be enough." Hill thought that the "White House was carrying out 'thru Meese' a 'carefully thought out strategy' to insulate the President and 'blame it on Bud [McFarlane].'"[80]

The president, Shultz said, was "in a steamy, angry mood clearly directed at me." He insisted, "we were right in what we were doing. Pounding the table, he said: "we are right...We had to take the opportunity! And we were successful! History will never forgive us if we don't do this!" To Shultz, the president was sending an "unmistakable message: understand me, and get off my back.... He was angry in a way I had never seen before."[81]

But Shultz would not be intimidated. In an unprecedented act, he got up from the table—and walked out. Shultz claimed that he "had to leave while the meeting was still going on for a previously scheduled appointment with South African Zulu Chief Buthelezi," but the plain fact is that he had figuratively dismissed the president.[82] The meeting ended a few minutes later. Shultz's answer

---

[76] Shultz, *Turmoil and Triumph*, 838; and Walsh, *Final Report of the Independent Counsel*, 1:542.

[77] Lawrence E. Walsh, *Firewall: The Iran-Contra Conspiracy and Cover-Up* (New York: Norton, 1997), 364. Although Regan later denied it, Meese evidently had prompted him to raise the issue before the meeting.

[78] "Regan Note, November 24, 1986," in Walsh, *Final Report of the Independent Counsel*, 1:512-13.

[79] Shultz, *Turmoil and Triumph*, 838.

[80] "Charles Hill Note, November 24, 1986," in Walsh, *Final Report of the Independent Counsel*, 1:543.

[81] Shultz, *Turmoil and Triumph*, 838.

[82] Ibid.

to the implied question of whether or not he would accept the interpretation put forward by Meese and support the president and his policy was an emphatic NO.

Reagan Surrenders Policy Control

Had Shultz caved in, the president could have weathered the storm, placed the blame for the Iran fiasco on conveniently retired McFarlane, and retained control of policy. Shultz's walkout and refusal to agree meant that the struggle would continue and intensify. The illegal aspects of the November Hawk deal would badly injure the president's credibility, and worse, if Shultz and the new world order faction leaked the diversion, it could easily have led to charges of a cover-up. Reagan, Meese and their closest confidants decided that the president's position had to be saved above all other considerations—and they had to act quickly.

Immediately after the NSPG meeting, Meese met with Poindexter for five minutes, ostensibly to find out what he knew about the diversion, but in reality, to signal that it was time for him to play his role and take responsibility. Poindexter dutifully admitted that he knew "what was going on, but that he had not inquired further." He had justified his inaction on the grounds that "he wanted the president and his staff to retain deniability." He also "knew that when the diversion became public, he would have to resign."[83]

Meese then joined Regan and the president for a brief meeting of sixteen minutes as Meese laid out for Regan's benefit what he knew about the diversion. According to Regan, Meese said that Iran had paid $30 million for arms and the CIA received $12 million. "Where the other $18 million had gone and what had been done with it, nobody seemed to know." Meese said, "North had admitted...that he had diverted some of these funds to the Nicaraguan contras," but there were questions about the location of the rest.[84]

The purpose of the meeting was to have a third party, Regan, verify that the president had no knowledge of the diversion and the chief of staff reacted perfectly. The president, he said, received Meese's report with "deep distress" and "he blanched when he heard Meese's words." Regan was convinced. "This guy I know was an actor, and he was nominated at one time for an Academy Award, but I would give him an Academy Award if he knew anything about [the diversion] when you watched his reaction to express complete surprise at this news."[85] Of course, the president was a good actor and he played his part well here (but he had never been nominated for an Academy Award).

Reagan asked, "did any Americans get their hands on that money?" and Meese told him North's lie that "no US person" had handled the money, which

---

[83] "John Poindexter Testimony," *Iran-Contra Investigation: Joint Hearings*, 100-8, 119-20.
[84] Regan, *For the Record*, 38.
[85] "Donald Regan Testimony," *Iran-Contra Investigation: Joint Hearings*, 100-10, 29-30.

had gone from Iranian to Israeli to Swiss bank accounts and then to the Contras. The question of Poindexter's fate came up and it was agreed that he would have to go, but North, oddly, was not mentioned.

Regan offered two suggestions. First, congressional leaders must be told forthwith, which should be followed by a press conference "to make sure the White House could announce the problem before it leaked." Second, the president should appoint a bipartisan commission "to establish the facts and make recommendations." There was also talk of an independent counsel, but Reagan, agreeing with this plan, emphasized that he wanted a commission, not an independent counsel, which would take too long. The president decided to "wait overnight and make a decision in the morning."[86]

The policy battle was finally over and Reagan had given up. The president would hand over policy control to Shultz and concentrate on preserving his position. Poindexter was tasked with conveying the news. A little over an hour after the NSPG meeting, he called Shultz's office and talked to Whitehead. The national security adviser's demeanor was "entirely different now":

> He wanted to assure Whitehead that the uproar over his testimony was no problem. Poindexter would tell the president it was okay. He said he hoped State would 'get involved' with Iran policy. 'State can take the lead if it wants to,' Poindexter said. In fact, he went on, 'I want to get out of it. I haven't been able to do anything else for weeks.'[87]

Shultz professed to be "stunned" at this news, hurriedly telling Whitehead to call Poindexter back to "firm up the details of how State would take charge of Iran policy and this operation." The secretary said, "we just crossed the Great Divide…Something dramatic must have happened. What, I did not know. I could not believe that Poindexter had simply had a change of heart or was putting this issue aside in order to attend to other matters. I was mystified but elated at this dramatic shift from the White House."[88]

That evening, while Shultz and the new world order faction were rejoicing over their victory, Meese and Regan were busy contacting their colleagues to tell them that the president would be making the results of the attorney general's investigation public the next day. Regan stopped by Casey's house on the way home to tell him of the plan. Casey objected strenuously, saying that it would probably mean the end of both the Iran and Contra programs. But Regan was adamant. "It's the only thing we can do."[89]

Poindexter and North commiserated with each other, realizing that the game was up, but not fully aware of what lay in store for them. Exchanging PROF

---

[86] Mayer and McManus, *Landslide*, 343.
[87] Shultz, *Turmoil and Triumph*, 839.
[88] Ibid.
[89] Mayer and McManus, *Landslide*, 344.

notes, Poindexter told him about his offer to resign and said that Meese was "one of the few beside the President that I can trust." He thought that if "we don't leave," perhaps North could be assigned as Casey's assistant. North said that he was "prepared to depart at the time you and the President decide it to be in the best interests of the Presidency and the country."[90] Clearly, neither man had an inkling they were about to become scapegoats for the president.

The next morning, November 25, Meese asked NSC counsel Paul Thompson "to do a search one more time of the presidential records to ascertain that the president had not seen or signed any memorandum dealing with Iran during the time period 1 April to the end of May, '86," a period that would encompass North's April 8 "diversion" memo, though Meese had not referred to it in his request. Thompson tasked staff member Brenda Reger to do the search, which turned up no evidence that the president had seen or signed any such memorandum.[91] Meese was now ready to announce the diversion and turn the Iran policy flap into the Iran-Contra scandal.[92]

Springing the Diversion

After briefing the NSPG and congressional leaders about the diversion and the dismissals of Poindexter and North, the president and Meese went to the White House briefing room. Reagan said that "after becoming concerned" about the inability of the national security staff to provide a "complete factual record with respect to the implementation of my policy toward Iran, I directed the attorney general to undertake a review of this matter over the weekend and report to me on Monday." Meese's report "led me to conclude that I was not fully informed on the nature of one of the activities undertaken in connection with this initiative."[93]

The president announced that the Department of Justice would be undertaking an investigation and that he would appoint a special review board to evaluate the "role and procedures" of the NSC staff in the conduct of foreign and national security policy. He said that he would share their findings with the Congress and American people. He then announced that Poindexter, "although not directly involved," had "asked to be relieved," and that North "has been relieved," but did not explain why. Then, as he attempted to turn the meeting over

---

[90] Draper, *Very Thin Line*, 534-35.

[91] "Paul Thompson Deposition," *Congressional Report on the Iran-Contra Affair*, Appendix B, vol. 26, 1076-86. Thompson, 1086, says that after the search of computer records was completed, he told Meese that "we found no record of any Presidential signature or Presidential review of any documents dealing with that issue during that time period."

[92] Don Oberdorfer and Walter Pincus, "Iran-Contra Connection Tipped the Scale: Meese's White House Revelation Turned a Flap into a Scandal," *Washington Post*, November 30, 1986, A1.

[93] "Reagan: 'I Was Not Fully Informed,'" *Washington Post*, November 26, 1986, A6.

to Meese, reporters shouted several times asking whether Shultz was also going to be let go, but Reagan ignored the questions, and left the room.

Meese then took over, saying that "all the information is not yet in," but he did want to "make available immediately what we know at the present time." He then proceeded to surprise everyone. Instead of laying the blame on McFarlane, as virtually everyone expected, especially Shultz, he introduced an entirely new issue, the diversion of Iran arms sale funds to the Contras, and placed the blame on North and Israel. Virtually everything he said skirted the edge of truth, or went over the line into clever obfuscation, but it all was designed to divert blame from the president and show that he was in charge of his administration.

The attorney general then laid out the story of the diversion, based in large part on his interview with North. "In the course of the arms transfers" to Iran, he said, "certain monies which were received in the transaction between representatives of Israel and representatives of Iran were taken and made available to the forces in Central America..." [94] He continued: "a certain amount of money was negotiated by representatives outside the United States with Iran for arms. This amount of money was then transferred to...representatives of Israel. They, in turn, transferred to the CIA, which was the agent for the United States government under a finding...signed by the president in January 1986. And, incidentally, all of these transactions . . . took place between January 1986 and the present time."

The Israelis paid the CIA "the exact amount...that was owed...for the weapons" and the CIA then repaid the Department of Defense. "All government property was accounted for and statements of that have been verified by us up to the present time...the difference between the money owed to the United States...and the money received from...Iran was then deposited in bank accounts which were under the control of representatives of the forces in Central America."

The general reaction, in the briefing room and across the nation, was shock and surprise at what was a bolt out of the blue. Then, the question and answer session began. Reporters asked over a hundred probing questions, a sampling of which is included below, in italics. Meese's answers to all but a handful regarding the diversion were either "we don't know yet, or we're still looking into it." Increasingly, the tone was one of general skepticism, verging on disbelief in the tale they were being told, which appeared to have no relevance to the Iran story.

How much money was involved? "We don't know the exact amount, yet. Our estimate is that it is somewhere between $10 million and $30 million." *How did you find out?* "In the course of a thorough review of a number of intercepts, and other materials . . . the hint of a possibility that there was (sic) some monies being made available for some other purpose came to our attention." *Did the president know?* "The president knew nothing about it until I reported it to him."

---

[94] "Transcript of Attorney General Meese's News Conference," *Washington Post*, November 26, 1986, A8-9.

*Were you looking for this when you began, or was this just something
that turned up in the course of the investigation?* "It turned up in the course of the
investigation." Reflecting McFarlane's view, one reporter asked: *We have been
told that the president was operating from the beginning of this operation in June
or July of 1985 on legal opinions—not written, but oral—from you. Are you sorry
that you gave that advice?* "The only legal opinion that was involved had to do
with the routine concurrence with the finding of January 1986."

Who knew that money was being transferred to the Contras? "The only
person in the United States Government that knew precisely about this, the only
person, was Lt. Colonel North. Adm. Poindexter did know that something of this
nature was occurring, but he did not look into it further." *What about Casey?* "CIA
Director Casey, Secretary of State Shultz, Secretary of Defense Weinberger,
myself, the other members of the NSC—none of us knew." Everyone was
innocent, Meese claimed. The only culprit was North. McFarlane was not
mentioned.

*Is it correct to say that we have heard "nothing new" from you about the
central questions that have been asked for the past three or four weeks about the
propriety of shipments to...Iran?* Meese answered in the affirmative: "we have
heard nothing new that hasn't been testified to essentially on the Hill." The
discovery of the diversion "does not drive to any of those other questions." *Was
what North did a crime? Will he be prosecuted?* "We are presently looking to the
legal aspects of it as to whether there's any criminality involved." *Is it time to
appoint a special prosecutor?* "No. If we find that there is any criminality...then
that would be the time to request an independent counsel."

What were the diverted funds used for? "I don't know. I don't know that
anyone does." *How did you discover it?* "There were some references to this in
one particular document that we found." *Did these transfers go through one
man—Colonel North? Were there no other people involved?* "No transfers of
money went through anyone. Bank accounts were established ... by
representatives of the forces in Central America. And this information was
provided to representatives of...Israel...and then these funds were put into the
accounts.... No American person actually handled any of the funds that went to
the forces in Central America."

*Have you done anything about the spectacle of top members of this
administration fighting one another like cats and dogs over policy, damaging the
president's credibility?* "I think...this would involve commenting on other
members of the administration, which I won't do.... I think anyone who is a
member of the president's...cabinet has an obligation either to support the policy
decisions of the president or to get out." *Where does that leave the Secretary of
State?* "I'm not talking about any particular person. Conclusions are your
business, not mine."

At what point did the president know about all this? "The president was
informed generally that there had been an Israeli shipment of weapons to Iran
sometime during the late summer, early fall of 1985, and then he later learned in
February of 1986 details about another shipment that had taken place in

November of '85." *If he didn't know, then why did he call Shimon Peres to thank him right after Benjamin Weir was released?* Surprised by the question, Meese stumbled through an answer: "Well, he thanked—he called—I don't know, because that's something I have not discussed with the president...but I think there was no question that the Israelis had been helpful in terms of their contacts with other people in regard to Weir."

Did the president authorize the September 1985 Israeli shipment to Iran? "Well, nobody—to my knowledge.... To my knowledge, nobody authorized that particular shipment specifically." *The Israelis did it on their own?* "That's my understanding, yes." *The Israelis claim they never did anything without the full knowledge, understanding and consent of the US Government.* "My understanding is that in terms of that particular shipment...it was done at their— on their own motion.... [But] after the fact, at least, it was condoned by the United States government."

What's to prevent an increasingly cynical public from thinking that you went looking for a scapegoat and you came up with this whopper, [which] doesn't have a lot to do with the original controversy? Meese's answer to this penetrating question was quite revealing, even though the mangled syntax. "The president felt that in the interests of getting the full story out, that he should make the statement that he did today and that I should appear before you and answer questions— which I think you will agree is doing everything we can do to be sure that there is no hint that anything is trying to be concealed."

How high did this go? Are we being asked to believe that a lieutenant colonel took this initiative and had these funds transferred, and that only Adm. Poindexter knew about it? How high did it go? Again, attempting to insulate the president, Meese answered: "To the best of our knowledge—and we have checked this rather extensively —it did not go any higher than that."

What did Colonel North actually tell you? Why did he do it, and where was the money deposited? Meese did not answer directly, but what he said, perhaps inadvertently, went well beyond North to the president, saying: "it was done during a time...that provisions had been made by Congress to permit the United States to seek funding...from third countries." As to where the money was deposited, "the bank accounts were in Switzerland."

Are you suggesting that Congress authorized what Colonel North did in seeking funds for the Contras from third countries? Meese hastily corrected himself and changed the subject, saying: "Congress never specifically authorized what Colonel North did. The question that has to be looked at, as a legal matter, is whether he committed any violation of law at the time he did that."

Was the $30 million owed to the US Government? "No, it was not owed to the US Government. All the money that was owed to the United States Government was paid to the United States Government." *Will you seek to recover the money that went to the Contras?* "We have no control over that money. It was never US funds, it was never the property of United States officials, so we have no control over that whatsoever." *If it wasn't US Government funds, whose money* *was it?* Meese's answer: "I think it would probably be the party that had sold the weapons to the Iranians."

Who set the price for the weapons? Was it North, or the Israelis? "My understanding is that all of that took place in negotiations between people...representing Israel and people representing Iran.... This was not done in the presence of, or with the participation of any American persons, to the best of my knowledge." *Was it North's idea to bid up the price the Iranians were paying?* "I don't know.... It's a matter that is still up for investigation."

How can so much of this go on and the president not know about it? "Because somebody didn't tell him, that's why.... No one in the chain of command was informed." The last question was about Eugene Hasenfus. *Was his fateful mission in any way funded by any of these diverted funds?* Meese's answer: "I have no knowledge and I doubt if we'll ever find out since we have no information about how those funds were used once they were ultimately received."

"Survival" of the President

Meese had quite deliberately left the impression that it had been North who diverted Iran surplus funds to the Contras and reporters jumped to that conclusion, but that is not what he had actually said. He said that North was the only person "that knew precisely about" the diversion, not that he had actually done it. Furthermore, he said, "no American person handled any of the funds." It had been "representatives of Israel" who put the money into Contra bank accounts.[95]

"People...representing Israel and people representing Iran" had determined prices. No American persons participated in that either. Meese had no idea what the diverted funds had been used for and didn't think "anyone" did. The money was not US money; it belonged to the "party that had sold the weapons," whom he never identified. His main point, reiterated several times, was that the president had been uninformed and that it had all happened without his knowledge because nobody told him. Once Meese informed him, he acted to correct the problem. It was imperative, he concluded, to rally around the president, to stand "shoulder to shoulder with him" in this time of crisis.

The "diversion" was a brilliant stratagem clumsily implemented, but it served its purpose of diverting attention away from the failed Iran policy and the president's political defeat. It changed the trajectory of inquiry from Iran to Contra, from policy failure to an apparent illegal transaction. Three investigations would focus on Reagan's policy toward Iran, the Contras, and their interconnections. The Tower Report and the Congressional Investigation were published in February and November 1987, while the Independent Counsel report

---

[95] Both the Israelis and Contra leaders immediately objected to Meese's thesis. See Glen Frankel, "Israel Denies Funding Contras," *Washington Post*, November 26, 1986, A1 and Julia Preston, "Contra Leaders Deny Receiving Funds," Ibid., A10.

would not be completed until five years after Reagan left office. Although unearthing valuable details, none of them even remotely addressed the central dynamic that conflicted the Reagan presidency from its outset—the continuous factional struggle for control over American strategy between the president and the new world order proponents.

The president emerged bloodied and weakened by the cumulative impact of the investigations, but the argument Meese laid out at his news conference that the president was uninformed and the victim of mismanagement by his aides held. No evidence was ever produced showing that Reagan knew about or authorized a diversion of funds. Indeed, Brent Scowcroft, one of the Tower board's principals, admitted: "we were unable to develop any clear independent evidence—either in terms of money in bank accounts with the Contras or in terms of flows of equipment—that the diversion had in fact taken place."[96]

The closest Reagan would come to acknowledging that his policy had been a mistake was in his speech to the nation on March 4, 1987 when, after reviewing the Tower Report, he said "what began as a strategic opening to Iran deteriorated, in its implementation, into trading arms for hostages."[97] The speech was not only an admission of policy failure, but it also masked what appeared to be his last feeble attempt to regain power.

In late January, on the 22nd, as the president was preparing for his appearance before the Tower Board on the 26th, he disclosed to Bush, Regan, Abshire, and Wallison, who were briefing him, that notes he had made on the briefing materials had come "from his diary." They were surprised because, up until that moment, no one had known that the president had kept a diary.[98]

Before the Tower Board four days later, the existence of the president's diary did not come up, but Reagan surprised everyone, including his briefers, when he declared that, although he was "still digging," he thought that he had approved the first Israeli arms shipment "in advance." He also said that "the Israelis had shipped the HAWKs without our permission." Wallison was dumbfounded; the president's testimony was contradictory and "muddled the record," as far as he knew it.

Attempting to determine how the president had come to these positions, which had differed from what he had said to them privately, Wallison realized that he had included copies of North's chronology of November 19 and

[96] Mary Belcher, "Tower Says Arms Proceeds Vanished 'Into a Black Hole,'" *Washington Times*, March 2, 1987, A1. See also Gaylord Shaw and James Gerstenzang, "Weinberger Skeptical Profits Were Diverted," *Los Angeles Times*, January 7, 1987, A11.

[97] "Address to the Nation on the Iran Arms and Contra Aid Controversy, March 4, 1987," *The Public Papers of Ronald W. Reagan*, Ronald Reagan Presidential Library, https://www.reaganlibrary.gov/archives/speech/address-nation-iran-arms-and-contra-aid-controversy-0.

[98] Peter J. Wallison, *Ronald Reagan: The Power of Conviction and the Success of His Presidency* (Boulder: Westview, 2003), 249.

McFarlane's testimony of December 11, but not apparently Regan's testimony of January 7, in the president's briefing materials, which contained these respective arguments. This explained for Wallison how the president thought he had approved the first Israeli shipment in advance and could say that the Israelis shipped the Hawks in November without his permission.[99]

When the president's testimony leaked, it was assumed that he was siding with McFarlane against Regan in the dispute over whether he had authorized the Israeli shipments in advance or not.[100] However, the president had in fact adopted the legal strategy developed by Meese that the earlier the president had approved of the Israeli shipments the better for the president, because all subsequent actions would be covered by what would have amounted to an oral finding.

News of the existence of the president's diary, or notes as they decided to call them, appeared in the *Washington Post* on February 1, provoking intense interest in what information the notes might hold. The clear implication was that they held the key to whether or not Reagan had authorized Israeli arms sales in advance. After discussions between Wallison and staff of the Tower Board to arrange for a second appearance, the president announced that he would turn over "relevant excerpts" from his notes to investigators.[101] In a statement he said he would "furnish copies of the relevant notes" to the Tower Board.[102]

McFarlane was scheduled to testify to the Tower Board on February 9 and the president on the 11th. As news of the president's notes trickled out the pressure on McFarlane mounted. He had to assume that the notes would show that the president had not authorized arms sales in advance and would thus expose the former national security adviser as having acted in contravention to the president's wishes. The implications for the new world order faction were equally grave, for it would give Reagan the leverage he needed to reclaim power.

There can be little doubt that either Tower or Scowcroft, close friends of McFarlane's, informed him of what the notes contained. McFarlane was faced with a major quandary. It was vital for him to avoid testifying first at the risk of being exposed as a liar two days later. The way out he chose was to take an overdose of Valium. McFarlane claimed that he had attempted suicide "for the wrong [he] believed [he] had done [his] country." The Iran-Contra scandal, he believed, was "all [his] fault." He had "disgraced [his] country."[103] That may be true. He may well have been guilt-stricken, but his action was also consistent with the need to avoid the president's public repudiation.

---

[99] Ibid., 252-53. Walsh, *Final Report of the Independent Counsel*, 1:521, omits the fact that Wallison included McFarlane's testimony in Reagan's briefing materials.

[100] John G. Tower, *Consequences: A Personal and Political Memoir* (New York: Little, Brown, 1991), 283-84.

[101] Steven Roberts, "Reagan Would Turn Over 'Excerpts' from Notes," *New York Times*, February 3, 1987, A14.

[102] Wallison, *Ronald Reagan*, 258.

[103] McFarlane, *Special Trust*, 3, 6, 8.

Although it is a common method to attempt suicide by taking an overdose of drugs, medical experts say that even taking "extremely large quantities" of Valium "is unlikely to cause death." McFarlane reportedly ingested between 30 and 40 tablets. "Experts said individuals had survived many times that amount."[104] McFarlane apparently took what would be a drug overdose on the night of February 8 and was rushed to the hospital the next morning, "two hours before he was scheduled to testify before the Tower Commission."[105]

President Reagan appeared before the Tower Commission on February 11 and reversed his earlier testimony. He now declared that he had *not* approved the Israeli arms shipments in advance, but there was no mention that the president had come to that conclusion based on a review of his notes. Wallison said that the president had actually read from a memorandum that he had prepared for him to use as a reference.[106]

The next day's press account, quoting an official who was in a position to know, reported that "they've got something," but subsequent accounts said he had reached the conclusion that he had not authorized the Israeli shipment in advance after "he and Regan talked at length about the issue following the first interview with the panel."[107] The impression left was that the president had been persuaded by Regan, not his own notes.

On February 19, Tower and Scowcroft met with McFarlane in the hospital for his interview. He admitted that in writing the November 18 memorandum he had laid out how the president could deny authorizing the Israelis shipment in advance, but continued to insist that he had given his "private approval" in advance.[108] This new position seemed to explain the president's own contradictory accounts and it was at this point that the president decided to end his struggle with the new world order faction.

The next day, Friday February 20, Reagan sent a note to the Tower Board "clarifying" his position. It read:

> I'm afraid that I let myself be influenced by others' recollections, not my own.... *I have no personal notes or records to help my recollection on the matter.* The only honest answer is that try as I might I cannot recall anything whatsoever about whether I approved an Israeli sale in advance, or whether

---

[104] Harold Schmeck, "Valium, Often a Suicide Step, Seldom Works," *New York Times*, February 11, 1987, A17.

[105] Susan Okie and Chris Spolar, "McFarlane Takes Drug Overdose," *Washington Post*, February 10, 1987, A1.

[106] Wallison, *Ronald Reagan*, 265-66 and Walsh, *Final Report of the Independent Counsel*, 1:521.

[107] Steve Roberts, "Tower Panel Data Said to Link N.S.C., Illicit Contra Aid," *New York Times*, February 12, 1987, A1 and "President Changed Statement on 1985 Iran Arms Approval," *Washington Post*, February 19, 1987, A1.

[108] Armstrong et al., *The Chronology*, 642.

I approved replenishment of Israeli stocks around August of 1985. My answer therefore—and the simple truth is, 'I don't remember—period.'[109]

In short, the president now *denied* that he had any "personal notes" to help his recollection, a statement that flew in the face of the facts, but which removed the role of the notes from the issue. If Reagan had hoped to use them to establish the truth about his decision he had failed.

Although the battle was over, it was nevertheless necessary for the new world order faction to make sure the notes, or any other evidence, would never appear at any future time to endanger their political victory. Their decision was to gain control of the paper flow to and from the president, which meant it was necessary to force out Regan and his counsel Wallison and replace them with their own men.

Nancy Reagan and George Bush now played key roles in the drama that unfolded, both demanding that Regan resign immediately.[110] For months, Nancy's contact with him had been solely by telephone, pressing him to leave. The president had staunchly defended his chief of staff all through the Iran-Contra crisis. Now, following resolution of the notes issue, the president had agreed to expedite Regan's departure and the chief of staff had agreed to depart after the Tower Board's report had been published. On February 23, however, Vice President Bush called him into his office and suggested that he speak to the president immediately "about your situation."[111]

Regan went to the president and asked directly when he should resign, and the president replied that "now" would be a good time. Flabbergasted, Regan exploded, demanding "better treatment than that." The president, taken aback, then asked when he thought he should leave. Regan thought the following Monday, March 2 would be appropriate, which would be after the publication of the Tower Board's report.

He would not last that long. Three days later, on February 26, the Tower Board briefed the president an hour before releasing its report. The report contained a harsh criticism of Regan, who had counted on the board to exonerate him of any wrongdoing.[112] Within hours of the report's release, Nancy Reagan had solicited the recommendations of influential "friends of Reagan," including Mike Deaver, Paul Laxalt, Republican party chairman Frank Fahrenkopf, and

---

[109] Mayer and McManus, *Landslide*, 378, emphasis added.

[110] Walter Pincus and George Lardner, "Shultz Sought Nancy Reagan as Iran-Contra Ally," *Washington Post*, February 20, 1993, A1. Nancy Reagan had been furious with Shultz, at first, for not supporting the president, but later came around to support him.

[111] Regan, *For the Record*, 96-97.

[112] David Hoffman and Dan Morgan, "Tower Panel Details Administration Breakdown, Blames Reagan, Top Aides for Failed Policies," *Washington Post*, February 27, 1987, A1.

pollster Richard Wirthlin. They all agreed that former Senator Howard Baker should immediately replace Regan.[113]

The next morning Baker was shown in to the president's private quarters and offered the job, which he accepted on the spot. However, the president did not want to announce the appointment until the following Monday, when it had been agreed Regan would leave. The first lady refused to wait and leaked word of Baker's appointment. When reporters called her office to confirm the rumors, her press secretary said that Mrs. Reagan wished Regan "good luck," and "welcomed Howard Baker."[114]

Regan was shocked. He had known nothing of the back-door dealings and appointment of Baker, and could not understand the urgency about his departure. However, as reports began appearing on the news wire confirming the appointment of Baker, he immediately resigned. His 22-word letter, dated February 27, 1987, read:

> Dear. Mr. President:
> I hereby resign as Chief of Staff to the President of the United States.
> Respectfully yours,
> Donald R. Regan.[115]

Baker immediately assumed the job of Chief of Staff and brought along with him his long-time aide A. B. Culvahouse as legal counsel replacing Wallison. Culvahouse now re-negotiated the rules regarding the president's notes. Instead of providing "copies of relevant notes" to congressional investigators, as agreed by Wallison, Culvahouse himself "copied verbatim" the president's notes.[116] According to Senators Daniel Inouye (D-HI) and Warren Rudman (R-NH) chairmen of the Senate Select Committee, Culvahouse "personally reviewed all of the president's handwritten diaries…and represented to us that he had copied all relevant entries."[117]

According to public agreement, "the excerpts would be typewritten, shown to Reagan for his approval and then shown to senior members of the House and Senate committees or designated staff aides."[118] This was an extraordinary and flawed procedure. What should have been done, of course, was to provide photocopies of the relevant portions of the president's handwritten notes

---

[113] Mayer and McManus, *Landslide*, 383.

[114] Ibid., 384.

[115] Regan, *For the Record*, 370-72.

[116] Lou Cannon, *President Reagan: Role of a Lifetime* (New York: Simon & Shuster, 1991), 616.

[117] *Congressional Report on the Iran-Contra Affair*, 637.

[118] David Espo, "Congressional Investigators to Get Reagan Iran-Contra Notes," *Associated Press*, April 8, 1987.

alongside the typewritten transcription. Instead, the typewritten excerpts were accepted as a matter of "faith."[119]

While the approach taken may have been politically expedient and satisfied Nancy Reagan, who objected to the release of any notes at all, the procedure introduced the obvious possibility of human error, if not outright tampering. In short, all of the president's typewritten "notes" must be considered to have been "tainted" for purposes of authenticity until verified against the original handwritten material. The notes, as "copied," played no further role in the Iran-Contra Affair. The president had lost his battle with the new world order faction. His speech of March 4, 1987 was his statement of surrender.

---

[119] Despite the president's promise of full cooperation, Culvahouse would staunchly refuse congressional committee requests for additional information from the White House. See *Congressional Report on the Iran-Contra Affair*, 639-40.

Epilogue

The four years following the promulgation of NSDD-75 in January 1983 witnessed President Reagan's victory over the Soviet Union in the Cold War, but it also saw his defeat at the hands of his domestic political opponents. These were not just congressional Democrats, but also Republicans in his own administration, particularly the secretary of state, who sought accommodation with Moscow over victory.

Policy toward Iran, a linchpin of containment that Reagan sought to restore, was a source of intense internal contention during his administration. Here, the differences between the president and Secretary Shultz of were serious and unconcealed. Amid a public scandal surrounding an alleged exchange of arms for hostages and the use of funds from arms sales to support rebels in Nicaragua, the Iran-Contra scandal, the president decided to relinquish control over foreign policy to Shultz. It was a momentous development. Shultz, in his effort to bring about détente with Moscow, set about reversing Reagan's transformational initiatives. He abandoned the shift to strategic defense; allowed relations with China to atrophy; terminated the policy of pursuing normalization of relations with Iran, ineffectually pressed against international terrorism, and negotiated "solutions" with Soviet client regimes that left them all in power.

Not a single US supported anti-Soviet resistance movement came to power—not in Nicaragua, Angola, Cambodia, Mozambique, Ethiopia, and not in Afghanistan. Throughout, Shultz and his supporters proclaimed that he and Reagan were in total agreement, but no one who followed American politics was fooled. Reagan had not suddenly seen the light; he had been defeated politically, kicked upstairs and out of power.

Shultz's decision to terminate the Iran Initiative had predictable consequences. Contrary to his view that "Iran needed the United States.... We didn't need to chase after the Iranians," a quite different outcome occurred.[1] With no effective source of support or weapons to counter Soviet-armed Iraq, Iran would suffer military defeat and move to an accommodation with Moscow, resulting in a *de facto* alliance that continues to the present. Indeed, the Russians adroitly parlayed withdrawal from Afghanistan into alliance with Iran.

The relationship with China, which Reagan had so carefully nurtured, atrophied once Shultz took power. A US-China alignment was contrary to the détente Shultz and the new world order faction sought with the Soviet Union. The

---

[1] George Shultz, *Turmoil and Triumph* (New York: Scribner, 1993), 841.

Tiananmen crisis in mid-1989 precipitated the removal of pro-American Chinese leaders and marked China's shift away from the United States toward closer ties to the Soviet Union. It would not be until the collapse of the Soviet Union in 1991—which dramatically altered the global strategic situation—that US-China relations improved again, and then arguably to an unhealthy extreme.

Consistent with the new world order strategy of dismantling the containment structure, both West Germany and Japan edged to the middle between American and Soviet power. In the two years Shultz controlled American foreign policy the Western Alliance, which President Reagan had labored so strenuously to rebuild, had loosened measurably. In part, this was due to what appeared to be Shultz's lone accomplishment—the INF Treaty to eliminate intermediate-range nuclear weapons.[2]

What appeared to be a successful demonstration of the fruits of détente simply returned the missile balance to what it had been before the deployment of the Pershing II in the fall of 1983, restoring Soviet leverage. Structurally, the outcome was closer to what Soviet leader Yuri Andropov had proposed than to what Reagan envisioned, to the consternation of allies and friends around the Eurasian landmass.[3]

The US withdrew the Pershing II missiles from West Germany, removing a major advantage in both strategic and intermediate-range weapons. While the Soviets removed most of the SS-20s, they hid others, perhaps as many as they had destroyed. They also replaced the SS-20 with weapons of similar or superior capacity. Some had shorter or longer ranges not proscribed by the treaty; others were *de facto* violations that went unchallenged.

The treaty prohibited weapons with ranges between 500 and 3,500 kilometers. Just before it was signed, however, the Soviets secretly rushed 73 SS-23 shorter-range missiles, which were explicitly prohibited by the treaty, into East Germany, Czechoslovakia, and Bulgaria.[4] When they were discovered in 1990 the State Department conducted a compliance review. The astounding conclusion was that "Soviet control over the SS-23 missiles did not constitute actual possession of them…. The missiles were the property of the three East European states. The presence of the missiles, therefore, was *not* a violation of the INF Treaty ban on all Soviet shorter-range missiles."[5]

The Russians also deployed the SS-25, which was classified as an ICBM, with a maximum range of 10,000km, and thus outside the scope of the INF Treaty. However, the SS-25 also could strike targets down to a range of 2,000km, well

---

[2] Angelo Codevilla and L. Francis Bouchey, "Bringing Out the Worst in European Politics," *Strategic Review* (Winter 1988): 14-23.

[3] For Andropov's proposal, see chap. 1.

[4] Kenneth Timmerman, "Russia's Hidden Nuclear Missiles," *World Net Daily*, June 5, 2000 and "Why Is Moscow Cheating on the INF Treaty and is Washington Minimizing the Implications?" *Center for Security Policy*, March 14, 1990.

[5] "Case Study: SS-23 Missiles in Eastern Europe," US Department of State, October 1, 2005, emphasis added.

within the prohibited range. By the end of 1988 the Soviets had deployed over 200 SS-25s, many at former SS-20 sites. The United States made no similar compensatory moves, nor voiced any complaint.

During Secretary Shultz's stewardship, as the price of détente, the United States allowed the Soviet Union's three main objectives, as described in this study, to be fulfilled. Moscow's strategic deterrent remained intact; there would be no treaty to reduce strategic weapons or shift to the strategic defensive. The Soviets reestablished nuclear weapons domination over the Eurasian landmass, with the withdrawal of the Pershing II missile from West Germany; and the Soviets drew Iran into their orbit, with the termination of the Iran initiative. This last would encourage a strong Soviet and later Russian drive to gain leverage over Middle East Oil.[6] Thus, not only would Iran be lost, but also American leverage over Middle Eastern oil would be sharply attenuated.

The Iran-Contra affair was also pivotal in a deeper sense, marking the end of a quarter-century struggle within the American political establishment, spanning Republican and Democratic administrations, over the transcendent issue of American strategy. On the question of whether to continue the strategy of anti-Soviet containment, known in the Reagan administration as the victory strategy, or to revert to a strategy of détente and accommodation with Moscow, the decision was to terminate the former and embrace the latter. The United States pursued an accommodationist course for the next thirty years.

It is profoundly disconcerting that American strategy was not decided by America's elected leaders, but by an unelected political elite, the left-of-center political establishment, many of whom were appointed to high office in Republican administrations, but none of whom was elected by the American people. Shultz claimed that as an appointed cabinet officer he was accountable, but by accountable he meant that he could be called to testify before Congress.[7] This form of "accountability" should not be confused with electoral accountability. According to the US Constitution, only the president *decides* strategy and policy, not appointed officials.

Both Presidents Nixon and Reagan had acted to defeat Soviet strategy, putting the United States in position to exploit victory and create beneficial outcomes for the West, and possibly for the Soviet Union too, through the regime change that invariably accompanies strategic defeat. At the moment of success in both cases, the new world order faction of the political establishment shrank from victory and, betraying their presidents, demanded negotiated settlements with the Soviets. Backed by the Democratic Party in control of both houses of Congress, the new world order faction employed the stratagem of entrapment to achieve political power and, once gaining power, changed course to seek accommodation with Moscow. The similarities of the political struggles between Nixon and Reagan and their political opponents are striking. In both cases, scandals led to

---

[6] See the author's "The US-Russian Struggle for World Oil, 1979-2010," in Alain Beltran, ed., *Le Pétrole et la Guerre* (Brussels: Peter Lang, 2012), 299-312.

[7] Shultz, *Turmoil and Triumph*, 919.

the defeat of the president, the transfer of power to the new world order faction's leaders, and the reversal of strategy. The exception was that Nixon resigned in the face of the Democratic-led impeachment threat, while Reagan caved in to that threat and remained in office. The outcome, however, was the same.

In the Orwellian world of Washington-speak, Reagan's defeat was hailed as a victory, the repudiation of his strategy its continuation, and Moscow's continued assault against the West through proxies and support of international terrorism indicated the blossoming of détente and the end of the Cold War. Failing even to identify the Russians as state supporters of international terrorism was perhaps the most grievous fault, which gave them a blank check in their long-term "death by a thousand cuts" strategy against the United States and the West.

Worst of all, Reagan's failure to clarify the fundamental issues in dispute permitted the new world order faction to blur the fact that a great strategic choice had been made. The United States, from late in 1986, embarked on a course of détente and accommodation with Moscow, and later with Beijing, that continued for three decades until the election of 2016. Who would argue that the country has been better off for it? As of this writing, the realignment begun four years ago appears to have been suspended, if not completely nullified.

In the immortal words of Pogo: "We have met the enemy and he is us."

Illustration Credits

Cover Image

"President Ronald Reagan Alone in the Oval Office," White House Photographic Office, National Archives catalog, https://catalog.archives.gov.

Optimum Location for Deployment of SS-20s to the Caribbean

Joanne Thornton
Drawn on map by Natural Earth (naturalearthdata.com).

Grenada and St. George's: Key Locations

Joanne Thornton
Drawn using Google Maps.

Soviet Phased-Array Radars

"Ballistic Missile Early Warning, Target-Tracking, and Battle Management Radars," *Department of Defense, Soviet Military Power, 1986* (Washington, DC: US Government Printing Office, 1986).

KAL 007's Probable Route

R.W. Johnson, *Shootdown: Flight 007 and the American Connection* (New York: Viking, 1986), 10.

Japan Defense Agency Map

Michel Brun, *Incident at Sakhalin: The True Mission of KAL Flight 007* (New York: Four Walls Eight Windows, 1995), 19.

Radar Track of Soviet MiG-23/Possible Director of KAL 007's Landing on Sakhalin

David Pearson, *KAL 007: The Cover-Up*: *Why the True Story Has Never Been Told* (New York: Summit Books, 1987), 81.

Ill-Fated Hawk Flight

Joanne Thornton
Google Earth
Image: Landsat/Copernicus
Data: SIO, NOAA, US Navy, NGA, GEBCO, IBCAO.

Iran-Iraq Battleground and Al Faw Campaign

Joanne Thornton
Drawn using d-maps (d-maps.com, map: South-West Asia, Hydrography, States) and Google Maps, adapted from image in Weapons and Warfare, "Iran-Iraq War II," https://weaponsandwarfare.com/2015/08/14/iran-iraq-war-ii/; and image "Operation Dawn 8: Iran's Capture of Fao," in Efraim Karsh, Essential Histories: The Iran-Iraq War 1980-1988 (Oxford: Osprey, 2002), 50.

Index

CPSIA information can be obtained
at www.ICGtesting.com
Printed in the USA
BVHW040933100521
606948BV00014B/350